Mechanisms of Language Acquisition

Mechanisms of Language Aquisition

edited by

BRIAN MACWHINNEY

LEA LAWRENCE ERLBAUM ASSOCIATES, PUBLISHERS
1987 Hillsdale, New Jersey London

Lawrence Erlbaum Associates, Inc., Publishers
365 Broadway
Hillsdale, New Jersey 07642

Library of Congress Cataloging-in-Publication Data

Mechanisms of language acquisition.

"These papers were presented in May of 1985 at the 20th Carnegie-Mellon Symposium on Cognition sponsored by the National Science Foundation and the Department of Psychology at Carnegie-Mellon University."—Pref.

Includes bibliographies and index.

1. Language acquisition—Congresses. 2. Learning, Psychology of—Congresses. I. MacWhinney, Brian. II. Carnegie-Mellon Symposium on Cognition (20th : 1985 : Carnegie-Mellon University) III. National Science Foundation (U.S.) IV. Carnegie-Mellon University. Dept. of Psychology.

P118.M397 1987 401'.9 86-32763

ISBN 0-89859-596-7

ISBN 0-89859-973-3 (pbk.)

Printed in the United States of America

10 9 8 7 6 5 4 3 2 1

Contents

Preface

Three decades of intensive study of language development have led to an enormous accumulation of descriptive data. But there is still no over-arching theory of language development that can make orderly sense of this huge stockpile of observations. Grand structuralist theories such as those of Chomsky, Jakobson, and Piaget have kept researchers asking the right questions, but they seldom allow us to make detailed experimental predictions or to formulate detailed accounts. The papers collected in this volume[1] attempt to address this gap between data and theory by formulating a series of mechanistic accounts of the acquisition of language.

In organizing the conference, it was my goal to invite representatives of all major approaches to language acquisition. Unfortunately, there were two areas that could not be included: the study of speech development in infancy and the detailed study of the impact of interaction with parents and siblings on language development. Despite these omissions, we did succeed in assembling an excellent group of speakers representing a great diversity of theoretical positions. Given this diversity, it was quite surprising to find out that virtually all of the speakers agreed on three major and important issues.

First, all of the papers in the volume assign a major role to *mechanism* as an

---

[1]These papers were presented in May of 1985 at the 20th Carnegie-Mellon Symposium on Cognition sponsored by the National Science Foundation and the Department of Psychology at Carnegie-Mellon University. Particular thanks to Betty Boal who helped organized the conference. Betty has been the organizer for each of the 20 CMU Symposia and her help across the years was recognized at this 20th Symposium.

important ingredient of accounts of language acquisition. In some papers we see proposals for a variety of interlocking mechanisms. Other papers propose single powerful mechanisms. Some of the mechanisms are innate constraints imposed on learning. Other mechanisms are pieces of the learning process itself. All of the mechanisms are proposed as parts of what will some day be a fuller and more explanatory account of the whole of language learning.

Second, the papers agree in the way in which they assess the fundamental problem of language acquisition. Each paper recognizes the importance of the "overgeneralization problem." How does the language learner steer a course between the Scylla of overgeneralization and the Charybdis of undergeneralization? If learners succumb to undergeneralization, how will they be able to acquire and produce new forms? If learners become trapped in overgeneralization, how can they then retreat from the errors which overgeneralization generates? Perhaps learners are guided by innate constraints that manage to guide them through these quagmires. If this is true, how did these innate constraints get there and what is their biological basis? Although the papers diverge widely in their answers to these questions, they all recognize the centrality of the overgeneralization problem.

Third, the papers are all remarkably unanimous in the conceptualization of the "negative instances problem." This problem focuses on evidence indicating that children do not learn by correction or "negative instances." In some formal accounts, the nonavailability of negative instances leads to major problems with demonstrating the learnability of language. Langley and Carbonell show that machine learning is facilitated when the program is given information about sentences that are not in the language. However, researchers also agree that such negative instances are not available to the child or at least are not utilized by the child. In the current papers we find rich and detailed proposals about ways in which language learning can proceed without reliance on negative instances. At the very least, these proposals demonstrate that the negative instances problem is not an insurmountable barrier to the formulation of accounts of language learning.

Just as the papers reflect these broad areas of agreement, so they differ sharply in terms of the theory of adult competence to which they subscribe. Among the major theories being defended are: Lexical Functional Grammar, Filter Theory, Parallel Distributed Processing, Government and Binding Theory, Generalized Phrase Structure Grammar, Production Systems, Autosegmental Phonology, and the Competition Model. Perhaps, some day, when the dust has settled, these theories will not seem so radically different from each other as they do today. Perhaps, viewed from the perspective of the 1990's, it will be the areas of agreement that turn out to be important, while the babble of alternative theories will appear to simply reflect the quaint style of the 1980's. Already, we can see that many of the papers sketch out ways in which apparently conflicting notational systems and apparently competing accounts can be brought into reconciliation and cooperation. But such attempts at reconciliation cannot be pushed too far until each position has been worked out in detail. Because of this, in the end, we must leave to the reader the final task of discerning the broad new theoretical synthesis which undoubtedly awaits our field.

Brian MacWhinney

I THE PROBLEM OF OVERGENERALIZATION

1 The Principle of Contrast: A Constraint on Language Acquisition

Eve V. Clark
Stanford University

Different words mean different things. That is, wherever there is a difference in *form* in a language, there is a difference in *meaning*. This is what, in 1980, I called the *Principle of Contrast*.[1] It is by virtue of this property that language maintains its usefulness as a medium of communication. As Bolinger put it, ''any word which a language permits to survive must make its semantic contribution'' (1977, p. ix). This applies as much to constructions as to words: ''the same holds for any construction that is physically distinct from any other construction'' (1977, p. ix-x).

In the present paper I focus on the acquisition of meaning in light of the Principle of Contrast. This principle makes specific predictions about acquisition that are supported by data from many different domains. It shapes the lexicon for immature and mature speakers alike. It also plays a role in establishing which forms are conventional and thus contributes a solution to why children give up over-regularizations in morphology and syntax. Finally, it helps account for individual variation during acquisition.

I begin in the first section with a statement of the Principle of Contrast together with its corollary, the Principle of Conventionality, and review its predictions about language use in general. In the next section I review the evidence for the Principle of Contrast in acquisition and show that children observe it in both expected and unexpected ways from the earliest stages in the acquisition of language. In the third section I look at the consequences of the Principle of Contrast for the acquisition of morphology and of syntax, and the

---

[1]See also Clark (1983a, 1983b), Clark and Berman (1984), Clark and Clark (1979), and Clark and Hecht (1982).

role it plays in children's getting rid of over-regularizations. I then show how this principle helps account for variations in the courses children follow during acquisition. In the last section I argue that this principle subsumes several other proposals to constrain language development in that they each constitute special cases of the Principle of Contrast.

THE PRINCIPLE OF CONTRAST

The Principle of Contrast states that any difference in **form** in a language marks a difference in **meaning.** The term *dog,* for instance, which differs in form from *horse* also differs from it in meaning. This principle can be stated as:

> *The Principle of Contrast:* Every two forms contrast in meaning.

This principle is a general one for speakers of a language. It is one that has been stated or assumed by virtually every linguist over the years.

The Principle of Contrast must be carefully distinguished from its converse, which I will call the Homonymy Assumption. This assumption is that every two meanings contrast in form. Under this view, one should never find two different meanings being carried by the same form, as in *bank* of a river versus a financial institution, or *bat,* a small flying mammal versus an instrument used in playing cricket or baseball. This assumption clearly doesn't hold in general for speakers of a language. But, within one level of a semantic field, where the words for two different meanings over time come to have the same form, the resultant homonymy may cause genuine confusion. Speakers then typically introduce another form to carry one of the meanings (see Orr, 1962). Aside from this special case, the Homonymy Assumption should be kept distinct from the Principle of Contrast because it may play little or no role in either adult language use or acquisition.

The Principle of Contrast is essential, though, because it helps maintain conventionality in language:

> *The Principle of Conventionality:* For certain meanings, there is a conventional form that speakers expect to be used in the language community.

If one wishes to talk about an instance of the category 'dog', one had better use the conventional word *dog* (and not *horse*), or no one will understand. Conventional terms used conventionally work best to convey speakers' intentions within the speech community. Conventional terms work in large part because speakers are *consistent* with the conventional meanings they assign to forms from one occasion to the next, and therefore maintain the *same* contrasts in meaning over time. Speakers of English use the word *dog* to denote dogs, not dogs one day, horses the next, and some other animal the day after. These two principles jointly constrain the choices speakers make in language use (e.g., Bolinger, 1977; Clark & Clark, 1979). Without them, languages simply wouldn't work.

If the Principle of Contrast (from now on, Contrast for short) is truly general in language, then a number of predictions follow:

1. Words contrast in meaning, so there are no true synonyms.
2. Established words have priority in the expression of meaning.
3. Innovative words fill lexical gaps and so may not be used in place of established words with the identical meanings.

The evidence for these predictions is extensive, so I will simply summarize some of the major findings before turning to the predictions Contrast makes about acquisition.

Contrast in Meaning

Evidence for the first prediction comes from the lexicon and from syntax. In both, differences in form make for contrasts in meaning. Meanings may overlap, of course, but they nonetheless contrast in at least some contexts. In the lexicon, many apparent synonyms are in fact not synonymous; they mark contrasts in dialect, in register, or in connotation. In syntax, differences in form mark differences in meaning, but some of these reflect subtle shifts in perspective or topicalization.

Lexical contrasts. Meaning differences, large and small, are characteristic of the lexicon. The study of such differences has traditionally been carried out within semantic fields where linguists have analyzed and characterized patterns of contrasts (e.g., Bierwisch, 1967; Lehrer, 1974; Lyons, 1963). While different lexical domains may be organized in a variety of ways, the property they all display is that each term within a domain or semantic field contrasts in meaning with all the others. The precise pattern of lexical contrasts will vary with the internal organization of a semantic field (for discussion, see Fillmore, 1978; Kay, 1971; Lehrer, 1974; Lyons, 1977).

Possible relations in lexical domains include those among *co-hyponyms* (terms contrasting at the same level). For example, *horse, dog, cat,* and *sheep* are all co-hyponyms of terms above them, hierarchically, like *mammal* or *animal.* This relation of hyponymy may hold across two or more levels. Thus *spaniel,* a co-hyponym of *boxer, Alsatian,* and *Labrador,* is a hyponym of and contrasts with *dog,* and *dog* in turn is a hyponym of and contrasts with *animal.*

Contrasts in meaning, then, may hold at the same level (among co-hyponyms) or across different levels.[2] Contrasts may also be orthogonal, between terms that potentially belong in more than one domain. *Dog,* for instance, is a hyponym of *animal* and also of *pet* (see further Fillmore, 1978; Lyons, 1977).

Analyses of specific lexical domains, then, have focussed on the contrasts inherent in the meaning relations within each domain. Many contrasts are obvious but others are more subtle. All languages contain numerous expressions whose meanings overlap. In many contexts these may be exchanged for each other, and it is this degree of overlap or partial synonymy that is exploited in dictionaries or thesauri, e.g., for the adjective *mature,* one finds *adult, ripe, perfect, due;* for the verb *govern: direct, control, determine, require;* or for the adjective *loose: inexact, free, relaxed, vague, lax, unbound, inattentive,* or *slack.* When the entry for each of these is inspected, one moves further and further away from the original word being "defined." What this shows, clearly, is that overlaps are not equivalent to synonymy. While two terms may be interchangeable in many contexts, they are not so in all, and it is the contexts where they are not equivalent that reveal their often subtle contrasts in meaning.

Dialect, register, and connotation. English, like most other languages, contains many apparent synonyms, but these typically contrast in meaning according to dialect or register choices, or according to emotive coloring, connotation. Terms that differ only in one of these dimensions have the same extensions: their intensions are different. It is this that may mislead. Such pairs are then perceived as synonyms and their meaning differences ignored.

Choice of a term from one dialect over another in many settings identifies the speaker's membership in a particular societal group. Dialect differences account for pairs such as *autumn* (UK) versus *fall* (Western UK and US), as well as for differences between pairs like *truck/lorry, pail/bucket, sack/bag,* and *cup/tassie* (Palmer, 1981). They also account for multiple terms with the same denotation such as *cowshed, cowhouse,* and *byre; haystack, hayrick,* and *haymow; tap, spigot,* and *faucet,* and so on. The contrasts between dialects are really no different from translation equivalents across languages like French and Hungarian or English and Hebrew. In many communities speakers may be unfamiliar with the original dialects while being familiar with some of these pairs from written sources. This, though, simply makes the pairs similar to equivalent terms from two distinct languages, e.g., *house* and *maison.*

Other apparent synonyms mark different registers (speech styles). Registers may differ in formality, e.g., the contrasts among *smell, effluvium, stink*

---

[2]The terms superordinate and subordinate are often used in place of hyponymy to talk about the relations among terms at different levels. However, they tend to suggest there is a fixed number of levels, typically three—superordinate, basic, subordinate—when in fact there are sometimes more and sometimes fewer.

(straightforward, pretentious, colloquial) or, on a similar continuum, *die, pass away, pop off*. Speakers often opt for Latinate vocabulary in English to mark a more formal register: compare *numerous* and *many, facilitate* and *ease, attempt* and *try, sufficient* and *enough* (Joos, 1961). Choices of lexical items may signal solidarity or identification with a particular social group, formality or informality, or politeness. The dimensions along which lexical choices can mark register are not clearcut, and the same choices may have different consequences on different occasions (Lakoff, 1973; Nunberg, 1978).

Yet other apparent synonyms differ in the emotive coloring or connotation each carries. That is, the speaker's choice of term can convey his attitude towards the person or event being described. Compare the choice of *politician* versus *statesman,* where the latter is laudatory and the former not (see also Orwell, 1950). Much the same contrast appears to underlie choices of *skinny* versus *slim, obstinate* versus *firm,* and *spendthrift* versus *generous.* The first term typically carries a negative connotation, while the second carries a positive one. Many apparent synonyms contrast in connotation.

Syntactic contrasts. Differences in form at the syntactic level also mark contrasts in meaning (e.g., Bolinger, 1977; Chafe, 1971). Consider the following pairs of sentences.

(1a) They pulled the ropes in.
(1b) They pulled in the ropes.
(2a) Jan taught Rob French.
(2b) Jan taught French to Rob.
(3a) Jo lit the fire.
(3b) The fire was lit by Jo.
(4a) Bees swarmed in the garden.
(4b) The garden swarmed with bees.

In (1), as Bolinger (1977) pointed out, the contrast is one of completion or achievement marked by the first form (the ropes were in) compared to non-completion in the second. Much the same contrast appears in (2): in the first, one infers that Rob learned some French; in the second, the outcome remains unspecified. In (3) and in (4), the first form in each pair focuses on the actor, while the second focuses on the object affected and the location respectively (see Salkoff, 1983).

Other constructional contrasts appear in lexicalized versus periphrastic causatives as in (5) and in descriptions of sequence as in (6):

(5a) Bill killed John.
(5b) Bill caused John to die.

(6a) He opened the door and he came in.
(6b) He opened the door and came in.

In (5), the contrast is one between direct (5a) versus indirect (5b) causation (McCawley, 1978; Shibatani, 1976), while in (6) there is a subtle contrast in meaning between (6a) where there are two distinct activities, and (6b) where there is only one (Bolinger, 1977).

Finally, in (7), adjectival modification offers further contrasts at the constructional level:

(7a) the blue cushion, the pale blue cushion
(7b) the green cushion, the pale green cushion
(7c) the red cushion, the pink cushion (*pale red)

Here the modification of adjectives by *pale* is blocked in the case of *red* because of the existence of the term *pink,* an adjective that picks out just the domain that would otherwise be designated by the construction *pale red* (see Gruber, 1976; Hofmann, 1982, 1983).

Contrasts in meaning, then, show up not only in the lexicon but also in the combinatorial options possible at the syntactic level.

In summary, differences in form mark differences in meaning at both the lexical and the syntactic levels. Furthermore, where languages contain a variety of apparent synonyms, these typically mark contrasts in dialect, in register or speech style, or in connotation. True synonyms probably do not exist: ". . . there are no real synonyms . . . no two words have exactly the same meaning" (Palmer, 1981, p. 89).

Priority of Established Forms

Evidence that established forms take priority comes from existence of suppletive forms in many otherwise regular paradigms in the lexicon as well as elsewhere in the language. The lexicon as a whole can be roughly organized into paradigms or groups of terms that share some element of form that marks an element of meaning shared by all the members of a paradigm. For example, many adjectives in English end in the suffix *-y,* an element of form marking any terms that carry it as adjectives with the meaning, roughly, 'having X' or 'being connected with X', e.g., *stony, dirty, watery.* Similarly, many agentive nouns end in *-er,* an element of form indicating agentivity, e.g., *builder, farmer, runner;* and many nouns for states end in *-ness,* a suffix indicating statehood, e.g., *closeness, ordinariness, roughness.* Such paradigms reflect the many regularities to be found in the lexicon.

But irregularities abound too. The lexicon as a whole combines regular and irregular forms in a complex patchwork. Irregular forms are often the remains of paradigms no longer in use, as when a suffix like nominal *-th* ceased to be productive several hundred years ago. Yet traces of *-th* remain in the lexicon in words like *warmth, width,* and *depth.* Other irregularities result from changes in the sound system that obscure the connections between forms that were originally related (e.g., *create* and *creature*), or from the borrowing of isolated forms to express special meanings (e.g., *hors d'oeuvres, sabotage*).

Irregular forms in the lexicon often fill slots in otherwise regular paradigms. These forms are *suppletive.* They pre-empt or block the use of the expected, regular form that would otherwise fill that slot. In morphology, for instance, the regular past tense **goed* (*unacceptability indicates) is pre-empted by suppletive *went,* the regular comparative adjective **gooder* is pre-empted by *better,* and the regular plural **foots* is pre-empted by *feet.* In the lexicon, the regular noun **gloriosity* (from *glorious*) is pre-empted by *glory,* the regular **longness* (from *long*) is pre-empted by *length,* the regular agentive **cooker* (from the verb *cook*) is pre–empted by the noun *cook,* and the regular denominal verb **to car* is pre-empted by *to drive.* In syntax, the regular causative construction **to disappear X* is pre-empted by *to make X disappear,* just as the regular phrase **to kick with his foot* (alongside *to bruise with his foot, to knock with his foot,* etc.) is pre-empted by *to kick,* and the regular phrase *on this day* (alongside *on the next day, on the second day, on that day*) is pre-empted by *today* on just those occasions when the speaker is referring to the actual time of utterance. In each instance, an established but irregular suppletive form with just the meaning required pre-empts or blocks use of the regular form one would expect there (see Aronoff, 1976; Clark & Clark, 1979; Gruber, 1976; Hofmann, 1982, 1983; Kiparsky 1983). Provided there is no contrast in meaning, established suppletive forms in the language take priority over regular ones that would convey the *same* meaning. This can be stated as a principle covering pre-emption by synonymy in general (Clark & Clark, 1979, p. 798):

> *Pre-emption by synonymy:* If a potential innovative word-form would be precisely synonymous with a well-established word, the innovative word is pre-empted by the well-established word, and is therefore considered unacceptable.

Such pre-emption is illustrated further for some verb and noun paradigms in English in Table 1 and Table 2 respectively. In Table 1 the paradigm is that of verbs formed from nouns, a highly productive option in English. Virtually all terms for vehicles, for instance, provide the source for the corresponding verbs, e.g., *to sled, to ski, to skateboard, to helicopter, to jet, to truck, to Chevy,* and *to bicycle.* Two possible verbs in this paradigm, **to car* and **to airplane,* though, are normally pre-empted by *to drive* and *to fly.* This is because these two terms are already established in the lexicon with just the meanings intended. In contexts where *to car* and *to airplane* contrasted in meaning with *to drive* or *to fly,* they would be perfectly acceptable verbs (Clark & Clark, 1979). The pre-empt-

TABLE 1
Pre-emption within the Lexicon: Verbs

Source	*Paradigm*	*Pre-empted*	*Pre-empter*
bicycle	to bicycle		
jet	to jet		
car		*to car	to drive
airplane		*to airplane	to fly
knee	to knee		
shoulder	to shoulder		
foot		*to foot	to kick
palm		*to palm	to slap
stable	to stable		
jail	to jail		
hospital		*to hospital	to hospitalize
prison		*to prison	to imprison
salt	to salt		
pollen		*to pollen	to pollinate
butcher	to butcher meat		
chauffeur	to chauffeur		
baker		*to baker bread	to bake
banker		*to banker money	to bank

ing terms pre-empt, then, because they already have just the meaning that the regular forms would carry within the pertinent paradigm. The same point applies to the nouns formed from adjectives and verbs listed in Table 2. Such pre-emption is a logical consequence of the Principles of Contrast and Conventionality. If different forms carry contrasting meanings, the starred forms in Tables 1 and 2 should differ in meaning from the established, suppletive terms.

Contrast in Innovative Forms

Evidence for the third prediction comes from the fact that speakers coin words freely and frequently, typically to fill gaps. These may be momentary gaps, as when one forgets the exact word for something, or long-term gaps, where there is no established word for that particular meaning. In either case, speakers make use of the word-formational resources available to construct a form appropriate for the meanings they wish to convey.[3] Speakers freely coin new verbs for specific actions. They construct these verbs, for instance, around terms for instruments: *to BART to Berkeley, to Concorde, to siren up to an accident* (said of the police), *to postcard someone, to Ajax the bath, to Windex the panes, to*

[3]In using an innovation speakers rely on their addressees to work out the intended meaning, given their mutual knowledge, the prior linguistic context, and any other pertinent information (see Clark & Clark, 1979; H. Clark, 1983).

bottle the police (meaning 'to throw bottles at'), *to toothpick the clam, to jaw the swimmer* (following the film *Jaws*), *to microwave the chicken, to crayon the walls, to x-and-m out a word,* or *to 86 a customer* (meaning 'to throw out for drunkenness according to Ordinance 86'). These represent only a minute sample of the range English-speakers use (see further Clark & Clark, 1979; Karius, 1985).

Speakers are equally free in coining new nouns for talking about new categories or subcategories of objects. One of the easiest ways is to create innovative noun + noun compounds, such as *apple-juice-chair* for the chair with the apple-juice nearest it, *earthquake-schools* for schools that would be unsafe in the event of an earthquake, *hedge-axe* for an axe for cutting down hedges, *banana-fork* for a fork for eating bananas, *giraffe-fence* for a fence for confining giraffes, *elf-shoes* for shoes to fit elves, or *bike-horn* for a horn on a bicycle (Downing, 1977). There are other ways too. People can construct a term to designate virtually any category they wish. What is crucial, as Bolinger (1975, p. 109) observed, is that:

> Words are not coined in order to extract the meanings of their elements and compile a new meaning from them. The new meaning is there FIRST, and the coiner is looking for the best way to express it without going to too much trouble.

In summary, evidence for the Principle of Contrast is widespread. The first prediction was that differences in form mark differences in meaning. The evidence for this comes from analysis of lexical contrasts, including contrasts between terms that differ in dialect, in register, and in connotation, as well as from

TABLE 2
Pre-emption within the Lexicon: Nouns

Source	*Paradigm*	*Pre-empted*	*Pre-empter*
curious	curiosity		
tenacious	tenacity		
glorious		*gloriosity	glory
furious		*furiosity	fury
polish$_V$	polisher		
sweep$_V$	sweeper		
drill$_V$		*driller	drill$_N$
bore$_V$		*borer	bore$_N$
ride$_V$	rider		
drive$_V$	driver		
cook$_V$		*cooker	cook$_N$
spy$_V$		*spyer	spy$_N$
apply		*applier	applicant
inhabit		*inhabiter	inhabitant

syntactic contrasts, where differences in form again mark contrasts in meaning. The second prediction was that established terms take priority (by virtue of their meaning) over regular terms designed to carry the *same* meaning. The evidence here was drawn from the presence of suppletive forms in otherwise regular paradigms in morphology, in the lexicon, and in syntax. The suppletive forms pre-empt or block the formation of regular forms to carry the requisite meanings. The third prediction was that lexical gaps—points where there are no established terms to convey particular meanings—are filled by lexical innovations. Here pre-emption no longer applies since the novel meanings have no conventional expressions already established. Speakers must therefore call on some other resource, and they do.

CONTRAST IN ACQUISITION

The general predictions of Contrast for children acquiring language parallel those for adult users of a language. If the notion of Contrast is inherent to the nature of language, then children should assume this principle from a very early point in acquisition (Clark, 1983a, 1983b). The major predictions for children, then, are similar to those for adults:

1. Children assume words contrast in meaning.
2. Children give priority to known words.
3. Children assign novel words that they hear to gaps in their lexicon, and, to fill such gaps, they coin new words themselves

But the kinds of evidence I shall draw on appear very different.

Different Forms Contrast in Meaning

For children, too, different forms contrast in meaning so they reject any apparent synonyms. Evidence for this first prediction comes from several sources: children narrow down over-extensions as they acquire new, contrasting vocabulary items; they build up each lexical field by adding new contrasts as they add new items; and they assign contrasting meanings to contrasting forms at the level of words, word-formational patterns, and multi-word constructions.

Narrowing down over-extensions. Some of the earliest evidence that children assume that words contrast in meaning comes from their narrowing down of lexical over-extensions. Suppose, in an over-extension, child A applies *dog* not only to dogs, but also to cats, sheep, and other four-legged mammals (Clark, 1973, 1978). When this child acquires *cat,* a word for part of this domain, he stops over-extending *dog* to cats. And when A acquires *sheep,* he stops over-extending *dog* to sheep. At this point, A relies on *cat* for designating cats, *sheep* for sheep, and *dog* for dogs and (possibly still over-extending it) for other small mammals excluding any for which he already has terms available. Each new term contrasts with the terms already known, rather than being treated as synonymous with one or more of them. Such patterns of narrowing are clearly illustrated in the detailed diaries kept by Leopold (1939, 1949), and Pavlovitch (1920) and in studies such as Mervis and Canada (1981).

Building up lexical fields. In narrowing down over-extensions, children simultaneously build up *lexical fields:* terms for animals, for birds, for vehicles, for people, for toys, and for furniture as well as for relations and dimensions (Clark, 1978). Each new term acquired contrasts in meaning with those already known.[4] Early uses of *big* and *small,* for example, become restricted with the addition of further contrasting adjectives like *tall/short* for objects with vertical extent, or *long/short* for ones with horizontal extent (e.g., Clark, 1972; Donaldson & Wales, 1970). Children follow a similar progression with orientational terms like *top* as they add *front, back,* and *side* (Clark, 1980; Kuczaj & Maratsos, 1975) and possession verbs like *give* as they add *take, buy, sell,* and *trade* (Gentner, 1975). Each term added contrasts with its neighbors.

Contrasting meanings for contrasting forms. Children assign contrasting meanings to distinct forms, but they don't always hit on the conventional adult contrasts. For example, in building up terms for birds, some children establish a three-way contrast quite early among *duck, bird,* and *chicken,* to group birds into those that go in the water, those that fly, and those that don't fly (Clark, 1978). Similarly, many children make use of the deictics *here* and *there* among their first 50 to 100 words, but they don't contrast these terms deictically. Instead, they typically use one term to mark transfers of possession, e.g., *Here* said as a child hands a rattle to his parent, and the other to mark completion of some activity, e.g., *There!* said as the child places the last block on a tower (Clark & Sengul, 1978). Such contrasts must often be revised as they learn more about the adult meanings.

Children may also assign idiosyncratic contrasts at the syntactic level. For example, in a study of early possessive constructions by Deutsch and Budwig (1983), children contrasted utterances containing their own name plus the term for some object, e.g., *Timmy book* with utterances containing a first person pronoun (*I, me, mine*) plus some object, e.g., *Me cookie*. The first type of utterance was used to describe current states—the object named was in the child's possession—while the second was used in situations where the child was

[4]Children do not necessarily identify the appropriate adult contrast, but they do impose *some* contrast. This may be modified later or even changed altogether as they learn more about the conventional meanings of all the terms in a particular domain.

laying claim to something not yet his (see also Budwig, 1985). Analogously, children acquiring Hungarian may contrast two different inflected forms of nouns to mark two different meanings. For instance, they may use the nominative or citation form in naming things and the accusative of the same nouns when talking about things they want to have (MacWhinney, 1985; Slobin, 1985b). In other words, even though they may not hit at first on the conventional contrasts adults use, children consistently assume that differences in form mark contrasts in meaning.

Finally, in assigning meanings to contrasting forms, children may tidy up the language by aligning one form with one meaning in a manner orthogonal to the match of meanings and forms in the adult language. In a study of Icelandic word-formation by Mulford (1983), some children used the suffix *-ari* (equivalent to English *-er*) only for agentive terms analogous to English forms like *worker,* and opted for a compound noun pattern (X + N) for instrument terms analogous to English *work-machine*. Icelandic-speaking adults, however, make use of both the suffix and the compound pattern for both agentive and instrumental nouns. Also a French child observed by his father (Vinson, 1915–16) took contracted *de* + article forms to be partitive in meaning, as in *du pain* for '[some] bread', and uncontracted forms to be possessive in meaning, as in *de la fille* 'of the girl, the girl's'. Contraction in fact occurs only when *de* is combined with masculine singular or with plural definite articles and appears in both partitive and possessive constructions. Vinson's son created a meaning contrast for contracted versus uncontracted forms that was orthogonal to the adult one. He then filled in the paradigm by constructing a contracted feminine form with partitive meaning, e.g., **da neige* '[some] snow', and using uncontracted masculine forms with possessive meaning, e.g., **de le garçon* for *du garçon* 'of the boy, the boy's.'

Children consistently act as if they assume different forms must have contrasting meanings. That is, they assume any new expressions contrast with those they already know.

Priority Goes to Known Words

In giving priority to words or expressions already familiar to them, children again reject apparent synonyms. The evidence for the second prediction comes from two main sources: early in language acquisition, children don't appear to realize that contrast operates both within and between levels for the lexicon and the grammar. Two- and three-year-olds consistently reject what appear to them to be multiple labels for the same thing. For instance, if an adult says of a dog, *There's an animal,* children object by saying, *No, it's a dog*. They act as if one cannot use *animal* because *dog* already carries the requisite meaning. They haven't yet recognized that there are contrasts between levels in the lexicon as well as within any one level. Young bilinguals also reject multiple labels across languages. Both within and across languages, children's reliance on form-meaning combinations already familiar to them leads them to reject further forms perceived as synonymous. Even in word-learning tasks, children reject synonyms.

Rejecting multiple labels within a language. Children aged two and three have long been known to reject multiple labels for things. Having learned one label for something, they are unwilling to accept a second even though it is superordinate or subordinate to the first (e.g., François, 1977; Macnamara, 1982; Mervis & Canada, 1981). These utterances from two-year-olds are typical:

(8) Not a plate, it a bowl. (upon being asked to take his plate off the table)
(9) That not a plane, that a jet-plane. (looking at a picture book)
(10) It's not a animal, it's a dog. (said of a toy)

What these children have not yet realized is that meanings may contrast in the levels of categorization being picked out. They act as if terms for the same domain all contrast at the same level. If the terms in these examples were at the same level, the pairs would have to be synonymous. Since the children already know one term for the object being referred to and don't accept synonymy, they reject the multiple labeling. Once they recognize that there is more than one level for labeling, such rejections vanish.

Rejecting multiple labels across languages. Young bilingual children face a similar problem. In the earliest stages of acquisition, they often accept only one label for a category despite exposure to a label from each language (e.g., Ervin-Tripp, 1974; Fantini, 1974; Taeschner, 1983). Knowing a term in one language appears to preclude use of the equivalent term from the second language, as in the following typical examples:

(11) English/Spanish: *leche* precludes *milk*
English/Spanish: *lupo* precludes *wolf*
English/French: *bird* precludes *oiseau*
German/Italian: *acqua* (water) precludes *Wassar*
German/Italian: *Beine* (legs) precludes *gambe*

The result, from the young child's point of view, is a single lexicon in which all the terms should contrast. This leads them to accept only one term (from whichever language they happen to pick up on first) for each category. The other is rejected. This typically lasts only a few months, until these children have a vocabulary of about 150 words (Taeschner, 1983). At that point, bilingual children begin to admit 'doublets', equivalent terms from both languages, e.g., *leche* and *milk,* into their vocabulary. This point may well coincide with the one at which young bilinguals also begin to distinguish their two languages on phonological grounds. Early on, they typically make use of a single phonological system as well as a single lexicon (e.g., Vogel, 1975). If young bilingual children at first believe they are dealing with a single language, their rejection of apparent synonyms follows directly from their assumption of contrast: different forms should carry different meanings. Bilingual children, however, start to accept equivalent terms in their two languages at a stage when monolingual children still reject as synonymous terms from a single level within their language. The only reason for young bilinguals to begin accepting equivalent terms across languages—essentially two labels for many of their categories—is their recognition that they are dealing with two distinct systems with the Principle of Contrast applying *within* each system, but not *across* systems. From that point on, they should only reject apparent synonyms within each language.

Children not only give priority to words already known and reject apparent synonyms within a language. They also do so across languages, but they reject apparent synonyms only until they realize they are dealing not with one but with two languages. Terms learned first, then, take priority over apparent synonyms, whether from within the same language or from another language. Where there is no synonymy, children simply add new terms and expressions to their growing repertoire.

Rejecting synonyms in word-learning tasks. Priority for known terms sometimes causes unanticipated problems. In 1950, Werner and Kaplan examined the difficulties children had in inferring the meanings of nonsense words used in a set of sentential contexts. Children found this a very difficult task. Most five-year-olds failed, and only some nine-year-olds did well. This occurred even though children add actual new words to their vocabulary at an average rate of nine a day from age two onwards (e.g., Carey, 1978; Templin, 1957). If children acquire real words so rapidly, why did they have such difficulty with Werner and Kaplan's task?

The task itself dealt in synonyms. To construct the sets of context sentences, Werner and Kaplan took English words like the noun *stick,* made up several sentences using the word *stick* (e.g., including the facts that sticks are used to walk with and burn easily), and then substituted a nonsense word like *corplum* for *stick* in each sentence. The children's task was to discover the meanings of the nonsense words—exact synonyms for English words they already knew.

This is indeed a major source of difficulty for children. In a replication of the Werner and Kaplan study by Braun-Lamesch (1962), French-speaking children were given sets of four sentences with a nonsense word substituted for a familiar French noun, verb, or adjective. (They were told the sentences had been produced by a second-language speaker who made some mistakes.) One hundred children (aged from five to nine) heard the sentences read one at a time and were asked to correct what was wrong in each set. As in Werner and Kaplan's original study, few of the younger children (under age seven) succeeded in supplying the target word across all four sentences in each set.

In Braun-Lamesch's second study (with five-, six-, and eight-year-olds), children heard similar sets of sentences, but with a pause in place of the target word. Under these conditions, six- and eight-year-olds found the task much easier than when they had to identify and correct the nonsense words. The youngest children also produced the appropriate target words more often. So if children aren't being asked to discover synonyms, they can make use of linguistic context to identify any words omitted. Gaps are easier to fill than places that are already taken.

In summary, when children are faced with apparent synonyms, they reject them. They do this within a language prior to discovering that terms at higher or lower levels of categorization are simply labels given at some other still contrasting level. They also do this across languages prior to discovering that they are working on two languages simultaneously. And, again for the same reason, they have difficulty in tasks where they have to discover exact synonyms for terms they already know.

Unfamiliar Words and Innovations Fill Gaps

Evidence for the third prediction comes from two sources. First, when children hear words new to them, they consistently assume these words designate kinds of things for which they lack terms themselves. They assign new terms to gaps in their lexicon. Second, when children themselves wish to talk about things for which they have no words, they often construct innovative terms on the spot.

Unfamiliar words fill gaps. When children hear an unfamiliar word, they appear to make some immediate inferences about what it might mean. This "rapid mapping," which appears to be the first step children take in figuring out what a word means, was first looked at experimentally by Carey and Bartlett (1978). In their study, nursery school children were exposed to one instance of an unfamiliar word in a color context (e.g., "Give me the chromium tray, not the red tray" in the presence of a red and an olive-green tray). A number of the children took *chromium* to be a color term, as Carey and Bartlett had intended, and remembered it as such a couple of weeks later, even if they got the target color wrong.

Do children hearing unfamiliar words consistently associate them with unfamiliar objects? In a follow-up study by Dockrell (1981), three- and four-year-olds were presented with a set of animals, three familiar (a cow, a pig, and a sheep) and one unfamiliar (a tapir), and then heard a novel word (*gombe*) in contrast to the familiar words for the known animals. All the children assumed the novel word picked out the novel animal.

The setting influences the inferences children make about unfamiliar words. For instance, children were given a set of solids of different colors, in two different linguistic contexts. In the shape context, children were asked for "the gombe one, not the square one or the round one." In the color context, they were asked for "the gombe one, not the green one or the red one." When the contrast was with known shapes, children consistently handed Dockrell the only solid unfamiliar to them. When the contrast was with color, they were more likely to select solids of an unusual color or with some pattern although some children still preferred shape.[5]

It has long been known that one- to two-year-olds attach new words they hear to unfamiliar objects (Vincent-Smith, Bricker, & Bricker, 1974). In a study by Golinkoff, Hirsh-Pasek, Lavallee, and Baduini (1985), two-year-olds were presented with a series of novel objects mixed in with familiar ones, and heard both familiar and unfamiliar labels. The children overwhelmingly selected a novel object as a referent for a novel word and an appropriate referent for a known word. Since all the objects in a set were equally familiar from prior handling and play, the children's assignments of labels could not be attributed just to the salience of a new object.

In the same study, two-year-olds also readily extended the novel word to a new exemplar from the same category. And, when given a choice (through the introduction of a second novel word with further novel objects from another category), these children preferred *not* to pair a second novel name with a novel object that had already been labeled. Instead, they assumed that the second novel name must refer to an as-yet-unnamed novel object. That is, these children assumed contrast rather than synonymy. Overall, these studies offer strong support for the hypothesis that children rely on contrast in their acquisition of the lexicon.

Gaps can be filled by innovative words. Young children typically have vocabularies much smaller than they need for talking about objects and activities. Yet this rarely limits what they talk about. To make do with the resources at their disposal, they stretch them. For example, they over-extend their words, they rely heavily on deictic terms like *that,* and they use general purpose verbs like *do* or *go.* They also construct innovative words (Clark, 1978, 1982a, 1983b).

Children's coinages appear from the earliest stages of acquisition on. Typical examples of innovative nouns, adjectives, and verbs, together with glosses of their intended meanings, are shown in Table 3. Children coin new verbs but only to talk about actions that contrast with those they already have words for. These

---

[5]The preference for shape in mapping the meanings of unfamiliar words may be a further reflection of the importance of shape in identifying instances of categories. In the overextensions used by one- and two-year-olds, the vast majority are based on similarities in shape (Clark, 1973; Thomson & Chapman, 1977).

TABLE 3
Some Spontaneous Coinages

Nouns:
a plate-egg vs. a cup-egg (2;0) = 'fried/boiled egg'
the car-smoke (2;6) = 'the car exhaust'
a tell-wind (2;6) = 'weather-vane'
plant-man (3;0) = 'gardener'
fix-man (3;0) = 'mechanic'
a driver (3;0) = 'ignition key'
a lessoner (4;0) = 'teacher'
Adjectives:
hay-y (3;3) = 'covered in hay'
salter (3;6) = 'saltier'
a windy parasol (4;0) = 'a parasol blown by the wind'
flyable (4;0) = 'able to fly' (of cocoons)
Verbs:
You have to scale it (2;4) = 'to weigh'
I'm darking the sky (2;6) = 'making dark/darkening'
How do you sharp this? (3;0) = 'sharpen'
String me up, mommy (3;2) = 'do up the string' (of a hat)
I'm crackering my soup (3;11) = 'putting crackers into'
We already decorationed our tree (4;11) = 'decorated'
I'm sticking it (5;7) = 'hitting with a stick'

actions are often very specific in that they involve particular instruments, places, or goals.[6]

They also coin nouns to talk about objects, and they again contrast these with terms they already know. English-speaking two-year-olds produce many innovative noun + noun compounds, e.g., *plate-egg* ('a fried egg') or *fire-dog* ('a dog like that found at the site of a local fire'). In a corpus of over 300 such compounds produced between age 2;2 and 3;2 (Clark, Gelman, & Lane, 1985), over two-thirds were used to mark explicit contrasts between subcategories, e.g., *tea-sieve* versus *water-sieve* (2;2) for a small and large strainer respectively, *snow-car* versus *race-car* (2;4) for pictures of a car with snow on it and a racing car respectively, and *car-truck* versus *cow-truck* (2;4) for pictures of a car-transporter and a cattle-truck respectively. In a follow-up elicitation task, two- and three-year-olds, like adults, relied on compounds far more often when they were labeling contrasting subcategories than when they were not (Clark, Gelman, & Lane, 1985). Finally, when presented with agentive and instrumental

[6]As in Dockrell's studies, when children are presented with verbs that contrast in form e.g., *walk* versus *make X walk*, or *kick* versus *foot*, they consistently interpret them as having contrasting meanings (Ammon, 1980; Clark, unpublished data).

TABLE 4
Examples of Illegitimate Innovations

Child Innovation	*Adult Pre-empter*
to broom	to sweep
to fire	to burn
to scale	to weigh
to babysitter	to babysit
to decoration	to decorate
a fix-man	a mechanic
a tooth-guy	a dentist
a lessoner	a teacher
a oarer	a rower
a locker	a lock

meanings for which there are no conventional terms available, young children freely coin innovative nouns upon demand (e.g., Clark & Berman, 1984; Clark & Hecht, 1982; Mulford, 1983).

The innovative terms children construct fill gaps in their lexicon. But since children have such a small vocabulary, many of their innovations express meanings for which there is already a conventional, established term in the language. What are gaps for children are often not gaps for adults. Children's innovations, then, can be divided into *legitimate* innovations that fill long-term gaps (innovations that could just as well have been produced by adults) and *illegitimate* ones that are actually pre-empted by established forms not yet acquired (see further Clark, 1981). Some examples of illegitimate innovations together with their pre-empters are given in Table 4. In each instance, children eventually have to give up their innovative form in favor of the conventional established one.

How do established forms take over from such innovations? Contrast again plays a crucial role. It is children's discovery that two forms do *not* contrast in meaning that leads to take-over by the established term. Imagine that children have expressed some meaning with term *a,* and this meaning is identical with the meaning expressed by *b,* the term consistently used by adults for that meaning. Since there is no contrast in meaning between *a* and *b,* children are faced with two different forms with a single meaning.[7] And this is a violation of Contrast. But since adults are consistent in using one form, *b,* in just the meaning slot children have assigned *a* to, the adult form takes priority over the child one. And children then give up their own form in favor of the established, conventional form for that meaning.

[7]Moreover, there are no phonological conditioning factors they can appeal to account for the difference in form, as there may be for case endings, say, where these can differ in form with the class of noun, for example, as well as with the number or gender of the stem (see further Slobin, 1985b).

In summary, children rely heavily on Contrast in filling gaps in their lexicon: unfamiliar words are assumed to denote categories for which they as yet have no words. At the same time, when they need to talk about categories for which they lack established words, they freely construct innovative terms for that purpose. In both cases, they are engaged in filling lexical gaps in accordance with Contrast.

THE ROLE OF CONTRAST IN MORPHOLOGY AND SYNTAX

Children replace their own coinages with established terms when they find no meaning contrast between the form they are using and the one adults use. The absence of a contrast in meaning leads them to choose one and eliminate the other. Since the form used by adults is already established in the lexicon, it takes priority. The same procedure applies with equal force in the acquisition of inflectional morphology and syntax.

Morphological Over-regularizations

Children are pattern-makers. And when they begin to acquire the inflections that mark tense, for instance, they typically take irregular verbs such as *break, bring,* and *go,* and treat them as if they belonged to the regular paradigm of *walk, open,* and *jump.* So the past tense of *break* is produced as *breaked, bring* as *bringed,* and *go* as *goed* (e.g., Berko, 1958; Cazden, 1968; Kuczaj, 1977). The initial basis for adding particular inflections and then for over-regularization appears to be semantic: verbs for change of state like *break* or *drop* are inflected for past tense before verbs for activity or state like *run* or *sleep* (Bloom, Lifter, & Hafitz, 1980). Moreover, the phonetic shape of the verb stem also affects the course of over-regularization. As Bybee and Slobin (1982) found, children first over-regularize verb stems that do not end in an alveolar stop (e.g., *break/breaked, bring/bringed, go/goed*). Verbs like *hit, ride,* or *eat* are left unchanged, because, argued Bybee and Slobin, they already conform to the past tense schema by ending with an alveolar stop (/t/ or /d/). It is only later, often after forms like *broke* and *went* have been mastered, that *hit* is over-regularized to *hitted* and *ride* to *rided.*

Once children have constructed over-regularized past tense forms, how do they get rid of them? Just as for the lexicon, the Principle of Contrast offers children crucial evidence for replacing regularized forms by irregular past tense forms. Suppose a child uses *breaked* as the past tense of *break* instead of *broke.* But that child hears only the *irregular* form *broke* from adults. He then notices that wherever he would use *breaked,* adults use *broke,* so his anticipations about the the form for a particular meaning are wrong. He realizes that the meaning conveyed by *broke* must be identical to the meaning of his own *breaked*. By the Principle of Contrast, different forms necessarily have different meanings. So if the meanings of two forms are the same, one form must be eliminated. The child therefore gives up his over-regularized form in favor of the established adult one (see also Platt & MacWhinney, 1983). Pre-emption works in morphology just as it does in the lexicon.

Children appear to extend rules to different verbs, for instance, on a rather gradual basis (Bloom et al., 1980). They presumably get rid of over-regularized forms in the same way. They should eliminate them one by one as they discover the absence of any difference in meaning between their own over-regularized forms and the forms adults use.[8] The evidence suggests that this is just what they do (e.g., Bybee & Slobin, 1982).

Syntactic Over-regularizations

Over-regularizations appear in syntax just as they do in morphology, though they are less well documented. The best examples, perhaps, come from Bowerman (1983). Bowerman classified the syntactic errors she observed in her two daughters' speech into several categories. One type consists of incorrect *Dative movement* with verbs like *say,* as in (12) and (13):

(12) (3;6) Don't say me that or you'll make me cry.
(13) (3;9) I do what my horsie says me to do.

or with verbs like *button,* as in (14):

(14) (3;4, asking to have the remaining snaps on her pajamas fastened) Button me the rest.

Further instances are documented by Mazurkewicz and White (1984). A second type of syntactic over-regularization involves *Passivization* with verbs like *fall:*[9]

(15) (4+) I don't like being falled down on!

---

[8]At the same time, children clearly set up routines for producing particular forms that may endure beyond the point where they distinguish the conventional form from their own, and will acknowledge, when pressed, that the conventional form is ''right'' or is the one grown-ups use (see Platt & MacWhinney, 1983; Slobin, 1978) even though they themselves do not yet produce the latter with consistency. Instances of over-regularization may well linger on after children have begun to produce the appropriate irregular past tense forms just because the children have become used to saying the past-tense form of a verb that way. After all, they have been doing so for three or four years.

[9]Part of the problem here may be with the prepositions allowed with passive verbs. Verbs with particles and prepositions tend to be less favored for passivization. My thanks to Dwight Bolinger for this observation.

A third involves *Causativization,* with such verbs as *disappear* or *ache* appearing incorrectly as causatives as well as correctly as intransitives:

(16) (6+) Do you want to see us disappear our heads?

(17) (5;3, as she climbs a long flight of stairs)
This is aching my legs.

A fourth type involves *Figure-ground reversals.* These are exemplified by the two patterns in "The garden swarmed with bees" and "Bees swarmed in the garden." They were used with verbs like *cover* or *spill* that normally appear in only one of the two patterns:

(18) (4;5) I'm going to cover a screen over me.
(for 'cover myself with')

(19) (5;0, of a salt shaker) Can I fill some salt into the bear?
(for 'fill the bear with salt')

(20) (4;11, after being asked if she was going to finish her toast)
I don't want to because I spilled it of orange juice.
(for 'spilled orange juice on it')

In all these over-regularizations, the children have extended a syntactic pattern to further instances that do not belong.[10]

Syntactic over-regularizations have also been documented by Mazurkewicz and White (1984) for verbs that do and don't allow dative alternation. Verbs that do allow it appear with their indirect object either adjacent to the verb (NP NP) or marked by the preposition *to* (NP PP) as in *Rob gave Jan the book/Rob gave the book to Jan,* while verbs with NP PP forms only do not allow alternation as in *Rob donated the picture to the museum/*Rob donated the museum the picture.* It has commonly been assumed that children learn which verbs do and don't take both constructions on an item-by-item basis through positive evidence alone (e.g., Baker, 1979).[11] However, as Mazurkewicz and White found, nine-, twelve-, and sixteen-year-olds[12] judged as grammatical many instances of NP

---

[10]One issue is whether these errors are lexical or syntactic. The decision appears to depend on one's grammatical frame of reference with some approaches including them in the syntax and others excluding them.

[11]The evidence that children receive no negative feedback tends to rest on a single study carried out by Brown and Hanlon in 1970. While parents may not directly approve or disapprove the syntactic forms their children produce, recent work shows that adults are more likely to repeat ungrammatical utterances from two-year-olds, with corrections, than they are grammatical utterances (Hirsh-Pasek, Treiman, & Schneiderman, 1984). The range of indirect, corrective (negative) feedback available to children at different ages and stages is badly in need of further documentation.

[12]Children younger than this are typically unfamiliar with many Latinate verbs of the type that appear to be over-regularized, e.g., *suggest, create,* or *capture* in *for*-dative constructions. The

NP constructions where only NP PP forms appear for adults. That is, these children over-regularized the syntactic paradigm of verbs like *give* to verbs like *donate*. Syntactic over-regularizations of *to*-dative verbs, according to Mazurkewicz and White, are eliminated by age 12;0, and those of *for*-datives verbs are virtually gone by age 16;0.

How do children arrive at the established, conventional forms? Part of the answer lies in their identification of semantic contrasts between pairs of successive configurations and their detection of the absence of pertinent contrasts. Let's take the intransitive verb *to disappear:* it is frequently over-regularized (from as young as age three) to a transitive structure, as in *I disappeared the box*. The transitive meaning, though, is conventionally expressed by a periphrastic construction, *to make X disappear*. Once children realize that there is no difference in meaning between their form and the adult one, they give up their form.[13] Absence of a contrast in such instances is as critical as presence of a contrast elsewhere. Take the case of *give* (NP NP and NP PP) and *donate* (only NP PP). One difference between them is that the indirect object of *give* verbs is both a goal and eventual animate possessor. It contrasts in meaning with *donate* which occurs with inanimate, indirect object goals or beneficiaries. In the case of *give,* children hear the verb with both configurations, NP NP and NP PP. In the case of *donate,* they hear it only with NP PP. But absence of a form on its own in the input is not enough to eliminate NP NP for *donate*. Children also discover, from their erroneous *anticipations* of NP NP that *donate* with NP PP is the only configuration adults use with *donate*. From this, they infer that there is no meaning contrast marked by dative-alternation for *donate,* and they therefore give up their over-regularization of *donate* with NP NP.

So far investigators have only just begun to explore over-regularizations in syntax.[14] Sometimes over-regularized constructions are pre-empted by other constructions conventionally used to express just the meaning children attempt to convey through regularization. At other times, they may result from missing a subtle contrast in meaning between two otherwise related construction types.

---

reason for this unfamiliarity is probably that the Latinate verbs differ in register from their non-Latinate counterparts. Latinate connotes a higher or more formal register of speech. In addition, a Latinate verb like *donate* is typically more specific in meaning than its non-Latinate counterpart *give*. As a result, the class of things one may donate is much more restricted than the class of things one may give. The greater specificity of Latinate verbs also shows up in the fact that idiomatic or metaphorical extensions typically stem from non-Latinate rather than Latinate forms. My thanks to Dan I. Slobin for discussion on these points.

[13]The exact nature of the mechanism at work has yet to be specified in detail, but to achieve this, children have to be able to monitor their own production as well as compare it continually against comprehension (see further Clark, 1982b; MacWhinney, 1978).

[14]Few researchers have observed or tested children over the age of 5;0 or 6;0, so there are few data available on syntactic over-regularizations. Two things are needed: longitudinal observations to a much later age to explore the range of spontaneous over-regularizations in syntax, and systematic elicitation of the pertinent forms.

Discovering these subtleties may take children a long time. In either case, contrast is a crucial ingredient in discovering which syntactic forms convey which meanings.

CONTRAST AND THE COURSE OF ACQUISITION

The Principle of Contrast also helps account for the different courses children follow in acquisition. Although there are many consistencies in the routes children follow, there is also much variation from child to child. Children necessarily build, as they learn more, on what they already know. But they vary in the particular expressions they are exposed to and hence in the stage at which they acquire such expressions. Equally, differences in exposure may lead children to different initial hypotheses about word meanings. These in turn may point children along different paths en route to the adult analysis.

Children with similar input, for example, may differ in the course they follow in organizing their lexicon. Consider their acquisition of terms for animals. Child A acquires the term *dog* as his first term at a point when his vocabulary totals 20 words. Child B acquires the same term, *dog,* as her fifth term for an animal (following *cat, horse, cow,* and *rabbit*), at a point where her vocabulary totals 150 words. The set of contrasts within the domain of animals for these two children is very different. Child A contrasts *dog* as the sole animal term with his other 20 words drawn from several domains. Child B contrasts *dog* with each of four other animal terms, and with the rest of her vocabulary, some five times larger than A's. In the lexicon, different points of acquisition for the same expression may lead to different lexical organizations from child to child. The general point in acquisition is this: What's already been acquired affects what gets acquired next.

When children are exposed to markedly different types of input, it seems less surprising that they might follow different courses. Such differences in input may stem from several sources—from adults, from older siblings, and from peers—and may vary in amount and in influence from culture to culture and even within cultures (e.g., Heath, 1983; Ochs, 1985; Schieffelin, 1985; Snow & Ferguson, 1977). Such differences should affect the initial "fast mapping" children make following their first encounter with a new word (Carey, 1978; Dockrell, 1981). For example, in the acquisition of the dimensional adjectives *tall* and *long,* children's initial meanings appear to depend directly on the kinds of objects they first hear the terms applied to—trees, fences, buildings, shelves, or pencils (Keil & Carroll, 1980; Gelman, Ravn, & Maloney, 1985). This in turn affects the pattern of contrasts they construct as they build up this lexical domain.

The routes children follow in getting to the adult meaning may also depend on the initial hypothesis they form about the meaning of a word. For example, once children begin to work out the deictic meanings of terms like *here* and *there,* some children opt for the hypothesis that *here* designates the place where the child is (ego-centered), while others identify *here* with where the speaker is (speaker-centered). These two starting points lead children to follow different routes as they work out the meaning relations conveyed by *here* and *there* (Clark & Sengul, 1978). These routes converge when children arrive at the adult meanings. But the hypotheses children start with, I suggest, depend on the contrasts they have already worked out for locative and deictic terms; it is what they already know that points them in one direction rather than another.

Whatever the variations in the courses children follow, the Principle of Contrast operates in the same way. What children already know at each step affects how they deal with each new form—in the lexicon, in morphology, and in syntax.

SPECIAL CASES OF CONTRAST

The Principle of Contrast appears in several more specific proposals designed to account for constraints children seem to observe during acquisition. The first of these is Slobin's (1973, 1985a) *Unifunctionality,* which assumes one-to-one mapping of forms and meanings. The second is Markman's (1984) *Mutal Exclusivity:* it assumes contrast among category labels at a single level. Another proposal is the *M-constraint* examined by Keil (1979), and the last proposal is *Uniqueness,* put forward in a learnability framework by Wexler and Culicover in 1980 and since then extended by others. Each of these proposals, I will argue, represents a special case of the Principle of Contrast.

Unifunctionality. In 1973, Slobin discussed several instances where children appeared to have adopted a one-to-one mapping of forms and meanings in language. He appealed to one-to-one mapping to account for children's over-uses of a single inflectional form to mark a particular meaning, e.g., instrumental *-om* in Russian added to all nouns regardless of gender, past tense *-ed* in English added to regular and irregular verbs alike. Under this view, children hold onto such unifunctional mappings until forced to give them up in light of many meanings with one form or many forms with one meaning.[15]

This Unifunctionality, Slobin (1985a) argued, is what leads children to maximize one-to-one mappings of forms and meanings. Slobin called on two kinds of evidence: first, the morphological over-regularizations children use where a single form marks a particular modulation in meaning; and second, the construction

[15]The latter is actually hard, if not impossible, to find. In case systems, the forms of inflections for a particular case can vary with gender, number, and person. Verb inflections to mark aspect or tense also vary with person and number, as well as mood or even negativity (Bybee, 1985). That is, different forms are not used to express the same meaning.

of additional forms to distinguish two closely allied meanings carried, for adults, by a single form.[16] For instance, French-speaking five- to seven-year olds sometimes construct additional forms to distinguish, for example, the numeral 'one' from the indefinite 'a' meaning of the indefinite article, e.g., *une voiture* 'a car' versus **une de voiture* 'one car' (Karmiloff-Smith, 1977, 1979).

Unifunctionality is actually a complex principle. It has two parts: *1*. Each form carries a different meaning, and *2*. Each meaning is carried by a different form. In other words, it combines the Principle of Contrast (no synonymy) with the Homonymy Assumption (no homonymy). This combination is necessarily more restricted in scope than Contrast alone because it requires not only Contrast but also the Homonymy Assumption. But as we saw earlier, this assumption doesn't hold in general. In fact, children violate the Homonymy Assumption from early on. In English, for instance, two-year-olds have no difficulty treating the inflection *-s* as marking plural on nouns (e.g., *dogs*), possessive on nouns (*the girl's*), and third person singular present on verbs (*goes*). From two or three on, children have no difficulty with *-er* appearing both as a nominal suffix on agent and instrument nouns (e.g., *rainer* 'someone who stops it raining' or *locker* 'a lock') and as a comparative suffix on adjectives (e.g., *gooder*). Nor do they appear to have any difficulty with such homonyms in the lexicon as *bank, bat, bee/be, pair/pear, sea/see,* or *two/too*. Yet children who tolerate homonyms do not tolerate synonyms.

Unifunctionality as a constraint on language acquisition, then, is only half correct: children do observe Contrast but they don't observe the Homonymy Assumption. So once we discard the second half of Unifunctionality, we are left with Contrast pure and simple. Unifunctionality, then, should be replaced by the Principle of Contrast.

Mutual Exclusivity. The second proposal is Markman's (1984) Mutual Exclusivity. As she put it (1984, p. 403), "Category terms will tend to be mutually exclusive." The labels children apply to categories are treated as mutually exclusive because this makes them more useful in picking out instances of different categories: "For example, an object cannot be a cat *and* a dog or a bird or a horse" (1984, pp. 403–404). Mutual Exclusivity, she argued, is needed to account for the discreteness of children's labels for object categories and for the fact that children assume unfamiliar words label instances of categories, e.g., kinds of dogs, rather than thematic groupings of related objects, e.g., a dog and a bone (Markman & Hutchinson, 1984). Since many of the labels children learn early are labels for basic-level categories, Mutual Exclusivity offers a useful way of characterizing how children use such labels. Once they realize that labels

[16]Slobin (1985a) puts this in the form of the following Operating Principle: "If you discover that a linguistic form expresses two closely related but distinguishable notions, use available means in your language to distinctly mark the two notions."

apply at different levels in a taxonomy, though, they must give up Mutual Exclusivity. So this constraint, Markman argued, applies for only a relatively brief period during acquisition.

Mutual Exclusivity, like Unifunctionality, is a complex principle. It consists of three distinct parts. The first is equivalent to the Principle of Contrast: different forms have different meanings. The second I will call the Principle of No Overlap: terms at one level in a semantic field (*dog, horse*) denote non-overlapping categories. This is a general assumption about terms in semantic fields, and it holds just as much for adults as for children. The third part is what I will call the Single Level Assumption: all terms are at only one level of the lexicon. So all contrasts are like *dog* versus *horse*. None are like *dog* versus *animal*. So what Markman argued, in effect, is that children have a Single Level Assumption, which they give up as they learn terms at different levels. Children do not give up either the Principle of Contrast or the Principle of No Overlap. So by recasting Markman's hypothesis in this form, we can see what assumption it is that children actually give up and what it is they retain.

While Mutual Exclusivity superficially appears to be equivalent to the Principle of Contrast, it actually embodies two other principles besides. And even when children leave off using that part of Mutual Exclusivity captured in the Single Level Assumption, they continue to rely on Contrast.

The M-Constraint. The so-called M-Constraint studied by Keil (1979) is a constraint on the predicates that apply to ontological categories. These categories, it is assumed, form a rigid hierarchy or tree structure. An M structure is one where two predicates apply to a single category, as follows:

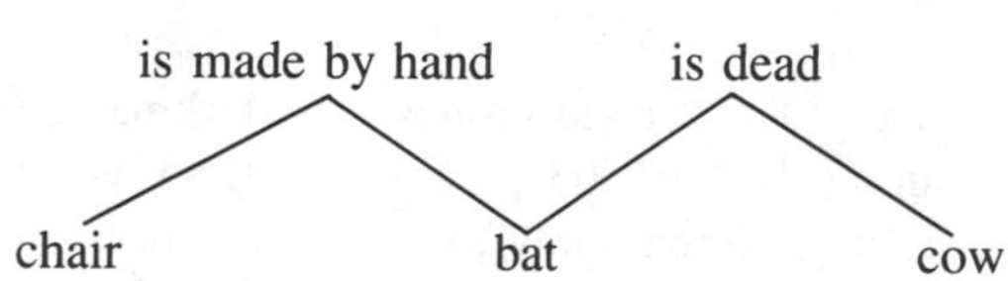

The assumption is that M structures are disallowed, so the term *bat* must be a homonym. It picks out both the instrument used in games and the small nocturnal mammal, two distinct categories. W structures like this one are also disallowed:

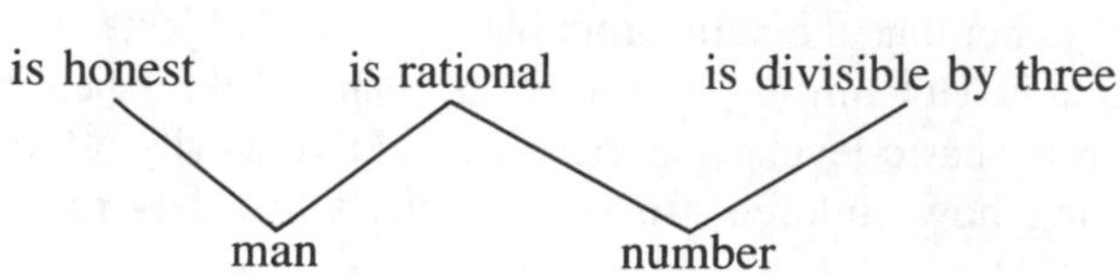

As a result, the predicate *is rational* must be a homonym with two distinct meanings, the first 'having reason' and the second 'is expressible as a fraction'.

M and W structures without ambiguous terms do not occur, according to the M-Constraint.[17] That is, the M-Constraint requires rejection of the Homonymy Assumption.

In language, according to Keil (1979, p. 168f.), the M-Constraint offers a source of information about the properties of referents for new words, and hence clues to word meaning. Suppose a child hears *The boojum is hungry,* he can then infer of boojums that they have mass and are animals (Keil, 1979, p. 168f.). That is, the new term *boojum* inherits all the predicates above it in the tree the child has constructed to date as well as *is hungry*. There is nothing in the M-Constraint itself that requires terms appearing with the same predicates to contrast, yet Contrast is needed for the scheme to work. For instance, when a child hears *The boojum is hungry,* nothing in the M-Constraint per se prevents the child from assuming that *boojum* is synonymous with *dog* or anything else that can be hungry. So although the M-Constraint correctly disallows the Homonymy Assumption, it doesn't require Contrast. Yet it cannot work without it. Not until children hear predicates applied that force a meaning difference, do they need assume any contrast between *boojum* and *dog,* and they might never hear pertinent evidence for this conclusion.

The M-Constraint (whether or not it holds on other grounds) requires that the Homonymy Assumption be rejected, and it requires *tacit* observance of Contrast, namely that any difference in form is taken to mark a difference in meaning.[18] Without the Principle of Contrast, the M-constraint does not work.

Uniqueness. The final proposal is the Uniqueness Principle, put forward by Wexler and Culicover (1980) and assumed necessary in learnability for the acquisition of syntax. Wexler and Culicover (1980) argued that children take each surface form in the input as the expression of a single 'deep structure', which corresponds to a single meaning, unless they hear evidence that the same form is used for more than one meaning. This constrains the surface structures a given deep structure can map onto. That is, the same meaning can't be expressed by two different forms. Without this, Wexler and Culicover argued, there is no way for children to work back from surface sentence structures to the underlying meanings.

Wexler and Culicover applied Uniqueness only to syntax, but it has been extended since by Grimshaw (1981), Pinker (1984), and Roeper (1981) to morphology. Like Platt and MacWhinney (1983), Pinker (1986) argued that Uniqueness is at work when children remove regularized forms from their own speech, as when they replace *breaked* with *broke:*

---

[17]This is equivalent to Bever and Rosenbaum's (1970) argument that daughter nodes in a tree structure cannot converge.

[18]Besides relying on the Principle of Contrast, it also appears to rely on the Principle of No Overlap.

> There may be at most a single realization of a given form [e.g., the past tense of *break*] in a language, unless there is direct positive evidence in the input for more than one form, in which case both forms may be retained (p. 71).

For *breaked* and *broke,* of course, the elimination of *breaked* by Uniqueness is equivalent to pre-emption by synonymy. However, for Uniqueness to be fully equivalent to Contrast, one would have to motivate such pre-emptions on semantic grounds. In Pinker's account, the constraint is simply stipulated.[19] Notice that Pinker allowed for more than one form if "there is direct positive evidence in the input for more than one form". But unless such forms have different meanings, this violates the Principle of Contrast. If the meanings are different, then this must be specified by Uniqueness. Otherwise, there is no way for children to tell that *came* and *went,* for example, aren't both realizations of the past tense of *come*. That is, the semantic motivation assumed by Wexler and Culicover is essential for Uniqueness to work. Without it, children would be unable to analyze forms in the input. And once Uniqueness is motivated semantically, it becomes equivalent to the Principle of Contrast. In other words, adherents of Wexler and Culicover's Uniqueness have in fact espoused the Principle of Contrast.

CONCLUSION

The Principle of Contrast is inherent in language. It is a principle essential both to skilled users of a language and to children who are just acquiring their first words. Yet, because Contrast is so basic, it is often taken for granted, and its power ignored. The Principle of Contrast offers a powerful tool to children acquiring language. It constrains the inferences they can make about possible meanings for new forms by distinguishing them from already familiar forms. The general predictions made by this principle fall under three headings: that differences in form make for differences in meaning, that established words take priority over innovations, and that gaps in the child's lexicon are filled by unfamiliar words on the one hand or can be filled by innovative ones on the other. Each of these predictions is strongly supported by the evidence. Moreover, the evidence suggests that the Principle of Contrast operates, for children, from very early in the process of acquisition.

The Principle of Contrast is important for another reason too: it helps account for differences in the course of acquisition across children. Children necessarily build in language on what they already know. But since they vary in when and how they are exposed to specific expressions, they differ in their points of

---

[19] In discussing the need for motivation, Pinker did suggest avoidance of synonymy might be a candidate (1986, p. 74).

acquisition. And, depending on their initial hypotheses about the meanings of new forms, children may follow quite different routes in arriving at the adult analysis.

Every theory of acquisition tacitly assumes that when children hear new forms—whether in phonology, morphology, syntax, or the lexicon—they infer that these forms carry new meanings. Every theory, then, subscribes to the Principle of Contrast. But Contrast also motivates children in acquisition itself. It motivates them to acquire new forms at every level in language. And it motivates them to get rid of unconventional, over-regularized forms, again at every level. As a tool for acquisition, the Principle of Contrast is invaluable.

ACKNOWLEDGMENTS

Preparation of this chapter was supported in part by a grant from the National Institute of Child Health and Human Development (NICHHD 5 R01 HD18908) and in part by the Sloan Foundation. I would particularly like to acknowledge my debt to Melissa Bowerman and Herbert H. Clark for many discussions of meaning and contrast over the years; to Thomas G. Bever, Frank Keil, and Ellen M. Markman for their questions about the scope of the present arguments; and to Dwight Bolinger for his helpful comments. Herbert H. Clark and Judith G. Hochberg offered invaluable criticisms and suggestions on an earlier draft.

REFERENCES

Ammon, M. S. H. (1980). Development in the linguistic expression of causal relations: Comprehension of features of lexical and periphrastic causatives. Unpublished PhD dissertation, University of California at Berkeley.

Aronoff, M. (1976). *Word-formation in generative grammar.* (Linguistic Inquiry Monograph 1.) Cambridge, MA: MIT Press.

Baker, C. L. (1979). Syntactic theory and the projection problem. *Linguistic Inquiry 10,* 533–581.

Berko, J. (1958). The child's learning of English morphology. *Word 14,* 150–177.

Bever, T. G., & Rosenbaum, P. S. (1970). Some lexical structures and their empirical validity. In R. A. Jacobs & P. S. Rosenbaum (Eds.), *Readings in English transformational grammar.* Waltham, MA: Ginn & Co., pp. 3–19.

Bierwisch, M. (1967). Some semantic universals of German adjectivals. *Foundations of Language 3,* 1–36.

Bloom, L., Lifter, K., & Hafitz, J. (1980). Semantics of verbs and the development of verb inflection in child language. *Language 56,* 386–412.

Bolinger, D. (1975). *Aspects of language* (2nd. ed.). New York: Harcourt Brace Jovanovich.

Bolinger, D. (1977). *Meaning and form.* London: Longman.

Bowerman, M. (1983). How do children avoid constructing an overly general grammar in the absence of feedback about what is not a sentence? *Papers & Reports on Child Language Development* [Stanford University] *22,* 23–35.

Braun–Lamesch, M. M. (1962). Le rôle du contexte dans la compréhension du langage chez l'enfant. *Psychologie Française 7,* 180–189.

Brown, R., & Hanlon, C. (1970). Derivational complexity and order of acquisition in child speech. In J. R. Hayes (Ed.), *Cognition and the development of language*. New York: John Wiley & Sons, pp. 11–53.

Budwig, N. (1985). I, me, my, and 'name': Children's early systematizations of forms, meanings, and functions in talk about the self. *Papers & Reports on Child Language Development* [Stanford University] *24*, 30–37.

Bybee, J. (1985). *Morphology: A study of the relations between meaning and form*. Amsterdam: John Benjamins.

Bybee, J., & Slobin, D. I. (1982). Rules and schemas in the development and use of the English past tense. *Language 58*, 265–289.

Carey, S. (1978). The child as word-learner. In M. Halle, J. Bresnan, & G. A. Miller (Eds.), *Linguistic theory and psychological reality*. Cambridge, MA: MIT Press, pp. 264–293.

Carey, S., & Bartlett, E. (1978). Acquiring a single new word. *Paper & Reports on Child Language Development* [Stanford University] *15*, 17–29.

Cazden, C. B. (1968). The acquisition of noun and verb inflections. *Child Development 39*, 433–448.

Chafe, W. L. (1971). Directionality and paraphrase. *Language 47*, 1–26.

Clark, E. V. (1972). On the acquisition of antonyms in two semantic fields. *Journal of Verbal Learning & Verbal Behavior 11*, 750–758.

Clark, E. V. (1973). What's in a word? On the child's acquisition of semantics in his first language. In T. E. Moore (Ed.), *Cognitive development and the acquisition of language*. New York: Academic Press, pp. 65–110.

Clark, E. V. (1978). Discovering what words can do. In D. Farkas, W. M. Jacobsen, & K. W. Todrys (Eds.), *Papers from the parasession on the lexicon*. Chicago, IL: Chicago Linguistic Society, pp. 34–57.

Clark, E. V. (1980a). Convention and innovation in acquiring the lexicon. (Keynote Address, Twelfth Annual Child Language Research Forum, Stanford.) *Papers & Reports on Child Language Development* [Stanford University] *19*, 1–20.

Clark, E. V. (1980b). Here's the *top:* Nonlinguistic strategies in the acquisition of orientational terms. *Child Development 51*, 329–338.

Clark, E. V. (1981). Lexical innovations: How children learn to create new words. In W. Deutsch (Ed.), *The child's construction of language*. London: Academic Press, pp. 299–328.

Clark, E. V. (1982a). The young word-maker: A case study of innovation in the child's lexicon. In E. Wanner & L. R. Gleitman (Eds.), *Language acquisition: The state of the art*. Cambridge, England: Cambridge University Press, pp. 390–425.

Clark, E. V. (1982b). Language change during language acquisition. In M. E. Lamb & A. L. Brown (Eds.), *Advances in developmental psychology*, vol 2. Hillsdale, NJ: Lawrence Erlbaum Associates, pp. 171–195.

Clark, E. V. (1983a). Convention and contrast in acquiring the lexicon. In Th. B. Seiler & W. Wannenmacher (Eds.), *Cognitive development and the development of word meaning*. Berlin & New York: Springer, pp. 67–89.

Clark, E. V. (1983b). Meanings and concepts. In J. H. Flavell & E. M. Markman (Eds.), *Handbook of child psychology*, vol. 3: *Cognitive development* (gen. ed. P. H. Mussen). New York: John Wiley & Sons, pp. 787–840.

Clark, E. V., & Berman, R. A. (1984). Structure and use in the acquisition of word formation. *Language 60*, 542–590.

Clark, E. V., & Clark, H. H. (1979). When nouns surface as verbs. *Language 55*, 547–590.

Clark, E. V., Gelman, S. A., & Lane, N. M. (1985). Noun compounds and category structure in young children. *Child Development 56*, 84–94.

Clark, E. V., & Hecht, B. F. (1982). Learning to coin agent and instrument nouns. *Cognition 12*, 1–24.

Clark, E. V., & Sengul, C. J. (1978). Strategies in the acquisition of deixis. *Journal of Child Language 5,* 457–475.

Clark, H. H. (1983). Making sense of nonce sense. In G. B. Flores d'Arcais & R. J. Jarvella (Eds.), *The process of language understanding.* New York: John Wiley & Sons, pp. 297–331.

Deutsch, W., & Budwig, N. (1983). Form and function in the development of possessives. *Papers & Reports on Child Language Development* [Stanford University] *22,* 36–42.

Dockrell, J. E. (1981). The child's acquisition of unfamiliar words: An experimental study. Unpublished doctoral dissertation, University of Stirling, Scotland.

Donaldson, M., & Wales, R. G. (1970). On the acquisition of some relational terms. In J. R Hayes (Ed.), *Cognition and the development of language.* New York: John Wiley & Sons, pp. 235–268.

Downing, P. (1977). On the creation and use of English compound nouns. *Language 53,* 810–842.

Ervin-Tripp, S. (1974). Is second language learning like the first? *TESOL Quarterly 8,* 111–127.

Fantini, A. E. (1974). *Language acquisition of a bilingual child: A sociolinguistic perspective (to age 5).* Brattleboro, VT: The Experiment Press.

Fillmore, C. J. (1978). On the organization of semantic information in the lexicon. In D. Farkas, W. M. Jacobsen, & K. W. Todrys (Eds.), *Papers from the parasession on the lexicon.* Chicago, IL: Chicago Linguistic Society, pp. 148–173.

François, D. (1977). Du pré-signe au signe. In F. François, D. François, E. Sabeau-Jouannet, & M. Sourdot, *La syntaxe de l'enfant avant 5 ans.* Paris: Librairie Larousse, pp. 53–89.

Gelman, S. A., Ravn, K. E., & Maloney, L. T. (1985). When "big" does not refer to overall size: Dimension adjectives in context. *Papers & Reports on Child Language Development* [Stanford University] *24,* 62–69.

Gentner, D. (1975). Evidence for the psychological reality of semantic components: The verbs of possession. In D. A. Norman, D. E. Rumelhart, & the LNR Research Group, *Explorations in cognition.* San Francisco, CA: W. H. Freeman, pp. 211–246.

Golinkoff, R. M., Hirsh-Pasek, K., Lavallee, A., & Baduini, C. (1985, October). What's in a word?: The young child's predisposition to use lexical contrast. Paper presented at the Boston University Conference on Child Language, Boston, Massachusetts.

Grégoire, A. (1937, 1947). *L'apprentissage du langage* (2 vols.). Paris: Droz.

Grimshaw, J. (1981). Form, function, and the language acquisition device. In C. L. Baker & J. J. McCarthy (Eds.), *The logical problem of language acquisition.* Cambridge, MA: MIT Press, pp. 165–182.

Gruber, J. (1976). *Lexical structures in syntax and semantics.* (North-Holland Linguistic Series 25.) Amsterdam: North-Holland Publishing Co.

Heath, S. B. (1983). *Ways with words: Language, life, and work in communities and classrooms.* Cambridge, England: Cambridge University Press.

Hirsh-Pasek, K., Treiman, R., & Schneiderman, M. (1984). Brown & Hanlon revisited: Mothers' sensitivity to ungrammatical forms. *Journal of Child Language 11,* 81–88.

Hofmann, T. R. (1982). Lexical blocking. *Journal of the Faculty of Humanities* [Toyama University, Japan] *5,* 239–250.

Hofmann, T. R. (1983). Lexical blocking II. *Journal of the Faculty of Humanities* [Toyama University, Japan] *6,* 119–145.

Joos, M. (1961). *The five clocks.* New York: Harcourt, Brace & World.

Karius, I. (1985). *Die Ableitung der denominalen Verben mit Nullsuffigierung im Englischen.* Tübingen: Niemeyer Verlag.

Karmiloff-Smith, A. (1977). More about the same: Children's understanding of post-articles. *Journal of Child Language 4,* 377–394.

Karmiloff-Smith, A. (1979). *A functional approach to child language.* Cambridge, England: Cambridge University Press.

Kay, P. (1971). Taxonomy and semantic contrast. *Language 47,* 866–887.

Keil, F. C. (1979). *Semantic and conceptual development: An ontological perspective*. Cambridge, MA: Harvard University Press.

Keil, F. C., & Carroll, J. (1980). The child's acquisition of ''tall'': Implications for an alternative view of semantic development. *Papers & Reports on Child Language Development* [Stanford University] *19,* 21–28.

Kiparsky, P. (1983). Word-formation and the lexicon. In F. Ingemann (Ed.), *Proceedings of the 1982 mid-America linguistics conference*. Lawrence, KS: University of Kansas, Department of Linguistics, pp. 47–78.

Kuczaj, S. A., II (1977). The acquisition of regular and irregular past tense forms. *Journal of Verbal Learning & Verbal Behavior 16,* 589–600.

Kuczaj, S. A., & Maratsos, M. P. (1975). On the acquisition of *front, back,* and *side*. *Child Development 46,* 202–210.

Lakoff, R. (1973). The logic of politeness, or minding your p's and q's. In C. Corum, T. C. Smith-Stark, & A. Weiser (Eds.), *Papers from the ninth regional meeting*. Chicago, Illinois: Chicago Linguistic Society, pp. 292–305.

Lehrer, A. (1974). *Semantic fields and lexical structure*. (North-Holland Linguistic Series 11.) Amsterdam: North-Holland Publishing Company.

Leopold, W. F. (1939–49). *Speech development of a bilingual child* (4 vols.). Evanston, IL: Northwestern University Press.

Lyons, J. (1963). *Structural semantics*. Oxford: Blackwell.

Lyons, J. (1977). *Semantics* (2 vols.). Cambridge, England: Cambridge University Press.

McCawley, J. D. (1978). Conversational implicature and the lexicon. In P. Cole (Ed.), *Syntax and semantics, vol. 9: Pragmatics*. New York: Academic Press, pp. 245–259.

Macnamara, J. (1982). *Names for things: A study of human learning*. Cambridge, MA: MIT Press.

MacWhinney, B. (1978). The acquisition of morphophonology. *Monographs of the Society for Research in Child Development 43* (Serial No. 174).

MacWhinney, B. (1985). Hungarian language acquisition as an exemplification of a general model of grammatical development. In D. I. Slobin (Ed.), *The crosslinguistic study of language acquisition (*vol. 2.) Hillsdale, N.J.: Lawrence Erlbaum Associates, pp. 1069–1155.

Markman, E. M. (1984). The acquisition and hierarchical organization of categories by children. In C. Sophian (Ed.), *Origins of cognitive skills: The 18th annual Carnegie symposium on cognition*. Hillsdale, NJ: Lawrence Erlbaum Associates, pp. 376–406.

Markman, E. M., & Hutchinson, J. (1984). Children's sensitivity to constraints on word meaning: Taxonomic vs thematic relations. *Cognitive Psychology 16,* 1–27.

Mazurkewich, I., & White, L. (1984). The acquisition of the dative-alternation: Unlearning overgeneralizations. *Cognition 16,* 261–283.

Mervis, C. B., & Canada, K. (1981, April). Child-basic categories and early lexical development. Paper presented at the Biennial Meeting of the Society for Research in Child Development, Boston, Massachusetts.

Mulford, R. C. (1983). On the acquisition of derivational morphology in Icelandic: Learning about *-ari. Islenskt mál og almenn málfraedi 5,* 105–125.

Nunberg, G. (1978). Slang, usage conditions, and l'arbitraire du signe. In D. Farkas, W. M. Jacobsen, & K. W. Todrys (Eds.), *Papers from the parasession on the lexicon*. Chicago, IL: Chicago Linguistic Society, pp. 301–311.

Ochs, E. (1985). Variation and error: A sociolinguistic approach to language acquisition in Samoan. In D. I. Slobin (Ed.), *The crosslinguistic study of language acquisition* (vol. 1). Hillsdale, NJ: Lawrence Erlbaum Associates, pp. 783–838.

Orr, J. (1962). *Three studies on homonymics*. Edinburgh: Edinburgh University Press.

Orwell, G. (1950). Politics and the English language. In *Shooting an elephant and other essays*. New York: Harcourt, Brace & World, pp. 77–92.

Palmer, F. R. (1981). *Semantics*. (2nd. ed.) Cambridge, England: Cambridge University Press.

Pavlovitch, M. (1920). *Le langage enfantin: Acquisition du serbe et du français par un enfant serbe*. Paris: Champion.

Pinker, S. (1984). *Language learnability and language development.* Cambridge, MA: Harvard University Press.

Pinker, S. (1986). Productivity and conservatism in language acquisition. In W. Demopoulos & A. Marras (Eds.), *Language learning and concept acquisition.* Norwood, NJ: Ablex, pp. 54–79.

Platt, C. B., & MacWhinney, B. (1983). Error assimilation as a mechanism in language learning. *Journal of Child Language 10,* 401–414.

Roeper, T. (1981). On the deductive model and the acquisition of productive morphology. In C. L. Baker & J. J. McCarthy (Eds.), *The logical problem of language acquisition.* Cambridge, MA: MIT Press, pp. 129–150.

Salkoff, M. (1983). Bees are swarming in the garden. *Language 59,* 288–346.

Schieffelin, B. (1985). Acquisition of Kaluli. In D. I. Slobin (Ed.), *The crosslinguistic study of language acquisition* (vol. 1). Hillsdale, NJ: Lawrence Erlbaum Associates, pp. 525–593.

Shibatani, M. (1976). The grammar of causative constructions: A conspectus. In M. Shibatani (Ed.), *Syntax and semantics,* vol. 6: *The grammar of causative constructions.* New York: Academic Press, pp. 1–40.

Slobin, D. I. (1973). Cognitive prerequisites for the development of grammar. In C. A. Ferguson & D. I. Slobin (Eds.), *Studies of child language development.* New York: Holt, Rinehart & Winston, pp. 175–208.

Slobin, D. I. (1978). A case study of early language awareness. In A. Sinclair, R. J. Jarvella, & W. J. M. Levelt (Eds.), *The child's conception of language.* Berlin & New York: Springer, pp. 45–54.

Slobin, D. I. (1985a). Crosslinguistic evidence for the language-making capacity. In D. I. Slobin (Ed.), *The crosslinguistic study of language acquisition* (vol. 2). Hillsdale, NJ: Lawrence Erlbaum Associates, pp. 1157–1260.

Slobin, D. I. (1985b, October). Developmental paths between form and meaning: Crosslinguistic and diachronic perspectives. Keynote Address, Tenth Annual Boston University Conference on Child Language, Boston, Massachusetts.

Snow, C. E., & Ferguson, C. A. (Eds.). (1977). *Talking to children: Language input and language acquisition.* Cambridge, England: Cambridge University Press.

Taeschner, T. (1983). *The sun is feminine: A study on language acquisition in bilingual children.* Berlin & New York: Springer.

Templin, M. C. (1957). Certain language skills in children: Their development and interrelationships. *University of Minnesota Institute of Child Welfare Monograph 26.*

Thomson, J. R., & Chapman, R. S. (1977). Who is 'Daddy' revisited: The status of two-year-olds' over-extended words in use and comprehension. *Journal of Child Language 4,* 359–375.

Vincent-Smith, L., Bricker, D., & Bricker, W. (1974). Acquisition of receptive vocabulary in the child. *Child Development 45,* 189–193.

Vinson, J. (1915–1916). Observations sur le développement du langage chez l'enfant. *Revue de Linguistique et de Philologie Comparée 48,* 1–39.

Vogel, I. (1975). One system or two: An analysis of a two-year-old Romanian-English bilingual's phonology. *Papers & Reports on Child Language Development* [Stanford University] *9,* 43–62.

Werner, H., & Kaplan, E. (1950). The acquisition of word meanings: A developmental study. *Monographs of the Society for Research in Child Development 15* (Serial No. 51).

Wexler, K., & Culicover, P. (1980). *Formal principles of language acquisition.* Cambridge, MA: MIT Press.

2 Simplicity and Generality of Rules in Language Acquisition

Janet Dean Fodor
Stephen Crain
University of Connecticut

THE PROBLEM

Languages like generalizations, and children like generalizations—a perfect harmony, but of course not an accidental one. Languages are shaped by their learners. It must be *because* children generalize that languages do. Pushing the quest for explanation back one step further, we can ask *why* children generalize. A standard answer rests on two assumptions. The first assumption is a least-effort principle, namely, that a language learner always formulates the simplest rule that will accommodate his data. The second assumption is that natural language grammars have the property that the simpler a rule is, the more general it is. In other words, children favor general rules because they are *easier* than restricted rules.

The simplicity or easiness that counts does not have to be formal simplicity (e.g., length of rules in number of symbols). As Chomsky has always emphasized (for example in *Aspects,* 1965), the evaluation metric which represents the preference ranking of alternative grammars and guides learners in forming hypotheses is something to be discovered by empirical investigation; it might bear little relation to what looks simple to our eyes as linguists. Nevertheless, there is a long tradition in generative linguistics of translating qualitative preferences into a uniform preference for formal simplicity of rules. That is, we try to develop a theory of the mental representation system in which grammars are encoded in people's heads such that the grammars that learners adopt are *literally* simpler (shorter) in this mental metalanguage than other grammars that learners reject. An excellent illustration of this appears in Morris Halle's (1962) paper arguing for the psychological reality of phonological features. A rule written in feature notation looks, on the page, more complex than a rule written in phoneme symbols, but Halle argued that it must be the feature notation that we have inside our heads because only this exhibits the proper *positive* correlation between simplicity and generality. (A rule referring to all front vowels is more general—expresses a "better" generalization—than a rule referring only to the front vowel /*i*/; in phonemes the more general rule is more complex, but in features it is simpler.) Exactly comparable points have been made for syntax, leading to a variety of claims about the format of syntactic rules (for example, that they can contain parentheses, essential variables, syntactic features, and so forth).

This is a very standard line of reasoning in linguistics, and the only problem with it is that it doesn't work. The generalizations that natural languages exhibit are *partial* generalizations only. In phonology there are rules that do things to consonants in the context of a *front* vowel or a *high* front vowel, but often not in the context of just *any* vowel (or just any *segment*). But of course, if children always pick the simplest rule, then—given that simplicity entails generality in a feature notation—they should opt immediately for the *maximal* generalization, i.e., for the "any vowel" or "any segment" context rather than for the more specific contexts.

In syntax, also, rules typically express only *partial* generalizations. In English, for example, we can topicalize a noun phrase, a prepositional phrase, or an untensed verb phrase, but not a tensed verb phrase. We can topicalize a phrase out of a main clause and out of an object complement clause, but not out of a relative clause or a subject complement clause. We can extrapose a clause only if it has an overt complementizer; we can invert auxiliary verbs but not main verbs. And so on and so on. Here too, just as in phonology, the standard assumption that simplicity of rules is positively correlated with generality predicts that learners should favor the wrong generalizations. We would expect them always to select the maximal generalizations, whereas, in fact, they hypothesize partial generalizations, and apparently just the *right* partial generalizations as exhibited in the adult language.

There are some standard ways out of this dilemma. One is to suppose that, though learners do select maximal generalizations whenever they can, they have access to data which tell them that the maximal generalizations are too strong and that they should formulate more complex grammars that are more restricted. The problem with this is that the data in question would have to be negative data providing information about what is *not* in the language, but it is widely held that little or no such information is available in language acquisition (see, e.g., Baker, 1979; Wexler & Culicover, 1980). We will return to this point below. Our goal for the moment is to set out the logic of the situation so that we can see clearly which assumptions about children and learning and grammars interact with which others to create the puzzle about the extent of grammatical generalizations.

The most familiar way out of the problem, on the assumption of no negative data, is to propose that the learner's tendency to overgenerate is held in check by innate constraints—constraints such as Subjacency, the Empty Category Principle, the Strict Cycle principle, the binding principles, and so forth (see e.g., Chomsky, 1981; for an introductory presentation, see Radford, 1981). It is important to see that these constraints *must* be innate. A constraint (at least as we shall use the term)[1] is a negative statement about a language, and negative statements cannot be learned if there are no negative data to learn them from. This leads immediately to the conclusion (see Chomsky & Lasnik, 1977) that *all* constraints, even those that are highly language-specific in application, are innate and hence are universal; they must be "unlearned," on the basis of positive data, by children exposed to a target language in which they do not apply. These constraints also count as *substantive,* in a sense that we will explain below, and there are reasons, as we will show, why one might prefer a theory without substantive innate constraints.

Let us summarize the situation in the form of an equation, presenting things in the starkest possible light so that we can see the full shape of the problem before we set about trying to solve it.

1. The overgeneralization puzzle:

a formal simplicity metric
+ a positive correlation between simplicity and generality of rules
+ a least-effort learning procedure
+ no negative data
+ no substantive innate constraints
→
maximal generalization by learners =
greater generalization than natural languages exhibit

Clearly, something has to go. Theories of language and language acquisition can be classified according to which of the elements of this equation they deny. We will now consider each in turn. The arguments pro and con will have to be highly compressed here, but we will suggest that the optimal point at which to insert a wedge in the problem has been overlooked by all current theories. The one assumption that is never queried is that simplicity and generality of rules go hand-in-hand.

[1]There are no standard definitions in linguistic theory distinguishing between constraints and rules. We suggest the following: a constraint is a statement in a grammar (possibly inherited from Universal Grammar) such that if it were deleted, the language generated by the grammar would become larger; a rule is a statement in a grammar (possibly inherited from UG) such that if it were deleted, the language generated would become smaller.

POSSIBLE SOLUTIONS

The Existence of Overgeneralization

We begin our evaluation of equation (1) by scrutinizing its conclusion, for if children do indeed overgeneralize, then it would obviously be a mistake to abandon any of the assumptions which combine to predict that they do. (Of course, there would then be another problem, which is how they eventually learn to withdraw from their youthful overgeneralizations, but this inevitably encroaches on the issue of negative data, so we will save discussion for a later section.)

Do children, in fact, tend to overgeneralize? The clearest sign that a learner has overgeneralized is that he overgenerates, i.e., that his grammar characterizes as grammatical a sentence which the target grammar characterizes as ungrammatical. Within this we may further distinguish three cases, depending on what a sentence is taken to be.[2] *1*. If a sentence is thought of as just a word string, then a child who overgenerates will utter different word strings than adults; we will refer to such cases as *string overgeneration*. *2*. If we think of a sentence instead as a word string with a certain syntactic structure, then a child could overgenerate without uttering any incorrect word strings, for he could utter correct word strings to which he assigns structures not assigned to them by the adult grammar; we will call this *structural overgeneration*. *3*. Finally, there is the possibility that the child uses an acceptable word string with the correct structure but assigns it an improper meaning; we dub this *semantic overgeneration,* but we will not discuss it further in this paper.

Obviously there can be instances of overgeneralization of rules which don't result in overgeneration in one or another of these senses, e.g., a case of overgeneralization of a structural rule which does not result in string overgeneration. Conversely, overgeneration may or may not be due to overgeneralization. We take overgeneralization to be acceptance of a rule which applies more broadly than the corresponding rule of the target grammar, either because the rule itself is too broadly formulated or because the rule is identical to that of the target grammar, but the grammar lacks some constraint which should block application of the target rule in some contexts. Clearly, a grammar may overgenerate even if none of the rules it contains are overgeneral in this sense, for it may contain a rule (or a lexical item) which has no counterpart in the target grammar at all. We will try to observe these subtle distinctions in our discussion, but complications arise when the terms are applied to particular examples because what counts as structural overgeneration depends on the rules that are assumed to be correct for the target language, and these may differ from one theory of syntax to another.

---

[2]In any or all of these cases, the child might simultaneously *under*generate in the relevant subsense, e.g., fail to assign the correct structure as well as assign an incorrect structure.

So now our question has become: do learners in fact tend to overgenerate? The acquisition literature contains many examples of morphological overgeneration errors (e.g., *foots; goed*), and some examples of lexico-syntactic overgeneration (e.g., *Who deaded my kitty cat?* from Bowerman, 1974). These kinds of errors are discussed in Fodor (1985) where it is suggested that they are not, despite appearances, the result of overgeneralization of lexical rules. In the present paper we will restrict discussion to 'pure' (non-lexical) syntactic phenomena, and there the incidence of overgeneration is surprisingly low.

What must be borne in mind is how many opportunities learners would have for syntactic overgeneration, if that were their wont. We will focus primarily in what follows on extraction phenomena. It is clear that, in principle, children could extract phrases of the wrong category (e.g., **Hat, I'm going to paint the— red*), they could extract phrases from the wrong local context (e.g., **Who did he say that—was at the door?*), and they could extract them over the wrong sorts of intervening material (e.g., **That's the boy that I forgot the fact that I didn't like—*). But such errors seem to be extremely rare, perhaps non-existent. Surely if they did occur, they would be noticeable enough to have been reported.[3]

However, the issue of overgeneration is so important that we should search energetically for examples before concluding that there aren't any. We will now review some of the few reported examples of string overgeneration and structural overgeneration.

String overgeneration. One classic error in children's speech is the absence of Subject Auxiliary Inversion (SAI) in root WH-questions in English. Bellugi (1965) gives the examples in (2), and many other examples can be found in the literature.

---

[3]Some striking errors not unlike these have been reported by Wilson & Peters (1984); some of the 17 examples that constitute their corpus are shown in (i).

(i) What are you cooking on a hot? (Answer: stove)
What are we going to look for some with Johnnie? (Answer: house)
What's Kathryn is my? (Answer: cousin)

However, Wilson & Peters do not regard these as overgeneralization errors characteristic of normal linguistic development. They emphasize that the speaker was an almost blind child (3+ years old) with unusually heavy reliance on verbal routines for maintaining communicative interaction, and was exposed to a high proportion of incomplete indirect questions (''three-dot sentences'') that he was supposed to complete, as illustrated in (ii).

(ii) Oh, that's a . . . (Completion: aleph (the Hebrew letter))
That's a nice . . . (Completion: other kaf (another letter))
Did you throw your . . . (Completion: keys)
B.J. went . . . (Completion: to Big Island and see her doggies)

Note that in several of these examples the interruption divides a noun phrase after the determiner (and sometimes, an adjective) and before the noun, just as the child's anomalous Wh-questions do.

(2) What he can ride in?
How he can be a doctor?
Where the other toe will drive?

What is going on here? Clearly it is a case of string overgeneration since the examples in (2) are not sentences of the adult language. Whether it is a case of overgeneralization is less clear. In a transformational framework it would be a failure to apply a transformation. But in a phrase structure framework, it would presumably have to be characterized as overgeneralization of the rule for NP Aux VP constituent order from certain legitimate contexts to the context of a fronted WH-phrase.[4] Since we will advocate a phrase structure approach in what follows, we should give serious attention to this as a potential instance of syntactic overgeneralization.

There is almost an embarrassment of alternative approaches to this error which succeed in removing its sting. The most familiar is Bellugi's account, which rejects the idea that the absence of SAI reflects a mistake in children's grammars. She proposed instead that it is a performance mistake attributable to the difficulty of applying two transformations in the same sentence derivation. Pinker (1984) has argued against this production overload account. He observes that children should be able to avoid a double transformation just as well by omitting WH-Movement and applying Subject Auxiliary Inversion, producing sentences such as *Can she see what?,* but in fact this is not a common error. However, the salience of the initial WH-word in a WH-question might be sufficient to explain why learners invariably retain this aspect of the target construction. Pinker also notes that children who sometimes fail to apply SAI in WH-questions also produce yes/no questions without SAI even though these involve no other transformations that would compete for processing resources. This is also not a conclusive objection, however, because yes/no questions without Subject Auxiliary Inversion (e.g., *The clown can't sing?*) are of course acceptable in English.[5] Thus, the fact that children do not always invert the auxiliary in yes/no questions without WH-Movement is understandable and is perfectly compatible with a production overload account of the WH-question errors.

---

[4]For the sake of comparison with other syntactic frameworks we represent Aux here as an immediate constituent of S, though this is not usual in a phrase structure approach; see, for example Gazdar, Klein, Pullum, and Sag (1985).

[5]Even if a child happened not to have encountered these, there are other sentences that adults use which can be construed as non-inverted questions even if the speaker's own mental representation of his utterance involved inversion. We have in mind elliptical questions as illustrated in (i).

(i) You want some milk? (reduction of: Do you want some milk?)
Bobby hurt your arm? (reduction of: Did Bobby hurt your arm?)

Because of various morphological accidents of English, a question with an elided initial inverted auxiliary may be indistinguishable from a question without inversion.

perfectly compatible with a production overload account of the WH-question errors.

A second possibility is that the error is a semantic error. The sentences in (3) are similar to those in (2), with a fronted WH-phrase but no SAI, and they are syntactically well-formed though they express exclamations rather than questions.

(3) What a good boy you are!
How wise the doctor is!
What dives he hangs out in! (Pinker, *op. cit.*)

It could be, then, that the syntactic component of the learner's grammar is just as it should be, but that he has somehow picked up the idea that sentences like (3) can be interpreted as questions. (Of course, this itself calls for some explanation; we don't know what the answer is, but it might be something as simple as inattention to the sequential positions of unstressed items.)

A third suggestion (see MacWhinney, 1982; Pinker, *op. cit.*) is that the error, though a matter of competence rather than performance and of form rather than meaning, involves lexical entries rather than 'pure' syntactic rules. There are clear lexical influences on the grammaticality of sentences with and without SAI. For instance, whether SAI is required in questions with WH-Movement depends on what is moved; *who, where* and *which movie* trigger SAI, but *how come* does not. Whether a root clause with WH-Movement must be a question with SAI or can be an exclamation without SAI also depends on what is moved; *who* and *what* can only be fronted in questions, but *how tall* can also appear in an exclamation. Since the Uniqueness Principle (see below) operates quite efficiently for lexical phenomena, a certain degree of overgeneration might be tolerable in the lexicon because it can be recovered from. (But see also Fodor, 1985, on lexical generalizations.)

A fourth possibility, and the one we would guess is most likely to be true, is that the learner does make an error of 'pure' syntax, but it is an error in his perception of the input rather than in his induction of syntactic rules from adequately perceived input. In particular, we note that the facts of English with respect to SAI are very complex. Correct discrimination between the NP Aux VP order and the Aux NP VP order depends on four factors: *1.* the distinction between root and non-root clauses (as in *Will he leave?* vs. *I wonder whether he will leave*); *2.* the distinction among 'normal' questions and other illocutionary types such as echo questions and exclamations (e.g., *Is Mary tall?* and *How tall is Mary?* vs. *Mary is HOW tall?* and *How tall Mary is!*); *3.* the distinction between sentences with and without an NP preceding the subject (as in *Who will Sam hug?* vs. *Who will hug Sam?*); *4.* the distinction between WH-phrases and non-WH-phrases (e.g., *Who will Sam hug?* vs. *Mary, Sam will hug*). The NP

Aux VP order is ungrammatical *only* in an interrogative root clause which has a fronted WH-phrase.[6] (Furthermore, the optionality of inversion in root yes/no questions means that acceptability of the Aux NP VP order cannot be taken as evidence of the unacceptability of the NP Aux VP order).

The relevant discrimination can thus be made only on the basis of four features of the construction. It doesn't seem implausible to suppose that an early learner may not yet have identified all of these features. If so, there will be a discrepancy between his input and his 'intake' (see Corder, 1967). The phrase markers from which he is inducing his rules will be defective, incomplete, since they will be lacking feature specifications that appear in the correct phrase markers for the target language. But then, inevitably, the rules that the young child derives from his incomplete phrase markers will lack these feature specifications too.

SAI errors, therefore, do not provide clear evidence that the rule induction mechanisms for language have an inherent bias towards overgeneralization. To show that the rule induction process is defective, it would be necessary to show that it results in incorrect rules even when it is applied to *correct* phrase markers, and that is what has not been established.[7]

Note that our approach to SAI errors is not novel; this is a standard form of explanation in language acquisition research. A child in the two-word stage is not normally accused of being unable to deduce the target rules from the target phrase markers. Rather, we assume that he has been able to process only a couple of words of what he hears. The rules he constructs from his effective data (intake) might be perfectly motivated, even though they are incorrect for the target language.

A comparable account can be offered for other familiar string overgeneration errors in children's speech, such as those in (4), cited by Baker (1979).

(4) I turned off it.
I gave Sally it.
Your books are bigger than my ones.

In all of these examples the error could be described as a failure to respect the distinction between pronouns and full lexical nouns or noun phrases. This *might* arise because children have an innate tendency to make their rules as general as

---

[6]There are also cases of obligatory inversion triggered by fronted negative elements (e.g., *Never would I borrow Brenda's boots*) which represent a further featural complication, but these are not colloquial in modern English and we will ignore them here.

[7]How children do eventually detect all the relevant features in their input is an important topic, but we will not pursue it here. (For discussion see Pinker, 1984.) Why a learner who has succeeded in identifying relevant features would be moved to include them in his rules is a question we will address later.

possible, but it might mean only that young children do not mark the ± pronominal distinction consistently in their phrase markers. This would indeed be an error, but once again it would merely be the kind of error that is the hallmark of early language; namely, simplification of the input, presumably due to an inability to perceive or remember all the details of adult sentences.

To summarize: Our concern in this paper is not overgeneration *per se,* but overgeneration only insofar as it reveals whether children's grammatical inference procedures are pressured by simplicity considerations toward rules that generalize far beyond the data on which they are based. The SAI and pronoun errors do constitute overgeneration, but their source has not (yet) been shown to be the rule induction process itself.[8] Pinning the problem instead on inadequacies in the learner's effective data base, as we have proposed, may look like a 'cheap' solution, but it does have empirical implications that could be tested. It could not be resorted to, for example, in cases where it could be shown on other grounds that learners do perceive the features or structural configurations that govern the adult rules. Whether or not such cases actually occur has not been the focus of studies on overgeneration and won't be easy to determine, but it is a question of considerable theoretical importance.

Structural overgeneration. Structural overgeneration without string overgeneration will not normally reveal itself in spontaneous production, but it can be probed for in comprehension experiments if assigning the incorrect structure to a word string causes assignment of an incorrect meaning. Some comprehension errors that have been reported are not relevant here since they reveal a tendency to *under*generate. For example, Solan (1983) and Tavakolian (1978) have argued that there is a stage at which children reject backward pronominalization including acceptable adult forms such as *That he kissed the lion made the duck happy.* (But see Crain & McKee, 1985). However, other studies could be regarded as demonstrating structural overgeneration by children's early grammars. For example, it has been claimed (Tavakolian, 1981) that 3- to 5-year-olds analyze (and hence interpret) relative clause constructions as conjoined clause constructions

[8]It's not absurd to suppose that errors occur in the process of inducing the rules. In terms of the phrase structure theory that we develop below, the child learning about SAI, for example, would acquire individual phrase structure rules imposing uninverted word order in clauses with fronted NPs, for all combinations of the features [± root],[± Q], [± WH], *except* for the combination [+ root, + Q, + WH]. In the process of collapsing these rules into a single rule schema, the learner might simply overlook the fact that one of the eight possible feature combinations is missing. Or he might slip up in performing the proper rule collapsing procedures designed to ensure that the resulting schema is equivalent to the original set of rules (see Pinker, 1984, Ch. 3). Neither of these possibilities, however, entails a systematic tendency in children to overgeneralize syntactic rules, as would be the case, for example, if learners were designed always to opt for the simplest available rule schema, and the schema collapsing eight feature combinations were significantly simpler than the one collapsing seven. See Fodor and Crain (to appear) for discussion of this latter possibility.

(for example, that they will construe a word string such as *The man was watching the cow that was eating* as having the structure of *The man was watching the cow and was eating*).[9]

The issue here is whether the experimental results that have been reported do in fact reveal properties of children's grammars. We believe that many studies of comprehension have underestimated children's knowledge. In all areas of psychology there is a serious problem of finding practicable experimental tasks which are sensitive only to the factor(s) under investigation. In the case of language, we can only observe linguistic competence as filtered through a host of performance complications. The subject has to parse the test sentence, i.e., apply his knowledge of the rules, in real time, to this particular input. Even adults make parsing errors, and it would hardly be surprising, given the limited memory and attention spans of children, to find that they do too. The child subject must also have and apply knowledge of word meanings and semantic composition principles. Here too, even adults are not above making occasional mistakes (e.g., computing the benign misinterpretation of *Your work fills a much-needed gap*). There are also pragmatic factors to attend to—the contextual fixing of deictic reference, the satisfaction of presuppositions, obedience to cooperative principles of conversation, and so forth. Finally, when the sentence has been parsed, comprehended, and related to the current context, the child must still plan and execute a series of actions by which his understanding or lack of it is demonstrated to the experimenter.

Over the last several years we have been gathering evidence indicating that many of children's failures in sentence comprehension experiments are due to one or another of these factors. For example, we have challenged (Crain & Fodor, 1984) the idea that children's misinterpretations of certain extraction constructions (see Otsu, 1981) are due to their being unaware of Subjacency. There are strong parsing pressures which can obscure the Subjacency-respecting analysis of the experimental sentences—and can do so for adults as well as children. We have shown that children perform very well on relative clause constructions (Hamburger & Crain, 1982) and on temporal adverb constructions (Crain, 1982) if the situation in which they are required to respond conforms to the presuppositions standardly associated with these constructions; for example, they very rarely adopt the conjoined clause analysis of relative clauses.[10] We also have experimental results (Hamburger & Crain, 1984) indicating that 4- and 5-year-olds assign the correct syntactic structure to modifier sequences such as

---

[9]It has been suggested (Sheldon, 1974; 1977) that children's misinterpretation of such strings is due to their analysing them as containing extraposed relative clauses. If so, this would be a case not of structural overgeneration but of structural undergeneration (failure to assign the alternative, non-extraposed structure).

[10]Even more convincing evidence of children's mastery of relative clause rules is that 4- and 5-year-olds will reliably produce relative clauses and in contexts which indicate that they associate correct meanings with them (Hamburger & Crain, *op. cit.*).

the second green ball and that their reported misinterpretations of these phrases (Matthei, 1982) were due to the complexity of the cognitive plans they had to formulate and execute in order to apply their correct interpretations to the instances presented in the experimental task (e.g., keeping track of the colors of the balls while simultaneously counting only some of them).

Obviously we cannot at present rule out all potential cases of structural overgeneration by language learners. But the results of recent experimental studies seem to be falling into line with impressionistic judgements based on conversational interaction with children; namely, that they have a great deal of the target grammar under their belts at an early age, even though they may fail to exhibit their knowledge consistently in challenging situations.

To summarize: The evidence for structural overgeneration, as for string overgeneration of the relevant kind, is quite weak at present. There are a great many imaginable errors that children do not make, and alternative explanations seem to be available for the errors they do make. For this reason we do not advocate resolving the overgeneralization puzzle by accepting its conclusion, namely, that overgeneralization is the norm in language acquisition.

Innate Constraints

We will also not accept the common assumption that the rules of both children's and adults' grammars are extremely general but do not overgenerate because they are held in check by innate constraints. We do accept the common view that it would be impossible to account for the uniformity of natural languages or for the efficiency of language acquisition without postulating extensive constraints on the class of possible languages, but that is quite different from the claim that grammars *contain* constraints.

Explicit constraints on grammatical structures or derivations are postulated by Government Binding Theory (see, for example, Chomsky, 1981), by Lexical Functional Grammar (see Bresnan, 1982), and by Generalized Phrase Structure Grammar (see Gazdar, Klein, Pullum, & Sag, 1985). Grammars that don't contain explicit constraints are nevertheless imaginable, and we believe that there are methodological reasons for aiming at a theory which postulates such grammars for all natural languages. The argument concerns the nature of innate linguistic knowledge, specifically the distinction between substantive knowledge and purely formal knowledge about possible grammars.[11]

Every theory must assume that humans are innately equipped with a mental 'metalanguage' for natural language, i.e., a medium of representation in which to encode their observations about the target language, the rules they hypothesize

[11]The points that follow are presented in greater detail in Fodor & Crain, to appear. But it should be especially noted here that the distinction we draw between formal and substantive knowledge is different from that of Chomsky, 1965, Ch. 1.

for it, the derivations generated by these rules, and so forth. A purely formal theory of innate linguistic knowledge assumes that this metalanguage is *all* that is innately specified, and that this is sufficient, in interaction with the learner's data, to constrain severely the set of grammars that he will contemplate. As a very simple illustration we may consider the possibility that the innate metalanguage contains no expression designating deletion. If so, then a child encountering a construction such as *He can sing but I can't* would be unable to accommodate it by adding a deletion rule to his grammar but would have to deal with it by some other means (e.g., a base-generated empty VP).

The currently familiar theories of language cited above are not purely formal theories. They assume substantive innate knowledge as well as the knowledge implicit in the innate metalanguage. By 'substantive knowledge' we mean knowledge of the *truth* of some proposition framed in the metalanguage. Informally, we can imagine a 'grammar box' inside each person's head in which is contained a representation of all the information he has about his target (natural) language. These facts are expressed by metalanguage sentences written down inside the box. A formal theory of innate linguistic knowledge claims that at birth the grammar box is empty; a substantive theory claims that at birth the grammar box already contains some statements in the metalanguage. Note that the very same information (or amount of information) could be encoded in both cases. The difference between the theories is not a matter of how *much* innate knowledge there is. It has to do with whether that knowledge is represented by explicit statements or whether it follows indirectly from the expressive power of the metalanguage.

The formal/substantive distinction is relevant to the puzzle about the extent of generalization in acquisition because the innate constraints that are commonly invoked as an antidote to the learner's tendency to hypothesize overgeneral rules can be shown to constitute substantive knowledge. Formal constraints deriving from the expressive power of the metalanguage will not do what is needed. They can restrict the hypotheses the learner is capable of formulating about his language, but they cannot force him to formulate one hypothesis rather than another (e.g., the Empty Category Principle as opposed to its denial). So if an infant is to be born knowing that certain constraints will hold of his language (despite the lack of evidence for them in his input), then this knowledge must take the form of metalanguage sentences already tagged as true, preinserted into his mental grammar box.

We don't claim that a substantive theory of innate knowledge must be false, but we do hold that it is methodologically inferior to a formal theory. One way to appreciate the special status of the formal approach is to consider how many degrees of freedom different theories have at their disposal for the purpose of capturing the linguistic facts. A theory which admits substantive innate principles can all too easily add another to the list, in response to a new observation about natural languages. For each of the possible sentences of the metalanguage, such a theory can stipulate either that it is, or that it is not, innately known to be true (present in the grammar box at birth). Depending on the size of the metalanguage, this provides a vast amount of descriptive freedom, limited only by internal consistency among the innate principles postulated. The differences here are by no means trivial. Consider any one of the imaginable metalanguages for natural language grammar representation. This metalanguage might contain anything from one to an infinite number of sentences. For illustration we will consider a metalanguage with exactly 100 distinct sentences. This defines a unique formal theory (since the humanly thinkable thoughts about natural languages are just the thoughts expressed by those 100 sentences), but it makes available 2^{100} distinct substantive theories, differing with respect to how many and which of these sentences they hold to be innately true. Of course, this isn't really a fair comparison, for even those who accept substantive principles are concerned about minimizing their number. However, the number would have to be very small indeed if the degrees of freedom are to be reduced to anything comparable to a formal theory. In our artificial example, there would be a unique formal theory, but 100 different theories with one substantive principle, 4950 different theories admitting two substantive principles, 161,700 different theories admitting three, and so on exponentially.

To summarize: A formal theory is stronger because it has much less room to maneuver. It would be a real achievement to devise a theory of the mental metalanguage from which all truths about the class of natural languages follow as theorems, and the unlikelihood of being able to do so would mean that one could have some confidence, if the project were successful, that this was because it was really on the right track.

Another methodological strength of the formal theory concerns the relationship between innateness and universality. As we noted earlier, a proposed innate substantive constraint isn't even required to be universally (or anywhere near universally) realized, because it can be claimed to be 'unlearnable' on the basis of positive data. By contrast, since no amount of linguistic experience could presumably alter the set of propositions expressable in the metalanguage,[12] a formal theory cannot assume 'unlearning' of innate principles, so it cannot take the easy way out and assume innate knowledge of any and all language-specific facts whenever it has trouble explaining how they could be learned.

For these reasons we think it is important at least to explore the possibility of a formal theory of innate linguistic knowledge. If it fails, it fails, but we would at least have learned a lot by discovering just where and how it is inadequate and needs enrichment. And it just might succeed. In what follows, therefore, we will

[12]It is doubtful that the innate metalanguage supplies the learner with a fixed set of possible syntactic features (see Pullum, 1984), so in this one respect learning could have an effect on what propositions about a language can be mentally formulated.

not appeal to substantive innate knowledge and this means that we cannot solve the overgeneralization problem by assuming that the patterns of partial generalization characteristic of natural languages are the result of the interplay, in sentence derivations, of innate constraints with highly general rules hypothesized by children on the basis of their positive data.

Negative Data

An obvious solution to the overgeneralization problem is to deny that children are limited to positive information about the target language. There have been several different proposals about where negative information might come from, and we will now review the main alternatives.

Parental Feedback

It has been suggested (Hirsh-Pasek, Treiman, & Schneiderman, 1984) that the commonly cited study by Brown and Hanlon (1970) underestimated the amount of feedback that parents provide because it overlooked cases in which an adult repeats and corrects a child's utterance before proceeding further with the conversation. However, the Hirsh-Pasek *et al.* study documents this kind of feedback only for two-year-olds from upper-middle class environments. Perhaps it occurs somewhat more extensively than this, but there remains the old objection that children who receive very little attention from parents or other caretakers also develop perfectly adequate and elaborate grammars. At least at present, then, it seems unlikely that repetition with expansion and correction constitutes a *general* solution to the overgeneralization problem.[13]

The Uniqueness Principle

The Uniqueness Principle of Wexler (1979) and its several close relations (see Clark, this volume, for a survey) have been proposed as an indirect source of negative information. The suggestion is that a learner makes the working assumption that there is only one surface structure derivable from each deep structure, or more generally, that there is only one way of expressing each possible

[13]Hirsh-Pasek *et al.* are careful to note that there is no evidence at present that learners detect or make use of parental repetitions as an indication of the ill-formedness of their utterances. In fact it might do more harm than good if they did, since well-formed sentences as well as ill-formed ones were repeated (12% well-formed repeated vs. 20% ill-formed repeated for 2-year-olds; 11% vs. 16% over all subjects, 2 through 5 years old), and in some cases these well-formed sentences were altered or expanded in the mothers' repetitions. One example given is *Where did you get them?* which was repeated as *Where did you get these things?* Another example was *What do you do with a wooden block?* which was repeated as *What do you do with a little wooden block?* It would be unfortunate if the child in this case inferred that the sentence was ungrammatical with *little* omitted.

message. This assumption can be overridden if the child receives sufficient positive evidence for the existence of alternative expressions of the same message; but except where this occurs, his positive evidence for the acceptability of one linguistic form will carry with it negative information about the non-acceptability of all other possible forms with which it is in competition (including those that the child may already mistakenly have hypothesized).

The Uniqueness Principle may very well be an important factor in the acquisition of phonology, and of lexical rules, and perhaps even of some 'pure' syntactic rules. But it fails for other important syntactic phenomena, including extraction. It is an intriguing fact about most of the constraints on extraction that the language doesn't systematically provide an alternative, well-formed sentence to express the meaning that would have been expressed by an extraction construction if there had been no constraint. For instance, there is no well-formed competitor for the ungrammatical sentence **Who did John overhear the statement that Mary had dinner with—yesterday?* (with the meaning 'John overheard the statement that Mary had dinner with who yesterday?'). But this means that there is no positive input that could drive out ill-formed sentences of this kind from the child's language if he were mistakenly to formulate rules for generating them.

It might be counter-argued that every ungrammatical sentence (including constraint-violating sentences) *must* have a well-formed paraphrase, on the grounds that any human thought can be expressed in all natural languages. However, this argument from 'effability' conflates different kinds of paraphrase relation. The Uniqueness Principle works well for alternative syntactic forms that express the same message, such as *It seems to me that John is angry* and **That John is angry seems to me*. The acceptability of the former could serve as an indication to the learner that the latter is ungrammatical.[14] For extraction violations, by contrast, the closest paraphrase often involves a restructuring of the message expressed. For example, the ungrammatical question cited above could be avoided by a reformulation such as *Who does John think that Mary had dinner with yesterday because he overheard someone talking about it?*, but this is not an exact paraphrase; it involves a slight distortion of the original content. But then the learner would have no reason to view the two sentences as competitors. It is surely not plausible to suppose that he would take every sentence he hears as evidence of the ungrammaticality of all other sentences that express nonidentical but related messages; natural languages are just too rich and subtle in their expressive power for this to be a useful working hypothesis.

We conclude that the Uniqueness Principle will not substitute for direct negative data in all the cases in which it would be needed if learners did have a systematic tendency to overgeneralize rules.

---

[14]Note that for other predicates, such as *troubles me*, the Uniqueness Principle would eventually have to be overridden by the weight of positive evidence for the existence of both alternatives.

Record of Attested Constructions

Another imaginable indirect source of negative information is some kind of case-by-case record of the constructions evidenced in the input, so that constructions which are *not* attested can be identified. The idea is that a learner takes stock at some point of the fact that he has not encountered a construction that his grammar generates, infers that it (probably) isn't part of the target language, and then restricts his grammar so as to block the generation of this construction. But what is the psychological mechanism for this grammar-testing procedure supposed to be? The possibilities can be grouped into two main classes, but one kind will not do what is required of it, while the other is implausibly complex. Chomsky (1981, Ch. 1) suggests that the learner will limit his generalizations "if certain structures or rules fail to be exemplified in relatively simple expressions, where they would be expected to be found." It turns out to make a considerable difference whether it is structures or rules that are assumed to be monitored, so we must consider both.

Let's suppose first that the focus is on rules. Then there is a quite plausible mechanism for rule rejection, comparable to that for the rejection of lexical items that a child may have mistakenly hypothesized. The frequency-sensitivity of lexical access times implies that speakers (i.e., adults, but presumably starting when they are children) keep track of the frequency with which they hear each lexical item. Since this carries no apparent computational cost, it is presumably an automatic consequence of accessing lexical entries; perhaps, as suggested by Morton (1970),[15] the threshold for activation of a lexical entry is lowered each time the entry is accessed so that less sensory stimulation is needed for subsequent accessing. The more a word is used, the more easily its entry is activated. But an entry that is accessed rarely will be more difficult to activate. Thus we could suppose that a lexical entry that is hypothesized but never subsequently confirmed by further input will eventually become inaccessible (at least relative to others) from lack of use—the lexical entry will in effect have withered away. Likewise for rules. If a rule is mistakenly hypothesized and thereafter never activated for the processing of input, it could just wither away, fade from long-term memory.

The problem with this suggestion is that non-use of rules can discriminate among legitimate and illegitimate constructions only to the extent that the child's rules discriminate among constructions. If, for instance, the child formulates the highly general rule *Move Alpha* for extraction, he will find confirmation of this rule in every extraction construction he hears, and it will not fade from lack of use. It is only if *different* rules are involved in *different* kinds of extraction that his rules for one kind will be strengthened and his rules for another kind will not. Thus 'unlearning' in response to nonattestation in the corpus would be effective, on this assumption about the psychological mechanism, only for a theory which

[15]But see also Morton (1982).

claimed that syntactic rules are quite specific. But of course such a theory would predict little overgeneralization in the first place (see example below). More familiar theories typically posit highly general rules and thus stand most in need of some source of negative information to curtail overgeneralizations, but it is precisely for these theories that the unlearning procedure is least effective.

Now let us suppose instead that the learner notices the non-existence of certain types of syntactic structures, where these do not necessarily stand in a one-to-one relation with his rules. Children are now pictured as behaving (albeit unconsciously) like linguists. A child does not merely *use* his rules, for parsing or producing sentences. He also finds occasions to compute out the various predictions that follow from his rules and to check that not just some but all of these predictions are confirmed by his positive data; if one is not, he will restrict the guilty rule to block generation of that construction.

There are two problems with this proposed mechanism. First, it assumes that a learner engages in a vast amount of labor 'on the side', that he does not stop work when he has constructed a set of rules that generate all the constructions he hears and uses. And there is no plausible evolutionary account of why children should be designed to engage in all this work. If you think about it, it would be just fine for a learner to skip it as long as previous generations of children learning the language did the same, for then the correct rules (established by earlier generations of speakers) would be just as general as his rules are, i.e., he wouldn't be *over*generalizing after all. Thus, these grammar-checking procedures have the curious property that nobody would need them if nobody had them.

The second problem is that what the child takes to be instances of the 'same' construction is absolutely crucial and yet, by hypothesis, he receives no guidance here from the rules of his grammar (which, assuming that they are very general, divide up the input much less finely than is needed for his rule-confirmation procedures). He must know, for example, that he doesn't have to have heard extraction of a singular NP from some context (e.g., sister to a preposition in a subordinate clause) as long as he has heard extraction of a plural NP from that context, or vice versa; either case would be sufficient to confirm the grammaticality of the extraction. By contrast, he must not take extraction of an NP from some position in a main clause as confirmation for a rule that also extracts NPs from that position in a subordinate clause (because some languages permit extraction only from main clauses, and such languages would then be unlearnable); these cases must count as *different* constructions from the point of view of the rule-testing procedures. It would, therefore, have to be assumed that children know not only what is a possible rule, but also, and quite independently, what counts as 'the same construction' for the purposes of testing rules.[16]

[16]It is not easy to avoid this assumption that learners group sentences into sub-types for the purposes of rule confirmation and disconfirmation. If they didn't, they would incorrectly construe the non-occurrence of a particular sentence (e.g., *His elephant is short-sighted*) as reason for abandoning

Construction-by-construction grammar checking thus involves unpalatable assumptions if very general rules can be hypothesized by children. If, on the other hand, the only possible rules are fairly specific, then they themselves could serve to parcel the corpus of sentences into just the right sub-types for confirmation and disconfirmation, without the need for any additional mental machinery. Thus, as before, it appears that the correction of overgeneralizations on the basis of non-attestation would be most effective where it is least needed; that is, it would be a plausible source of negative data only for a theory whose admissible rule types had little tendency to overgeneralize in the first place.

Is there any other account of rule disconfirmation which might work even for very general rules? Chomsky's reference to the learner's expectations (see above) suggests a subtler scenario, in which the detection of mismatches between grammar and data is more focused. On some occasion the child observes that a speaker uses sentence S1 where he (the child) would have used, and so would have expected to hear, sentence S2. He assumes that the reason the speaker didn't use S2 is that S2 is ill-formed, and so he sets about restricting his rules so that they no longer generate S2.

This expectation approach is closer to the Uniqueness Principle approach discussed earlier than to the non-attestation approach, and it is susceptible to some of the objections we have already raised. It presupposes, for example, that the range of felicitous utterances at some point in a discourse is so restricted that a child could expect to hear *Who did John overhear the statement that Mary had dinner with yesterday?* as opposed to *Who does John think that Mary had dinner with yesterday because he overheard someone talking about it?*, and thus could infer the ungrammaticality of the former from the occurrence of the latter. But it is hard to believe that discourse expectations are so refined. The expectation approach also implies either that the child imposes the maximally complex restriction on his rules so as to exclude only the one sentence that was expected but didn't occur or that he imposes a simple restriction which also excludes a host of other sentences many of which he will probably have to reinstate later. Furthermore, any theory which holds that negative evidence (direct or indirect) is essential for language acquisition must also hold that the negative evidence in question is so abundant that every normal child will encounter every bit of it that is needed to limit every one of his possible overgeneralizations (see Lasnik &

---

or restricting one or more of the rules involved in its generation. One might simply embrace this suggestion, but note that the child would then have to relearn many rules after wrongly rejecting them; acquisition would consist of a constant back-and-forth between overgeneralization and undergeneralization on the way to eventual equilibrium. (Berwick, 1985 Ch. 3, considers an idealized learning situation in which *all* sentences of the target language up to some degree of complexity are included in the learner's data base. Then non-occurrence of a string would be *valid* evidence for its ungrammaticality, and the child would modify his rules only where modification was appropriate. But a realistic model of acquisition must obviously allow for extensive gaps in the corpus; see Pinker, 1984 Ch. 8.)

Crain, 1985). But the negative evidence provided by the failure of particular discourse expectations seems to be too chancy to be relied on.

For these reasons, we see little hope at present that the right solution to the overgeneralization puzzle is to assume that learners do have access to some variety of negative data.

No Least-Effort Principle

In our equation representing the overgeneralization puzzle we have assumed that a language learner is naturally lazy, in that he will always select the simplest modification of his previous grammar that will accommodate some new (positive) datum. But suppose we drop this assumption now and assume that the learner's highest priority is not to save himself trouble but to formulate rules which fit his positive data very snugly, generating the fewest possible constructions over and above the one that motivated the introduction of each rule in the first place. Then there should be little danger of his overgeneralizing. Indeed, the less experience he has, the *fewer* constructions his grammar would generate. The course of acquisition would consist of a gradual extension of his initially undergenerating rules, driven forward by more and more positive data.

This picture of how grammars develop is certainly not incoherent, but it interacts with the assumption of a formal simplicity criterion and the assumption that simple rules are general rules to predict—quite implausibly—that children must always formulate the most *complex* rules compatible with their positive data. Snug rules are complex rules because they must include highly specific contextual restrictions and rich featural specifications of affected categories.

Of course, it might be proposed that learners don't go all the way with these possible complications but select some middle level of rule complexity which leads to some, though not too much, generalization over the input. Pinker (1984) offers an acquisition model of this kind, assuming that learners obligatorily engage in a great deal of information processing whose outcome is the construction of rules that are complex enough to avoid illicit prediction beyond the motivating data. Like the earlier suggestion about checking for the non-occurrence of predicted constructions, this proposal creates a puzzle about *why* humans should be designed to go to all this trouble, given that languages would be just as learnable without it as long as all generations of learners abjured it equally. (See Fodor, 1985, for further discussion.)

Moreover, assuming that a learner's corpus at any (pre-final) stage of acquisition will be consistent with a variety of different possible natural languages, whose rules are similar but slightly different in extension, it would be impossible even for this kind of labor-intensive acquisition mechanism to hit on exactly the right degree of generalization at a first attempt, therefore. Gradual adjustments in response to further data would be necessary. But these would have to be adjustments in the direction of greater generality. It would then follow that a child's rules are more complex than those of an adult, and that the younger he is, the more complex his rules will be. In view of the limited working memory and processing capacity of young children, this strikes us as a hypothesis to be invoked only when more plausible alternatives have been exhausted.

A Non-Formal Evaluation Metric

Suppose, then, that the learner's choice of hypotheses has nothing to do with simplicity at all, that the innate evaluation metric is qualitative rather than quantitative. We will deal with this idea briefly.

First, this means that the evaluation metric, which is an aspect of the child's innate knowledge of language, constitutes substantive knowledge and thus falls under our argument that a substantive theory is methodologically less desirable than a formal theory as long as there is some hope that the latter can be made to fit the facts.

A second methodological disadvantage of a qualitative evaluation measure is that it is less comprehensive than a formal metric insofar as it does not offer a *general* principle for choosing between any two hypotheses compatible with the learner's input, so that the preference in each case must be independently specified by the theory. A general principle has been proposed, *viz.* the Subset Principle (Berwick, 1985). This is designed precisely to solve the problem of overgeneralization in the absence of negative data by ensuring that the learner always hypothesizes the least general of the grammars available, the one that generates the smallest language. But the Subset Principle is a guiding principle for linguists to follow in devising theories. It is not, presumably, a principle that a learner can abide by in constructing his grammar—at least not unless we suppose that he is capable of computing, every time he is faced with a choice between grammars, which languages they generate and whether these stand in a subset relation.[17]

Finally, as long as rules of the usual sort are assumed with a positive correlation between simplicity and generality, the substantive evaluation metric would have to be more or less the exact inverse of a formal symbol-counting simplicity metric. This is suspicious. It wouldn't be so bad if formal simplicity were utterly irrelevant, orthogonal to the learner's preference ranking. But the fact that it is relevant but in an upside-down fashion suggests that something has gone awry.[18]

---

[17]Sometimes the computation is straightforward, as for example in the case of a choice between bounding node A and bounding nodes A and B. But what of the choice between A and C? Or between an addition to the bounding nodes and a restriction on landing sites, etc.?

[18]Parameter theory (Chomsky, 1981; Hyams, 1983) offers the learner a choice not between whole rules but between very specific, localized aspects of rules or of otherwise innately given constraints, and in some cases the alternative values for a parameter may be equally simple. Howev-

SIMPLICITY AND GENERALITY RECONSIDERED

There is only one factor in our equation left to be considered, and that is the assumption that simpler rules are invariably more general rules. If we were to relinquish this assumption, we could reconcile the idea that learners favor simple rules with the idea that their rules exert no pressure towards overgeneralization, and so don't need to be limited either by substantive innate constraints or by negative data.

To give up the familiar simplicity/generality correlation means revising our notions of what sorts of rules grammars contain. For one thing, they mustn't be context-sensitive, for a context-sensitive rule can always be simplified by omission of part or all of its context specification with the result that it will apply in a broader set of contexts than it should. This precludes Standard Theory type transformations. Also precluded, of course, is the rule *Move Alpha* of Government and Binding Theory, since this overgenerates massively without the benefit of substantive constraints (such as Subjacency, the binding principles, etc.), and yet it is simpler than any other imaginable transformation (except *Affect Alpha*, see Lasnik & Saito, 1984) and so would be postulated by any child encountering any extraction phenomenon at all.

A feature analysis, as is standardly assumed for syntax following Chomsky (1970), is also a potential danger, just as it is in phonology. On closer examination, though, the severity of the features problem turns out to be dependent on other properties of rules. An overly simple feature specification will overgenerate and be uncorrectable on the basis of positive data if its role is to identify the context or the affected term in a transformation; but it will undergenerate and will be correctable on the basis of positive data if it governs the construction of a phrase marker "from scratch," as a context free phrase structure rule does, for it will then fail to assign the correct phrase markers to sentences in the learner's data base. For example, a transformational rule that didn't mention the feature [+ finite] would apply to constructions containing [+ finite] and to constructions containing [− finite], and thus would be more general in application than a target rule which did include the feature [+ finite], but a phrase structure rule that didn't mention [+ finite] would not generate phrase markers containing the

---

er, when there *are* complexity differences, it is still generally the case that the learner must initially favor the more complex choice e.g., both S and S′ as bounding nodes rather than either one alone; or the requirement that an anaphor be bound in its governing category rather than just that it be bound (see Hong, 1985). Though it undeniably has other merits (e.g., minimization of the amount of data processing learners must be assumed to engage in), parameter theory is thus not immune to all the points we have been raising. The reason we have not discussed it in detail in this paper is that it falls under the exclusion in the section above on innate constraints, because it is necessarily a substantive theory. (See Ch. 4 of Fodor & Crain, to appear, for discussion).

feature [+ finite], and thus would fail to generate all the phrase markers generated by a target rule that did include [+ finite].[19]

It is of interest to explore possible modifications of the format for transformational rules which would free them of these characteristics that associate generality with simplicity. But the properties we are seeking are already at hand in context free phrase structure rules (CFPS rules). As we have seen, the feature notation does not misbehave in these rules. They are also safe inasmuch as they contain no context specifications. Or rather, they contain a sort of built-in context specification that can't be tampered with. A CFPS rule identifies a local tree (i.e., a mother-and-daughters node configuration), and thus it necessarily introduces a node into a very specific context. As an illustration (highly oversimplified), consider the distribution of adjectives. An adjective is introduced beneath an NP node and as (left or right) sister to an N node (or: beneath an N′ node and as sister to another N′ node). The format requirements on CF rules do not allow the specifications of the mother and sister nodes to be omitted, so a 'least effort' learner who is constrained to formulate CF rules will be in no danger of simplifying his grammar by omitting crucial context specifications. So he will be in no danger of overgeneralizing his rule for adjectives so that it positions them in contexts other than those in which he has observed them. It would take a more complex CF grammar, not a simpler one, to put adjectives in additional positions in phrase markers.

To summarize this point: Each CF rule is responsible for a very small 'bite' of sentence structure; and these rules do not lend themselves to oversimplification leading to overgeneralization. It would be satisfactory, then, if we could claim that language acquisition consists of formulating CF rules. The child would postulate them one by one in response to his positive data (reading them off the trees assigned to input sentences). Such a child would learn about each local construction in his language individually and would not predict the existence of constructions which he hadn't heard attested.

The obvious weakness of this phrase structure approach is that CF grammars have been held for years to be inadequate for natural languages. There is no point in solving the acquisition problem if the grammars acquired are not the right ones. But *are* CF grammars inadequate? Traditional CF grammars, as discussed by Chomsky (1957), cannot account for unbounded dependencies. But the theory of Generalized Phrase Structure Grammar (as presented by Gazdar, 1981, Gazdar, Klein, Pullum and Sag, 1985, and in related works) has solved this problem of observational adequacy by introducing 'slash categories'. A slash

[19]This is a rough and ready description of the difference, omitting various technical details concerning rule schemata and feature instantiation algorithms; see Fodor and Crain (to appear) for more detailed discussion. Note also that we are presupposing here that learners do somehow eventually know which features appear where in phrase markers even though, as we noted above, they may fail to identify some features at early stages.

feature on a node encodes the information that the constituent that the node dominates must contain a 'gap' or trace of a specified category. In (5), for example, the label "S/NP" denotes a sentence (clause) containing an NP trace, associated with the NP antecedent or 'filler' that is the sister of the S/NP node.[20]

(5)

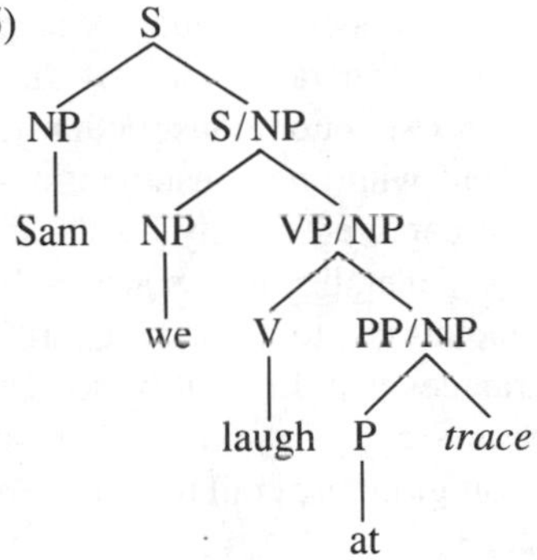

The slash annotation is 'passed down' by the rules onto successively lower nodes, carrying the information that a trace is needed down to the lexical level. Thus in (5), the VP/NP node beneath the S/NP indicates that the trace associated with *Sam* will appear within the verb phrase of the clause; the PP/NP node indicates that it will appear in the PP complement to the verb.

The rules needed to generate (5) are shown in (6).

(6) S → NP S/NP
S/NP → NP VP/NP
VP/NP → V PP/NP
PP/NP → P *trace*

These rules jointly have the same effect as standard base rules plus a topicalization transformation. But note that despite the slash annotations, they are perfectly ordinary CF rules. They are, therefore, compatible with our proposal that language acquisition consists of building up a CF grammar in small steps in response to positive input. For instance, a child encountering sentence (5) would postulate the rules in (6) but would not postulate additional rules for 'extracting' from subordinate clauses (e.g., VP/NP → V S/NP) until he actually encountered extraction from subordinate clauses.

The observational adequacy problem for CF grammars is solved (at least for extraction phenomena) by 'slash rules' like those in (6). (Note that it doesn't take

---

[20]To keep this illustration as simple as possible we have used traditional category labels rather than the variant of X-bar notation employed by Gazdar *et al.*, and the "/" symbol of Gazdar (1981) rather than the feature notation of later versions of the theory.

an infinite number of slash rules to account for unbounded extraction because the rule system can be recursive.)[21] But descriptive and explanatory problems remain. Each CF rule expresses an extremely modest generalization about a language. Why, then, do natural languages consistently exhibit broader generalizations than this? Consider, for example, the fact that extraction constructions are typically just like non-extraction constructions in the same language except for the position of the extracted constituent. This is a generalization that falls out naturally in a transformational system, where an extraction construction just *is* the corresponding non-extraction construction but with one constituent moved. But this 'correspondence generalization' is *not* captured merely by the use of slash categories. The rules in (6) *abide* by the generalization, since each one happens to be identical, except for its slash annotations, to a 'basic' CF rule for English. But nothing we have said so far guarantees that this will be so. Thus it looks as if CF grammars explain why children's early grammars don't overgeneralize at the cost of predicting that even adult grammars fail to capture many of the significant generalizations in the language.

To solve this problem, we need some way of predicting that natural language grammars are not *random* subsets of the set of possible CF rules. We need to explain how the existence of one rule in a grammar could facilitate the inclusion of formally related rules, but not the inclusion of other rules unrelated to it. GPSG theory has met this challenge by postulating (originally) metarules or (later) feature instantiation mechanisms, which create slash rules as systematic elaborations of basic rules. A metarule generates natural language grammar rules from natural language grammar rules. Given, for example, the basic rule S → NP VP, it creates a new rule by adding slash annotations to the mother node and one of the daughter nodes, as in the second rule in (6). Feature instantiation principles take skeletal rule schemata without features, and add features such as slash features in specified positions. Either mechanism will guarantee the kind of correspondence between extraction and non-extraction constructions that is characteristic of natural languages.[22] And either mechanism will serve to reduce the number of rules in a grammar to within plausible limits, since it will no longer be

[21]For natural languages that are not CF (see Shieber, 1985) an infinite number of CF rules would be required. This entails a recursive metagrammar (see below) or infinite rule schemata. We will not address this point here, but it does pose a potential threat to the model we are proposing and should be considered seriously. We would need to establish somehow that learners will posit these powerful mechanisms only where they are correct for the target language.

[22]This correspondence need not be absolute if slash rules can also be present in a grammar without being derived from basic rules. Correspondence is then merely the unmarked case, on the assumption that these specifically listed rules 'cost' more than derivable rules. But a markedness approach is surely correct. Note that this is also acknowledged in a transformational framework, given the possibility that one transformation (e.g., Subject Auxiliary Inversion) may be obligatory following another (e.g., Wh-Movement).

necessary to list each slash rule individually.[23] Thus GPSG captures at the level of the metagrammar generalizations that are too powerful to be captured by the CF 'object-level' grammar which actually generates the phrase markers for the language.

Unfortunately, this standard GPSG solution is unacceptable for our purposes because it leads straight back into overgeneralization in acquisition, overgeneralization that is just as severe as that predicted by transformational grammars in the absence of substantive constraints. The metagrammatical mechanisms for generating CF rules serve to encourage the learner to formulate generalizations about his target language. But they go too far, just as transformational rules do, for these same mechanisms also encourage the learner to formulate *over*generalizations, e.g., to generate additional slash rules for which he has no direct evidence and which may not in fact be in the target grammar.

Fortunately, there is another way of achieving generality in a CF grammar besides rule generation. The alternative is rule collapsing. Familiar abbreviatory conventions for rules, such as parentheses, simplify grammars by combining rules that are formally related. But the generalizations that they thereby express are not *predictive* generalizations, but *post hoc* generalizations. It is not assumed, for example, that a learner will insert parentheses in a rule unless his data require him to do so. If he has encountered evidence for VP → V NP and none as yet for VP → V, he will formulate VP → V NP and not VP → V (NP). (Again, this isn't offered as a realistic example, only as a simple illustration.) In fact the parenthesis notation is very cleverly designed to interact with the formal simplicity metric to predict that learners will generalize only *after* acquiring each instance separately. The rule schema VP → V (NP) is simpler than the combination of the two rules that it collapses, which explains why learners will formulate it. But note that the schema is more complex than either rule alone, and this explains why learners don't run ahead of their data, why they don't formulate the more powerful schema on the basis of evidence that supports only one of the specific rules. Abbreviatory conventions thus simplify grammars and capture generalizations *without* predicting overgeneralization in acquisition.

For the case of extraction, parentheses are insufficient, but angle brackets will do the job. The basic rule S → NP VP and the slash rule S/NP → NP VP/NP can be collapsed into the schema (7), where the angle brackets indicate linked options.

(7) S⟨/NP⟩ → NP VP⟨/NP⟩

---

[23]Neither linguistics nor psychology provides any evidence about the *absolute* size of grammars. At most we have evidence (e.g., from the direction of language change) about *relative* grammar size. Strictly speaking, therefore, it is not an argument against traditional CF grammars for natural languages that they would have to contain an enormous number of rules. The real argument is that their large size reflects their failure to capture psychologically real generalizations.

As in the case of parentheses, the schema is more complex than either rule alone, so the simplicity metric will not trick a learner into inventing a slash rule corresponding to every basic rule in his grammar; adding a slash rule still carries some cost and so must be motivated by positive data. But adding a slash rule now carries *very little* cost as long as it can be incorporated into an independently needed basic rule; it is less costly than adding a completely unrelated, non-corresponding, non-collapsible, slash rule.

There are two distinct senses in which natural languages could be said to favor generalizations. One sense is that it is 'cheaper' to represent a superset of phenomena than to represent a subset. This is a familiar assumption, but it is what creates the overgeneralization problem in language acquisition. The other sense is that it is 'cheaper' to represent a set of phenomena that exhibit a common pattern than a similar sized set where the member phenomena are arbitrary and unrelated. This is the sense that is captured by the rule collapsing approach that we have outlined. And since it does not drive grammars inexorably onwards toward *maximal* generality, it appears to do justice to the existence of generalizations in natural languages without creating acquisition problems.

All sorts of further elaborations of the rule-collapsing proposal are possible. For instance, we could incorporate into schema (7) the rule for extracting prepositional phrases from verb phrases. As it stands, (7) is equivalent to the two rules in (8).

(8)
$$\begin{aligned} S &\rightarrow NP\ VP \\ S/NP &\rightarrow NP\ VP/NP \end{aligned}$$

If we add PP into the angle brackets, as shown in (9), the schema becomes equivalent to the three rules in (10).[24]

(9)
$$S/\left\langle \begin{matrix} NP \\ PP \end{matrix} \right\rangle \rightarrow NP \quad VP/\left\langle \begin{matrix} NP \\ PP \end{matrix} \right\rangle$$

(10)
$$\begin{aligned} S &\rightarrow NP \quad VP \\ S/NP &\rightarrow NP \quad VP/NP \\ S/PP &\rightarrow NP \quad VP/PP \end{aligned}$$

[24]Notice that we have left the slash sign outside of the angle brackets here with the result that the full expansion of (9) is not really (10); it has S/ in place of S. Obviously S/ must be construed as equivalent to S. Adopting this convention makes the angle bracket notation work a little more smoothly, and there seems to be no harm in it. In any case, these implementation details change as one moves to a feature notation for slash annotations, as in Gazdar *et al.* (*op. cit.*), in a way that allows the angle brackets to be dispensed with. (For example, they are not really essential in (12) below, because it is no longer necessary to establish a link between slash annotations in two different places in a rule).

The angle bracket notation reduces the size of the grammar and captures the similarities between PP extraction and NP extraction.

Another possibility would be to establish a general convention to the effect that the contents of linked pairs of angle brackets must be identical (in syntax, though perhaps not in phonology). Then the content of the second pair of brackets in (10) would be redundant and so these brackets could be left empty as in (11).

$$\text{(11)} \quad \mathrm{S}/\left\langle \begin{matrix} \mathrm{NP} \\ \mathrm{PP} \end{matrix} \right\rangle \rightarrow \mathrm{NP} \quad \mathrm{VP}/< \;\; >$$

Even more interesting is the possibility of finding general principles that will predict the distribution of slash features in the angle brackets on the right hand sides of rules (at least in the unmarked case), so that even the empty angle brackets that encode their position can be omitted. For example, the Head Feature Convention of Gazdar *et al.* (*op. cit.*) entails that slash features on the S in (11) will pass to the VP daughter; thus, the empty brackets in (11) are redundant and so (11) can be further streamlined as in (12).

$$\text{(12)} \quad \mathrm{S}/\left\langle \begin{matrix} \mathrm{NP} \\ \mathrm{PP} \end{matrix} \right\rangle \rightarrow \mathrm{NP} \quad \mathrm{VP}$$

Schema (12) is still equivalent to the three rules in (10), but implicit in it (together with the conventions for construing it) are generalizations that (10) misses, about universal properties of the routes by which slash features can pass down through phrase markers from one node to another. Note that we are supposing that a learner would acquire the rules in (10) individually, and then collapse them into (12) (and likewise for other subsets of rules in the grammar). This sequence of events gives learners the best of both worlds: conservative generalization from attested forms until all the rules have been acquired, but simplicity and generality in the eventual grammar.

It is clear in principle how to extend this rule collapsing approach to other syntactic phenomena, but we don't have space here to work through more examples. (See Fodor and Crain, to appear.) We propose to stop here, with one last comment. Nothing we have said *proves* that this approach will be successful. It is founded on the premise—the speculation—that all valid syntactic generalizations can be cast as formal similarities among CF rules, similarities of the kind that will permit them to be combined into rule schemata with consequent simplification of the grammar. Establishing whether or not this is so will require a great deal of work, reanalyzing familiar phenomena and investigating new ones. But there doesn't seem to be any *principled* reason why it shouldn't succeed. And it is certainly worth trying, in view of the elegance of the solution it offers to the central puzzle about the extent of generalization in language acquisition.

ACKNOWLEDGMENTS

This research was supported in part by NSF Grant BNS 84–18537. Parts of it were completed while the first author was at the Center for the Study of Language and Information at Stanford University, supported by funds from the System Development Foundation. We would like to thank Eve Clark, Brian MacWhinney and Cecile McKee for their helpful comments on an earlier draft.

REFERENCES

Baker, C. L. (1979). Syntactic theory and the projection principle. *Linguistic Inquiry 10,* 533–581.

Bellugi, U. (1965). The development of interrogative structures in children's speech. In K. Riegel (ed.), *The development of language functions,* Report No. 8, 103–138. University of Michigan Language Development Program, Ann Arbor, MI.

Berwick, B. (1985). *The acquisition of syntactic knowledge.* Cambridge, MA: MIT Press.

Bowerman, M. (1974). Learning the structure of causative verbs: A study in the relationship of cognitive, semantic and syntactic development. In E. Clark (ed.), *Papers and reports on child language development,* No. 8, 142–178. Stanford University Committee on Linguistics.

Bresnan, J. (ed.). (1982). *The mental representation of grammatical relations.* Cambridge, MA: MIT Press.

Brown, R. and C. Hanlon (1970). Derivational complexity and order of acquisition in child speech. In J. R. Hayes (ed.), *Cognition and the development of language.* New York: Wiley.

Chomsky, N. (1957). *Syntactic structures.* The Hague: Mouton.

Chomsky, N. (1965). *Aspects of the theory of syntax.* Cambridge, MA: MIT Press.

Chomsky, N. (1970). Remarks on nominalization. In R. A. Jacobs and P. S. Rosenbaum (eds.), *Readings in english transformational grammar.* Waltham: Ginn, 184–221.

Chomsky, N. (1981). *Lectures on government and binding.* Dordrecht, Holland: Foris Publications.

Chomsky, N. and H. Lasnik (1977). Filters and control. *Linguistic inquiry* 8, 425–504.

Corder, S. P. (1967). The significance of learner's errors. *International review of applied linguistics in language teaching 5,* 161–170.

Crain, S. (1982). Temporal terms: mastery by age five. In *Papers and reports on child language development.* Proceedings of the Fourteenth Annual Stanford Child Language Research Forum.

Crain, S. and J. D. Fodor (1984). On the innateness of subjacency. In *Proceedings of the first eastern states conference on linguistics.* 191–204, Ohio State University, Columbus, OH.

Crain, S. and C. McKee (1985). Acquisition of structural constraints on anaphora. Paper presented at The North Eastern Linguistic Society, XVI, Montreal, Canada.

Fodor, J. D. (1985). The procedural solution to the projection problem. Paper presented at the Boston University Conference on Language Development, Boston, MA.

Fodor, J. D. and S. Crain (In press). *On the form of innate linguistic knowledge.* Cambridge, MA: Bradford Books.

Gazdar, G. (1981). Unbounded dependencies and coordinate structure. *Linguistic inquiry* 12, 155–184.

Gazdar, G., E. Klein, G. Pullum and I. Sag (1985). *Generalized phrase structure grammar.* Cambridge, MA: Harvard University Press.

Halle, M. (1962). Phonology in generative grammar. *Word 18,* 54–72.

Hamburger, H. and S. Crain (1982). Relative acquisition. In S. A. Kuczaj II (ed.), *Language development: Vol. 1. syntax and semantics.* Hillsdale, NJ: Lawrence Erlbaum.

Hamburger, H. and S. Crain (1984). Acquisition of cognitive compiling. *Cognition 17,* 85–136.

Hirsh-Pasek, K., R. Treiman and M. Schneiderman (1984). Brown and Hanlon revisited: Mothers' sensitivity to ungrammatical forms. *Journal of child language 11*, 81–88.

Hong, S. (1985). *A and A' Binding in Korean and English: Government-Binding parameters.* Unpublished Ph.D. dissertation, University of Connecticut, Storrs, CT.

Hyams, W. M. (1983). *The Acquisition of parameterized grammars.* Unpublished doctoral dissertation, The City University of New York.

Lasnik, H. and S. Crain (1985). On the acquisition of pronominal reference. *Lingua 65*, 135–154.

Lasnik, H. and M. Saito (1984). On the nature of proper government. *Linguistic inquiry 15*, 235–289.

MacWhinney, B. (1982). Basic processes in syntactic acquisition. In S. A. Kuczaj II (ed.), *Language development: Vol. 1. Syntax and semantics.* Hillsdale, NJ: Lawrence Erlbaum Associates.

Matthei, E. M. (1982). The acquisition of prenominal modifier sequences. *Cognition 11*, 301–332.

Morton, J. (1970). A functional model of memory. In D. A. Norman (ed.), *Models of human memory.* New York Academic Press.

Morton, J. (1982). Disintegrating the lexicon: An information processing approach. In J. Mehler, E. Walker, and M. Garrett (eds.) *Perspectives on mental representation.* Hillsdale, NJ: Lawrence Erlbaum.

Otsu, Y. (1981). *Universal grammar and syntactic development in children: Toward a theory of syntactic development.* Unpublished Ph.D. dissertation, MIT.

Pinker, S. (1984). *Language learnability and language development.* Cambridge, MA: Harvard University Press.

Pullum, G. (1984). How complex could an agreement system be? In *Proceedings of the first eastern states conference on linguistics.* 79–103, Ohio State University, Columbus, OH.

Radford, A. (1981). *Transformational syntax: A student's guide to Chomsky's extended standard theory,* Cambridge, England: Cambridge University Press.

Sheldon, A. (1974). The role of parallel function in the acquisition of relative clauses in English. *Journal of verbal learning and verbal behavior 13*, 272–281.

Sheldon, A. (1977). On strategies for processing relative clauses: A comparison of children and adults. *Journal of psycholinguistic research* 6.4, 305–318.

Shieber, S. (1985). Evidence against the context-freeness of natural language. *Linguistics and philosophy 8*, 333–343.

Solan, L. (1983). *Pronominal reference: Child language and the theory of grammar.* Dordrecht, Holland: D. Reidel: Dordrecht.

Tavakolian, S. (1978). Children's comprehension of pronominal subjects and missing subjects in complicated sentences. In H. Goodluck and L. Solan (eds.), *Papers in the structure and development of child language.* U. Mass Occasional Papers in Linguistics, Vol. 4, 145–152.

Tavakolian, S. (1981). The conjoined-clause analysis of relative clauses. In S. Tavakolian (ed.), *Language acquisition and linguistic theory.* Cambridge, MA: MIT Press.

Wexler, K. (1979). Untitled presentation at the Workshop on Learnability, Laguna Beach, California, June 4–8.

Wexler, K. and P. Culicover (1980). *Formal principles of language acquisition.* Cambridge, MA: MIT Press.

Wilson, B. and A. M. Peters (1984). What are you cookin' on a hot?: A blind child's 'violation' of universal constraints. Paper presented at the Boston University Conference on Language Development, Boston, MA.

3 What is Learned in Acquiring Word Classes—A Step Toward an Acquisition Theory

Martin D. S. Braine
New York University

There is a classic tension in discussions of word classes, perhaps as old as the topic itself, between semantic and distributional conceptions of what word classes are. The semantic conception postulates semantic properties as the basis of word classes, e.g., nouns are names of places, persons, things, verbs represent actions, adjectives represent properties, etc. According to this approach, the acquisition of word classes by children is primarily a matter of associating the semantic property with the class, either by a process presumed to be one of discovery (e.g., Brown, 1957) or because the association is taken as inborn (e.g., Grimshaw, 1981). The distributional approach, on the other hand, emphasizes the privileges of occurrence of the words of the class, e.g., they occur in particular positions in phrases or sentences, are marked in particular morphophonemic ways, or co-occur (agree) with particular morphemes. Thus, in the distributional approach, the common property shared by the words of a class is distributional, not semantic, and it would be this property that children discover in acquiring word classes (e.g., Maratsos & Chalkley, 1980).

A purely distributional approach cannot be sufficient because distributional criteria are language specific, whereas some classes (noun, at least) appear to be linguistic universals. For any universal class, there must be some nondistributional property that marks it that is valid across languages. Another problem with a purely distributional approach is the complexity of the distributional analysis that would be demanded of the learner. Any reader can readily convince him or herself of the difficulty of the task by imagining that they are confronted by text in some language they are completely ignorant of and faced with the requirement of identifying the nouns or verbs in the text. (The real-life learner's task would be more complicated than this because the text would be received auditorily and consequently would disappear before it could be more than cursorily inspected.)

On the other hand, as Maratsos and Chalkley (1980) have shown, the semantic approach is also seriously problematic, at least as regards the semantic features most commonly ascribed to classes—''object'' to noun, ''action'' to verb, and ''property'' to adjective. These features do not fit the classes at all exactly, there is much overlap, and the properties themselves are fuzzy—much fuzzier than the distributional properties. Moreover, there is a dearth of evidence for errors made by children—misassignments of words to classes—based on these semantic properties. Also, of course, when semantic and distributional properties conflict for a word, it is invariably the distributional properties that determine the class of the word. Finally, there are classes that are virtually semantically arbitrary like the gender classes of many languages, the shape-based classes of some American Indian languages, and the declension and conjugation classes of inflected languages. These must be discovered wholly or largely on a distributional basis, and the existence of such classes argues that language learners do in fact have some fairly substantial ability to make distributional analyses and indeed exercise that ability. Thus, both approaches lead to the problem of defining the learner's ability to make distributional analyses.

I do not reject the idea there there is a place for semantics in an acquisition theory for word classes. Indeed, one broad semantic contrast—between 'predicate' and 'argument'—will be crucial to the theory presented. However, Maratsos and Chalkley have convinced me that it would be advisable to start by considering the distributional properties of word classes and to be particularly sceptical about properties like 'object,' 'action,' etc., marking grammatical classes, or being crucially important in the learning of them. So I shall begin with the idea that the classes the child acquires are to a great extent distributionally determined and see where that leads.

This starting point leads instantly to the question: What distributional analyses does the child make? However, before tackling this question, it will be useful to consider a prior question to which both approaches lead as noted above: What evidence is there about the kind of competence that people have for making purely distributional analyses?

Obviously, the distributional analyses that children make will be limited by the distributional analyses that they can make. Thus, an acquisition theory that postulates that the learner makes distributional analyses can be theoretically well-founded (i.e., not ad hoc) only if it is consistent with evidence on the learner's competence for making distributional analyses. Otherwise, there is a danger of postulating mechanisms that are too strong or of the theory's failing to take advantage of resources that are available to the learner.

I begin, therefore, by reviewing laboratory evidence on people's competence for making purely distributional analyses. The evidence indicates that certain kinds of distributional patterns are very easy to acquire, and others much more difficult. A theory of what is learned in acquiring noun, verb, and adjective classes is then presented, which accounts for the relative universalities and speeds of acquisition of these classes in a way consistent with the evidence on the relative difficulties of different kinds of distributional patterns. The acquisition of arbitrary subclasses of these categories is then discussed, taking gender subclasses of nouns as a prototypical case. Although the evidence on competence for making distributional analyses predicts that such classes should be hard to acquire, an artificial language experiment indicates factors that may be operative in such acquisitions and suggests how the theory should be extended to this kind of word class.

WHAT ASPECTS OF DISTRIBUTION ARE EASY TO ACQUIRE AND WHICH ARE HARD?

Competence for making purely distributional analyses must, of course, be considered relative to a particular condition of utterance reception. When the old-fashioned structural linguists did distributional analyses (e.g., Harris, 1951), they were able to survey a large corpus that was written down and to compare the utterances one with another systematically. Children, however, never see an entire input corpus at once but have to do their analysis of distribution on utterances received seriatim, with most utterances being processed and presumptively forgotten before the next one is received. So the competence which concerns us is the ability to register features of distribution under this condition of serial presentation.

In the sixties, beginning in the period when syntax was fashionable and semantics was considered a subject too fuzzy to be worthy of the serious attention of linguists, there was a brief spate of experimental studies of the learning of miniature, artificial, semantically-empty, language-like systems (e.g., Braine, 1963, 1965, 1966, 1971; Reber, 1967, 1969; Reber & Lewis, 1977; Segal & Halwes, 1965, 1966; Smith, 1966, 1969; Smith & Gough, 1969). The work soon adopted a paradigm (called the "verbal constructive memory" paradigm in Braine [1965] and Smith [1969]) that was as follows. One first dreamed up a miniature grammar the learning of which was of interest to study. The words were arbitrary tokens (English nonsense words, letters of the alphabet). Some proper subset of the strings generated by the grammar were assigned as input corpus and these were presented one after the other to subjects who listened to them on tape, or read them, or both listened and read. Subjects were sometimes children, more often adults. (No dramatic age differences are suggested by the work.) At various points subjects were tested to see what patterns of string formation they had acquired. For example, they might be asked to try to remember what they had heard. Since there would be too much material for it all to be recalled by rote, the "memory" is in part reconstruction. Alternatively, subjects would be presented with test strings (often ones they had not heard) and asked to say whether they were on the tape. In both cases, subjects would often "remember" material which they had not heard, and these "errors" indicate which distributional features were registered.

In general, this work demonstrated that certain distributional properties are quickly and easily registered by subjects. Subjects readily learn the positions of words (e.g., first, last) in short phrases (e.g., Braine, 1963; Smith, 1966); they learn the positions of words or phrases defined with respect to a marker, thought of as analogous to a function word (first after the marker; second after the marker) (Braine, 1966, 1971). They also readily learn dependencies (co-occurrences) between individual morphemes (e.g., Braine, 1965).

The work also indicated an important distributional feature which is extremely difficult for subjects to discover under these conditions (i.e., serial presentation of strings, no similarity relation among the words of a class other than their privileges of occurrence). Smith (1966, 1969) studied a miniature system with four grammatical classes, arbitrarily labeled M, N, P, and Q. Their privileges of occurrence were given by the rules $S \rightarrow M + N$, $S \rightarrow P + Q$. That is, all strings were two words long; M-words and P-words occurred first; N-words occurred second, but only after M-words; and Q-words occurred second but only after P-words. In Smith (1969), the string list was repeatedly presented, and at no point between initial exposure and complete rote learning was there any indication that subjects registered the dependency between the M–N and P–Q classes. The only pattern subjects learned was that M- and P-words went first, and that N- and Q-words went second, i.e., they "remembered" the "ungrammatical" MQ and PN strings as readily as the MN and PQ strings they had not heard. In sum, this laboratory work indicates that there is a huge gap between the ease with which subjects register simple positional properties and inter-morpheme co-occurrences, and the difficulty of registering the class dependencies of the MN/PQ structure.

Note that in the case of learning co-occurrences, the difference in difficulty has to do with whether the co-occurring items are morphemes or classes. Learning co-occurrences between morphemes is easy, between classes, difficult. (We are still talking, of course, of classes whose members share no common property other than where they appear in phrases or sentences—if there is a perceptible common property, that property can be taken as a morpheme, and then class co-occurrence learning reduces to morpheme co-occurrence learning.) While the relative difficulty may interact with the distance between the co-occurring items, learning co-occurrences between morphemes can be very easy even between nonneighboring items (Braine, 1965, 1966), whereas learning co-occurrences of classes has not been found in the laboratory work even in the ideally simplest case (the MN/PQ structure), where the co-occurring classes are adjacent.

If this difference in ease of acquisition found in the laboratory is true of native language acquisition, then we have an important constraint on language acquisition models. A number of current models (e.g., Anderson, 1983; MacWhinney, 1978; Pinker, 1984) build in learning mechanisms capable of acquiring arbitrary MN/PQ structures, and thus may be improperly powerful in this respect.

Natural languages contain features formally similar to the MN/PQ structure. We discuss some later. In an effort to bridge the gap between natural language acquisition and the results of studies of semantically empty systems, Moeser and Bregman (1972) used an artificial system that contained a reference world, and they varied the relations between the system and the world. They found, among other things, that certain class dependencies are easily acquired if they exactly mirror dependences between corresponding attributes in the reference world. This result has provided some fuel for the idea that a semantic basis is important for the acquisition of word classes and not just distribution. The class dependencies they studied were not precisely of the MN/PQ type, but there is no reason to doubt that the conclusion (that such dependencies would be easily acquired if they mirrored dependencies in the reference world) would be generalizable to the MN/PQ type. However, the bearing of this conclusion on ordinary language acquisition is uncertain because in some of the best natural language analogs of the MN/PQ type structure, there is only very meager mirroring in the language of real-world attributes, e.g., consider the typical poor quality of the correlation between masculine and feminine gender categories of nouns with male and female in the reference world. Studies of the acquisition of gender systems (e.g., Karmiloff-Smith, 1978; Levy, 1983; MacWhinney, 1978) do not suggest that the partial real-world correlate is the child's mode of entry into the system.

Based on another artificial language experiment with a reference world, Morgan and Newport (1981) have recently argued, against Moeser and Bregman, that the reference world functions in grammar acquisition primarily by clarifying constituent structure and indicating the boundaries of constituents, not by any more direct mirroring in the world of dependencies in the language. Their general point seems well taken, but the work, like other interesting recent artificial language work (e.g., MacWhinney, 1983), does not further clarify the basis of the learning of MN/PQ type structures in natural languages.

In sum, the laboratory work indicates that simple positional and co-occurrence relations are easy to pick up on a distributional basis, and that class dependencies of the MN/PQ type are quite hard.

With these considerations as background, let us consider the main word class categories, focusing on English.

NOUN, VERB, AND ADJECTIVE

Following a prior discussion (Braine, 1983), I make the assumption that we can take the notions "predicate" and "argument" for granted. I shall assume that the child's conceptual apparatus sees concepts and relations as made up of predicates and arguments, i.e., at the time of acquiring language, children see the world as having objects that bear properties and are related to other objects, and they distinguish the objects from their properties, and relations from the entities related. Thus, our acquisition theory is not going to account for the origins of these cognitive categories.

The parts of a sentence that identify arguments are the NPs that serve as subject, object, etc., of the verb, and the part of a sentence that communicates the predicate is what I shall call the "verbal phrase," i.e., the verb or predicate adjective or noun, together with their auxiliary morphemes. I shall take my assumption to mean that these phrases—at any rate a sufficient number of them—come to the learning mechanism marked with their function. They do not come labeled as NP and Verbal Phrase as such, of course, but as identifying arguments and predicates. What this means is that the child's distributional analysis mechanism does not have to discover that there are argument phrases and predicate phrases in sentences, nor, for a sufficient number of sentences, where the boundaries between them lie. Thus, the distributional analysis mechanism is going to analyze within NPs to discover nouns, and within Verbal Phrases to discover verbs and distinguish them from adjectives.

Parenthetically, I would note that the main work that the Predicate/Argument distinction does in the theory presented here is to legitimate the move away from whole sentences as the unit for distributional analysis, to NPs and Verbal Phrases as units considered separately. It does not seem feasible to me that the child could have a distributional analysis mechanism that would work on whole sentences and discover the noun, verb, and adjective categories. It does seem feasible that the child should have a distributional analysis mechanism that analyses NPs and discovers nouns and analyzes Verbal Phrases and discovers verbs and predicate adjectives. Any assumption that would permit this move from whole sentences as the unit of analysis to separate analysis of NPs and Verbal Phrases would serve the needs of the theory presented almost as well as the Predicate/Argument distinction.[1]

Nouns

The distributional structure of English NPs is shown in Figure 3.1. The structure is quite simple, consisting of slots for determiner and noun with optional slots before and after the noun for modifiers. The structure of the great majority of the NPs that a young child hears is even simpler, consisting of just the determiner in first position and the noun second without the modifiers. Registering the posi-

[1]However, the Predicate/Argument distinction accounts for the universality of the noun category, whereas other assumptions might not.

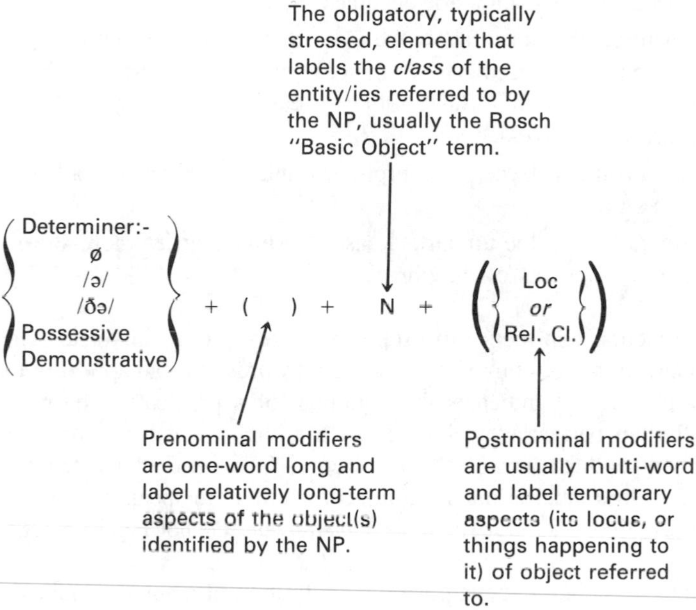
The obligatory, typically stressed, element that labels the *class* of the entity/ies referred to by the NP, usually the Rosch "Basic Object" term.
Determiner:-
ø
/ə/
/ðə/
Possessive
Demonstrative
+ (   ) +   N +
Loc
or
Rel. Cl.
Prenominal modifiers are one-word long and label relatively long-term aspects of the object(s) identified by the NP.
Postnominal modifiers are usually multi-word and label temporary aspects (its locus, or things happening to it) of object referred to.

FIGURE 3.1. The Structure of the English Noun Phrase, showing the four positions within it, and their typical content and function. The parentheses around the second and fourth positions indicate their optionality.

tional structure and marking the words that occur in the position that we call the Noun-slot would call for no abilities to register features of distribution that have not been demonstrated to be quite simple in artificial language experiments. Any mechanism capable of discovering positions in short strings would discover the Noun-slot easily.

Not only is the distributional analysis formally quite simple, but in fact the acquisition task is made even easier by the fact, indicated in Figure 1, that each position within the NP has distinct semantic functions. That is, an argument phrase consists of a word labeling the class of the entity or entities one is talking about, with a determiner preceding it (in speech to young children, commonly either /ə/, /ðə/, or a possessive). The class word can be preceded or followed by modifiers: preceding modifiers label relatively lasting properties of the entity, usually by means of a single word; following modifiers label temporary properties (locus, things happening to it), usually using several words to do so (e.g., a prepositional phrase or relative clause). Thus, the noun labels the class of the argument and the modifiers narrow the range of possibilities within that class.

In general, the Noun-slot within an NP presents a confluence of properties:

1. Structural: The Noun-slot occupies a particular position in the phrase.[2]
2. Semantic: The noun labels the class of the entity or entities that are the argument of the predicate; in the case of definite NPs, the label is almost always the Rosch "Basic Object" class label (Rosch, Mervis, Gray, Johnson, & Boyes-Braem, 1976).
3. Obligatoriness: Except for pronouns and proper names, all NPs have a Noun-slot.
4. Prominence: In the unmarked case, the noun carries more stress than the other components of the phrase.

This particular confluence of properties appears to be universal. That is, the nouns of any language comprise the set of all words that can appear in the Noun-slot of a phrase that indicates the argument of a predicate. The Noun-slot is universally that particular position in such a phrase that labels the class of the entity or entities that comprise the argument. (Note, incidentally, that to speak of a noun as a class label is much more accurate than to speak of it as naming an object: nouns like *earthquake, week, smell, war,* do not label objects, but are class terms.)

Given the simplicity of the positional definition of a noun combined with the clarity of its semantic function, it is predictable that children would acquire the category very early in language development.

The universality as well as the ease of acquisition are to be expected on the basis of the view developed. The universality depends, first, on the postulate that the predicate-argument distinction is available at the outset of language acquisition. This postulate, taken with the fact that most sentences express predicate-argument relations (whatever else they express), guarantees the universality of the NP, i.e., of phrases that identify arguments. The convenience of identifying an argument by making some reference to the class of the entity or entities that constitute the argument then brings about the universality of the Noun-slot within the NP. Further, the fact that the human concept learning mechanism is apparently built to preferentially extract concepts at a particular level of generality (the Rosch "basic object" level) makes it likely that this is the level used most of the time in identifying arguments.

Claims about the universality of the Noun category are usually vague as to whether it is the Noun-slot that is claimed to be universal, or whether it is the word class. It would be logically possible for a language to have Noun-slots without nouns as a word class (i.e., without earmarking words in the mental dictionary for appearance in Noun-slots). Indeed, Chinese has been suggested as such a language (e.g., Herdan, 1964). In the present theory the Noun-slot is logically prior to the Noun-class, and any universality of the Noun-class would

---

[2]In inflected languages, it is also the element with which other items in the phrase are in concord.

be secondary to the universality of the Noun-slot. On the present view, the noun as a word-class, i.e., as a tag on a word in the mental dictionary, would come from a tendency, amply demonstrated in the artificial language work reviewed above, for the learner to tag words for the string position in which they appear.

Verbs and Adjectives

Verbs and predicate adjectives are clearly marked as different from the auxiliary elements in verbal phrases both positionally and semantically. Positionally, they occur after the auxiliaries. Semantically, they are the words that communicate the main predicate, as opposed to the auxiliaries which express time features that are relevant for the predication. Thus, acquiring the distinction of verb or adjective from auxiliary would be expected to be an extremely simple distributional-analysis task, rendered even easier by a correlated, clear, semantic-role distinction.

Distinguishing distributionally between verb and predicate adjective is a more complex task, since, because of the similarity of their positions in verbal phrases, the distinction cannot be made solely on the basis of position in short strings. Nevertheless, there is a rather straightforward distributional difference. Unlike verbs, predicate adjectives are always immediately preceded by one or other of a very small group of verbs, including notably *be* and *get* (in the sense of 'become'—*become* itself, of course, also belongs to the group although it is much rarer than *get* in conversational English). In the case of verbs, the verb inflexions (*-ing, -ed, -en*) go on the verb itself; in the case of adjectives, these inflexions go on the *be* or *get* that precedes the adjective, not on the adjective itself.[3]

The distinctive marking with *be* or *get* is present in all kinds of phrases that accept both verbs and predicate adjectives, e.g., in infinitives and imperatives:

$$\text{to [verb]} \quad \textit{vs.} \quad \text{to} \begin{Bmatrix} \text{be} \\ \text{get} \end{Bmatrix} \text{[adjective]}$$

$$\text{(Don't) [verb]!} \quad \textit{vs.} \quad \text{(Don't)} \begin{Bmatrix} \text{be} \\ \text{get} \end{Bmatrix} \text{[adjective]!}$$

In main verbal phrases, the same difference is presented in underlying structure:

$$\text{Aux [verb]} \quad \textit{vs.} \quad \text{Aux} \begin{Bmatrix} \text{be} \\ \text{get} \end{Bmatrix} \text{[adjective]}$$

---

[3]Predicate nominals and locatives are, of course, like adjectives in taking preceding *be* (though not *get*). However, they both contain distinctive marking—nominals by a preceding article, and locatives by their preposition + NP structure. So registering the difference among predicate adjectives, nominals and locatives demands very little from a distributional analysis mechanism.

However, in surface structure the *be* often appears in a form (e.g., *is, was*) with no phonological resemblance to *be*. No doubt this complicates the distributional-analysis task somewhat, since to discover the underlying *be* the child has to come to understand that *is* = 'present' + *be* and *was* = 'past' + *be*. Nevertheless, the kind of distributional learning that is demanded falls within the kinds found to be simple in the artificial language work. No MN/PQ type structures are involved. The learner has to learn (a) co-occurrences between neighboring items (that certain words—i.e., adjectives—require a preceding *be* or *get* when they are inserted in verbal phrases), and (b) the position of the inflexions (that *-ing, ed, -en* go on the *be* or *get,* not on the following adjective).

It follows from this analysis that the distinction between verbs and predicate adjectives should be relatively easy for a child to acquire, though somewhat harder than the noun category because the distributional properties that distinguish verbs and predicate adjectives are nevertheless a little more complex than those that mark nouns.

It seems to be the case that in acquiring the distinction between verb and predicate adjective, the learner can get little help from the semantic correlates of the classes. As Maratsos and Chalkley (1980) point out, although most adjectives are stative, some have an actional component in their meaning; and although many verbs express actions, there are also many stative verbs. Moreover, if one compares actional verbs, stative verbs, and adjectives in respect to the auxiliaries that typically occur with them, one finds that the adjectives lie between the action and stative verbs, i.e., action and stative verbs differ more from each other in their co-occurring auxiliaries than either differs from adjectives. For example, progressive forms are very common for action verbs (e.g., *He is jogging*), ungrammatical for stative verbs (**He is knowing*), and typically possible but uncommon for adjectives (e.g., *He is being serious*). Thus, unlike noun, where we find a clear semantic as well as distributional correlate of the class, the acquisition of the distinction between verb and predicate adjective seems likely to be wholly based on distributional analysis. This conclusion is consistent with the fact that the verb-adjective distinction appears not to be universal (e.g., Chinese is said not to have it [Li and Thompson, 1981]); moreover, among the many languages that do make the distinction, a given concept may not always be assigned to the same class (e.g., Hebrew has a verb for 'to be late' whereas English has only the adjective).[4]

---

[4]Some qualifications to this analysis may be necessary. First, other possible semantic correlates than action/state could be relevant. For example, adjectives are commonly susceptible to degree modifiers like *very, quite, rather,* etc., and that is presumably because they express properties that can vary in degree. (However, all-or-nothing adjectives like *present-absent* do not take degree modifiers, and, on the other hand, some verbs also label attributes that intrinsically vary in degree, e.g., *hurt, ache, bend, clean.*)

Second, adjectives, but not verbs, occur as prenominal noun modifiers, whereas both verbs and adjectives occur as postnominal modifiers in relative clauses. This distributional difference could be

Segmentation Errors in the Input

It is to be expected that from time to time children will make mistakes in assigning boundaries to argument phrases and verbal phrases. For instance, a child hearing *The old hated to hit it* might construe *The old hated to* as the argument phrase and thus /hetɨdtʊ/ as the word for whatever was ''old'' that hit what *it* referred to; /hetɨdtʊ/ might then be tagged as a noun.

Any language acquisition model must be robust against occasional errors in the input, whether these come from adult ungrammaticalities or disfluencies or from children's misunderstanding of what is said to them. In general, such robustness can be accomplished by arranging that learning is gradual; no simple input by itself has much of an affect on what is learned, for good or ill, and certainly no decisive effect. Thus, /hetɨdtʊ/ may indeed be weakly registered as a noun on some occasion, but since it does not repeat in the input in contexts leading to construal as the head of an argument phrase, it will soon be forgotten and have no permanent effect on what is learned.

The problem of input error is a general problem for acquisition models; it arises for virtually any specific theory of any aspect of language acquisition, and demands a solution that transcends specific theories. The problem is extensively discussed in Braine (1971, 1983), and these papers propose a general kind of model (called a ''sieve memory'' model in Braine [1983]) that is capable of acquiring grammatical rules despite a certain amount of input error. The model is perfectly compatible with the theory of word class acquisition proposed here. That language learners are in fact able to acquire grammatical patterns from input containing unsystematic errors is demonstrated for the acquisition of an artificial language in Braine (1971).

GENDER AND OTHER ARBITRARY SUBCLASSES OF NOUNS AND VERBS

I take gender subclasses of nouns as a prototypical example of an arbitrary subclass, and consider this in some detail, ending with some discussion of declension and conjugation classes in inflected languages.

Noun gender categories differ from the main word classes in that they present to the learner a distributional problem with some formal similarity to the MN/PQ structure. Figure 3.2 schematizes the problem structure. $M(m_1, m_2, \ldots m_m)$

---

relevant to the acquisition of the verb-adjective distinction. However, prenominal adjectives and predicate adjectives are not exactly the same class. There are many predicate adjectives that do not occur prenominally, e.g., *ready, okay, asleep, ahead, alive;* similarly, not every prenominal modifier can occur predicatively; finally, there are words that have both uses, but with quite different meanings in each use, e.g., *late.* So it is not at all clear that occurrences of verbs and adjectives in NPs must be relevant to the acquisition of the distinction between Verb and Predicate Adjective.

$$\left\{\begin{array}{c}\text{Determiner } (=n_i)\\ \text{Determiner } (=n_j)\\ \text{—}\end{array}\right\} + \left\{\begin{array}{c} m_1\\ m_2\\ \cdot\\ \cdot\\ \cdot\\ \cdot\\ m_m\end{array}\right\} + \left[\begin{array}{c}\text{Adjectival}\\ \text{modifier}\\ \text{or}\\ \text{verb}\end{array}\right] - \left\{\begin{array}{c}\text{affix } (=n_1)\\ \text{affix } (=n_2)\\ \text{—}\\ \text{—}\end{array}\right\}$$

$$\left\{\begin{array}{c}\text{Determiner } (=q_i)\\ \text{Determiner } (=q_i)\\ \text{—}\end{array}\right\} + \left\{\begin{array}{c} p_1\\ p_2\\ \cdot\\ \cdot\\ \cdot\\ \cdot\\ p_n\end{array}\right\} + \left[\begin{array}{c}\text{Adjectival}\\ \text{modifier}\\ \text{or}\\ \text{verb}\end{array}\right] - \left\{\begin{array}{c}\text{affix } (=q_1)\\ \text{affix } (=q_2)\\ \text{—}\\ \text{—}\end{array}\right\}$$

FIGURE 3.2. A Schematization of a Typical "Gender" Problem Space. Note—M ($m_1, \ldots m_m$) are the "masculine" nouns, P ($p_1, \ldots p_n$) the feminine nouns. We have assumed a language in which determiners precede the noun and adjectival modifiers follow it, but the linear order of these elements is immaterial to the formal structure.

and $P(p_1, p_2, \ldots \mathrm{p_n})$ are the masculine and feminine nouns, respectively. $N(n_1, n_2, \ldots)$ is the class of all the affixes that co-occur ("agree") with the members of M, and $Q(q_1, q_2, \ldots)$ is the class of the affixes that co-occur with the members of P. Alternatively (or in addition), N and Q may be classes of determiners the selection of which depends on whether the noun is masculine or feminine.

Natural gender systems have two properties which are not brought out clearly in Figure 3.2 and which were not present in Smith's (1966, 1969) system but which may be relevant to understanding how such categories are acquired. One of these is the statistical imbalance in the sizes of the classes: The N and Q (affix) classes are closed classes with very few members relative to the enormous size of M and P. There is some experimental evidence from work on the old "acquired stimulus equivalence paradigm" that such a size imbalance could facilitate learning the class dependencies (Foss & Jenkins, 1966).

The other property lies in the partial phonological cues that are often present in natural systems. Thus, in Italian, masculine nouns very often end in *-o* and feminine in *-a*. In Hebrew, nouns ending in *-a* and *-t* are usually feminine, and other nouns usually masculine. However, these rules are merely statistical; there are many exceptions. It is also common that affixes on adjectives or verbs that agree with the nouns are phonologically similar to the statistically favored noun endings. Thus, in Hebrew, the singular feminine affixes are the suffixes *-a, -et, -at, -t* (*-it* vs. masculine *-i*), infixed *-t-* (e.g., *alta* vs. masculine *ala* 'went up'), and prefixed *t-* (e.g., *taale* vs. masculine *yaale* 'will go up'); the statistically favored feminine noun endings are *-a, -et, -at, -it, -ut;* modifiers frequently rhyme with the noun they agree with, and there is evidence for rhyming strategies in children and in rapid adult speech (Levy, 1983b).

One would predict that the child's first steps in acquiring gender would be the formation of associations between small elements (e.g., between noun endings and adjective endings, between endings and articles), and of particular nouns with particular articles or with particular endings of adjectives or verbs. There is, in fact, abundant evidence for the acquisition of such inter-item dependencies at early stages of development before the gender categories as such are acquired. Thus, in Hebrew, the feminine plural ending *-ot* first appears on nouns ending in *-a:* The rule, change *-a* to *-ot,* is attested by errors of overgeneralization, and *-ot* is later extended to various classes of nouns ending in *-t* (Levy, 1983a). In French, children learn early the associations between articles and endings like /-õ/, leading to errors like **le maison* (Karmiloff-Smith, 1978). It is likely that adjective contrasts like *bon-bonne, brun-brune* contribute to the acquisition of the association of *le* with nasalized vowel ending and *la* with nasal consonant ending, and, more generally, the contrast between masculine vocalic and feminine consonantal endings is very common in French adjectives (*le beau-la belle, mauvais mauvaise,* etc.). There is similar evidence for acquisition of dependencies between small elements for other languages (see Levy, 1983b, and MacWhinney, 1978, for examples).

However, at some point the child must go beyond acquisition of inter-item dependencies to the formation of the gender categories themselves, and that requires solving the problem of the MN/PQ structure. How that is done is still obscure.

Many years ago, I did a miniature artificial language experiment with Philip Arnsfield that may throw some light on the problem. It provides a laboratory demonstration of gender class acquisition that includes acquisition of class dependencies of the MN/PQ type. Its purpose was to explore whether gender class acquisition would be facilitated by the existence of a similarity relation among a subset of each gender class. Thus, we compared two formally equivalent miniature languages (in one of which there was such a partial similarity relation and in the other not) to see whether the first would be significantly easier to learn than the other.

A Miniature-Language Experiment on Gender Classes

The experiment was done well before the recent developmental work on gender categories, and at the time I considered that the most plausible partial similarity relation underlying gender categories would be natural sex. (As discussed later, I now think that the most plausible partial similarity relations are phonological, not semantic.) Thus, in one language (the experimental language) half the "masculine'' nouns designated males, and half the ''feminine'' nouns designated females. (The other nouns designated inanimate objects.) In the other (control) language, both classes were equivalent in composition (the designata being 25% male, 25% female, and 50% inanimate). The question was whether the semantic consistency of a subset of each class would help the learner discover the existence of the classes in the language.

The Languages. Both languages contained nouns and number words; every ''sentence'' consisted of a noun followed by a number word, and together they described a picture, stating what the items in the picture were, and how many there were. The words were pronounceable nonsense words.

Each language contained the same 24 nouns, 12 designating things (e.g., chair, rifle) and 12 designating kinds of people, 6 male (e.g., soldier, baseball player) and 6 female (e.g., nurse, airline stewardess). The nouns were divided into two classes: ''M'' and ''P.'' Half the things were randomly assigned to the M-class and half to the P-class. In the experimental language the six males were assigned to the M-class and the six females to the P-class, whereas in the control language three males and three females were assigned to each class. (Thus, the only difference between the languages is that the M—P distinction is correlated with natural sex in the experimental language, but not in the control.) The number words had to ''agree'' with the class of the noun. That is, there were two words for 'one' or 'singular,' one used when the noun was an M-word and the other if it were a P-word; similarly, there were two words for 'two' (or 'dual'), one used with M-nouns and the other with P-nouns; and likewise two words for 'plural' (i.e., more than two). (Thus, there were 72 possible sentences—24 nouns combinable with three numbers—and 72 pictures, one describable by each sentence.) There were no partial phonological similarities among the six number words. They were all monosyllabic, and no number word shared any vowel or consonant with any other.

Procedure. The languages were taught by means of a paired-associated technique with the pictures as stimuli. The experiment consisted of three stages.

In the first stage, the subjects learned to a criterion the vocabulary of 24 nouns as one-word responses to pictures of the items.

In the second stage, two-word sentence responses had to be given to the pictures, telling what the item was, and how many there were. A set of 48 pictures was used. Each item (and therefore each noun) appeared twice: for one third of the items the numbers were 'one' and 'two,' for one third 'one' and 'plural,' and for the remaining third 'two' and 'plural.' After an initial study trial, the pictures (in random order) were presented and represented until subjects reached the learning criterion of generating the right description of each picture. The few subjects who were still making errors at the tenth trial were discontinued.

The third stage was a test stage including a generalization test. The subjects were exposed once to all 72 pictures and had to generate a description of each. The pictures included the 48 learned in the second stage, plus the 24 that had been left out and which the subjects had not seen before; these 24 comprised the generalization test.

Subjects. Each language was taught to 18 college students.

Results. A criterion was set for "solving" the generalization test that involved essentially perfect command of the system: correct naming of 11 of the 12 new people pictures and also 11 of the 12 new object pictures. In general, subjects tended either to give correct responses throughout the generalization test, or else to obtain scores no better than chance on the 24 new people and object pictures.

In the experimental language 17 of the 18 subjects reached the second stage learning criterion and 13 of them solved the generalization test. Two other experimental subjects showed some partial command of the system in that they solved the people items of the generalization test but failed to assign gender to new object items. In the control language, 16 of the 18 subjects reached the second stage learning criterion, but only six of them solved the generalization test. None of the other subjects obtained scores on either the people or the object items of the test that were significantly better than chance, thus showing no evidence of partial command of the system. These subjects never discovered that the "nouns" of the language were divided into two classes.

In sum, 13 of 18 subjects acquired the gender classes of the experimental language as against 6 of 18 for the control. The difference is significant (chi-square [1 d.f.] = 5.5, $p < .02$) indicating that the partial semantic correlate of the classes of the experimental language made it easier to discover the existence of the classes. Interestingly, interviews with the few subjects who mastered the control language indicated that some of them had manufactured some ad hoc semantic correlate for the classes.

Discussion. The experiment provides a demonstration that learning the class dependencies of an MN/PQ type structure is made easier when there is a partial correlate of the classes, i.e., when there is a similarity relation among a subset of each of the contrasting classes.

It seems to me that the results argue that the learning that occurred in the experimental language in this experiment is an associative process in which the foci of associations are not just lexical items, but also features. Thus, subjects begin by registering co-occurrences not just among items, but also co-occurrences of items with features. The first co-occurrences relevant to the class learning are those of the number words with the features 'male' and 'female' present in half the nouns of each set. Thus, the number words of one set become marked with the feature [co-occurs with 'male'] and those of the other set with [co-occurs with 'female']. Once the number words have acquired these new features, the features themselves become available for association back upon the nouns. Thus, the ''masculine'' nouns, including particularly those that designate objects, acquire the feature [co-occurs with number word bearing the feature (co-occurs with 'male')], and the ''feminine'' nouns acquire the feature [co-occurs with number word bearing the feature (co-occurs with 'female')]. The learning is then complete. The subject has two classes of nouns each marked as cooccurring with one of two classes of number words.

Application to Gender and Other Arbitrary Subclasses of Nouns and Verbs in Natural Languages

In the preceding experiment, the use of the features 'male' and 'female' is almost certainly not crucial to the learning. No doubt we could have made half the objects of one class striped, and half of the objects of the other class spotted, and achieved the same results. The available evidence reviewed earlier suggests that the relevant partial correlate is usually phonological, not semantic, for natural language gender classes. That is, the phonological correlates play much the same role in nature as the semantic correlates in this experiment.

The associations that are most relevant to the formation of gender categories are those of which the correlate is the focus, i.e., co-occurrences between the correlate and affixes, articles, etc. These associations are of course made easier to learn if there are phonological similarities between the correlate (noun ending) and the affixes, such, for instance, as give rise to rhyme (as in Hebrew). Learning would also be facilitated (by reducing the number of associations to be acquired) if there were real phonological similarities among the affixes, or among subsets of them, as there usually are. Note that at the end of learning, new exceptional nouns can be handled easily since hearing the exception with one article or affix marks which other articles or affixes must be used.

The theory presented would predict differences in ease of acquisition of arbitrary subclasses as a function of properties of the partial correlates, such as their salience, their relative frequency of occurrence in the subclass, and the number of correlates that mark the subclass. Thus, since phonological associates of noun gender are more consistently and more simply marked in Italian and Spanish nouns than in French and more in French than in German, the theory would predict that children would more easily acquire the gender categories in Italian and Spanish than in French and more easily in French than in German.[5] However, the fine-grained data needed to check such a prediction are lacking.

---

[5]MacWhinney has suggested to me in personal communication that German may have more phonological aids than is apparent to the inspection of a nonnative nonspeaker (see also Kopcke and Zubin, 1983).

Declension and Conjugation classes. In applying this line of analysis to declension and conjugation classes, the relevant affixes are the case endings in declension classes and endings for person, number, and tense in conjugation classes. In the languages I am familiar with, the stem classes are marked phonologically (e.g., by the final vowel or consonant of the stem), and that phonological feature plays the role of associational focus. The approach leads to a simpler view of the acquisition of inflectional systems than some other theories in the literature (e.g., Pinker, 1984; Anderson, 1983). To concretize discussion of the differences between their approaches and the present one, I will take the inflectional classes of Latin nouns as example.[6] Representative examples from the five declensions (singular number only) are set out in the top part of Table 1 for reference.

The first issue, a crucial one, concerns the segmentation of stems from endings. Pinker posits that the child examines all case forms of a noun and takes what is held in common among them as the stem (Pinker, 1984, Procedure 14, p. 188). This leads to the segmentations shown in the middle rows of Table 1 (cf. Pinker, 1984, Fig. 5.1, p. 174). This segmentation causes the thematic vowels (e.g., the first declension *-a-*) to be taken as part of the ending, not of the stem, and means that there are about as many endings for any given case as there are declensions, e.g., for the nouns represented in Table 1, there would be seven different nominative endings and five different accusative endings across the five declensions. (Pinker's procedure is problematic in other ways, too, e.g., for the many third declension nouns like *ordo, ordin-em, -is,* etc., and *miles, milit-em,* etc., the procedure would deliver absurd stems like *ord-* and *mil-*, rather than the correct *ordin-, milit-*.)

The present approach, which stresses associative (co-occurrence) learning, would take the thematic vowels as part of the noun stem. This leads to the segmentations shown in the lower third of Table 1. Note that this segmentation greatly reduces the variety of endings for each case. If we except the deviant nominatives of the neuter nouns (*bellum* in Table 1), there are never more than two case forms for any case. Apart from the accusative (where there is just one form common to all the declensions), the child has only to learn which of two possible forms is to be used with a noun stem. Moreover, the choice of which form to use is contingent on the final phoneme of the noun stem, so virtually the entire learning task reduces to the psychologically simple mechanism of associating case signals with the final phoneme of the noun stem. The learning is not

[6]I take Latin as example because I have some acquaintance with it (from having been obliged to study it in my youth). Since the purpose is to discuss principles and contrast the mechanisms of theories, the example will serve. The reader should be warned, however, that there is evidence that many spoken dialects of Latin departed from the classical forms even in classical times, and my reading in this area (e.g., Elcock, 1960; Palmer, 1961) suggests that it is not certain that there was ever a generation of children that learned precisely the classical forms as their native spoken language.

TABLE 1
The Latin Declension Classes (singular forms only).

Case	*Class I a-stem*	*Class II o-stem*[1]		*Class III Consonant & i-stem*			*Cl's IV u-stem*	*Cl's V e-stem*	*No. of endings*
	Representative examples								
Nom.	insula	annus	bellum	urbs	pater	ignis	manus	res	—
Acc.	insulam	annum	bellum	urbem	patrem	ignem	manum	rem	—
Gen.	insulae	annī	bellī	urbis	patris	ignis	manus	reī	—
Dat.	insulae	annō	bellō	urbī	patrī	ignī	manui	reī	—
Abl.	insulā	annō	bellō	urbe	patre	igne	manu	rē	—
	Pinker's segmentation								
Nom.	insul-a	ann-us	bell-um	urb-s	pater-ø	ign-is			7
Acc.	-am	-um	-um	-em	patr-em	-em			5
Gen.	-ae	-i	-i	-is	-is	-is	etc.		5
Dat.	-ae	-o	-o	-i	-i	-i			4
Abl.	-a	-o	-o	-e	-e	-e			5
	Segmentation with vowel in stem								
Nom.	insula-ø	an $\frac{u}{o}$-s	bell $\frac{u}{o}$-s	urb-s	patr-ø	igni-s			ø, -s, -m
Acc.	-m	-m	-m	-m	-m	(i→e)-m			-m[4]
Gen.	-i[2]	$\frac{u}{o}$→i	$\frac{u}{o}$→i	-(i)s	-(i)s	-s	etc.		-i, -s[4]
Dat.	-i[2]	-:[3]	-:	-i	-i	-:			-:[3], -i
Abl.	-:[3]	-:	-:	-e	-e	i→e			-:, -e

[1]Class II nouns are consistently called *o*-stems in the linguistic literature. Old Latin had *o* in the nom. and acc., as did many spoken dialects of late Latin or early Romance (Kent, 1946; Elcock, 1960). In the nom. and acc., the /u/ reflects a morphophonemic rule raising /o/ to /u/ in these forms, operative in the classical dialect.

[2]/ai/ = *ae.*

[3]: = length.

[4]Acc. *-m* and gen. *-s* are syllabic and require an intercalated vowel after a consonant.

always a process of *adding* a case signal to a stem. For instance, in the second declension genitive, the *-i* ending replaces the stem vowel rather than follows it; for the accusative *-m* and genitive *-s* signals, a vowel has to be intercalated for consonantal stems to keep the ending syllabic, and the child would have to learn which vowel. There are also morphophonemic rules needed to generate some of the surface forms, e.g., in some third declension nominatives, e.g., *patr* + ø = *pater*. However, none of these details disturb the conception of the learning process as associative in nature.

There are some parts of the Latin system where the present analysis predicts difficulty because the associations that have to be posited become complex, e.g., the fact that the nominative is the same as the accusative in neuter nouns (e.g., *bellum* in Table 1). However, from early stages of Latin, evidence from graffiti and from Plautus (Elcock, 1960; Palmer, 1961) indicates for the spoken language both that neuter nouns of the pattern of *bellum* often had nominatives with -s (like *annus*) and that the fourth declension *u*-stems were assimilated to the second declension (again like *annus*). These are the major points where an associative learner would be expected to encounter difficulty. Neither the neuter gender nor the fourth declension survived into early Romance. Certain other forms that this analysis would predict to occur readily are also attested in Latin, e.g., *-im* as the accusative of third declension *i*-stems (e.g., forms like *ignim* in place of *ignem* in Table 1) (e.g., Kent, 1946).

Note that under this analysis the problem of accounting for the acquisition of arbitrary subclasses largely disappears. One does not have to postulate that the child possesses a learning mechanism powerful enough to provide a general solution of the MN/PQ problem. Languages with complex declension and conjugation classes seem always to have thematic stem vowels and consonants, and the present analysis explains why: These phonological elements are needed as associative foci; languages without them would be filtered out as human languages by the learner's failure to learn.

It might be objected that I have not proposed any mechanism whereby a child might arrive at the segmentation proposed. My suggestion would be that at the beginning of learning the child takes the most frequent form of a noun heard as the stem (usually, no doubt, the nominative), and initially computes case forms as changes on this initial form. Then, as soon as some productive case-forming rules have been acquired, stems would be arrived at by back formation. The most likely first productive case-forming rule is the addition of *-m* to form the accusative, since that is frequent and the same across all declensions; moreover, the accusative rule could be very readily learned from the common first declension nouns as a simple addition of *-m* to the nominative as stem. Most stems would then be formed by subtracting the accusative *-m*.

This analysis of Latin is quite similar to MacWhinney's (1978, 1985) analysis of Hungarian, both in general spirit and in a number of details. For example, MacWhinney assigns thematic vowels and consonants to noun and verb stems and allows a deletable segment in an underlying representation to control the choice of affix. Moreover, the data of MacWhinney (1978) indicate that an account of the type proposed here for Latin works well for a language for which quite detailed developmental data have been obtained.

We have seen that Pinker's segmentation procedure puts the thematic vowel in the ending rather than the stem and thus assigns the vowel no role in the learning. Because of this and because he sets up declension classes as independent paradigms, he is forced to provide his model with a learning mechanism capable of a general solution of the MN/PQ problem, i.e., of discovering such classes even when they lack any semantic or phonological correlates (Pinker, 1984, Procedures I8 and I9, pp. 197–8, which are quite similar in logic to a last-resort procedure of MacWhinney's model [cf. MacWhinney, 1978, p. 111]). The procedure assumes that a child's long-term memory has some self-editing capability, i.e., when children find competing sets of affixes for the same set of cases, they are able to survey and compare word-specific paradigms that already exist in long-term memory to see which sets of affixes occur with which stems; they then set up arbitrary class labels for each set of stems that take a distinct set of affixes so that the affix-sets no longer compete. Anderson's (1983) model also assumes that the child has a general method of solving the MN/PQ problem for classes without semantic or phonological correlates. The method also uses a long-term memory with self-editing capability; the memory continually self-edits for economy by collapsing similar rules, creating word classes when their creation would simplify the rule system (Anderson, 1983, pp. 282–284).

Both the laboratory learning studies and the actual structure of natural inflectional systems make it doubtful that the child has a learning mechanism capable of solving the MN/PQ problem for classes without either semantic or phonological partial correlates. Thus, the models of Pinker and Anderson are probably inappropriately powerful. I would also urge that postulation of a long-term memory with a self-editing capability is an overly rich addition to a language acquisition model's innate structure; parsimony would prefer a model without that capability.

SUMMARY AND CONCLUSIONS

The theory outlined in this paper is a theory of *what* is learned in acquiring word classes. It is not a model of *how* learning takes place. Although the theory has a natural fit with my sieve-memory acquisition model (Braine, 1971; 1983), it would no doubt be quite compatible with other models of the acquisition process and is therefore open for borrowing. It could be incoporated into models like Pinker's, Anderson's, or MacWhinney's (1978) with little change to the components of these models which are not aimed specifically at word-class acquisition.

The theory is a special case of what Pinker (1984) has called a ''bootstrapping'' theory. It differs from prior theories by taking 'predicate' and 'argument' as the primitive semantic notions that ultimately underlie the main word classes, rather than 'object' and 'action' as Grimshaw (1981) and Pinker (1984) do. It also assigns a somewhat larger role to distributional analysis mechanisms in the acquisition of word classes than other boot-strapping theories have done. It thus expands the range of options within this family of models.

In general, the paper shows that if we take the distinction between a predicate and its arguments for granted as a primitive notion that is within the child's cognitive competence at the outset of language acquisition, then it is possible to build a theory of the acquisition of word classes that is based primarily on the child's sensitivity to the distribution of elements in argument phrases and predicate phrases.

The theory's merits include the following:

1. The assumptions made about the child's ability to register properties of distribution are rooted in laboratory evidence about human pattern-learning abilities for linguistic or language-like material. There is laboratory evidence that the postulated abilities exist, and for a crude, easy-to-difficult, learnability metric.
2. The theory predicts the relative order of difficulty as Noun, Verb vs. Adjective, and Gender Classes—an order that seems to conform with observation.
3. The theory delivers an account of the basis of "noun" that explains both the basicness and universality of that category.
4. In the acquisition of subclasses, the theory's emphasis on associative learning (i.e., the learning of contingencies or co-occurrences, especially with phonological elements) accords well within the evidence for the widespread existence of such elements as possible foci of associations in natural declension and conjugation systems.

ACKNOWLEDGMENTS

Preparation of this paper was partially supported by a fellowship at the Institute for Advanced Studies of the Hebrew University of Jerusalem. The paper profits from discussions of the general topic with Michael Maratsos, Yonata Levy, Izchak Schlesinger, Mary-Anne Chalkley, and Anat Ninio during the time the first draft was written. I thank Brain MacWhinney for useful comments on the penultimate draft.

REFERENCES

Anderson, J. R. (1983). *The architecture of cognition*. Cambridge, MA: Harvard University Press.
Braine, M. D. S. (1963). On learning the grammatical order of words. *Psychological Review, 70*, 323–348.

Braine, M. D. S. (1965). The insufficiency of a finite state model for verbal reconstructive memory. *Psychonomic Science, 2,* 291–292.

Braine, M. D. S. (1966). Learning the positions of words relative to a marker element. *Journal of Experimental Psychology, 72,* 532–540.

Braine, M. D. S. (1971). On two types of models of the internalization of grammars. In D. I. Slobin (Ed.), *The ontogenesis of grammar.* New York: Academic Press.

Braine, M. D. S. (1983). *Modeling the acquisition of linguistic structure.* Ms.

Brown, R. W. (1957). Linguistic determinism and part of speech. *Journal of Abnormal & Social Psychology, 55,* 1–5.

Elcock, W. D. (1960). *The romance languages.* London: Faber & Faber.

Foss, D. J., & Jenkins, J. J. (1966). Mediated stimulus equivalence as a function of the number of converging stimulus items. *Journal of Experimental Psychology, 71,* 738–745.

Grimshaw, J. (1981). Form, function, and the language acquisition device. In C. L. Baker and J. J. McCarthy (Eds.), *The logical problem of language acquisition.* Cambridge, MA: MIT Press.

Harris, Z. S. (1951). *Methods in structural linguistics.* Chicago, IL: University of Chicago Press.

Herdan, G. (1964). *The structuralist approach to Chinese grammar and vocabulary.* The Hague: Mouton.

Karmiloff-Smith, A. (1978). The interplay between syntax, semantics, and phonology in language acquisition processes. In R. Campbell & P. Smith (Eds.), *Recent advances in the psychology of language.* New York: Plenum.

Kent, R. G. (1946). *The forms of Latin: A descriptive and historical morphology.* Baltimore, MD: The Linguistic Society of America.

Köpcke, K. & Zubin, D. (1983). Die kognitive Organisation der Genuszuweisung zu den einsilbigen Nomen der Deutschen Gegenwartssprache. *Zeitschrift fur germanistische Linguistik 11,* 166–182.

Levy, Y. (1983a). The acquisition of Hebrew plurals—the case of the missing gender category. *Journal of Child Language, 10,* 107–121.

Levy, Y. (1983b). It's frogs all the way down. *Cognition, 15,* 75–93.

Li, C. N., & Thompson, S. A. (1981). *Mandarin Chinese: A functional reference grammar.* Berkeley, CA: University of California Press.

MacWhinney, B. (1978). *The acquisition of morphophonology. Monographs of the Society for Research in Child Development, 43,* 1–2 (Serial No. 174).

MacWhinney, B. (1983). Miniature linguistic systems as tests of the use of universal operating principles in second-language learning by children and adults. *Journal of Psycholinguistic Research, 12,* 467–478.

MacWhinney, B. (1985). Hungarian language acquisition as an exemplification of a general model of grammatical development. In D. Slobin (Ed.) *The cross-linguistic study of language acquisition.* Hillsdale, NJ: Lawrence Erlbaum.

Maratsos, M. P., & Chalkley, M. A. (1980). The internal language of children's syntax: The ontogenesis and representation of syntactic categories. In K. Nelson (Ed.), *Children's language* (Vol. II). New York: Gardner Press.

Moeser, D. S., & Bregman, A. S. (1972). The role of reference in the acquisition of a miniature artificial language. *Journal of Verbal Learning and Verbal Behavior, 11,* 759–769.

Morgan, J. L., & Newport, E. L. (1981). The role of constituent structure in the induction of an artifical language. *Journal of Verbal Learning and Verbal Behavior, 20,* 67–85.

Palmer, L. R. (1961). *The Latin Language.* London: Faber & Faber.

Pinker, S. (1984). *Language learnability and language development.* Cambridge, MA: Harvard University Press.

Reber, A. S. (1967). Implicit learning of artificial grammars. *Journal of Verbal Learning & Verbal Behavior, 5,* 855–863.

Reber, A. S. (1969). Transfer of syntactic structure in synthetic languages. *Journal of Experimental Psychology, 81,* 118–119.

Reber, A. S., & Lewis, S. (1977). Implicit learning: An analysis of the form and structure of a body of tacit knowledge. *Cognition, 5,* 333–361.
Rosch, E., Mervis, C. B., Gray, W. D., Johnson, D. M., & Boyes-Braem, P. (1976). Basic objects in natural categories. *Cognitive Psychology, 8,* 382–439.
Segal, E. M., & Halwes, T. G. (1965). Learning of letter pairs as a prototype of first language learning. *Psychonomic Science, 3,* 451–452.
Segal, E. M., & Halwes, T. G. (1966). The influence of frequency of exposure on the learning of a phrase structure grammar. *Psychonomic Science, 4,* 157–158.
Smith, K. H. (1966). Grammatical intrusions in the recall of structured letter pairs: Mediated transfer or position learning? *Journal of Experimental Psychology, 72,* 580–588.
Smith, K. H. (1969). Learning cooccurrence restrictions: Rule learning or rote learning? *Journal of Verbal Learning and Verbal Behavior, 8,* 319–321.
Smith, K. H., & Gough, P. B. (1969). Transformation rules in the learning of miniature linguistic systems. *Journal of Experimental Psychology, 79,* 276–282.

4 A Study in Novel Word Learning: The Productivity of the Causative

Michael Maratsos
University of Minnesota

Poldi Gerard-Ngo
University of Minnesota

Roxane Gudeman
Macalester College

Ganie DeHart
University of Minnesota

INTRODUCTION: THE PROBLEM OF THE CAUSATIVE

For nearly two decades, one of the central problems of both linguistics and psycholinguistics has been semi-productive constructions. By these we mean constructions for which the pattern of the language offers much justification, but which also seem not to apply as productively or widely as their most general formulation would predict. Among these, the causative construction has figured prominently in linguistic and psycholinguistic discussions ever since Lakoff's 1965 paper in which relations among expressions like "it's red," "it reddened" and "she reddened it" were analyzed (Bowerman, 1974; Chomsky, 1965, 1970; Fodor, 1970; Gergeley & Bever, 1982; Lakoff, 1965; Lord, 1976; Maratsos, 1982; McCawley, 1968; Pinker, 1984). Since Lakoff's proposals for treating the causative transformationally, linguists have argued over whether the causative is really productive, whether it should be treated transformationally or by lexical redundancy rules, and a host of other such questions. Psycholinguists have had similar questions.

What are the basic facts about the construction? They are straightforward enough on initial inspection, though they grow very complicated rather quickly. A small number of stems seem to have adjective, intransitive verb, and transitive verb forms which refer to a state, a change of state, and a caused change of state respectively (e.g., "it is open," "it opened," "the girl opened it."). For a somewhat larger group of terms, one can find a change-of-state intransitive verb and a caused-change-of-state transitive verb (e.g., "it melted," "the boy melted it."). For these related forms, the subject of the intransitive constructions denotes what changes, while the subject of the transitive form denotes the causer of the change, the thing that changes being denoted by the grammatical object. Similar kinds of constructions (often marked morphologically) relate intransitive and transitive verb forms in many languages, sometimes without the restriction that the verbs denote changes of state.

A fairly large group of related change-of-state and causative terms can be found in English. But there are also many exceptions. Intransitive change-of-state terms that do not have a phonologically identical, transitive causative counterpart include *die, disappear, go, come, bloom,* and many others. Even larger is the set of transitive causative verbs that has no intransitive counterpart, e.g., *paint, destroy, convince,* and many others. Because of the pattern of these irregularities, Lakoff (1970) proposed that the derivation works in the direction intransitive-to-transitive and that, furthermore, undergoing the transformation from intransitive to transitive should be marked as an exceptional property on the verbs which take the property, much as taking an irregular past tense has to be marked on verbs which take it.

Another species of difficulties is that the semantic relation of the transitive form to the intransitive form is irregular. For example, it is plausible to relate intransitive and transitive forms of *grow* by the causative. But although there exist both ''the plants grew'' and ''he grew the plants,'' it is not plausible to predict ''he grew children'' from ''children grew'' (Chomsky, 1965).

On the other hand, the causative has had defenders of its stateability and productivity as have many other partially productive constructions. Pinker (1984) gives a good summary of these various attempts to give the causative a properly focused productive statement. He contends that whether or not an intransitive change-of-state verb will have a transitive causative counterpart is more predictable than it seems. For usually when there is no phonologically identical or similar form, there is a *suppletive* form, that is, another word which fills the apparent gap. For example, there is no causative *die* to complement the intransitive form, as shown by the unacceptability of ''he died the bug.'' But there is a transitive verb ''kill'' which fills the role of causative ''die.'' Similarly, transitive ''bring'' is the suppletive for intransitive ''come'' and transitive ''take'' is the suppletive for transitive ''go.'' Not all lexical transitive gaps can be filled in this way. For example, there does not seem to be a suppletive transitive for ''disappear,'' ''vanish,'' ''bloom,'' or ''faint''—but a great many apparent exceptions can be so accounted for. Thus, the causative rule might be amended: the transitive causative form can be predicted if there is not already a phonologically distinctive transitive causative form that has similar meaning.

Another emendation is that transitive causatives (whether suppletive forms like ''kill'' or forms related to intransitives) have a number of further semantic conditions that must be satisfied. First, they must involve direct physical causation by the agent. Thus, one cannot say that Harry killed Sam by putting him into a car with a psychopathic killer on a cross-country journey. Second, the reference must be to a stereotypical manner of causation peculiar to the particular verb. Thus, "paint" does not just mean "to apply paint to" because one would not say a painter was painting the brush he used to paint a wall, even though he is causing the brush to be covered with paint. Finally, only a change-of-state intransitive verb can give rise to a phonologically identical, transitive causative.

But such conditions suggest the causative could be something of a peripheral construction. For all of them present problems for both analysis and actual use by a speaker of English. We now consider some of these difficulties:

1. Suppletive forms as gap fillers. The idea that gaps in a predictive pattern can be filled by alternative forms is not an odd one. For example, it applies to cases like the past tense construction in which the presence of an irregular form precludes the possibility of applying the otherwise productive *-ed* ending. But in the case of the past tense, the suppletive form is at least nearly always phonologically related (e.g., *run-ran*). This is obviously not so in the case of the causative: *kill,* for example, has no phonological similarity to *die*. We do not know about the analyzability of the relation of such phonologically different forms to the initial forms, but it may well be problematic for language learners.

2. The one-way nature of the relation. As noted above, many causatives have no corresponding change-of-state intransitive. Most often, in fact, The intransitive form for transitive causatives is a passive (e.g., "He painted the wall"; "The wall got painted.") In effect, the overt periphrastic causative *get* combines with a passive participle to produce a change-of-state intransitive form. This state of affairs seems likely to combine with the next characteristic to be discussed in such a way as to produce problems.

3. Problems with the semantics of causatives. These fall into a number of subproblems.

a. The idiosyncracy of the relation of the transitive form to the intransitive form. This problem was mentioned above but deserves a fair number of examples. For *grow,* one can say "tomatoes grow here" and "John grows tomatoes." But one cannot say "children grow here" and "John grows children." The idiosyncracy is shown by the fact that if one could imagine Swift's well-known suggestion being carried out, it would be reasonable to say "Harold grew children for market." Similarly, one can walk a dog, but this is much different from causing a dog to walk by some kind of direct physical causation (in fact, it can mean just accompanying the dog and keeping a watch on it). To dance someone across the room is a very constrained, only partially causative sense of "cause to dance." For *move,* it seems reasonable to say that "the animal moved" means either that it stirred in place, or that it actually changed locations. But saying that "Mary moved the animal" clearly means she caused it to change position. One can speak of two people marrying and of someone marrying two people. But the transitive does not mean "to cause them to marry each other" though it does have some sense of the agent being causally implicated. Flying an airplane means steering it rather than causing it to fly *per se*. The same idiosyncracies show up in so-called suppletive causatives like *kill* or *take*. (See Fodor, 1970, for detailed discussion of *kill*.) *Take* seems to be the causative of "go," but to take a child to school is not the same a causing them to go to school. On the other hand, pushing someone through a doorway constitutes physically direct means of causing them to go through it but would not usually count as taking them through the doorway. It is not even clear that all causatives have highly stereotyped meaning. For example, one can freeze something by putting it outside on a cold day, putting it in the refrigerator, or by putting it against very cold skin (a fairly novel circumstance which nevertheless seems appropriate for the word meaning). In fact, even the requirement of direct physical causation does not seem invariably applied. It seems reasonable enough to say that someone who pays other people to plant orange trees and pick oranges under his direction and then markets them "grows oranges in the Imperial Valley." It is possible to kill someone by throwing him to sharks, even if the sharks do the job. In some of the cases discussed above, like walking a dog, one is often not directly causing the dog's walking at all. At least some transitive-intransitive alternations involve change and causation, but no particular physical causation, e.g., "our profits increased," "we increased our profits," "his morals improved," "we improved his morals."

b. Lack of clarity of the change-of-state requirement. For some intransitive-transitive pairs, it is clear enough that the acted on patient does undergo a fairly long lasting change of state, e.g., *rip, tear, crumble, freeze,* or *melt.* But what about others? When a door opens or closes, has the state of the door been particularly effected? When a plane is flown, is it changed after the flying is over? There is considerable variation among causatives in how much change actually occurs.

These various problems seem considerable, and perhaps the most problematic of them is the semantic idiosyncracy of the causative transitive's relation to corresponding intransitives. Consider one difficulty in using the causative productively that arises from this idiosyncracy. Because of it, coining a novel causative transitive is, in effect, making up a novel word meaning. It is not making up a new word meaning in the same way as adding *-ed* to a verb or *-ness* to an adjective. For in the latter cases, the meaning of the derived form is novel but specified generally by the rule of derivation. In the case of the causative, there are some usual effects of deriving the new form, but the conventional meaning of the form cannot be reliably predicted because of the partially idiosyncratic meaning of the form.

The idiosyncratic nature of the transitive causative could also have effects on whether the relationship between the transitive and intransitive pairs is analyzed in development. For example, it may not be worthwhile to bother to analyze the causative relation at all since learning a transitive causative meaning requires a great deal of idiosyncratic learning for each transitive verb anyway. Or as more of the detailed meaning of individual transitive forms is learned over time, the tendency to analyze the transitives as forms which are separated from the intransitive would also grow. Because of such problems, this semantically idiosyncratic nature of the transitive causative is probably the weakest point in the construction.[1]

Perhaps, however, such questions only serve to show the drawing power of the causative as a formation point for syntactic analysis. In a well-known paper, Bowerman (1974) discusses the development of the use of novel causatives in her own children. Both children, according to Bowerman, at first produced only conventionally available intransitive and transitive forms. But later on, when they began to use periphrastic causative complements (e.g., "I make her go"), novel transitives like "he fall me" and "stay it there" began to appear. One child produced over 100 novel causatives over a period of about three years. At first the novel forms were not restricted to good change-of-state terms, but with time they came to be. The forms were never very frequent, but Bowerman holds that their sudden onset shows the child's underlying analysis of a productive form.

Since Bowerman published her analyses, other analysts have disagreed both about the nature of the generalization that children capture (e.g., see Lord, 1976 and Pinker, 1984 for various disagreements) and about the productivity of the causative, both at the outset and later. We shall have a little to say about the nature of the captured generalization later. The problem of productivity plays a more central role in our paper. For analysts have disagreed both about how robust the productivity of the construction is and its eventual fate in development. Bowerman (1974, 1983) holds that the timing and nature of the novel forms show real productivity, and Pinker (1984) concurs, partly because he feels we have little reason to believe children are conservative. But others (e.g., Baker, 1979; Maratsos, 1979, 1983) have held that productivity of the causative and similar constructions may be *nil* or marginal; Bowerman herself (1974) noted that the rate of novel causative production was low. Maratsos (1979, 1982) estimated that, in fact, if Bowerman recorded her examples from a sample of two hours a day (a modest estimate, since the chief subjects were Bowerman's own children), the effective sample size from which over 100 errors were recorded in about three years could be around 750,000 utterances. As a possible baseline corpus, this is too high, for only a minority of utterances would offer an oppor-

[1](One might also guess that the lack of any distinctive grammatical marking for the English causative would inhibit its clear productivity. In Tagalog, however, there are two causative morphological changes verbs can undergo. One of these gives a semantically idiosyncratic physical causation causative, the other a periphrastic or permission causative meaning (e.g., the relation of "make him sit" to "he sits"). The first, however, is applicable only to a restricted set of verbs, while the second is quite productive (Schachter, 1972).

tunity for causative use at all; but it still indicates a very low error rate. Maratsos (1982) looked at 74 hours of transcripts of children who were advanced enough grammatically to produce novel causatives (55 hours being from the longitudinal sample of one child). Only 1 or 2 possible novel causatives were found, (It was not clear the errors were causative ones, e.g., "I exploded those men" was one, which could easily be related to "I exploded the bomb," not "those men exploded". We note in passing that transitive "explode" is another example of very idiosyncratic causative meaning.) Maratsos (1983) concluded that the chronology Bowerman reports makes it likely that some kind of productive process is going on but that it may be a highly marginal productivity.

What all these considerations point to is how hard it is to gauge the productivity of the construction. Adult intuitions or feelings about the construction do not seem uniform, and the data from children's naturalistic speech are only clear in some particulars. Nor are the prospects for cross-sectional naturalistic investigation encouraging since a very large corpus is needed to serve the purpose. Samples of one or two hours a week show novel causatives so infrequently that there is practically nothing to analyze. So questions as to whether children (or adults) find the causative a productive construction are hard to answer. If one takes any errors at all to mean productivity, then it is; but given the infrequency of the novel causatives, such evidence gives little comfort. At this point, experimental investigation suggests itself as an option. Experiments, of course, have their own very considerable hazards of interpretation. But given the circumstances, experimentation seems like a reasonable thing to try.

*FUD*DING: AN EXPERIMENTAL STUDY

What is called for is to introduce children to a novel verb, such that the syntactic and semantic nature of the verb and the circumstances of its use encourage the child's use of the causative form of the verb. The verb we made up is called *fud*, and we think it has the required characteristics. It is an intransitive verb which refers to the change of state that clay or doughlike substance undergoes when put into a machine that converts it into strands. These strands are used by creatures called Beamers (that live in Beamerland) who use them for food and to make pottery to hold the food. In the intransitive form, the subject of the verb is the clay or dough. Examples of sentences with intransitive *fud* are "the dough's fudding" or "the dough wouldn't fud" or "the dough finally fudded for him." As will be seen, in the standard referential situation we set up, a beamer was trying to get the dough to fud or succeeding in doing so, so there was a natural causative agent who carried out the action by direct physical causation (putting the dough through the machine and turning the handle). We also attempted to set up the situation such that children would have plenty of chances to use the verb but would be using it in reasonably natural circumstances. A more detailed account of the nature of the subjects and the procedures now follows.

Subjects. Our subjects were children from a number of nursery schools and day care centers in the Minneapolis area. They ranged in age from 4;6 through 6;2 with all but a couple falling in the 4;6 to 5;6 range. Bowerman reports the causative is productive for children after they have begun to produce causative periphrastic complements. According to the available literature, 4;6 should be old enough for children to have passed this point (see Brown, 1973 and Limber, 1973). The transcripts show the children were indeed sufficiently advanced. Thus for most of the children in the study, the causative should have been in their repertoires for some time if it was productive for them. The subjects were half male and half female. Since sex of the children did not seem to be related to any results, we shall not refer to it in discussion.

Procedures. In general, we wanted to familiarize the children with the procedures and also give them a great deal of time to produce uses of *fud.* So the children were seen over seven sessions, spaced approximately a week apart. In the first session the children were each introduced to the types of procedures to be used later. They were shown pictures of simple actions (like a boy watering a flower with a hose), asked what was happening, and asked to complete sentences with the various actors in the picture as subjects (e.g., "in this picture, the flowers . . ."). Then each child was given a Berko morpheme test with real verbs such as *skate* (e.g., "In this picture, this boy is skating; yesterday he . . ."). Results from these initial procedures do not seem to bear much on the experimental performance of the children, so we will not discuss them any further.

The main testing sessions began the next time the experimenter saw each child. At the beginning of this session, the child was told about creatures called Beamers who live in Beamerland. The child was given a Beamer doll to hold. These were stuffed animals that basically resemble teddy bears with some changes, e.g., noodle-like ears (they are more attractive than they sound). Then the child was told how Beamers get food by using the machine to make clay and dough fud. This was demonstrated. Then the main elicitation procedures began.

The first main procedure was called Stories. There were three stories about Beamers. The main characters of each story were two young Beamers called Bim and Bobo (a girl and boy Beamer) and their mother. The first story was about Bim and Bobo trying to get fudding to work. The second story was about them seeing who could do it faster to get pottery. In the third story, the concern was for getting food and pottery for a party. All three stories revolved around sibling rivalry to a considerable extent. The stories were long and fairly complicated so that rote imitation was impossible. On the average a story had *fud* used in it 20 or 21 times.

At the beginning of the six testing sessions, each child heard one story, and each story was told with accompanying pictures. Then the child was asked to retell the story as best he or she could. If the child could not retell the whole story, the child was told that part of the story was all right or that the child could make up a story. The stories were told in the constant order Session 1 - Story 1,

Session 2 - Story 2, Session 3 - Story 3, Session 4 - Story 1, Session 5 - Story 2. Session 6 - Story 3. This order was chosen because our intuition was that Story 1 was the least complicated story and Story 3, the most complicated.

In each session, after hearing and telling a story, the child was asked to demonstrate to a baby Beamer how fudding worked. It was explained that this was important for the baby Beamer to learn, since this was where all the food in Beamerland came from. The child was allowed to use the dough and the machine to do this. (It was probably not a good idea to repeat this test all six days, for a number of children remarked that if the baby Beamer had not learned how fudding worked after three or four demonstrations, it probably was not about to learn.)

The Stories and Demonstrations were the main source of the spontaneous speech use of *fud.* After these procedures were carried out in the sixth and final testing session, there were two more major tests. The first of these was a fill-in-the-blank procedure in which the child completed various types of lead-ins; that is, the task was a Sentence Completion test. Finally, the child was shown 25 pictures of activities which resembled the original fudding situation in varying degrees. For each picture, the child was asked if it showed fudding. We will discuss the Sentence Completion and picture comprehension tasks in more detail after discussing the results from the Stories and Demonstrations procedures.

In all, we saw 41 children. One child's results were omitted immediately for reasons to be discussed, leaving 40 children. These were assigned to one of 4 groups.

Group I (N=11; it was supposed to be N=10, but one child was assigned to it rather than another group by mistake). This group was a control or comparison group to the children in the main study. The children in Group I always heard *fud* used as a full transitive verb in sentences like "Bobo finally fudded the dough." The sentence subject was an animate causative agent like Bobo half of the time and the inanimate machine instrument the other half (e.g., "the food machine fudded the dough.")

Group II (N=10). These children heard *fud* used consistently as an intransitive in sentences like "it finally fudded" or "the dough wouldn't fud."

Group III (N=9). The sentences were intransitives like those of group II, but they contained either a benefactive or locative prepositional adjunct phrase with the animate beneficiary or the machine referred to, e.g., "the dough finally fudded for Bim," or "the dough's fudding in the machine."

Group IV (N=10). These subjects also heard *fud* used in simple intransitive sentences, e.g., "the dough finally fudded." To explain the difference between Group IV and the other groups, we have to say more about the general procedures.

In general, we were trying to reach a compromise between the natural use of the novel verb, and, we thought, the elicitation of enough uses from each child to be able to give a useful statistical profile of the individual subject. So we used story telling and demonstrations as what we hoped were reasonably natural elicitation procedures. However, we also decided we would try to encourage the children to use *fud*. The children were thus urged at the beginning of the procedures to try to figure out what the word was about and to use it at the beginning of each procedure. Other devices were used, too. During demonstration procedures, for example, the children were told the experimenter was marking down each time they used *fud* and they would get stickers which could be stuck onto cards depending on how often they used the verb. There were also prompts like "what's happening?" or "what are you doing?" which were used mostly in the Demonstrations procedures at the experimenter's discretion.

Obviously some of this was a little heavy-handed, and we could not be sure it would just increase the number of uses without changing the nature of children's responses as well. Therefore we also ran a last condition, Group IV, in which children were told they were going to learn about fudding, but no mention was made of *fud* as a word. Nor were the children urged to use the word during the procedures. Its use was not kept track of in any obvious way, and the children were not rewarded contingently for using it. We called this condition the "no frills" condition.

We should further note two important aspects of the procedures. First, children's exposure to *fud* came about solely through the experimenters' use of the word in the Stories. The experimenters did not use it otherwise. Second, the actual situation of usage remained uniform for all conditions, in the sense that fudding always took place in a stereotypical way in the stories: it always referred to an event (or possible event) in which a Beamer caused the substance to emerge in strands from a machine by handling it directly and working the machine. Thus, situationally, there was always a causative agent and machine; the Groups I–IV received different grammatical input but identical situational input. We were trying to set up a situation in which productive transitive causatives would be pragmatically useful, so we set up a situation with both a substance undergoing a change of state and an agent that caused the change. We should also mention that neither the Group I nor the Group II–IV subjects ever hear *fud* used in a periphrastic causative like "I can't get this dough to fud" or "he was trying to make the machine fud the dough." Thus no indirectness of causation was implied by grammatical usage (see Pinker, 1984, for discussion of possible results of periphrastic causative use).

Results of Stories and Demonstrations. Our procedures elicited uses of *fud* with varying success. The range over the six sessions was from a low of eight uses in one child to 107 at the high end. Actually, we must qualify these numbers as referring to *verb* uses, because to our surprise, the children did not confine their use of *fud* to main verb uses. Some of their other uses were ones related to verb uses, such as forming a participle modifier referring to the *fudding machine*. But uses of *fud* as a noun referring to the substance undergoing the change or the product of the change were reasonably common. Twenty-one of the 41 original subjects used the word *fud* at least once to refer to the substance itself in one of these two ways. On the whole, such uses were not frequent. In the whole sample of 41 children, the median number of such uses was 1; and among the 21 children who used *fud* as a noun referring to the substance, the median number of such uses was still only 2. But at least a few subjects very frequently used *fud* as a noun; there was one subject who used *fud* as a concrete noun 32 times, and used it as a verb only once or twice (one could not be sure). This subject was dropped from further tabulation. Among the remaining subjects, a small group used *fud* both as noun and verb fairly frequently: the top five number of concrete noun uses were 26, 15, 14, 13, and 8 uses; these subjects continued to use *fud* as a concrete noun throughout the study with no drop off.

These last results have some interest in themselves. Clearly the fudding situation creates a kind of referential vacuum which we only partly filled: we gave a unique name to the process itself, but no name to the substance which underwent or resulted from the process. At least half the children felt the need to have a unique name for the substance itself at least once, and, of course, the main one at hand to refer to this new situation was *fud;* some used this new word quite often.

Aside from the one subject who used *fud* only as a noun, we retained subjects in the study for analysis even if they used *fud* as a noun frequently. (We should note here, however, the dropping of one Group IV subject. This subject was dropped because two independent scorers of the transcripts agreed the experimenter had pushed her to produce *fud,* contrary to the general procedure in this condition. Thus the revised N for Condition IV is N=9).

Use of the verb was very low in the initial testing session. For example, the average number of *fud* uses in retelling the stories was just 1.4 uses per child the first day, and nearly half of the subjects did not use it at all in either the Story or Demonstration procedures during session 1. The average number of uses rose to 3.2, 3.2, 5.9, 3.6, and 3.9 in the Story procedure on succeeding days, and the Demonstration procedure frequencies show similar trends. Over the six sessions, the total number of verb uses was as below in the Story and Demonstration tasks, given separately by input condition.

Input Condition	Story Task	Demonstrations	Total
I (transitives)	22.7	16.8	39.5
II (intransitives)	24.4	14.3	38.7
III (intransitives with prepositional adjuncts)	22.9	16.0	38.9
IV (''no frills'' intransitives)	19.9	17.8	37.7

The most striking result in these findings is that the much stronger pressure that was applied to children in conditions I, II, and III had no effects on usage at all, compared to the children in the Group IV "no frills" condition. Nor did the usage curves for condition IV subjects rise any more slowly. These results were surprising to us, but are taken as a good sign. They suggest that there is something in the children's learning processes that is stable across this much of a difference in experimental manipulation.

We are now ready to discuss the main issue of interest, the nature of the children's verb uses. In particular, how often did the children of groups II–IV, who received wholly intransitive input, produce novel transitives? In fact, all three intransitive groups contained children who produced causatives. But before we can give more of the results, we have to discuss two important scoring decisions. First, children in all four conditions frequently omitted the syntactic object from their causative transitive utterances. That is, they very frequently produced sentences like "Bobo's fudding" instead of "Bobo's fudding the dough" or "Bobo's fudding it." Group I subjects omitted the object thirty percent of the time, even though all the transitive sentences they heard contained a syntactic object. This tendency to omit the object was constant over the course of the study showing no change at all from session 1 to session 6. The children in Groups II–IV also omitted the object, somewhat more frequently, in fifty percent of the novel causatives they produced. (The difference between these frequencies is statistically reliable, $t(28) = 2.90$, $p < .02$; it seems likely the transitive input subjects of Group I recorded something of the surface transitivity of the input.) We scored these objectless transitives as underlying transitive causatives since their subjects were causative agents. In the remainder of the paper, we shall refer to all sentences with animate or inanimate agents as transitives, whether or not such sentences have overt objects.

The second scoring decision arose from a problem in pronominal ambiguity. The pronoun for referring to either the dough substance or the machine is *it*. Thus, sentences like "it finally fudded" are ambiguous in meaning. The way we scored these sentences was to infer the likely proportions of substance vs. machine reference for each child according to the reference of the grammatical subject in the child's unambiguous sentences. For example, suppose a child used "it" as the grammatical subject five times. Suppose the same child used "the dough" or "the clay" as grammatical subject four times, and "the machine" as subject once. Then four of the five ambiguous "it" references would be scored as referring to the clay or dough and one as referring to the machine. The overall results are very much the same if the ambiguous responses are not scored at all, so we felt justified in using this procedure to retain them.

Using these procedures, we find that the Group I subjects, who consistently received full transitives as input, produced transitive sentences 98% of the time: 98% in the Story condition, and 97% in the Demonstration condition. Despite this resemblance to the input, this result does not reflect simple input modeling. For as noted above, they omitted the direct object 30% of the time, and it was never omitted in the model sentences. They also used an animate agent grammatical subject 80% of the time, compared to 50% in the modeled input.

The main results of interest, though, are how often the children of Groups II–IV, who received intransitives as input, produced intransitives vs. novel transitives as output. We give the proportions below for each condition and in each procedure:

	%Transitives in	
Input Condition	Stories	Demonstrations
Group II	23	37
Group III	27	23
Group IV	21	30

Overall, the children usually produced intransitives. But they also produced novel transitives about 26% of the time overall. This result indicates some productivity of the causative construction and thus supports Bowerman's claims that the causative does commonly become productive in children. (We note that 80% of the causatives had animate agents as grammatical subjects, and 20% the inanimate machine, thus matching exactly the proportion found in the Group I subjects.)

Again no reliable difference was found among the various intransitive input conditions. No group differences even approach statistical reliability. Most importantly, giving children encouragement to use *fud* had no effects, quantitatively or qualitatively, on the children's verb usage. We shall proceed by reporting the results for all 28 children of Groups II–IV as one group, Group II. There are no group differences in our results, but a closer inspection shows that there were very strong individual differences. As can be seen from Figure 1, about two-thirds of the subjects seem to fall into a range of 16% to 71% production of novel causatives with a mode of about 20% to 30%. But there were also 10 subjects who consistently stuck to the intransitive form of the verb and produced novel transitives only 0% to 7% of the time.

Are these, however, true individual differences in response or statistical artifacts? Perhaps the true mean for the whole group really is 26%; but since subjects at the low end of the curve cannot go any lower than 0%, there is a statistical pile up of subjects at the low end of the curve that is nothing more than a statistical floor effect. We were able, however, to collect enough data over the sessions for each subject to eliminate this statistical interpretation. For example, one subject never used *fud* as a transitive in 43 verb uses. The probability that the "true mean" for this subject was 26%, but the probability that he never produced a novel transitive in 43 responses is well below .00001% by exact test. It would be unusual to find even one subject this extreme in a random distribution around 26%. But in fact, these 10 subjects, whom we might call "constant

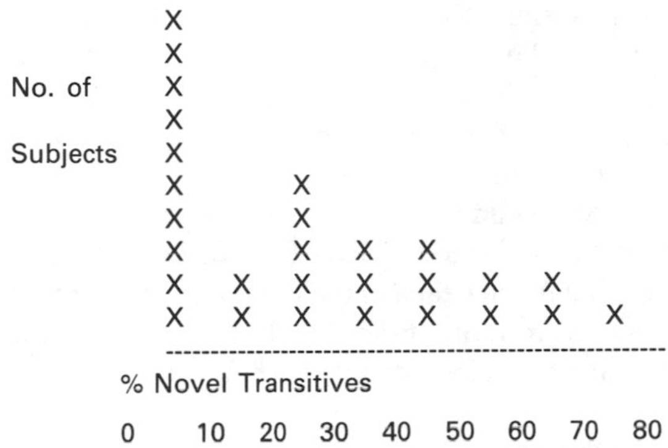

FIGURE 4.1. Distribution of Intransitive Input Subjects by % Novel Transitives

intransitive'' subjects, used *fud* as a verb between 8 and 76 times overall. For each of these subjects, the probability of being so far below 26% by chance is less than 05% (or much less), with the exception of one subject for whom the probability was $.05 < p < .10$ (by two-tailed exact test). The probability that so many subjects belong to a curve with a true mean of .26 yet randomly have such low proportion scores is statistically negligible. (A similar analysis indicates that many of the children who frequently produced novel causatives did so at a ''true'' rate considerably higher than the mean of 26%.)

There is another analysis that supports taking these individual scores as measures of some stable, individual response to the task. This analysis is subject stability over the six sessions. For each subject we compared the proportion of novel causative responses in sessions 1–3 to the same proportion in sessions 4–6. The correlation is .75 for which $t(27) = 5.67$; $p < .0001$. Obviously much of this correlation is due to the ''constant intransitive'' subjects, who produced novel causatives in neither the first nor the second halves. But even if we eliminate these 10 subjects from the analysis, the split-half correlation is .54, for which $t = 2.49$, $p < .02$. Thus, there was considerable stability in subjects' responses over the course of the experiment, and this was so even for subjects who used a mixture of intransitives and transitives. Stable individual differences thus appear to be a major finding of the study. A last question is whether children's productions showed some overall qualitative change over time beyond increasing in frequency. For example, the overall proportion of novel causatives could have changed over the sessions even if individual children preserved their rank relative to other children (the latter being what our split-half reliability analysis indicates). In fact, aside from the increase in how often children used *fud*, little else changed. There was a peak in the use of *fud* on the fourth testing day, and this peak was associated with a higher proportion of intransitive use (see

Maratsos, Gudeman, Gerard-Ngo, DeHart, and Glicksman, 1984), but the research design does not allow explanation of this result. No overall change occurred in the proportion of intransitives versus causatives. One intransitive input subject did seem to change from producing many novel causatives (7 of 13 verb uses) in the first three sessions to using none (0 out of 11 verb uses in the second half), but this is the only child to show such a change; in a group of 28 subjects, such a finding might be expected by chance alone. Even if we take a very crude overall measure like tabulating each child's first *fud* use, we find fhat 7 of these were causatives, and the rest, intransitives, which is very close to the overall rate of 26% novel causatives obtained over the whole six sessions.

A small side experiment. These Story and Demonstration results comprise our main experimental findings, though results from the Sentence Completion and Picture Comprehension tasks will also prove relevant. One of the interpretive problems we found, however, was that we could not say what the baseline is against which the results might be compared. Is the baseline response for the situation a random one, transitive or intransitive being equally likely? We ourselves believed we had set up a situation in which transitives were a natural response since *fud* was consistently used to describe a situation in which an animate agent caused the relevant changes to occur. But one cannot be sure of this, and it is important. For example, suppose the random baseline response to our situation is truly random (50% transitives, 50% intransitives). Our results would show the causative relation to be highly directional, since the intransitive input subjects often produced novel causatives, while transitive input subjects only rarely produced novel intransitives. To find out about this, we performed an experiment with a small group of adults and children.

Our question was what the default syntactic use of *fud* is when there is no modeling of any syntactic use in the input, but one knows that *fud* refers to the demonstrated situation. In the small study we ran, 6 adults (most of them highly educated) and 6 children of preschool age were asked to describe pictures of the fudding situation when they only knew that *fud* describes the relevant actions. To get them used to the task, subjects were first shown pictures of actions described by real verbs, e.g., ''push,'' ''fall,'' and ''break'' for one picture, then ''burn,'' ''pop,'' and ''tear'' each with separate pictures. (These verbs were selected according to transitivity: ''push'' must be a transitive, ''fall'' has to be an intransitive, and ''break'' can be either in a picture which has both an agent and a patient.) ''Burn,'' ''pop,'' and ''tear'' are like ''break.'' The subject was told something like ''in this picture, there is falling going on; can you make up a sentence with *fall* in it to describe what is going on here?'' All the subjects managed this part without difficulty. (In fact, they always used a transitive form when it was an option). Then the subjects were introduced to the Beamers and their machines and the clay and were shown pictures of the fudding situation. It was explained that the pictures showed fudding. Each subject was then asked to make up sentences using "fud." All the pictures used to elicit sentences showed the animate agent, the machine, and the substance turning into strands. Each subject was shown 8 pictures, the first two being introduced by "now in this picture . . ." and the other 6 being introduced by sentences taken from the Sentence Completion Test (which will be discussed shortly).

The six adults each produced sentences with "fud" as main verb for all eight trials. Nearly all of their sentences were transitives in which the subject was an animate agent. Two subjects produced two sentences each in which the substance being turned into strands provided the grammatical subject. Interestingly, like the children in the main experiment, they often omitted the syntactic objects: two subjects always omitted the object, one produced both full and truncated transitives, and three always supplied the object for an overall object omission rate of 39%.

One of the preschool age subjects only used *fud* as a noun, but the other five used it as a main verb an average of 4.6 trials out of 8. Without exception, their sentences had animate agents as subjects. The children also frequently omitted the grammatical object; the rate of omission was 40%, almost exactly the same as the adult rate. (They were not, however, as individually consistent).

The referential circumstances of this little side experiment cannot be assumed to be identical to those of the main experiment. For example, the subjects in the main experiment used an inanimate agent (the machine) as subject 20% of the time, while the subjects of the default reference study never did so. Nevertheless the results support our conjecture that the natural grammatical form for talking about the fudding situation was a transitive. This is appropriate, since one sets up a situation in which past tense usage, for example, is reasonable if one is testing to see if children use the past tense productively. In our case, the demonstration is that many subjects for whom syntactic input is consistently intransitive will produce novel causatives in a referentially appropriate situation. At the same time, establishment of the transitive as the natural default response indicates how strong the resistance to producing novel causatives was in our "constant intransitive" subjects. Finally, establishment of the high transitivity of the baseline response indicates we should not take too seriously the failure of the Group I transitive input subjects to produce novel intransitives since the situation had such a strong skew towards transitive reference.

Other results from the main study: We have two other sets of results from the main experiment that are worth reporting on. 1) The first result comes from the Sentence Completion task that was given to children after the Demonstration task in the last testing session. In this task, children were asked to produce or complete sentences using *fud* as a verb, after a few introductory sentences given by the experimenter. The children were first given a few Berko morphology tests with real verbs to get them used to the idea. Then they were told they would be making up sentences with *fud* to go with various pictures. The introductions to the child's productions set up four kinds of completion:

1. Full Sentence Production. The child produced a full sentence with *fud*, for example: Experimenter: "In this picture, now. . . ."
2. Sentence Completion with Patient as Subject: e.g., "Before the Beamers can eat, the dough. . . ."
3. Sentence Completion with Instrument as Subject: e.g., "Everytime dough is in the machine and the handle is pushed, the fudding machine. . . ."
4. Sentence Completion with Agent as Subject: e.g., ". . . If she turns the handle now, Bim. . . ."

Each elicitation condition had four test stimuli, and the order of presentation was always as above (Full Sentence Completion, Patient as Subject, Instrument as subject, Agent as Subject). The context-setting sentences before the child's responses were always constructed from the four above (e.g., "In this picture now . . . ," "Before the Beamers can eat," "Everytime dough is in the machine and the handle is pushed," and ". . . if she turns the handle now . . .") For the Full Sentence Productions these were used with no further material supplied. For each of the other conditions, an appropriate subject for the child's response was supplied. Children were encouraged to use *fud* in their completions. But if the child simply used another main verb or did not respond, this was accepted. Sometimes children started the sentence over (e.g., Experimenter: "if she turns the handle now, Bim . . ." Child: "it will fud.") These were also accepted.

We will concentrate here on the results from the Intransitive Input children, referring to the results for the Transitive Input children as these seem appropriate.

Full Sentence Production. In this condition, there was a strong and interesting consistency with children's performance in the Story and Demonstration tasks. Children who produced a higher proportion of intransitives in the Story and Demonstration tasks also did so in the Full Sentence Production task, $r = .70$, $p < .0001$. This correlation was comprised of independent correlations with the Story and Demonstration tasks. The correlation of the subjects' Story intransitive scores with their Full Sentence Production intransitive scores was .40, as was the correlation of Demonstration scores with Full Sentence Production scores, both correlations being significant at the .05 level. Interestingly, Story and Demonstration scores did not correlate significantly to each other ($r = .20$, $p > .10$), so they seem to have acted as independent measures of some underlying competence which predicted the Full Sentence completions very strongly.

When a sentence subject was supplied, however, the results were quite different, and the correlation with Story and Demonstration task performance was disrupted. Not surprisingly, Intransitive Input subjects were quite willing to complete the Patient-as-Subject sentences as simple actives so that 92% of their scoreable responses were intransitives. There was no correlation with Story and Demonstration performance since the scores were at a ceiling. More peculiar were the children's responses to the Instrument-as-Subject sentences. They were again quite willing to accept the given subject and complete it as a simple active (e.g., Experimenter: "If she turns the handle now the food machine. . . ." Child: "fuds!") Fully 87% of the children's responses were thus scored by our usual criteria as underlying transitives. One wonders, though, if these really are underlying transitives as far as the children are concerned. Like the substance, the machine was always acted on by the animate agent, so it is inanimate and, in a way, a patient. Hearing the machine suggested by the experimenter as a subject immediately after doing the Patient-as-subject sentences, children may have thought it was enough of a patient to be an appropriate intransitive subject of *fud*. This possibility is supported by some results from the Transitive Input subjects. Ten of 11 of these subjects had frequently (37% of the time) finished the Patient-as-subject sentences as passives (e.g., Experimenter: "In this picture, the dough. . . ." Child: "needs to be fudded"). This was of course a good way to finish patient-initial sentences and maintain the underlying transitivity of the verb. Interestingly, 5 of the 11 Transitive Input subjects also finished the Instrument-as-subject sentences as passives at least once (e.g., Experimenter: Before the Beamers can eat, the food machine . . ." Child: "hasta—be fudded"). Only three passives of this latter kind were produced by the Group I subjects over the entire course of the Story and Demonstration tasks, so this kind of use looks to have been a special function of the Sentence Completion task. Very likely the intransitive input children's performance was a partial function of the same type of predisposition produced by the Sentence Completion task.

The final condition was the Agent-as-Subject condition. Group II Children's scoreable responses were transitive completions 50% of the time. But again there was no correlation of Sentence Completion performance with story and Demonstration performance (r = .23, $p < .10$). High intransitive children produced causative completions slightly less often, 40% vs. 67% for the other children, but this difference was statistically negligible. Interestingly, the Group II children sometimes produced one construction characteristic of an Intransitive orientation. It was the periphrastic causative as exemplified by the following completion sequence. Experimenter: "In this picture now, Bim . . ." Child: "is turning the handle and making yellow clay fud." Overall 10 of the 28 Intransitive Input children used a periphrastic causative at least once, such usage being evenly split between the "constant intransitive" and other children. Such periphrastic causatives did not appear in the Transitive Input children's responses.

Overall, then, there are a number of main points from the Story Completion results. First, the results from the Full Sentence Production condition confirm the consistency in response to "constant intransitive" versus other Intransitive Input children. Second, the results from the remaining sentence completion conditions indicate something about the effects resulting from the experimenter's actually supplying a sentence subject for the child's completion. On the one hand, revealing results were obtained, such as the Group I children's characteristic use of passives vs. the use of periphrastic causatives by the Intransitive Input children. On the other hand, some of the other results seem to show various kinds of disruption or peculiarity. Results that show such disruption include the very high proportion of transitives given by non-"constant intransitive" children in the Full Sentence Completions, the treatment of Instrument-as-subject completions by all groups, and the disruption of the cross-task consistency of response by Intransitive Input children in the Agent-as-subject condition. The interpretive problems of experimental tasks such as comprehension, judgment, and imitation are fairly well known (e.g., Bowerman, 1979; De Villiers & De Villiers, 1974; Maratsos, 1983). It seems that production tasks, despite their advantages for some purposes, also can have interpretive difficulties. As with the use of other experimental methods, it seems necessary to have converging methods for studying a problem rather than assuming the results from one procedure in isolation can tell what is going on.

Other results from the main study: Comprehension results reveal one last finding from the main study pertinent to our central findings. We have to consider the possibility that the "constant intransitive" children may have been children who were simply very concerned to match the situations modeled to them in the experiment. Perhaps their strong tendency to stick to intransitive forms represents task conservatism among these children rather than underlying linguistic orientation.

There are a number of reasons to doubt this. First, 10 of the 11 children in the Transitive Input condition produced objectless transitives in fair proportion throughout the experiment, even in the face of the experimenter's resolutely consistent supply of the syntactic object. Judging from this result, the desire to imitate modeled input exactly does not appear to be very high in this population. Second, it will be recalled that whether or not we strongly urged and prodded children to produce *fud* made little difference to the frequency or nature of the Intransitive Input in children's responses. This is why the original conditions 2, 3, and 4 could be collapsed. Such urging should have had stronger differential effects if sensitivity to implied experimenter demand was stronger in a sizeable group of children. Finally, we can cite a brief portion of the results from the Picture Comprehension task given at the end. In this task, each child was shown

25 pictures; each more or less resembled the original fudding situation. Four or five of the pictures were almost exactly identical to it, while in others, the changes ranged from small to fairly radical (e.g., the absence of the fudding machine) to very radical (e.g., a picture of a Beamer sifting sand into streams or a spider extruding webbing). The pictures were shown in random order. The child was asked whether each picture showed fudding. Thus, the fewer pictures a child accepted, the closer a match the child made to the original fudding situation. The Transitive Input children formed a normal curve around a mode of 9 pictures accepted. The Intransitive Input children seemed to form a curve with two modes, one around 9 pictures accepted, the other around 15. If our ''constant intransitive'' subjects had simply been generally conservative in requiring a match to the original situation, their scores should have clustered around the lower end of the distribution, but this did not occur: they accepted 18, 18, 17, 17, 15, 15, 8, 6, and 5 pictures out of 25 (one subject's responses are partly missing because of a tape accident, so his score is not available). There is no evidence here of a general conservatism in observing experimental input.[2]

INDIVIDUAL DIFFERENCES: CORROBORATION FROM NATURALISTIC RESULTS

The central question in our experiment was whether the causative is or is not productive for fairly advanced preschool age children. What we seem to have found is individual differences: it is for some children and is not for others, at least under fairly ideal eliciting circumstances. Given the hazards of experimental research in language, it would be useful to have corroborating naturalistic evidence as well. In fact, the available diary studies, Lord (1976) and Bowerman (1983), already imply individual differences in the pattern of novel intransitive

---

[2]There is another possibility for accounting for the ''constant intransitive'' subjects; the possibility that they may have been doing true exception learning or negative learning. That is, they heard *fud* used as an intransitive 21 times in the first story to describe an agentive situation. Thus perhaps they learned that *fud* is an exception to the general rule of causative formation by hearing it not used as a transitive in a situation in which it could have been. This is possible, but seems unlikely for a number of reasons. First, intransitives can indeed be used in situations in which there was an agentive cause, e.g., ''it broke'' to refer to a glass after someone dropped it (and thus broke it), or ''it fell'' after someone pushed something over. So the situation of use is a possible one. Second, the children's initial low frequency of use shows they were still becoming familiar with the verb. It is doubtful they processed it more than a fraction of the time it was used. One imagines children hear some irregular verbs used more often than this during the time they are still likely to overregularize them, judging from Kuczaj's (1977) finding that overregularization can persist for individual verbs for months or years. Finally, if negative instance learning were an active process in the study, one would expect change over time toward giving intransitives in a number of children, as more and more failures for *fud* to be used as a transitive verb were registered. But only one subject, as reported above, showed any such tendency.

vs. novel transitive use. We can add more naturalistic evidence, again from anecdotal diary recordings. The relevant data come from diary recordings of a child Jessica, currently 5;0. The senior author of this paper and his wife, Mary Anne Chalkley, have taken down all of Jessica's utterances in which the verb had a novel transitivity. Jessica was not around her parents all the time during the day, so the recorded utterances by no means comprise a complete sample. But they constitute a fairly large sample base nonetheless.

Jessica produced both intransitives and full transitives from 1;11 on, but no novel transitives (or intransitives) were observed until 2;6. Then both periphrastic causatives and novel causatives appeared nearly simultaneously, as Bowerman (1974) reported for her children. Jessica's first novel causative, in fact, appeared the day after she attempted her first periphrastic causative, a garbled use with *make:* "you make close the shirt?" The next day she produced "Punkin fall me" and "I'll go mine right here." In the next two weeks, more causatives were recorded: "you talk it" ('turn on the sound on the television'), "don't eat him" ('don't make him eat'; this, by the way, was the only novel transitive Jessica produced in which the original form was a transitive; she otherwise observed the restriction that the novel forms are derived from intransitives), "stay them in there," "you felled it," and "I stay him outside." Coming after a long period with no such forms recorded, these novel transitives do point to the emergence of some generalization into some kind of productive status. In the period 2;6–2;11, 22 novel causatives with a wide variety of verbs were recorded. Many more were no doubt produced but unrecorded.

This period did not, however, see the exclusive emergence of novel causatives. The day after her first novel causative was recorded, J. M. produced her first novel intransitive, saying "it's not losing" of a balloon tied to a stroller to prevent its being blown away. Eleven such novel intransitives were recorded in the first six months. They were probably more frequent than this since novel intransitives are not generally as striking to the ear as novel causatives; for the first six months, in fact, all of the recorded novel intransitives were taken down by the senior author. The chronological evidence suggests Jessica noted the alternation between transitive and intransitive forms and inferred the possibility of changing transitivity more generally, rather than interpreting the causative-noncausative relation as a one-way relation.

After the first six months, novel forms appeared much more slowly. There were just six more novel causatives produced in the next year, and only one more in the year after that (age = 4;0). There have been none in the last five months, the last being "you laugh me up" ('you make me laugh') at the age of 4;7. Intransitives actually persevered longer; 12 more were recorded in the year after Jessica was 3;0, and 12 more in the year after 4;0. There have been none recorded in the last five months, however (the last being "But then it losed," at 4;7). It is doubtful she will produce no more forms with novel transitivity since they are a natural result of certain kinds of speech errors. But for all practical purposes, the productivity of the construction seems to have dropped to zero. This last result contrasts with the results Bowerman reports for her subjects, who seem to have gradually narrowed the range of their novel causatives to true change of state verbs over the next years. J. M. never narrowed the semantic range in this way (her last novel causative was ''you laugh me up'' = 'you make me laugh'), and she seems instead to have dropped the construction from productive status.

The comparison of Jessica's data to those of Christy and Eva gives us strong naturalistic evidence for the presence of individual differences in children's analysis of transitive-intransitive alternations. It is likely that for other children, the pattern never attains much productive status at all (B. MacWhinney tells us, for example, that one of his children was heard to produce only 2–3 novel transitives in total; a number so small indicates the transitive-intransitive alternation never attained much productive status for this child).

SUMMARY AND DISCUSSION

Our experimental and naturalistic results reinforce and complement each other in a number of ways. In one way, the experimental results provide a stronger demonstration of the dubious status of the productivity of the causative. For in the naturalistic cases that are relevant, the causative does not exist in a vacuum. There are other constructions which provide competing expressive force. For example, a child may learn the suppletive causative for some intransitives. Or a child has available competing causative constructions such as periphrastic causatives with ''make'' or ''get'' in cases where certain knowledge is lacking; these may also be increasingly learned as the appropriate forms for some meanings. Thus the causative might remain as a productive device, but over time, it would be used less as other alternatives are learned or become stronger competition for some other reasons. Such processes do not seem as though they could explain zero levels of use such as MacWhinney's child had or Jessica attained, but they might mitigate one's certainty about the estimate. In the experimental situation there was no possible competing suppletive transitive modeled, nor were periphrastics modeled (or used very much by children in the Story and Demonstration tasks). The differences among the children thus indicate individual differences in children's analysis of the productivity of the construction *per se*. On the other hand, the naturalistic results show us we should not interpret the experimental differences as arising only from differential rates of progress through the same stages of development, for the differences between Jessica, Christy, Eve, and MacWhinney's child are qualitative, not simply differentially progressive through an identical sequence. Finally, naturalistic results have a methodological simplicity that experiments of course do not; results from the latter are always subject to various kinds of intelligent doubt. But the presence of individual differences in both the experimental and naturalistic findings serves to reinforce both kinds of data.

Both kinds of results support another conclusion, too: that productivity with the causative is not an all-or-none phenomenon. In the experimental results, we found stable individual differences in the willingness to use the causative productively even among the Intransitive Input children who produced novel transitives. In the naturalistic results, Jessica produced 22 recorded causatives in the first 6 months, then just 6 in the following year. Should we interpret those 6 uses as indicating the construction was completely nonproductive or as indicating it was completely productive but other constructions now competed more successfully? It may be reasonable to conclude that neither of these was true, that instead the construction was going down in productivity, but was rated neither fully productive nor fully unproductive. Jackendoff (1972) discusses at length the prospect that productivity of many derivational processes receives some kind of graded analysis, and his proposal strikes us as likely to be correct.

The causative is only one of a number of constructions which have caused controversy about productivity in some respect—whether or not the construction is productive for adults and whether or not it attains or retains productivity for children. Analysts who interpret the data conservatively typically believe that children themselves are conservative, whether because of general predisposition (Maratsos & Chalkley, 1980) or specific linguistic predispositions for certain types of constructions (Baker, 1979). Such analysts typically point to the small number of errors that attest the productivity of such constructions and point to the doubious aspects of the construction in adult grammar (e.g., Baker, 1979; Maratsos, 1982). On the other hand, other analysts typically favor a view that errors, even if few in number, point to full productivity (e.g., Clark, 1982 for the use of nouns as verbs or Pinker, 1984 for a variety of constructions). But underlying most of these discussions is the view that children are uniform in how they accord productive status to the relevant constructions. What our results indicate for the causative is that in this sample of older preschool children, some do make productive use of the causative, and others do not. Bowerman herself, in fact, has speculated (1982) that there may serious individual differences in the acquisition (or not) and productivity (or not) of a number of constructions. Though the causative is not one mentioned, it is a likely candidate for the list. Why, though, should some constructions be more liable to such individual differences than others? It is not that, for example, they have many exceptions. Children overregularize past tensing with *-ed* at a time when the irregular verbs in their vocabulary outnumber the regular ones; irregular verbs are usually commonly used verbs as well (Slobin, 1973). In the introduction we listed a number of possible difficulties of the causative including the presence of suppletive verbs as exceptions, rather than phonologically similar verbs and the presence in English of a great many transitive causatives that have no corresponding intransitive (e.g., *throw, destroy, fix*). For these, the truncated passive is used instead (e.g., "it got fixed"). But we think a likely general candidate is the third factor mentioned: the semantic irregularity of the relation of the causative to the intransitive, the fact that transitive causatives typically have much idiosyncratic or stereotyped meaning distinguishing them from the intransitive beyond the addition of causativity and direct physical causation (the latter not being completely reliable itself). As we wrote there, this could affect both the analysis of the productivity of the construction and the willingness to use it in a number of ways:

1. If the transitive was idiosyncratic meaning compared to the intransitive, it may be that the child will not believe them to be related in the first place.
2. Even if the generalization has been analyzed, it may be registered as being used relatively infrequently. For in producing the transitive causative, the child may as well just look up the transitive directly rather than referring the use to the intransitive since the transitive requires specific lookup for its idiosyncratic properties anyway. Similarly, in comprehension there is so much specific to the transitive that its analysis may not be referred to the intransitive.
3. Suppose a child has analyzed the idiosyncracy of the relation of the transitive to the intransitive in a fair number of cases, so that his analytic system has implicitly or explicitly stored the relationship as idiosyncratic. This means that when occasion arises in which one might produce a novel transitive, one is in effect coining a new meaning for the stem. If the child's internal system has some notion of "risk," making up a new causative is a greater risk, say, than adding *-ed* to a verb stem. The latter operation results in a new word meaning, but one specified completely by the general description of the construction. Making up a new causative is venturing into unknown territory. (Perhaps there is actually another, unknown meaning for the transitive causative altogether.) Difficulties like this might manifest themselves in a child's analysis of a construction at different times, depending on when the child analyzes and has easy access to the extra idiosyncratic meanings of a number of transitive causatives.

As was also noted in the introduction, the semantic idiosyncracy of transitive causatives can combine with other factors—use of suppletive transitive forms, intransitives with no corresponding causative form at all, the presence of great numbers of transitives which have no corresponding intransitive at all (except the passive), the presence of competing forms which can express causation novelly—to cause further uncertainties. Of these, however, the semantic idiosyncracy of the causative seems to us to have a special explanatory role. Since this particular property of the causative is a common one of word derivation processes, we can more generally hypothesize that all other things held equal, derivational processes that involve an idiosyncratic, unpredictable extra addition of meaning to the stem will be comparatively less productive than those which add meaning in a completely predictable way. (See Aronoff, 1976, for discussion of the same general thesis with respect to the productivity of suffixes which convert adjectives into nouns.) This does not mean, obviously, that such processes will never become productive in any way or degree. Both the naturalistic data and our experimental data indicate children for whom the causative (or some other aspect of the transitive-intransitive alternation) becomes productive. But the data also indicate children for whom the causative never becomes productive, or for whom the productivity of the construction becomes marginal at best. Obviously many properties of constructions may affect the degree to which they inspire similar kinds of variation. But for the causative in particular, and probably for a number of others, unpredictability in the meaning of derived forms will prove, we think, one powerful predictor of individual variation in development and adult use as well.

ACKNOWLEDGMENTS

This research was conducted while the authors were being supported in part by the following grants: M. Maratsos and R. Gudeman: NICHD HD05027-14, P. Gerard-Ngo and G. DeHart: NICHD T32HD07151.

REFERENCES

Aronoff, M. (1976). Word formation in generative grammar. *Linguistic Inquiry Monographs,* No. 1.

Baker, C. L. (1979). Syntactic theory and the projection problem. *Linguistic Inquiry 10:* 533–581.

Bowerman, M. (1974). Learning the structure of causative verbs: a study in the relationship of cognitive, semantic and sy tactic development. In E. Clark, ed., *Papers and reports on child language development,* No. 8, pp. 142–178. Stanford University Committee on Linguistics.

Bowerman, M. (1976). Semantic factors in the acquisition of rules for word use and sentence construction. In D. M. Morehead & A. E. Morehead, eds., *Normal and deficient child language.* Baltimore, MD: University Park Press.

Bowerman, M. (1982). Reorganizational processes in lexical and syntactic development. In E. Wanner & L. R. Gleitman, eds., *Language acquisition: the state of the art.* Cambridge: Cambridge University Press.

Bowerman, M. (1983). Evaluating competing linguistic models with language acquisition data: Implications of developmental errors with causative verbs. *Semantica, 3,* 1–40.

Brown, R. (1973). *A first language: the early stages.* Cambridge, MA: Harvard University Press.

Chomsky, N. (1965). *Aspects of the theory of syntax.* Cambridge, MA: MIT Press.

Chomsky, N. (1970). Remarks on nominalization. In R. Jacobs & P. Rosenbaum, eds., *Readings in English transformational grammar.* Waltham, MA: Ginn.

Clark, E. V. (1982). The young word maker: a case study of innovation in the child's lexicon. In E. Wanner & L. R. Gleitman, eds., *Language acquisition: The state of the art.* Cambridge, MA: Cambridge University Press.

de Villiers, J. G. & de Villiers, P. A. (1974). Competence and performance in child language: are children really competent to judge? *Journal of Child Language, 1,* 11–22.

Fodor, J. A. (1970). Three reasons for not deriving "kill" from "cause to die." *Linguistic Inquiry 1,* 429–438.

Gergely, G., & Bever, T. G. (1982). The mental representation of causative words. Unpublished manuscript. Columbia University.

Jackendoff, R. F. (1972). *Semantic interpretation in generative grammar.* Cambridge, MA: MIT Press.

Kuczaj, S. A., II (1977). The acquisition of irregular past tense forms. *Journal of Verbal learning and Verbal Behavior, 16,* 589–600.

Lakoff, G. (1965). *Irregularity in syntax.* Doctoral Dissertation, University of Indiana.

Lakoff, G. (1970). *Irregularity in syntax.* New York: Holt, Rinehart, and Winston.

Lord, C. (1976). Valence changing operations in children's speech. Stanford: *Papers and reports in child language,* No. 13.

Maratsos, M. P. (1979). How to get from words to sentences. In D. Aaronson and R. Reiber, eds., *Psycholinguistic research: Implications and applications.* Hillsdale, N.J.: Erlbaum Associates.

Maratsos, M. P. (1983). Some current issues in the study of the acquisition of grammar. In P. Mussen, ed., *Carmichael's manual of child psychology,* fourth edition. New York: John Wiley and Sons.

Maratsos, M. P. & Chalkley, M. A. (1980). The internal language of children's syntax: The ontogenesis and representation of syntactic categories. In K. Nelson, ed., *Children's language,* Vol. II. New York: Gardner Press.

Maratsos, M., Gudeman, R., Gerard-Ngo, P., DeHart, G., & Glicksman, M. (1984). An experimental study of the causative. Presented at the Boston conference in language development, Boston, MA.

McCawley, J. (1968). The role of semantics in grammar. In E. Bach & J. Harms, eds., *Universals in linguistic theory.* New York: Holt, Rinehart, and Winston.

Pinker, S. (1984). *Language learnability and language development.* Cambridge, MA: Harvard University Press.

Schachter, P. (1972). *A Tagalog reference grammar.* Berkeley, CA: University of California Press.

5 Language Acquisition and Machine Learning

Pat Langley
University of California, Irvine
Jaime G. Carbonell
Carnegie-Mellon University

INTRODUCTION

Despite the apparent complexity of language, nearly every human being masters its use in the first ten years of life, and as scientists we would like some theory to explain this phenomenon. Ideally, such a theory should explain the *processes* that lead from naive to sophisticated language use, just as chemical theories explain the processes involved in reactions. The natural places to turn for such process descriptions are the fields of artificial intelligence (AI) and cognitive science. In particular, one should look to machine learning, the subfield of artificial intelligence concerned with computational approaches to learning—i.e., with processes that lead to improved performance over time.

Over the past two decades, machine learning researchers have made considerable progress in understanding the nature of learning mechanisms, and many of their results are relevant to models of human behavior. In this paper, we examine these results and their implications for theories of language acquisition. We begin by reviewing four basic learning tasks that have been the focus of the machine learning work, describing each in terms of a common framework. We then turn to the task of grammar learning, comparing and contrasting it with other learning tasks. After this, we review some earlier computational models of grammar learning and consider some drawbacks of these models. Finally, we outline a new approach to the modeling of language acquisition that we hope will overcome these limitations.

AN OVERVIEW OF MACHINE LEARNING RESEARCH

In order to give the reader a better feel for the nature of machine learning research and its implications for models of language acquisition, let us begin by considering some common tasks that researchers in this field have addressed. We will consider the tasks in roughly historical order, based on the periods at which they first drew the major attention of machine learning researchers. Using this ordering, we have the tasks of learning from examples, learning search heuristics, conceptual clustering, and learning macro-operators. This list is not exhaustive, but the majority of AI learning research has focused on these tasks.

Considerable work has also been carried out on the task of learning grammars. Interest in this area emerged early in the history of machine learning and has remained active until the present. Despite its early role in the field, we will delay our discussion of grammar learning (and thus violate our historical ordering) so we can better see its relation to other work. However, before moving on to specific tasks, let us first present a general framework within which each task can be viewed.

The Components of Learning from Experience

Any attempt to define *learning* is as doomed to failure as attempts to define *life* and *love*. One can certainly generate a formal definition, but others can always find intuitive examples that fall outside the specified conditions or find counterexamples that fall within them. Rather than trying to define learning in general, we will focus on the more constrained issue of learning from experience. Most of the research in machine learning has focused on this class of problems, as opposed to learning by being told or learning by deduction from known facts. We will not attempt to define the task of learning from experience; instead, we will specify some components or subproblems which must be addressed by any system that learns from experience.

As we will see, these components are designed to characterize the five basic learning tasks that we consider in the following pages. It is possible that additional dimensions are required, but we will not know this until someone formulates a new learning task that forces expansion of the framework. Of course, other frameworks are possible that divide the learning problem along orthogonal dimensions. However, we will see that the current framework leads to useful insights about the nature of the language acquisition task, making it sufficient for our present goals. The four basic components of learning from experience are:

- *Aggregation*. The learner must identify the objects from which he will form rules or hypotheses: i.e., he must determine the appropriate *part-of* relations.[1] For instance, in understanding a visual scene, the viewer must identify the basic objects and their components. Similarly, in language acquisition, one must first group utterances into component sound-sequences (words). Thus, one may aggregate over either spatial or temporal descriptions.

- *Clustering*. The learner must identify which objects or events should be grouped together into a class: i.e., he must determine the appropriate *instance-of* relations, or generate an *extensional* definition of the rule or hypothesis. For example, a concept learner must divide objects into instances and non-instances of the concept being learned.
- *Characterization*. The learner must formulate some general description or hypothesis that characterizes instances of the rule; i.e., he must generate an *intensional* definition of the rule or hypothesis.[2] For instance, the task of language acquisition requires one to move beyond specific sentences, and to formulate general rules or grammars.
- *Storage/Indexing*. The characterization of the rule must be stored in some manner that lets one retrieve it when appropriate. For example, one may store an acquired problem-solving heuristic in some form of discrimination network.

As we proceed, we will see examples of these components in concept learning, in procedural learning, and in grammar learning. All learning tasks include the components in one form or another, and all learning systems must address them in some sense.

However, in many tasks one or more components have been idealized out; that is, the solution to a subproblem is either provided by some outside source or can be effectively ignored. For instance, the programmer may divide the learner's input into distinct objects, thus solving the aggregation problem. Similarly, the learner may acquire only a few characterizations, so that storage issues are not significant. We will see examples of these and other simplifications shortly, but Table 1 summarizes the basic results of this analysis, listing the relevant components of the five learning tasks we will consider.

---

[1]Some readers will prefer the term *segmentation* to the term *aggregation*, but this is simply a matter of perspective. One can view part-of relations as being established in either a top-down or a bottom-up manner.

[2]This is often called the *generalization* problem. We will avoid this term because it has has two distinct meanings within machine learning. The first sense includes the process of moving from a specific hypothesis to a more general one and is the opposite of *discrimination* learning. The second sense includes *any* process for constructing a general rule from data and encompasses both discrimination and the first sense of *generalization*. We intend the term *characterization* to replace this second (more general) sense.

TABLE 1
Relevant Components of Machine Learning Tasks

Learning task	*Relevant components*
Learning from examples	characterization
Learning search heuristics	clustering, characterization
Conceptual clustering	clustering, characterization, storage
Learning macro-operators	aggregation
Grammar learning	aggregation, clustering, characterization, storage

Learning from Examples

The task of learning concepts from examples is the most widely studied problem in machine learning. Research on this task addresses the question of how one forms concepts from examples presented by a tutor. The general version of this task may be stated:

- *Given:* One or more classes or concepts, along with a set of instances or examples for each class, e.g., one might be given instances and non-instances of the concept *uncle*.
- *Find:* Some description or rule that correctly predicts the class to which each instance should be assigned. In the *uncle* example, one would hypothesize some general description of this concept.

In other words, given an extensional definition of one or more concepts, one must generate intensional definitions for each of those concepts. These descriptions must satisfy two constraints—each instance of a class must be covered by the description of that class, and no instance of a class may be covered by the description of any other class. Michalski (1983) has called the first of these the *completeness* condition and the second of these the *consistency* condition. In general, the description is expected to correctly classify instances that were not in the training set, so the learner must move beyond simple summaries of the original data.

The simplest version of learning from examples involves formulating a description for a single concept. In this case, we use the term *positive instances* for all examples of the concept and the term *negative instances* for all non-examples. Let us consider a simple task in which objects can be described in terms of only two attributes—*size and shape*. The learner might be told that *a large circle* and *a large square* are positive instances of the concept to be learned, while *a small circle* is a negative instance. One hypothesis that accounts for these data (though not the only one) is that the concept is simply *large:* this description covers the positive instances but not the negative instance. Concept learning tasks of this type were widely studied in psychology (e.g., Bruner, Goodnow, & Austin, 1956) before they were adopted by the machine learning community.

The task of learning multiple concepts from examples can be reduced to the simpler problem of learning a single concept, repeated a number of times. Focusing on one of the classes, we label all objects associated with this class as positive instances, and label all objects associated with other classes as negative instances. The task of learning this single concept involves formulating some description which covers all positive instances but none of the negative instances. Suppose we repeat this process for each of the other classes, in each case producing a set of positive and negative instances and generating a concept description for that class. The result of this scheme is a set of concept descriptions, each complete and consistent with respect to the others.[3] Since the multiple concept learning task can be subdivided in this manner, most researchers have focused on the task of learning single concepts, and we will do so here as well.

Learning from examples can be viewed as an idealized version of the general task of learning from experience. Since the tutor provides the basic objects upon which rules or descriptions are based, the aggregation subproblem is bypassed. Since the tutor assigns instances to classes for the learner, the clustering subproblem is trivialized. Finally, since only a few concepts are learned, the resulting descriptions can be stored in a simple list, thus avoiding the subproblem of storage and indexing.

In other words, the task of learning from examples can be viewed as "distilled" characterization, and it is undoubtedly for this reason that it proved so popular in the early days of machine learning research. Focusing on this simplified task let researchers deal with characterization issues to the exclusion of complicating factors, much as the early physicists ignored nuisances like air resistance. This strategy led to a variety of interesting methods for formulating general descriptions from positive and negative instances (Winston, 1975; Hayes-Roth & McDermott, 1978; Mitchell, 1982; Anderson, 1983), which later proved invaluable in studying more complex learning tasks.

Since these characterization methods have been widely used in the work on more complex learning tasks, we should briefly review the set of methods that have been developed. The vast majority of methods rely on the insight that the set of descriptions or hypotheses considered during the characterization process can be partially ordered according to their generality. However, since this is only a *partial* ordering, multiple paths exist through the space of hypotheses, and this leads to *search*. Even very simple spaces are only partially ordered along the dimension of generality; e.g., Figure 5.1 shows the space for the size/shape task

[3]This approach assumes that classes must be disjoint; this assumption is not necessary, but is very common among machine learning researchers.

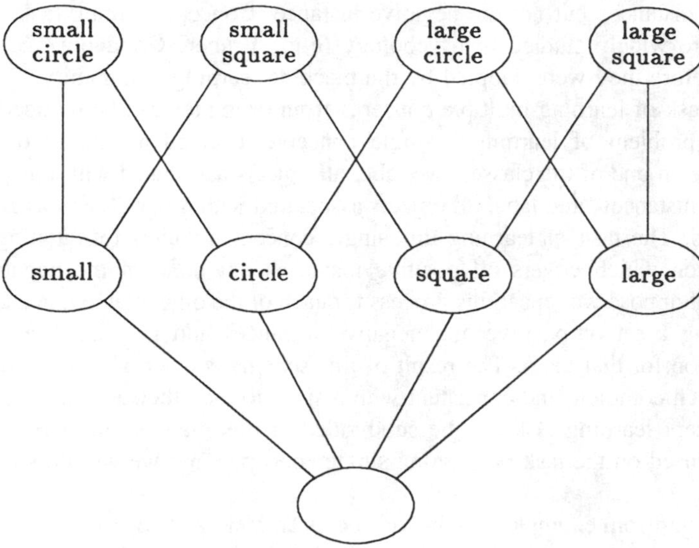

FIGURE 5.1. A partially ordered space of hypotheses.

described above. As a result, most characterization methods carry out a systematic search through the hypothesis space, but they differ widely in the details of this search.

For instance, one can start with very specific hypotheses and gradually make them more general until an acceptable description is found (specific-to-general search), or one can begin with very general hypotheses and gradually make them more specific (general-to-specific search). One can even search in both directions simultaneously (the version space method). These approaches have different implications for the nature of the resulting description; for example, specific-to-general strategies will arrive at more specific characterizations than general-to-specific methods. However, all will generate descriptions that are both consistent and complete over the given instances, provided certain assumptions are met, such as the absence of noise (misclassified instances). We will see examples of both approaches in our review of grammar learning methods.

Characterization methods also vary in their processing of the instances they are given. Some approaches incorporate data one instance at a time; these are usually called incremental learning methods. Other approaches examine all of the instances simultaneously, often using statistical techniques to direct their search for useful hypotheses. These are typically called *nonincremental* learning methods. Naturally, the former are more plausible models of the human learning process, while the latter are more analogous to scientific data analysis. Most of the grammar learning systems we examine later are incremental, but we will see one example of the nonincremental approach.

Finally, characterization methods differ in the *operators* that they employ for moving through the space of hypotheses. Some systems use operators that require only the current hypothesis as input. These techniques use some knowledge of the domain to transform the current description into one or more new hypotheses, and use the data only to test these hypotheses. We will call these *model-driven* methods. Other systems employ operators that require both the current hypothesis and a new instance as input; such techniques use the new data to transform the current description into one or more new hypotheses. We will call these *data-driven* methods. Historically, there has been a strong association between data-driven and incremental approaches, and a similar correlation between model-driven and nonincremental approaches, though exceptions to these trends exist. All of the grammar learning systems we will consider are data-driven in nature.

Within the data-driven approach, we find two quite different classes of operators. The first of these finds *common structure* between instances and/or hypotheses and is always combined with specific-to-general methods. For instance, suppose one's current hypothesis states that all members of some concept are *large, red,* and *square,* and that one observes the new positive instance *large, blue,* and *square.* Since the hypothesis fails to match the new example, we know it is overly specific and should be made more general. In this case, the technique would generate the revised hypothesis that all examples of the concept are *large* and *square,* since these features are held in common between the old hypothesis and the new instance. Such methods are usually conservative in that they generalize only enough to cover the new instance and no more.

One interesting aspect of the ''finding common structures'' operator is that, given a simple attribute-value representation involving a single object (like the one above), no search is required through the hypothesis space. Given relational or structural representations (in which predicates take two or more arguments), one description may be mapped onto another in multiple ways so that competing hypotheses must be considered and search carried out. However, to the extent that one can represent one's hypotheses entirely in terms of attributes and their values, the characterization task will be greatly simplified.[4]

In relational cases involving search, there must be some way to distinguish good hypotheses from bad ones, and this is where negative instances come into play. If hypothesis H covers any of the known negative instances, we know it is overly general: thus, we can remove H from consideration and concentrate on the alternatives. Another important aspect of these operators is that they generate hypotheses containing those features held in common by all positive instances.

---

[4]A number of researchers, including MacWhinney (1978), Berwick (1979), and Wexler (personal communication), have applied this approach to grammar learning. Given the inherent relational nature of language, this seems counterintuitive, but their success speaks for itself. Hedrick (1976) employed a relational version of the common structures method in his grammar learning system.

This is desirable if the concept can be described as a conjunction, but if a disjunction is required, the approach will lead to overly general hypotheses that cover some negative instances. Note that if the concept can be expressed in terms of an attribute-value scheme and if we know the concept is conjunctive in form, then *we can determine the correct concept description using only positive instances*.

The second type of data-driven operator finds *differences* between instances and/or hypotheses, and is always combined with general-to-specific characterization methods. For instance, suppose one's current hypothesis is that all members of some concept must be *red*, and that the last positive instance of this concept was *small, red,* and *circle*. Further suppose that the next negative instance is *small, red,* and *square*. Since the current hypothesis matches this counterexample, we know the hypothesis is overly general and should be made more specific. In this case, a better hypothesis would be *red* and *circle*.

We can generate more specific hypotheses by finding the differences between the positive and negative instances and using these differences to further constrain the hypothesis. Thus, each difference leads to an alternative description, each more specific than the one we started with. In this case, the only difference is that the positive instance is a circle while the negative instance is a square. Winston (1975) has used the term *near miss* to refer to such one-difference negative instances. They are important because they eliminate search for difference-based methods. One can still make progress with *far misses,* but alternative hypotheses must be considered.[5] As with specific-to-general techniques, these methods are conservative in that they discriminate only enough to ensure that the negative instance will not be covered.

The majority of research on learning from examples has employed *empirical* methods like those we have just considered, which rely on many instances to induce an adequate characterization. We will see that these methods have been widely used in other machine learning tasks, including grammar learning. However, recently some researchers have explored another approach that generates descriptions on the basis of a single positive instance.

These have been called *analytical* methods, since they reason about why the instance belongs to the specified class. They have also been called *explanation-based* methods, since they construct justifications for the instance's classification. For example, one might be given a functional specification of the concept *cup*—that it must contain liquids, that it can be lifted, and so forth. If one is then given a specific coffee cup labeled as a positive instance, one can *prove* that the physical features of this object satisfy the functional definition of cup. Thus, the

[5]Langley (1980, 1982) and Anderson (1981) have employed difference-based methods in their models of first language acquisition. Unfortunately, since parents do not carefully plan their presentation of sample sentences, we cannot assume that the first language learner relies on near misses to eliminate search.

cup's handle lets it be lifted, its concavity lets it contain liquid, etc. This proof identifies the relevant features of the instance, and these features can be used to formulate a general structural description of the concept.

We do not have the space to describe such analytical approaches in detail, but later we will see that some of the work on grammar acquisition fits into this framework, rather than the empirical one. We direct interested readers to Mitchell, Keller, and Kedar-Cabelli (1986) for an excellent review of explanation-based learning methods.

Learning Search Heuristics

One of the central insights of AI is that intelligence requires the ability to search, and another is that expertise involves the ability to direct search down useful paths. This search occurs within the context of some *problem space,* which can be defined as a set of problem states together with operators for moving between those states. Each operator has an associated set of legal conditions that specify when it can be applied, but these are not enough to let one discover the goal state without search. For this one needs additional *heuristic* conditions on each operator that suggest the optimal move at each point in the problem-solving process.

Naturally, researchers in machine learning are concerned with how such heuristics might be learned from experience. The task of learning search heuristics may be stated as follows:

- *Given:* A problem space defined in terms of an initial state and set of legal operators,
- *Given:* A test to determine when the goal has been reached and a search strategy for selecting operators and states,
- *Find:* Heuristic conditions for each operator that will reduce or eliminate search.

For example, Mitchell, Utgoff, and Banerji (1983) have examined heuristics learning in the domain of symbolic integration. In this case, problem states take the form of integral expressions, such as $\int 6x^2dx$ and $2x^3$, and the goal is to find some state in which no integral sign occurs. Similarly, operators take the form of rules for transforming one state into another, such as $\int a \cdot bx^n dx \rightarrow a \int bx^n dx$. Fifty such operators commonly occur in solving simple integration problems, and the search space generated by these operators is quite large.

As with learning from examples, researchers have explored a variety of different methods for automatically generating heuristics. However, each such method must respond to an issue that makes the heuristics learning task more difficult than the task of learning from examples. This is known as the *credit assignment* problem.

Minsky (1963) was the first to identify the difficulty of assigning credit and blame in procedural learning. This issue arises in situations where the learner receives feedback only after it has taken a sequence of actions. In order to improve its performance, the learner must assign *credit* to desirable actions and *blame* to undesirable ones. For instance, if one loses a chess game, the final move is seldom responsible for checkmate. Usually, some other (much earlier) move led to this undesirable state, but identifying this move may be very difficult.

Significant progress in heuristics learning occurred only when researchers identified effective methods for assigning credit and blame. The most obvious of these methods involves waiting until one finds the goal state through search and then using the complete solution path to distinguish desirable moves from undesirable ones. For the integration problem $\int 6x^2dx$, the optimal solution path would be $\int 6x^2dx \Rightarrow 2 \int 3x^2dx \Rightarrow 2x^3$. Any move lying directly along this path to the goal state is marked as desirable, while any move leading one step off the solution path is marked as undesirable. Sleeman, Langley, and Mitchell (1982) have called this method *learning from solution paths*. Later, we will see that Berwick (1979) has employed a very similar approach to learn grammar rules.

An alternative method involves assigning credit and blame during the search process itself. Rather than waiting until a complete solution has been found, one may note regularities in the search tree as it is generated. For instance, one might notice that an existing state has been revisited. This may result from a loop or from a longer path to that state, but in either case the move that led to the state is undesirable. (In integration, loops can easily occur when integration by parts is attempted.) Similarly, moves that lead to dead ends should be avoided if possible. Anzai and Simon (1979) and Langley (1985) have called this approach *learning while doing*, since it lets one assign credit and blame while search is being carried out.

Once a credit assignment technique has been used to label moves as desirable or undesirable, one can easily identify positive and negative instances of each operator. These can be passed to a characterization method, which in turn generates general descriptions of the conditions under which each operator should be applied. When the heuristic conditions associated with an operator are used to determine when that operator should be applied, search is reduced or even eliminated. Langley and Ohlsson (1984) have called this basic method the *problem reduction approach to heuristics learning*, since it involves separately identifying the heuristic conditions for each operator and then recombining them into a system that requires little or no search. The vast majority of research on heuristics learning has taken this approach, though there has been considerable variation in both the credit assignment methods and characterization methods employed.

Like the task of learning from examples, the heuristics learning problem is an idealized case of the general task of learning from experience. Since the problem space is provided by the programmer, the basic objects upon which rules are based (the problem states) are given at the outset. As a result, there is no significant aggregation problem. Since the problem spaces that have been examined seldom have more than a few operators (the 50 that Mitchell et al. examined was very unusual) and since no more than a few heuristics are learned for each operator, there is no significant storage or indexing problem.

However, the heuristics learning task differs from learning from examples in that the programmer does not provide the clusters from which descriptions (in this case heuristics) are generated. The learning system must of its own accord cluster instantiations of each operator into groups of positive and negative instances, using complete solution paths or some other credit assignment method. In fact, within the context of learning search heuristics, the subproblem of clustering is identical to the problem of assigning credit and blame. Once the system has determined the positive and negative instances for each operator, it must still employ some characterization method to determine the heuristic conditions for that operator. However, the same methods that have proven so useful in learning from examples can also be applied in this situation. To summarize, the task of heuristics learning involves less idealization than the task of learning from examples, since the former requires one to address issues of both clustering *and* characterization.

Conceptual Clustering

We associate the notion of taxonomies with biology, but many (if not all) of the sciences progressed through a stage of taxonomy formation before moving on to discovering laws and theories. The task confronting scientists in this stage can be stated:

- *Given:* A set of objects and their associated descriptions.
- *Find:* A hierarchical classification tree that covers all objects and which places similar objects in the same classes.

For instance, one might observe many different species of plants and animals and then attempt to formulate a taxonomy which places similar species in the same categories. The most frequent examples come from biology, but taxonomies have also played an important role in astronomy (classifying stars and galaxies) and chemistry (classifying substances).

At first glance, this task appears quite similar to the problem of learning from examples. However, it differs from the simpler task on three dimensions. First, objects are not assigned to classes by a tutor, so that a distinction between positive and negative instances is not inherent in the data. Second, the goal is to generate extensional definitions of each class rather than general descriptions (intensional definitions). Finally, since a taxonomy is hierarchical, one must discover concepts at multiple levels of abstraction, as contrasted with the single level concepts that occur in learning from examples.

Despite the apparent complexity of the taxonomy formation task, statisticians and biologists have developed computational methods for automating this process. These techniques share the general names of *cluster analysis* and *numerical taxonomy,* and a variety of them have been proposed (Everitt, 1980). Most of the methods employ some measure of the *distance* between objects or clusters in a N-dimensional feature space, attempting to group together objects that are close to each other. Unlike most statistical methods, cluster analysis and numerical taxonomy have little theoretical justification and are largely heuristic in nature. Moreover, different methods tend to produce radically different taxonomies unless the data are very regular, and the resulting hierarchies are often difficult to interpret.

In response to these limitations, Michalski and Stepp (1983) have formulated a related task they call *conceptual clustering*. This task differs from the traditional taxonomy formation task in two respects:

- In addition to generating a hierarchy containing clusters of objects, one must also *characterize* those clusters.
- In evaluating potential clusters, one should consider the characterizations of these clusters as well as the objects they contain.

The authors argued that by including characterizations in the evaluation process, the resulting clusters will be easier to understand than those generated by traditional methods. Given this revised framework, it is not surprising that Michalski and Stepp used established characterization methods as subroutines in their approach to taxonomy formation. Other methods for conceptual clustering (Langley & Sage, 1984; Fisher, 1984) differ in various respects, but all take advantage of standard characterization techniques in some manner.

Methods for conceptual clustering can be viewed in terms of three different levels of search, each involving a different problem space. The first of these involves search for clusterings or groupings of objects at a given level of the hierarchy.The second involves search for descriptions or characterizations of object clusters; this is identical to the search carried out by systems that learn from examples. The final search is through the space of possible hierarchies within which the clusters and their descriptions are contained.

Methods for dealing with each of these subproblems can vary along a number of dimensions. For instance, we have already seen some varieties of characterization methods, and similar variations exist in the search for clusterings and hierarchies. One may search for clusterings exhaustively or one may use heuristic search techniques; in particular, Michalski and Stepp employed a hill-climbing method to find useful clusterings. Similarly, one may construct hierarchies from the top down or from the bottom up; Michalski and Stepp used a top-down approach, while most numerical taxonomy methods operate in a bottom-up fashion.[6] The interested reader is directed to Fisher and Langley (1985) for a more detailed discussion of conceptual clustering methods in these terms.

The conceptual clustering task can be viewed as another variant on the general problem of learning from experience. Like the task of learning from examples, it ignores the problem of *aggregation,* since the basic objects and their descriptions are given to the learner. However, it differs from the simpler task in that it explicitly addresses the problem of *clustering* objects into groups without aid from a tutor. Unlike traditional clustering techniques, it also addresses the *characterization* problem, since one must form general descriptions for each cluster. Finally, it begins to deal with the *storage/indexing* problem, since objects and classes are stored in a hierarchy that can be used in classifying novel objects.

In other words, conceptual clustering forces one to address three of the four components of learning from experience, more than either learning from examples or heuristics learning. Late in the paper, we will see that the clustering problem also arises in the grammar learning task, and we will examine some responses to this problem by several grammar learning systems.

Learning Macro-Operators

The notion of *chunks* was originally proposed by Miller (1956) to explain short-term memory phenomena. The term *chunk* denotes some familiar pattern that one can remember or manipulate as a single entity. Chunks can be perceptual or action-oriented, and can involve either spatial or sequential relations. In practice, machine learning researchers' interest in issues of procedural learning has led them to emphasize sequential action structures.

Like the work on heuristics learning, the chunking research has focused on learning in the context of search through some problem space. In this case, the goal is to discover sequences of operators, or *macro-operators,* that achieve useful results in the problem space (e.g., bringing one closer to the goal). Since relatively little work has been done on the acquisition of spatial or perceptual chunks, we will focus on macro-operators here.[7]

A number of mechanisms for generating macro-operators have been described in the literature, though they have not always been cast in these terms. For example, Lewis (1978) and Neves and Anderson (1981) discuss a process called *composition* that combines two production rules into a single, more powerful rule whenever the original rules apply in sequence. They have used this to explain the Einstellung effect, in which problem solvers prefer a well-practiced solution to

---

[6]Researchers in numerical taxonomy (Everitt, 1980) use the term *divisive* for top-down methods and *agglomerative* for bottom-up approaches.

[7]However, later we will see that sequential chunks also arise in the grammar learning task where they correspond to structures such as noun phrases and verb phrases.

some problem even when more efficient solutions are possible. More recently, Anderson (1983) has described a more selective version of composition that combines only those rules used to achieve a common goal.

Korf (1982) has described a quite different method for generating macro-operators that involves the notion of decomposable subgoals, while Iba (1985) has employed a third method that combines rules when it notes peaks in a numeric evaluation function. Finally, Laird, Rosenbloom, and Newell (1986) have described a method called *chunking* that is evoked only when a goal is achieved: however, this method differs from Anderson and Neves' composition in that it constructs the resulting macro-operator from memory elements involved in the goal, rather than from the rules used to reach the goal.

Despite the differences in these approaches to forming sequential chunks, some common themes have emerged. First, most of the work has occurred within a heuristic search framework in which macro-operators are composed from primitive legal operators. Second, goals play a central role in determining when most of the chunking methods are evoked. For this reason most of the methods are embedded within a means-ends analysis framework like that used by Newell, Shaw, and Simon's GPS (1960) which allows intelligent generation of subgoals.

The task of forming macro-operators can be viewed as another variant on the general task of learning from experience. In this case, the structure to be learned is some configuration of actions or operators—a sequential chunk. Methods for learning macro-operators directly address the *aggregation* issue, since they decide which components to include as parts of the higher level structure. In most chunking methods, the *characterization* problem is made trivial, since new rules are based directly on existing rules, for which the level of generality is already known. Even in methods that address issues of characterization (such as Laird, Rosenbloom, & Newell's approach), chunks are based on single instances, so that the *clustering* problem is bypassed. Finally, none of the research in this area explicitly addresses storage issues, though much of the work is embedded within production system frameworks like Anderson's ACT (1983) which have implications for how knowledge is indexed in long term memory.

Grammar Learning

Now that we have considered a number of machine learning tasks, let us turn to the problem of language acquisition. The overall task of language acquisition is very complex and involves many levels, including learning to recognize and generate words, learning the meanings of words, learning grammatical knowledge, and learning pragmatic knowledge. Each of these subproblems is interesting in its own right, but since the majority of AI work on language acquisition has dealt with grammar learning, we will focus on this issue in the current section.

Some of the earliest work in machine learning addressed the problem of grammar acquisition, and this is still an active area of research in the field. The basic task may be stated in the following manner:

- *Given:* A set of grammatical sentences from some language.
- *Find:* A procedure for recognizing and/or generating all grammatical sentences in that language.

The learned procedure may take many different forms such as a set of rewrite rules, an augmented transition network, or a production system. Note that one is given only legal sentences from the language to be learned and that no "negative instances" are presented. Solomonoff (1959) carried out some of the earliest AI work on this problem, followed by Knowlton (1962), Garvin (1967), and Horning (1969). Wolff (1978, 1982) and Berwick (1979) have described more recent grammar learning systems in this tradition.

However, we know from the child language data that the human learner does not hear sentences in isolation: rather, the sentences usually describe some event or object in the immediate environment. This observation leads to a different formulation of the grammar learning task, which may be stated:

- *Given:* A set of grammatical sentences from some language, each with an associated meaning.
- *Find:* A procedure for mapping sentences onto their meanings or vice versa.

This view of grammar acquisition differs significantly from the first one we examined. Grammatical knowledge may again be represented in a variety of ways, but it must contain more than information about sentence structure—it must also relate this structure to meaning. We will see that the second view of grammar learning leads to quite different models of the learning process. Kelley (1967), Siklóssy (1968), and Klein and Kuppin (1970) carried out the earliest work in this "semantic" tradition. More recent systems have been described by Hedrick (1976), Reeker (1976), Anderson (1977), Selfridge (1981), Sembugamoorthy (1981), Langley (1982), Smith (1982), and Hill (1983).

Since we review some of the earlier work on grammar learning in detail in the following section, we will not delve deeply into particular methods here. However, we should note that both versions of the grammar learning task can be viewed as further variants on the general problem of learning from experience. However, they differ from the other four tasks in an important respect. Like the chunking task, they address the problem of *aggregation,* since the grammar learner must form sequential chunks such as noun phrase and verb phrase. Like the conceptual clustering task, they address the *clustering* problem, since one must group words into disjunctive classes like noun and verb without the aid of a tutor.

The opportunity for *characterization* also exists in the second (semantic) version of the task since semantic features can often be used to predict when a class like noun or verb is appropriate. Finally, most representations of grammatical knowledge (such as ATNs and production systems) have implications for the *storage/indexing* problem, and this carries over into the work on grammar learning. In other words, the task of grammar learning is the only task that forces one to address all four components of learning from experience, making it (in principle, at least) the most challenging of the problems we have examined.

MACHINE LEARNING RESEARCH ON GRAMMAR ACQUISITION

Now that we have reviewed the types of tasks that machine learning researchers have focused on, let us consider some examples of AI systems that address the grammar learning process. Considerable work has been done in this area, and we will not have time to cover it all here. Instead, we will examine four specific systems that we feel will clarify the nature of this work and its relation to other problems in machine learning. The interested reader is directed to reviews by McMaster, Sampson, and King (1976), Pinker (1979), and Langley (1982).

We will examine four AI systems that implement quite different approaches to grammar learning: Wolff's SNPR (1978, 1982), Berwick's LPARSIFAL (1979, 1980), Anderson's LAS (1977), and Langley's AMBER (1980, 1982). We will see that these systems differ on a variety of dimensions, the most important involving whether they learn from isolated sentences or from sentence-meaning pairs. In each case, we describe the inputs and outputs of the system, its representation of acquired grammatical knowledge, its learning mechanisms, and the relation of these mechanisms to the four components of learning from experience. We close with some comments on the role of negative instances in grammar learning.

Wolff's SNPR System

Wolff (1978, 1982) has developed SNPR, a program that acquires grammatical knowledge in a very data-driven manner. The system begins with a sequence of letters and generates a phrase structure grammar (stated as rewrite rules) that summarizes the observed sequence. SNPR is not provided with any punctuation or with any pauses between words or sentences; it must determine these boundaries on its own. The program processes the strings in a semi-incremental manner, first examining a subset of the data, then processing another segment, and so forth.

One of SNPR's strategies is to look for common sequences of symbols, and to define *chunks* in terms of these sequences. For example, given the sequence *thedogchasedthecatthecatchasedthedog* . . . , the program might define chunks like *the, dog, cat,* and *chased*. This example is somewhat misleading, since the system always builds chunks from pairs of symbols, but it conveys the basic idea. Whenever a chunk is created, the component symbols are replaced by the symbol for that chunk. In this case, the sequence *the-dog-chased-the-cat-the-cat-chased-the-dog* would result. This process can be applied recursively to generate hierarchical chunks.

In addition, when SNPR finds a number of different symbols (letters or chunks) that precede or follow a common symbol, it may define a disjunctive class in terms of the first set. For instance, in the above sequence we find the subsequences *the-dog-chased* and *the-cat-chased.* Based on this regularity, Wolff's program might define the disjunctive class *noun* = {*dog, cat*}. It would then substitute the symbol for this new class into the letter sequence for the member symbols. In this case, the sequence *the-noun-chased-the-noun-the-noun-chased-the-noun* would be generated. Additional classes such as 'verb' and 'determiner' would be defined and replaced in the same manner.

These two basic methods are applied recursively, so that chunks can be defined in terms of disjunctive classes. This leads to constructs such as noun phrases, prepositional phrases, verb phrases, and ultimately to sentences. Thus, the interleaving of chunks and disjuncts leads SNPR to construct phrase structure grammars which summarize the letter sequences it has observed.

From this description we see that Wolff's learning system employs two operators—one for forming disjunctive classes such as noun, and another for defining chunks or conjunctive structures, such as dog. SNPR also includes operators for generalization (by discarding some data) and recursion, but we will not focus on them here. The system employs a numeric evaluation function to determine which of its operators should be applied in a given situation. This function measures two features of the grammar that would result—the *compression capacity* (the degree to which a given grammar compresses the original data) and the *size* of the grammar. At each point in its learning process, SNPR selects that step which gives the greatest improvement in compression capacity per unit increase in size. Thus, the system can be viewed as carrying out a hill-climbing search through the space of possible phrase structure grammars.

Now that we have described Wolff's SNPR in process terms, let us re-examine the system in terms of the four components of learning from experience. The first operator is clearly responsible for generating sequential chunks and thus addresses the *aggregation* problem. Similarly, the second operator is responsible for forming disjunctive classes or extensional definitions and thus addresses the *clustering* component. The most interesting feature of SNPR is that these operators both compete for attention through the evaluation function and interact in that chunks are later used in disjunctive classes, which are in turn used in higher level chunks. Thus, the solution to both aggregation and clustering is inherently intertwined, with both using co-occurrence statistics to determine which step to take. Note that this data-intensive approach to chunking differs radically from the work on macro-operators in which chunks are determined on the basis of a single instance.

Wolff's system is also interesting in that it makes no explicit attempt to characterize its disjunctive classes (e.g., noun and verb) after they have been extensionally defined. However, the interaction between aggregation and clustering can lead to multiple chunks which reference the same disjunctive class. For instance, the symbol *noun* may occur in the rewrite rules for *noun phrase* and *prepositional phrase*. Taken together, one can view the set of chunks that refer to *noun* as an intensional definition or characterization of that class. Thus, SNPR arrives at characterizations of a sort, though it does so indirectly.

Similarly, Wolff does not explicitly address the details of the storage process, but the notion of efficient storage is a major motivation behind his work. Rewrite rules are commonly used within computer science to store grammars for compilers, and recent versions of the AI programming language Prolog incorporate efficient implementations of such rewrite rules. Moreover, although SNPR's heuristics are concerned with efficient storage rather than efficient access and retrieval, the two measures are certainly correlated. Now that we have considered SNPR's relation to the components of learning, let us turn to some incremental approaches to grammar acquisition.

Berwick's LPARSIFAL System

Berwick (1979, 1980) has described LPARSIFAL, a system that learns grammars from a sequence of legal English sentences. The program incrementally modifies its grammar after each input sentence, unless that sentence can already be parsed by the grammar. The input sentences differ from Wolff's in that each one is composed of a sequence of separate words, and the sentences themselves are separated from each other. No meanings are associated with either words or sentences. Grammatical knowledge is represented as a set of rules, but ones quite different from the rewrite rules used by Wolff's SNPR. In order to understand the nature of these rules, we must review Marcus' (1980) PARSIFAL, the natural language system upon which Berwick's work is based.

PARSIFAL differs from most AI natural language systems in that it employs a look-ahead method to avoid the need to backtrack on the vast majority of sentences. The system employs two data structures—a buffer containing the words in the sentence (the input) and a stack of nodes representing phrase structures (the output). The conditions of rules can examine only the first three items in the buffer and the top item in the node stack. There are four available actions:

1. *Create* a node and push it onto the stack,

2. *Remove* the top node on the stack and put it in the buffer, pushing existing items to the right,
3. *Attach* the first buffer item to the top node on the stack, moving the remaining items in the buffer to the left,
4. *Switch* the first and second items in the buffer.

The first of these actions can be instantiated in different ways. For instance, one rule may create a noun-phrase node while another may create a verb-phrase node. However, the last three actions are completely determined by the situation in which they apply. PARSIFAL operates in cycles, applying the first rule that matches, altering the stack and buffer accordingly, applying the next rule that matches, and so forth. This process continues until the sentence has been completely analyzed and a parse tree has been constructed.

Now let us return to Berwick's LPARSIFAL, which operates within this framework. The system begins with a knowledge of $\bar{X}$ theory and an interpreter for applying grammar rules to parse sentences. Although the program can learn rules "from scratch," our discussion will be simplified if we assume that LPARSIFAL has already acquired a few rules for parsing simple sentences, such as active statements like *The boy bounced the ball*.

When given a new sentence, LPARSIFAL attempts to parse it using the existing rules. If it encounters some problem, the system attempts to create a new rule that will handle the problem-causing situation. The program determines the action on this rule using a generate and test strategy, first seeing if *attach* will let it continue parsing the sentence, and if this fails, seeing if *switch* will suffice. Assuming one of these ultimately leads to a successful parse, the program constructs a new rule containing that action.

The conditions of the new rule are based on the state of the parse when the impasse was encountered. This includes the top of the stack and the contents of the input buffer, including lexical features associated with the words in the buffer. Upon adding the new rule to memory, the system checks to see if any existing rules have identical actions. If there are none, the rule is inserted at the beginning of the rule list.

However, if a rule with the same action and the same $\bar{X}$ context is found, LPARSIFAL compares the two condition sides to determine what they hold in common. The resulting mapping is used to construct a more general rule with the same action. Differing conditions are dropped from the resulting general rule or, in some cases, lead to the creation of syntactic classes like nouns and verbs. In the latter case, the words that differ in the two conditions are replaced by the name of the class, and the words are stored as members of that class. If the old rule contains a class where the new rule contains a word, the word is added to that class.

The reader will note that LPARSIFAL's method for combining rules is identical to one of the data-driven characterization operators we considered in the context of learning from examples. This is the "finding common structures" operator, which is often used in conjunction with specific-to-general strategies for learning concepts from examples. There are three interesting aspects to Berwick's use of this method.

First, the system decides for itself into which of the existing rules it should incorporate the new "instance" (a given buffer-node combination). LPARSIFAL determines this by examining the action and the $\bar{X}$ context associated with existing rules and the new situation, much as a system that learns from examples uses the name of the class associated with an instance. Second, the system represents instances and condition sides purely in terms of attribute-value pairs. As a result, there is never more than one way to incorporate a new instance into an existing rule, so that absolutely no search through the rule space is required. This leads directly to the third point. Since no search problem exists, the program does not require negative instances to prune the search tree, and LPARSIFAL can learn grammars without computing such negative instances.[8]

However, recall that the "finding common structures" approach relied on an important assumption—that there exists a conjunctive characterization of the data. If an adequate description requires a disjunct of some form, then this approach will lead to an overly general characterization, and only negative instances will reveal the difficulty. Thus, Berwick's approach relies on the assumption that each action/$\bar{X}$ context combination has at most one associated set of conditions. If this assumption were violated, his system would acquire overly general grammatical rules, though it would never realize this fact.

Now let us reconsider LPARSIFAL's approach to grammar acquisition as it relates to the four components of learning from experience. We have seen that the system addresses the issue of *clustering,* since it decides which instances (combinations of buffer items and nodes) to compare to one another. We have also seen that it attempts to *characterize* the resulting clusters by finding common features. The system's response to the *storage* problem is to create rules that are indexed for easy retrieval, a common approach that we have seen in other contexts. However, the program does not form any new sequential chunks beyond those it starts with so that it bypasses the *aggregation* problem.

Upon reflection, LPARSIFAL feels quite different not only from Wolff's SNPR, but from every other grammar learning system that has been proposed. The reason for its distinctiveness becomes apparent when we recall another class of learning problems that addresses clustering and characterization but not aggregation—the task of *heuristics learning.* We would argue that Berwick has successfully transformed the grammar learning task into the task of learning search heuristics, a counterintuitive (but apparently useful) approach.

---

[8]Berwick's system could identify negative instances of each action using the *learning from solution paths* method described earlier. Later, we will see another approach to "constructing" negative instances from grammatical sentences.

The relation will become apparent if we consider a conservative approach to the heuristics learning task. Suppose one begins with a set of heuristic rules that are overly specific, and which thus lead to a state in which no move is proposed. At this point, one falls back on those operators whose legal (but not heuristic) conditions are met. If applying one of these operators eventually leads to the goal state, then a new heuristic rule is created based on the successful move. This specific rule may then be combined with other rules that involve the same operator. The operators correspond to Berwick's four actions, and the learned heuristics correspond to his acquired grammar rules. This analogy is not as forced as it appears at first glance. Ohlsson (1983) has described UPL, a heuristics learning system that uses a nearly identical strategy to learn rules for puzzles like the Tower of Hanoi.[9]

Although Berwick's approach is an elegant one, it clearly addresses different issues in grammar learning than other systems. For instance, Wolff's SNPR generates sequential chunks like noun phrase and verb phrase, while LPARSIFAL does not. Similarly, Berwick's program learns the conditions under which to apply specific "parsing" operators, while other systems do not. The main overlap lies in the formation of syntactic classes like nouns and verbs, which both SNPR and LPARSIFAL (and many other systems) define. What is interesting about the latter system is that it *clusters* objects at two entirely different levels—the level of instances of each operator and the level of words that should be grouped into one syntactic class.

Anderson's LAS System

Anderson (1977) has developed LAS, a program that learns to understand and generate sentences in both English and French. The system accepts legal sentences and their associated meanings as input, with meaning represented in terms of a semantic network. The goal is to acquire a *mapping* from sentences onto their meanings and vice versa, rather than simply learning to recognize grammatical utterances. LAS represents grammatical knowledge as an augmented transition network (ATN) with both semantic and syntactic information stored on each link.

In addition to this basic information, LAS is provided with additional knowledge that constrains the learning process. This information includes:

- Connections between concepts and their associated words;
- The main topic of each sentence;
- Knowledge that some concepts (like shapes) are more significant than

[9]We should note that Berwick reported the first version of LPARSIFAL in 1979, when very few results had been achieved in heuristics learning.

others; the words for these concepts eventually develop into the class of nouns;

- The *graph deformation condition,* which roughly states that if two words occur near each other in a sentence, the concepts associated with those words must occur near each other in the meaning of that sentence.

These sources of information are sufficient to enable LAS to determine a unique parse tree for any given sentence-meaning pair. For instance, suppose the system is given the sentence *The big dog chased the red ball* and its associated meaning. We can represent this meaning using node-link-node triples with each triple specifying a connection in a semantic network: (*event-1 action chase*), (*event-1 agent agent-1*), (*agent-1 type dog*), (*agent-1 size big*), (*event-1 object object-1*), (*object-1 type ball*), (*object-1 color red*).[10] Given this information, LAS would generate the parse [The (big) dog] chased [the (red) ball]), where parentheses indicated the level of the tree. Figure 5.2 presents a graphic version of this parse tree.

Let us consider the graph deformation condition in somewhat more detail. Stated more formally, this says that the parse tree for a sentence must be a graph deformation of the network representing that sentence's meaning and that the branches in this parse tree must not cross each other. This assumption constrains the space of grammars that LAS considers, but it does not eliminate search by itself. Given the same meaning representation as above, a variety of associated sentences would satisfy the constraint. These include *The dog big chased the ball red, The red ball chased the dog big,* and *Chased the big dog the red ball.* If LAS observed any of these sentences paired with the same meaning, it would find them acceptable and generate their parse trees. Since the parses would be different, the system would acquire a different ATN in each case.

However, the sentence *The big ball chased the red dog* violates the graph deformation condition. When one orders the words in this fashion, there is no way to redraw the tree from Figure 5.2 so that the lines do not cross. As Figure 5.3 shows, the agent *dog* is too far from the agent node and the object *ball* is too far from the object node for this to be possible. As a result, LAS would reject this sentence as unacceptable, and would never consider learning a grammar which generated such sentences.

Given the parse tree for a sentence, it is a simple matter to generate an augmented transition network that will parse that sentence. For instance, suppose LAS is given the parse tree ([*The (big) dog*] *chased* [*the (red) ball*]), shown graphically in Figure 5.2. Using the knowledge it has been given (including the graph deformation condition), the program can transform this structure directly into the (initial) ATN shown in Figure 5.4.

---

[10]LAS actually used a different set of links in its network representation, but we have used mnemonic ones for the sake of clarity.

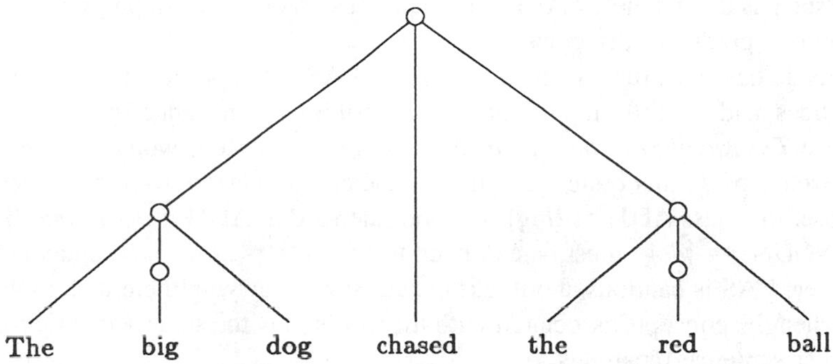

FIGURE 5.2. Inferred parse tree for a simple sentence.

Since the parse tree has three branches at the top level, LAS would generate a top-level ATN with three links—one for the first structure [*The (big) dog*], one for the second structure *chased,* and one for the third [*the (red) ball*]. Since the first and third components themselves contain internal structure, LAS would build a sub-ATN for both of these, each with three links. For example, the first sub-ATN (call it NP1) would have links for *The*, (*big*), and *dog*. Similarly, since the second element for each of the sub-ATNs has internal structure, LAS would create even lower level ATNs for these, each having one link (in one case for *big* and in the other for *red*).

In other words, there is a direct mapping from a parse tree to an ATN for generating that parse tree. Note from Figure 5.4 that specific words are never used as tests on the ATN's links. Instead, LAS defines a word class that initially has a single member and uses this class in the test. Also note that the initial grammar employs different subnetworks for constructs that we view as equiv-

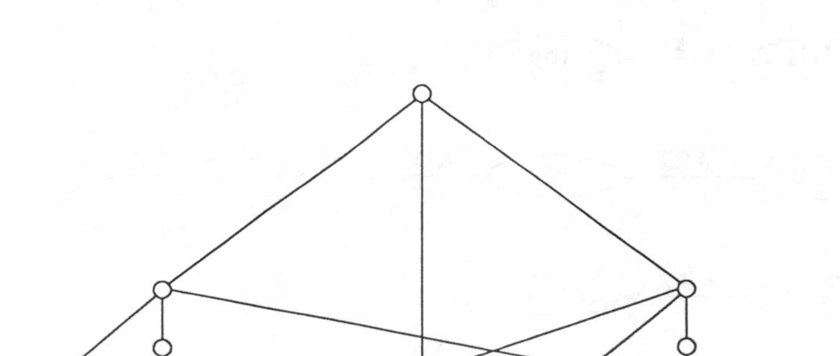

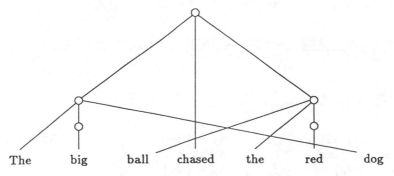

FIGURE 5.3. A sentence that violates the graph deformation condition.

alent, such as the two networks for noun phrases. As the system progresses, such distinctions gradually disappear.

After it has constructed an initial ATN, LAS attempts to incorporate new parse trees with as little modification as possible. For instance, given the new sentence *The small cat chased the long string*, the system would note that its ATN would parse this quite well, if only the certain classes were expanded. In this case, the class ADJ1 = {*big*} must be extended to ADJ1 = {*big, small*}, the class NOUN1 = {*dog*} must be extended to NOUN1 = {*dog, cat*}, and so forth. However, LAS is cautious about taking such steps, carrying them to completion only when the concepts associated with the words play the same semantic role as in earlier sentence meanings.

In addition to expanding word classes, LAS employs two other mechanisms for producing more general grammars. First, when the system finds two word classes that share a significant number of elements, it combines them into a single class. Second, if LAS finds two sub-ATNs to be sufficiently similar, it combines them into a single subnetwork. A special case of this process actually leads to recursive networks for parsing noun phrases, so that arbitrarily deep embeddings can be handled. These steps occasionally lead the system to learn overly general ATNs which generate constructions such as *foots* instead of *feet*, and it has no mechanisms for recovering from such errors.

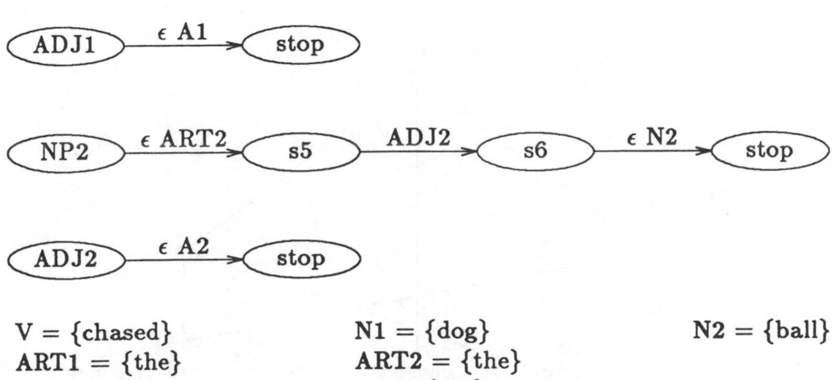

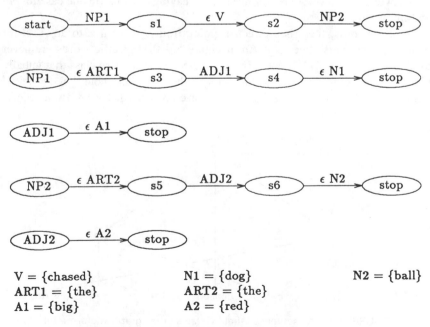

V = {chased} N1 = {dog} N2 = {ball}
ART1 = {the} ART2 = {the}
A1 = {big} A2 = {red}

FIGURE 5.4. Initial ATN based on a single sentence.

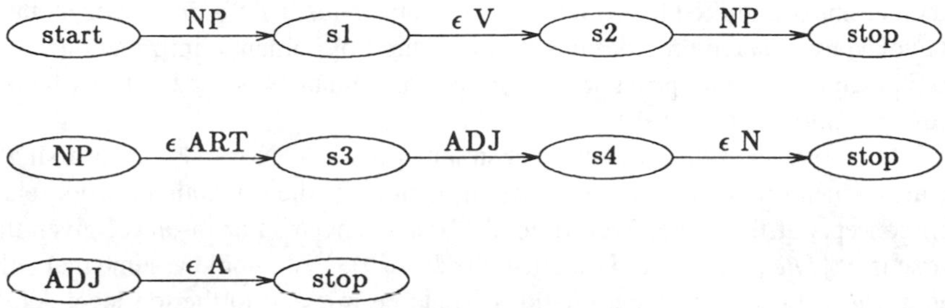

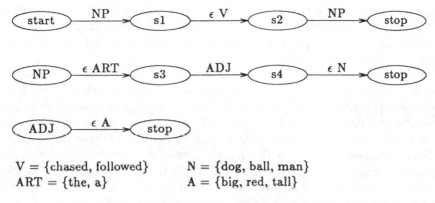

V = {chased, followed} N = {dog, ball, man}
ART = {the, a} A = {big, red, tall}

FIGURE 5.5. Revised ATN after a second sentence.

Figure 5.5 presents a revised ATN that LAS might construct after hearing the second sentence *A tall man followed the big dog*. In this case, the word *followed* has been added to the syntactic class V. Moreover, the two classes N1 and N2 have been combined into the single class N with members *dog, ball,* and *man.*[11] Similarly, the classes ART1 and ART2 have been collapsed, as have the classes A1 and A2. More important, the two noun phrase ATNs have been combined into the single ATN NP, based on their similar structure and components. An analogous combination has occurred for the ADJ1 and ADJ2 networks, generating a much simpler grammar than we had after the first example.

Now let us reconsider Anderson's LAS in terms of the four components of learning from experience. First, we see that the system employs the meanings of sentences, their main topic, and the graph deformation condition to determine a unique parse tree. This in turn determines an augmented transition network, which can be viewed as a hierarchically organized set of *sequential chunks*. In other words, LAS used the above information to solve the *aggregation* problem for each sentence it is given. Note that this approach is quite different than chunking methods that have been used for building macro-operators, employing knowledge about language to determine the chunks.

Anderson's approach to the clustering problem also differs from methods used for conceptual clustering. LAS uses a bottom-up (agglomerative) approach to form disjunctive word classes, but this process operates in two stages. In the first stage, the system extends its word classes incrementally, expanding them whenever required to parse new sentences. In the second stage, it combines classes (nonincrementally) if they have enough common members. Moreover, both

[11]This combination could occur after dog had been added to N2 causing the two sets to have a 50% overlap. Actually, we doubt that LAS would collapse word classes on the basis of such slim evidence, but we have assumed that it would for the sake of simplicity.

mechanisms are limited by semantic constraints. Thus, LAS's *clustering* method is evoked by syntactic regularities, but is filtered by semantic information. Syntax is used to generate possible clusters, while semantics is used to test whether they are appropriate.

LAS determines the semantic constraints on its ATN's links from a single sentence-meaning pair, assuming that all portions of the semantic network relating concepts at the same level in the ATN are relevant. For instance, given the parse tree ([*The (big) dog*] *chased [the (red) ball*]), LAS would assume that only the agent, action, and object relations would be relevant to the top-level ATN. Thus, Anderson's response to the *characterization* problem also differs from the traditional approaches, producing a general rule from a single instance. In this sense, it is similar to the *explanation-based learning* methods that have recently been formulated by Mitchell, Keller, and Kedar-Cabelli (1986) and others.

Finally, Anderson's decision to use augmented transition networks constitutes a response to the *storage* issue. The use of ATNs have implications for retrieval, since the connecting arcs act as direct pointers to successor states, giving them a top-down, expectation-driven flavor. Assuming the system has parsed the first part of a sentence, the most likely following steps can be easily retrieved. In addition, LAS combined sub-ATNs whenever possible. Although this was primarily intended as an induction technique, it also led to an efficient storage of grammatical knowledge. This is another dimension on which Anderson's work differs from other machine learning efforts, but this is not surprising considering that ATNs were designed to handle linguistic phenomena.

Langley's AMBER System

Langley (1980, 1982) has described AMBER, a cognitive simulation of the early stages of child grammar acquisition. Like LAS, the system accepts sentence/meaning pairs as input, using a semantic network to represent meaning. Again, the goal is to learn a mapping, in this case from meanings to sentences. AMBER represents this grammatical knowledge as production rules for generating sentences, including both semantic constraints and information about what has already been said in the conditions of rules.

AMBER is also similar to LAS in that it requires knowledge of the meanings of content words (like *small, ball,* and *bounce*), as well as information about the main topic of each sentence. In addition, the system assumes that utterances having no associated meaning (like *the* and *ing*) are function words and that these play a different role from content words. Although AMBER does not assume Anderson's graph deformation condition, we will see that something analogous arises from the system's strategy for generating sentences.

The reader will recall that LAS used each sample sentence-meaning pair to generate a parse tree, which formed the basis for its ATN. Instead, AMBER employs information about the main topic of the sentence to transform the semantic network representation of meaning into a tree in which the top node corresponds to the main topic. Consider the following sentences:

The big dog chased the red ball
The red ball was chased by the big dog.
The dog that chased the red ball was big.

Although these sentences describe the same event, they differ in their main topic. In the first construction, the chasing action is emphasized; in the second, the ball is highlighted; and in the final sentence, the dog is emphasized. In each case, AMBER transforms the network representation of the meaning into a different tree structure.

Based on the resulting tree, AMBER proceeds to generate an utterance to describe the structure. In doing so, it employs the notion of goals and subgoals. The system's top level goal is to describe the entire tree. In order to achieve this high level goal, it creates subgoals to describe nodes lower in the tree. At the outset, AMBER can handle only one subgoal at a time, leading the system to generate one-word "sentences." Much of the system's learning consists of acquiring rules that let it deal with multiple subgoals and then identifying the relative order in which those subgoals should be achieved.

However, even in its early stages AMBER places two important constraints on this process. First, it never creates a goal at level L while another goal at the same level is still active. Second, once it has deactivated a given goal, it cannot reactivate it for the current utterance. Thus, in describing an event in which a big dog chased a red ball, AMBER might not mention all aspects of the event; for instance, it might fail to mention that the dog was big or that the action involved chasing. However, it would never say *dog*, followed by *chase,* and then return to *big,* since the concepts *big* and *dog* occur in the same subtree. As a result of this goal-processing strategy, AMBER is guaranteed to generate only utterances which obey Anderson's graph deformation condition even though this constraint is not explicitly included in the system.

AMBER begins with the ability to say one content word at a time. Based on differences between these utterances and the sample sentences it is given, the system generates new rules that let it generate combinations of words and phrases in the correct order. For instance, upon describing the shape of an object (say *ball*) without mentioning its color (say *red*), AMBER would acquire a rule stating that it should only describe shape after it had described color. Such rules must be constructed a number of times before gaining enough "strength" to take control from the default rules. Similarly, if the agent was omitted entirely from the system-generated sentence while the object was described, the system would construct a rule stating that the object should only be described once the agent had been mentioned. This last situation leads AMBER to constructions like Daddy ball in which the action is omitted. Of course, such omissions eventually disappear as the system progresses.

Whenever AMBER successfully predicts all of the content words in an adult sentence, it turns its attention to function words like *is, the,* and *ing*. In the early stages, the system simply omits these terms and creates rules to produce them in the future. However, these initial rules include only limited conditions based on the semantic role played by the associated content word. For instance, *ing* would only be produced following an action word, but no additional constraints are included. Once such rules gain sufficient strength, they begin to generate errors of commission by applying in inappropriate situations. In these cases, AMBER invokes a discrimination learning mechanism to identify differences between positive and negative instances of the overly general rule. This creates more conservative rules with additional conditions, which (after gaining sufficient strength) eliminate the errors of commission.

Now let us reconsider Langley's system in light of our four components of learning. First, we see that AMBER uses the meaning of a sentence, together with the main topic, to determine a tree structure that is very similar to a parse tree. In fact, this tree contains all of the information in a parse tree except the word order, which is available from the sentence itself. As in LAS, this tree structure tells AMBER which basic chunks it should form, solving the *aggregation* problem.

Although their basic response to this problem is the same, the two systems differ in their implementation details. In particular, Langley's system does not require an explicit statement of the graph deformation condition, since this falls out of the model's mechanisms for processing goals.[12] In this sense, AMBER's approach to chunking is similar to Anderson's (1983) composition learning method, which creates chunks based on goal trees.

Unlike the other language acquisition systems we have discussed, AMBER does not formulate explicit syntactic word classes. Rather, the system states its "grammar" entirely in terms of semantic roles like *agent, action, color,* and *shape.* This corresponds to children's early utterances, though eventually they move beyond the semantic stage to more abstract syntactic classes like nouns and verbs. In any case, this means that AMBER has no explicit response to the *clustering* problem for content words. The system does have to group sentences into positive and negative instances for each function word, but this is easily done by seeing whether each word occurs in the expected position.

Langley's model has two distinct responses to the *characterization* problem. Once it has identified positive and negative instances for the various function

---

[12]Anderson's (1981) ALAS employs a very similar response to the chunking problem and to modeling first language acquisition in general. The two systems employ quite similar representations and learning mechanisms though AMBER accounts for somewhat earlier stages than ALAS.

words, AMBER invokes a discrimination mechanism to determine the semantic conditions for each word. We discussed this method earlier in the context of learning from examples. Basically, it is a data-intensive technique that begins with general hypotheses and generates more specific ones as errors of commission occur, using a differencing technique to determine new conditions. Anderson (1983) and Langley (1985) have used similar methods for other domains, including learning from examples and heuristics learning. AMBER combines the discrimination process with a strengthening mechanism that serves to direct search through the space of hypotheses, as well as modeling the gradual nature of children's mastery of function words.

In contrast, AMBER employs a quite different strategy to identify conditions on rules for content word order. In this case the system learns from a single instance, rather than relying upon a method that requires multiple observations. Learning occurs when the system correctly generates one content word but omits another content word it should have produced. To determine the relevant conditions, the system finds the *path* through the semantic network that connects the two content words and includes all links along this path as conditions in the new production rule. Although the details differ, this strategy is similar to that used by LAS in that the system reasons about the meaning of a sample sentence to decide which conditions are relevant. Although AMBER must relearn the resulting rules many times before they affect behavior, the same conditions would be determined in each case. Thus, Langley's system uses a simple form of explanation-based learning to acquire rules for content words, rather than the empirical method it uses for function words.

Although it makes no explicit response to *storage* issues, AMBER is implemented as a production system model. Newell and Simon (1972) have argued that production systems are a viable model of human long term memory, accounting for a variety of robust phenomena exhibited in human cognition. Moreover, Forgy (1979) has proposed a method for efficiently storing large numbers of production rules that takes advantage of shared features and for efficiently matching against these rules by retaining partial matches. AMBER is implemented in PRISM (Langley & Neches, 1981), a production system architecture that employs Forgy's storage and matching methods to provide reasonable performance even when large numbers of rules are involved. Thus, the system provides a plausible response to issues of the storage and retrieval of grammatical knowledge.

Negative Instances in Grammar Learning

Before concluding our review, we should add a few words about the role of negative instances in grammar learning. In an earlier section, we saw that many learning methods rely on negative instances to direct their search through the space of hypotheses. Characterization methods that find common structure employ such instances to determine when a description is overly general and thus should be eliminated. Characterization methods that find differences use negative instances to determine how overly general descriptions should be made more specific. We found that negative instances are heavily used in learning from examples, where they are provided by the tutor. However, they are also used in heuristics learning and conceptual clustering, where they must be generated by the learning system itself.

Only one of the grammar learning systems we discussed (Langley's AMBER) actually employs negative instances, but a number of other systems have also used this type of information, including Reeker's PST (1976) and Anderson's ALAS (1981). At first glance, the use of negative instances may seem odd, since these models are given only examples of *legal* sentences. However, AMBER and its relatives are not dealing with positive and negative instances at the level of the entire sentence. Rather, they are learning the conditions on rules or networks that deal with only *parts* of sentences.[13] Moreover, they are not acquiring the ability to judge grammaticality, but to *map* sentences onto their meanings and vice versa.

The presence of sentence meanings makes a major difference. Since a particular word or phrase may fail to occur in the presence of a particular meaning, negative instances become possible. As a result, one can use difference-based characterization methods such as discrimination (Langley, 1985) that require comparisons between positive and negative instances. Let us consider a brief example of how this can occur. Suppose the learner knows that *ed* may occur after a verb or action word but does not know exactly when. Each case in which the ending does occur is marked as a positive instance of *ed,* while each case in which it fails to occur is marked as a negative instance. Based on this clustering, one can systematically search the space of characterizations to determine which semantic conditions best predict the occurrence of the ending. Similar methods could be used for content words or larger structures such as phrases.

Let us repeat that we do *not* mean that children receive negative evidence in the form of ungrammatical sentences. However, we do mean that one can *generate* negative instances from sentences paired with their meanings and use this information in the grammar learning process. The ability to do this relies on an important assumption that has not been clearly stated in earlier papers taking this approach: there must be a one-to-one mapping between sentences and meanings.[14] If this *uniqueness* assumption does not hold, then one cannot infer that a

---

[13]Berwick (1979) could also have employed negative instances at the rule level by noting which actions failed to allow a successful parse. However, LPARSIFAL did not employ this information, since its search for rules was already sufficiently constrained.

[14]We direct the reader to other chapters in this volume for a fuller treatment of the uniqueness assumption. In particular, the chapters by Clark, by Pinker, and by MacWhinney and Sokolov all make use of this assumption, though not always by the same name. For example, Clark calls it the *principle of contrast.*

missing word or phrase implies a negative instance; the construct might be perfectly acceptable, but the speaker has simply decided to describe the meaning another way.

Thus, the uniqueness assumption guarantees that a missing construct constitutes a negative instance of that construct. This considerably simplifies the learning task, since one can then use the inferred negative instances to eliminate overly general rules or to formulate more specific ones. Of course, learning mechanisms that can handle noise (such as strength-based methods) might still learn if this assumption is not met, and in this case, more frequent constructs would come to be preferred. Still, the greater the degree to which the assumption is violated, the more difficult the grammar learning task will become.

A RESEARCH PROPOSAL

Our review of computational approaches to language acquisition would not be complete without some evaluation of this work and some suggestions for future efforts. For instance, we might evaluate various systems in terms of the psychological and linguistic validity, but this would not really be fair. Of the four grammar learning systems we have examined, only Langley's AMBER (1980, 1982) is intended as a psychological model of first language acquisition and thus makes a serious attempt to account for child language data. Other models have been proposed by Kelley (1967), Reeker (1976), MacWhinney (1978a, 1983), Selfridge (1979), and Hill (1983), but the majority of AI research on language learning has not attempted to explain the observed phenomena. We would like to encourage more work of this sort, but even ignoring this issue, the existing systems suffer on other dimensions. In this section, we consider their limitations and outline an alternative approach that we are using in our own work.

Limitations of Previous Research

One problem with the existing work is its focus on grammar learning to the exclusion of other aspects of language acquisition. A few systems, such as Siklóssy's ZBIE (1968) and Selfridge's CHILD (1979), learn to associate words with concepts, but the majority assume that these connections are present at the outset. Wolff's SNPR (1978, 1982) acquires words as well as grammars, and Mac Whinney (1983) has modeled the development of morphophonology, but these are distinct exceptions to the rule. In addition, all existing systems focus on generating or understanding *correct* sentences rather than *interesting* ones. We know of no system that acquires pragmatic knowledge for determining what one should talk about in a given context. Ultimately, we would like an integrated theory of language acquisition that incorporates all of the above components.

The previous work has also ignored interactions between the process of language acquisition and other aspects of cognition, such as concept formation. Thus, it fits well with the traditional machine learning focus on isolated tasks like those we reviewed earlier in the paper. However, it is clear that concept learning has major implications for language acquisition, and a complete model would take their interaction into account. One can make similar arguments for other components of intelligence.

A more subtle criticism concerns only those systems that learn mappings between sentences and their meanings. However, this assumption holds for all psychological models of grammar learning, an important class of learning systems. The problem is that the representation of meaning is provided by the programmer, and this leaves considerable room for hand-crafting the input. Similar problems arise for other machine learning tasks, but the nature of the grammar learning task emphasizes the issue. There are two ways in which such "cheating" can be embedded in the meanings presented to a model of language acquisition.

First, one may employ concepts and features that are well-suited to the language being learned. For instance, some systems allow a *progressive* feature to be associated with the action of an event. This considerably simplifies the acquisition of the English *ing* construct, while the progressive concept is useless for other languages that make orthogonal distinctions. Second, one may include in the meaning representation only those features that are relevant to the learning task. This lets one avoid modeling the process of focusing attention on important aspects of the environment. All existing cognitive models of language acquisition suffer from such hand-crafting: the "kludges" have moved out of the models (which are often quite general) and into the inputs.

An Alternative Approach to Modeling Language Acquisition

We have been somewhat unfair in criticizing machine learning's emphasis on isolated, idealized tasks, and equally unfair in criticizing models of grammar learning for their carefully crafted inputs. Simplifying assumptions are always helpful when one is first attempting to understand a problem area, and the simplifications that occurred were natural ones. However, the history of artificial intelligence reveals a recurring trend—after the components of a problem are reasonably well understood, more "complex" problems may become easier to solve than the original "simple" ones.

An example from vision research should clarify the trend. Early work in this area focused on the idealized problem of constructing three-dimensional models from very well-lit scenes. Methods for solving this problem involved considerable computation and search. However, when the "harder" task of working with shadowed scenes was attempted, many of the difficulties disappeared. In retrospect, the reason is obvious: the presence of shadows provided constraints that were absent in the original, idealized task, and this significantly reduced the space of possible interpretations.

We believe that research on computational models of language acquisition would benefit from similar strategy. Since this work is still in its early stages, we will spend the remainder of the paper on the constraints we have set ourselves, rather than on solutions to them. Such constraints can occur at two distinct levels. First, one can make the modeling problem more difficult for oneself by using the resulting constraints to direct search through the space of possible models. Second, one can make the language acquisition task more difficult for the learning system by providing additional constraints for the system to use itself. We plan to use both of these strategies in our work on language acquisition.

One way to constrain our search for mechanisms of language acquisition is to model human behavior in this domain. In addition to the intrinsic interest of this endeavor, human children are still our best examples of language learning systems, making them obvious objects of study. MacWhinney (1978b) has proposed nine criteria that should be satisfied by computational models of human language acquisition. Here we will list only four broad classes of constraints that our model should meet, but each of these is sufficient to rule out many of the approaches that have been previously explored.

First, it is clear that children acquire language in an incremental fashion, so our learning mechanisms must have this characteristic as well. Second, it is clear that humans learn not only to judge the grammaticality of sentences, but to map sentences onto their meanings, and our model must do the same. Third, the model should be consistent with our knowledge of the human cognitive architecture. For instance, Newell and Simon (1972) and Anderson (1983) have argued that production systems are central to human cognition; this makes production systems an obvious framework to consider, though certainly not the only one. Finally, children progress through clearly identifiable stages during their acquisition of language, and our model should account for these stages. Thus, the model should progress from the one word stage, through a telegraphic stage, and eventually produce complete adult sentences. We have not decided the level of detail we should strive to explain, but even the highest levels significantly limit the space of models.

Towards an Integrated Model of Learning

In addition to developing a psychologically plausible model of first language acquisition, we hope to develop a more complete model that moves beyond grammar learning in isolation. The planned system must learn to recognize and generate words like *bounce* and *ball,* and it must also associate these words with particular concepts. The model will have to learn the mapping between combinations of words (sentences) and their meanings and to acquire heuristics for generating useful sentences. Moreover, these different components must be integrated into a single model of the language acquisition process.

The advantage of this approach is that the various learning tasks should feed into each other, thereby reducing the learner's reliance on carefully crafted inputs. For instance, the model will initially learn the meanings of words based on repeated situations in which a given word and concept co-occur. This knowledge can then be used to aid the grammar learning process much as existing grammar learning systems use word meanings. However, once an initial grammar has been acquired, this can be used in turn to learn new word meanings from context (Granger, 1977). Such positive feedback would let the system move away from its initial reliance on sentence-meaning pairs.

We also hope to integrate the language acquisition process with a model of both concept formation and problem solving. It is clear that children have many concepts in memory before they associate words with them; this concept formation process must account for their origin. Presumably, some concepts will be acquired later than others, and this may account for the fact that certain words are learned relatively late. Thus, the model of concept formation may contribute to explaining phenomena that appear entirely linguistic at first glance. The causal arrow may point in the other direction as well, since language may be used to communicate new concepts once it has advanced sufficiently.

We believe the problem-solving process is also important to language acquisition since it is responsible for the generation of goals and for the creation of plans to achieve these goals. Many of children's early utterances seem to revolve around goals such as easing hunger and getting attention. If we hope to explain these utterances, we must account for the origin of these goals and thus the need for a model of problem solving. Also, it seems quite likely that an explanation of pragmatic rules and their acquisition will revolve around goals, and a full account must explain how these goals originate.

Learning in a Reactive Environment

Machine learning researchers have traditionally focused on abstract, symbolic tasks like learning from examples and heuristics learning. Not surprisingly, they have attempted to cast the task of language acquisition in the same mold by providing well-defined inputs such as sentence-meaning pairs and expecting clean, categorical rules or grammars as outputs. However, humans learn language in the context of a complex physical world, and our model of the acquisition process should reflect this fact.

In the World Modelers Project, we have implemented a complex simulated environment in which our learner will perceive and act, much as a human child does in the real world. There are three central motivations for using this simulated environment: (*1*) to provide our learning model with (qualitatively) the same class of inputs as a human learner might find in the real world rather than some mathematical abstraction of preselected information with no surrounding context; (*2*) to investigate reactive learning so that the learner can experiment with different ways of generating language or action and directly observe the behavioral consequences of its linguistic or physical acts; and (*3*) to provide situations in which learning can be guided by the pursuit of goals instead of being an end in itself.

The simulated environment supports three-dimensional objects (such as furniture and toys), and these objects obey standard physical laws involving gravity, friction, and torque. The learner itself has a (simplified) physical body that lets it move around and affect its surroundings, as well as senses that let it observe these surroundings. Carbonell and Hood (1985) describe the simulated environment in more detail, but the important point is that it has much the same flavor as the environment in which a child learns language. To date, we have constructed only very simple agents, but our long-term goal is to develop an integrated model of learning (including the acquisition of language) within this environment.

The planned agent will perceive its surroundings through various senses (sight and hearing) and store the resulting descriptions in memory. This has important implications for the language acquisition task, since it means that the programmer need no longer spoonfeed the meanings of sentences to the model. In fact, such direct transfer of information is explicitly forbidden; the learner will have access *only* to what it can see and hear.

This will force us to deal explicitly with two issues we raised earlier: giving the model hand-crafted features like *progressive* to ease the learning task, and limiting the agent's attention by presenting only relevant aspects of an event. Let us consider some responses to these issues that we plan to explore in our model of learning in a reactive environment.

Rather than provide the system with arbitrary high-level features, we must show how these concepts arise naturally out of an integrated cognitive architecture. For instance, any system that interacts with a physical world must have some representation for time and be able to use this in describing events. The system must be able to distinguish between events that are currently occurring and those which are not. Thus, such a system will already have one of the features needed to state progressive rules (like the English *ing*), which are used only in describing ongoing events. However, this feature arises naturally from the architecture itself and has many uses, rather than being given by the programmer specifically for the grammar learning task. We believe that most other features can be handled in an analogous manner.

Similarly, we should not simplify the grammar learning task by providing only the relevant features of an event. Instead, we must model the process by which the learner focuses on relevant information and ignores other features, and this requires a model of *attention*. We believe that existing concepts and schemas generate goals and expectations and that humans use these expectations to filter the overwhelming information provided by their senses. Attention is initially focused by specific object and procedural concepts such as *ball* and *bounce,* since the child's early interactions with the world lead to such concepts. This bias helps account for the dominance of content words in early speech. Only later, after he has mastered content words, does the child turn to function words. If the learner is unable to account for these with existing schemas, he must "loosen up" his filter and examine other features that he previously ignored. Different features will prove useful in different languages, and this is the point at which grammar can influence the learner's knowledge structures in significant ways.

In addition, placing the learner in a physical world should lead naturally to a variety of goals, such as easing hunger. If the agent has only limited manipulation capabilities (e.g., an object may be out of reach), then it will have significant motivation to communicate its goals, in the hope that another agent (e.g., a parent) will satisfy them. Thus goals will play a central role not only in our model of problem solving and concept formation, but in our model of language use as well. In general, the agent will talk about what it wants, rather than describing random objects and events. Such goal-driven focus of attention should constrain the otherwise combinatorially intractable problem of correlating linguistic utterances with physical objects or actions. Moreover, these goals will arise naturally from the learner's interaction with the world instead of being provided by the programmer.

This opens the way to modeling the development of discourse strategies. We expect that the learner will usually be accompanied by an "adult" which has both sophisticated language skills and a repertoire of actions available to it. (This agent will be directly controlled by the programmer so that we can "put words into its mouth.") Thus, the learner will be able to make demands, ask questions, and exhibit a variety of linguistic behaviors beyond simple declarative sentences. Different types of sentences can be used to satisfy different goals, and the model must acquire the proper distinctions from experience.

Also, the presence of world knowledge provides an explanation for why understanding often *appears* to precede production (generation). Although the process of concept formation leads to knowledge of the world without need for language, this does not mean that the knowledge cannot be used in linguistic contexts. Upon hearing a sentence that it only partly understands, the agent may well take the appropriate action based on its previous experience.

For example, suppose the child hears *Go to the door,* but only knows the meaning of *door.* Since moving towards an object is a common strategy used to explore one's surroundings, the child may perform the desired action, even with no knowledge of syntax and little knowledge of semantics. Selfridge (1981) has used a similar approach in his model of first language acquisition. However, he provided the learner with the necessary knowledge structures, rather than modeling the process through which this knowledge is acquired, as we plan.

Of course, to the extent that such non-linguistic strategies are useful, the child will have little reason to learn word meanings and grammar. But in many cases, this approach will lead to behaviors that the adult does not desire, and the learner will observe his displeased response. For example, the above strategy would produce the same response to *Close the door* (the child would go to the door), but in this case it would be incorrect. At this point, the parent might demonstrate his intention by closing the door and repeating the word *close*. Only in a reactive environment can such interaction be modeled and exploited for learning.

This approach to language learning should work in the opposite direction as well. Suppose the child says *ball* to request that an adult bounce the ball to him, and then sees the adult place the ball in his pocket. This is a violated expectation, and as we described earlier, such failures can be used to generate the negative instances that are so useful to learning mechanisms. Experiences of this type will encourage the child to use complete sentences to achieve his goals, rather than isolated words or telegraphic sentences.

We can say little more about the model at this point, since it exists only in the most abstract terms. In fact, we have said more about the task we have set ourselves than the model. However, we feel the nature of this task is central, since it will force us to deal with issues that have been ignored (or at least postponed) in previous work on language acquisition. We feel that the goals of modeling human behavior, developing an integrated model of learning, and examining learning in a reactive environment will lead us down paths that have never been traversed, but which are essential if we hope to understand the full nature of language acquisition.

Summary

In closing, let us briefly review the main points of the paper. We have seen that the field of machine learning has addressed a number of distinct tasks, including learning from examples, heuristics learning, conceptual clustering, and learning macro-operators. Significant work has also been carried out on the problem of learning grammars from sample sentences. We described each of these tasks in terms of four components or subproblems—aggregation, clustering, characterization, and storage. We found that only the grammar learning task forces one to address all four of the components, making it the most complex of the learning problems we examined.

We also saw that in the area of language acquisition, machine learning researchers have focused almost exclusively on grammatical knowledge, and we reviewed four systems that acquire such knowledge. These systems differed along a number of dimensions, including their representation of grammars, their reliance on sentence meanings, and the actual learning mechanisms they employed. Each system also had its own response to the four components of learning given above. Finally, we discussed some problems with existing computational approaches to language acquisition, and outlined an alternative approach in which we plan to integrate different aspects of the learning process, and in which we plan to model learning in a complex, reactive environment.

We have no illusions that developing an integrated model of language learning will be easy. Nor do we believe that we will succeed in any absolute sense. However, we do believe that the attempt to construct such an integrated model will lead to questions that have never before been asked and to some tentative answers that future researchers will expand and improve upon. In the long run, we expect that this strategy will lead to our common goal—a fuller understanding of the mechanisms that underlie language acquisition.

ACKNOWLEDGMENTS

We would like to thank Brian MacWhinney and Jeff Sokolov for their comments on an early draft of the chapter. We also thank Doug Fisher and Dan Easterlin for discussions that led to our framework for research in machine learning.

This research was supported by Contract N00014-84-K-0345 from the Information Sciences Division, Office of Naval Research. Approved for public release; distribution unlimited. Reproduction in whole or part is permitted for any purpose of the United States Government.

REFERENCES

Anderson, J. R. (1977). Induction of augmented transition networks. *Cognitive Science, 1,* 125–157.

Anderson, J. R. (1981). A theory of language acquisition based on general learning principles. *Proceedings of the Seventh International Joint Conference on Artificial Intelligence* (pp. 165–170). Vancouver, B.C., Canada.

Anderson, J. R. (1983). *The architecture of cognition.* Cambridge, MA: Harvard University Press.

Anzai, Y., & Simon, H. A. (1979). The theory of learning by doing. *Psychological Review, 86,* 124–140.

Berwick, R. (1979). Learning structural descriptions of grammar rules from examples. *Proceedings of the Sixth International Conference on Artificial Intelligence* (pp. 56–58). Tokyo, Japan.

Berwick, R. (1980). Computational analogues of constraints on grammars: A model of syntactic acquisition. *Proceedings of the 18th Annual Conference of the Association for Computational Linguistics* (pp. 49–53). Toronto, Ontario, Canada.

Bruner, J. S., Goodnow, J. J., & Austin, G. A. (1956). *A study of thinking.* New York: Wiley.

Carbonell, J. G., & Hood, G. (1985). The world modelers project: Objectives and simulator architecture. *Proceedings of the Third International Machine Learning Workshop* (pp. 14–16). Skytop, PA.

Clark, E. (1986). The principle of contrast: A constraint on language acquisition. In B. MacWhinney (Ed.), *Mechanisms of language acquisition.* Hillsdale, N.J.: Lawrence Erlbaum Associates.

Everitt, B. (1980). *Cluster analysis.* Heinemann Educational Books, Ltd.

Fisher, D. (1984). *A hierarchical conceptual clustering algorithm.* (Technical Report) Department of Information and Computer Science, University of California, Irvine.

Fisher, D., & Langley, P. (1985). Approaches to conceptual clustering. *Proceedings of the Ninth International Joint Conference on Artificial Intelligence* (pp. 691–697). Los Angeles, CA.

Forgy, C. L. (1979). *On the efficient implementation of production systems.* Dissertation, Department of Computer Science, Carnegie-Mellon University, Pittsburgh, PA.

Garvin, P. I. (1967). The automation of discovery procedure in linguistics. *Language, 43,* 172–178.

Granger, R. H. (1977). Foul-Up: A program that figures out words from context. *Proceedings of the Fifth International Joint Conference on Artificial Intelligence* (pp. 172–178). Cambridge, MA.

Hayes-Roth, F., & McDermott, J. (1978). An interference matching technique for inducing abstractions. *Communications of the ACM, 21,* 401–410.

Hedrick, C. (1976). Learning production systems from examples. *Artificial Intelligence, 7,* 21–49.

Hill, J. A. C. (1983). *A computational model of language acquisition in the two-year-old.* Dissertation, Department of Computer Science, University of Massachusetts, Amherst, MA.

Horning, J. J. (1969). *A study of grammatical inference.* (Technical Report, No. CS 139) Computer Science Department, Stanford University, Stanford, CA.

Iba, G. (1985). Learning by discovering macros in puzzle solving. *Proceedings of the Ninth International Joint Conference on Artificial Intelligence* (pp. 640–642). Los Angeles, CA.

Kelley, K. L. (1967). *Early syntactic acquisition.* (Technical Report P-3719) The Rand Corporation, Santa Monica, CA.

Klein, S., & Kuppin, M. A. (1970). *An interactive, heuristic program for learning transformational grammars.* (Technical Report No. 97) Computer Sciences Department, University of Wisconsin, Madison.

Knowlton, K. (1962). *Sentence parsing with a self-organizing heuristic program.* Dissertation, Massachusetts Institute of Technology, Cambridge, MA.

Korf, R. E. (1982). A program that learns to solve Rubik's cube. *Proceedings of National Conference on Artificial Intelligence* (pp. 164–167). Pittsburgh, PA.

Laird, J. E., Rosenbloom, P. S., & Newell, A. (1986). SOAR: The anatomy of a general learning mechanism. *Machine Learning, 1,* 11–46.

Langley, P. (1980). A production system model of first language acquisition. *Proceedings of the Eighth International Conference on Computational Linguistics* (pp. 183–189). Tokyo, Japan.

Langley, P. (1982). Language acquisition through error recovery. *Cognition and Brain Theory, 5,* 211–255.

Langley, P. (1985). Learning to search: From weak methods to domain-specific heuristics. *Cognitive Science, 9,* 217–260.

Langley, P., & Neches, R. T. (1981). PRISM User's Manual. (Technical Report) Computer Science Department, Carnegie-Mellon University, Pittsburgh, PA.

Langley, P., & Ohlsson, S. (1984). Automated cognitive modeling. *Proceedings of the National Conference on Artificial Intelligence* (pp. 193–197). Austin, TX.

Langley, P., & Sage, S. (1984). Conceptual clustering as discrimination learning. *Proceedings of the Fifth Biennial Conference of the Canadian Society for Computational Studies of Intelligence* (pp. 95–98). London, Ontario, Canada.

Lewis, C. H. (1978). *Production system models of practice effects.* Dissertation, Department of Psychology, University of Michigan, Ann Arbor, MI.

MacWhinney, B. (1978a). The acquisition of morphophonology. *Monographs of the Society for Research in Child Development, 43.*

MacWhinney, B. (1978b). Conditions on acquisitional models. *Proceedings of the Annual Conference of the Association for Computing Machinery.* New York, NY.

MacWhinney, B. (1983). Hungarian language acquisition as an exemplification of a general model of grammatical development. In D. I. Slobin (Ed.), *The cross-linguistic study of language acquisition*. Hillsdale, N.J.: Lawrence Erlbaum Associates.

MacWhinney, B., & Sokolov, J. (1986). Acquiring syntax lexically. In B. MacWhinney (Ed.), *Mechanisms of language acquisition*. Hillsdale, N.J.: Lawrence Erlbaum.

Marcus, M. (1980). *A theory of syntactic recognition for natural language*. Cambridge, MA: MIT Press.

McMaster, I., Sampson, J. R., & King, J. E. (1976). Computer acquisition of natural language: A review and prospectus. *International Journal of Man-Machine Studies, 8,* 367–396.

Michalski, R. S. (1983). A theory and methodology of inductive learning. In R. S. Michalski, J. G. Carbonell, & T. M. Mitchell (Eds.), *Machine learning: An artificial intelligence approach*. Palo Alto, CA: Tioga Press.

Michalski, R. S., & Stepp, R. (1983). Learning from observation: Conceptual clustering. In R. S. Michalski, J. G. Carbonell, & T. M. Mitchell (Eds.), *Machine learning: An artificial intelligence approach*. Palo Alto, CA: Tioga Press.

Miller, G. A. (1956). The magical number seven, plus or minus two. *Psychological Review, 63,* 81–97.

Minsky, M. (1963). Steps toward artificial intelligence. In E. A. Feigenbaum & J. Feldman (Eds.), *Computers and thought*. New York: McGraw-Hill, Inc.

Mitchell, T. M. (1982) . Generalization as search. *Artificial Intelligence, 18,* 203–226.

Mitchell, T. M., Keller, R. M., & Kedar-Cabelli, S. (1986). Explanation-based generalization: A unifying view. *Machine Learning, 1,* 47–80.

Mitchell, T. M., Utgoff, P., & Banerji, R. B. (1983). Learning problem solving heuristics by experimentation. In R. S. Michalski, J. G. Carbonell, & T. M. Mitchell (Eds.), *Machine learning: An artificial intelligence approach*. Palo Alto, CA: Tioga Publishing Co.

Newell, A. Shaw, J. C., & Simon, H. A. (1960). Report on a general problem-solving program for a computer. *Information Processing: Proceedings of the International Conference on Information Processing* (pp. 256–264).

Newell, A., & Simon, H. A. (1972). *Human problem solving*. Englewood Cliffs, N.J.: Prentice-Hall, Inc.

Neves, D. M., & Anderson, J. R. (1981). Knowledge compilation: Mechanisms for the automatization of cognitive skills. In J. R. Anderson (Ed.), *Cognitive skills and their acquisition*. Hillsdale, N.J.: Lawrence Erlbaum Associates.

Ohlsson, S. (1983). A constrained mechanism for procedural learning. *Proceedings of the Eighth International Joint Conference on Artificial Intelligence* (pp. 426–428). Karlsruhe, West Germany.

Pinker, S. (1979). Formal models of language learning. *Cognition, 7,* 217–283.

Pinker, S. (1986). The bootstrapping problem in language acquisition. In B. MacWhinney (Ed.), *Mechanisms of language acquisition*. Hillsdale, N.J.: Lawrence Erlbaum Associates.

Reeker, L. H. (1976). The computational study of language acquisition. In M. Yovits & M. Rubinoff (Eds.), *Advances in computers,* Volume 15. New York: Academic Press.

Selfridge, M. (1981). A computer model of child language acquisition. *Proceedings of the Seventh International Joint Conference on Artificial Intelligence* (pp. 92–96). Vancouver, B.C., Canada.

Sembugamoorthy, V. (1981). A paradigmatic language acquisition system. *Proceedings of the Seventh International Joint Conference on Artificial Intelligence* (pp. 106–108). Vancouver, B.C., Canada.

Siklóssy, L. (1972). Natural language learning by computer. In H. A. Simon & L. Siklóssy (Eds.), *Representation and meaning: Experiments with information processing systems*. Englewood Cliffs, NJ: Prentice Hall.

Sleeman, D., Langley, P., & Mitchell, T. (1982). Learning from solution paths: An approach to the credit assignment problem. *AI Magazine, 3,* 48–52.

Smith, D. E. (1982). *Focuser: A strategic interaction paradigm for language acquisition*. Dissertation, Department of Computer Science, Rutgers University, New Brunswick, NJ.

Solomonoff, R. (1959). A new method for discovering the grammars of phrase structure languages. *Proceedings of the International Conference on Information Processing.*

Winston, P. H. (1975). Learning structural descriptions from examples. In P. H. Winston (Ed.), *The psychology of computer vision.* New York: McGraw Hill.

Wolff, J. G. (1978). Grammar discovery as data compression. *Proceedings of the AISB/GI Conference on Artificial Intelligence* (pp. 375–379). Hamburg, West Germany.

Wolff, J. G. (1982). Language acquisition, data compression, and generalization. *Language and Communication, 2,* 57–89.

II COMPETITION

6 Competition, Variation, and Language Learning

Elizabeth Bates
University of California, San Diego
Brian MacWhinney
Carnegie-Mellon University

The problem of accounting for the acquisition of language can be decomposed into two smaller problems: how to account for what is universal in language development and how to account for what is variable. We have seen a number of elegant and detailed accounts of universal processes in language acquisition. But these models have not yet taken seriously the existence of two significant aspects of variation in the acquisition process: *1.* variation across natural languages and *2.* variation between individual learners within a particular language. In this paper we discuss a model of language acquisition that has attempted to deal with the first type of variation. We then indicate how this model will have to be elaborated in order to deal with the second form of variation, i.e. variation between individual learners. The development of a detailed mechanistic account for variation is particularly important for those who are interested in a biologically-based theory of language learning. By looking at variation, we are addressing a fundamental issue in the biological sciences, the plasticity of developing systems. How many different forms can a biological system take under normal and abnormal conditions?

The data currently available (Slobin, 1985) provide little evidence for a single, universal sequence in the acquisition of basic grammatical forms. This means that, in order to construct a universalist account of the acquisition of grammar, one must introduce concepts that extract universal patterns out of what appear to be particularistic data. One way of doing this is to think in terms of the nativist concept of ''parameter-setting'' (e.g. Chomsky, 1982; Lightfoot, 1982). According to a parameter-setting analysis, natural languages vary too much in their basic structure to permit a definition of universals entirely in terms of some *intersect,* i.e. the set of structures that *every* language has to have. Rather than obeying categorical universals, languages are governed by ''implicational universas,'' a pool of structural possiblities in which any choice carries important structural consequences of the ''If X, then Y'' variety. Each individual language has charted a path through this set of possibilities. However, given the many implicational constraints within the system, the total set of possible pathways is finite, and rather small. According to this view, language acquisition can be viewed as a process of the successive setting of parameters in a way that allows the system to live with the preordained consequences of each setting. Biology provides the universal parameters; language input triggers a set of constrained choices within that pool of possibilities.

The problem with parameter setting as a model of cross-language variation is that it predicts sudden and all-or-none decisions, carried out in a single specified order, with essentially no opportunity to turn back once a parameter is set. Furthermore, the model is based on the assumption that the adult ''steady state'' can be modelled in terms of the presence or absence of certain structural types. We will present cross-linguistic evidence to suggest that languages vary not only in their end points (as a parameter-setting theory would predict) but also in the initial hypotheses that children hold about their grammar. This evidence indicates that the sequence of ''parameter testing'' is apparently not universal. Furthermore, the passage from initial states to end states is a gradual one. Two competing tendencies may coexist for prolonged periods of time, cycling in and out as though the child were unable to make up her mind. Finally, the ''steady state'' reached by adults also contains patterns of statistical variation in the use of grammatical structures that cannot be captured by discrete rules. This kind of cross-linguistic variation is difficult to capture with an all-or-none model.

Recognizing many of the problems we have just noted, Pinker (this volume) attempts to modify the parameter-setting model by encoding the parameters themselves in probabilistic terms. But this approach underestimates the depth of the problem. Any model that rests exclusively on universalist principles will fail to provide veridical accounts of the variable facts of language acquisition. Any model that rests solely on variation would also fail to provide coherent explanations for universal patterns. What is needed, instead, are models that are fundamentally capable of expressing both the universal and the variable aspects of language acquisition.

We have called the model that we will be presenting the Competition Model. Like other data-driven, connectionist models, the Competition Model allows statistical properties of the input to play a major role in determining order of acquisition as well as the nature of the final state. In this way the fundamental mechanisms of the model provide us with a way of understanding variability in particular words, segments, or constructions. This emphasis on ways in which the organism can adapt to the shape of the input allows us to apply our model to the study of cross-linguistic variation.

The other major type of variation that we will consider is variation in the contour of the learning process. Here, the major source of variability is the child herself. It has become increasingly clear in recent years that children can acquire English in radically different ways—at least in the early stages of language learning (Nelson, 1981; Bretherton, McNew, Snyder & Bates, 1983; Bates, Bretherton & Snyder, 1985). Furthermore, these differences are apparently not due to variation in the child's linguistic input, although environmental factors can serve to discourage or enhance a particular linguistic "style" once it becomes apparent (Nelson, 1973; Furrow & Nelson, 1984; Goldfield & Snow, in press). Bates et al. (1985) show that individual differences in language development can be brought about by the differential strength and/or differential timing of two or more underlying mechanisms responsible for language acquisition and language processing. We are thinking of dissociable processes as faculties in the sense of abilities or skills. For example, one child may have a well-developed faculty for memorizing strings with detailed phonology, whereas another child may make greater use of a faculty for analyzing these same strings into their component parts. Differences in the patterns of development between these two children can then be seen as a reflection of differential use of these basic faculties. One major goal of our work with the Competition Model is to delimit a set of fundamental processing mechanisms whose strength at a given point in development varies across learners in a way that can eventually be linked to fundamental differences between the learners.

In the first part of our paper, we will consider the treatment of data on cross-linguistic variation in language learning provided by the Competition Model. In the second part of the paper, we will consider evidence for individual variation in the acquisition of English. We will then consider some suggested modifications that could be added to the competition model or any other connectionist/lexicalist theory to account for these patterns of variation.

VARIATION ACROSS LANGUAGES

Here we will examine the problem of accounting for the details of the differences in the course of language acquisition between children learning different languages. We will provide a sketch of the Competition Model, with emphasis on the principle of cue validity and the predictions that it makes for cross-linguistic differences in language learning. Then we will present the cross-linguistic evidence for and against a simplistic version of the model leading to the postulation of two kinds of developmental constraints on cue validity: functional readiness and cue cost.

The Competition Model

The competition model is a particular instantiation of a general functionalist approach to language performance and language acquisition. As defined by

MacWhinney, Bates, and Kliegl (1984, p. 128), functionalism is the belief that ''The forms of natural languages are created, governed, constrained, acquired and used in the service of communicative functions.''

From this point of view functionalism is the natural alternative to theories that postulate a severe separation between form and function in the grammars of natural languages. The idea that grammars routinely and generally spawn and proliferate forms that play no role in facilitating communication is foreign to the functionalist position. While recognizing that some systems, such as the gender-case marking of German article declension, may have lost much of their original function, we believe that language works continually to find functions for forms that have lost their original use. There are, of course, many versions of the functionalist approach with different kinds of claims requiring different kinds of evidence:

- at the diachronic level where functions play a role in the evolution of a particular language,
- at the synchronic level where functions continue to constrain linguistic forms in real time comprehension and production,
- at the developmental level where children use communicative functions as a guide in the acquisition of forms,
- at the level of formal grammar where rules in the grammar make direct reference to semantic and pragmatic symbols.

The competition model makes functionalist claims at the first three of these four levels. In other words, it is not offered as a formal model of **linguistic competence** but rather as a model of **linguistic performance.** This concentration on performance has one particularly important implication: in modelling the differences among natural languages, our goal is to provide an explicit account not only for the kinds of discrete ''yes or no'' phenomena that play a role in traditional linguistic models but also for the probabilistic differences between natural languages that are observed in real-time language use. In other words, **we are focussing on cross-linguistic variation in the mapping between form and function in language comprehension, production and acquisition.**

Before we describe the current version of the competition model, let us first consider some illustrative contrasts between two of the languages that we have studied in greatest detail, Italian and English. We will concentrate on a small but very important aspect of the grammar: the structural phenomena associated with the form of ''sentence subject'' as they relate to basic functions such as agent/actor and patient/object.

In both Italian and English, the ''basic'' or pragmatically-neutral word order is Subject-Verb-Object (SVO). There are no case inflections to mark semantic relations, except for some remnants of case in the pronoun system (e.g., the contrast between *I* and *me*). These are both Indo-European languages, and they share a large number of cognates and word-formation patterns. But despite such formal similarities, Italian and English behave quite differently in everyday use.

First of all, Italian permits a great deal of pragmatic variation in basic constituent order. In fact, every logical order of subject, verb and object can be found in informal speech. This is illustrated in the following excerpt from Bates, MacWhinney and Smith (1983):

1. SVO: lo mangerei un primo. (I would eat a first course.)
2. OSV: La pastasciutte Franco la prende sempre qui. (Pasta Franco it orders always here.)
3. VSO: Allora, mangio anche io la pastasciutte. (Well then, am eating also I pasta.)
4. VOS: Ha consigliato la lasagna qui Franco, no? (Has recommended the lasagna here Franco, no?)
5. OVS: No, la lasagna l'ha consigliata Elizabeth. (No, the lasagna it has recommended Elizabeth.)
6. SOV: Allora, io gli spaghetti prendo. (In that case, I the spaghetti am having.)

The flexibility of word order is compounded still further by the fact that Italian is a "pro-drop" language, i.e., a language in which subject omission is a perfectly legal and very common option (occurring in approximately 70% of the clauses in informal speech among adults, according to Bates, 1976). As a result, the most frequent form in Italian discourse is not SVO, but (S)VO or O(S)V. Given this combination of word order variation plus ellipsis, the identity of subject and object is not at all predictable in Italian by word order information alone.

How do Italians get away with such behavior? For one thing, they can often rely on a richly marked system of verb morphology to let them know "who did what to whom." This contrasts markedly with the degraded system of verb morphology in English, as illustrated below:

1. lo mangio. I eat.
2. Tu mangi. You-informal-singular eat.
3. Lui/Lei mangia. He/She/You-informal-singular eat.
4. Noi mangiamo. We eat.
5. Voi mangiate. You-informal-plural eat.
6. Loro mangiano. They/You-formal-plural eat.

In these present tense examples, the only available contrast in English is provided by the third person singular "'s." The other forms are entirely ambiguous.

Although ambiguities do occur in Italian (e.g., between third person and the second person formal), they are relatively infrequent. In a sense, then, Italians can make a "case-like" use of verb agreement and other aspects of morphology (e.g., the system of pronominal object clitics that agree with the object in person, gender and number) as primary cues to semantic role relations. Quite simply, Italians can "trust" morphology more than they can "trust" word order—precisely the opposite of the patterns expected and observed in English.

There are some other contrasts between English and Italian in the way the subject system works, contrasts that are particularly hard to capture in terms of the presence or absence of structures and/or rules. For example, Italians seem to have an aversion for constructions with an indefinite subject, even though such constructions are perfectly "grammatical" in the strict sense (Devescovi and Taeschner, 1985). To avoid indefinite subjects, they often make use of complex, syntactic structures that an English speaker prefers to avoid. For example, given a picture of a monkey eating a banana, English speakers from 2 to 90 years of age are likely to say,

A monkey is eating a banana.

Given exactly the same picture, Italians as young as 2 years of age are six to seven times more likely to say something like,

There is a monkey that is eating a banana.

These facts are really not mysterious when we remember that Italians are making extensive use of word order variation as a pragmatic device. In the terminology of functional grammar, we would say that Italian is a relatively *topic-dominant* language (Li & Thompson, 1976; Schachter, 1976). The subject system is associated more strongly with the functional notion of discourse topic, and hence it is more likely to be used to talk about given or established information. Insofar as an indefinite determiner is used to mark new information, indefinite subjects represent a violation of "topichood." In the Philippine languages described by Schachter, indefinite subjects are not only avoided, they are entirely ungrammatical. To convey the information contained in our monkey/banana picture, these Philippine speakers would be required to begin by introducing the monkey in some kind of existential clause, adding the verb comment only after the subject is established in discourse (e.g., "There is a monkey, and he is eating a banana," or "I see a monkey that is eating a banana"). From this point of view, the Italian hatred for indefinite subjects and love of relative clauses suggest that Italian represents a statistical midpoint between the subject system of English and the subject system of Philippine languages.

We can use these performance facts about English and Italian to "walk through" the main features of the competition model as we currently understand it. The model can be summarized in terms of the following list of claims.

Direct Mapping

Only two levels of processing are specified in this performance model: a *functional* level (where all the meanings and intentions to be expressed in an utterance are represented) and a *formal* level (where all the surface forms or expressive devices available in the language are represented). Mappings between these levels are said to be direct. The notion of language as a system of mappings between form and function is the basic insight underlying the linguistics of de Saussure. In this sense, much of our work can be seen as an application of the Saussurian framework to the domain of performance or *parole*.

The principle of direct mapping does *not* require that the relationships between form and function stand in a one-to-one relation. Rather, direct mapping means that it is possible for languages to integrate on a single level cues that refer to different data types. In sentence comprehension, the parser is able to consider compounds or configurations of lexical semantic cues (e.g., animacy), morphological cues (e.g., agreement markers), word order cues (e.g., preverbal position), and intonational cues (e.g., contrastive stress). As we will see later, the parser may also take into account low-level acoustic/phonetic information about the "perceivability" and hence the "trustworthiness" of particular markers. In sentence production, the same configurations can be retrieved and assembled together, as a block. This contrasts with modular theories in which each distinct data type is handled by a separate processor (Fodor, 1983; Garrett, 1981).

In this paper, we will talk about the elements at each level in essentially "pretheoretical" terms, using global notions like "topic" and "agent" to describe the level of function and theory-neutral terms like "subject-verb agreement" and "contrastive stress" to describe the level of form. MacWhinney (this volume) will provide a more formal and explicit characterization of these two levels in terms of a system of lexical items (to describe the level of form) and a propositional notation (to describe the level of function). At this point, however, it is probably worth pointing out that the principle of direct mapping is basically a *lexicalist claim*. Like Saussure, we focus on the relation between the sign and the signified as the central structure controlling language processing. Extending Saussure's notion of lexically-based syntagmatic relations, we show how the native speaker learns to map phrasal configurations onto propositions, using the same learning principles and representational mechanisms needed to map single words onto their meanings.

Cue Validity

The major predictive construct in the competition model is cue validity. Following Brunswik (1956), we argue that human beings possess psychological mechanisms that bring them in tune with the validity or information value of cues in their ecology. This means that validity is an objective property of the cue itself, i.e., a property of the perceptual environment relative to some organismic state.

MacWhinney (1978) and MacWhinney, Pleh, and Bates (1985) have analyzed cue validity into two components: **cue availability** (i.e., how often is this piece of information offered during a decision making process?), and **cue reliability** (i.e., how often does the cue lead to a correct conclusion when it is used?). McDonald (1984) has tested some alternative methods for calculating cue validity.

1. *Availability* in McDonald's scheme is best expressed numerically as the ratio of the cases in which the cue is available over the total number of cases in a given task domain. For example, the availability of preverbal position is very high in English but relatively low in Italian. This reflects the fact that subjects are frequently omitted in Italian leaving many verbs in sentence-initial position.
2. *Reliability* can be expressed numerically as a ratio of the cases in which a cue leads to the correct conclusion, over the number of cases in which it is available. For example, preverbal position is a highly reliable cue in English where it is almost always assigned to the agent of a transitive action; it is a very unreliable cue in Italian (when it is available at all), since OV and SOV constructions are both possible and likely.
3. *Validity* is defined as the product of availability times reliability. Given the reliability and availability calculations described above, this necessarily means that the cue validity of preverbal position is very high in English and very low in Italian—a fact that is reflected in the performance of English and Italian listeners in the experiments described below. Insofar as validity is a property of the environment relative to some organismic state or goal (e.g., the communicative function of "agent"), we can calculate validity directly from samples of the linguistic input to children.

Cue Strength

To model the organism's knowledge about the validity of information, we postulate a subjective property of the organism called **cue strength.** This is a quintessentially connectionist notion, referring to the probability or weight that the organism attaches to a given piece of information relative to some goal.

In our psycholinguistic instantiation of this idea, each link between a given surface form (e.g., a nominative case marking) and an underlying function (e.g., the agent role) is given a weight or strength. With this kind of mechanism no sharp line is drawn between probabilistic tendencies and deterministic rules. An obligatory relationship between form and function is nothing other than a connection whose strength approaches unity. This permits us to capture statistical differences between adult speakers of different languages, e.g., the tendency for

English listeners to "trust" word order more than their Italian counterparts. It also permits us to capture facts about language change (in language history and/or in language learning) in gradual and probabilistic terms; we are not forced to postulate a series of all-or-none decisions, i.e., moments where parameters are definitively set and rules are added or dropped.

However, cue strength is not completely isomorphic with cue validity. Calculations of cue strength require some specification of the size and frequency of the task domain. For example, in our research we have calculated cue validity from one language to another within the domain of sentences that require a decision about who did what to whom, i.e., the domain of transitive sentences. Some tasks—like this one—are very frequent; others—like some of the tasks used in Piagetian studies of scientific reasoning—rarely come up. Cue strength will be a function of *both* cue validity and task frequency. In practical terms, it is of course quite difficult to estimate the frequency of a task with any precision. Sometimes, the best that we can do is to offer an *ordinal* prediction that cues for highly infrequent tasks will be learned relatively late as compared with cues for frequent tasks. However, within a specified task domain, the major determinant of order of acquisition and eventual cue strength should be cue validity. This leads to a series of very strong and falsifiable claims about language learning.

Horizontal and Vertical Correlations

We do not believe that mappings can only be between forms and functions. Rather, in the Saussurian system of forms and functions, three types of correlations are possible.

1. There may be direct *vertical correlations* between forms and functions. For example, the form of preverbal positioning in English is correlated with the function of expressing the actor role.
2. There may be correlations between forms themselves. These are *horizontal correlations* on the level of form.
3. There may be correlations between functions. These are *horizontal correlations* on the level of function.

In Bates and MacWhinney (1982) we focus our attention on the role of vertical correlations in language learning. However, we also recognize the importance of horizontal correlations. We speak of horizontal correlations on the level of function in terms of systems of competition between functions governed by "divide the spoils" and "peaceful coexistence" solutions. We speak of horizontal correlations on the level of form in terms of ossified forms. Maratsos (1982, 1983) is correct in pointing out that the relegation of form-form correlation detection to the bone pile of language history is an overly strong application of functionalism. We have been persuaded by his emphasis on the detection of correlation as a fundamental process in language acquisition. However, we also believe that the child does not consider *all* possible correlations between *all* items in *all* sentences in acquiring an accurate set of form-form correlations. Rather, following MacWhinney (1975, 1978, 1982, 1984) and Braine (1976, this volume), the child appears to be guided by two principles in deciding what to correlate with what. One principle is that of semantic connectedness. The other is positional patterning. Together, these two principles tightly delimit the scope of the co-occurence patterns that the learner considers. At the same time, by examining formal correlations between items that are positionally connected and semantically related, the learner can acquire the basic form-form correlations of the language. The fact that children have no trouble picking up discontinuous forms such as "call . . . up" as well as long-distance dependencies such as subject-verb agreement should not be interpreted as indicating that all correlations between all forms are tracked all the time. For such discontinuous forms there are also continuous versions in which the two parts of the construction occur next to each other (e.g. "call up" or "we are") and these nondiscontinuous variants can serve as initial guides to the formation of the systems of horizontal and vertical correlations.

It is important to remember that, although the system is capable of acquiring a complex set of horizontal correlations, the mappings that drive the system are the vertical correlations. Horizontal correlations are acquired in the service of supporting the system of vertical correlations. Vertical correlations are mappings between devices and the functions that they cue and the acquisition of these mappings is driven by the principle of cue validity (MacWhinney et al., 1985). By relating our principle of cue validity to this view of horizontal and vertical correlations, we have moved toward an integration of the functionalism of Bates and MacWhinney (1982) with the correlational learning of Maratsos (1982).

Coalitions as prototypes. In natural languages, mappings of a single form onto a single function are quite rare. Rather, languages make extensive use of polysemy, thereby producing grammatical systems in which the same form can map onto several functions, while the same function can map onto several forms. Taken together, these many-to-many mappings comprise a series of subsystems which we refer to as *coalitions*. The paradigm case of a coalition, exploited in most of our experimental work, is the organization of "sentence subject." In our view, "subject" is neither a single symbol nor a unitary category. Rather, it is a coalition of many-to-many mappings between the level of form (e.g., nominative case marking, preverbal position, agreement with the verb in person and number) and the level of function (e.g., agent of a transitive action, topic of an ongoing discourse, perspective of the speaker). Notice that the entries at the level of form include both "obligatory" and "defining" devices such as subject-verb agreement and "optional" correlates such as the tendency for subjects to be marked with definite articles. This is precisely what we mean when we argue that there is no sharp line between obligatory rules and probabilistic tendencies.

When we say that a mature speaker "knows" the set of connections of the subject coalition, we mean that he "knows" the internal composition of a **prototypic subject** in his native language. It is the system of horizontally and vertically weighted correlations that underlies our view of grammatical categories as prototypes (Bates and MacWhinney, 1982). All of the critical predictions of prototype theory follow from this claim.

- *Family resemblance.* In less-than-ideal communicative situations (where the proposition to be expressed does not contain a prototypic subject), the set of surface forms that comprise "subject" in this language will be assigned by family resemblance, i.e., by "best fit" or "maximum overlap" with the prototypic subject. Hence membership in the subject category is a matter of degree.
- *Heterogeneous membership.* A grammatical category will contain members that overlap with the prototype but not with one another (e.g., a subject that is a non-topicalized agent versus a subject which is a non-agentive topic).
- *Maximum distance from other categories.* Grammatical knowledge involves reciprocal relations among neighborhoods of categories, where category assignment is the joint product of *maximum overlap* with the category that is ultimately assigned and *minimum overlap* with competing categories that could have been assigned. Hence assignment of the subject role involves not only a calculation of goodness-of-fit to a prototypic subject but also a calculation of goodness-of-fit to other grammatical categories (e.g., prototypic object).

Through generations of experience with the competition process, languages have evolved to exploit natural coalitions whenever it is possible to do so. Nevertheless, it does occasionally happen that functions which prototypically "go together" have to be split apart and assigned to different items in order to express an idea adequately. To illustrate, consider what happens when the coalition between agency and topicality breaks down in English and Italian. This can occur, for example, when we need to topicalize "the ball" even though "John" did the hitting. In such cases the grammar has to determine which of the two elements should "win" access to devices like preverbal positioning and verb agreement. We have classified solutions to this problem into two basic types: "compromise" or "divide the spoils."

A typical compromise solution, provided by both English and Italian, is selection of the passive; the patient/topic "ball" wins access to the major subject devices, but the agent is placed in a special "by clause" that signals its continued semantic role. In terms of prototype theory, this is the kind of "hedging" and category-mixing that often occurs when categorization decisions have to be made for peripheral members. In a sense, it is a sentence-level analogue to word-level expressions like "an ostrich really is a bird," designed to mark explicitly the peripheral status of a category assignment.

Topicalization is an illustration of a typical "divide the spoils" solution. In topicalization in Italian, preverbal position is assigned to the topicalized patient, but verb agreement is still assigned to the agent. In other words, the set of surface devices comprising "subject" is simply split and assigned to separate elements. This kind of splitting rarely occurs in English, although we do find informal constructions like "Now that I'd really love to see!" The highly-correlated subject devices in English tend to be assigned as a block, while the lower correlations among the same devices in Italian permit the coalition to be split up for non-prototypical situations.

The point is that a series of compromises are made in both sentence comprehension and sentence production. The ideal situation does not always hold. In fact, the fully prototypical instance of a category such as "subject" may actually be fairly rare (like the "ideal member" that is extracted but never taught in studies of artificial category learning such as Posner and Keele, 1968). This is possible because our knowledge of a "prototypic subject" is the emergent property of a great many weightings between individual forms and functions. It is the result of a lifetime of distributional analysis and not a template derived from any single instance of grammatical learning.

Competition. The model assumes dynamic control of the mapping of form onto function in comprehension, and the mapping of function onto form in production. This mapping is understood to be governed by a system of parallel activation with strength-based conflict resolution much like that found in word-level processing models such as Thibadeau, Just and Carpenter (1982) or McClelland and Rumelhart (1981). The competition model extends these word-based models to the sentential level to account for assignment to grammatical roles and other parsing decisions in comprehension.

To illustrate what we mean, consider the kind of word-recognition system modelled by McClelland and Rumelhart to account for experimental findings by Glushko (1979). People know how to pronounce a "new" or non-existent string like *mave,* even though they have never seen it before. Usually they will pronounce it to rhyme with *cave,* but occasionally they will pronounce it to rhyme with *have*. Glushko suggested that speakers make their decisions *not* by applying an abstract set of phonological rules but by a process of analogy. Specifically, when the letter string *mave* appears, all of the existing words that overlap partially with this nonsense string are activated simultaneously. Each of the real world candidates has a basic activation level reflecting (at least in part) its baseline frequency in the language. The decision on how to pronounce this nonsense input and the time taken to reach that decision emerge out of the competition among all of these partially overlapping "demons": *have* as well as *cave, save, rave, mane, mate, cane,* etc. In the case of *mave,* the high frequency candidate *have* does occasionally win out, but it is usually overwhelmed by the greater number of word candidates with a long "a" pronunciation. Hence decisions are a combined product of the number of different types in the competition pool, and the activation weights associated with each type.

A syntactic analogue to this process can account for a number of robust phenomena in our cross-linguistic sentence comprehension data. In a series of studies with children and adults, we have presented listeners with simple sentences comprised of two concrete nouns and a transitive action verb. The sentences always represent some orthogonal combination of lexical semantic, pragmatic, grammatical and/or phonological cues: different word orders (NVN, VNN, NNV), presence of contrastive stress or presence of topicalization information for one of the two nouns, subject-verb agreement, case marking, etc. In some of our studies in some languages, the resulting list of stimuli includes a mixture of grammatical and "semi-grammatical" sentences, e.g.,

- The dog are kicking the cows.
- The pencil the horse is pushing.
- Is eating the ELEPHANT the tiger.

As we will present in more detail below, there are massive differences between languages in the way that listeners respond to such stimuli. Most of these differences follow directly from calculations of cue validity as described above. For example, Italians make greater use of both semantic contrasts and subject-verb agreement than their English counterparts; English listeners make greater use of word order than any other cue.

In addition, however, we have also uncovered some interesting new information about the specific strategies used in different languages to deal with combinations of word order and stress information. For example, English listeners have not only an overwhelming SVO strategy to deal with NVN sentences, but they also have very strong and reliable VOS and OSV strategies to deal with the two respective non-canonical word order types. Italians have a rather weak SVO bias for NVN stimuli. But they have no bias at all for NNV or VNN word orders. In fact, Italians can make use of word order information only in the presence of certain characteristic order/stress configurations: SVO applies consistently only if the NVN sentence has default stress; a weak but reliable SOV bias appears if the second noun is stressed in an NNV; a weak but reliable VOS bias is applied only if the first noun is stressed. For every language that we have looked at, we have discovered some set of word order biases that do not follow in any straightforward or obvious way from known facts about basic word order types in the language. That is, the word order biases cannot be attributed to any single word order "model."

However, we discovered that word order and/or order/stress biases *can* be accounted for by the parallel activation of *all* the partially-overlapping word order types in the language. That is, if a syntactic analogue to the *mave* example is going on, we should get exactly the results that we have obtained in all of the languages examined so far. Suppose, for example, that we line up all the possible syntactic patterns for talking about "John hit the ball" in English. Ignoring morphology and looking only at the "islands" of constituent ordering (e.g., treating a cleft sentence like "The one who *hit* the *ball* was *John*" as a VOS), it is clear that SVO is the statistically predominant ordering in English, followed by OSV and VOS. Carrying out a similar exercise in Italian, we find a much weaker bias toward SVO with essentially random probabilities for SOV versus OSV, VOS versus VSO—unless we take stress into account. For French, alternative word orders are possible only in the presence of a complex set of clitic markers. And yet, in our experiments, French listeners behave almost exactly like Italians, distrusting word order and making decisions primarily on the basis of semantic and morphological cues even though, in our sentence stimuli, we did not provide clitics to "release" word order variation. Their behavior with respect to word order alternatives makes sense only if they are engaged in some kind of competition process that involves a competition among *partially* as well as *completely* overlapping word order candidates. That is, the French listener's behavior is influenced by partially activated cliticized phrase structures, even when no clitics appear in the input.

Ongoing updating. In order to control the real-time interaction of the various cues participating in the competition, we believe that the parsing system engages in an ongoing updating of assignments of nouns to case roles. For example, when parsing a sentence such as "The dogs are chasing the cat," the assignment of "dogs" as the agent is first promoted by its appearance as the initial noun. Then the fact that "are chasing" agrees with "dogs" in number further supports this assignment. Finally, when the singular noun "cat" appears post-verbally, its binding to the object case role further supports the candidacy of "dogs" as the agent. Thus, at each point in sentence processing the mapping from the lexical item "dogs" to the agent role is updated. In this particular case, each updating increased the strength of this assignment. In other cases—particularly in languages that permit a great deal of word order variation—assignments may wax and wane in strength across the course of sentence processing.

Having reviewed the basic claims of the model, let us note some ways in which the model relates to some older models of the learning process. Within our model, language learning is viewed as a process of acquiring coalitions of form-function mappings, and adjusting the weight of each mapping until it provides an optimal fit to the processing environment. This is quite similar to the process that Gibson (1966) describes as "detection of invariance" and/or "acquired distinctiveness of cues." Remember, however, that it is the organism who determines the set of functions to be mapped onto forms. In this sense, then, our connectionist model has little in common with passive associationist theories of the Hullian variety. Instead, it might be more appropriate to label this kind of learning theory as a "neo-Tolmanian" approach, insofar as (a) the goals and expectations of the organism play a major role in determining what will be learned, and (b) form-form, function-function, and form-function connections can be observed and pondered in their own right whether or not the organism is currently being driven to meet some primary need.

Evidence for Cue Validity in Acquisition

The major developmental prediction of the Competition Model is that cue validity will determine the order in which grammatical devices are acquired. Cues differ widely in their validity across languages, and the model predicts that these differences in cue validity will be reflected in differences in the course of use of the cues in language acquisition. The prediction is that children should be sensitive from the beginning to the information value of particular perceptual patterns, and will go to work first in those forms that promise a greater "payoff." This is most assuredly a **minimalist claim,** i.e., a hypothesis that is offered with the hope and conviction that it will be falsified. It is, however, a claim that accounts for a great deal of variation in language learning across natural languages.

To illustrate, let us consider two would-be universals that have been disproven by cross-linguistic evidence:

1. Semantic cues to agent-object relations will be acquired before word order cues.
2. Word order cues to agent-object relations (and to other sentence roles) will be acquired before grammatical morphology.

Semantics before word order.

Bever (1970) proposed that three-year-old children will rely primarily on semantic strategies in comprehending simple declarative sentences, whereas four year-olds make primarily use of word order. A related "semantics first" hypothesis has been offered by Strohner and Nelson (1974). Chapman and Kohn (1978) provided some qualifications on this proposal differentiating between abstract semantic contrasts like "agent/patient" and "probable event" relationships between the protagonists in certain well-known events (e.g., mother and baby in "The mother feeds the baby"). They suggested that probable event strategies would precede the application of word order principles, but abstract semantics might be rather late. In either case, however, the main idea is that some kind of semantic information would be used by all children in all languages in advance of the grammatical information in word order.

Although the "semantics first" hypothesis has gained rather wide acceptance, it has not held up under cross-linguistic tests. In French, Sinclair and Bronckart (1972) found that reliance on SVO word order increased from two- to seven-years of age. But interpretations based on event probabilities were also strong at all ages. In English, SVO word order eventually dominates over any alternative strategy. In contrast, at no point in this study of French children did SVO word order "defeat" a probable event strategy when the two were placed in competition. A recent study by Hakuta (1982) provides still clearer evidence regarding the status of lexical semantic strategies in languages other than English. Hakuta's stimuli were created by random assignment of nouns such as "tiger," "goat," "chair" and "banana" to verbs like "push" and "chase." When word order and lexical semantics were placed in direct competition in Japanese, lexical semantics dominated quite clearly.

Of course, when data are presented for only one language, we can always argue that the results are stimulus-specific, and probably would have created the same effects in *any* language. For this reason, we have tested the relationship between abstract lexical semantics and word order in several different languages, looking at adults as well as children to determine the "end state" of development in each language.

First, notice a certain anglocentric bias in the previous experiments on children, i.e., the assumption that word order *ought to* dominate in a mature listener. In the competition model, there is no pressure toward the licensing of such biases. Instead, the relative strengths of word order and lexical cues are a function of the relative validity or information value of those cues in each language. In languages like Italian (as well as French and Japanese), word order variation for pragmatic purposes is very common. A mature listener would do well to "trust" semantics over word order in many situations. And that is exactly what we find in studies of adults. In all of these languages, an abstract animacy contrast between two nouns wins out over word order relations when the two pieces of information are placed in direct competition. This includes studies of Italian (Bates, McNew, MacWhinney, Devescovi & Smith, 1982; MacWhinney, Bates & Kliegl, 1984), French (Kail & Combier, 1983), and Japanese (Ito, in press), as well as German (MacWhinney, Bates & Kliegl, 1984), Serbo-Croatian (Smith & Mimica, 1984), Mandarin Chinese (Xiao-Chun, 1981), and several other languages—although the magnitude of this semantic bias varies from one language to another in accord with language-specific differences in the cue validity of word order information. It actually seems fair to conclude at this point that English is an exotic language with a word order bias that has so far failed to appear with equivalent strength in any other language.

If cue validity is a major determinant of the acquisition of forms across languages and if the same or equivalent stimuli are used in each language, then we should expect to find an early SVO word order bias in English children, contrasting with an early semantic bias in languages like Italian or Serbo-Croatian. We recently tested this hypothesis with English and Italian children between two and seven years of age (Bates et al., 1984). The stimuli, like those used in studies of adults, were all simple, active, declarative sentences with two concrete nouns and a transitive action verb. All three word orders were tested (NVN,

NNV, VNN) in orthogonal combinations of animacy (first noun animate and second inanimate; first noun inanimate and second animate; both nouns animate) and contrastive stress (first noun stressed; second noun stressed; default stressed only). The results were clearcut: SVO word order was the first cue to have a significant effect on sentence interpretation for English children (starting at two years of age), and animacy was the first cue to have a significant impact on Italians (again, at two years of age). At no point in the English data did an animacy strategy dominate over word order; at no point in the Italian data did word order dominate over animacy. Instead, children tended to veer closer and closer to the adult end point with more and more variance accounted for by the most valid cue in the child's language. There were certain ''minor'' deviations from this ''major'' trend, to be discussed in more detail below. In general, however, the data provide a remarkably clear confirmation of the role of cue validity in language acquisition. Very similar findings, with appropriate language-specific variations in timing and magnitude, have also been reported for French (Kail & Combier, 1983), Hungarian (MacWhinney, Pleh & Bates, in press), Mandarin Chinese (Miao, 1981) and Serbo-Croatian (Smith, personal communication).

Word order before morphology. Pinker (1982) offered this proposed universal in this form:

> For case-inflected languages, children will utter sentences in the dominant word order, and will use the dominant word order as a cue in comprehending sentences, before they have mastered their language's morphology.

Around the same time, however, Slobin and Bever (1982) offered a rather clear counter-example to Pinker's claim, in data on sentence interpretation by Turkish children. The Turkish system of case inflections is perhaps the most regular, semantically transparent, and unambiguous system in the world. In our terminology, the cue validity of nominative/accusative case marking as a guide to semantic relations approaches 100%, and hence should be the first cue adopted by Turkish children. Indeed, Slobin and Bever showed that Turkish children have completely mastered the use of these case contrasts by two years of age; by contrast, they show little or no sensitivity to word order contrasts until around the age of four, and even then they apply word order only to ''aberrant'' sentences in which case information is ambiguous. Independent information on language production suggests that these contrasts also appear very early in expressive language, perhaps even in the one word stage (thus providing a considerable complication for our notion of a ''single word utterance'').

Gleitman and Wanner (1982) have provided a counter-argument to Slobin and Bever, in an effort to salvage the ''word order first'' hypothesis. They note that the case markers of Turkish can receive full stress, very much like a free-standing lexical item. They do not, then, qualify as "clitics," i.e. as word- and phrase-building morphemes that can neither stand alone nor receive full stress. If children are innately endowed to perceive only unstressed clitic forms as elements of grammatical morphology, then they would end up treating Turkish case inflections as full lexical items. As such, the apparent precocity of case morphology in Turkish would not really constitute a counter-example to the "word order first" hypothesis.

However, more recent information on the acquisition of Hungarian (Pleh, 1981; MacWhinney et al. 1985) and Polish (Weist & Konieczna, 1985) suggests that children can also acquire unstressed case inflections before they demonstrate systematic use of word order patterns, in comprehension or production. To be sure, these children do not seem to acquire case with the lightning speed evidenced by their Turkish counterparts—nor would we expect them to, since the Polish and Hungarian case systems are somewhat more irregular than Turkish. However, they use morphological marking before they use word order, unlike children acquiring the nightmarish inflectional systems of Russian (Gvozdev, 1961) or Serbo-Croatian (Radulovic, 1975).

To summarize, the relative timing of semantic, syntactic and morphological developments is at least a partial function of cue validity. There is no universal schedule that determines the order in which children will acquire these surface forms. However, we cannot conclude that order of acquisition is determined *entirely* by the information value of cues. There are a number of other processing constraints that interfere. This brings us to the important issue of **constraints on cue validity.**

Before we proceed, we need to make a few statements about our philosophy of science. We do not consider the competition model a theory. A theory is a set of inter-related hypotheses that can be directly tested and rejected by some line of evidence. They can be found in areas such as particle physics and cellular genetics. In areas such as psychology, we must generally be satisfied not with theories, but with models such as the competition model. A model has much less internal coherence, insofar as it reflects an open-ended or "bottom up" attempt to describe or simulate aspects of the world. For this reason, it cannot be falsified in the strict sense; it can only be confirmed or disconfirmed in pieces. We can always "fix" a model by adding new constraints and principles to account for new findings and by dropping specific claims that cannot stand up to the evidence. How, then, do we ever decide that a model should be rejected? We suggest that models fail to be useful when they become circular, that is when new principles or constraints are added just to save the old ones, with no independent justification. When a model undergoes too many *ex post facto* repair attempts, it finally becomes a patchwork of assumptions that has no architectural center. When this architectural inadequacy becomes evident to all, the model collapses.

In the next section, we would like to point out some places where the minimalist principle of cue validity has failed to account for cross-linguistic variation.

In each case, these failures have led us to add new constraints to the model. Each of the new constraints that we have added so far does have a "life of its own", leading to a new and different set of empirical tests. We will discuss two classes of constraints here: **functional readiness** and **cue cost.**

The Importance of Functional Readiness

Cue validity apparently does play a major role in determining the sequence of acquisition. However, in our studies to date we have found some interesting and consistent exceptions. These exceptions arise when the language makes use of a form to express a function that the children have not yet acquired. In such cases we can say that the function itself is not "ready." This occurs most obviously in those areas where functions play roles that are determined by complex discourse structures. If the child has not yet developed sufficient control of narrative and expository styles to understand the uses of these functions, it will be difficult for her to learn to make correct use of the forms that express these functions.

One set of patterns which is particularly delayed in acquisition are the kinds of secondary word order stress patterns we discussed earlier. These patterns include

- VOS and OSV "second noun strategies" in English
- word order and stress configurations in Italian

Although these patterns are quite reliable in adults, showing up in several different studies, Italian and English children show no apparent use of these adult patterns until somewhere between seven and nine years of age. In fact, children in both languages show a small but reliable tendency in the first years to choose the stressed element as the subject—exactly the opposite of the adult pattern. We have suggested elsewhere (MacWhinney & Price, 1980) that in this case children are using an essentially non-linguistic strategy: if you don't know what else to do, choose the noun that the experimenter said loudest. This pattern of results indicates that children can certainly hear the stress manipulation. We believe that they fail to make consistent use of them because they are not yet ready to acquire the underlying functions.

Because they cannot make effective use of these patterns, Italian children develop a secondary strategy of their own. They generalize the first noun strategy derived from SVO to other word order types. This strategy starts between four and five years of age and does not drop out until after the age of nine when we finally see reliable use of stress to interpret NNV and VNN sentences. During this period of "word order overgeneralization," Italian children make *more* use of word order and *less* use of animacy than their adult counterparts (although word order never actually "wins out" over lexical semantics). One way of understanding this overgeneralization is to say that children are overgeneralizing the pattern they do understand rather than making use of patterns whose function they do not understand.

Kail and Combier (1983) and Kail and Hernandez-Charvillat (1983) have obtained almost identical results in a comparison of children and adults in French. A much weaker version of ''first noun overgeneralization'' has also been noticed in Hungarian and Serbo-Croatian (Pleh, 1981c; MacWhinney et al., 1985; Slobin and Bever, 1982; Smith, personal communication). In these studies the overgeneralization of first noun choice also starts around four years of age, although it drops out considerably earlier than it does in Italian or French. Similar results can be found in Miao's (1981) study of Chinese children. And a very small bias to attend to word order seems to get off the ground around four years of age in Slobin and Bever's (1982) study of Turkish.

No such overgeneralization occurs in our data on English children. Other investigators have reported a tendency for English children to generalize SVO strategies to the passive—a strategy which, interestingly, peaks between ages four and five. But the first noun bias is apparently not extended to NNV and VNN constructions in our research. Bates et al. (1984) suggest that the first noun tendency is somehow *blocked* in English, because the English children are sensitive at some level to the factors that create VOS and OSV biases in adults. We will return shortly to an explanation of how this might occur.

In any case, we do seem to be confronted here with a consistent cross-linguistic exception to the role of cue validity in determining acquisition of word order and other grammatical forms. To the extent that these patterns of ''first noun dominance'' vary markedly in size, range, and time of offset, we would not want to argue that they are universal. And it is possible that they reflect very different principles from one language to another. For example, Bever (1975) has reported that first noun strategies in the interpretation of the passive are correlated with degree of left-hemisphere bias in a dichotic listening task, among a sample of English four- to six-year-olds. Pleh (1981) carried out a similar study in Hungarian and found diametrically opposed results: to the extent that a child imposed a word order strategy in interpreting case-marked sentences in Hungarian, that child was significantly *less* likely to show a left-hemisphere bias on a dichotic listening task. Both authors suggest that degree of lateralization can be taken as an index of linguistic maturity. If they are correct, then word order biases are *more* mature in English and *less* mature in Hungarian. Nevertheless, the fact that they can exist at all needs to be explained in a performance model like the Competition Model.

To explain these phenomena we invoke a principle called **functional readiness.** Functional readiness means that children will not acquire a complex form until they can assimilate it, directly or indirectly, to an underlying function. This principle was used by Brown (1973), MacWhinney (1975), and Slobin (1973) to account for the acquisition of grammatical markers. However, here we are extending it to account for aspects of syntactic development. Following MacWhinney (1978) we can distinguish between the acquisition of forms, the acquisition of functions, and form-function mappings.

- **The acquisition of functions:** When the child uses and perceives new concepts and patterns, these new patterns become integrated into mental processing as new functions. For example, after a visit to a farm, a child may begin to develop the concept of a "cow." This concept is then a function which the child may seek to express.
- **The acquisition of forms:** A form is assimilated without being bound to a function when the child does not understand what it is for, but learns by rote that it is associated with other forms that he does understand and wants to use (e.g., the morphology associated with gender may be picked up by necessity as the child acquires lexical items that are marked for gender).
- **Form-function mappings:** By relating forms to functions, the child ties a function to a form, and thus gives motivation for that form. For example, when the child learns that subject-verb agreement signals topic/agent roles, she has acquired a new form-function mapping.

Karmiloff-Smith (1982) has argued that children do not acquire the inter-sentential functions of surface forms until seven years of age or older. Her conclusions are based upon a variety of facts about the way that children use and talk about pronouns and determiners in French and English. If Karmiloff-Smith is correct, then the same principle could account for delays in the acquisition of secondary word order patterns and order/stress configurations in our data. The analysis we are proposing can be outlined as follows:

- In adults, the application of these secondary strategies depends upon the presence of complex and low frequency phrase structure types in the "competition pool."
- These phrase structure types are governed by underlying discourse cohesion functions that span several propositions.
- Young children do not yet understand these inter-sentential discourse functions.
- Therefore, they cannot assimilate the complex phrase structure configurations directly (i.e., they cannot map them on to appropriate functions).
- They also fail to pick up complex syntactic patterns by indirect assimilation, i.e., by rote association with things that they do understand, perhaps because they are not exposed to enough exemplars.
- As a result, the process of sentence comprehension in very young children involves competition among a much smaller pool of sentence patterns.
- The small competition pool can result in temporary patterns of first-noun overgeneralization. These are similar to the temporary overgeneralizations

observed in the acquisition of morphology (see Rumelhart and McClelland, this volume). They peak when a certain proportion of subject-initial phrase structures have accumulated and drop again as further evidence comes in.

The last point leads to the prediction that similar overgeneralizations will be observed in comprehension and production. We do not yet know whether this is the case. It is certainly true that preschool children use only a subset of the possible syntactic patterns in their language. However, we need more evidence about such things as the range and frequency of order/stress configurations in child speakers in ''free word order'' languages like Italian and Hungarian (cf. Bates, 1976).

We also need to explain why English children fail to overgeneralize SVO to the same extent as children in the other languages studied to date. If they do not have the phrase structures responsible for the OSV and VOS biases of English adults, then why should any ''blocking'' occur at all? We may have to postulate a ''two-tiered'' membership in the competition pool of either word or phrase structure candidates. Active members in the pool are members that have been functionally assimilated (as defined above). These candidates exert the greatest force in a parsing decision. However, the child may well retain some memory of sentence types that he heard but failed to understand. If enough of these exceptions accumulate, they may serve to block certain generalizations that would be possible in their absence. This ''second tier'' notion is similar to the ''waiting room'' idea discussed by Ammom and Slobin (1979) and to the ''file of unknown forms'' in MacWhinney (1978).

The functional readiness principle can handle a variety of exceptions to cue validity. It is really a very simple notion, tantamount to ''What you don't know can't hurt you.'' Furthermore, applied to the contrast between sentence-level and discourse-level functions, the principle has a certain amount of independent justification (e.g., the research by Karmiloff-Smith). But just how powerful is this principle? Are there findings that it *cannot* explain? In a word, yes. In the next section we turn to some exceptions that require a very different kind of explanation (if they are to be explained at all).

The Role of Cue Cost

The concept of cue cost did not originate with us. It is discussed by Carroll (1978) as a source of constraints on cue validity in sentence interpretation. Simply stated, a very informative cue may be used less than we would otherwise expect, because the processing costs involved in using that cue are unusually high. We have found it useful to break this general notion down into two distinct components: perceivability and assignability.

Perceivability. We use the term "perceivability" to refer to the extent to which a listener encounters difficulty in trying to detect a cue for use in sentence processing. Consider, for example, the extreme example of subject-verb agreement in spoken French, e.g., the contrast between

Elle mange	She eats

and

Elles mangent	They-feminine eat

For most verbs in conjugations, the clear-cut written difference between the singular and plural form of the verb is entirely inaudible. Even though the agreement contrast is distributed quite faithfully through written texts of French, it is an imperceptible cue in the oral language. Cue validity means very little if a cue cannot be heard at all.

MacWhinney, Pleh, and Bates (1985) have shown that less drastic differences in the perceivability of cues can also have a significant impact on the way those cues are used in sentence interpretation. In Hungarian, case contrasts are very high in cue validity. However, some case suffixes are easier to hear than others. The nominative/accusative contrast can involve a strong vowel contrast plus the addition of a final /t/ (kutya—kutya't), or it may simply involve the addition of the final /t/ (mokus—mokust). When the /t/ follows a dental or alveolar consonant, it is difficult to identify with certainty. In sentence interpretation experiments with adults and children, this difference in the perceivibility of cues interacted with cue validity in determining the probability that a Hungarian listener will rely on case information. If case competed with other cues (e.g., word order and semantics), the strong vowel form of the suffix quite clearly "won" the competition; but if the weaker consonant form was involved, listeners would often (though not always) take the "conspiracy" of order and semantics into consideration in making their decision. MacWhinney et al. suggest that this is a morphological version of the "phoneme restoration effect" of Warren and Warren (1976), e.g., the tendency to hear a stimulus like "(cough) eel" as "wheel" or "meal", depending on the sentence context. Another way of putting it is that a lifetime of not being sure whether a case contrast is there or not has led listeners to "distrust" that cue, even in those instances when it is perceived.

We are currently pursuing some extensions of the perceivability notion in studies of the acquisition of clitic particles in Italian and French. There are a number of places where a preverbal object marker is equally informative in both these languages. However, the respective French and Italian markers differ in their perceptual salience, depending on such factors as the kind of verb that follows. For example, if the clitic precedes a participial construction, as in the French "Les ont fait" versus the Italian "Li hanno fatto," the fact that a consonant is pronounced between the clitic and the auxiliary should make the French clitic relatively more salient. We are interested in determining the extent to which subtle phonological factors like these influence the acquisition of clitic forms as a cue to underlying semantic relations. Obviously this complicates any predictions based on cue validity, since a whole catalogue of phonological factors would have to be taken into consideration. But if that is the way things are, so be it. Interactions between phonology and syntax may be hard to handle theoretically, but they are certainly testable.

Assignability. The second class of cue cost factors have to do not with perception but with memory. "Assignability" refers to the ease with which a given cue can be assigned to a role. A cue which can be utilized as soon as it is perceived is maximally high in assignability. In a language like Turkish, with a completely unambiguous case system, case suffixes have this status. The semantic role of a noun is assigned as soon as the suffix on that noun can be classified. This is what Ammon and Slobin (1979) and Johnston and Slobin (1979) refer to as a "local cue." By contrast, a cue which spans two or more disparate and perhaps discontinuous elements can be referred to as a "global cue." These cues are low in assignability, because the listener has to wait until several pieces of information are in before an assignment can be made. If the processing system is under stress and/or if the processor has limited auditory storage, global cues may become so costly to handle that they are abandoned despite their information value.

We have used the principle of assignability to explain another kind of anomaly in our developmental cross-linguistic data. As we have already pointed out, Italian adults use the information in subject-verb agreement in the same way that speakers of case-marked languages use case inflections: as a very powerful, almost deterministic cue to sentence meaning. Agreement is not maximally high in validity, because it is occasionally ambiguous (e.g., when both the subject and the object noun phrase are third person singular or third person plural). However, if cue strength does depend on cue validity to the extent that we believe it does, then reliance on agreement in Italian should be as strong as reliance on case in languages like German and Serbo-Croatian (where case is also ambiguous, to approximately the same extent). The adult data support this interpretation. But the developmental comparison looks very different. Serbo-Croatian children begin to make systematic use of case information by three years of age (Smith, personal communication). And according to some analyses we were allowed to carry out on Slobin and Bever's data, 2 year-old Yugoslavians may already have at least some sensitivity to case marking.

On grounds of cue validity alone, we should expect similar behavior by Italian children in the use of subject-verb agreement. Devescovi and Caselli (1985) tested this hypothesis in study of Italian children between three and nine years of age, varying three factors: word order, animacy, and number agreement between the verb and one of the two nouns. Results for word order and animacy replicated our findings in previous studies on Italian in every respect. So there is no reason to think that, just this once, we did something wrong. Nevertheless, findings for verb agreement were very surprising. The agreement factor did not become the dominant cue until the age of seven—three to four years after a similar level was reached by Yugoslavian children using the "best" morphological cue in their language. There are no "functional readiness" principles to account for this discrepancy since agreement maps onto basic sentence-level event structures in exactly the same way that case signals meaning in Serbo-Croatian and word order signals meaning in English. Nor can we turn to principles involving the perceivability of cues. The singular/plural contrast on verbs is very salient, involving an additional consonant/vowel syllable on the plural form (e.g., mangia/mangiano). Furthermore, we know on the basis of other data that Italian children mark some forms of verb agreement in their productive language by the age of two, with the singular/plural contrast in the third person coming in at least by the age of three (Bates, 1976). Thus children have this surface form in production; they simply are not using it in comprehension.

These data can be explained if we assume that a global agreement cue places too much load on the young child's limited memory system. To use agreement correctly in the third person, the child must store *1.* the noun that will ultimately agree with the verb, *2.* the verb itself, and *3.* one or more competing noun phrases which could also agree with the verb (thereby rendering agreement information ambiguous and useless). But do we have any independent evidence that the "low assignability" of agreement creates a delay in acquisition? This idea was tested again in a recent study of sentence interpretation in French adults and children (Kail and Combier, 1983; Kail and Hernandez-Charvillat, 1983). These authors used two agreement markers as variables (subject-verb agreement and clitic-object agreement) with word order and animacy. In adults, both agreement markers played a major role in sentence interpretation. But in children, neither of the agreement cues were used to any significant degree until after five years of age. This is, at the very least, a replication and extension of the anomaly posed by Devescovi and Caselli. But it also suggests that the late acquisition of agreement markers is a fairly general phenomenon, in contrast with various studies on the acquisition of case. So the "assignability" hypothesis is rendered more credible.

A final bit of support for the role of assignability comes from a comparison between children and adult aphasics in the same kinds of experiments. We would expect the two cue cost variables (perceivability and assignability) to play a role in language processing in aphasia, since the performance of brain-damaged patients is presumably the reflection of a system under stress. However, there is less reason to expect the developmental principle of functional readiness to affect the performance of brain-damaged adults. Processing may be under stress, but knowledge of how language works—once it is acquired—should not easily go away. Some of our preliminary cross-linguistic findings in aphasia provide support for this view. For example, the second noun strategies shown by normal adults in English are still detectable in English aphasics, even though such strategies are not apparent at all in the performance of English children under five. However, a comparison of Italian and Serbo-Croatian aphasics shows that the assignability contrast does play a role when the adult system is under stress. Both case and agreement are impaired in these patients relative to normals in the same two languages. However, the "damage" done to case is measurably smaller than the "damage" done to agreement. In other words, "local" morphological cues are more resistant to brain damage than distributed, "global" morphology that is low in assignability.

In short, we think that the two principles of functional readiness and cue cost serve not only to constrain the competition model, but also to enrich it. The two principles are fully in accord with our emphasis on form-function mappings and the role of competition in processing. These principles are non-circular, motivated by independent lines of evidence, and they are testable. The competition model continues to assist us in studying variation in the acquisition process across natural languages by both accounting for old data and stimulating new research. However, we are less sure how the model will stand up to data on individual differences within a single language, which we will now confront.

INDIVIDUAL DIFFERENCES

The literature on individual styles of language acquisition has grown considerably in the last decade, although the results pertain almost exclusively to English. Our purpose here is simply to indicate the *kinds* of variation that have to be accounted for by acquisition theories. The reader is referred elsewhere for more detailed reviews (Kempler, 1980; Nelson, 1981; Bates, Bretherton, & Snyder, in press; Bretherton et al., 1983).

At the lexical level, the parameters of variation were first set out by Nelson (1973), in a study of the first 50 words acquired by 18 children in the second year of life. She described a dimension of variation ranging from *referential style* (i.e., vocabularies with a high proportion of common object names) to *expressive style* (i.e., heterogeneous vocabularies containing items from a variety of form classes including some frozen phrases like "Stop it" and "I love you."). The term "referential" is based on the tendency for children at this end of the continuum to focus on the process of object naming. The term "expressive" captures the tendency for children at the other extreme to focus more on the social/regulatory uses of language. This dimension was quantified through simple proportion scores (total object names divided by total vocabulary), resulting in a normal distribution with most children falling somewhere in the middle. In other words, this is not a bimodal categorization of children into distinct language types. Nevertheless, for children at the extreme ends of the continuum, linguistic behavior looks so strikingly different that it seems to reflect the operation of qualitatively different acquisition mechanisms and/or linguistic environments. The range of variation observed in Nelson's study has now been replicated many times over. Furthermore, Snyder, Bates and Bretherton (1981) have shown that the referential/expressive split occurs in comprehension as well as production, beginning as early as 13 months of age when vocabularies average only 10–12 words. This is, then, a very general phenomenon that spans the period from first words to sentences.

At the grammatical level, the first major report on individual differences was offered by Bloom, Lightbown and Hood (1975). In a longitudinal study of four children, these authors introduced a contrast between *nominal style* (i.e., multiword constructions composed primarily of nouns and other content words), and *pronominal style* (i.e., multiword constructions in which the same meanings are conveyed with non-specific pronominal forms). All of the children in the Bloom et al. study produced some "pivot-open" constructions like NO + X, MORE + X, or ANOTHER + X. However, to encode semantic relations involving action, location and possession, two of the children produced "telegraphic" combinations of content words: KATHRYN SOCK, TOUCH MILK, etc. In particular, they tended to refer to themselves by name. To express the same meanings, the other two children were more likely to use non-specific forms of reference: I finish, my truck play it. In particular, these children were more likely to refer to themselves with first person pronouns. The terms "nominal" and "pronominal" are based on the striking difference between the two types in first person reference. Note, however, that this particular difference occurred only in the first stages of grammatical development; by the time all four children had attained a Mean Length of Utterance of 2.5 morphemes, contrasts in noun and pronoun use had disappeared.

The nominal/pronominal dimension has been replicated in several other studies of English children, including a large-sample study by Bretherton et al. (1983). These investigators also showed that the noun/pronoun distinction is only one manifestation of a more general contrast involving presence or absence of grammatical morphology during Stage I. Children at the extreme nominal end of the continuum produce the kinds of uninflected telegrams that were once believed to constitute a universal starting point for grammatical development. However, children at the other end never pass through a telegraphic stage; their first word combinations are already heavily inflected with a large number of free standing function words. Like referential/expressive style, this nominal/morphological dimension is normally distributed. That is, most children cluster around a midpoint in the distribution, using a mixture of sentence types. For example, it is quite common for children in Stages I and II to vacillate between two or more forms of first person reference (e.g., Bates' 23 month old daughter, who produced the single utterance "I do that. . . . Julia do that . . . me do that"). Again, however, children at the extreme ends of the distribution look so different from one another that it is hard to believe that they have the same "theory" of their native language.

Although the nominal/morphological contrast itself has a short half-life, we now know that it is linked to other dimensions of variation throughout language acquisition. For example, there is a connection between referential/expressive style in the one word stage, and nominal/morphological contrasts in early multiword speech. As one might expect, referential children are more likely to start their grammatical careers with telegraphic speech; expressive children, who have heterogeneous vocabularies from the very beginning, also have heterogeneous mixes of content and function words in their very first sentences. Furthermore, Horgan (1981) suggests that the nominal/referential children are "noun lovers" who continue to emphasize the development of noun phrases and their associated morphology in the more advanced stages of language acquisition; by contrast, pronominal/expressive children can be characterized as "noun leavers," who spend more time elaborating verb phrase morphology across the following months and years of language learning.

There are, then, stylistic links between lexical and morphological development throughout the early stages of language acquisition. Other evidence suggests that the same stylistic dimensions can be found in the development of phonology. It has been noted for some time that pronominal/expressive style is associated with a greater tendency to imitate at both the word and sentence levels. But the imitation tends to be imprecise, focussing on the suprasegmental/intonational "packaging" of a target rather than its phonetic details. In fact, several studies of lexical and grammatical development have noted that the speech of pronominal/expressive children is difficult to understand and transcribe—a tendency that Horgan refers to as "mushmouth." Researchers at the Stanford Child Phonology Project have tried to explicate this notion of intelligibility. Researchers at the Stanford Child Phonology Project (Vihman, 1985; Vihman, Ferguson, & Elbert, in press) have tried to explicate the notions of intelligibility and phonological style. At one year of age, style revolves around the number and identifiability of consonants in babbling and speech. This measure is associated with phonological consistency at age 3, i.e., whether a child pronounces a given word in the same way across instances. Most important, the dimension of *phonological* consistency at 3 is significantly correlated with *syntactic* consistency in the same children. In other words, the same mechanisms may be responsible for individual differences in phonology and grammar.

There is a great irony in these findings on consistency and variation in phonology and grammar. As Goldfield and Snow (in press) point out, the language acquisition literature of the 1960's left us with the impression that all children pass through a universal course of development from naming, to telegraphic speech, to grammar. We know that this is, at best, an optional route to language acquisition. Why did we miss the other half of the story for so long? In the first classic longitudinal studies of language acquisition, there was absolutely no reason to believe that variation in phonology would bear any relation at all to semantic or grammatical development. Children were chosen for inclusion in the studies on the basis of several criteria, including the relative intelligibility of their speech (Bellugi, personal communication). The purpose of this selection criterion was obviously to facilitate the lengthy process of tape transcription. But it also influenced our theories of language acquisition for at least a decade.

A number of studies are now underway to determine whether linguistic variation is correlated with dimensions outside of language proper: cognitive styles in problem solving and symbolic play, aspects of personality or temperament, and a host of social/environmental factors including social class, birth order, and maternal style. For example, preliminary findings suggest that children at the pronominal/expressive end of the continuum are a bit more sociable, and that they are interested in trying to act and sound like other people as much and as often as possible (a tendency that is frequently manifested in immediate imitation of adult speech). There are also differences in the way that adults respond to these contrasts in style, reactions which can either augment or damp an initial tendency by the child to follow a particular path into language acquisition (Goldfield and Snow, in press). Nevertheless, the differences that have been observed in linguistic input—for some children some of the time—do not seem to be sufficient to account for the robust and reliable patterns of variation that result. For example, if we factor social/environmental variables out of the language data, correlations among variables in the referential/expressive "strands" of language development are relatively unaffected (Bates et al., 1985). We do not know whether these strands of variation are unique to language, or whether they represent linguistic versions of a more general cognitive style. However, we can conclude that these differences originate in the child.

CAN OUR MODELS DEAL WITH THESE DATA?

The data on individual variation mentioned above constitute a major challenge to current models of language acquisition. For one thing, it is difficult to defend a universal and stage-like passage from reference, to predication, to grammar. Certainly, naming does precede *productive* control over grammatical rules, even in children at the extreme pronominal/expressive of the continuum. In fact, Bates et al. (1985) have presented evidence suggesting that rate of lexical development at one year of age is an excellent predictor of grammatical development in the third year. But the passage is apparently neither simple nor linear. For example, we might have expected to find that children who start out early in collecting and using inflections and function words would have a headstart in the analysis and mastery of grammatical morphology. However, Bates et al. report that the ratio of closed class elements in the child's speech at 20 months is significantly and *negatively* correlated with the same measure at 28 months. In other words, the children who ultimately make more progress in the use of grammatical morphology are the referential/nominal/telegraphic children who studiously leave those elements *out* of their speech during the phase of first word combinations. This suggests, among other things, that the use of grammatical morphology in Stage I is based primarily on rote, unanalyzed expressions and not on "rules" of any sort. In any case, the first appearance of a grammatical form is in no way a harbinger of its eventual mastery. At least at first glance, these non-linear and contradictory patterns of acquisition seem to present problems for a data-driven, connectionist model of language learning—particularly if, as seems to be the case, these variations are not caused by differences in the language environment. From the point of view of the competition model, successive stages in language acquisition should be shaped by the information value of form/function mappings in the linguistic input—modulated, as we have noted, by such factors as functional readiness and cue cost. As the model is presently constituted, there are no mechanisms for predicting these consistent patterns of individual variation.

The individual differences data also provide little comfort for proponents of a nativist, modular theory of language acquisition. If parameters are set by "input triggers," then the intermediate stages of acquisition should look the same for all children within a given language—assuming that the linguistic environment is in fact the same on all the relevant dimensions.

One possible solution for a modular theory is to argue that distinct components of language processing can mature at different rates. Hence the different profiles that we obtain across children exposed to the same language would derive from an asynchrony between modules in the parameter-setting process. In fact, we suggest that this is the most workable solution to the problem of variation within a language: individual differences are brought about by the differential strength and/or differential timing of two or more mechanisms for processing and learning language. The question is, what kinds of modules can be said to underlie the dissociations observed in early language development? Most of the existing nativist models would predict dissociations corresponding to independent levels of linguistic analysis: phonology, syntax, morphology, and the lexicon. These are the "vertical faculties" discussed by Fodor (1983) in his treatise on modularity, i.e., faculties that have evolved to deal with particular kinds of content or data types. These can be contrasted with "horizontal faculties," i.e., mechanisms like short-term memory or reasoning ability that cut across content domains.

However, as we have already pointed out, the dissociations observed in early language do not respect the boundaries of traditional "vertical modules" for language. Instead, patterns of early language style affect all aspects of phonology, grammar, the lexicon, and perhaps social and cognitive domains outside of language-proper. Bates et al. (1985) characterized a set of pathways of variation in language development from first words to grammar in a sample of 27 children studied between the ages of 10 and 28 months. A wide variety of linguistic measures were included in this study, chosen to reflect aspects of variation proposed by earlier investigators. They include both receptive and expressive measures from structured testing, free speech, and parental report. Traditional measures like vocabulary totals and MLU were supplemented with detailed analyses of the flexibility and productivity of both lexical and grammatical structures. There was, then, a fair chance for dissociations between grammar and the lexicon to emerge. Nevertheless, there was no evidence for asynchrony between these hypothetical components of language. Instead, variation in language was distributed along such "horizontal modules" as rote versus analytic behavior, and comprehension versus production.

The picture is considerably more complex than the "two strand" approach in the individual difference literature might lead us to expect. At 10 to 13 months two factors emerged: an *analytic factor* (including comprehension vocabulary, referential style in both comprehension and production, and flexibility in the use of common object names) and a *rote factor* (based primarily on spontaneous speech with comprehension factored out). At 20 months, we now find three factors: *analyzed production* (including the range of meanings expressed in single and multiword speech), *rote production* (including a precocious overuse of inflections and function words, and a tendency to imitate a novel word taught in the laboratory), and a newly-emerging separate factor for *pure comprehension* (reflected in a variety of receptive language indices). By 28 months, we are back to two factors only: *production* (cutting across both lexical and grammatical measures) and *comprehension* (again including both lexical and grammatical tests). The cross-age correlations among these factors are also complex; comprehension at one age weaves back in to production at the next, and rote learning seems (at least temporarily) to lead nowhere at all after 20 months.

There are, then, at least *four* kinds of mechanisms involved in the dissociations observed in early language development: analytic learning (what MacWhinney [1978] refers to as "analysis" and what Peters [1983] refers to as "segmentation"), rote learning (what MacWhinney [1978] refers to as "amalgam acquisition" and Peters refers to as "extraction of forms for later analysis"), comprehension, and production. As far as we can determine from the Bates et al. study and related studies by other investigators, these four horizontal factors affect all the major components of language: word order, grammatical morphology, phonology, and lexical semantics. It is of course quite possible that other dissociations will emerge later in development, including a separation between grammar and the lexicon. Linguistic modules may have to be constructed and developed over time before they can attain a modular status (c.f.

Karmiloff-Smith, 1985). But they do not seem to play a role in the early stages—or, more precisely, they do not play any obvious role in creating the dissociations that underlie individual differences in language learning.

There is a rather inelegant clash between the detailed albeit contrasting models of language learning we find in the current volume, and the rather vague and old-fashioned notions of analytic versus rote and comprehension versus production. These characterizations of individual variation have more discriptive than explanatory value. How can existing theories be modified to take these findings into account? We suggest that all of the models discussed here (including the competition model) have so far ignored some essential aspects of information processing and learning: perception, memory, attention and motivation. To preserve the computer metaphor that motivates so many current models, we might think of these in terms of the ''peripherals'' that subserve the language learning device, or mechanisms that select, preprocess and transfer the data on which the learner will operate. Individual differences in children may derive from variation in the status of these data-transfer systems.

First, at the perceptual level, all of the models discussed so far assume that the sentence strings input to the learner are exactly the same for the child as they are for the observer. In our elucidation of the competition model, we showed that cue cost factors like ''perceivability'' can influence language learning. But we have treated ''perceivability'' as a property of the stimulus. Certainly this must be true, to a considerable extent. There are psychoacoustic realities that enter into a determination of which cues to meaning will be learned first. But these will undoubtedly interact with both ''software'' and ''hardware'' properties of the perceiver. Consider a finding in the adult psycholinguistics literature (Pollack and Pickett, 1964): when words uttered in a conversation between adults are taken out of context and presented in a list format, only 47% are recognizable to other adult listeners. In other words, complete perception of the elements in a sentence stimulus presupposes the lexical, grammatical and pragmatic knowledge necessary to disambiguate individual elements. But even in the most radical nativist theories, children cannot be assumed to have such knowledge at the beginning of language acquisition. The sentence strings input to the learner must surely be perceived—at least initially—as strings of incomprehensible noise punctuated by islands of familiarity. Among other things, there may be individual differences in the absolute acuity of the auditory system making it possible for some children to literally hear more of the stimulus prior to an analysis of its meaing. We know, for example, that ''hyperacousis'' is a characteristic of Williams Syndrome in children who are retarded but have surprisingly advanced language. Like Radar O'Reilly in *Mash,* these children can reportedly hear a helicopter coming long before anyone else nearby. Even in the normal range, production may move ahead of comprehension, and rote strings may outnumber analyzed strings in children who quite simply hear better.

By the same line of argument, the strings input to the learner presumably have to be held in some kind of memory buffer long enough for "on-line analysis" and/or storage to take place. We suggested earlier that the operation of cue validity in acquisition is tempered by the cue cost factor of "assignability"—once again, viewed as a property of the stimulus. The ability to hold elements in memory long enough to make an assignment and/or to store the form for later consideration, may also be a variable property of the learner herself. The claim that so-called pronominal/expressive children are particularly good at early prosody provides some support for this notion, suggesting that these children perceive and maintain the "intonational envelope" of a sentence that carries many of the otherwise incomprehensible phonetic units with it. Similarly, in some reports of retarded children with exceptionally good expressive language (e.g., Curtiss, Yamada & Kempler, 1981), the children seem to have exceptionally good auditory short term memory spans, at or above their age level and far ahead of their performance on cognitive tasks.

Attention is another domain that must be involved in determining the shape of language learning. The "inner searchlight" discussed by some investigators may focus on different parts of the linguistic signal with important results for the kinds of form/function correlations that will be noticed. We know from studies of eye movement monitoring that there are individual differences in the nature of the scanning process in visual pattern perception. Some analogue to scanning must play a role in language as well in order to determine which parts of the input will actually be learned, and when the learning will occur. As Bowerman (this volume) has pointed out, the models discussed here have been fairly agnostic about exactly when all this learning takes place. Does it happen "on line," as the stimulus comes in? Or does the child re-present stimuli to herself later on, changing her system in the process? The so-called referential/analytic child may actually be more attentive, spending more time focussing on the segmentation of utterances both inside and outside of the real-time process of communication. Such a difference in the distribution of attention could account for several facts about referential/nominal/analytic style:

1. referential style tends to be associated with precocity in language development overall;
2. referential children tend to produce more overgeneralizations in grammatical morphology (a result which would occur if analyses are being forced at an early point in development when the competition pool is still rather small);
3. referential children are more consistent in their apparent rule systems (or whatever the analogue to rules may be in parallel distributed processing systems) as though they were continually trying to "clean things up" and eliminate exceptions.

Finally, we may want to consider the role of motivation in the tendency for children to focus their attention on particular kinds of language, start up conversations on particular kinds of topics, and demand particular kinds of linguistic data from their conversational partners. We now have several lines of evidence to suggest that referential/analytic children play more with objects and use objects to interact with adults even during the prespeech phase (e.g., Nelson and Furrow, 1984; Goldfield and Snow, in press). Perhaps for this reason they also tend to elicit more object-oriented, nominal language from their partners. Hence the initial predisposition of a child to focus on the world of reference may set up a benign cycle of language-about-objects that feeds into an increasingly consistent language style. Similarly, expressive/morphological/rote styles of learning typically involve a great deal of immediate imitation of adult input. These children tend to be more sociable overall; they engage in a wider variety of social/regulatory speech acts, and seem to want to jump into the game of conversation without going through the tedious process of figuring out the linguistic pieces first. As several investigators have suggested, they learn "the tune before the words." Such an imitative style will insure that the child has a larger and more heterogeneous array of elements stored in the linguistic anteroom, awaiting further analysis. The nature of the "competition pool" will be very different for this child than it is for her more reflective and analytic counterpart.

In short, we cannot assume that the data input to the learner is the same for every child—even though it may look the same from our point of view. The learning systems described by the contributors to this volume—whether they are nativist or empiricist, deterministic or probabilistic—are necessarily embedded within a much more complex, multi-component system for selecting, shaping and delivering both the input and output of learning. This will of course make it more difficult to model the language learning process, since more components must be modelled. But if we can account in a principled way for variation in language learning, we can be much more comfortable in concluding that we have verged on something like the truth.

REFERENCES

Ammon, M. S., & Slobin, D. I. (1979). A cross-linguistic study of the processing of causative sentences. *Cognition, 7,* 3–17.

Bates, E. (1976). *Language and context: Studies in the acquisition of pragmatics.* New York, NY: Academic Press.

Bates, E., Bretherton, I., & Snyder, L. (in press). *From first words to grammar: Individual differences and dissociable mechanisms.* New York: Cambridge University Press.

Bates, E., MacWhinney, B., Caselli, C., Devescovi, A., Natale, F., & Venza, V. (1984). A cross-linguistic study of the development of sentence interpretation strategies. *Child Development, 55,* 341–354.

Bates, E., MacWhinney, B., & Smith, S. (1983). Pragmatics and syntax in psycholinguistic research. In S. Felix & H. Wode (Eds.), *Child language at the crossroads.* Tubingen: Gunter Narr.

Bates, E., McNew, S., MacWhinney, B., Devescovi, A. & Smith, S. (1982). Functional constraints on sentence processing: A cross-linguistic study. *Cognition, 11,* 245–299.

Bever, T. G. (1970). The cognitive basis for linguistic structures. In J. R. Hayes (Ed.), *Cognition and the development of language*. New York, NY: Wiley.

Bever, T. (1975). Cerebral asymmetries in humans are due to the differentiation of two incompatible processes: holistic and analytic. *Annals of the New York Academy of Sciences, 263,* 251–262.

Bloom, L., Lightbown, P., & Hood, L. (1975). Structure and variation in child language. *Monographs of the Society for Research in Child Development, 40,* whole no. 2.

Braine, M. (1976). Children's first word combinations. *Monographs of the Society for Research in Child Development, 41,* Whole No. 1.

Bretherton, I., McNew, S. Snyder, L., & Bates, E. (1983). Individual differences at 20 months: Analytic and holistic strategies in language acquisition. *Journal of Child Language, 10,* 293–320.

Brown, R. (1973). *A first language: The early stages*. Cambridge, MA: Harvard University Press.

Brunswik, E. (1956). *Perception and the representative design of psychology experiments*. Berkeley, CA: University of California Press.

Carroll, J. M. (1978). Sentence perception units and levels of syntactic structure. *Perception and Psychophysics, 23,* 506–514.

Chapman, R. S., & Kohn, L. L. (1978). Comprehension strategies in two- and three-year-olds. Animate agents or probable events? *Journal of Speech and Hearing Research, 21,* 746–761.

Chomsky, N. (1982). *Lectures on government and binding*. New York, NY: Foris.

Curtiss, S., Kempler, D., & Yamada, J. (1981). The relationship between language and cognition: Theoretical framework and research design. *UCLA Working Papers in Cognitive Linguistics, 3,* 1–60.

Devescovi, A., & Caselli, C. (1985). *Acquisition of subject-verb agreement by Italian children*. Manuscript, University of Rome.

Devescovi, A., & Taeschner, T. (1985). Strategie di uso del pronome in eta' scolare. Manuscript, University of Rome, Faculty of Psychology.

Furrow, D., & Nelson, K. (1984). Environmental correlates of individual differences in language acquisition. *Journal of Child Language, 11,* 523–534.

Gibson, J. J. (1966). *The senses considered as perceptual systems*. Boston, MA: Houghton Mifflin.

Gleitman, L., & Wanner, E. (1982). Language acquisition: the state of the state of the art. In E. Wanner and L. Gleitman (Ed.), *Language acquisition: the state of the art*. New York, NY: Cambridge University Press.

Glushko, R. (1979). The organization and activation of orthographic knowledge in reading words aloud. *Journal of Experimental Psychology: Human Perception and Performance, 5,* 674–691.

Goldfield, B., & Snow, C. (in press). Individual differences in language acquisition. In J. Gleason (Ed.), *Language development*. Columbus, OH: Merrill.

Gvozdev, A. N. (1961). *Voprosy izucheniya detskoy rechi*. Moscow: Akademija Pedagogika Nauk RSFSR.

Hakuta, K. (1982). Interaction between particles and word order in the comprehension of simple sentences in Japanese children. *Developmental Psychology, 18,* 62–76.

Horgan, D. (1981). Rate of language acquisition and noun emphasis. *Journal of Psycholinguistic Research, 10,* 629–640.

Ito, T. (In press). Universal and particular in sentence processing. In B. MacWhinney and E. Bates (Ed.), *Cross-linguistic studies of sentence processing*. New York, NY: Cambridge University Press.

Johnston, J., & Slobin, D. (1979). The development of locative expressions in English, Italian, Serbo-Croatian and Turkish. *Journal of Child Language, 6,* 529–545.

Kail, M., & Combier, C. (1983). Role des indices pragmatiques, lexico-semantiques et syntaxiques dans la comprehension de phrases simples dans une perspective genetique et interlangue. Master's degree, University Rene Descartes.

Kail, M., & Hernandez-Charvillat, A. (1983). Role des indices syntaxiques, semantiques et pragmatiques dans les strategies de comprehension chez les adultes francais. Master's degree, University Rene Descartes.

Kempler, D. (1980). Variation in language acquisition, UCLA Working Papers in Cognitive Linguistics. UCLA Linguistics Department.

Li, C., & Thompson, S. (1976). Subject and topic: a new typology of language. In C. Li (Ed.), *Subject and topic*. New York, NY: Academic Press, Inc.

Lightfoot, D. (1982). *The language lottery*. Cambridge, MA: MIT Press.

MacWhinney, B. (1975). Rules, rote, and analogy in morphological formations by Hungarian children. *Journal of Child Language, 2,* 65–77.

MacWhinney, B. (1975). Pragmatic patterns in child syntax. *Stanford Papers And Reports on Child Language Development, 10,* 153–165.

MacWhinney, B. (1978). The acquisition of morphophonology. *Monographs of the Society for Research in Child Development, 43,* Whole no. 1.

MacWhinney, B. (1984). Grammatical devices for sharing points. In Schiefelbusch, R., & Pickar, J. (Ed.), *The acquisition of communicative competence*. Baltimore, MD: University Park Press.

MacWhinney, B., Bates, E., & Kliegl, R. (1984). Cue validity and sentence interpretation in English, German, and Italian. *Journal of Verbal Learning and Verbal Behavior, 23,* 127–150.

MacWhinney, B., Pleh, Cs., & Bates, E. (1985). The development of sentence interpretation in Hungarian. *Cognitive Psychology, 17,* 178–209.

MacWhinney, B., & Price, D. (1980). The development of the comprehension of topic-comment marking. In D. Ingram, C. C. Peng, & P. Dale (Eds.), *Proceedings of the First International Congress for the Study of Child Language*. Lanham: University Press of America.

Maratsos, M. (1982). The child's construction of grammatical categories. In Wanner, E., & Gleitman, L. (Ed.), *Language acquisition: The state of the art*. New York, NY: Cambridge University Press.

Maratsos, M. (1983). Some current issues in the study of the acquisition of grammar. In Flavell, J., & Markman, E. (Ed.), *Handbook of Child Psychology: Vol. 3*. New York, NY: Wiley.

McClelland, J., & Rumelhart, D. (1981). An interactive activation model of context effects in letter perception: Part I. An account of basic findings. *Psychological Review, 88,* 375–408.

McClelland, J., & Rumelhart, D. (1986). A PDP Model of the Acquisition of Morphology. In B. MacWhinney (Ed.), *Mechanisms of language acquisition*. Hillsdale, N.J.: Lawrence Erlbaum.

Nelson, K. (1973). Structure and strategy in learning how to talk. *Monographs of the Society for Research in Child Development, 38,* Whole Nos. 1–2.

Nelson, K. (1981). Individual differences in language development: Implications for development and language. *Developmental Psychology, 17,* 170–187.

Peters, A. (1983). *The units of language acquisition*. New York, NY: Cambridge University Press.

Pinker, S. (1982). A theory of the acquisition of lexical-interpretive grammars. In J. Bresnan (Ed.), *The mental representation of grammatical relations*. Cambridge, MA: MIT Press.

Plèh, Csaba. (1981). Kūlōnbōzō szòrendü mondatok èrtelmezèse ès a dichotikus hallàsi aszimmetriàk 3-6 èves gyermekeknèl. *Pszichològia, 1,* 365–393.

Pleh, Cs. (1981). The role of word order in the sentence interpretation of Hungarian children. *Folia Linguistica, 15,* 331–343.

Pollack, I., & Pickett, J. M. (1964). Intelligibility of excerpts from fluent speech: Auditory vs. structural context. *Journal of Verbal Learning and Verbal Behavior, 3,* 79–84.

Posner, M., & Keele, S. (1968). On the genesis of abstract ideas. *Journal of Experimental Psychology, 77,* 353–363.

Radulovic, L. (1975). *Acquisition of language: Studies of Dubrovnik children*. Doctoral dissertation, University of California at Berkeley.

Schachter, P. (1976). The subject in Philippine languages: Topic, actor, actor-topic, or none of the above. In C. Li (Ed.), *Subject and topic*. New York, NY: Academic Press, Inc.

Sinclair, H., & Bronckart, J. (1972). SVO—a linguistic universal?: A study in developmental psycholinguistics. *Journal of Experimental Child Psychology, 14*, 329–348.

Slobin, D. (1985). *The cross-cultural study of language acquisition*. Hillsdale, NJ: Lawrence Erlbaum Associates, Inc.

Slobin, D., & Bever, T. (1982). Children use canonical sentence schemas: A crosslinguistic study of word order and inflections. *Cognition, 12*, 229–265.

Slobin, D. I. (1973). Cognitive prerequisites for the development of grammar. In C. A. Ferguson & D. I. Slobin (Eds.), *Studies of child language development*. New York, NY: Holt, Rinehart, & Winston.

Smith, S., & Mimica, I. (1984). Agrammatism in a case inflected language. *Brain and Language, 21*, 274–290.

Snyder, Lynn S., Bates, Elizabeth, & Bretherton, Inge. (1981). Content and context in early lexical development. *Journal of Child Language, 8*, 565–582.

Strohner, H., & Nelson, K. E. (1974). The young child's development of sentence comprehension: Influence of event probability, nonverbal context, syntactic form, and their strategies. *Child Development, 45*, 567–576.

Thibadeau, R., Just, M., & Carpenter, P. (1982). A model of the time course and content of reading. *Cognitive Science, 6*, 157–203.

Vihman, M. (1985). Individual differences in babbling and early speech: Predicting to age 3. In B. Lindblom & R. Zetterstrom (Eds.), *Precursors of early speech*. Basingstroke, Hampshire: MacMillan.

Vihman, M., Ferguson, C., & Elbert, M. (in press). Phonological development from babbling to speech: Common tendencies and individual differences. *Applied Psycholinguistics*.

Warren, R., & Warren, N. (1976). Dual semantic encoding of homographs and homophones embedded in context. *Memory and Cognition, 4*, 586–592.

Weist, R. & Konieczna, E. (1985). Affix processing strategies and linguistic systems. *Journal of Child Language, 12*, 27–36.

Xiao-chun, M. (1981). Word order and semantic strategies in Chinese sentence comprehension. *International Journal of Psycholinguistics, 8*, 23–33.

7 Learning the Past Tenses of English Verbs: Implicit Rules or Parallel Distributed Processing?

David E. Rumelhart
University of California, San Diego
James L. McClelland
Carnegie-Mellon University

THE ISSUE

Scholars of language and psycholinguistics have been among the first to stress the importance of rules in describing human behavior. The reason for this is obvious. Many aspects of language can be characterized by rules, and the speakers of natural languages speak the language correctly. Therefore, systems of rules are useful in characterizing, at least approximately, what they will and will not say. Though we all make mistakes when we speak, we have a pretty good ear for what is right and what is wrong, and these judgments of correctness are generally even easier to characterize by rules than actual utterances are.

Since the early work of Chomsky (1957), a great deal of progress has been made by viewing language structure in terms of a system of rules. It seems likely that this approach will continue to lead to insights about the nature of language and the nature of the language processing and acquisition tasks. These insights clearly contribute to what Marr (1982) has called the *computational theory* of language—an abstract description of language itself and of the tasks facing the language learner and user.

But what of the actual representations and procedures used in language processing and language learning? Do the processing mechanisms actually consult a set of rules, and do the acquisition mechanisms actually formulate, evaluate, and/or modify members of the set? We take the view that the answer may be "no." We suggest instead that implicit knowledge of language may be stored in connections among simple processing units organized into networks. While the behavior of such networks may be describable (at least approximately) as conforming to some system of rules, we suggest that an account of the fine structure of the phenomena of language use and language acquisition can best be formulated in models that make reference to the characteristics of the underlying networks.

In our network models, the mechanisms that process language are constructed in such a way that there are no rules anywhere in them. Acquisition occurs by a simple process of adjusting connections between units. The behavior of the models is lawful (as lawful, we would argue, as the human behavior it simulates), but it is not based on the formulation or consultation of rules.

This kind of thing is of course extremely frequent in nature. One example, which we take from Bates (1979), is provided by the honeycomb. The regular structure of the honeycomb arises from the interaction of forces that wax balls exert on each other when compressed. The honeycomb can be described by a rule, but the mechanism which produces it does not contain any statement of this rule.

Our approach to the question of language representation and learning does not arise from within the tradition of linguistic theory. We are not linguists, but psychologists who have discovered that a new class of models based on highly parallel processing architectures appears to provide rather good accounts of a number of aspects of cognition. We call these models *Parallel Distributed Processing* (PDP) models. Several members of this class of models are described in two forthcoming volumes (Rumelhart & McClelland, 1986; McClelland & Rumelhart, 1986).

More specifically, our thinking about issues in language representation and learning grew out of our earlier work with a model called the interactive activation model of word perception (McClelland & Rumelhart, 1981; Rumelhart & McClelland, 1981, 1982). Initially, we intended the model as a mechanism for capturing perceptual facilitation of letters in familiar words. The model consisted of a set of word units, (one for each word), a set of letter units, and a set of feature units. There were bi-directional excitatory connections between each word unit and the units for the letters of the word, and between each letter unit and units for features of the letter. When some or all of the units for the letters in a word received excitation from the feature level, they would activate the corresponding word, which would in turn provide feedback support for the letters. In this way we were able to account for perceptual facilitation and disambiguation of letters in words compared to letters in isolation or in random strings.

There were no units in the model for common letter clusters and no explicit provision for dealing differently with orthographically regular letter sequences (strings that accorded with the rules of English) as opposed to irregular sequences. Yet we discovered that the model did show perceptual facilitation for orthographically regular nonwords (such as MAVE) but not for random letter strings (such as XMPQ). The reason, in brief, was that the sequence of letters in a regular nonword partially activated many words sharing several letters in common with the nonword, and these partially activated word units caused the letters to receive some feedback support. The random letter strings activated few if any words to any significant degree, and so the letters in them received little or no feedback support. The model simulated rather closely a number of results in the word perception literature relating to the finding that subjects perceive letters in orthographically regular letter strings more accurately than they perceive letters in random letter strings. Thus, the behavior of the model was lawful, even though it contained no explicit rules of orthography.

Some people may be tempted to argue that the behavior of the model shows that we can do without rules entirely (for this case, at least). We prefer, however, to view the matter in a slightly different light. There is no denying that a system of rules can still provide an approximate description of which letter strings will produce perceptual facilitation and which letter strings will not. More generally, rule systems have shown considerable power in providing a characterization of the structure of linguistic objects of various types and constraints that exist on these structures. Such descriptions are extremely useful for describing the basic patterns found in language, and in characterizing the human behaviors that conform to these patterns. We would only suggest that PDP models may provide mechanisms that can capture the fine structure of human language use and acquisition in an appealing and succinct way.

We anticipate two kinds of arguments against this kind of claim. The first kind would state that although certain types of lawful behavior might emerge from PDP models, such models as a class simply lack the computational power needed to carry out certain essential operations which can be easily handled by systems using rules. We believe that this argument is mistaken. We discuss the issue of computational power of PDP models in Rumelhart and McClelland (1986) and consider specifically the issues that arise in applying PDP models to sentence processing in McClelland and Kawamoto (1986). The second kind of argument would be that the details of language behavior and, indeed, the details of the language acquisition process would provide evidence that would be better captured by postulating the acquisition of rules than by a PDP model.

It is this latter kind of argument we wish to address in the present article. We begin by describing a phenomenon that is often taken to demonstrate the acquisition of a linguistic rule, namely, the ''over-regularization'' of irregular words that occurs during the acquisition of the past tense of English. We then describe a parallel distributed processing model that simulates this phenomenon. From there, we go on to show that the model provides an account of a number of detailed aspects of the performance of children in the use of the past tense in English and makes several new predictions about the kinds of errors one might expect to observe during past-tense acquisition.

THE PHENOMENON

The phenomenon we wish to account for is actually a sequence of three phases in the acquisition of the use of the past tense by children learning English as their native tongue. Descriptions of development of the use of the past tense may be found in Brown (1973), Ervin (1964), and Kuczaj (1977). Here we describe what we take to be the high points of this literature. In later sections we will delve into aspects of it in greater detail.

In Stage 1, children use only a small number of verbs in the past tense. Such verbs tend to be very high-frequency words, and the majority of these are irregular. At this stage, children tend to get the past tenses of these words correct if they use the past tense at all. For example, a child's lexicon of past-tense words at this stage might consist of *came, got, gave, looked, needed, took,* and *went.* Of these seven verbs, only two are regular—the other five are generally idiosyncratic examples of irregular verbs. In this stage, there is no evidence of the use of the rule; it appears that children simply know a small number of separate items.

In Stage 2, evidence of implicit knowledge of a linguistic rule emerges. At this stage, children use a much larger number of verbs in the past tense. These verbs include a few more irregular items, but it turns out that the majority of the words at this stage are examples of the *regular* past tense in English. Some examples are *wiped* and *pulled.*

The evidence that the Stage 2 child actually has a linguistic rule comes not from the mere fact that he or she knows a number of regular forms. There are two additional and crucial facts:

- The child can now generate a past tense for an invented word. For example, Berko (1958) has shown that if children can be convinced to use *rick* to describe an action, they will often say *ricked* when pressed to use the word in the past tense.
- Children now *incorrectly* supply regular past-tense endings for words which they used correctly in Stage 1. These errors may involve either adding *ed* to the root as in *comed* /k^md/, or adding *ed* to the irregular past tense form as in *camed* /kAmd/[1] (Ervin, 1964; Kuczaj, 1977).

Such findings have been taken as fairly strong support for the assertion that the child at this stage has acquired the past-tense "rule." To quote Berko (1958):

> If a child knows that the plural of *witch* is *witches,* he may simply have memorized the plural form. If, however, he tells us that the plural of *gutch* is *gutches,* we have evidence that he actually knows, albeit unconsciously, one of those rules which the descriptive linguist, too, would set forth in his grammar. (p. 151)

In Stage 3, the regular and irregular forms coexist. That is, children have regained the use of the correct irregular forms of the past tense, while they

---

[1]The notation of phonemes used here is somewhat nonstandard. It is derived from the computer-readable dictionary containing phonetic transcriptions of the verbs used in the simulations. A key is given in Table 5.

continue to apply the regular form to new words they learn. Regularizations persist into adulthood. In fact, there is a class of words for which either a regular or an irregular version are both considered acceptable. But for the commonest irregulars such as those the child acquired first, regularizations tend to be rather rare. At this stage there are some groups of exceptions to the basic, regular past-tense pattern of English. Each group includes a number of words that undergo identical changes from the present to the past tense. For example, there is a *ing/ang* cluster, an *ing/ung* cluster, an *eet/it* cluster, etc. There is also a group of words ending in /d/ or /t/ for which the present and past are identical.

Table 1 summarizes the major characteristics of the three stages.

Variability and Gradualness

The characterization of past-tense acquisition as a sequence of three stages is somewhat misleading. It may suggest that the stages are clearly demarcated and that performance in each stage is sharply distinguished from performance in other stages.

In fact, the acquisition process is quite gradual. Little detailed data exists on the transition from Stage 1 to Stage 2, but the transition from Stage 2 to Stage 3 is quite protracted and extends over several years (Kuczaj, 1977). Further, performance in Stage 2 is extremely variable. Correct use of irregular forms is never completely absent, and the same child may be observed to use the correct past of an irregular, the base+ed form, and the past+ed form within the same conversation (Kuczaj, 1977). Furthermore, mastery of the regular pattern, as evidenced by generalization to novel forms, may be far from complete; Berko (1958) found that even children in kindergarden and first grade were considerably more likely to use the past tense correctly with familiar than with unfamiliar verbs.

Other Facts About Past-Tense Acquisition

Beyond these points, there is now considerable data on the detailed types of errors children make throughout the acquisition process, both from Kuczaj (1977) and more recently from Bybee and Slobin (1982). We will consider aspects of these findings in more detail below. For now, we mention one intrigu-

TABLE 1
Characteristics of the Three Stages of Past Tense Acquisition

Verb Type	*Stage 1*	*Stage 2*	*Stage 3*
Early Verbs	Correct	Regularized	Correct
Regular	—	Correct	Correct
Other Irregular	—	Regularized	Correct or Regularized
Novel	—	Regularized	Regularized

ing fact: according to Kuczaj (1977), there is an interesting difference in the errors children make to irregular verbs at different points in Stage 2. Early on, regularizations are typically of the base+ed form, like *goed;* later on, there is a large increase in the frequency of past+ed errors, such as *wented*.

While the basic over-regularization phenomenon and the ability of children to correctly regularize novel words are certainly well captured by postulating the acquisition of the past-tense rule, such a characterization of the acquisition of the past tense of English leaves out a great deal of detail. In what follows, we will see that our PDP model can capture the same basic phenomena as well as most of the details.

THE MODEL

The goal of our simulation of the acquisition of past tense was to simulate the three-stage performance summarized in Table 1 and to see whether we could capture other aspects of acquisition. In particular, we wanted to show that the kind of gradual change characteristic of normal acquisition was also a characteristic of our distributed model, and we wanted to see whether the model would capture detailed aspects of the phenomenon, such as the change in error type in later phases of development and the differences in error patterns observed for different types of words.

We were not prepared to produce a full-blown language processor that would learn the past tense from full sentences heard in everyday experience. Rather, we have explored a very simple past-tense learning environment designed to capture the essential characteristics necessary to produce the three stages of acquisition. In this environment the model is presented as learning experiences with pairs of inputs—one capturing the phonological structure of the root form of a word and the other capturing the phonological structure of the correct past-tense version of that word. The behavior of the model can be tested by giving it just the root form of a word and examining what it generates as its "current guess" of the corresponding past-tense form.

Structure of the Model

Overview. The basic structure of the model is illustrated in Figure 7.1. The model consists of three basic parts: (a) a fixed encoding network that generates feature representations from input strings of phonemes, (b) a *pattern associator* network similar to those studied by Kohonen (1977, 1984) which learns the relationships between the base form and the past-tense form, and (c) a decoding network that converts a featural representation of the past-tense form into a phonological representation. All learning occurs in the pattern associator; the

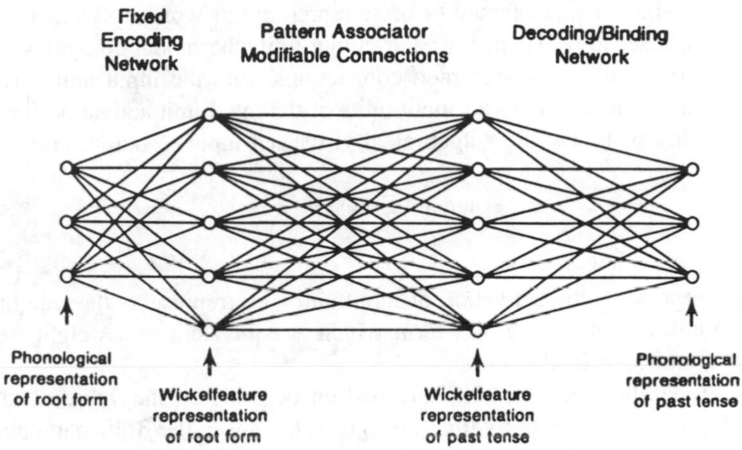

FIGURE 7.1. The basic structure of the model.

decoding network is simply a mechanism for converting a featural representation which may be a near miss to any phonological pattern into a legitimate phonological representation. In this section we focus on the pattern associator. We discuss the details of the encoding and decoding in later sections.

Units. The pattern associator contains two pools of units. One pool, called the input pool, is used to represent the input pattern corresponding to the root form of the verb to be learned. The other pool, called the output pool, is used to represent the output pattern generated by the model as its current guess as to the past tense corresponding to the root form represented in the inputs.

Each unit stands for a particular feature of the input or output string. The particular features we used are important to the behavior of the model, so they are described in a separate section below.

Connections. The pattern associator contains a modifiable connection linking each input unit to each output unit. Initially, these connections are all set to 0 so that there is no influence of the input units on the output units. Learning, as in other PDP models, involves modification of the strengths of these interconnections, as described below.

Operation of the Model

On test trials, the simulation is given a phoneme string corresponding to the root of a word. It then performs the following actions. First, it encodes the root string as a pattern of activation over the input units. The encoding scheme used is described below. Node activations are discrete in this model, so the activation values of all the units that should be on to represent this word are set to 1, and all the others are set to 0. Then, for each output unit, the model computes the net input to it from all of the weighted connections from the input units. The net input is simply the sum over all input units of the input unit activation times the corresponding weight. Thus, algebraically, the net input to output unit i is

$$net_i = \sum_j a_j w_{ij} + \beta_i$$

where a_j represents the activation of input unit j, w_{ij} represents the weight from unit j to unit i, and β_i is a bias term which is equivalent to a weight from an additional unit that is always on.

The probability that the unit is turned on depends on the value of this net input. The *logistic* probability function is used here as in the Boltzmann machine (Ackley, Hinton, & Sejnowski, 1985) to determine whether the unit should be turned on. The probability is given by

$$p(a_i = 1) = \frac{1}{1 + e^{-net/T}} \qquad (1)$$

where T represents the temperature of the system. The logistic function is shown in Figure 7.2.

Since the pattern associator built into the model is a one-layer net with no feedback connections and no connections from one input unit to another or from one output unit to another, iterative computation is of no benefit. Therefore, the

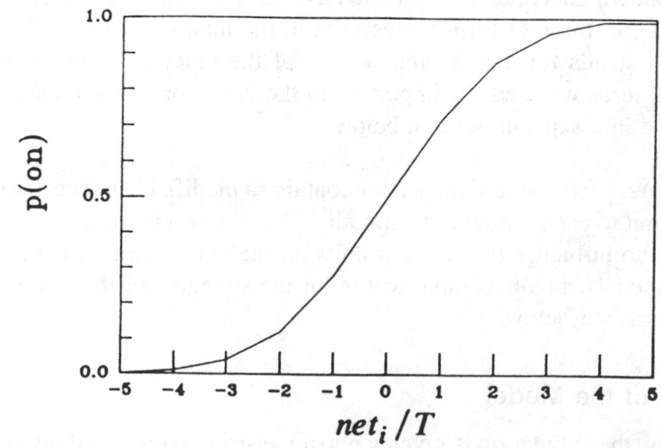

FIGURE 7.2. The logistic function used to calculate probability of activation. The x-axis shows values of net_i/T, and the y-axis indicates the corresponding probability that unit i will be activated.

processing of an input pattern is a simple matter of first calculating the net input to each output unit and then setting its activation probabilistically on the basis of the logistic equation given above. The temperature T determines the variability of the response of the output units; a fixed value of T was used throughout the simulations.

To determine how well the model did at producing the correct output, we simply compare the pattern of output Wickelphone activations to the pattern that the correct response would have generated. To do this, we first translate the correct response into a target pattern of activation for the output units, based on the same encoding scheme used for the input units. We then compare the obtained pattern with the target pattern on a unit-by-unit basis. The target specifies that some of the output units should be 1, and some should be 0. Cases in which the output should be 1 and is 1 are called *hits,* following the conventions of signal detection theory (Green & Swets, 1966). Cases in which the output should be 0 and is 0 are called *correct rejections.* Cases in which there is a 1 in the output but not in the target are called *false alarms,* and cases in which there is a 1 in the target but not in the output are called *misses.*

Based on the bit-wise hit, miss, false-alarm, and correct rejection data, a variety of measures of performance can be computed. We can measure the percentage of output units that match the correct past tense, or we can compare the output to the pattern for any other response alternative we might care to evaluate. This allows us to look at the output of the system independently of the decoding network. We can also employ the decoding network and have the system synthesize a phonological string, as described in detail below. We can measure the performance of the system either at the featural level or at the level of strings of phonemes. We shall employ both of these mechanisms in the evaluation of different aspects of the overall model.

Learning

On a learning trial, the model is presented with both the root form of the verb and the target. As on a test trial, the pattern associator network computes the output it would generate from the input. Then, for each output unit, the model compares its answer with the target. Connection strengths are adjusted using the classic *perceptron convergence procedure* (Rosenblatt, 1962). The exact procedure is as follows: we can think of the target as supplying a teaching input to each output unit, telling it what value it ought to have. When the actual output matches the target output, the model is doing the right thing and so none of the weights on the lines coming into the unit are adjusted. When the computed output is 0 and the target says it should be 1, we want to increase the probability that the unit will be active the next time the same input pattern is presented. To do this, we increase the weights from all of the input units that are active by a small amount η. At the same time, the bias is also increased by η. When the computed output is 1 and the target says it should be 0, we want to decrease the probability that the unit will be active the next time the same input pattern is presented. To do this, the weights from all of the input units that are active are reduced by η; the bias term is also reduced by η. In all of our simulations, the value of η is simply set to 1. Thus, each change in a weight is a unit change, either up or down. For nonstochastic units, it is well known that the perceptron convergence procedure will find a set of weights that will allow the model to get each output unit correct, provided that such a set of weights exists. For the stochastic case, it is possible for the learning procedure to find a set of weights that will make the probability of error as low as desired. Such a set of weights exists if a set of weights exists that will always get the right answer for nonstochastic units.

Learning Regular and Exceptional Patterns in a Pattern Associator

In this section, we present an illustration of the behavior of a simple pattern associator model. The model is a scaled-down version of the main simulation described in the next section. We describe the scaled-down version first because in this model it is possible to actually examine the matrix of connection weights and from this to see clearly how the model works and why it produces the basic three-stage learning phenomenon characteristic of acquisition of the past tense. Various aspects of pattern associator networks are described in a number of places (Anderson, 1973, 1977; Anderson, Silverstein, Ritz, & Jones, 1977; Kohonen, 1977, 1984; Stone, 1986). Here we focus our attention on their application to the representation of rules for mapping one set of patterns into another.

For the illustration model, we use a small network of eight input and eight output units and a set of connections from each input unit to each output unit. The network is illustrated in Figure 7.3. The network is shown with a set of connections sufficient for associating the pattern of activation illustrated on the input units with the pattern of activation illustrated on the output units. (Active units are darkened; positive and negative connections are indicated by numbers written on each connection). Next to the network is the matrix of connections abstracted from the actual network itself with numerical values assigned to the positive and negative connections. Note that each weight is located in the matrix at the point where it occurred in the actual network diagram. Thus, the entry in the *i*th row of the *j*th column indicates the connection w_{ij} from the *j*th input unit to the *i*th output unit.[2]

---

[2]In the examples we will be considering in this section, the biases of the units are fixed at 0. Bias terms add an extra degree of freedom for each output unit and allow the unit to come on in the absence of input, but they are otherwise unessential to the operation of the model. Computationally, they are equivalent to an adjustable weight to an extra input unit that is always on.

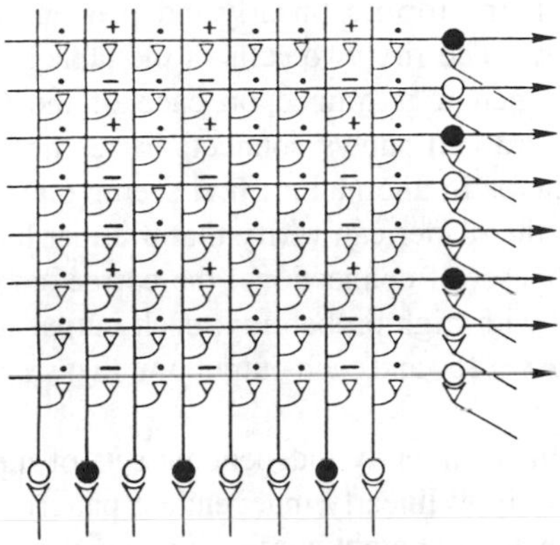

.	+15	.	+15	.	.	+15	.
.	−15	.	−15	.	.	−15	.
.	+15	.	+15	.	.	+15	.
.	−15	.	−15	.	.	−15	.
.	−15	.	−15	.	.	−15	.
.	+15	.	+15	.	.	+15	.
.	−15	.	−15	.	.	−15	.
.	−15	.	−15	.	.	−15	.

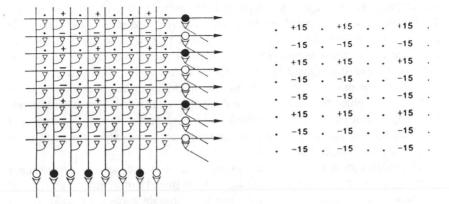

FIGURE 7.3. Simple network used in illustrating basic properties of pattern associator networks; excitatory and inhibitory connections needed to allow the active input pattern to produce the illustrated output pattern are indicated with + and −. Next to the network is the matrix of weights indicating the strengths of the connections from each input unit to each output unit. Input units are indexed by the column they appear in; output units are indexed by row.

Using this diagram, it is easy to compute the net inputs that will arise on the output units when an input pattern is presented. For each output unit, one simply scans across its rows and adds up all the weights found in columns associated with active input units. (This is exactly what the simulation program does!) The reader can verify that when the input pattern illustrated in the left-hand panel is presented, each output unit that should be on in the output pattern receives a net input of +45; each output unit that should be off receives a net input of −45. Plugging these values into Equation 1, using a temperature of 15,[3] we can compute that each output unit will take on the correct value about 95% of the time. The reader can check this in Figure 7.2; with the net input equal to +45 and $T = 15$, the value of net/T is 3; and with the net input equal to −45, net/T is −3. These correspond to activation probabilities of about .95 and .05, respectively.

One of the basic properties of the pattern associator is that it can store the connections appropriate for mapping a number of different input patterns to a number of different output patterns. The perceptron convergence procedure can accommodate a number of arbitrary associations between input patterns and

[3]For the actual simulations of verb learning, we set the value of T equal to 200. This means that for a fixed value of the weight on an input line, the effect of that line being active on the unit's probability of firing is much lower than it is in these illustrations. This is balanced by the fact that in the verb learning simulations, a much larger number of inputs contribute to the activation of each output unit. Responsibility for turning a unit on is simply more distributed when larger input patterns are used.

output patterns, as long as the input patterns form a linearly independent set. Table 2 illustrates this aspect of the model. The first two cells of the table show the connections that the model learns when it is trained on each of the two indicated associations separately. The third cell shows connections learned by the model when it is trained on both patterns in alternation, first seeing one and then seeing the other of the two. Again, the reader can verify that if either input pattern is presented to a network with this set of connections, the correct corresponding output pattern is reconstructed with high probability; each output unit that should be on gets a net input of at least +45, and each output unit that should be off gets a net input below −45.

The restriction of networks such as this to linearly independent sets of input patterns is a severe one since there are only N linearly independent patterns of length N. That means that we could store at most eight unrelated associations in the network and maintain accurate performance. However, if the associations between input and output patterns conform to a general rule, the network can respond correctly to a much larger number of patterns. For example, the set of connections shown in Table 2D is capable of processing all of the patterns defined by what we call the *rule of 78*. The rule is described in Table 3. There are 18 different input/output pattern pairs corresponding to this rule, but they present no difficulty to the network. Through repeated presentations of examples of the rule, the perceptron convergence procedure learned the set of weights shown in cell D of Table 2. Again, the reader can verify that it works for any legal association fitting the rule of 78. (Note that for this example, the "regular" pairing of (1 4 7) with (1 4 8) was used rather than the exceptional mapping illustrated in Table 3).

We have, then, observed an important property of the pattern associator: if there is some structure to a set of patterns, the network may be able to learn to respond appropriately to all of the members of the set. This is true, even though the input vectors most certainly do not form a linearly independent set. The model works anyway because the response that the model should make to some of the patterns can be predicted from the responses that it should make to others of the patterns.

Now let us consider a case more like the situation a young child faces in learning the past tenses of English verbs. Here, there is a regular pattern, analogous to the rule of 78. In addition, however, there are exceptions. Among the first words the child learns are many exceptions, but as the child learns more and more verbs, the proportion that are regular increases steadily. For an adult, the vast majority of verbs are regular.

To examine what would happen in a pattern associator in this kind of a situation, we first presented the illustrative 8-unit model with two pattern-pairs. One of these was a regular example of the 78 rule [(2 5 8) → (2 5 7)]. The other was an exception to the rule [(1 4 7) → (1 4 7)]. The simulation saw both pairs 20 times, and connection strengths were adjusted after each presentation. The re-

TABLE 2

Weights in the 8-Unit Network After Various Learning Experiences

A. Weights acquired in learning (2 4 7) → (1 4 6)

.	15	.	15	.	.	15	.
.	−16	.	−16	.	.	−16	.
.	−17	.	−17	.	.	−17	.
.	16	.	16	.	.	16	.
.	−16	.	−16	.	.	−16	.
.	17	.	17	.	.	17	.
.	−16	.	−16	.	.	−16	.
.	−17	.	−17	.	.	−17	.

B. Weights acquired in learning (3 4 6) → (3 6 7)

.	.	−16	−16	.	−16	.	.
.	.	−17	−17	.	−17	.	.
.	.	17	17	.	17	.	.
.	.	−16	−16	.	−16	.	.
.	.	−17	−17	.	−17	.	.
.	.	16	16	.	16	.	.
.	.	17	17	.	17	.	.
.	.	−17	−17	.	−17	.	.

C. Weights acquired in learning A and B together

.	24	−24	.	.	−24	24	.
.	−13	−13	−26	.	−13	−13	.
.	−23	24	1	.	24	−23	.
.	24	−25	−1	.	−25	24	.
.	−13	−13	−26	.	−13	−13	.
.	13	13	26	.	13	13	.
.	−25	24	−1	.	24	−25	.
.	−12	−13	−25	.	−13	−12	.

D. Weights acquired in learning the rule of 78

61	−37	−37	−5	−5	−3	−6	−7
−35	60	−38	−4	−6	−3	−5	−8
−39	−35	61	−4	−5	−4	−7	−6
−6	−4	−5	59	−37	−37	−8	−7
−5	−5	−4	−36	60	−38	−7	−7
−5	−4	−6	−37	−38	60	−8	−7
.	1	.	1	.	.	−50	51
.	.	−1	−2	1	.	49	−50

TABLE 3
The Rule of 78

Input patterns consist of one active unit from each of the following sets:	(1 2 3) (4 5 6) (7 8)
The output pattern paired with a given input pattern consists of:	The same unit from (1 2 3) The same unit from (4 5 6) The other unit from (7 8)
Examples:	2 4 7 → 2 4 8 1 6 8 → 1 6 7 3 5 7 → 3 5 8
An exception:	1 4 7 → 1 4 7

sulting set of connections is shown in cell A of Table 4. This number of learning trials is not enough to lead to perfect performance, but after this much experience the model tends to get the right answer for each output unit close to 90 percent of the time. At this point, the fact that one of the patterns is an example of a general rule and the other is an exception to that rule is irrelevant to the model. It learns a set of connections that can accommodate these two patterns, but it cannot generalize to new instances of the rule.

This situation, we suggest, characterizes the situation that the language learner faces early on in learning the past tense. The child knows, at this point, only a few high-frequency verbs, and these tend, by and large, to be irregular, as we shall see below. Thus each is treated by the network as a separate association, and very little generalization is possible.

But as the child learns more and more verbs, the proportion of regular verbs increases. This changes the situation for the learning model. Now the model is faced with a number of examples, all of which follow the rule, as well as a smattering of irregular forms. This new situation changes the experience of the network and thus the pattern of interconnections it contains. Because of the predominance of the regular form in the input, the network learns the regular pattern, temporarily "overregularizing" exceptions that it may have previously learned.

Our illustration takes this situation to an extreme, perhaps, to illustrate the point. For the second stage of learning, we present the model with the entire set of eighteen input patterns consisting of one active unit from (1 2 3), one from (4 5 6), and one from (7 8). All of these patterns are regular except the one exception already used in the first stage of training.

At the end of 10 exposures to the full set of 18 patterns, the model has learned a set of connection strengths that predominantly captures the "regular pattern." At this point, its response to the exceptional pattern is *worse* than it was before the beginning of Phase 2; rather than getting the right output for Units 7 and 8, the network is now *regularizing* it.

TABLE 4
Representing Exceptions: Weights in the 8-Unit Network

A. After 20 exposures to (1 4 7) → (1 4 7), (2 5 8) → (2 5 7)								B. After 10 more exposures to al 18 associations							
12	−12	.	12	−12	.	12	−12	44	−34	−26	−2	−10	−4	−8	−8
−11	13	.	−11	13	.	−11	13	−32	46	−27	−11	2	−4	−9	−4
−11	−11	.	−11	−11	.	−11	−11	−30	−24	43	−5	−5	−1	−2	−9
12	−12	.	12	−12	.	12	−12	−1	−7	−7	45	−34	−26	−4	−11
−11	11	.	−11	11	.	−11	11	−8	−3	−3	−31	44	−27	−7	−7
−11	−12	.	−11	−12	.	−11	−12	−6	−8	−3	−31	−28	42	−7	−10
12	11	.	12	11	.	12	11	11	−2	−6	11	−2	−6	−35	38
−11	−13	.	−11	−13	.	−11	−13	−9	−4	7	−13	1	6	36	−42
C. After 30 more exposures to all 18 associations								D. After a total of 500 exposures to all 18 associations							
61	−38	−38	−6	−5	−4	−6	−9	64	−39	−39	−5	−4	−5	−7	−7
−38	62	−39	−6	−5	−4	−8	−7	−39	63	−39	−5	−5	−5	−7	−8
−37	−38	62	−5	−5	−3	−7	−6	−39	−40	64	−5	−5	−5	−8	−7
−4	−6	−6	62	−40	−38	−8	−8	−5	−5	−5	64	−40	−39	−8	−7
−5	−5	−4	−38	62	−38	−7	−7	−5	−5	−5	−39	63	−39	−7	−8
−6	−4	−5	−38	−39	62	−8	−7	−5	−5	−5	−39	−39	63	−8	−7
20	−5	−4	22	−5	−6	−50	61	71	−28	−29	70	−28	−28	−92	106
−19	8	5	−18	5	7	54	−60	−70	27	28	−70	27	28	91	−106

The reason for this behavior is very simple. All that is happening is that the model is continually being bombarded with learning experiences directing it to learn the rule of 78. On only one learning trial out of 18 is it exposed to an exception to this rule.

In this example, the deck has been stacked very strongly against the exception. For several learning cycles, it is in fact quite difficult to tell from the connections that the model is being exposed to an exception mixed in with the regular pattern. At the end of 10 cycles, we can see that the model is building up extra excitatory connections from input Units 1 and 4 to output Unit 7 and extra inhibitory strength from Units 1 and 4 to Unit 8, but these are not strong enough to make the model get the right answer for output Units 7 and 8 when the (1 4 7) input pattern is shown. Even after 40 trials (panel C of Table 4), the model still gets the wrong answer on Units 7 and 8 for the (1 4 7) pattern more than half the time. (The reader can still be checking these assertions by computing the net input to each output unit that would result from presenting the (1 4 7) pattern.)

It is only after the model has reached the stage where it is making very few mistakes on the 17 regular patterns that it begins to accommodate the exception. This amounts to making the connection from Units 1 and 4 to output Unit 7 strongly excitatory and making the connections from these units to output Unit 8 strongly inhibitory. The model must also make several adjustments to other connections so that the adjustments just mentioned do not cause errors on regular patterns similar to the exceptions, such as (1 5 7), (2 4 7), etc. Finally, in panel D, after a total of 500 cycles through the full set of 18 patterns, the weights are sufficient to get the right answer nearly all of the time. Further improvement would be very gradual since the network makes errors so infrequently at this stage that there is very little opportunity for change.

It is interesting to consider for a moment how an association is represented in a model like this. We might be tempted to think of the representation of an association as the difference between the set of connection strengths needed to represent a set of associations that includes the association and the set of strengths needed to represent the same set excluding the association of interest. Using this definition, we see that the representation of a particular association is far from invariant. What this means is that learning that occurs in one situation (e.g., in which there is a small set of unrelated associations) does not necessarily transfer to a new situation (e.g., in which there are a number of regular associations). This is essentially why the early learning our illustrative model exhibits of the (1 4 7) → (1 4 7) association in the context of just one other association can no longer support correct performance when the larger ensemble of regular patterns is introduced.

Obviously, the example we have considered in this section is highly simplified. However, it illustrates several basic facts about pattern associators. One is that they tend to exploit regularity that exists in the mapping from one set of patterns to another. Indeed, this is one of the main advantages of the use of distributed representations. Second, they allow exceptions and regular patterns to coexist in the same network. Third, if there is a predominant regularity in a set of patterns, this can swamp exceptional patterns until the set of connections has been acquired that captures the predominant regularity. After that, further gradual tuning can occur that adjusts these connections to accommodate both the regular patterns and the exception. These basic properties of the pattern associator model lie at the heart of the three-stage acquisition process, we claim, and account for the gradualness of the transition from Stage 2 to Stage 3.

The presentation up to this point has focused on basic properties of the model. The next two sections go into detail about our particular choice or representation and about the assumptions we have made about generating overt responses. These sections may be skipped by readers interested in gaining a general understanding of the behavior of the model, although both contain detailed information about aspects of the model that influence its adequacy to capture the phenomena of interest.

Featural Representations of Phonological Patterns

The preceding section describes basic aspects of the behavior of the pattern associator model and captures fairly well what happens when a pattern associator is applied to the processing of English verbs, following a training schedule similar to the one we have just considered for the acquisition of the rule of 78. There is one caveat, however: the input and target patterns—the base forms of the verbs and the correct past tenses of these verbs—must be represented in the model in such a way that the features provide an adequate basis for capturing the regularities embodied in the past-tense forms of English verbs. Basically, there were two considerations:

- We needed a representation that permitted a differentiation of all of the root forms of English and their past tenses.
- We wanted a representation that would provide a natural basis for generalizations to emerge about what aspects of a present tense correspond to what aspects of the past tense.

We hasten to add that these criteria are clearly not sufficient to provide a basis for capturing all phonological generalizations. They are sufficient for present purposes, and so is the representation that we have hit upon. But we believe that a richer distributed representation than the one we have developed here would be required to capture a wider range of phonological phenomena. In particular, the code will in general have to be sensitive to syllable structure and stress pattern, among other things, in ways that the present representation is not.

In any case, returning to our criteria, a scheme which meets the first but not the second is the scheme proposed by Wickelgren (1969). He suggested that words could be represented as sequences of context-sensitive phoneme units which represent each phone in a word as a triple consisting of the phone itself, its predecessor, and its successor. We call these triples *Wickelphones*. Notationally, we write each Wickelphone as a triple of phonemes consisting of the central phoneme, subscripted on the left by its predecessor and on the right by its successor. A phoneme occurring at the beginning of a word is preceded by a special symbol (#) standing for the word boundary; likewise, a phoneme occurring at the end of a word is followed by #. The word /kat/, for example, would be represented as ${}_{\#}k_{a}$, ${}_{k}a_{t}$, and ${}_{a}t_{\#}$. Though the Wickelphones in a word are not strictly position specific, it turns out that (a) few words contain more than one occurrence of any given Wickelphone, and (b) there are no two words we know of that consist of the same sequence of Wickelphones. For example, /slit/ and /silt/ contain no Wickelphones in common.

One nice property of Wickelphones is that they capture enough of the context in which a phoneme occurs to provide a sufficient basis for differentiating between the different cases of the past-tense rule and for characterizing the contextual variables that determine the subregularities among the irregular past-tense verbs. For example, the word-final phoneme that determines whether we should add /d/, /t/ or /^d/ in forming the regular past. And it is the sequence ${}_{i}N_{\#}$ which is transformed to ${}_{a}N_{\#}$ in the *ing* → *ang* pattern found in words like *sing*.

The trouble with the Wickelphone solution is that there are too many of them, and they are too specific. Assuming that we distinguish 35 different phonemes, the number of Wickelphones would be 35^3, or 42,875, not even counting the Wickelphones containing word boundaries. And, if we postulate one input unit and one output unit in our model for each Wickelphone, we require rather a large connection matrix (4.3×10^4 squared, or about 2×10^9) to represent all the possible connections.

Obviously, a more compact representation is required. This can be obtained by representing each Wickelphone as a distributed pattern of activation over a set of feature detectors. The basic idea is that we represent each phoneme, not by a single Wickelphone, but by a pattern of what we call *Wickelfeatures*. Each Wickelfeature is a conjunctive or context-sensitive feature, capturing a feature of the central phoneme, a feature of the predecessor, and a feature of the successor.

Details of the Wickelfeature representation. For concreteness, we will now describe the details of the feature coding scheme we used. It contains several arbitrary properties, but it also captures the basic principles of distributed representation described in Hinton, McClelland, and Rumelhart (1986); that is, it provides an example of a coarse, conjunctive coding scheme for representing the internal structure of words. First, we will describe the simple feature representation scheme we used for coding a single phoneme as a pattern of features without regard to its predecessor and successor. Then we describe how this scheme can be extended to code whole Wickelphones. Finally, we show how we "blur" this representation, to promote generalization further.

To characterize each phoneme, we devised the highly simplified feature set illustrated in Table 5. The purpose of the scheme was (a) to give as many of the phonemes as possible a distinctive code, (b) to allow code similarity to reflect the similarity structure of the phonemes in a way that seemed sufficient for our present purposes, and (c) to keep the number of different features as small as possible. The coding scheme can be thought of as categorizing each phoneme on each of four dimensions. The first dimension divides the phonemes into three major types: interrupted consonants (stops and nasals), continuous consonants (fricatives, liquids, and semivowels), and vowels. The second dimension further subdivides these major classes. The interrupted consonants are divided into plain stops and nasals, the continuous consonants into fricatives and sonorants (liquids and semivowels are lumped together), and the vowels into high and low. The third dimension classifies the phonemes into three rough places of articulation—front, middle, and back. The fourth subcategorizes the consonants into voiced vs. voiceless categories and subcategorizes the vowels into long and short. As it stands, the coding scheme gives identical codes to six pairs of phonemes, as indicated by the duplicate entries in the cells of the table. A more adequate scheme could easily be constructed by increasing the number of dimensions and/or values on the dimensions.

Using the above code, each phoneme can be characterized by one value on each dimension. If we assigned a unit for each value on each dimension, we would need 10 units to represent the features of a single phoneme since two dimensions have three values and two have two values. We could then indicate the pattern of these features that corresponds to a particular phoneme as a pattern of activation over the 10 units.

TABLE 5
Categorization of Phonemes on Four Simple Dimensions

		Place					
		Front		*Middle*		*Back*	
		V/L	*U/S*	*V/L*	*U/S*	*V/L*	*U/S*
Interrupted	Stop	b	p	d	t	g	k
	Nasal	m	—	n	—	N	—
Cont. Consonant	Fric.	v/D	f/T	z	s	Z/j	S/C
	Liq/SV	w/l	—	r	—	y	h
Vowel	High	E	i	O	^	U	u
	Low	A	e	I	a/α	W	*/o

Key: N = ng in *sing;* D = th in *the;* T = th in *with;* Z = z in *azure;* S = sh in *ship;* C = ch in *chip;* E = ee in *beet;* i = i in *bit;* O = oa in *boat;* ^ = u in *but* or schwa; U = oo in *boot;* u = oo in *book;* A = ai in *bait;* e = e in *bet;* I = i_e in *bite;* a = a in *bat;* α = a in *father;* W = ow in *cow;* * = aw in *saw;* o = o in *hot.*

To represent Wickelphones, we constructed units that detect what we call *Wickelfeatures*—triples of features, one from the central phoneme, one from the predecessor phoneme, and one from the successor phoneme.

Using this scheme, each Wickelfeature unit is activated when the word contained a Wickelphone containing its particular combination of three features. Since each phoneme of a Wickelphone can be characterized by 11 features (including the word-boundary feature) and each Wickelphone contains three phonemes, there are 11 × 11 × 11 possible Wickelfeature detectors. Actually, we are not interested in representing phonemes that cross word boundaries, so we only need 10 features for the center phoneme.

Though this leaves us with a fairly reasonable number of units (11 × 10 × 11 or 1,210), it is still large in relation to what will easily fit in available computers. However, it is possible to cut the number down still further without much loss of representational capacity since a representation using all 1,210 units would be highly redundant; it would represent each feature of each of the three phonemes in each Wickelphone 16 different times, one for each of the conjunctions of that feature with one of the four features of one of the other phonemes and one of the four features of the other.

To cut down on the number of units required, we simply eliminated all those Wickelfeatures specifying values on two different dimensions of the predecessor and the successor phonemes. We kept all the Wickelfeature detectors for all combinations of different values on the same dimension for the predecessor and successor phonemes. It turns out that there are 260 of these (ignoring the word-boundary feature), and each feature of each member of each phoneme triple is still represented four different times. In addition, we kept the 100 possible Wickelfeatures combining a preceding word-boundary feature with any feature of the main phoneme and any feature of the successor; and the 100 Wickelfeatures combining a following word boundary feature with any feature of the main phoneme and any feature of the successor. All in all then, we used only 460 of the 1,210 possible Wickelfeatures.

Using this representation, a verb is represented by a pattern of activation over a set of 460 Wickelfeature units. Each Wickelphone activates 16 Wickelfeature units. Table 6 shows the 16 Wickelfeature units activated by the Wickelphone ${}_{k}A_{m}$, the central Wickelphone in the word *came*. The first Wickelfeature is turned on whenever we have a Wickelphone in which the preceding contextual phoneme is an interrupted consonant, the central phoneme is a vowel, and the following phoneme is an interrupted consonant. This Wickelfeature is turned on for the Wickelphone ${}_{k}A_{m}$ since /k/ and /m/, the context phonemes, are both interrupted consonants and /A/, the central phoneme, is a vowel. This same Wickelfeature would be turned on in the representation of ${}_{b}i_{d}$, ${}_{p}\hat{\ }_{t}$, ${}_{m}a_{p}$, and many other Wickelfeatures. Similarly, the sixth Wickelfeature listed in the table will be turned on whenever the preceding phoneme is made in the back, and the central and following phonemes are both made in the front. Again, this is turned on

TABLE 6
The Sixteen Wickelfeatures for the Wickelphone ${}_{k}A_{m}$

Feature	*Preceding Context*	*Central Phoneme*	*Following Context*
1	Interrupted	Vowel	Interrupted
2	Back	Vowel	Front
3	Stop	Vowel	Nasal
4	Voiced	Vowel	Unvoiced
5	Interrupted	Front	Vowel
6	Back	Front	Front
7	Stop	Front	Nasal
8	Voiced	Front	Unvoiced
9	Interrupted	Low	Interrupted
10	Back	Low	Front
11	Stop	Low	Nasal
12	Voiced	Low	Unvoiced
13	Interrupted	Long	Vowel
14	Back	Long	Front
15	Stop	Long	Nasal
16	Voiced	Long	Unvoiced

because /k/ is made in the back and /A/ and /m/ are both made in the front. In addition to ${}_{k}A_{m}$ this feature would be turned on for the Wickelphones ${}_{g}i_{v}$, ${}_{g}A_{p}$, ${}_{k}A_{p}$, and others. Similarly, each of the sixteen Wickelfeatures stands for a conjunction of three phonetic features and occurs in the representation of a large number of Wickelphones.

Now, words in this representation are simply lists of Wickelphones. Thus, words can be represented by simply turning on all of the Wickelfeatures in any Wickelphone of a word. Thus, a word with three Wickelphones (such as *came*, which has the Wickelphones ${}_{\#}k_{A}$, ${}_{k}A_{m}$, and ${}_{a}m_{\#}$) will have at most 48 Wickelfeatures turned on. Since the various Wickelphones may have some Wickelfeatures in common, typically there will be less than 16 times the number of Wickelfeatures turned on for most words. It is important to note the temporal order is entirely implicit in this representation. All words, no matter how many phonemes in the word, will be represented by a subset of the 460 Wickelfeatures.

Blurring the Wickelfeature representation. The representational scheme just outlined constitutes what we call the *primary* representation of a Wickelphone. However, we actually allowed partially matching Wickelfeatures to be active as well. This served to further blur the representation of each word. Thus, in addition to the 16 primary Wickelfeatures, we also turned on a randomly selected subset of the Wickelfeatures having the same value for the central feature and one of the two context phonemes. That is, whenever the Wickelfeature for the conjunction of phonemic features f_1, f_2, and f_3 is turned on, each

Wickelfeature of the form $<?f_2 f_3>$ and $<f_1 f_2?>$ could be turned on as well. Here "?" stands for "any feature." This causes each word to activate a larger set of Wickelfeatures, allowing what is learned about one sequence of phonemes to generalize more readily to other similar but not identical sequences.

To avoid having too much randomness in the representation of a particular Wickelphone, we turned on the same subset of additional Wickelfeatures each time a particular Wickelphone was to be represented. Based on subsequent experience with related models (McClelland & Kawamoto, 1986), we do not believe this makes very much difference.

There is a kind of trade-off between the discriminability among the base forms of verbs that the representation provides and the amount of generalization. We need a representation which allows for rapid generalization while at the same time maintaining adequate discriminability. We can manipulate this factor by manipulating the probability p that any one of these similar Wickelfeatures will be turned on. In our simulations we found that turning on the additional features with fairly high probability (.9) led to adequate discriminability while also producing relatively rapid generalization.

Although the model is not completely immune to the possibility that two different words will be represented by the same pattern, we have encountered no difficulty decoding any of the verbs we have studied. However, we do not claim that Wickelfeatures necessarily capture all the information needed to support the generalizations we might need to make for this or other morphological processes. Some morphological processes might require the use of units that were further differentiated according to vowel stress or other potential distinguishing characteristics. All we claim for the present coding scheme is its sufficiency for the task of representing the past tenses of English verbs and the importance of the basic principles of distributed, coarse (what we are calling blurred), conjunctive coding that it embodies (Hinton, McClelland, & Rumelhart, 1986).

Generating Overt Responses

The pattern of activation over the output units is a static spatial pattern containing a large number of distinct features that are activated. Due to its probabilistic and deliberately blurred nature this representation is inherently noisy; it nearly always contains features that are not part of the correct response, and there are nearly always features that are part of the correct response that are not activated. Given this state of affairs, some readers may wonder whether there is any sense in which the model could ever be said to generate the "correct" response. More generally, it is important to specify exactly how these patterns of activation are to be related to possible overt responses.

To address this issue we needed a scheme for translating patterns of activation over the output units into responses and associated probabilities. The scheme we used is based on a special kind of PDP network called a *binding network*.

Roughly speaking, a binding network is a scheme whereby a number of response units *compete* for a set of available features. Through the competition, the response units finally attain a strength that is proportional to the number of features the units account for. We proceed by first describing the idea behind the binding network, then describing its application to produce the set of Wickelphones implicit in the Wickelfeature representation, and finally by producing the set of phonological strings implicit in the Wickelfeatures.

The basic idea is simple. Imagine that there are a set of specification features and a set of response features. In general a response can be characterized by some set of response features. Each response feature is consistent with certain of the specification features, inconsistent with certain other of the specification features, and neutral about still others of the specification features. The idea is to find a set of response features that accounts for as many as possible of the specification features while minimizing the number of specification features accounted for by more than one response feature. Thus, we want each of the response features to *compete* for specification features. The more specification features it *captures,* the stronger its position in the competition and the more claim it has on the features it accounts for.

We apply this idea to the generation of a representation of the set of output Wickelphones that are represented in the pattern of activation over the model's output Wickelfeature units. In this case, the specification features are the Wickelfeatures of the output representation, and the response features are units that stand for entire Wickelphones. Essentially, then, the idea is that the Wickelphones compete among one another for the available Wickelfeatures. When a particular Wickelphone "captures" a particular Wickelfeature, that specification feature no longer provides support for other Wickelphones. In this way, it is possible to come up with a set of more or less nonoverlapping Wickelphones which account for as many as possible of the available Wickelfeatures. This means that if two Wickelphones have many Wickelfeatures in common (e.g., ${}_{k}\hat{}_{m}$ and ${}_{k}A_{m}$) but one of them accounts for more features than the other, the one that accounts for the most features will remove nearly all of the support for the very similar response feature which accounts for few if any specification features uniquely. The binding network described below has the property that if two response units are competing for a set of specification features, each will attain a strength proportional to the number of specification features uniquely accounted for by that response feature divided by the total number of specification features uniquely accounted for by any response feature.

The Wickelphone binding network we used contained a set of Wickelphone response units consisting of all of the Wickelphones that occurred anywhere in the entire corpus of verbs we studied (see below). The network computed the activation of Wickelphone response units as follows. Each active Wickelfeature specification unit has a fixed amount of activation (in our case we assumed that it had a total activation value of 1) to be distributed among the response units consistent with that specification feature. The Wickelfeature unit distributes its activation in proportion to the strength of the Wickelphone response unit to which it is connected. Thus, this is a network of units with dynamic weights on its connections. The weight from specification unit j to response unit i is given by

$$w_{ij} = \frac{a_i}{\sum_{k_j} a_{k_j}}$$

where k_j ranges over the set of response units consistent with specification unit j. The total strength of response unit k at time t is a linear function of its inputs at time $t - 1$ and is thus given by

$$a_k(t) = \sum_{j_k} i_{jk} w_{kj_k}(t) = \frac{\sum_{j_k} i_{j_k} a_k(t-1)}{\sum_{l_{j_k}} a_{l_{j_k}}(t-1)}$$

where j_k ranges over the set of specification features consistent with response feature k, l_{j_k} ranges over the set of response features consistent with specification feature j_k, and i_j takes on value 1 if specification feature j is present and is 0 otherwise.

The computation of the activation of the Wickelphone units is iterative. It begins with all of the Wickelphone response units at an equal initial activation of 1 and ends with each unit having an activation that reflects the number of Wickelfeatures it has "claimed credit" for or "bound" to itself. In general Wickelfeatures can remain divided between two Wickelphones, so the activation each unit ends up with may include some fractions of features. These activations are then normalized when divided by the number of features that are consistent with the Wickelphone so that they range from 0 to 1.0.

We used this Wickelphone binding network to find the set of Wickelphones which gave optimal coverage to the Wickelfeatures in the specification. The procedure was quite effective. In general, we found that the correct Wickelphones were always stronger than any others when the output pattern had 80 percent or more of the Wickelfeature activations correct. Performance dropped off as the percentage of correct Wickelfeatures dropped. Still when as few as 50 percent of the Wickelfeatures were correct, the correct Wickelphones were the strongest most of the time. Sometimes, however, a Wickelphone not actually in the input would become strong and push out the "correct" Wickelphones. If we added the constraint that the Wickelphones had to fit together to form an entire string (by having response features mutually activate other response features that they are consistent with, as ${}_{k}\hat{\ }{}_{m}$ and ${}_{\hat{}}m_{\#}$ are consistent), we found that when more than 60 percent of the output Wickelfeatures were correct the correct Wickelphones were more active than any of the incorrect Wickelphones on more than 90 percent of the trials.

These experiments with the binding network demonstrate that the accuracy of the response that can be generated from the output Wickelfeature representation is far higher than a raw measure of the accuracy of the pattern of Wickelfeature activations would tend to suggest. The reason is simply that the Wickelfeature representations are extremely redundant. The correct Wickelfeatures of $_{\mathrm{k}}\hat{}_{\mathrm{m}}$ are each represented four times in the set of core Wickelfeatures that represent this Wickelphone. If any one of these is not active and even if a few others are spuriously active, the correct Wickelphone will still receive many more votes than any other possible Wickelphone.

Still, in our discussion to this point we have not specified a way of measuring the relative probabilities of several possible alternative responses that the model might make. Even when all the correct Wickelphones are the most active, random factors might lead to incorrect responses some fraction of the time, and in some cases (the most interesting ones considering the kinds of errors we see in the developmental data) particular, incorrect Wickelphones will be activated that would lead to interesting error responses.

To assess the overt responses the model would make accurately would require an explicit mechanism for translating the pattern of Wickelphone activations into an overt response. We have not yet developed such a mechanism. In lieu of this, we used the following application of the binding network idea to assess the relative strength of possible alternative whole-string responses. In this *whole-string* binding network, there is a single response unit for each candidate whole response alternative. For example, in assessing the model's tendency to produce *went, goed,* or *wented* as responses to *go,* we constructed response units for each of these three entire response alternatives. In this case, specification features that are present but not consistent with a given response alternative can count against that response alternative. Thus, in this case we allowed the Wickelfeature specification units to *excite* consistent response units according to the rule given above and to inhibit inconsistent response units. In this case, then, we used the following activation rule:

$$a_k(t) = \sum_{j_k} i_{j_k} w_{kj_k}(t) - \sum_{l_k} i_{l_k}$$

Where l_k indexes the specification features that are inconsistent with response unit k, and where the w_{kj} are computed as before. This method of assessing relative strength of different responses is used extensively in the analysis of the results of the simulations, described below.

Of course, the child who is making overt responses does not have at his disposal an n-alternative forced-choice situation like the one we have given the binding network here. Rather, the child must construct a response by effectively choosing from all of the possibilities. To assess how well the model could perform in this kind of unconstrained choice situation, we developed an unconstrained choice procedure that worked as follows. We began by considering as candidate response alternatives all of the strings of less than 20 phonemes which could be generated from the set of Wickelphones that occurred anywhere in the entire corpus of verbs. Since this amounts to a very large number of response alternatives, it was computationally infeasible to simulate the operation of the binding network on all of these. We therefore eliminated a candidate response unit from the actual binding network competition if any of its Wickelphones has a strength of less than .2 after a preliminary run of the Wickelphone binding network described above. The remaining set of candidate responses were then considered as response alternatives in the whole-string binding network. The set of strings with a resulting strength of .2 or greater were taken to characterize the set of responses that might be generated from the pattern of activation over the Wickelfeatures.[4]

It should be emphasized that we are not proposing that some procedure such as this is actually used by human speakers to generate responses. Rather, we believe that some sort of sequential readout process is applied to read out a pattern of activation from the atemporal Wickelfeature representation, or perhaps from a Wickelphone representation such as that generated as the output of our Wickelphone binding network. The whole-string binding network is simply a way of assigning response strengths that approximate the strengths that we assume such a readout mechanism would assign.

We use the unconstrained response procedure just described because it is exceedingly computationally intensive for a serial computer. While it would actually occur quite quickly in a real hardware implementation of this highly parallel algorithm, it is simply too slow for practical purposes given the computers that are available today. If the unconstrained response procedure had been run on each presentation of a verb to the model throughout the course of training, the simulations would have taken over three years of computer time, rather than the 260 hours it took for the main learning experiment described below. We did, however, use this procedure in assessing the performance of the model on verbs it had not seen in training. The results of these tests are described in detail below.

Summary of the Structure of the Model

In summary, our model contains two sets of 460 Wickelfeature units, one set (the input units) to represent the base form of each verb and one set (the output units) to represent the past-tense form of each verb.

---

[4]The Wickelphone cutoff value of .2 was chosen to be liberal in allowing strings to enter the binding network competition without including excessive numbers of strings that had little chance of achieving a whole-string strength of .2 or greater.

The model is tested by typing in an input phoneme string which is translated by the fixed encoding network into a pattern of activation over the set of input units. Each active input unit contributes to the net input of each output unit by an amount and direction (positive or negative) determined by the weight on the connection between the input unit and the output unit. The output units are then turned on or off probabilistically, the probability increasing with the net input according to the logistic activation function. The output pattern generated in this way can be compared directly with the feature patterns corresponding to various alternative possible output patterns, such as the correct past-tense form or some other possible response of interest, using the whole-string binding network. Or the output pattern can be applied to the whole-string binding network to give response strengths associated either with a set of prespecified alternatives or with all possible response alternatives.

The model is trained by providing it with pairs of patterns consisting of the base pattern and the target (or correct) output. Thus, in accordance with common assumptions about the nature of the learning situation that faces the young child, the model receives only correct input from the outside world. However, it compares what it generates internally to the target output. When it gets the wrong answer for a particular output unit, it adjusts the strength of the connection between the input and the output units so as to reduce the probability that it would make the same mistake the next time the same input pattern is presented. The adjustment of connections is an extremely simple and *local* procedure, but it is sufficient to capture what we know about the acquisition of the past tense, as we shall see in the next section.

THE SIMULATIONS

The simulations described in this section are concerned with demonstrating three main points:

- That the model captures the basic three-stage pattern of acquisition.
- That the model captures most aspects of differences in performance on different types of regular and irregular verbs.
- That the model is capable of responding appropriately to verbs it has never seen before, as well as to regular and irregular verbs actually experienced during training.

In the sections that follow we will consider these three aspects of the model's performance in turn.

The corpus of verbs used in the simulations consisted of a set of 506 verbs. All verbs were chosen from the Kucera and Francis (1967) word list and were ordered according to frequency of their gerund form. We divided the verbs into three classes: 10 high-frequency verbs, 410 medium-frequency verbs, and 86 low-frequency verbs. The ten highest frequency verbs were *come* (/k^m/), *get* (/get/), *give* (/giv/), *look* (/luk/), *take* (/tAk/), *go* (/gO/), *have* (/hav/), *live* (/liv/), and *feel* (/fEl/). There is a total of 8 irregular and 2 regular verbs among the top 10. Of the medium-frequency verbs, 334 were regular and 76 were irregular. Of the low-frequency verbs, 72 were regular and 14 were irregular.

The Three-Stage Learning Curve

The results described in this and the following sections were obtained from a single (long) simulation run. The run was intended to capture approximately the experience with past tenses of a young child picking up English from everyday conversation. Our conception of the nature of this experience is simply that the child learns first about the present and past tenses of the highest frequency verbs; later on, learning occurs for a much larger ensemble of verbs, including a much larger proportion of regular forms.

Although the child would be hearing present and past tenses of all kinds of verbs throughout development, we assume that he or she is only able to learn past tenses for verbs already mastered fairly well in the present tense. This is because the real learning environment does not, in fact, present the child with present-tense/past-tense pairs. Rather, it presents the child with past-tense words in sentences occurring in real-world context. The child would therefore have to generate the appropriate present tense form internally with the aid of the entire sentence and context, and this, we suppose, requires that the child already know the present tense of the word. Just how the child comes to know such things is of course an interesting and central issue but is not the focus of the present investigation.

To simulate the earliest phase of past-tense learning, the model was first trained on the 10 high-frequency verbs, receiving 10 cycles of training presentations through the set of 10 verbs. This was enough to produce quite good performance on these verbs. We take the performance of the model at this point to correspond to the performance of a child in Phase 1 of acquisition. To simulate later phases of learning, the 410 medium-frequency verbs were added to the first 10 verbs, and the system was given 190 more learning trials with each trial consisting of one presentation of each of the 420 verbs. The responses of the model early on in this phase of training correspond to Phase 2 of the acquisition process; its ultimate performance at the end of 190 exposures to each of the 420 verbs corresponds to Phase 3. At this point, the model exhibits almost errorless performance on the basic 420 verbs. Finally, the set of 86 lower frequency verbs were presented to the system and the transfer responses to these were recorded. During this phase, connection strengths were not adjusted. Performance of the model on these transfer verbs is considered in a later section.

We do not claim, of course, that this training experience exactly captures the learning experience of the young child. It should be perfectly clear that this training experience exaggerates the difference between early and later phases of learning as well as the abruptness of the transition to a larger corpus of verbs. However, it is generally observed that the early, rather limited vocabulary of young children undergoes an explosive growth at some point in development (Brown, 1973). Thus, the actual transition in a child's vocabulary of verbs would appear quite abrupt on a time-scale of years so that our assumptions about abruptness of onset may not be far off the mark.

Figure 4 shows the basic results for the high frequency verbs. What we see is that during the first 10 trials there is no difference between regular and irregular verbs. However, beginning on Trial 11 when the 410 midfrequency verbs were introduced, the regular verbs show better performance. It is important to notice that there is no interfering effect on the regular verbs as the midfrequency verbs are being learned. There is, however, substantial interference on the irregular verbs. This interference leads to a dip in performance on the irregular verbs. Equality of performance between regular and irregular verbs is never again attained during the training period. This is the so-called U-shaped learning curve for the learning of the irregular past tense. Performance is high when only a few high-frequency, largely irregular verbs are learned, but then performance drops as the bulk of lower frequency regular verbs are learned.

We have thus far shown only that performance on high-frequency irregular verbs drops; we have said nothing about the nature of the errors. To examine this question the response strength of various, possible response alternatives must be

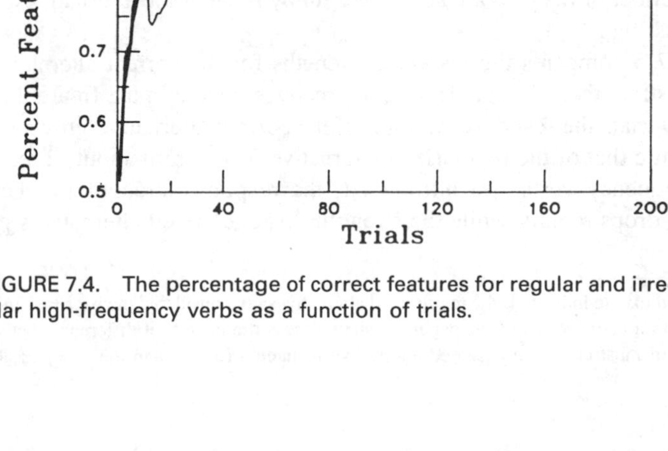

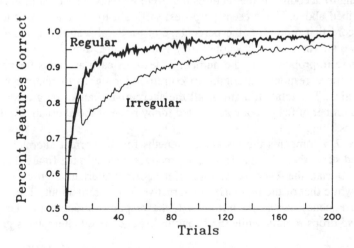

FIGURE 7.4. The percentage of correct features for regular and irregular high-frequency verbs as a function of trials.

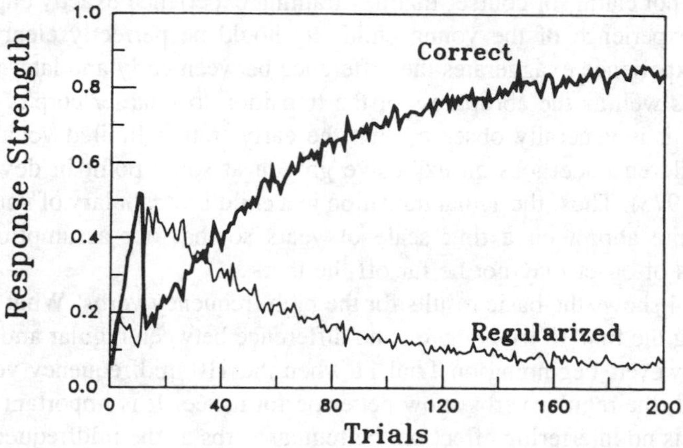

FIGURE 7.5. Response strengths for the high-frequency irregular verbs. The response strengths for the correct responses are compared with those for the regularized alternatives as a function of trials.

compared. To do this, we compared the strength of response for several different response alternatives. We compared strengths for the correct past tense, the present, the base+ed and the past+ed. Thus, for example with the verb *give* we compared the response strength of /gAv/, /giv/, /givd/, and /gAvd/. We determined the response strengths by assuming that these response alternatives were competing to account for the features that were actually turned on in the output, as described above. For present purposes, suffice it to say that each alternative gets a score that represents the percentage of the total features that it accounts for. If two alternatives both account for a given feature, they divide the score for that feature in proportion to the number of features each accounts for uniquely. We take these response strengths to correspond roughly to relative response probabilities. The total strength of all the alternatives cannot be greater than 1, and if a number of features are accounted for by none of the alternatives, the total will be less than 1.

Figure 7.5 compares the response strengths for the correct alternative to the combined strength of the regularized alternatives.[5] Note in the figure that during the first 10 trials the response strength of the correct alternative grows rapidly to over .5 while that of the regularized alternative drops from about .2 to .1. After the midfrequency verbs are introduced, the response strength for the correct alternative drops rapidly while the strengths of regularized alternatives jump up.

---

[5]Unless otherwise indicated, the regularized alternatives are considered the base+ed and past+ed alternatives. In a later section of the paper we shall discuss the pattern of differences between these alternatives. In most cases the base+ed alternative is much stronger than the past+ed alternative.

From about Trials 11 through 30, the regularized alternatives together are stronger than the correct response. After about Trial 30, the strength of the correct response again exceeds the regularized alternatives and continues to grow throughout the 200-trial learning phase. By the end, the correct response is much the strongest with all other alternatives below .1.

The rapidity of the growth of the regularized alternatives is due to the sudden influx of the medium-frequency verbs. In real life we would expect the medium-frequency verbs to come in somewhat more slowly so that the period of maximal regularization would have a somewhat slower onset.

Figure 7.6 shows the same data in a slightly different way. In this case, we have plotted the ratio of the correct response to the sum of the correct and regularized response strengths. Points on the curve below the .5 line are in the region where the regularized response is greater that the correct response. Here we see clearly the three stages. In the first stage, the first 10 trials of learning, performance on these high-frequency verbs is quite good. Virtually no regularization takes place. During the next 20 trials, the system regularizes and systematically makes errors on the verbs that it previously responded to correctly. Finally, during the remaining trials the model slowly eliminates the regularization responses as it approaches adult performance.

In summary, then, the model captures the three phases of learning quite well, as well as the gradual transition from Phase 2 to Phase 3. It does so without any explicit learning of rules. The regularization is the product of the gradual tuning

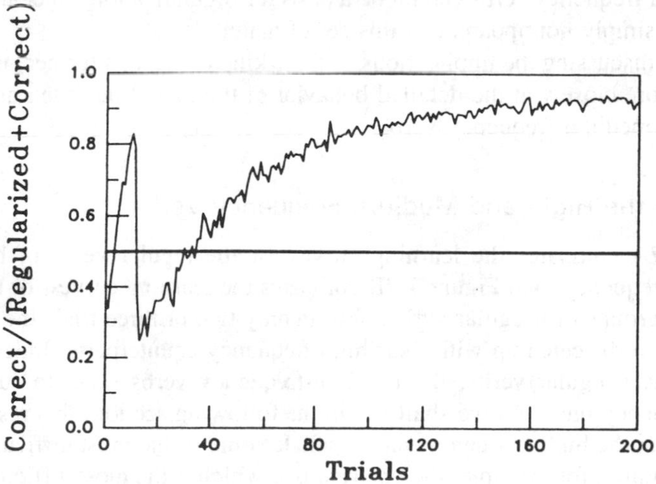

FIGURE 7.6. The ratio of the correct response to the sum of the correct and regularized response. Points on the curve below the .5 line are in the region where the regularized response is greater than the correct response.

of connection strengths in response to the predominantly regular correspondence exhibited by the medium-frequency words. It is not quite right to say that individual pairs are being stored in the network in any simple sense. The connection strengths the model builds up to handle the irregular forms do not represent these items in any separable way: they represent them in the way they must be represented to be stored along with the other verbs in the same set of connections.

Before turning to a detailed discussion of the patterns of errors made by the model, a brief consideration of the relation between our account of the three-stage acquisition process and other accounts may be in order. First of all, it can be seen that the performance of the model in Phase 1 essentially amounts to "rote" learning. In Phase 2 it appears heavily rule-based, and in later phases its performance amounts to what might be described as a blend of rule-based, analogy-based, and rote-based. MacWhinney (1982) has proposed just these three processes. Here, however, we see that a single, homogeneous learning mechanism is all of these different forms of learning.

There is one aspect of our acquisition scenario that might be quibbled with. This is our assumption that even in the earliest phase, the child is learning to associate the present and past tense forms of each word. Another possibility is simply that at this stage the high-frequency past tense words are treated as separate items, totally divorced from their base forms. We do not wish to claim that this kind of thing does not occur at all; we simply observe that the assumptions we have made provide an alternative account of this early phase of the learning process. The model captures the simple fact that learning based only on the highest frequency verbs cannot be a basis for regularization, since the regular pattern is simply not apparent in this set of materials.

Before discussing the implications of these kinds of results further, it is useful to look more closely at the detailed behavior of the model, as it learns both the high- and medium-frequency verbs.

Learning the High- and Medium-Frequency Verbs

Figure 7.7A compares the learning curves for the regular verbs of high- and medium-frequency, and Figure 7.7B compares the learning curves for the corresponding groups of irregular verbs. Within only two or three trials the medium-frequency verbs catch up with their high-frequency counterparts. Indeed, in the case of the irregular verbs, the medium-frequency verbs seem to surpass the high-frequency ones. As we shall see in the following section, this results from the fact that the high-frequency verbs include some of the most difficult pairs to learn including, for example, the *go/went* pair which is the most difficult to learn (aside from the verb *be,* this is the only verb in English in which the past and root form are completely unrelated). It should also be noted that even at this early stage of learning there is substantial generalization. Already on Trial 11, the very first exposure to the medium-frequency verbs, between 65 and 75 percent of the

(A)

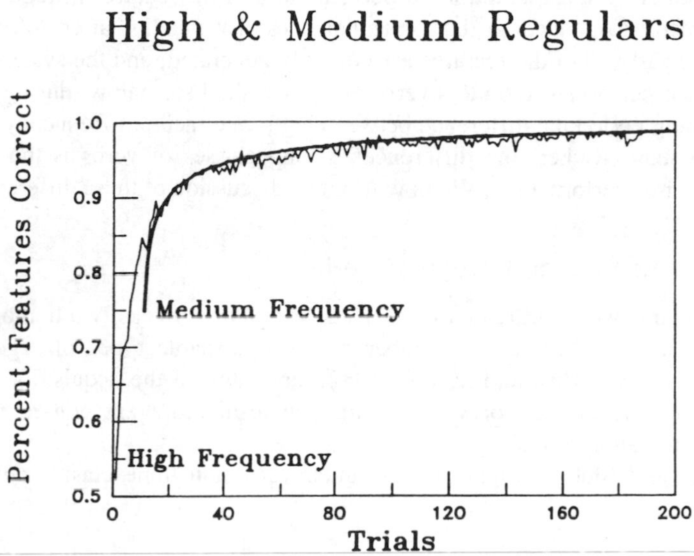

(B)

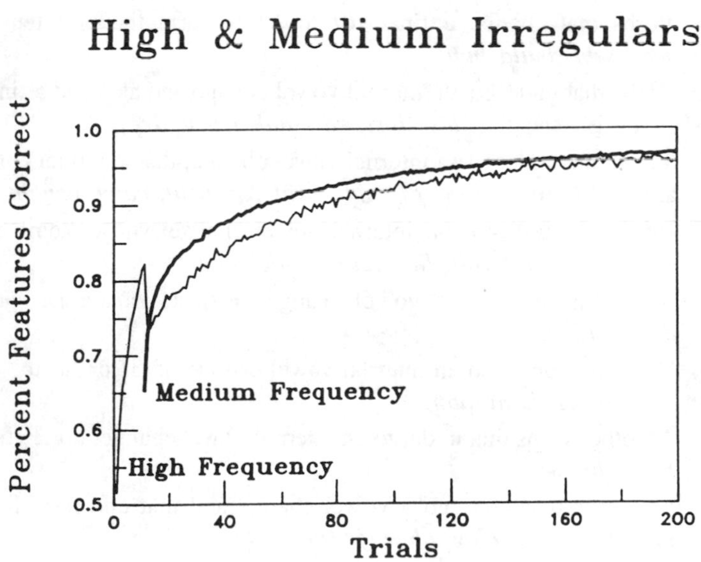

FIGURE 7.7. The learning curves for the high- and medium-frequency verbs.

features are produced correctly. Chance responding is only 50 percent. Moreover, on their first presentation 10 percent more of the features of regular verbs are correctly responded to than irregular ones. Eventually, after 200 trials of learning nearly all of the features are correctly generated, and the system is near asymptotic performance on this verb set. As we shall see below, during most of the learning period the difference between high- and medium-frequency verbs is not important. Rather, the differences among classes of verbs is the primary determiner of performance. We now turn to a discussion of these different types.

Types of Regular and Irregular Verbs

To this point, we have treated regular and irregular verbs as two homogeneous classes. In fact, there are a number of distinguishable types of regular and irregular verbs. Bybee and Slobin (1982) have studied the acquisition of each type of verb. In this section we compare their results to the responses produced by our simulation model.

Bybee and Slobin divided the irregular verbs into nine classes defined as follows:[6]

- I. Verbs that do not change at all to form the past tense, e.g., *beat, cut, hit*.
- II. Verbs that change a final /d/ to /t/ to form the past tense, e.g., *send/sent, build/built.*
- III. Verbs that undergo an internal vowel change and also add a final /t/ or /d/, e.g., *feel/felt, lose/lost, say/said, tell/told.*
- IV. Verbs that undergo an internal vowel change, delete a final consonant, and add a final /t/ or /d/, e.g., *bring/brought, catch/caught.*[7]
- V. Verbs that undergo an internal vowel change whose stems end in a dental, e.g., *bite/bit, find/found, ride/rode.*
- VIa. Verbs that undergo a vowel change of /i/ to /a/, e.g., *sing/sang, drink/drank.*
- VIb. Verbs that undergo an internal vowel change of /i/ or /a/ to /^/, e.g., *sting/stung, hang/hung.*[8]
- VII. All other verbs that undergo an internal vowel change, e.g., *give/gave, break/broke.*
- VIII. All verbs that undergo a vowel change and that end in a dipthongal sequence, e.g., *blow/blew, fly/flew.*

---

[6]Criteria from Bybee and Slobin, 1982, pp. 268–269.

[7]Following Bybee and Slobin, we included *buy/bought* in this class even though no final consonant is deleted.

[8]For many purposes we combine Classes VIa and VIb in our analyses.

A complete listing by type of all of the irregular verbs used in our study is given in Table 7.

In addition to these types of irregular verbs, we distinguished three categories of regular verbs: (a) those ending in a vowel or voiced consonant, which take a /d/ to form the past tense, (b) those ending in a voiceless consonant, which take a /t/, and (c) those ending in /t/ or /d/, which take a final /ˆd/ to form the past tense. The number of regular verbs in each category, for each of the three frequency levels, is given in Table 8.

Type I: No-change verbs. A small set of English verbs requires no change between their present- and past-tense forms. One factor common to all such verbs is that they already end in /t/ or /d/. Thus, they superficially have the regular past-tense form—even in the present tense. Stemberger (1981) and Menn and MacWhinney (1984) point out that it is common in inflectional languages not to add an additional inflection to base forms that already appear to have the inflection. Not all verbs ending in /t/ or /d/ show no change between present and past (in fact the majority of such verbs in English do show a change between

TABLE 7
Irregular Verbs

Type	Frequency: High	Medium	Low
I		beat fit set spread hit cut put	thrust bid
II		build send spend	bend lend
III	feel	deal do flee tell sell hear keep leave sleep lose mean say sweep	creep weep
IV	have make	think buy bring seek teach	catch
V	get	meet shoot write lead understand sit mislead bleed feed stand light find fight read meet hide hold ride	breed wind grind
VIa		drink ring sing swim	
VIb		drag hang swing	dig cling stick
VII	give take come	shake arise rise run become bear wear speak brake drive strike fall freeze choose	tear
VIII	go	throw blow grow draw fly know see	

TABLE 8
Number of Regular Verbs of Each Type

Type	Suffix	Example	Frequency High	Medium	Low
End in dental	/^d/	start	0	94	13
End in voiceless consonant	/t/	look	1	64	30
End in voiced consonant or vowel	/d/	move	1	176	29

present and past tense), but there is a reasonably large group—the Type I verbs of Bybee and Slobin—that do show this trend. Bybee and Slobin (1982) suggest that children learn relatively early on that past-tense verbs in English tend to end in /t/ or /d/ and thus are able to correctly respond to the no-change verbs rather early. Early in learning, they suggest, children also incorrectly generalize this "no-change rule" to verbs whose present and past tenses differ.

The pattern of performance just described shows up very clearly in data Bybee and Slobin (1982) report from an elicitation task with preschool children. In this task, preschoolers were given the present-tense form of each of several verbs and were asked to produce the corresponding past-tense form. They used the set of 33 verbs shown in Table 9.

The results were very interesting. Bybee and Slobin found that verbs not ending in *t/d* were predominately regularized and verbs ending in *t/d* were predominately used as no-change verbs. The number of occurrences of each kind is shown in Table 10. These preschool children have, at this stage, both learned to regularize verbs not ending in *t/d* and, largely, to leave verbs ending in *t/d* without an additional ending.

Interestingly, our simulations show the same pattern of results. The system learns to regularize and has a propensity *not* to add an additional ending to verbs already ending in *t/d*. In order to compare the simulation results to the human data we looked at the performance of the same verbs used by Bybee and Slobin in our simulations. Of the 33 verbs, 27 were in the high- and medium-frequency

TABLE 9
Verbs Used by Bybee & Slobin

Type of Verb	Verb List
Regular	walk smoke melt pat smile climb
Vowel change	drink break run swim throw meet shoot ride
Vowel change + *t/d*	do buy lose sell sleep help teach catch
No change	hit hurt set shut cut put beat
Other	go make build lend

TABLE 10
Regular and No Change Responses
to *t/d* and other Verbs
(Data from Bybee & Slobin, 1982)

Verb Ending	*Regular Suffix*	*No Change*
Not *t/d*	203	34
t/d	42	157

lists and thus were included in the training set used in the simulation. The other six verbs (*smoke, catch, lend, pat, hurt,* and *shut*) were either in the low frequency sample or did not appear in our sample at all. Therefore, we will report on 27 out of the 33 verbs that Bybee and Slobin tested.

It is not clear what span of learning trials in our simulation corresponds best to the level of the preschoolers in Bybee and Slobin's experiment. Presumably the period during which regularization is occurring is best. The combined strength of the regularized alternatives exceeds correct response strength for irregulars from about Trial 11 through Trials 20 to 30 depending on which particular irregular verbs we look at. We therefore have tabulated our results over three different time ranges—Trials 11 through 15, Trials 16 through 20, and Trials 21 through 30. In each case we calculated the average strength of the regularized response alternatives and of the no-change response alternatives. Table 11 gives these strengths for each of the different time periods.

The simulation results show clearly the same patterns evident in the Bybee and Slobin data. Verbs ending in *t/d* always show a stronger no-change response and a weaker regularized response than those not ending in *t/d*. During the very early stages of learning, however, the regularized response is stronger than the no-change response—even if the verb does end with *t/d*. This suggests that the generalization that the past tense of *t/d* verbs is formed by adding /^d/ is stronger than the generalization that verbs ending in *t/d* should not have an ending added.

TABLE 11
Average Simulated Strengths of Regularized and
No-Change Responses

Time Period	*Verb Ending*	*Regularized*	*No Change*
11-15	not *t/d*	0.44	0.10
	t/d	0.35	0.27
16-20	not *t/d*	0.32	0.12
	t/d	0.25	0.35
21-30	not *t/d*	0.52	0.11
	t/d	0.32	0.41

However, as learning proceeds, this secondary generalization is made (though for only a subset of the *t/d* verbs, as we shall see), and the simulation shows the same interaction that Bybee and Slobin (1982) found in their preschoolers.

The data and the simulations results just described conflate two aspects of performance, namely, the tendency to make no-change *errors* with *t/d* verbs that are not no-change verbs and the tendency to make *correct* no-change responses to the *t/d* verbs that are no-change verbs. Though Bybee and Slobin did not report their data broken down by this factor, we can examine the results of the simulation to see whether in fact the model is making more no-change errors with *t/d* verbs for which this response is incorrect. To examine this issue, we return to the full corpus of verbs and consider the tendency to make no-change errors separately for irregular verbs other than Type I verbs and for regular verbs.

Erroneous no-change responses are clearly stronger for both regular and irregular *t/d* verbs. Figure 7.8A compares the strength of the erroneous no-change responses for irregular verbs ending in *t/d* (Types II and V) versus those not ending in *t/d* (Types III, IV, VI, VII, and VIII). The no-change response is erroneous in all of these cases. Note, however, that the erroneous no-change responses are stronger for the *t/d* verbs than for the other types of irregular verbs. Figure 7.8B shows the strength of erroneous no-change responses for regular verbs ending in *t/d* versus those not ending in *t/d*. Again, the response strength for the no-change response is clearly greater when the regular verb ends in a dental.

We also compared the regularization responses for irregular verbs whose stems end in *t/d* with irregulars not ending in *t/d*. The results are shown in Figure 7.8C. In this case, the regularization responses are initially stronger for verbs that do not end in *t/d* than for those that do. Thus, we see that even when focusing only on erroneous responses, the system shows a greater propensity to respond with no change to *t/d* verbs, whether or not the verb is regular, and a somewhat greater tendency to regularize irregulars not ending in *t/d*.

There is some evidence in the literature on language acquisition that performance on Type I verbs is better at an earlier stage than for irregular verbs involving vowel changes—Types III thorough VIII. Kuczaj (1978) reports an experiment in which children were to judge the grammaticality of sentences involving past tenses. The children were given sentences involving words like *hit* or *hitted* or *ate* or *eated* and asked whether the sentences sounded "silly." The results (averaged over three age groups from 3;4 to 9;0 years) showed that 70 percent of the responses to the no-change verbs were correct whereas only 31 percent of the responses' to vowel-change irregular verbs were correct. Most of the errors involved incorrect acceptance of a regularized form. Thus, the results show a clear difference between the verb types, with performance on the Type I verbs superior to that on Type III through VIII verbs.

The simulation model also shows better performance on Type I verbs than on any of the other types. These verbs show fewer errors than any of the other irregular verbs. Indeed the error rate on Type I verbs is equal to that on the most

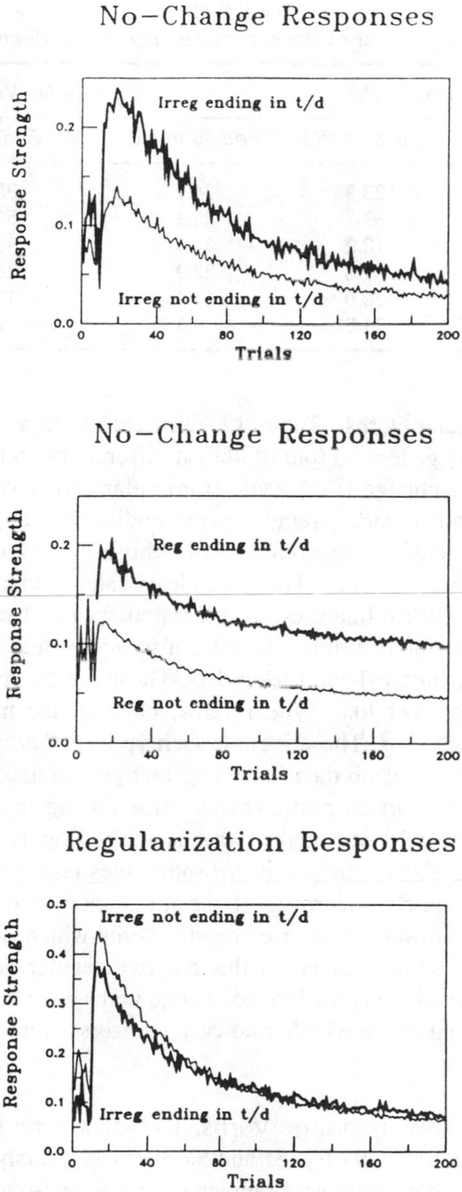

FIGURE 7.8. *A:* The strength of erroneous no-change responses for irregular verbs ending in a dental versus those not ending in a dental. *B:* The strength of erroneous no-change responses for regular verbs ending in a dental versus those not ending in a dental. *C:* The strength of erroneous regularization responses for irregular verbs ending in a dental versus those not ending in a dental.

TABLE 12
Average Number of Wickelfeatures Incorrectly Generated

Trial Number	*Irregular Verbs*		*Regular Verbs*		
	Type I	*Types III-VIII*	*Ending in* t/d	*Not Ending in* t/d	CVt/d
11-15	89.8	123.9	74.1	82.8	87.3
16-20	57.6	93.7	45.3	51.2	60.5
21-30	45.5	78.2	32.9	37.4	47.9
31-50	34.4	61.3	22.9	26.0	37.3
51-100	18.8	39.0	11.4	12.9	21.5
101-200	11.8	21.5	6.4	7.4	12.7

difficult of the regular verbs. Table 12 gives the average number of Wickelfeatures incorrectly generated (out of 460) at different periods during the learning processes for no-change (i.e., Type I) irregular verbs, vowel-change (i.e., Type III-VIII) irregular verbs, regular verbs ending in *t/d,* regular verbs not ending in *t/d,* and regular verbs ending in *t/d* whose stem is a CVC (consonant-vowel-consonant) monosyllable. The table clearly shows that throughout learning, fewer incorrect Wickelfeatures are generated for no-change verbs than for vowel-change verbs. Interestingly, the table also shows that one subset of regulars are no easier than the Type I irregulars. These are the regular verbs which look on the surface most like Type I verbs, namely, the monosyllabic CVC regular verbs ending in *t/d*. These include such verbs as *bat, wait, shout, head,* etc. Although we know of no data indicating that people make more no-change errors on these verbs than on multisyllabic verbs ending in *t/d,* this is a clear prediction of our model. Essentially what is happening is that the model is learning that monosyllables ending in *t/d* sometimes take no additional inflection. This leads to quicker learning of the no-change verbs relative to other irregular verbs and slower learning of regular verbs which otherwise look like no-change verbs. It should be noted that the two regular verbs employed by Bybee and Slobin which behaved like no-change verbs were both monosyllables. It would be interesting to see whether no-change errors actually occur with verbs like *decide* or *devote.*[9]

Types III-VIII: **Vowel-change verbs.** To look at error patterns on *vowel-change* verbs (Types III-VIII) Bybee and Slobin (1982) analyzed data from the spontaneous speech of preschoolers ranging from one-and-one-half to five years of age. The data came from independent sets of data collected by Susan Ervin-

---

[9]Though the model does not explicitly encode number of syllables, monosyllabic words are distinguished from multisyllabic words by the fact that the former contain no Wickelphones of the form $_{V}C_{V}$. There are no no-change verbs in English containing such Wickelphones.

TABLE 13
Percentage of Regularization by Preschoolers
(Data from Bybee & Slobin, 1982)

Verb Type	*Example*	*Percentage Regularizations*
VIII	blew	80
VI	sang	55
V	bit	34
VII	broke	32
III	felt	13
IV	caught	10

Tripp and Wick Miller, by Dan Slobin, and by Zell Greenberg. In all, speech from 31 children involving the use of 69 irregular verbs was studied. Bybee and Slobin recorded the percentages of regularizations for each of the various types of vowel-change verbs. Table 13 gives the percentages of regularization by preschoolers ranked from most to fewest erroneous regularizations. The results show that the two verb types which involve adding a *t/d* plus a vowel change (Types III and IV) show the least regularizations, whereas the verb type in which the present tense ends in a diphthong (Type VIII) shows by far the most regularization.

It is not entirely clear what statistic in our model best corresponds to the percentage of regularizations. It will be recalled that we collected response strength measures for four different response types for irregular verbs. These were the correct response, the no-change response, the base+ed regularization response, and the past+ed regularization response. If we imagine that no-change responses are, in general, difficult to observe in spontaneous speech, perhaps the measure that would be most closely related to the percentage of regularizations would be the ratio of the sum of the strengths of the regularization responses to the sum of the strengths of regularization responses and the correct response—that is,

$$\frac{(base + ed + past + ed)}{(base + ed + past + ed + correct)}$$

As with our previous simulation, it is not entirely clear what portion of the learning curve corresponds to the developmental level of the children in this group. We therefore calculated this ratio for several different time periods around the period of maximal overgeneralization. Table 14 shows the results of these simulations.

The spread between different verb classes is not as great in the simulation as in the children's data, but the simulated rank orders show a remarkable similarity

TABLE 14
Strength of Regularization Responses Relative to Correct Responses

Rank	Data		Trials 11-15		Trials 16-20		Trials 21-30		Average Trials 11-30	
Order	Type	Percent	Type	Ratio	Type	Ratio	Type	Ratio	Type	Ratio
1	VIII	80	VIII	.86	VIII	.76	VIII	.61	VIII	.71
2	VI	55	VII	.80	VII	.74	VII	.61	VII	.69
3	V	34	VI	.76	V	.60	IV	.48	V	.56
4	VII	32	V	.72	IV	.59	V	.46	IV	.56
5	III	13	IV	.69	III	.57	III	.44	III	.53
6	IV	10	III	.67	VI	.52	VI	.40	VI	.52

to the results from the spontaneous speech of the preschoolers, especially in the earliest time period. Type VIII verbs show uniformly strong patterns of regularization whereas Type III and Type IV verbs, those whose past tense involves adding a *t/d* at the end, show relatively weak regularization responses. Type VI and Type VII verbs produce somewhat disparate results. For Type VI verbs, the simulation conforms fairly closely to the children's speech data in the earliest time period, but it shows rather less strength for regularizations of these verbs in the later time periods and in the average over Trials 11-30. For Type VII verbs, the model errs in the opposite direction: here it tends to show rather greater strength for regularizations of these verbs than we see in the children's speech. One possible reason for these discrepancies may be the model's insensitivity to word frequency. Type VI verbs are, in fact, relatively low-frequency verbs, and thus in the children's speech these verbs may actually be at a relatively earlier stage in acquisition than some of the more frequent irregular verbs. Type VII verbs are, in general, much more frequent—in fact, on the average they occur more than twice as often (in the gerund form) in the Kucera-Francis count than the Type VI verbs. In our simulations, all medium-frequency verbs were presented equally often and the distinction was not made. A higher fidelity simulation including finer gradations of frequency variations among the verb types might lead to a closer correspondence with the empirical results. In any case, these verbs aside, the simulation seems to capture the major features of the data very nicely.

Bybee and Slobin attribute the pattern of results they found to factors that would not be relevant to our model. They proposed, for example, that Type III and IV verbs were more easily learned because the final *t/d* signaled to the child that they were in fact past tenses so the child would not have to rely on context as much in order to determine that these were past-tense forms. In our simulations, we found these verbs to be easy to learn, but it must have been for a different reason since the learning system was always informed as to what the correct past tense really was. Similarly, Bybee and Slobin argued that Type VIII verbs were the most difficult because the past and present tenses were so phonologically different that the child could not easily determine that the past and present tenses of these verbs actually go together. Again, our simulation showed Type VIII verbs to be the most difficult, but this had nothing to do with putting the past and present tense together since the model was always given the present and past tenses together.

Our model, then, must offer a different interpretation of Bybee and Slobin's findings. The main factor appears to be the degree to which the relation between the present and past tense of the verb is idiosyncratic. Type VIII verbs are most difficult because the relationship between base form and past tense is most idiosyncratic for these verbs. Thus, the natural generalizations implicit in the population of verbs must be overcome for these verbs, and they must be overcome in a different way for each of them. A very basic aspect of the mapping from present to past tense is that most of the word, and in particular everything up to the final vowel, is unchanged. For regular verbs, all of the phonemes present in the base form are preserved in the past tense. Thus, verbs that make changes to the base form are going against the grain more than those that do not; the larger the changes, the harder they will be to learn. Another factor is that past tenses of verbs generally end in /t/ or /d/.

Verbs that violate the basic past-tense pattern are all at a disadvantage in the model, of course, but some suffer less than others because there are other verbs that deviate from the basic pattern in the same way. Thus, these verbs are less idiosyncratic than verbs such as *go/went, see/saw,* and *draw/drew* which represent completely idiosyncratic vowel changes. The difficulty with Type VIII verbs, then, is simply that, as a class, they are simply more idiosyncratic than other verbs. Type III and IV verbs (e.g., *feel/felt, catch/caught*), on the other hand, share with the vast bulk of the verbs in English the feature that the past tense involves the addition of a *t/d*. The addition of the *t/d* makes these verbs easier than, say, Type VII verbs (e.g., *come/came*) because in Type VII verbs the system must not only learn that there is a vowel change, but it must also learn that there *is not* an addition of *t/d* to the end of the verb.

Type VI verbs (*sing/sang, drag/drug*) are interesting from this point of view, because they involve fairly common subregularities not found in other classes of verbs such as those in Type V. In the model, the Type VI verbs may be learned relatively quickly because of this subregularity.

Types of regularization. We have mentioned that there are two distinct ways in which a child can regularize an irregular verb: the child can use the base+ed form or the past+ed form. Kuczaj (1977) has provided evidence that the proportion of past+ed forms increases relative to the number of base+ed forms as the child gets older. He found, for example, that the nine youngest children he studied had more base+ed regularizations than past+ed regularizations whereas four out of the five oldest children showed more past+ed than bas+ed regularizations. In this section, we consider whether our model exhibits this same general pattern. Since the base form and the past-tense form are identical for Type I verbs, we restrict our analysis of this issue to Types II through VIII.

Figure 7.9 compares the average response strengths for base+ed and past+ed regularizations as a function of amount of training. The results of this analysis are more or less consistent with Kuczaj's findings. Early in learning, the base +ed response alternative is clearly the stronger of the two. As the system learns, however, the two come together so that after about 100 trials the base+ed and the past+ed response alternatives are roughly equal. Clearly, the simulations show that the percentage of regularizations that are past+ed increases with experience, just as Kuczaj found in children. In addition, the two curves come together rather late, consistent with the report by Kuczaj (1977) that these past+ed forms predominate for the most part in children who are exhibiting rather few regularization errors of either type. Of the four children exhibiting more past+ed regularizations, three were regularizing less than 12% of the time.

A closer look at the various types of irregular verbs shows that this curve is the average of two quite different patterns. Table 15 shows the overall percentage of regularization strength due to the base+ed alternative. It is clear from the table that the verbs fall into two general categories, those of Types III, IV, and VIII which have an overall preponderance of base+ed strength (the percentages are all above .5) and Types II, V, VI and VII which show an overall preponderance of past+ed strength (the percentages are all well below .5). The major variable which seems to account for the ordering shown in the table is the amount the ending is changed in going from the base form to the past-tense form. If the

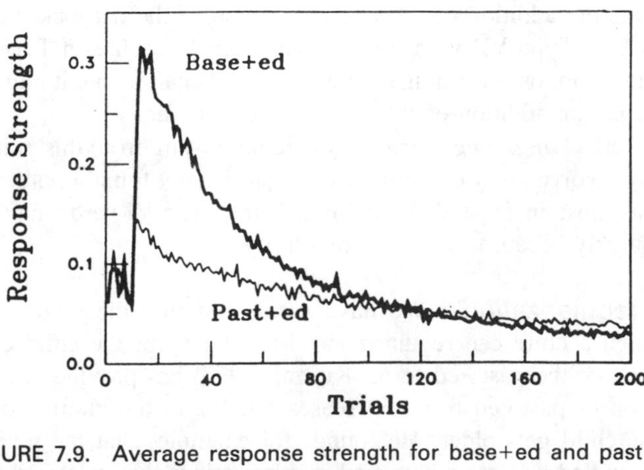

FIGURE 7.9. Average response strength for base+ed and past+ed responses for verb Types II through VIII.

TABLE 15
Percentage of Regularization Strength
Due to Base+ed

Verb Type	*Percent base+ed*	*Examples*
III	0.77	sleep/slept
IV	0.69	catch/caught
VIII	0.68	see/saw
II	0.38	spend/spent
VII	0.38	come/came
V	0.37	bite/bit
VI	0.26	sing/sang

ending is changed little, as in *sing/sang* or *come/came*, the past+ed response is relatively stronger. If the past tense involves a greater change of the ending, such as *see/saw*, or *sleep/slept*, then the past+ed form is much weaker. Roughly, the idea is that to form the past+ed for these verbs *two operations* must occur. The normal past tense must be created, and the regular ending must be added. When these two operations involve very different parts of the verb, they can occur somewhat independently and both can readily occur. When, on the other hand, both changes occur to the same portion of the verb, they conflict with one another and a clear past+ed response is difficult to generate. The Type II verbs, which do show an overall preponderance of past+ed regularization strength, might seem to violate this pattern since it involves some change to the end in its past-tense form. Note, however, that the change is only a one feature change from /d/ to /t/ and thus is closer to the pattern of the verbs involving no change to the final phonemes of the verb. Figure 7.10A shows the pattern of response strengths to be base+ed and past+ed regularizations for verb Types II, V, VI, and VII which involve relatively little change of the final phonemes from base to past form. Figure 7.10B shows the pattern of response strengths to base+ed and past+ed for verb Types III, IV, and VIII. Figure 7.10A shows very clearly the pattern expected from Kuczaj's results. Early in learning, base+ed responses are by far the strongest. With experience the past+ed response becomes stronger and stronger relative to the base+ed regularizations until, at about Trial 40, the past+ed response begins to exceed the base+ed regularization. Figure 7.10B shows a different pattern. For these verbs the past+ed form is weak throughout learning and never comes close to the base+ed regularization response. Unfortunately, Kuczaj did not present data on the relative frequency of the two types of regularizations separately for different verb types. Thus for the present, this difference in type of regularization responses remains an untested prediction of the model.

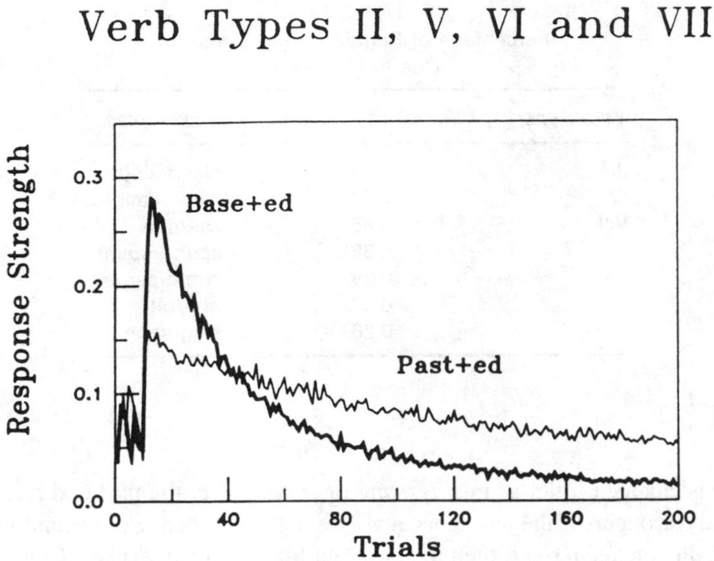

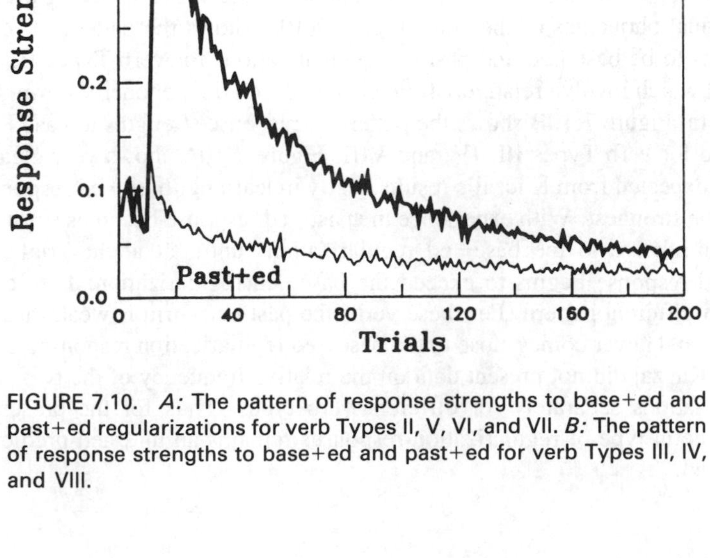

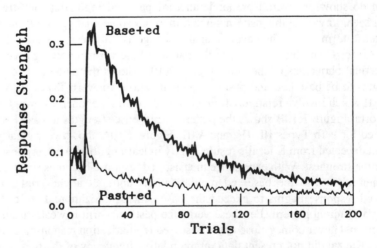

FIGURE 7.10. *A:* The pattern of response strengths to base+ed and past+ed regularizations for verb Types II, V, VI, and VII. *B:* The pattern of response strengths to base+ed and past+ed for verb Types III, IV, and VIII.

Transfer to Novel Verbs

To this point we have only reported on the behavior of the system on verbs that it was actually taught. In this section, we consider the response of the model to the set of 86 low-frequency verbs which it never saw during training. This test allows us to examine how well the behavior of the model generalizes to novel verbs. In this section we also consider responses to different types of regular verbs, and we examine the model's performance in generating unconstrained responses.

Overall degree of transfer. Perhaps the first question to ask is how accurately the model generates the correct features of the new verbs. Table 16 shows the percentage of Wickelfeatures correctly generated, averaged over the regular and irregular verbs. Overall, the performance is quite good. Over 90 percent of the Wickelfeatures are correctly generated without any experience whatsoever with these verbs. Performance is, of course, poorer on the irregular verbs, in which the actual past tense is relatively idiosyncratic. But even there, almost 85 percent of the Wickelfeatures are correctly generated.

The results from the free-generation test are quite consistent with our expectations from the constrained alternative phase, though they did uncover a few interesting aspects of the model's performance that we had not anticipated. In our analysis of these results we have considered only responses with a strength of at least .2. Of the 86 test verbs, there were 65 cases in which exactly one of the alternatives exceeded .2. Of these, 55 were simple regularization responses, four were no-change responses, three involved double marking of regular verbs, (e.g., *type* was responded to with /tIpt^d/), and there was one case of a vowel change (e.g., *slip/slept*). There were 14 cases in which two alternatives exceeded threshold and one case in which three exceeded threshold. Finally, in six cases, no response alternative exceeded threshold. This occurred with the regular verbs *jump, pump, soak, warm, trail,* and *glare*. In this case there were a number of alternatives, including the correct past-tense form of each of these verbs, competing with a response strength of about .1. Table 17 shows the responses generated for the 14 irregular verbs; the responses are very clear. All of the above-threshold responses made to an irregular verb were either regularization responses, no-change responses (to Type I and V verbs as expected), or correct

TABLE 16
Proportion of Wickelfeatures
Correctly Generated

Regular	.92
Irregular	.84
Overall	.91

TABLE 17
The Model's Responses to Unfamiliar, Low-Frequency, Irregular Verbs

Verb Type	*Presented Word*	*Phonetic Input*	*Phonetic Response*	*English Rendition*	*Response Strength*
I	bid	/bid/	/bid/	(bid)	0.55
	thrust	/Tr^st/	/Tr^st^d/	(thrusted)	0.57
II	bend	/bend/	/bend^d/	(bended)	0.28
	lend	/lend/	lend^d/	(lended)	0.70
III	creep	/krEp/	/krEpt/	(creeped)	0.51
	weep	/wEp/	/wEpt/	(weeped)	0.34
			/wept/	(wept)	0.33
IV	catch	/kaC/	/kaCt/	(catched)	0.67
V	breed	/brEd/	/brEd^d/	(breeded)	0.48
	grind	/grInd/	/grInd/	(grind)	0.44
	wind	/wInd/	/wInd/	(wind)	0.37
VI	cling	/kliN/	/kliNd/	(clinged)	0.28
			/kl^N/	(clung)	0.23
	dig	/dig/	/digd/	(digged)	0.22
	stick	/stik/	/stikt/	(sticked)	0.53
VII	tear	/ter/	/terd/	(teared)	0.90

vowel-change generalizations. The fact that *bid* is correctly generated as the past for *bid,* that *wept* is correctly generated as the past for *weep,* and that *clung* is correctly generated as a past tense for *cling* illustrates that the system is not only sensitive to the major, regular past-tense pattern but is sensitive to the subregularities as well. It should also be noted that the no-change responses to the verbs *grind* and *wind* occurs on monosyllabic Type V verbs ending in *t/d* again showing evidence of a role for this subregularity in English past-tense formation.

Of the 72 regular verbs in our low-frequency sample, the six verbs mentioned above did not have any response alternatives above threshold. On 48 of the remaining 66 regular verbs, the only response exceeding threshold was the correct one. The threshold responses to the remaining 18 verbs are shown in Table 18.

Note that for 12 of the 18 verbs listed in the table, the correct response is above threshold. That means that of the 66 regular verbs to which any response at all exceeded threshold the correct response exceeded threshold in 60 cases. It is interesting to note, also, that the model never chooses the incorrect variant of the regular past tense. As shown in Table 8, verbs ending in a /t/ or /d/ take /^d/ in the past tense; verbs ending in unvoiced consonants take /t/, and verbs ending in vowels or voiced consonants take /d/. On no occasion does the model assign a strength greater than .2 to an incorrect variant of the past tense. Thus, the model has clearly learned the substructure of the regular correspondence and adds the correct variant to all different types of base forms. These results clearly demonstrate that the model acts in accordance with the regular pattern for English verbs and that it can apply this pattern with a high level of success to novel as well as familiar verbs.

In addition to the regular responses, five of the responses were no-change responses. In three cases the no-change response was to a verb ending in *t/d*. Four of the responses followed the pattern of Type III verbs, modifying the vowel and adding a final /t/. Thus, for example, we have the past of *sip* rendered

TABLE 18
System Responses to Unfamiliar, Low-Frequency, Regular Verbs

Verb Type	*Presented Word*	*Phonetic Input*	*Phonetic Response*	*English Rendition*	*Response Rendition*
End in *t/d*	guard	/gɑrd/	/gɑrd/	(guard)	0.29
			/gɑrd^d/	(guarded)	0.26
	kid	/kid/	/kid/	(kid)	0.39
			/kid^d/	(kidded)	0.24
	mate	/mAt/	/mAt^d/	(mated)	0.43
			/mAd^d/	(maded)	0.23
	squat	/skw*t/	/skw*t^d/	(squated)	0.27
			/skw*t/	(squat)	0.22
			/skw*kt/	(squawked)	0.21
End in unvoiced consonant	carp	/kɑrp/	/kɑrpt/	(carped)	0.28
			/kɑpt^d/	(carpted)	0.21
	drip	/drip/	/dript^d/	(dripted)	0.28
			/dript/	(dripped)	0.22
	map	/map/	/mapt^d/	(mapted)	0.24
			/mapt/	(mapped)	0.22
	shape	/SAp/	/SApt/	(shaped)	0.43
			/Sipt/	(shipped)	0.27
	sip	/sip/	/sipt/	(sipped)	0.42
			/sept/	(sepped)	0.28
	slip	/slip/	/slept/	(slept)	0.40
	smoke	/smOk/	/smOkt^d/	(smokted)	0.29
			/smOk/	(smoke)	0.22
	snap	/snap/	/snapt^d/	(snapted)	0.40
	step	/step/	/stept^d/	(stepted)	0.59
	type	/tlp/	/tlpt^d/	(typted)	0.33
End in voiced consonant or vowel	brown	/brWn/	/brWnd/	(browned)	0.46
			/br*nd	(brawned)	0.39
	hug	/h^g/	/h^g/	(hug)	0.59
	mail	/mA^l/	/mA^ld/	(mailed)	0.38
			/memb^ld/	(membled)	0.23
	tour	/tUr/	/tUrd^r/	(toureder)	0.31
			/tUrd/	(toured)	0.25

as *sept,* presumably on the model of *sleep/slept, keep/kept, sweep/swept,* etc. Interestingly, three of the four cases involved verbs whose base form ended in /p/ just as in the models listed above. Even though these last responses are, strictly speaking, incorrect, they all indicate a sensitivity to the regular and subregular patterns of the English past tense.

Perhaps the most surprising result evident from the table is the occurrence of a double past marker on the responses to seven of the verbs. Although we know of no references to this phenomenon in the literature, we expect that children (and adults) do occasionally make this kind of error. It is interesting, and possibly significant, that all seven of these responses occurred to verbs whose correct past tense is the addition of a /t/. It would be interesting to see whether children's errors of this type follow a similar pattern.

Finally, there were just four responses that involved the addition or modification of consonants. These were *maded* as a past tense of *mate, squawked* as a past tense for *squat, membled* as a past tense for *mail,* and *toureder* as a past tense for *tour*. It is unlikely that humans would make these errors, especially the last two, but these responses are, for the most part, near threshold. Furthermore, it seems likely that many of these responses could be filtered out if the model incorporated an autoassociative network of connections among the output units. Such a network could be used to clean up the output pattern and would probably increase the tendency of the model to avoid bizarre responses. Unfortunately, we have not yet had the chance to implement this suggestion.

Summary. The system has clearly learned the essential characteristics of the past tense of English. Not only can it respond correctly to the 460 verbs that it was taught, but it is able to generalize and transfer rather well to the unfamiliar, low-frequency verbs that had never been presented during training. The system has learned about the conditions in which each of the three regular past-tense endings are to be applied, and it has learned not only the dominant, regular form of the past tense, but many of the subregularities as well.

It is true that the model does not act as a perfect rule-applying machine with novel past-tense forms. However, it must be noted that people—or at least children, even in early grade-school years—are not perfect rule-applying machines either. For example, in Berko's classic study (1958), her kindergarten and first-grade subjects did often produce the correct past forms of novel verbs like *spow, mott,* and *rick,* but they did not do so invariably. In fact, the rate of regular past-tense forms given to Berko's novel verbs was only 51 percent.[10] Thus, we see little reason to believe that our model's "deficiencies" are significantly greater than those of native speakers of comparable experience.

---

[10]Unfortunately, Berko included only one regular verb to compare to her novel verbs. The verb was *melt*. Children were 73 percent correct on this verb. The two novel verbs that required the same treatment as *melt* (*mott* and *bodd*) each received only 33 percent correct responses.

CONCLUSIONS

We have shown that our simple learning model shows, to a remarkable degree, the characteristics of young children learning the morphology of the past tense in English. We have shown how our model generates the so-called U-shaped learning curve for irregular verbs and that it exhibits a tendency to overgeneralize that is quite similar to the pattern exhibited by young children. Both in children and in our model, the verb forms showing the most regularization are pairs such as *know/knew* and *see/saw*, whereas those showing the least regularization are pairs such as *feel/felt* and *catch/caught*. Early in learning, our model shows the pattern of more no-change responses to verbs ending in *t/d* whether or not they are regular verbs, just as young children do. The model, like children, can generate the appropriate regular past-tense form to unfamiliar verbs whose base form ends in various consonants or vowels. Thus, the model generates an /^d/ suffix for verbs ending in t/d, a /*t*/ suffix for verbs ending in an unvoiced consonant, and a /d/ suffix for verbs ending in a voiced consonant or vowel.

In the model, as in children, different past-tense forms for the same word can coexist at the same time. On rule accounts, such *transitional* behavior is puzzling and difficult to explain. Our model, like human children, shows a relatively larger proportion of past+ed regularizations later in learning. Our model, like learners of English, will sometimes generate past-tense forms to novel verbs which show sensitivities to the subregularities of English as well as the major regularities. Thus, the past of *cring* can sometimes be rendered *crang* or *crung*. In short, our simple learning model accounts for all of the major features of the acquisition of the morphology of the English past tense.

In addition to our ability to account for the major *known* features of the acquisition process, there is also a number of predictions that the model makes which have yet to be reported. These include:

- We expect relatively more past+ed regularizations to irregulars whose correct past form *does not* involve a modification of the final phoneme of the base form.
- We expect that early in learning, a no-change response will occur more frequently to a CVC monosyllable ending in *t/d* than to a more complex base verb form.
- We expect that the double inflection responses (/dript^d/) will occasionally be made by native speakers and that they will occur more frequently to verbs whose stem ends in /p/ or /k/.

The model is very rich and there are many other more specific predictions which can be derived from it and evaluated by a careful analysis of acquisition data.

We have, we believe, provided a distinct alternative to the view that children learn the rules of English past-tense formation in any explicit sense. We have shown that a reasonable account of the acquisition of past tense can be provided without recourse to the notion of a "rule" as anything more than a *description* of the language. We have shown that, for this case, there is no *induction problem*. The child need not figure out what the rules are, nor even that there are rules. The child need not decide whether a verb is regular or irregular. There is no question as to whether the inflected form should be stored directly in the lexicon or derived from more general principles. There is not even a question (as far as generating the past-tense form is concerned) as to whether a verb form is one encountered many times or one that is being generated for the first time. A uniform procedure is applied for producing the past-tense form in every case. The base form is supplied as input to the past-tense network and the resulting pattern of activation is interpreted as a phonological representation of the past form of that verb. This is the procedure whether the verb is regular or irregular, familiar or novel.

In one sense, every form must be considered as being derived. In this sense, the network can be considered to be one large rule for generating past tenses from base forms. In another sense, it is possible to imagine that the system simply stores a set of rote associations between base and past-tense forms with novel responses generated by "on-line" generalizations from the stored exemplars.

Neither of these descriptions is quite right, we believe. Associations are simply stored in the network, but because we have a *superpositional* memory, similar patterns blend into one another and reinforce each other. If there were no similar patterns (i.e., if the featural representations of the base forms of verbs were orthogonal to one another) there would be no generalization. The system would be unable to generalize and there would be no regularization. It is statistical relationships among the base forms themselves that determine the pattern of responding. The network merely reflects the statistics of the featural representations of the verb forms.

We chose the study of acquisition of past tense in part because the phenomenon of regularization is an example often cited in support of the view that children do respond according to general rules of language. Why otherwise, it is sometimes asked, should they generate forms that they have never heard? The answer we offer is that they do so because the past tenses of similar verbs they are learning show such a consistent pattern that the generalization from these similar verbs outweighs the relatively small amount of learning that has occurred on the irregular verb in question. We suspect that essentially similar ideas will prove useful in accounting for other aspects of language acquisition. We view this work on past-tense morphology as a step toward a revised understanding of language knowledge, language acquisition, and linguistic information processing in general.

ACKNOWLEDGMENTS

This research was supported by ONR Contracts N00014-82-C-0374 and N00014-79-C-0338, by a grant from the System Development Foundation, and by a Research Scientist Career Development Award MH00385 to the second author from the National Institute of Mental Health.

REFERENCES

Ackley, D., Hinton, G., & Sejnowski, T. (1985). Boltzmann machines: Constraint satisfaction networks that learn. *Cognitive Science, 9,* 113–147.

Anderson, J. A. (1973). A theory for the recognition of items from short memorized lists. *Psychological Review, 80,* 417–438.

Anderson, J. A. (1977). Neural models with cognitive implications. In D. LaBerge & S. J. Samuels (Eds.), *Basic processes in reading: Perception and comprehension* (pp. 27–90). Hillsdale, NJ: Lawrence Erlbaum Associates.

Anderson, J. A., Silverstein, J. W., Ritz, S. A., & Jones, R. S. (1977). Distinctive features, categorical perception, and probability learning: Some applications of a neural model. *Psychological Review, 84,* 413–451.

Bates, E. (1979). *Emergence of symbols.* New York: Academic Press.

Berko, J. (1958). The child's learning of English morphology. *Word, 14,* 150–177.

Brown, R. (1973). *A first language.* Cambridge, MA: Harvard University Press.

Bybee, J. L., & Slobin, D. I. (1982). Rules and schemas in the development and use of the English past tense. *Language, 58,* 265–289.

Chomsky, N. (1957). *Syntactic structures.* Mouton: The Hague.

Ervin, S. (1964). Imitation and structural change in children's language. In E. Lenneberg (Ed.), *New directions in the study of language.* Cambridge, MA: MIT Press.

Green, D. M., & Swets, J. A. (1966). *Signal detection theory and psychophysics.* New York: Wiley.

Hinton, G. E., McClelland, J. L., & Rumelhart, D. E. (1986). Distributed representations. In D. E. Rumelhart, J. L. McClelland, & the PDP research group (Eds.), *Parallel distributed processing: Explorations in the microstructure of cognition. Volume I.* Cambridge, MA: Bradford Books.

Kohonen, T. (1977). *Associative memory: A system theoretical approach.* New York: Springer.

Kohonen, T. (1984). *Self-organization and associative memory.* Berlin: Springer-Verlag.

Kucera, H., & Francis, W. (1967). *Computational analysis of present-day American English.* Providence, RI: Brown University Press.

Kuczaj, S. A. (1977). The acquisition of regular and irregular past-tense forms. *Journal of Verbal Learning and Verbal Behavior, 16,* 589–600.

Kuczaj, S. A. (1978). Children's judgements of grammatical and ungrammatical irregular past-tense verbs. *Child Development, 49,* 319–326.

MacWhinney, B. (1982). Basic processes in syntactic acquisition. In S. A. Kuczaj II (Ed.), *Language development: Vol. 1. Syntax and semantics.* Hillsdale, NJ: Lawrence Erlbaum Associates.

Marr, D. (1982). *Vision. A computational investigation into the human representation and processing of visual information.* San Francisco: CA: W. H. Freeman and Company.

McClelland, J. L., & Kawamoto, A. H. (1986). Mechanisms of sentence processing: Assigning roles to constituents. In J. L. McClelland, D. E. Rumelhart, & the PDP research group (Eds.), *Parallel distributed processing: Explorations in the microstructure of cognition. Volume II.* Cambridge, MA: Bradford Books.

McClelland, J. L., & Rumelhart, D. E. (1981). An interactive activation model of context effects in letter perception: Part 1. An account of basic findings. *Psychological Review, 88,* 375–407.

McClelland, J. L., Rumelhart, D. E., & the PDP Research Group (1986). *Parallel distributed processing: Explorations in the microstructure of cognition. Volume II.* Cambridge, MA: Bradford Books.

Menn, L., & MacWhinney, B. (1984). The repeated morph constraint: Toward an explanation. *Language, 19,* 519–541.

Rosenblatt, F. (1962). *Principles of neurodynamics.* Washington, DC: Spartan.

Rumelhart, D. E., & McClelland, J. L. (1981). Interactive processing through spreading activation. In A. M. Lesgold & C. A. Perfetti (Eds.), *Interactive Processes in Reading.* Hillsdale, NJ: Lawrence Erlbaum Associates.

Rumelhart, D. E., & McClelland, J. L. (1982). An interactive activation model of context effects in letter perception: Part 2. The contextual enhancement effect and some tests and extensions of the model. *Psychological Review, 89,* 60–94.

Rumelhart, D. E., & McClelland, J. L. (1986). Discussion and preview. In D. E. Rumelhart, J. L. McClelland, & the PDP research group (Eds.), *Parallel distributed processing: Explorations in the microstructure of cognition. Volume I.* Cambridge, MA: Bradford Books.

Rumelhart, D. E., McClelland, J. L., & the PDP Research Group (1986). *Parallel distributed processing: Explorations in the microstructure of cognition. Volume I.* Cambridge, MA: Bradford Books.

Stemberger, J. P. (1981). Morphological haplology. *Language, 57,* 791–817.

Stone, G. O. (1986). An analysis of the delta rule and learning statistical associations. In D. E. Rumelhart, J. L. McClelland, & the PDP research group (Eds.), *Parallel distributed processing: Explorations in the microstructure of cognition. Volume I.* Cambridge, MA: Bradford Books.

Wickelgren, W. A. (1969). Context-sensitive coding, associative memory and serial order in (speech) behavior. *Psychological Review, 76,* 1–15.

8 The Competition Model

Brian MacWhinney
Carnegie-Mellon University

In order to learn a language, a child must have available a rich representational system and flexible ways of deciding between representations. The child's framework must be rich enough to enable him to represent the intricate set of roles, positional patterns, cues, and conditions that constitute the grammar of any possible natural language. Since the child has no idea at the outset which of the many possible natural language structures he will need to learn, his approach to language learning must be extremely flexible. The model presented in this paper, the Competition Model, uses a small set of general cognitive principles to provide the learner with the power and flexibility to support reliable and input-sensitive language learning. This article is a companion piece to the article by Bates and MacWhinney (this volume). The article by Bates and MacWhinney provides an overview of the model and discusses the cross-linguistic work conducted within the Competition Model framework. The current article provides a description of the mechanisms of the model. For a full understanding of the Competition Model approach, both articles should be read together.

A major goal of the Competition Model is the building of bridges between child language research and cognitive science in general. If this is not done, there is a real danger that many of the advances made in the area of child language research will be lost. Roger Brown (1977) articulated the worry in this way:

> Developmental psycholinguistics has enjoyed an enormous growth in research popularity . . . which, strange to say, may come to nothing. There have been greater research enthusiasms than this in psychology: Clark Hull's principles of behavior, the study of the Authoritarian personality, and, of course, Dissonance theory. And in all these cases, very little advance in knowledge took place. . . . A

> danger in great research activity which we have not yet surmounted, but which we may surmount, is that a large quantity of frequently conflicting theory and data can become cognitively ugly and so repellent as to be swiftly deserted, its issues unresolved.

Heeding Brown's warning, child language researchers have been working to avoid conceptual fragmentation. In particular, many researchers have attempted to deepen the grounding of language acquisition theory in principles of linguistic analysis (Berwick, this volume; Macken, this volume; Pinker, this volume; Roeper, this volume; Wexler & Culicover, 1980). This work has dramatically broadened our understanding of the complexity of the task of language acquisition. Unfortunately, much of this linguistically-grounded work has not made contact with central issues in psychological approaches to the study of human cognition. Some researchers working in the linguistic tradition like to think of language as special and different from other forms of human mental activity. These ''modularists'' (Chomsky, 1980; Fodor, 1983) see language as a special ''organ of the mind'' obeying its own laws and agenda, rather than that of cognition in general. One problem with this approach is that, if we try to look at language as something entirely different from cognition in general, we run the risk of ignoring insights that can be derived from other studies of cognitive processes. Language is indeed special in the sense that it, more than any other system, utilizes virtually every major aspect of higher cognition, as well as many aspects of sensory and motor systems. This pervasive utilization of other cognitive structures by the linguistic function makes it all the more likely that language processing should be governed by many of the same basic principles that govern other aspects of cognitive processing and that the acquisition of language can be explained in terms of general learning principles placed at the service of communicative intentions.

The Competition Model adopts a research strategy that relates language to general cognitive principles. In doing this, we are guided by a ''minimalist'' approach that avoids making assumptions whenever possible. This minimalism emphasizes the extent to which cognitive processes needed by other areas of cognitive functioning can also be involved in language processing. To be sure, any attempt to place language into the Procrustean Bed of ''general cognition'' must eventually fail when it runs up against aspects of language that are specific adaptations to the task of communicating between human organisms. When the minimalist approach fails, there will then be solid reason to suspect that the skills involved are specific to language.

The current chapter sketches out an account of the mechanisms underlying language processing and acquisition. The discussion deals with three major facets of the model:

1. **The representational principles** of the model emphasize the importance of the lexicon as an organizer of auditory, semantic, allomorphic, polysemic, and role-relational (i.e. syntactic) knowledge.
2. **The processing principles** of the model emphasize the ways in which lexical items compete with each other during comprehension and production. It is this competition that gives the model its name. Our research group has produced a variety of empirical studies that focus on this facet of the model (see Bates & MacWhinney, this volume), particularly in regard to the competition of nouns for grammatical roles.
3. **The learning principles** of the model work to isolate lexical items and to shape connections between items and their properties on the basis of positive instances. The system uses competition as a way of enforcing the principle of contrast or non-synonymy. Competition guarantees that the child's representations will continually come closer to adult-like lexical representations.

In this paper, the Competition Model is offered as a general theory of the acquisition of grammar. The three critical points made in this paper are that:

1. a grammar in which all knowledge is represented by connections in the lexicon can provide a descriptively adequate and theoretically productive base for child language research,
2. competition between lexical items provides a good characterization of the ways in which children and adults process sentences, and
3. using learning based on competition, the child can acquire adult-like lexical items and shape the connections of these items to auditory, semantic, articulatory, polysemic, and role-relational properties.

The sketch presented here is a preliminary to a computational implementation of the model. Although parts of the model have been implemented, the implementation will not be discussed in this paper.

REPRESENTATION IN THE COMPETITION MODEL

One of the major lessons we have learned from cognitive science is the importance of developing a clear set of representational assumptions. Taking this lesson to heart, this section will be dedicated to outlining in detail the representational structures embedded in the Competition Model.

The core representational structure in the Competition Model is the lexical item—an association between external form and internal function (Bates & MacWhinney, 1982, this volume; Saussure, 1915). The form of the lexical item is represented as a set of auditory properties. The function of the lexical item is a set of semantic properties. In the next two sections we will look at these two sides of the lexical item—the auditory properties and the semantic properties that characterize the form and the function of the lexical item.

Auditory Properties

The auditory properties of lexical items specify their external form. In comprehension, auditory properties such as voicing onset time, formant frequencies, and noise bursts (Ladefoged, 1975, 1980) work together as cues to activate particular lexical items. It is common in phonological analysis to think of these cues as occurring in bundles as phonemes or segments (Jakobson, Fant, & Halle, 1963). For example, in the bundle of cues for a /k/, there is quiescence followed by a burst and then a high second formant transition. Although it is true that auditory properties cooccur in time, the Competition Model does not introduce a separate level of phonemic analysis to account for this cooccurrence. Rather, following Klatt (1980), the model assumes that word recognition works directly off of auditory properties.

In the Competition Model, the temporal positions of specific auditory properties are characterized by associating to each set of segmental properties a further set of positional properties. The absolute position of segments is coded as occurring within a hierarchy of four slot types: 1) position in the group of tone units, 2) position in the tone unit, 3) position in the syllable, and 4) position in the cluster. Groups contain syllables; syllables contain clusters, and clusters contain segments. Each of these four levels codes positions as "pre," "center," and "post."

In the word "springing," the positions of the seven segments can be coded in this way:

Segment	**Group**	**Tonic**	**Syllable**	**Cluster**
s	center	center	pre	pre
p	center	center	pre	center
r	center	center	pre	post
i	center	center	center	center
N	center	center	post	center
i	center	post	center	center
N	center	post	post	center

In this type of analysis, there is no single set of properties that holds for all occurrences of a segment. Rather, for the segment /s/, there is one set of properties for syllable and cluster initial quasi-randomness in fricatives such as

/s/ in "split" and "sit." There is another set of properties for syllable final but cluster initial quasi-randomness as in the /s/ of "cast." There is yet another set of properties for syllable final and cluster final quasi-randomness as in the /s/ of "bats." Each unique combination of tone group position, syllable position, cluster position, and segmental information is connected to all the words that contain it. For example the property combination [tonic, onset, beginning, /s/] that we find at the beginning of "springing" is also found at the beginning of "split," "slip," and "spill."

Articulatory form is also represented in this way. In fact, the assumption is that articulatory structure is a mapping right off of auditory structure, and that articulatory learning focuses not on the acquisition of representations, but upon the acquisition of a system for converting auditory/articulatory representations to motor commands. Child phonologists (Macken & Ferguson, 1983; Smith, 1973) believe that children possess essentially adult-like auditory representations for words. But knowing how a word sounds does not automatically tell the young child how to say that word. The child must develop a mapping from auditory forms to articulatory actions. Once this mapping is constructed, the processor uses the auditory shape of the item as a cue to its articulation. Although the actual shapes of motor commands are entirely different from the shapes of auditory properties, there is no reason to believe that the child maintains a full set of articulatory representations alongside a full set of auditory representations.

Semantic Properties and Concepts

We noted above that the basic representational structure in the Competition Model is the lexical item, which is essentially a connection between units of form and units of function. The previous section sketched out a picture of the level of lexical form in terms of auditory properties. This section examines the level of function, where lexical representations are connected to a set of semantic properties.

One of the major difficulties facing the study of lexical semantics is the fact that it is extraordinarily difficult to come up with a fixed set of semantic properties even for a single language, let alone for all human languages. Even if such a set could be devised, it would not be reasonable to imagine that the child is born with knowledge of all these many semantic properties. The problem seems to be that, although the languages of the world are sensitive to a rich array of semantic cues, there is not much evidence indicating that these cues are universally available to children at the beginning of language learning.

The Competition Model addresses this problem in two ways. First, it distinguishes semantic properties from semantic concepts. Semantic properties are basic percepts that often relate to particular experiences, individual objects, or episodes (Miller & Johnson-Laird, 1976; Medin & Smith, 1984). Concepts, on the other hand, are constructs which derive from generalization across experiences, objects, episodes, and lexical items. As the child discovers that properties of a particular experience can be generalized to other experiences, the set of generalized properties takes on a life of its own as a concept. Consider the semantic properties underlying the operator of "plurality." Early on, the child notes that there are often several tokens of a given type. In an egg carton, he sees several eggs. In a bag of carrots, he sees several carrots. He sees that these items can be picked up separately and that each is, in most important ways, equivalent to the others. From these experiences, he develops a general concept of plurality. This concept is not yet mapped onto a lexical item, but it can nonetheless be used in the child's thinking. Similarly, when the child first encounters a balloon, it provides him with a relatively unique experience. But, when he sees more and more balloons, he comes to form a general concept of "balloon." Even proper nouns develop in this way. When the child first sees a playmate called "Bill," he has a unique experience of Bill. Later, after playing with Bill on many different occasions, he develops a more general concept of "Bill." Whenever the child can superimpose experiences and extract a common core, that common core becomes a new concept.

However, by itself, the distinction between properties and concepts is not enough to explain certain conceptual reorganizations that occur in mid-childhood. For example, Bowerman (1982) has shown how English-speaking children develop a concept of causality under the impact of certain grammatical regularities in the formation of the causative in English. It appears to be the case that the child uses grammatical regularities as a basis for abducing the semantic shapes of at least some grammatical constructs (Bowerman, 1982, Markman, 1984, Keil & Batterman, 1984; Schlesinger, 1982; Wittgenstein, 1953; Whorf, 1967).

Work based on the Competition Model has focused primarily on the acquisition of grammar. However, our functionalist account places heavy emphasis on ways in which meaning guides the child in the acquisition of grammar. Because of this, we must pay careful attention to the nature of those concepts which guide grammatical acquisition. Using a corpus of child-mother interaction collected by Jacqueline Sachs (1983) that is entered in the Child Language Data Exchange System database (MacWhinney & Snow, 1985) at Carnegie-Mellon University, Jeffrey Sokolov and I have developed a coding system to notate the basic conceptual structure of situations described in discourse. The coding system tracks concepts and roles for which there is evidence of productive use by two-year-olds. For example, we are not coding for properties such as causative or honorific, since there is no evidence that the properties in these markers have been abstracted out as concepts (as opposed to properties) until the fourth year of life or later. In coding data from older children, we will begin to add codes for concepts acquired later in the preschool period. This section presents the various concepts which we are coding.

The basic types of items. There is a fundamental conceptual distinction between words that name objects and words that name actions or processes. This conceptual distinction is recognized by all the languages of the world. It is true that languages such as Navajo and Salish often seem to blur the distinction between nominals and verbs. For example, in Navajo, a chair is "on-it-you-sit." Technically, this word looks more like a verb than a noun. However, once constructed in this way, the word for "chair" behaves as a nominal. Something similar happens in English when we take the verb "visit" and the noun "relatives" and form the complex nominal "visiting relatives." Often there is no unique morphological marker that distinguishes nouns from verbs. In English, the word "hit" can be either a noun or a verb, depending on the context. But, given the context, it is clear when "hit" is functioning as a noun and when it is functioning as a verb. Although languages provide ways of making nouns into verbs and verbs into nouns, the basic distinction between nouns and verbs is always recognized in some way. Young children appear to have access to the concepts of object, action, and process which characterize nouns and verbs. Certainly, the ability to distinguish objects from actions is fundamental to cognition. Without such an ability, we would not be able to believe in object permanence and could not understand any sort of physical causation. In practice, there are many concepts that are on the border between the nominal and the verbal. It is true that nouns such as "lightning" and "rain" really describe processes. However, by virtue of their use as nouns in role-relational frames, they come to be treated as objects.

In addition to nominals and verbals, all languages have items that modify nouns and verbs. We will call these "operators." Nouns, verbs and operators are all connected to a rich variety of specific semantic properties as well as to a much smaller set of grammaticalized concepts. In this section we focus our attention on these grammaticalized concepts.

Concepts describing nominals. Concepts which describe nominals have a very major impact on the role structure of clauses and sentences. Pronouns use concepts describing nominals as identifying cues for coreference. In a sentence such as "The cat chased the dogs because it was growling" we know that the cat was growling because "it" agrees with "the cat" in terms of the concept of number. Verbs use concepts on nominals to control verb-noun agreement. In a sentence such as "the dogs are chasing the cat," we know that the dogs did the chasing since they agree in number with the auxiliary "are." In many Indo-European languages, adjectives use markings on nominals to control adjective-noun agreement. In a Spanish sentence like "*La muchacha no quiere a los hombres pobres*" ("The girl doesn't like poor men"), one cue that helps us to know that "*pobres*" "poor" modifies "*hombres*" "men" is the fact that "*pobres*" agrees in number and gender with "*hombres*" and not "*muchacha*" "girl." A great deal of the relational structure of clauses depends on nominal markings and the ways in which they are used as cues for placing items into particular roles.

The basic function of nominals is referential (MacWhinney, 1984a). The nominal can be either a pronoun, a common noun, a proper noun, or a dummy element (as in "It is raining"). Common nouns work by identifying a set of referents that are members of a general class of things. When we hear the word "mug," we know that the things being discussed have the properties that are activated by the word "mug." In order to further delineate the referent, common nouns can be characterized by concepts such as "singular," "plural," and "dual." They can also be characterized for "definiteness," "indefiniteness," and a variety of quantifiers. Finally, common nouns can be characterized by individuation concepts such as "mass," "count," "group," or "collection." Together, these various characterizations allow us to select out of the possible set of referents those that match the common noun to which the speaker is currently referring. In other words, when we say "this mug," the word "mug" is a cue to the consideration of all possible mugs, but the word "this" provides a further cue that rapidly narrows the possible referents down to the one currently in front of us. There are many studies indicating that, by the age of two, children understand many of the concepts expressing definiteness, number, and individuation.

Some languages focus on a division of nominals into semantic classes. For example, some Navajo verbs require that the subject be classified as flat or round, straight or flexible, hard or mushy and so on. Navajo word order and morphology is also sensitive to relative position on an eight level animacy hierarchy (Perkins, 1978): human > intelligent animals > medium-sized animals > small animals > insects > natural forces > plants and inanimates > abstractions. In languages like Chinese (Chao, 1968), nouns are classified into types such as "human," "animal," and so on. Languages of the Far East often use distinctions in honorific status to code agreement marking and pronominal marking. English distinguishes between masculine and feminine animates in its pronominal system, although many languages make no such gender distinction. Of these various semantic class distinctions, the two recognized earliest in development appear to be animacy and semantic gender (Gelman, Spelke, & Meek, 1984). Although young children can make these two distinctions, other distinctions made in these systems are quite subtle and go undetected by the child for many years (Hollos, 1977; Clancy, 1986; MacWhinney, 1978). For many of these concepts, acquisition is late and occurs only under the pressure of the fact that the markings expressing the concepts are needed to control the grammar. The full control of formal gender marking of the type that occurs in German is a slow development. MacWhinney (1978) found that, for real nouns, children display nearly adult-like performance by 6. However, in terms of generalization to nonce forms, adult-like use of this system is not attained until age 12. Such learning depends not on the extraction of a concept, but on the development of a complex set of interrelated cues which we will discuss later in the section on allomorphic processing.

Concepts describing pronominals. Pronouns provide instructions for the listener to look for referents by looking elsewhere. It is not enough to just tell the listener to look elsewhere for the referent. The listener must also be given some cues about where to look. The cues that are typically found in pronouns are much the same as the cues that are used to supplement common nouns: definiteness, indefiniteness, number, and quantifiers such as "some," "each," and "every." Pronouns also make use of person (first, second, and third) to facilitate the finding of the referent. The person cue is particularly helpful in the first and second persons, since the referent of "I" and "you" is usually quite clear.

The types of coreference that are possible include anaphoric reference (pointing to previous discourse), exophoric reference (pointing to the external situation), cataphoric reference (pointing to following discourse), and metaphoric reference (pointing to the entire speech act) (MacWhinney, 1984a). Together, these various types of reference can be called "phoric reference" and the pronouns that signal phoric reference can be called "phoric devices" or simply "phorics." To call all cases of phoric reference "anaphors" is incorrect, since many of them involve cataphora, metaphora, and exophora. This is important since, as Karmiloff-Smith (1979) and Maratsos (1976) have shown, exophoric reference is present in two-year-olds, but full anaphoric reference is not acquired until age four or later.

Pronouns can also mark certain locative concepts. The pronoun "here" can be understood as meaning "at a place close to the proximal area of reference." The pronoun "there" can be understood as meaning "at a place close to a distal area of reference." Marking locative pronouns in this way helps provide cues for the identification of the antecedent of the pronoun. Of course, what counts as proximal and distal is a relative matter and the learning of standard ways of encoding areas in relation to the speaker and the hearer is a difficult task for the child (Tanz, 1980).

Concepts describing verbals. The main impact of verbal properties is not upon agreement or coreference, but upon the selection of adverbial elements relating to the verb itself. For the noun, high frequency concepts include elements such as number and definiteness. Low frequency nominal concepts are usually coded as adjectives. For the verb, high frequency concepts include tense, aspect, and the modals. Low frequency verbal concepts are usually coded as adverbs.

Bybee (1985) has conducted a cross-linguistic analysis of the ways in which languages express mood, aspect, and tense. Her results show that aspect and mood are less free, in morphological terms, than tense. In languages such as Polish that make aspectual distinctions fundamental, there is evidence that children can use aspect early on (Weist, Wysocka, Witkowska-Stadnik, Buczowska, & Konieczna, 1984). The Polish evidence and that of Antinucci and Miller (1976) show that children use aspect as a property, but not that they have extracted it as an concept. The grouping of verbs into aspectual types is made difficult by the fact that the exact interpretation of aspect or verb type varies from verb to verb. Markings for verb class such as the causative are even less productive. When such markings are expressed morphologically, they are usually derivational rather than inflectional and lower in morphological productivity (Bybee, 1985). This is not to say that the properties underlying "causative" cannot eventually be wrapped up into a causative concept. But, as Maratsos et al. (this volume) show, the extraction of the causative concept is a late, weak, and variable process.

Another major group of verbal concepts is the group of modality markers. These markers are often expressed as affixes or auxiliaries on the verb. Some of these concepts express the speaker's belief status vis a vis the clause (certain, conditional, counterfactual, desiderative, dubitative, inferential, necessary, negative, potential, possible). Others express the illocutionary force (declarative, emphatic, imperative, intentional, interrogative, obligatory, prohibitive, presumptive) of the clause. Of these several modality concepts, the ones which are most clearly available to the two-year-old are negative (Choi, 1986), interrogative, and imperative (Ervin-Tripp, 1977). However, many of the other modality concepts begin to emerge during the third and fourth years of life. Kuczaj (1981) documents the acquisition of the conditional concept. However, other concepts such as the reportative and dubitative seem to come in much later. In languages which express non-basic concepts by affixes on the verb, there is a pressure to acquire the morpheme even before its function is clearly understood. Thus, in Turkish (Aksu & Slobin, 1986), there is a single affix *mis-mas* expressing the reportative/evidential. For some time, this concept is used in a not clearly reportative fashion. In Lhasa Tibetan (DeLancey, 1985), there are four evidentials which differ in respect to the part of the action (initiator, product, activity, report) being used to make the inference. Unfortunately, data on the acquisition of the Tibetan system are not yet available.

Eventually, all normal children acquire means of expressing all of these modals, although not necessarily as single morphemes. For example, English uses phrases such as "I heard tell that . . ." to express the meaning of the reportative in Turkish. English uses phrases such as "I see you had eggs for breakfast" when what is meant is "I infer from the result which is unfortunately spread all over your shirt that you had eggs for breakfast." Given the low functional frequency of such concepts, it is not surprising to find that they are acquired rather late.

Connectives. Connectives play a very specific role by joining together items and groups of items. Connectives may either come in pairs (if-then, both-and, either-or, although-nonetheless) or singles (and, or, but, but not). In the coding of the Sachs data, the set of possible connectives is essentially the set of logical connectives.

Concepts describing other concepts. Finally, we should note that there are a few important operators that describe other operators. For example, in the word "happier," the comparative operator depends on the adjective "happy" which is itself an operator. Apart from the comparative and superlative, operators such as "more" and "very" also behave in this way. Of course, adverbs may modify adjectives, as in "slightly dizzy" or "entirely finished." However, these kinds of constructions are quite rare in the speech addressed to two-year-olds and have few consequences for relational structure. When they occur in the Sachs data, they are coded by using the full adverb as an operator.

Summary of codings. In summary, the discussion in this section has indicated early availability of the following concepts:

1. Major item type: nominal, verbal, operator, and connective.
2. Nominal status: common, proper, pronoun, and dummy.
3. Number: singular, plural, and dual.
4. Person: first, second, third, and fourth (nominals are always third).
5. Quantification: definite, indefinite, some, each, every, and all.
6. Individuation: mass, count, group, and collection.
7. Location: proximal, medial, and distal.
8. Nominal class: masculine, feminine, neuter, animate, and inanimate.
9. Tense: present, past, future, generic, and nonpast.
10. Aspect: inchoative, terminative, continuative, iterative, punctual, and durative.
11. Modality: negative, imperative, and interrogative.

Grammatical Roles

We have now completed our brief examination of the auditory and semantic systems. The discussion of the semantic system focused on those concepts which play a role in grammatical processing. These two systems provide a basic skeleton for language. However, by themselves, lexical items are not enough to express complex meanings. There must be a way of showing how meanings relate to one another. Without a way of indicating these relations, our verbalizations would be an unstructured set of unrelated words. To solve this problem, language has developed a system of grammatical roles that use cues to place lexical items into relation with one another (Tesniere, 1959). Like the form-function relations expressed in lexical items, grammatical roles are also form-function relations. In relational structure, the forms are the surface word order patterns and morphological markings that cue particular relations; the functions are the underlying meaningful relations without which semantic interpretation could not proceed. If we were just to utter lexical items one after another, we would have only a vague notion of how to fit these words together into ideas. Grammatical roles provide us with a way of knowing what goes with what. This is their function. In the work of the transformational school (Chomsky, 1980), syntax is taken as a purely formal object. In the Competition Model, as in other work in the functionalist school (Dik, 1978; Givon, 1979), role-relational structure (i.e. syntax) is viewed as a way of expressing relational functions.

Relational structure connects lexical items to each other by means of grammatical roles. Roles are "opened up" by predicates (verbs and operators) and "filled" by arguments (nominals). We can schematize the opening up of a role in this way:

predicate ---- role ----> argument

For example, the opening up of a role for a subject by the verb "goes" can be diagrammed as:

goes --- S ---> argument

Here the "S" stands for "subject" which is the role played by the argument vis a vis the predicate. In this way, the sentence "John goes" can be diagrammed as:

goes---S---> John

Often predicates can take several arguments, but in such cases each argument is bound to the central predicate by its own relation.

In order to understand how roles work to build up dependency structure in Competition Model terms, it may be helpful to first take a look at an simple example of a dependency structure. Consider the sentence "The cute puppy always likes bones" which has the following structure:

```
<----H---  /s/
|
like ---S--->(the  ---  H--->(cute --H-->puppy))
|
|      O---> (plural  ---H--> bone)
|
<----H---   always
```

S = subject
O = object
H = head

In this structure, The phrase "the cute puppy" is bound to the subject role; "bones" is bound to the object role; "always" is bound as an adjunct with the verb as its head. The items "the" and "cute" are bound as operators to their head "puppy." This section will explain the meanings of these various roles and how they are assigned.

Verbs have connections to one, two, or three central argument roles. The central argument roles to which verbs may be connected are: subject, object, indirect, oblique, and result. These roles are not formal objects, rather each entails a specific functionalist interpretation. If there is only one argument to a verb, it is the subject. If there are two, they are the subject and the object. If there are three arguments, they must be subject, object, and result ("John put the lamp on the table") or subject, object, and indirect ("John gave Bill the lamp").

MacWhinney (1977) argued that, from a functionalist perspective, the role of subject is that of the argument from whose point-of-view the sentence is interpreted. He called this the role of the "perspective." Although the word "perspective" is a better description of this role, there is no reason to discard the term "subject," as long as the reader understands that it is being used here to refer to the functionalist concept of perspective. Similarly, from a functionalist perspective, the role of the object is that of the argument which is maximally involved in or changed by the action of the verb. Descriptively, it would be better to call this the role of the "affected." However, to avoid terminological unfamiliarity, the term "object" is used to refer to the element most affected by the activity of the verb.[1] The role of indirect (Ertel, 1977) is that of the secondary perspective—the participant that by virtue of being a beneficiary or recipient engages in a secondary action. The role of result is that of end result or goal. It appears with verbs like "paint" as in "Bill painted the wall red." The role of oblique occurs with transfer verbs such as "put" as in "Bill put the lamp on the table."

---

[1] It is important for the reader to that the following traditional terms have theory-dependent definitions within the Competition Model: subject, object, head, predicate, noun, verb, role, concept, cue, cue validity, reliability, availability, and competition. Words coined expressly for the current paper are: "exohead," "relhead," and "phoric."

Verbs can take up to three central arguments. For example, the verb ''put'' takes a subject, an object, and an oblique, as in ''John put the lamp on the table.'' Sometimes English verbs come in homophonous pairs, one member of the pair takes one argument and one takes two arguments. For example, the same auditory form is used for the two different verbs in ''the door closed'' and ''John closed the door.''

Of the four central roles, only that of the subject is fully obligatory. In some languages, there are subjectless verbs like ''rain'' and ''be hot.'' In English, such verbs take dummy subjects. On the other hand, there are no verbs for which the indirect is obligatory. We can say ''John gave the present'' or ''Mary sent the letter'' without using the indirect, but it is harder to omit required objects and finals. Under some fairly strange set of circumstances, one might say ''The speaker addressed until his breath gave out'' or ''John put the plate.'' But such omissions are highly marked and prompt a search for the missing argument.

For each argument role that it activates, the verb also activates one or more case roles. For example, the verb ''hit'' takes either an agential subject, as in the sentence ''John hit the ball'' or an instrumental subject, as in the sentence ''The ball hit the window.'' In such cases, the alternative case roles are in competition with one another. There are only four central argument roles, but there are dozens of possible case roles and some speakers may actually make finer case role distinctions than others.

In addition to the five central argument role slots for verbs, there are nine additional roles in the Competition Model account:

1. **Head:** Operators open up slots for heads. Modality elements, logical operators, articles, and adjectives serve as predicates that modify a single argument which is their head. The arguments of these operators can be verbals, nominals, or other operators. What makes the head role particularly powerful is the fact that the head may itself be a complex structure. For example, adverbial operators can take clusters of other operators as their head, as in ''a not so very bright light'' which has the structure (a ((not (so (very (bright)))) (light))). Adjectives may nest in the same way. The phrase ''my red wooden hammer'' has the structure: (my (red (wooden (hammer)))). Nominal adjuncts may also attach to other nominals through the head relation as in ''the cat on the table,'' where the adjunct ''on the table'' attaches to ''the cat.'' Prepositions can also take complex clusters as their heads as in the phrase: (with (my (red (wagon)))).
2. **Exohead:** Prepositions take two arguments. One argument is the head of the prepositional phrase. This argument is called the ''head.'' The other argument is the verb or noun which the whole prepositional phrase modifies. This second argument is called the ''exohead.'' When the prepositional phrase is an adjunct of the verb, the verb is the exohead. When the prepositional phrase modifies a noun, the noun is the exohead. In a sentence such as ''they

discussed the dogs on the beach,'' the exohead of ''on the beach'' could be either ''the dogs'' or ''discussed.''

3. **Coordinate:** Like prepositions, coordinate conjunctions take two arguments. One argument is the ''coordinate'' and the other is the ''head.'' Verbals, nominals, or operators can all serve as coordinates. In the English phrase ''Mary and John,'' ''Mary'' is the head and ''John'' is the coordinate. The whole phrase plays the role played by the head. Since verbs are the centers of clauses, there is no difference between verbal coordination and clausal coordination. In strings of coordinates such as ''the duck, the turkey, and the goose'' each of the nouns is bound to the head as a coordinate. Coordinates can also come in pairs, as in ''both John and Mary'' or ''if you like butter, then you will love these cookies.'' In pairs such as ''both-and'' or ''if-then,'' the material preceding the conjunction is its head and the other conjunction is the coordinate.

4. **Topic:** In many languages, clause-initial nominals are treated as topics by default. The topic is like the adjunct in that it can be a ''free'' argument to the verb. When no cues indicate any further role for the nominal, it simply retains its role of topic. This is frequent in languages such as Chinese that encourage the placement of unmarked nominals in clause initial position. Depending on the nature of the grammar, nominals may either preserve or lose their topic role when they take on a central role (subject, object, indirect, final). The most common central role for the topic is that of subject (MacWhinney, 1977). A common cue to topic assignment is the presence of an intonational break before or after the nominal. The topic is related to the rest of the clause by the topic-comment relation.

5. **Focus:** The counterweight to the role of topic is the role of focus (MacWhinney, 1977, 1982, 1985). The focal argument is the one which conveys some sort of contrastive presupposition. Like the topic, the focus is an optional argument of the verb. Like the topic role, the focus role can combine with any of the central roles. However, association of focus with the object is the default (Bates and MacWhinney, 1982).

6. **Antecedent:** Phoric forms (pronouns, definite NP's, ''too,'' ''so'') open up slots for antecedents. The antecedent serves as an argument and the phoric form is the predicate.

7. **Relhead:** The most complex grammatical role is that of the head of a relative clause. For brevity, we will call the head of a relative clause the ''relhead.'' The relhead plays a role both in the main clause and in the relative clause. In the main clause, the relhead serves as an argument of the verb or an adjunct of the verb. In the lower clause, the relhead also serves as an argument of the verb. It does this by filling what would otherwise be a ''gap'' in the argument structure of the verb. For example, in the sentence ''the man I saw chased Bill,'' the ''man'' is the subject of ''chased'' in the main clause

and the object of "saw" in the relative clause. The relhead also serves as the "head" in the modification relation which holds between it and the relative clause as a whole. This analysis also assumes that verb complements are actually arguments of the verb with dummy heads. Thus, the logical structure underlying "John said he wanted to go" is "John said it that he wanted to go."

8. **Description:** The role of predicate adjectives and nominals.
9. **Appositive:** The role of the appositive phrase.

Together with the five central argument roles, these nine roles constitute the basic set of grammatical roles.

Examples of items. Let us now take a look at the role and case connections for a few example lexical items. First consider the argument and case role connections for the verb "hit."

```
                                      |----instrument   --* inanimate
                                      |
          |--------> subject      ----C----actor        --* animate
          |          |  |  |          |
hit------R           *  *  *          |----patient      --* passive morphology
          |        pre agree N
          |-------->
                     object       ----C----patient
                     |    |
                     *    *
                   post   N
```

The letter "R" indicates the set of connections to the major grammatical roles (subject and object). The letter "C" represents connections to competing case role assignments. The connections ending in asterisks indicate cues for roles and cases. For this verb there are two arguments—the subject and the object. The agreement and preverbal positioning cues support the candidacy of a noun as the subject. The postverbal positioning cue supports the candidacy of a noun as the object. Following the two major roles, are the possible case role interpretations of each argument. When the verb is in the active mood, the subject can have either an actor or an instrument case role interpretation. The actor interpretation is favored when the N is animate and the instrument interpretation is favored when the N is inanimate. When the verb is in the passive mood, the subject plays the case role of patient. The cues to this case role selection are the inflectional cues for passive morphology on the verb.

The set of connections characterizing the subject of "hit" together with all of its case role interpretations is a very common set of connections. Verbs like "strike," "break," and "crack" have an identical subject structure. Rather than forming a set of connections for these additional verbs, it is possible to have them activate the same set of connections used by "hit." During development, the child comes to control such recurring patterns of connections between roles and cues by separate nodes connected to lexical items. Such nodes or "grammogens" can take on a certain life of their own. For example, Bock (1986a, 1986b) has shown that, in adults, role types can be primed by previous sentences.

Verbs like "sink" that have both transitive/causative and intransitive readings can be represented by two competing lexical entries. Omitting the notations for the cues we have already discussed, the lexical role representation for transitive "sink" is:

```
                                  | ---- actor
             | ---- subject ---- C ---- instrument
sink ---- R                       | ---- patient
             |
             | ---- object  ---- C ---- patient
```

The role clusters found in "hit" also occur here with the same cues. The lexical role representation for intransitive "sink" is:

sink ---- R ---- subject ---- C ---- patient

Maratsos (this volume) shows how the transitive and intransitive forms differ along a variety of dimensions besides their causality. These differences indicate that it is indeed correct to analyse these verbs in terms of two separate lexical entries. This is not to say that some relations between the transitive and intransitive entries of this type cannot be detected. Rather, these relations arise as a secondary fact with the lexical entries themselves being primary. Competitive processing must resolve the choice between these two forms of "sink." The presence of nominals to fill both of the slots specified by the transitive "sink" will make that form win out in its competition with the intransitive "sink" for lexical activation.

Unlike verbs, adjectives take a single argument. They are operators that open up a slot for a head. An adjective such as "big" has this role structure:

big --- R --- head --- C --- modified

In English, nouns can fill the head role slot if they occur in a position after the operator. In languages such as French or Spanish, modifiers occur in both pre and post position, but there is also often a semantic difference between the two positions and a morphological difference between the words in the two slots.

So far we have discussed two types of items: 1) verbs which take several nominal arguments and 2) operators which take only one argument. Prepositions work in a somewhat different way. In regard to their heads, they work like operators. For example, in a phrase like "into the box," the preposition "into" attaches to its head "box." At the same time, the preposition "into" also opens up a slot for a head to which the whole phrase "into the box" can attach. This is the preposition's exohead. The exohead to which the prepositional phrase attaches may be a nominal exohead or a verbal exohead and these two attachments are in competition. In a sentence such as "she moved the clothes on the rack" there is a competition between the attachment of "on the rack" to the verb "move" and the attachment of the prepositional phrase to the noun "clothes."

The possessive marker also takes a head and an exohead. In English, the possessive can be marked either by the preposition "of" or by the suffix /s/. In either case, the head of the preposition is the possessor and the exohead is the possession. The entry for the suffix is:

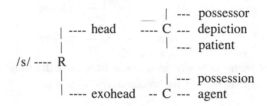

```
                                  | --- possessor
             | ---- head     ---- C --- depiction
             |                    | --- patient
             |
    /s/ ---- R
             |                    | --- possession
             | ---- exohead  --   C --- agent
```

The exact semantic role of the head of the possessive is often ambiguous. In a phrase such as "the statue of Venus," it could be that Venus is depicted by the statue or that she owns the statue. When there are additional cues on the exohead, the head may also take on the role of a patient. For example, Roeper (this volume) notes that we can speak of *the robber of the bank* and *the cooking of the stew,* but not *the thief of the bank* and *the cook of stew*. Roeper argues that the affixes *-er* and *-ing* provide a trigger for thematic inheritance. In the language of the Competition Model, we would say that these morphemes serve as cues supporting a patient role interpretation for the head of the preposition "of."

The *-er* on "robber" in the phrase "the robber of the bank" is an example of an item that has its effect on the interpretation of both its head and the phrase of which its head is the exohead (i.e. "of the bank"). The third person singular present tense affix on the verb in English (i.e. -/s/) works in much the same way. It marks the tense of its head verb. It also signals that any noun which is attempting to be a subject of its verb must be singular.

The nature-nurture issue and grammatical roles. The developmental psychologist will be quick to ask whether one must assume that these eleven grammatical roles are learned or innate. Schlesinger (1982) gives a thorough analysis of three plausible answers to this query. One approach is to say that the roles are learned during the period preceding the onset of multi-word utterances on the basis of exposure to perceptual regularities. For example, it is reasonable to imagine that the relation of coordination is learned early on when the infant scans his visual environment and discovers pairings of similar objects that move in a common trajectory or which share a common fate (Bower, 1978; Haith, 1980). There are probably also early antecedents of the topic and head relations in the figure-ground organization of infant perception. Perception may not be the only basis for the development of these relations in infancy. In action, the infant also works with recurrence, focusing, and modification. Thus, both perception and action may provide recursors to grammatical relational structure.

A second approach holds that at least some aspects of these roles are acquired during the period of language learning, possibly under the impact of language learning itself. For example, the three-year-old understands how to use agents and even instruments as subjects. However, taking the perspective of the patient in a transitive verb is more difficult. Perhaps it is the case that children only consider taking such a strange perspective when they find a linguistic device (the passive) that encourages them to see a patient as a subject.

A third approach to this issue is to claim that all of the roles are part of the biological inheritance of the human species. One version of this approach sees this inheritance as specifically linguistic. Another version sees it as generally cognitive. Although there is some *prima facie* evidence for such a nativist position, the untestability of such a position makes it one that we should accept only as a last resort. On the other hand, the two learning accounts have the advantage of forcing us to make detailed accounts that can be tested empirically. Because of this, we must favor the learning accounts over the nativist account.

Competition and phrase-structure. How does the Competition Model account of grammatical structure relate to traditional phrase structure analysis? In the work of child language researchers such as Brown (1973), Bloom (1970), and Pinker (1984), phrase structure plays a role as the central organizer of all of syntactic development. Accounts that focus more on the patterns governing relations between individual items have been offerred by Braine (1976), MacWhinney (1975b), and Schlesinger (1977).

The most powerful argument supporting the analyses of those who believe in the early presence of full phrase-structure competence is that, since adult performance is controlled by phrase-structure rules, children must eventually acquire these rules in full form and that it is better to have the child start off on this task early on. To start the child off on the path of language learning with lexically-based formulas, according to this view, is to start him off with an incorrect hypothesis from which he must eventually retreat. The Competition Model approach we are offerring here undercuts this argument. In the Competition Model, the connections between lexical items and roles learned by the child are the same connections used by the adult. Because children are learning the same types of things they will need as adults, they are not exploring a dead end along the route to learning the language. Rather, they are moving incrementally and monotonically toward the adult state. Given this, one cannot argue that the learning of the role-relational structure of particular lexical items is a grammatical cocoon that must later be sloughed off by the language learner.

Models that require that the child acquire phrase structure right at the beginning of language learning must deal with a number of tough problems. In such accounts the acquisition of languages with VSO word order is problematic, since this order breaks up the "verb phrase." In the Competition Model this is not a problem, since the model does not group the object and verb into a separate phrase. All that is necessary for processing of VSO order is use of either morphological or positional cues that clearly mark the object. The fact that children have no trouble learning VSO languages like Welsh supports the Competition Model analysis and calls the standard phrase-structure analysis into question. The acquisition of non-configurational languages such as Warlpiri (Bavin, in press) and Hungarian (MacWhinney, 1986) would also appear to be a problem for phrase-structure analyses. Such languages differ from configurational languages only in that the morphological cues are so well developed that they need not be supplemented by positional cues. The cue-based processor of the Competition Model is ideally suited for dealing with non-configurational cue processing, since it allows affixes on stems to directly cue the roles of those stems.

Pinker (1984) presents a number of further problems that phrase-structure analyses must address. For each of these issues, Pinker proposes a series of strategies that can acquire the necessary competence. However, in few cases is there independent evidence for these strategies. Rather, we need to believe in Pinker's principles P1, P2, P3, P4, P5, P6, and L1 largely because, if we do not believe in them, it is not clear how phrase structure could be learned. In the Competition Model, on the other hand, phrase structures are epiphenomena, with the core of the grammar being composed of the arguments entered on particular predicates. By relating arguments to predicates, the listener builds up something that looks like a parse tree, but this construction is from the bottom up and is promoted by competition between alternative attachments. There is no top-down parsing of the type proposed by Marcus (1980) or Wanner and Maratsos (1978). In this way, there is no need for a separate encoding of phrase-structure rules, since the correct patterns emerge from the operation of predicate-argument relations.

Connectionism and Roles. The Competition Model shares much with current "connectionist" proposals in cognitive psychology. The various connectionist models differ in their assumptions, but there is one way in which the Competition Model deviates from any current connectionist account. This is in its treatment of grammatical roles. In the Competition Model, each predicate is connected to roles which are in turn connected to cues that support the correct assignment of lexical items to those roles. However, the cues themselves are connected only to the roles, not to the items that fill those roles. We can think of the situation in terms of the following diagram:

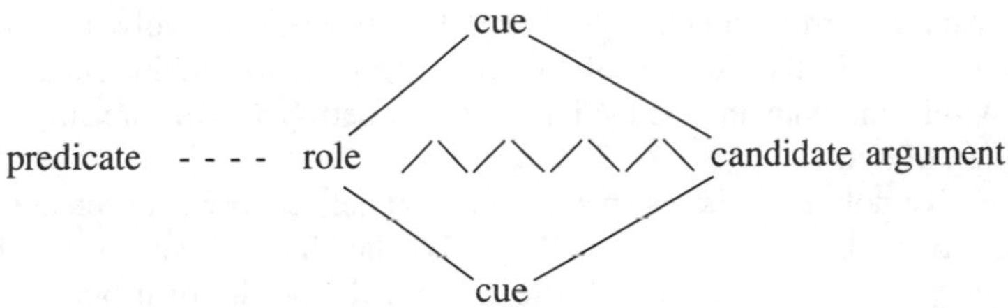

Up to the point of the zig-zagged line, the account of roles is much like that given in the interactive activation model of McClelland and Rumelhart, 1981. However, in the Competition Model, the connection between the role and the candidate argument is not hard-wired in the lexicon, but is formed dynamically during processing. This dynamic connection is indicated by the /\/\/\/\ connection. The assignment of arguments to roles could conceivably be handled in a standard connectionist fashion by linking every word in the lexicon to every possible role (Cottrell, 1985; Dell, 1985). This is the "binding nodes" solution. There are serious problems with the binding nodes solution. In a sentence such as "The big dog and the little dog both ate the ham," there would have to be two bindings of the item "dog" to the subject role node. This would require that there be connections not only from "dog" to the subject role but to a second copy of the subject role. There is no limit in principle on the number of similar nouns that can be coordinated. Thus, there would be no limit on the number of additional binding nodes that would have to be added to such a system. Another connectionist solution to this problem might be the "programmable blackboard" of McClelland (1985). In this solution, units need not be dedicated to particular positions, since they can be programmed during processing. Perhaps this approach could be extended to the problem of role assignments, but it is not immediately clear how this extension would work.

In the architecture of the standard digital computer, the linking of the candidate to the role is not a problem at all. The whole matter is simply handled by pointers and addresses. However, a pointers-and-addresses architecture is not appropriate as a model of the fundamentally parallel neuronal hardware of the brain. The problem of passing variables in parallel hardware is fairly severe in the general case, but it would be a mistake to think that the brain has no way of implementing variable binding for a small set of grammatical roles. In the long run, researchers must be able to devise a way in which connectionist hardware can be wired up to compute a dynamic relation between the role and the item filling the role.

Polysemy

The lexical item is basically a way of mapping functions onto forms. However, as Bates and MacWhinney (this volume) point out, language is more than just a set of mappings from function to form. Language also involves patterns or correlations within the domain of function and patterns within the domain of form. Within the domain of function, patterns between items are important in resolving polysemy.

To resolve polysemy, items specify cues that help choose between alternative readings. If we hear that "the needle pricked her finger" we assume that the needle in question is a sewing needle and not the needle of a pine tree. The semantic features of sharpness and penetration which are contained in "prick" are cues to the activation of the proper polyseme of "needle." These connections are indeed the same ones that would be postulated in many theories of semantic memory (Anderson, 1983). By activating words related to a target polysemic item, we spread activation to that item and help it win out over its competitors (Cottrell, 1985). MacWhinney (1984a) provides a more detailed discussion of the exact cues used to choose between the various interpretations of devices such as the definite article and personal pronouns.

Allomorphy

Within the domain of form, the speaker must be able to resolve allomorphic competitions such as the conflict between "drove" and "*drived." Often these conflicts are between an irregular form that must be learned by rote and a regular form that can be produced by combination (MacWhinney, 1978). In order to resolve such conflicts, the speaker must rely on a series of cues. Sometimes these cues are properties of the morpheme itself; sometimes the cues are other morphemes. Every item that undergoes allomorphic variation must have connections both to the competing allomorphs and to those cues whose activation helps choose between these allomorphs. Schematically, the connections are of this form:

```
           |--- allomorph ---* cue
item ---A
           |--- allomorph ---* cue
```

In this diagram, the letter "A" indicates connections to competing allomorphs. The problem that arises in relational structure of binding items to roles does not arise in allomorphy. Each allomorph is "hard-wired" to its parent item. And each cue is also wired to the allomorph it supports. For example, the inessive suffix in Hungarian uses the allomorph /-ban/ when the stem has a back vowel. When the stem has a front vowel, the allomorph is /-ben/. These connections can be diagrammed as follows:

```
                  |--- ban --- *pre, nucleus, a/o/u
 "inessive" ----A
                  |--- ben --- *pre, nucleus, e/i/u''/o''
```

In German, the choice of feminine allomorph *die* of the nominative definite article is influenced by many cues. One particularly strong cue is the presence of a final -e on the stem. Whole affixes may also serve as cues in these competitions. For example, the derivational suffixes *-keit* and *-lein* are cues to the selection of the article in German.

PROCESSING IN THE COMPETITION MODEL

This section will examine the way in which competition works during sentence processing. First, we will consider the general principles governing competition and then we will look at how competition operates in terms of audition, articulation, role assignment, polysemy, and allomorphy.

Basic Assumptions

The model assumes that lexical elements and the components to which they are connected can vary in their degree of activation. Activation is passed along connections between nodes. During processing, items are in competition with one another. In auditory processing, the competition is between candidate lexical items that are attempting to match input data. In allomorphic processing, the competition is between candidate allomorphs. In the processing of role relations, the competition is between candidate items for bindings to argument slots. In polysemy, the competition is between candidate readings of polysemous or homophonous items. In each of these competitions, the item that wins out in a given competition is the one with the greatest activation. An item must dominate over its competitors sufficiently strongly and for a sufficiently long period to emerge as a winner. When two items continue to have a closely matched activation, no clear winner can be discerned and ambiguity results. However, the competition system is designed to minimize such instances of close competition. There are four ways in which the activation of an item can be raised or lowered: cue support, completeness, domination, and previous activation.

1. **Cue Support:** The connection between cues and the items or roles they support vary in *strength.* When a cue is strongly activated and when it has a strong connection to a role, then that role is also strongly activated. For example when a noun is clearly in preverbal position in English, it is a strong candidate for the subject role, because the connection from preverbal positioning to the subject role is strong. The more cues that a given candidacy

receives, the stronger it becomes. Cue support is assumed to be additive. In lexicalization, support is also assumed to favor "specificity" in that one large item receiving support from several cues will dominate over two items that depend on the same set of cues even though the combined strength of the opponents equals that of the large form. This occurs because the strong single item is opposed to each competitor separately in a "divide-and-conquer" fashion. Thus, "party" dominates over "par tee" when the input cues are /parti/. Similarly, *cat* is better than *at* when the input cues are /kaet/, since *cat* receives support from three bundles of cues and *at* only receives support from two. Similarly, *bunny* is better than *bun* and *knee* when the input is /buni/. When receiving activation from connections to semantic cues, portmanteau forms are superior to their analytic counterparts. In French, both *du* and *de* + *le* compete for the masculine partitive. However, because *du* has more matches than *de* or *le* separately, it gets more activation. It is generally the case that rote forms and combined forms dominate over analytical forms (MacWhinney, 1978, 1986). In role processing, a candidate for subject that receives support from both agreement and animacy cues is superior to one that receives support from only animacy. However, if there is a single cue that is particularly strong, the item it supports may dominate over an item supported by two weak cues.

2. **Completeness:** Most competitions can be resolved simply through using cues to support items. However, sometimes the winning "slate" of candidates does not provide as good an overall match as does some alternative slate whose individual members narrowly lost out in their respective competitions. For example, if the items "tension" and "Ulster" were lexicalized out of an input which was actually "attentional stir" the lexicalization would be incomplete, since the initial vowel of "attentional" would not be recognized. When the failure is noticed, the failure decrements the candidacy of the winning items. This lets the losers gain enough collective activation to eventually win out and hence provide a more complete solution.

3. **Previous Activation:** Frequent items have a higher resting activation than less frequent items. However, when an item is activated by the current context (Warren and Warren, 1976), by previous mention (Bock, 1986a) or by other lexical items (Bock, 1986b), it receives still further activation. For example, it is unlikely that we would lexicalize the input /parti/ as "par tee" unless we were talking about golf or had already primed the words "tee" and "par." However, once "par" and "tee" have attained some pre-activation, they can compete successfully with the more specific form "party" for lexicalization.

4. **Resolution:** The competitive processor attempts to select a single candidate for each competition, although sometimes the resolution of the competition is not completed in time. In auditory processing, this means that the processor attempts to have each segment participate in one winning lexical item. However, sometimes a single segment may end up as a component of two winning items (Stemberger and MacWhinney, 1986). In articulatory

processing, the processor attempts to have only one word controlling a given output syllable, although occasionally blends arise (Stemberger, 1982). In semantics, the processor tries to have only one reading for a given lexical item, although sometimes ambiguities remain. In role assignment, the processor strives to have only one argument bound to each argument slot, although sometimes attachments remain ambiguous (Kurtzman, 1985; Sokolov, 1983). In order to maximize the resolution of competitions, the processor uses a winner-take-all strategy which makes "the rich get richer and the poor get poorer" in that good guesses are supported and poor guesses are eliminated (McClelland and Rumelhart, 1981) through excitatory and inhibitory feedback. The actual decision to go with one competitor over another is based on the extent to which that competitor dominates over the other competitors. As one candidate begins to emerge as clearly stronger than the others, it also starts to have dominant effects on processing throughout the system.

The four factors we have discussed operate at different points in the competition. The previous activation of an item is determined before the current stimulus is excited. Auditory cues begin to work as soon as they are detected. Cues for roles begin to work as soon as the lexical items controlling them are recognized. However, cues for role assignments cannot have their effect until the candidate for the role is also recognized. Completeness only comes into play when some assignment has not been successful. Resolution works throughout the period of competition with the goal of deriving a single result for each competition.

The Control of Processing

The goal of language processing is the extraction of meaning in comprehension and the communication of meaning in production. However, in order to achieve these goals, processing must focus on the activation of lexical items and the establishment of relations between these items. In comprehension, competition begins on the auditory side. As a lexical item starts to win out in the auditory competition, its lexical strength increases. If the item is a predicate, as its strength grows, it generates expectations for arguments. As an item has its arguments satisfied, this gives it further support in its competition with homophonous forms. For example, when we hear the word "saw," we activate both the verb and the noun, but when the slots of the verb "saw" turn out to be correctly filled by nominals, the nominal reading of "saw" is suppressed and the verbal reading begins to dominate.

Auditory Competition

Competition in auditory processing is between alternative possible lexicalizations of stretches of auditory information. The lexicon is, in effect, the major controller of the segmentation of the speech stream. When enough cues accumulate to support a given item, that item effectively segments off a part of the speech stream as "known." Many approaches to the segmentation problem (Cole, Jakimik, & Cooper, 1980; Cooper & Paccia-Cooper, 1980; Morgan, 1986; Wolff, 1983) in child language focus on the issue of the availability of juncture cues to perceptual segmentation. Although these cues can certainly assist in segmentation, it would be a mistake to think that there are enough juncture cues in the input to achieve a full segmentation of speech. Where juncture cues fail, the lexicon itself steps in as a powerful controller of segmentation. As cues for a given item accumulate, that item crosses over threshold and begins to dominate over its competitors. The item then sends information back to its cues telling them that they have already succeeded in finding a lexical match and that there is no need for them to further activate items. This "commits" the cues to the winning item. However, those cues that are not matched continue to send out activation in search of lexical matches.

Consider the segmentation of the phrase /ɨzdaedikʌmiŋ/ "is daddy coming?" Let us imagine a child lexicon which includes the lexical items /ɨz/ "is" and /daedi/ "daddy", but not /kʌmiŋ/ "coming." The item /iz/ will match segments 1 and 2. The item /daedi/ will match correctly and without competition for segments 3 to 6. The remaining material will be tagged as not lexicalized and the child will attempt to learn its meaning to add to his lexicon. Schematically:

ɨ	z	d	ae	d	i	k	ʌ	m	i	ŋ
iz			daedi				unknown			

A more difficult example might be recognition of /bʌni/ "bunny". Here, the child might have the lexical items /bʌn/ "bun" and /ni/ "knee" and could conceivably segment /bʌni/into /bʌn/ and /ni/. However, because "bunny" derives activation from all the cues that support both "bun" and "knee," it is stronger than any single competitor and can therefore defeat the competition.

As a final, much more complex example, consider an adult's segmentation of the input phrase /malnerbEr/. In this case, there is activation of "mine," "Minor," "miner," "herb," "herbal," and "beer." "minor" and "miner" will be in competition with "mine" since they are all candidate items for the same syllable. "Herbal" is in competition with "beer." "Herbal" has segments that do not match the input and is penalized for these mismatches and is defeated by "beer." "Minor" and "miner" defeat "mine" because they score more matches. The combined use of "mine" and "herb" fails to provide a match for the final /-er/ and is defeated by "minor" or "miner" and "beer." The competition between "minor" and "miner" is not resolved in auditory processing, but is left for polysemic competition. Studies of lexical priming (Seidenberg, Tanenhaus, Leiman, & Bienkowski, 1982) show that items such as "herbal" and "mine" that lose in this competition are indeed forced below their normal activation levels for a short refractory period.

Because the system is being dominated by the attempt to detect full lexical items, it is fairly robust against noise. It will hear a stimulus such as /tuθpeIst/ as "toothpaste" even though there is a misarticulation of the last consonant of "tooth." If form /tuθpeIst/ is placed into a context in which "toothpaste" is also semantically primed, it will be even more quickly perceived as "toothpaste." This is because there is no competing word "toofpaste." However, where two words compete closely, such as "present" and "pleasant," the role of context will be relatively weaker and the competition will be based more exclusively on the actual auditory input.

Articulatory Competition

In production, grammatical roles open up slots for groups of syllables in the articulatory buffer. The exact shape of these slots is not determined until particular items try to fill them. Transposition and stranding errors (Garrett, 1975; Stemberger, 1982; MacWhinney & Anderson, 1986) occur when items are sent to the wrong role slots.

Once a lexical item is activated, it begins to open up a set of syllable slots within the group slot opened up by relational structure. If an item is a head, it opens up its own set of syllable slots. If an item is an operator, it can open up slots in relation to the slots of the head. Suppose the child wants to say "a hippopotamus." When the item "hippopotamus" is activated, it opens up two groups of syllables—one for "hippo" and one for "potamus." The item "a" does not open up its own syllable group, but attaches before the first group of the head. If the item "a" is lexicalized before the noun is lexicalized, it cannot open up a syllable slot, since it only opens up a slot once a center has been established. Once that center is established, it then opens up a position that is "pre" in the group "a hippo." When the articulatory compiler is ready to output speech it simply reads off these activations syllable by syllable. Rumelhart and Norman (1982) have suggested one way in which such read-off can occur. This is to set up each syllable position as having a level of activation and then reading off actions by their activation levels.

Sometimes two forms that are both targeted for the same articulatory slots are so close in activation that neither has won by the time it is necessary to send information to the articulatory buffer. Blends such as *flavor* + *taste* = *flaste* arise from such head-on competition. Other competitions are not so direct. For example, in English, there is a competition between the three allomorphs of the plural /s/, /z/, and /ɨz/. However, thihs competition is not equal between the three forms. In errors such as "dogses" the /z/ allomorph wins out in the competition for final position in the final cluster of the head. The allomorph /ɨz/, on the other hand, is competing for a position which is post-head. So there is no direct conflict between these two sets of articulatory actions. The Competition Model can provide a good account for many of the most important types of speech errors. For details on how this account is constructed, consult MacWhinney and Anderson (1986), Menn and MacWhinney (1984), and Stemberger (1982).

Role Competition

Role competition begins with the activation of a predicate. As the predicate becomes activated, it awakens expectations for items to fill its role slots. For example, the verb "chase" specifies a slot for subject and object. Once these slots are opened, nominals begin to compete for these roles. In doing this, they use cues of the type analysed by Bates and MacWhinney (this volume). These cues include word order, agreement, case-marking, and grammatical prosody. In a sentence such as "the dogs are chasing the cat" the cues supporting "the dogs" as subject are preverbal positioning and agreement. There are no cues supporting "the cat" as subject and its postverbal positioning makes it a good candidate for the object slot.

Clustering. A major problem facing role competition is the fact that argument slots can be filled either by simple arguments or by complex arguments. A simple argument is a single lexical item. A complex argument is composed of several lexical items. In the sentence "Mary likes Bill" the object of "likes" is the simple argument "Bill." In the sentence "Mary likes a young soldier" the object of "likes" is the complex argument "a young soldier." The term "clustering" will be used to refer to the process which links two items such as "a" and "young soldier" into a cluster which can then be assigned as a unit to a role.

In order to see how this works, let us work through a trace of the processing of "Mary likes a young soldier."

Item	**Roles**	**Cues**	**Links**
Mary	—	—	—
likes	Subject	Pre,N,Anim,Sg	Mary <--S-- likes
	Object	Post,N	
a	Head	Post,N,Sg	
young	Head	Post,N	
soldier	—	—	young --H--> soldier
			a --H--> (young --> soldier)

Final: Mary --S--> likes --O--> (a --H--> (young --H--> soldier)))

Traces of this type are designed to reflect the major decisions made by the processor as it works on-line to accept incoming auditory material. Since these traces are designed to illustrate role competition, they do not reflect details of auditory competition. Let us walk through this trace. First the child lexicalizes "Mary." Since "Mary" is a noun and since nouns have no arguments, no links are built and no roles are expected. Then the child lexicalizes "likes." This verb expects a subject in pre position and an object in post position. Since "Mary" is a noun in pre position, it is bound as the subject of "likes." There is no competition for this role, so the binding is fairly strong. Next the child lexicalizes "a" which expects a following noun. Since the form which follows ("young") is not a noun, no binding can occur. After lexicalizing "soldier," however, all the unfulfilled expectations can be fulfilled. First "young" binds to "soldier," because it is in pre position. Then the nominal cluster "young soldier" binds to "a." Finally, the nominal cluster "a young soldier" fills the post verbal slot for an object. At this point, all the slots are filled and all items are attached.

When a cluster such as "young soldier" is formed from the combination of "young" and "soldier," it inherits the nominal properties of the head. A similar inheritance occurs within strings of operators. In a phrase such as "a not very clearly described pathway," the initial operators are clustered on the operator "described" and the resultant product also serves as an operator. This principle of inheritance from nominal heads is a basic notion of traditional linguistic analysis which has been recently reflected in the X-bar principle of Jackendoff (1977).

Clusters are established when simple structures fail to make proper assignments during sentence processing. There are three ways in which clustering can be triggered:

1. **Unfulfilled expectation:** If a predicate specifies that an argument should appear in a positional slot and the item in that slot does not match the cue expectations for a head, no role assignment is made. In the case of "Mary likes a soldier" the item following "likes" is "a." However, by itself "a" cannot be the object of "likes," since it is not a noun. This unfulfilled expectation leads the processor to hold off on attachment of "a" to any role. By holding off on attachment, the processor provides an opportunity for "a" to attach to "soldier" as a cluster. Then the whole cluster "a soldier" becomes a complex noun which then can serve as the object of the verb "likes."
2. **Unassigned item:** Sometimes the item in the head slot matches the cue expectations for a head, but assigning it as head will leave some other nominal unassigned. Consider a sentence such as "Bill has a toy dog," Initially, "toy" is a good candidate for the role of the head of "a." However, this reading fails to assign "dog" to any role. The alternative, and usually weaker, polysemic reading of "toy" is as an adjective. In order for the adjectival polyseme of "toy" to dominate, the nominal polyseme must be decremented by the failure of "dog" to receive any attachment.

3. **Cluster occupies slot:** In left-branching constructions, a cluster may already have been formed by the time the operator is lexicalized. Consider a phrase such as "the former Queen of England's hat." In this phrase, the possessive suffix /s/ is an operator which takes a head to its left. However, /s/ cannot take "England" as its head, since "England" is already a part of the cluster "the former Queen of England." The head cluster may be a phrase of arbitrary complexity. We could have "the former Queen of England's butler's hat" or "the former Queen of England's butler's dog's hat." In each of these cases, the attachments of elements within the head cluster are largely complete by the time that the operator is lexicalized. This makes it so that the only reasonable candidate for the head is the cluster itself.

The principles of clustering outlined for the head role also operate for the other roles. A subject may be a cluster, as may a topic. In a sentence such as "The dog the cat chased ate the meat," the whole structure "the dog the cat chased" functions as the subject of the verb "ate."

Flat structures and rebracketing. Adults tend to impose a hierarchical structure on phrases more than do children. The literature on adjective ordering (Martin & Molfese, 1971, 1972; Richards, 1979, Scheffelin, 1971; Schwenk & Danks, 1974) shows that children do not have clear ideas of the logical relations encoded by variations in adjective ordering. Hill (1983) argues that children initially compose relations such as "a big cat" from flat structures rather than hierarchical structures. In other words, children may code "a big cat" as the flat structure:

a -H-> cat <-H- big

rather than as the hierarchical structure:

a -H-> (big -H-> cat)

Adult may also make occasional use of flat structures, but it is clear that children must eventually learn to hierarchicalize clusters.

If hierarchical clustering is imposed, the exact bracketing of clusters can be a matter for competition. When clustering "a young soldier," no competition between attachments occurs, since "a" cannot attach to anything until the cluster "young soldier" is constructed. However, the corresponding phrase in Spanish cannot be processed without rebracketing. In Spanish, the adjective follows the noun, although the article precedes it. The phrase "un soldado joven" reads, word for word, as "a soldier young." If assignments are made from left to right, "soldado" will first be put in the role of the head of "un." This cluster would then serve as a head for "joven" and the final structure would be ((a soldier) young) or ((un soldado) joven). This is not correct, since the structure should be (un (soldado joven)). The rebracketing procedure takes an element that follows a cluster and attaches it closer to the head than the competitors.

Anticipation. In our discussion of clustering, we noted that sentences like "Mary likes a soldier" involve an unfulfilled expectation. The expectation is that the object of "likes" should follow it immediately. This anticipation is not immediately fulfilled. At the same time, the operator "a" anticipates that a nominal should follow it. Such anticipations establish weak attachments to items even before they are actually detected. Such links are particularly important in structures with strings of prepositions or prefixed adpositions. For example, English verbs can be preceded by long strings of auxiliaries and adverbs such as "might not have always been." English nouns can be preceded by strings of adjectives as in "my two big square red blocks." In Navajo, up to 12 prefixes may precede the verb stem. In such situations, the information-processing load can be decreased by allowing these preposed operators to all attach to the anticipated head that will follow them. This anticipated element is set up as an abstract unit in relational structure to which the other items attach. When it is finally lexicalized, its attachments to operators are already activated.

Gaps and relative clause clustering. In relative clauses in English, the head of the relative clause, or "relhead," is used in two ways. On the one hand, it is the item which the relative clause modifies. The whole relative clause is treated as a single cluster which follows the noun which it modifies. On the other hand, the relhead also works as a "filler" for the "gap" that occurs within the relative clause.[2]

During processing, the listener must decide when a noun should be judged to be a relhead. In English, this can be done in two ways. When a relativizer ("that") follows a noun, the noun is taken to be a relhead. A noun can also be judged to be a relhead when rebracketing is forced by the verb that follows the relative clause. Once a noun has become a candidate for the role of relhead, it also becomes a candidate for some role within the clause that modifies the relhead. If there is a missing argument or "gap" within that clause, the relhead fills the gap.

Let us consider the processing of a center-embedded relative clause such as "the dog the cat chased ate the bone." First, the units "the dog" and "the cat" are built. The next item is "chased" which opens up argument slots for a subject and an object. The only real candidate for the subject role is "cat" which is in preverbal position and gets bound to this role. Then the processor encounters

---

[2]In languages with resumptive pronouns in the relative clause, the processor has to compute the antecedent role, but does not have to use the relhead to fill a gap.

''ate'' which opens up slots for a subject and an object. There is no simple item in preverbal position, so clustering works to take all the material in preverbal position as a unit. To do this, ''the dog'' is taken as relhead. Finally, the item ''bone'' receives support from the postverbal positioning cue and wins out with no competition for the role of object of the verb ''ate.'' The trace for ''the dog the cat chased ate the bone'' is as follows:

Item	**Roles**	**Cues**	**Links**
the	Head	post,N	the --H--> X
dog	—	—	the --H--> dog
the	Head	post,N	the --H--> X
cat	—	—	the --H--> cat
chased	Subject	pre,N,Sg,Anim	(the --> cat) --S--> chased
	Object	post,N	
ate	Subject	pre,N,Sg,Anim	relative clustering
	Object	Post,N	

Clustering: ((the --> dog) <--RH-- (the cat <--S-- chased --O-->RH)) <--S-- ate

the	Head	post,H	the --H--> X
bone	—	—	the --H--> bone

Final: ((the --> dog) <-- ((the --> cat) <--chased--> RH)) <-- ate --> (the --> bone)

Alternative attachments. The process of attachment of elements to other elements or clusters is often ambiguous. Given a series of items A, B, and C, we could have the structures (A (B C)) or ((A B) (C)). The study of alternative attachments of prepositional phrases and reduced relative clauses has been a major topic in psycholinguistics in the last ten years (Clifton, Frazier, & Connine, 1984, Ford, Bresnan, & Kaplan, 1982; Frazier, 1985; Frazier & Fodor, 1978). Consider a sentence such as ''The women discussed the dogs on the beach.'' The cluster ''on the beach'' can attach itself either to the cluster ''the dogs'' or to the main verb. In the Competition Model framework, the cluster ''on the beach'' can have either a verb (discussed) or a noun (dogs) as its head. Both relations are being opened by the same item, so they must be in competition with one another. The one with the most cue support will be the winner.

Alternative attachments are in competition in the sentence ''I have a list of 300 people who are Communists that I can send to you.'' The head of ''that I can send to you'' could be either 1) ''300 people who are Communists,'' or 2) ''a list of 300 people who are Communists.'' Usually, a relative will attach to a single noun. In this particular case, however, we realize after awhile that it is unlikely that the speaker is really proposing to send 300 Communists and that the head of ''that I can send to you'' must be ''list.''

Many studies have looked at the processing of reduced relative clauses such as in ''the horse raced past the barn fell.'' From the viewpoint of the Competition Model, the processing of these sentences involves a competition rather than the full retracing implied by the term ''garden-pathing''. It is clear that the major interpretation of ''the horse raced'' is the one which assigns ''horse'' as the subject of ''raced.'' However, in an experiment rich with reduced relatives, adult subjects might also be able to establish a possible modification relation between ''raced'' and ''horse.'' They can maintain this competition for some time, until encountering information later in the sentence that leads to the victory of one of these interpretations over the other (Clifton et al, 1984; Kurtzman, 1985). The Competition Model provides the following trace for ''the horse raced past the barn fell.''

Item	**Roles**	**Cues**	**Links**
the	Head	Post,N	the --H--> X
horse	—	—	the --H--> horse
raced-1	Subject	Pre,N	(the --> horse) <--S-- raced
raced-2	Subject	Pre,N	(the --> horse) <--S-- raced
	Object	Post,NonHuman	
past	Head	post,N	
	Exohead	pre,V or N	(the-->horse) <--raced <--E-- past
the	Head	Post,N	the --H--> X
barn	-	-	(the --H--> barn)
fell	Subject	Pre,N	relative clustering

Final: ((the --> horse) <--RH-- (X <--S-- raced <--E-- past --H--> (the barn))) <--S-- fell

The relative clustering process here begins in the same way as the relative clustering that occurs in ''the dog the cat chased fell.'' The phrase ''the horse'' is taken as the head of a relative clause in which it will play the role of object. This means that ''raced-2'', the transitive polyseme of ''raced,'' must be chosen, since the head has to play the role of the object of the verb of the relative clause. What is tricky here is that the relative has an ellipsed subject. This requires yet another filling—this time by a general subject X.

Visitors. Some of the most complex grammatical patterns that the child has to learn involve the role assignment of raised elements. These raised elements will be called ''visitors.'' Visitors are elements which are related not to elements in the "foreign" clause where they appear but to elements in a "home" clause. Visitors take up temporary roles in the foreign environment, but their candidacy for further roles is maintained by "helper" cues along the way, until they can eventually be attached to a role in their home clause.

Let us consider a sentence such as "What did John say you ate?" The interrogative auxiliary "did" serves as a cue to the fact that the element following it is the subject. When the verb "say" is lexicalized, it opens up a slot for a subject and an object. The word "John" wins out as the candidate for subject since it is in preverbal and postauxiliary position. The interrogative "what" serves temporarily as the object of "say," but both the presence of a nominal after "say" and the fact that "say" is a cognitive verb serve as cues to maintain the candidacy of "what" as a visitor in search of a role as an object back home. The next item ("you") is in preverbal position *vis a vis* "ate" and wins the competition for the subject of "ate." However, "ate" also opens up a slot for an object and there is no word in postverbal position to fill that slot. But since the candidacy of "what" has been maintained by the verb "say", it can now fill that slot. Then, the cluser of "you ate" plus the visitor falls into postverbal position and serves as the object of "say." With this, each nominal is bound to a slot, every slot is filled, and the role competition is completed.

Competition Model analyses can be constructed for the most important types of raisings. Unfortunately, space is limited here and presentation of analyses of the various types of raisings and the cues that support each must wait for another occasion.

What determines how complex the competition gets?. One possible approach to the parsing problem would be to imagine that all possible parses of a sentence get built in parallel all the time (Kurtzmann, 1985). The Competition Model takes a different approach to this problem by focusing on the bottom-up construction of fragments of parses. There are two ways in which alternative parses can be generated. The most important source of competing parses is lexical polysemy. Consider a sentence like "He bought her waffles." The item "her" could be either the possessive or the indirect pronoun. The two competing parses of this sentence are both controlled off of this polysemic competition. The other major source of alternative parses is the competition between local and non-local attachment. The default attachment for heads, exoheads, and relheads are the items in the "standard" position. In English, the default head of an adjective is in post position; the default exohead of a preposition is in immediate pre position; and the default relhead of a relative clause is in pre position. However, when such attachments seem incorrect because of other cues, non-local attachments become strong competitors. Together these principles of polysemic control and failure of local attachment are the determiners of the generation of alternative parses.

Role competition in production. So far, our discussion of role competition has focused on comprehension. However, roles are also important in terms of controlling the order of items in production. When a verb or preposition becomes activated in production, it opens up a slot in the articulatory buffer for itself. It then also opens up slots for each of the nominal arguments related to it. When the nominal slot is opened up, it is then possible for the operators on the noun to open up further slots vis a vis the nominal head. Transpositions such as "closets in his skeleton" can be understood as nominals moving to the wrong slot around the preposition. In such errors, the operators are targeted separately and often end up at their correct targets, even though the heads have been transposed. For a further discussion of these various error types, see MacWhinney and Anderson (1986).

Ill-formedness and error. The Competition Model accounts for ill-formedness or ungrammaticality in terms of unassigned material. If a string of auditory cues goes unrecognized, the processor signals that there is an error. Children are accustomed to such errors and often treat them as ways of learning new words. Adults are more confident about their abilities and assume that it is the signal and not their grammar that is at fault. Ill-formedness can also be detected on the level of relational structure. If an item is lexicalized, but not attached to any other items through a role relation, there is an error. This can occur when an item expects another item and fails to find it. For example, the string "Bill had a big" is ill-formed because "big" expects a head and no head is available. Ill-formedness can also arise when there is simply an extra unattached noun, as in "John gave Fred the package Bill." This way of characterizing ill-formedness is very different from the systems of filters and constraints used in transformational grammar. Sometimes there may be both a missing expectation and an extra element. The speaker might think that the listener could somehow match up the extra element with the unfilled slot. However, there may be no cues to activate the match. For example, At the age of 5 years and 3 months, my son Mark was sitting in the kitchen eating a peanut sandwich. Out of the blue, he remarked, "Dad, next time when it's Indian Guides and my birthday, what do you think a picture of should be on my cake?" Some listeners have trouble processing such sentences. When they encounter a "what" before an auxiliary, they treat it as a "visitor" and search for its home environment. the major cue to that environment is the presence of a verb that takes an object and which is not a cognitive or communication verb such as "believe" or "say." In Mark's sentence, this cue is missing and it is hard to bind the visitor to a role slot. A somewhat better sentence would be "What do you think we should have a picture of on my cake?" Here the visitor fills a slot in the cluster which serves as the object. What makes this situation better is that the cue of the transitive verb keeps the slot active while the cluster with "picture of" is being formed and then the visitor fits into this cluster. When "picture of" is in subject position, the visitor is not activated to look for a home while the cluster is being formed.

Immediacy of processing. Note that this system is designed to handle grammatical information as it enters into the auditory buffer. In this sense, the system implements the principle of "immediacy of processing" espoused by Thibadeau, Just, and Carpenter (1982) and Marslen-Wilson and Tyler (1981). For example, each noun in a clause is a possible candidate for assignment to the role of subject. Cues serve to strengthen or weaken the candidacy of each noun for this role. For example, when parsing a sentence such as "the dogs are chasing the cat," the assignment of "dogs" as the subject is first promoted by its appearance as the initial noun. Then the fact that "are chasing" agrees with "dogs" in number further supports this assignment. Finally, when "cat" appears post-verbally, its candidacy as the object further supports the candidacy of "dogs" as the subject. Thus, at each point in the processing of the sentence the strength of the candidacy of "dogs" is updated. Because the language designs the cues to permit ongoing updating, the need for backtracking is minimized.

Allomorphic Competition

Competition also arises between allomorphs of a given item. In order to resolve allomorphic competition, the system uses a series of auditory and semantic cues. Unlike the model for inflectional processing presented by Rumelhart and McClelland (this volume), the Competition Model allows for a great deal of rote lexicalization. As in the accounts of Bybee (1985), Jackendoff (1975), MacWhinney (1975, 1978, 1982, 1986), Menn and MacWhinney (1985), Stemberger and MacWhinney (1985), and Vennemann (1972), many inflected forms are stored as whole lexical items. All irregular forms are stored in this way. So, "went," "geese," and "has" are all stored as complete items. In addition, high frequency regular forms such as "jumped," "wants," and "cats" are also stored as single lexical items.

Although the model of MacWhinney (1975, 1978, 1982, 1986) allowed for *rote* lexical storage, it also recognized the importance of *analogic processes* in forming inflected words, particularly forms using novel stems. Rumelhart and McClelland (this volume) provide an excellent characterization of the way this underlying analogic processing could occur in connectionist hardware. In the Rumelhart and McClelland "verb learning" model, the child uses the "Wickelfeatures" in the stem of the present tense as cues to the activation of phonological markings for the past tense. For example, the use of /a/ in syllable center position is cued by the presence of a final velar nasal, as in "sing-sang" and "ring-rang." The presence of a final /t/ is a weak cue to use of no inflection at all, as in "cut-cut" or "put-put." However, if none of these cues are activated strongly enough, the formation of the past by "-ed" wins out. In the

Competition Model, the underlying analogic (Brooks, 1978), property-based computation of the Rumelhart and McClelland model runs in parallel with rote lexical access. When rote access is weak, the underlying process wins out. Thus, a child may, at first, use the underlying analogic process to produce "*breaked" as the past tense of "break." While producing "*breaked," he is also learning the rote form "broke" and strengthening its representation. As "broke" grows in strength, the child finds it increasingly easier to retrieve. However, the analogic form does not disappear and continues to place some pressure on the system. Finally, in order to solidify the retrieval of the correct form, the child strengthens a specific inhibition of "*breaked" by "broke."

Gender and case marking languages such as German provide interesting examples of allomorphic competitions. In German, "der," "die," and "das" are all entered under the nominative singular definite article. For well-learned nouns, there are direct connections to the correct definite article. However, as with the English past tense, there is an underlying analogic cue-based process which selects the correct allomorph when rote retrieval fails. Final /e/, final fricative plus /t/, and a variety of other terminations are cues to activation of the various "feminine" markers including: "die (nominative, accusative)," "der (dative, genitive)," "-e (adjectival)," "ihr" (dative, genitive)," and "sie (nominative, accusative)." There are also full morphemes such as *-keit*, *-heit*, and *-in* which serve as cues to activation of the feminine markers. Finally, the feminine markers also receive activation from a series of semantic cues. Names for trees and ships are usually feminine as are names for humans and domestic animals of feminine biological gender. Köpcke and Zubin (1983) have explored the determination of gender in German through both phonological and semantic cues and shown that a cue integration model correctly accounts both for assignment of real nouns to gender in the language and for subjects assignments of nonce nouns to gender class in experiments. Just as high frequency past tense forms such as "went" and "had" resist the regular pattern in English, so high frequency nouns such as "Knie" and "Bier" are exceptions to the cue patterns worked out by Köpcke and Zubin. Such forms have direct connections to articles to yield "das Knie" and "das Bier."

In languages such as Hungarian, the underlying analogic process is a very accurate determiner of inflected forms and few forms need to be stored by rote. The choice between either /ban/ or /ben/ as the inessive suffix on the noun depends on whether the noun stem has either a back vowel such as /a/, /o/, or /u/ or a front vowel such as /e/, /i/, or /o''/ in its last syllable. If the stem is /ablak/ the final vowel is /a/ and the inessive is /ablakban/. If the stem is /keret/ the final vowel is /e/ and the inessive is /keretben/. Connections lead from each of the possible auditory cues to activation of the corresponding articulatory forms in the output.

An interesting problem in Hungarian is whether the variation between forms is handled on the level of whole morphemes, i.e. a selection between /ban/ and

/ben/, or whether there is a more local competition between just /a/ and /e/. The generality of the pattern supports the solution that focuses on the competition between /a/ and /e/. However, the fact that the child does not automatically extend the pattern to all suffixes equally (MacWhinney, 1978) indicates that the morphemes also play a controlling role. We can understand these two effects by assuming that the child must acquire the competition set (e.g. /ban/ vs. /ben/) separately for each suffix. However, once acquired, the competition is between /a/ and /e/. All the cues that are relevant to the competition between /a/ and /e/ for one suffix are automatically relevant to the competition between these segments for other suffixes, once the allomorphs of those other suffixes are learned.

Polysemic Competition

In order to resolve polysemy, the processor must look at two types of cues. One type of cue derives from differences in patterns of role attachment. In a sentence such as "the boy got fat fried" the causative polyseme of "got" wins out because of the failure of the non-causative to provide for attachment of "fried." However, most competitions between polysemes are resolved not on the basis of parsing cues, but on the basis of the priming of meanings by other meanings. Much recent work has focused on the extent to which contextual effects prime one polyseme over its competitors. Many studies have shown facilitative effects of context on word recognition. For example, Tulving, Mandler, and Baumal (1964) find that context can facilitate identification of an impoverished stimulus. More recently, studies by Seidenberg, Tanenhaus, Leiman, and Bienkowski (1982), Swinney (1979), and Tanenhaus, Leiman, and Seidenberg (1979) have failed to find significant priming of the contextually appropriate polyseme. However, detailed examination of these results indicates that in seven of the eight experiments involved in these three reports, there are effects in the direction of facilitation of contextually appropriate forms. In one experiment in Seidenberg et al. the effect was significant. From this we can conclude that, whereas contextual priming is real and available right at the beginning of lexicalization, it is a fairly weak effect. It makes sense, after all, that priming should be weak and have little impact at first, since otherwise the listener would run the danger of mishearing words entirely. However, this research provides little evidence in support of the view that the lexicon is somehow encapsulated in a way that prevents it from making use of contextual or relational information.

LEARNING IN THE COMPETITION MODEL

According to the account of sentence processing sketched out above, the language-learning child must acquire four types of representational structures:

1. The child must be able to code data in terms of the specific semantic and auditory cues and grammatical roles utilized by lexical items.
2. The child must acquire associations between auditory cues, semantic cues, and lexical items.
3. For verbs and operators, the child must add information about the roles they specify and the cues that promote the candidacy of items for those roles.
4. The child must also represent competitions between allomorphs and polysemes and the cues that decide these competitions.

This section examines the ways in which children acquire these structures. Learning of forms moves through four stages. First, the child develops a function to express. We will call this *functional acquisition.* Then the child makes a first stab at a way of mapping the function onto a form. We will call this *jumping in.* Then a period of *competition* ensues during which the range of the form is narrowed or widened. Finally, for some forms, a period of *conflict learning* works to block residual erroneous uses of the form.

Functional Acquisition

Before the child acquires language, he develops a set of things he wants to talk about. These are the functions that underly the forms of language. Lexical acquisition is initially driven by the child's interest in expressing some meaning. As Brown (1973) and MacWhinney (1975, 1978, 1984, 1986) have argued, the child usually develops an interest in the concept expressed by a word before actually acquiring that word. Bates and MacWhinney (this volume) refer to such pre-digestion of the semantics of lexical items as *functional readiness.* In connectionist terms, the acquisition of the function underlying a potential lexical item is achieved by strengthening the links between a set of semantic cues and a central concept node. Later, when the child strengthens the connections of this node to auditory cues, the node that was at the center of the earlier function becomes the central node of the lexical item.

There are a variety of ways in which the child can develop functional readiness for an item. The one-year-old child may have developed a concept of "dog" from repeated encounters with dogs. The child may find that being able to categorize a new animal as a dog is useful in that it helps predict a variety of actions that animals may take, such as barking, jumping, licking, and sniffing. Some months later, the same child may have learned enough language to be able to use terms such as "want" and "gimme." He sees a small stuffed dog among a collection of other stuffed animals and says "gimme." The parent is not sure which animal he wants and says "doggie?" while handing him the stuffed dog. The child is elated. At the same time, he learns to associate the sound "doggie" with the concept of "dog" that he has used for some months. Or the three-year-old child may be playing the game of naming colors and have just been presented a new color for which he will soon learn a new name. In this case, the gap between the acquisition of the form and the acquisition of the function is much shorter.

In both of these cases, the function is ready before the form is acquired. Seeing a concept realized in the current situation and hearing a sound being produced in association with that concept, the child then associates that sound to that concept. It is important to realize that the child is not searching blindly for forms to express the already-prepared function. He only needs to pay attention to forms when he understands that the adult is focusing on a function for which he does not yet have a name. In the case of the "doggie" example, the child recognized that the stuffed dog was present and that the parent was looking at the dog. If the parent had instead given the child the stuffed alligator he would not have attempted to associate the word /dawg/ to the concept "alligator." The child appears to be assuming that language is constructed so that it provides forms for the ideas that children have in their heads. Clark (this volume) calls this the principle of "conventionality" and holds that the child realizes that "for certain meanings, there is a conventional word or word-formation device that should be used in the language community." Mervis (1984) talks of such meanings as "child-based concepts" and holds that they are often major determinants of the scopes of the meanings of early words. She also shows that such first guesses at word meanings are often too broad. Fortunately, it is not necessary that the ideas in the child's mind exactly match the concepts sanctioned by the adult community. As long as the function is mapped onto a form that is of the right general type, competition will eventually force each concept into its adult-like shape. If the child mistakenly associates the concept "dog" to the form /alligalter/, this association will simply die out altogether and be replaced by the association of "dog" to /dawg/.

Jumping-In

As Carey (1982) has argued, the process of item acquisition is remarkably quick at first. These rough-and-ready "fast mappings" may be inaccurate in many ways, but by "jumping in" to a lexical domain the child is able to make a reasonable first guess that can be fixed up by later learning. The acquisition of a lexical item is the acquisition of a set of connections between auditory cues and semantic cues to a single lexical node. Since every item begins as an auditory-semantic association, the question becomes: How does the child know which auditory features to associate with which semantic features?

Quine (1960, 1977) views this problem as the fundamental problem in language acquisition. If a language learner hears a hunter say "gavagai" while aiming at a rabbit, what is the learner to infer? Should the sound /gavagai/ be associated with the concept "rabbit" or could it refer to the act of shooting? Might it refer only to a part of the rabbit or the hunter's dismay in not having been able to aim soon enough to have hit the rabbit? How does the child solve this problem? There is no single solution to the problem, but that a variety of factors work together to guide the child toward accurate learning. These factors include: 1) functional readiness on the part of the child, 2) the use of known items as a way of discovering the shape of new unknown items, and 3) the use of competitive learning to weed out incorrect hypotheses. If the child agonized about Quine's problem too much, he might never venture to make lexical associations at all. However, by "jumping in" he establishes a beachhead in unfamiliar territory which can be widened and strengthened by competition.

Finding the unknown within the known. The basic technique that the child uses to make an initial fast mapping of sound to meaning is to attempt to isolate out a part of the incoming signal that is unknown. The child can never be sure that the item he is learning rerers to exactly the referent that he has in mind. Nor does he know in advance exactly how much of the input should be matched to the item he is trying to form. In the worst case, the child must simply connect a whole audition with a complex meaning. For example, given the string *Mommy is coming* or /mamiyɨzkʌmiŋ/ as the first input to the simulation and the propositional structure: (present - -H- -> come - -S- -> Mommy), the child will associate the sound to the meaning and pick up the following lexical item:

Phonology: /mamiyɨzkʌmiŋ/
Semantics: (present - -H- -> come - -S- -> Mommy)

Such early amalgams blur the distinction between the word and the sentence. This is precisely what should happen, since the child has no idea at the outset whether he is trying to learn English with its emphasis on combinations of items into sentences or Greenlandic Eskimo with its emphasis on combinations of items into words.

Because the child does not know how much of the input corresponds to the item he is trying to acquire, the mapping of sound to meaning can be not only fast, but also quite sloppy. As MacWhinney (1975, 1978, 1982, 1986) and Peters (1983) have shown, early forms are full of superfluities, contradictions, and redundancies that come from connecting too much auditory material to a given meaning.

Often the child can use lexical forms he has already acquired to perform a fairly complete analysis of the sentence and thereby make a close guess at the length of the auditory form of a lexical item. If the child has already learned the word "Mommy," then he will directly acquire the item "is coming" from "Mommy is coming." The principle is simple. Because the lexical item "Mommy" rapidly reaches full activation with no competing forms, it is able to "commit" the auditory cues that led to its activation. The lexical item also commits the semantic cues corresponding to "Mommy." The remaining auditory cues are /yɨzkʌmiŋ/ and the remaining semantic cues are: (come <- -H- - present)). If the child is sufficiently interested in the semantic remainder, he associates it with the auditory remainder and acquires a new lexical item.

Note that, when associating auditory material with a new item, the child will assign ambiguous material to both the known lexical item and the new. For example, in Hungarian, there is a linking vowel that joins the stem to the suffix. In a form such as /ablakot/ the stem /ablak/ "window" can also have a final /o/ attached as in /ablako/. This does not preclude also attaching the /o/ to the final /t/ "accusative" to form /ot/. As Braine (this volume) argues, children appear to maximize the size of the stem in order to gain a maximum ability to predict allomorphic variation. They maximize not only the stem, but also the suffix. This is to say that material between a stem and a suffix is treated as ambimorphemic. The tendency of the perceptual system to treat one auditory group as part of two components is discussed in Menn and MacWhinney (1984) and Stemberger (1982).

Parents can make use of the child's ability to pick up the new within the frame of the old. If the child has learned a few simple sentence frames such as "that's a X" and "look, the man is X-ing that", the parent can rely on this knowledge to present new forms within the context of old. Because the child already understands the old forms, all he has to do is associate the new part of the semantics of the message with the new auditory forms. The more well-learned the frame, the smoother this process. However, it is generally true that the child can use familiar context to delimit the scope of the material for a new item.

Of course, adults can also help the child out by presenting forms in isolation. In such cases, the task of isolating the new is facilitated. If the child only wants to learn the word for "dog" and the parent knows this, an efficacious way of teaching the new form is to present it in isolation as /dawg/. Such a mode of presentation is not necessarily the best. When a form is presented in a frame such as "That's a X," the child can see quite clearly that the new form is a nominal and that it is a common noun. As Katz, Baker, and Macnamara (1974) have shown, children are quite sensitive to the cooccurrence specifications that operate in such frames.

What happens with incompletely analysed forms such as /mamiyɨzkʌmiŋ/ or /yɨzkʌmiŋ/? As MacWhinney (1978, 1986) has argued, such forms will be maintained only if they are useful in terms of lexical processing. Non-analytic or combined forms have a certain advantage over analytic forms in that they are more specific and match more cues than their analytic competitors. However, if they occur too rarely, their connections to cues will be so low that the specificity advantage will not be great enough for them to dominate over their analytic competitors. This means that learners retain rote patterns whenever they are used frequently enough. This is exactly what Stemberger and MacWhinney (1986) have shown for experimental tasks and speech error analyses with adults.

Competition in Learning

In the section on processing, we saw how competition works to choose lexical items with strong cue support over lexical items with weaker cue support. The same principle of competition also applies to the long-term development of strength in the connections between cues and lexical items. Connections which activate items that win in competitions become stronger and connections to items that lose in competitions become weaker. Connections that are pivotal in determining the correct output are the ones that are favored most by competitive learning.

Competition and Contrast. The Principle of Competition provides us with a powerful way of understanding the control of lexical acquisition. Much like Clark's (this volume) Principle of Contrast or Pinker's (this volume) Uniqueness principle, the Principle of Competition guarantees that the language will not tolerate a situation in which two different forms express exactly the same meaning. Because of competition, full synonymy is not possible. This relation between form and meaning was first proposed by Bolinger (1965) who noted that "when I say two different things I mean two different things by them." Clark (this volume) presents a wide array of evidence showing that children work within the context of this principle of contrast. Clark's analysis seems fundamentally sound. However, there are many times when forms appear to be in free variation in some environments. The competition principle predicts that some variation will occur at the boundaries between forms and in those areas where the cues governing the competition have not yet been discovered. The Competition Model analysis differs from Clark's mainly in the way it allows for predictable deviations from the principle of contrast. Clark views contrast as a constraint on language acquisition, but she does not attempt to explain how this constraint could be implemented in processing terms. In this sense, the Competition Model supplements Clark's analysis by allowing us to understand the processing mechanisms that support the Principle of Contrast.

The Uniqueness Principle and the Principle of Contrast are reflections of a more general principle—the Principle of Competition. Consider a multidimensional grid in which the points in the grid represent a particular combination of values on the semantic cues of the system. For example, one set of cues such as "utensil," "for drinking," "handle," and "cylindrical" might activate the item "mug" in the adult language. If the child codes this intersect of cues with the form "cup," he will place the incorrect form "cup" into competition with the correct form "mug." The correct extension of "mug" will be reinforced during comprehension. Eventually, after repeated presentation and occasional use in conflict cases, "mug" will come to dominate over the use of "cup" for this particular conjunction of cues. For other areas in the semantic cue space, it is "cup" that will come to dominate over "mug." A similar competition will lead to the elimination of errors in role assignment. The part of semantic space that is used to activate the form "*goed" is also used to activate the form "went." Since the latter form receives more reinforcement in the input, it will eventually come to dominate over the erroneous form "*goed."

The situation is much like that in population genetics. If two species of birds are competing for exactly the same ecological niche, one of the two species will win out and the other species will move into another niche or die out altogether. The niche of the losing species may overlap partly with that of the winning species, but it cannot be an exact overlap. Why must this be true? Because the two species are genetically different, they must also differ in one or more phenotypic characteristics. Each difference has some level of impact on the survivability of the species in each microenvironment of its niche. In some cases the impact will be small, in others it will be large. Each impact will be felt in terms of the ability of the species to compete in a given microenvironment. To the degree the species loses out in many major microenvironments, its overall survival can be threatened. Or, while losing out against its original competitor, it may shift over to competing against new competitors and its entire niche will change significantly. If one species has a thicker beak, it will be able to eat seeds with a tougher shell or husk, perhaps coming to dominate in areas around certain species of trees. However, this thickness of the beak may be a disadvantage in catching small insects and the other species will dominate in areas around ponds and meadows where insects abound.

A similar situation arises in language. Consider two possible past tenses of the verb "weave." We say that the Navajo mother "wove" a blanket for her child. But we say that the basketball player "weaved" his way down the court. The competition between "weaved" and "wove" is paralleled throughout the irregular past tenses. In such situations, allomorphic patterns give rise to competing formations. As Butler and MacWhinney (1983) and Stemberger and MacWhinney (1985) have shown, there is a good chance that even erroneous forms like "keeped" will be stored as lexical items along with forms like "kept." Once they are stored, competition places pressure upon these forms to differentiate semantically.

Competition and cue strength. The initial acquisition of a new lexical item is often just a preliminary first guess at the shape of that item. Both the auditory and semantic connections to that item may be inaccurate in various ways. The child may have only a vague idea about the way the word sounds and what it means. Over time, the child must prune from and graft onto these representations in order to reach forms that emulate the performance of the adult target (Wittgenstein, 1956). In the Competition Model, the gradual tuning of the connections to lexical items is a fundamental aspect of the developmental process. Unlike models such as those proposed by Anderson (1975) and Pinker (1984), which can learn major sections of the grammar on the basis of only a few examples, learning in the competition model proceeds by small increments, as it does in the child. If the item's shape is basically correct, any remaining inaccuracies can be shaped by competition. If the child finds that "raccoon" competes successfully for referents that he would have called "cat," he learns to restrict the range of "cat" by strengthening connections to "raccoon." Competition serves to strengthen those connections between cues and items that lead to successful usage. As these connections are strengthened, their competitors become weakened by comparison. If the form of an item has been so badly characterized that the item cannot be recognized auditorily or cannot be accessed semantically, then that item will fall into disuse because of the growth of other items.

Cue validity and cue strength. From the viewpoint of developmental psychology and learning theory, the most important claim of the Competition Model is that the primary determinants of cue strength are cue validity and task frequency (MacWhinney, Pleh, and Bates, 1985). Following Brunswik (1956), the Competition Model argues that human beings possess psychological mechanisms that bring them in tune with the validity of cues in their ecology. Cue validity is assessed within a given task domain. For example, the validity of a cue to assignment to the object role is assessed within the domain of sentences that require a decision regarding who did what to whom. This is the domain of transitive sentences. Note that some tasks are very frequent tasks and others are very infrequent. The task of deciding which of two sides of a balance scale has more weight is an infrequent task. The task of deciding who was the actor in a transitive sentence is a much more frequent task. Cue strength will be a function of both task frequency and cue validity in that cues for highly infrequent tasks will be learned later. However, within a given task domain, the major determinant of order of acquisition and eventual cue strength should be cue validity.

MacWhinney (1978) and MacWhinney et al. (1984) analyze cue validity into two components: cue availability and cue reliability. If a cue is there whenever you need it, it is maximally high in availability. McDonald (1984) notes that availability can be expressed numerically as the ratio of the cases in which the cue is available over the total cases in the task domain. If a cue always leads you to the correct conclusion when you rely on it, it is maximally high in reliability. Reliability can be expressed numerically as the ratio of the cases in which the cue is reliable (leads to correct assignments) over the cases in which it is available. Validity can then be defined as the product of reliability times availability. Following McDonald, the Competition Model represents cases where the cue is not available as A, cases where the cue is available but not reliable as B, and cases where the cue is available and reliable as C. Then availability is the ratio of

B + C divided by A + B + C. Reliability is the ratio of C divided by B + C. Validity is then defined as the product of availability times reliability. Since the B + C term cancels out when multiplying reliability times validity, validity becomes the ratio of C divided by A + B + C. This is precisely the way one wants to define validity, since this is the ratio of cases that are available and reliable over the total cases.

These notions can be illustrated by looking at how validity works for the cue of preverbal positioning in English. This cue is an excellent guide to assignment of a noun phrase as the subject. The cue is present in almost all sentences and almost always correct (except in structures like the passive). The cue of agreement with the verb is not so highly valid. It is only available when there is a competition between two nouns and when those two nouns differ in number, as in ''The dogs are chasing the cat''. As MacWhinney (1978), MacWhinney et al. (1984), Sokolov (1986), and McDonald (1984) demonstrate, both availability and reliability can be calculated from studies of the input of the language learner.

Learning on conflict. So far, we have painted a picture of a child who focuses only on what is right, hoping thereby that errors will be choked out by correct forms. For the young child, this picture is generally accurate. However, as learning progress, it is clear that the child pays more and more attention to the conflicts between clues. Both McDonald (1986) and Sokolov (1986) find that, for young children, cue validity is an excellent predictor of cue strength. However, this prediction is best during the initial stages of cue learning. As learning progresses, the best predictor of learning becomes what McDonald (1984) has called conflict validity, rather than simple cue validity. Conflict validity is the validity of the cue in those particular instances where it conflicts with other cues to the same role. For example, case-marking conflicts with word order in a sentence such as ''the dogs saw she.'' In English, this conflict is resolved in favor of word order and the sentence is given an SVO interpretation, but in Dutch the corresponding sentence is resolved in favor of case-marking and is given an OVS interpretation. Such conflicts between case-marking and word order are rare even in Dutch. Because they are so rare, it is difficult to estimate their frequency from text counts. Because children have not yet been exposed to many such conflicts, the strength of cues in their system is more determined by overall cue validity than by conflict validity. Indeed, Sokolov (1986) has shown that the intial strength of cues to identification of the object in Hebrew correlates at .96 with overall cue validity but that the strength of these cues in adults and older children correlates better with conflict validity.

Let us distinguish two basic types of learning: *positive learning* and *conflict learning*. Positive learning simply involves the strengthening of individual forms. If, by their nature, strong forms come to dominate over weaker forms, this is simply a by-product of positive learning. For example, in a garden one can plant ivy and nasturiums. Because the ivy grows so vigorously, it will eventually choke off sunlight to the nasturiums. In this way it will come to dominate without there being any direct "blocking" relation between the two plants. In conflict learning, on the other hand, there child learns a specific link between two forms such that, when form A occurs, the use of form B is specifically blocked. This occurs because activation is siphoned off from form B to form A. For example, if the child has learned a blocking relation between "*breaked" and "broke", then when underlying analogic system for past tense formation produces "*breaked," the specific connection between "*breaked" and "broke" siphons activation off from "*breaked" to "broke." In this way, the child does not have to rely solely on the strength of "broke" as a way of preventing usage of "*breaked."

Alternatives to conflict. When the child is faced with competition between two forms, he must either set up a way of blocking one of the forms or try to find a use for it. When the child first hears the word "animal" used to refer to a dog, he initially senses a conflict between the words "animal" and "dog." In the Competition Model, this conflict leads to a period of free variation. During this period, the child is receptive to any data that can distinguish the two forms. In this particular case, the child will also hear "animal" being used to refer to cats, mice, and horses. During this period, the word "animal" is competing with a variety of forms. However, it is also gaining strength from those features with are shared by cats, mice, dogs, and horses. This then leads to the formation of a concept which expresses the shared features, but which loses out when the child wishes to express more detailed features. In this way, the child uses competition to acquire superordinates (Callanan, 1982; Rosch, 1977).

Conflict can also arise between a subordinate term such as "dachshund" and a basic-level term such as "dog." Again, the child allows the forms to coexist for some time as variants. During this period of probation, the form "dachshund" gains support from features such as "short" and "long-eared." This allows the form to carve out a niche *vis a vis* "dog," so that when the child sees a dog that is clearly a dachshund and wishes to emphasize its exact identity, he uses "dachshund" rather than "dog." However, if the child is talking to a friend, and the friend has only one dog, he asks, "What's your doggie's name?" rather than "What's your dachshund's name?"

Teaching and competition. Competition is at the heart of the didactic interactions that occur between children and their parents. Recent work by Bohannon, Stanowicz, Ness, and Warren-Leubecker (1986), Hirsh-Pasek, Trieman, and Schneiderman (1983), Demetras and Snow (1986), and Ninio (1986) indicates that parents are indeed quite sensitive to the well-formedness of their children's speech. Ill-formed utterances are more likely to elicit recasts and repetitions of a variety of types. The exact shape of the recasting depends upon the nature of the error in the ill-formed utterance. It appears that the parent's didactic method is based on the application of the Principle of Contrast. When the child makes a phonological error, the parent can usually retrieve the meaning of the utterance. The parent can then repeat the utterance in the correct shape. This reinforces the correct pronunciation of the form and, by competition, decrements all alternative pronunciations. When a referent is named by the wrong nominal, the parent again often knows what the real referent is and can simply rename it with the correct term. In the competition framework, by providing one positive instance for the correct form-function mapping, the parent implicitly provides many negative instances.

The parent's problem is somewhat more serious when the child makes a complex error or when he makes several errors in one sentence. In such cases, the parent may not be able to retrieve the child's meaning at all. Without retrieving the meaning, it would be risky to recast the child's form, since that might amount to teaching the child the wrong form-function mapping. In practice, when there are several errors or when there is a complex error, adults do not recast the child's sentence, but instead use clarification attempts in order to make sure what it was that the child meant to say (Bohannon et al., 1986).

Problems for competition. Bowerman (this volume) points out several possible problems for a Competition Model account of language learning. First, Bowerman wonders how the Competition Model can account for the emergence of the understanding that a form such as ''*breaked'' is incorrect and that the correct form is ''broke.'' Perhaps Bowerman is suggesting that the child does not simply beef up the strength of ''broke'' on the basis of positive instances, but also actively suppresses ''*breaked.'' In fact, the Competition Model recognizes the importance of learning based on conflict, particularly in the later stages of the acquisition of precise distinctions between forms and meanings. As MacWhinney (1978) and McDonald (1986) point out, at least some aspects of learning must be driven on the basis of the detection of error. However, young children's intuitions regarding the correctness of competitors such as ''*breaked'' and ''broke'' are often very vague. From the age of 3 until the age of 6, my son Mark could not reliably distinguish correct from incorrect past tense forms of irregular verbs and made many errors in past tense usage in spontaneous speech. After age 6, he continued to make some errors, but his ability to judge a particular form as correct was close to the adult level. As Bowerman suggests, it may be experience with conflicts between the forms that leads to the firming up of judgments of acceptability. Such conflicts are recognized by the Competition Model as fundamental for learning (MacWhinney, 1978).

Bowerman also cites some erroneous forms for which she believes there are no real competitors. She claims there is no well-formed competitor to ''*Who did John overhear the statement that Mary kicked?'' Although there may be some debate on this matter, many speakers would use the sentence ''John overheard the statement that Mary kicked WHO?'' to express this meaning. Perhaps the problem here is that it is hard to imagine when one would ever want to say anything like this. But, if people did start saying things like this, listeners would simply have to learn to treat "overhear" in the same way they treat "believe" and "say," i.e. as cues to the continuation of the search of a "visitor" for a role in its home clause.

Along a similar line, Bowerman wonders how children ever decide to stop using "disappear" as a causative, since she believes that the conventional way of saying this ("make disappear") is not in direct competition with causative "disappear." Here, the problem is that, in fact, the semantic range of a periphrastic form such as "make stand up" actually includes that of a lexical causative such as "stand up." Whenever we say that we "stand the doll up" we can also say that we "make the doll stand up." The reverse is not the case. For a lexical causative to dominate over the periphrastic causative, it must be continually reinforced by being heard in the input. If it is not, the periphrastic will simply take over, much as grass will take over an untended flower bed. Bowerman claims that "*unsqueeze" has no direct competitor, although forms like "release" and "ease up" overlap on its semantic domain. Again, here is a situation where the range of the competitors is so wide (particularly that of "release") that, without reinforcement from the input, the erroneous form "*unsqueeze" will simply die out. The problem of "unlearning" errors in Dative Movement is basically the same as the other problems Bowerman raises. The child may say "I said her no" or "I'll brush him his hair." But, for these forms to survive the child must record the indirect as a central argument of the verb. In fact, the input does not support this addition to the lexical items "say" and "brush" and the child's innovation will die out like a flower that is not watered. Bowerman is correct in pointing out that a full suppression of these errors may require more than simply positive instances. Whenever a child makes an error that is not supported in the input, he does so on the basis of some regularities that he perceives in the lexicon. These underlying pressures will always be there and they may well lead to a continuing attempt to produce the overgeneralization. When other forms compete less directly, it may be necessary for the child to go to some extra work to block production of these overgeneralizations, as suggested by MacWhinney (1978) and McDonald (1986). The crucial point is that the child's initial approach is to rely on overall cue validity as a way of organizing language. But, the Competition Model emphasizes that in some areas, the child will eventually have to rely on conflict validity rather than overall cue validity.

The Acquisition of Role Structure

In order to acquire the role structure of predicates, the child must establish and strengthen (1) the connections between predicates and the roles they specify, (2) the connections between predicates and specific case relations, and (3) the connections between cues and the roles and cases they support. The first two types of learning are "role acquisition" and the third type of learning is "cue acquisition."

Role acquisition. Consider the verb "give." The child must establish and strengthen a connection between "give" and the subject, object, and indirect roles. He must also learn connections from "give" to specific case roles such as "giver," "transferred," and "recipient." For the passive and the dative passive, the subject role takes the case role of "transferred" or "recipient." When the child hears "Bill gave a tomato," he sees Bill giving a tomato to Hank and assumes that "Bill" is the subject and that "tomato" is the object. He also judges "Bill" to be the "giver" and the "tomato" to be the "transferred." In the Competition Model framework, the acquisition of roles is not a particularly difficult matter. The child uses situational cues to guess at the role for each nominal. The first few such guesses set up a connection from the predicate to its arguments. The acquisition of case roles occurs in a similar fashion.

Psycholinguistics has paid a great deal of attention to the acquisition and use of the passive. In the Competition Model account, the child faces two problems in learning the passive. One is that of isolating a discontinuous morpheme with two parts that both show extreme allomorphic variation. The second problem is that of associating the use of this cue with the correct case role or set of case roles for the noun that precedes the auxiliary. When learning the passive, the child has to learn a case interpretation that always competes directly with the standard actor interpretation of the subject. He must connect the passive morphemes to this alternative case role interpretation to insure that it can win in the competition. In the dative passive ("John was given a flower by Fred."), the child must learn that the subject can also be a recipient. These additional case roles for the subject must be entered one-by-one into each lexical form. The conservativeness of the generalization of verb frame patterns process in language acquisition is well-documented (Fodor and Crain, this volume; Maratsos, this volume; Roeper, this volume; Mazurkewich and White, 1984). Thus, it appears reasonable to suppose that these case role options are connected to each verb one-by-one. At the same time, it is clear that verbs form semantic groups in terms of the argument types they take. In our current account, these semantic groups exert an underlying pressure on the system which tends to keep individual verbs in line with the overall pattern. However, the child is also careful to note the grammatical and case role combinations for each verb individually. If a particular argument has not yet been encountered, the child could comprehend its use by reference to the underlying semantically-based system. But, in production, he would be guided chiefly by information stored on the verb itself.

Like Wexler and Culicover (1980) and Pinker (1984), The Competition Model assumes that the child has some representation of the meaning of the sentence that guides him in acquiring grammar. However, these other authors must assume that the child has complete trees of phrase-structure representations of the entire base or deep structure for each input sentence. This strong assumption is probably not defendable. Although the child may well construct some semantic assignments on the basis of his understanding of the situation, it is not clear that he continually builds complete dependency trees or that the representations he does build look much like deep structure. The Competition Model account makes fewer assumptions about such unobserved processes going on in the child. It only assumes that the child can at least occasionally assign arguments to roles. The assignment of a single argument to a role does not require the building of a complete tree for the entire clause. It only requires a link between the argument and its predicate.

Cue acquisition. The acquisition of connections between cues and roles is a more difficult task. The problem with cues is that the child does not know initially what should count as a cue. Potentially, anything in the clause could be a cue. Indeed, there could be cues that would involve all sorts of bizarre combinations such as "the nucleus of the second syllable on the word three before the candidate word if there is a /p/ at the end of the word at the end of the clause." In fact languages never make use of such bizarre cues. If the language did make use of such a cue, the child might not be able to learn it. In other words, the system for cue learning is structured so that only certain types of cues can be learned. As suggested by MacWhinney (1978a, b), cue acquisition occurs through the sifting out of commonalities that is the hallmark of competition. In other words, whenever the child encounters a competition that needs to be predicted by cues, he records the cue environment of each positive instance. Those cues which are repeatedly encountered across instances are the ones which survive the competition and become strong.

The recording of the cue environment of each positive instance is the computational bottleneck of the cue acquisition process. To streamline movement through this bottleneck, the child classes cues into four types:

1. **Positional Cues:** The child records the position of the argument vis a vis the head.
2. **Auditory Cues:** The child records the segmental and suprasegmental phonological properties of the argument.
3. **Semantic Cues:** The child records the semantic concepts that describe the argument (as discussed earlier).
4. **Lexical cues:** The child records the lexical identity of all the operators on the argument as well as all the operators on any predicate to which the argument is bound.

The child is trying to figure out how to identify a given argument and he is tracking cues that can be used to identify that argument. For example, the child is learning that stressed words are likely to take the focus role or that animate nouns are strong candidates for the subject role. Only in the case of lexical cues is the child tracking not just information about the argument itself, but also information attached to the predicate to which the argument attaches. If the child were not tracking such secondary lexical information, he could not acquire agreement cues.

Allomorphic Acquisition

The child must also acquire competing allomorphs and the cues for selection between allomorphs. When the child finds that a single meaning takes on two articulatory forms, he associates each articulatory form to the meaning. Each phonological variant that appears in the surface is stored in its full surface form. Just as in syntactic learning, the cue acquisitionl mechanisms must acquire cues to determine the choice of one allomorph over the other. These cues can be:

1. **Auditory cues:** The mechanism records the auditory cues of the item and of its head. For example, the presence of a final /e/ on a stem in German activates choice of feminine markers.
2. **Semantic cues:** The mechanism records the semantic cues of the item and of its head. For example, the presence of the semantic feature or cue "tree" on a stem activates choice of feminine markers.
3. **Lexical cues:** The mechanism records the lexical items attached to the head. For example, when the suffix "-keit" is attached to the head, this activates feminine articles, pronouns and suffixes in German.

As in the learning of cues to roles, the learning of cues to allomorph selection requires that the child be keeping track of these three basic types of predictors. The only difference between articulatory cue tracking and role cue tracking is that there is no need to track the shape of arguments of the head for allomorphic decisions.

Underlying Pressure

Both the selection between allomorphs and the use of particular arguments on the verb can be influenced by underlying pressures in the lexicon. Even if the speaker has never used an indirect argument with the verb "tap," he could say "LeMieux tapped Johnson the puck" when describing a hockey game. Similarly, after we have learned a new verb such as "obfuscate," we can immediately produce a past tense form such as "obfuscated" without having firmed up a direct connection between "obfsucate" and "-ed." This kind of role and allomorphic productivity is based upon an underlying system of connections of the type described by Rumelhart and McClelland (this volume) for allomorphy and McClelland and Kawamoto (1986) for roles.

Form-Driven Learning

In general, functional learning precedes formal learning. However, this is not always the case. As the child's vocabulary grows, he starts to comprehend more and more of the speech he hears. As this known material grows, the size of the unknown begins to shrink. This means that unknown material begins to stand out more clearly. When a small stretch of auditory is clearly unknown, the child may then provisionally think of that auditory material as a lexical item to which he has not yet connected a set of semantic cues.

Having decided entered this new lexical item, the child can then proceed directly to attempt to figure out what the item means and what arguments it takes. To do this, he looks at the role frames for the item in the current clause. For example, given a sentence such as "The man niffed the plate at the fence," coocurrence learning can abduce facts about the arguments of "niff" and some of its semantics. The child does this by attending to the underlying system of connections between semantics and verb frames described by McClelland and Kawamoto (1986). This system tells us that "niff" takes a subject and an object and that the action of the subject on the object is like that in "hit" and "slam."

The importance of a mechanism of this type has been stressed by MacWhinney (1978), Maratsos and Chalkley (1980), Bowerman (1982), and Schlesinger (1977). Bates and MacWhinney (1982) stressed the importance of functional characterizations of role-relational classes. There is evidence that even very young children are able to infer the class of a word from cooccurrence data. For example, Katz, Baker, and Macnamara (1976) found that, beginning around 17 months, girls who were given a proper name for a doll learned this name better than girls who were given a common noun. In the proper noun frame, girls were told that the doll was called "Zav"; in the common noun frame they were told that the doll was "a zav." Thus, even at this early age, children seem to realize that names with articles are common nouns and names without articles are proper nouns. This ability to infer the semantics of words on the basis of cooccurrence continues to develop. By age 8, Werner and Kaplan (1950) were able to show in their classic "corplum" experiment that children could acquire many aspects of the semantics of abstract nouns from highly abstract sentence contexts.

This chapter has shown how the Competition Model provides an account of the acquisition of the grammar and the lexicon. The account has focused on the ways in which cues interact to determine competitions between lexical items in auditory, semantic, relational, articulatory, allomorphic, and polysemic processing. The key constructs in the model have been *competition* and *cues*. The notion of grammar presented by the model is a not the standard account of generative transformational theory. However, from the viewpoint of psycholinguistics and cognitive psychology, the account is fairly orthodox. It would be a mistake to think of the Competition Model as a "performance model" distinct from some other, more formal "competence model." Rather, we should think of the Competition Model as a "processing model"—one which focuses on the psychological status of sentence processing.

We have attempted to keep the model consistent with the facts of both linguistic analysis and psychological experimentation. If we are correct in claiming that the processes used in language acquisition and language processing are not unique to language, then it should be possible to extend the Competition Model to other areas of cognitive development. This would be the major pay-off of our attempt to achieve cognitive generality. In fact, the developmental and cognitive literature is rich with competition-like models and accounts. The strategy-choice analyses of Siegler (Siegler 1986, Siegler & Shrager, 1984) and the information-integration approach of N. Anderson (Anderson & Cuneo, 1978) can be seen as applications of competition-type models to non-linguistic domains. Competition accounts are fundamental in much of the research on prototypes and fuzzy categories (Rosch & Mervis, 1975; 1976). One can find competition in infant search behavior (Sophian, 1984), visual-auditory cross-modal processing (Massaro, 1985) phonological processing (Massaro and Cohen, 1983, Menn & MacWhinney, 1984; Scott & Cutler, 1984), and competition can provide a useful characterization of data from studies of concept identification (Palermo & Eberhart, 1968). Well-articulated understandings of competition or both stimuli and responses can be found throughout the perceptual literature and the conditioning literature. The phenomenon of response competition is common to many associationist accounts such as those of Hull (1943) and Hebb (1949). Early cognitive Competition Models can be found in Herbart (1816) and Freud (1898). It is clear that the Competition Model has firm roots in psychological theory.

Although we see many parallels to the Competition Model elsewhere in cognitive development and psychology as a whole, few of these models use exactly the same constructs presented in the current paper. In extending the model to these new domains, there are particular questions to ask. How can we construct a task analysis of these other domains that properly reveals the types of cues the child uses in learning and decision-making? Can one construct competition-based accounts for highly ''serial'' skills such as computer programming or long division? Will the Competition Model be able to provide ways of dealing with strategy selection and hypothesis testing? By extending the model in these ways we will learn much about these new tasks and we will learn a great deal about the model itself.

ACKNOWLEDGMENTS

Jeffrey Sokolov worked closely with me on many aspects of the current project, particularly those relating to competitive aspects of the parsing mechanism. An earlier version of many of these competitive processes was offered by Sokolov (1983). Kevin Kelly provided explanations of the relation of psychological theory to formal semantics and learnability theory. Jay McClelland taught us about connectionist models. Many aspects of the semantic and syntactic analysis derive from work by Carl Pollard, Dan Slobin, and Charles Fillmore. Some of the learning mechanisms proposed are similar to those proposed by John Anderson and Martin Braine, both of whom helped outline the shape of the learning problem. The basic notions of cue strength and competition have been developed in collaboration with Elizabeth Bates and Janet McDonald. Joseph Stemberger provided ideas on activation in speech production and the relation between articulation and audition. Liz Bates, Neil Bohannon, Kevin Kelly, Klaus-Michael Kopcke, Jay McClelland, Janet McDonald, Mark St. John, and Roman Taraban provided helpful critical readings of an earlier draft.

REFERENCES

Aksu, A. and Slobin, D. I. (1986). The acquisition of Turkish. In D. I. Slobin (Ed.), *Cross-linguistic studies of language development*. Hillsdale, N.J.: Lawrence Erlbaum Associates.

Anderson, J. (1983). *The architecture of cognition*. Cambridge, Mass.: Harvard University Press.

Anderson, N., & Cuneo, D. (1978). The height + width rule in children's judgments of quantity. *Journal of Experimental Psychology, General, 107*, 335–378.

Antinucci, F., & Miller, R. (1976). How children talk about what happened. *Journal of Child Language*, pp. 167–189.

Bates, E., & MacWhinney, B. (1982). Functionalist approaches to grammar. In E. Wanner, & L. Gleitman (Eds.), *Language acquisition: The state of the art*. New York: Cambridge University Press.

Bloom, L. (1970). *Language development: Form and function in emerging grammars*. Cambridge: MIT Press.

Bock, K. (1986a). Syntactic persistence in language production. *Cognitive Psychology, 18*.

Bock, K. (1986b). Meaning, sound, and syntax: Lexical priming in sentence production. *Journal of Experimental Psychology: Learning, Memory, and Cognition, 12*, 575–586.

Bohannon, N., Stanowicz, L., Ness, J., Warren-Leubecker, A. (1986). Sentence error analysis: evidence from a limited information processor.

Bolinger, D. (1965). The atomization of meaning. *Language, 41*, 555–573.

Bower, T. G. R. (1974). *Development in infancy*. San Francisco: Freeman.

Bowerman, M. (1982). Reorganizational processes in lexical and syntactic development. In E. Wanner, & L. Gleitman (Eds.), *Language acquisition: The state of the art*. New York: Cambridge University Press.

Brooks, L. (1978). Nonanalytic concept formation and memory for instances. In Rosch, E., & Lloyd, B. (Ed.), *Cognition and categorization*. Hillsdale, N.J.: Lawrence Erlbaum.

Brown, R. (1973). *A first language: The early stages*. Cambridge, Mass: Harvard University Press.

Brown, R. (1977). Word from the language acquisition front.

Brunswik, E. (1956). *Perception and the representative design of psychology experiments*. Berkeley: University of California Press.

Butler Platt, C., & MacWhinney, B. (1983). Error assimilation as a mechanism in language learning. *Journal of Child Language, 10*, 401–414.

Bybee, J. (1985). *Morphology: A study of the relation between meaning and form*. Amsterdam: John Benjamins.

Callanan, M. (November 1982). *Parental input and young children's acquisition of hierarchically organized concepts*. Doctoral dissertation, Stanford University,

Carey, S. (1982). Semantic development: The state of the art. In E. Wanner, & L. Gleitman (Ed.), *Language acquisition: The state of the art*. New York: Cambridge University Press.

Chafe, W. (1971). *Meaning and the structure of language.* Chicago: University of Chicago Press.

Chao, Y. R. (1968). *A grammar of spoken Chinese.* Berkeley, California: University of California Press.

Choi, S. (May 1986). *The acquisition of negation in English, French, and Korean.* Doctoral dissertation, State University of New York at Buffalo.

Chomsky, N. (1980). On binding. *Linguistic Inquiry, 11,* 1–46.

Clancy, P. (1986). The acquisition of Japanese. In D. I. Slobin (Ed.), *Cross-linguistic studies of language development.* Hillsdale, N.J.: Lawrence Erlbaum Associates.

Clifton, C., Frazier, L., & Connine, C. (1984). Lexical expectations in sentence comprehension. *Journal of Verbal Learning and Verbal Behavior, 23,* 696–708.

Cole, R., Jakimik, J., & Cooper, W. (1980). Segmenting speech into words. *Journal of the Acoustical Society of America, 67,* 1323–1331.

Cooper, W., & Paccia-Cooper, J. (1980). *Syntax and speech.* Cambridge, MA: Harvard University Press.

Cottrell, G. (May 1985). *A connectionist approach to word sense disambiguation.* Doctoral dissertation, University of Rochester,

DeLancey, S. (1985). Evidentiality and volitionality in Tibetan. In W. Chafe and J. Nichols (Ed.), *Evidentiality: The Linguistic Coding of Epistemology.* Norwood, N.J.: Ablex.

Dell, G. S. (1984). Representation of serial order in speech: Evidence from the repeated phoneme effect in speech errors. *Journal of Experimental Psychology: Learning, Memory and Cognition, 10,* 222–233.

Demetras, M., Post, K., & Snow, C. (1986). Feedback to first language learners: the role of repetitions and clarification responses.

Dik, S. (Ed.). (1978). *Functional grammar.* Amsterdam: North-Holland.

Ervin-Tripp, S. (1977). ''Wait for me, roller skate''. In S. Ervin-Tripp & C. Mitchell-Kernan (Eds.), *Child discourse.* New York: Academic Press.

Ertel, S. (1977). Where do the subjects of sentences come from? In S. Rosenberg (Ed.), *Sentence production: Developments in research and theory.* Hillsdale, N.J.: Lawrence Erlbaum Associates.

Fodor, J. (1983). *The modularity of mind: An essay on faculty psychology.* Cambridge, MA: M.I.T. Press.

Ford, M., Bresnan, J., & Kaplan, D. (1982). A competence-based theory of syntactic closure. In Bresnan, J., & Kaplan, R. (Ed.), *The mental representation of grammatical relations.* Cambridge, MA: MIT Press.

Frazier, L. (1985). Syntactic complexity. In Dowty, D., Karttunen, L, & Zwicky, A. (Ed.), *Natural language parsing.* New York: Cambridge University Press.

Frazier, L., & Fodor, J. (1978). The Sausage Machine: a new two-stage parsing model. *Cognition, 6,* 291–325.

Freud, S. (1958). *Psychopathology of everyday life.* New York: New American Library, Mentor.

Gelman, R., & Gallistel, C. R. (1978). *The child's understanding of number.* Cambridge, MA: Harvard University Press.

Gelman, R., Spelke, E., & Meek, E. (1983). What preschoolers know about animate and inanimate objects. In Roger, D., & Sloboda, J. (Ed.), *The acquisition of symbolic skills.* New York: Plenum.

Givòn, T. (1979). *On understanding grammar.* New York: Academic Press.

Haiman, J. (1978). Conditionals are topics. *Language, 54,* 564–589.

Haith, M. (1980). *Rules that newborn babies look by: the organization of newborn visual activity.* Hillsdale, N.J.: Lawrence Erlbaum Associates.

Hebb, D. (1949). *The organization of behavior.* New York: Wiley.

Herbart, J. F. (1891). *A text-book in psychology.* New York: Appleton & Co.

Hill, J. (1983). A computational model of language acquisition in the two-year old. *Cognition and Brain Theory, 6,* 287–317.

Hirsh-Pasek, K., and Trieman, R., Schneiderman, M. (1984). Brown and Hanlon revisited: mother sensitivity to grammatical form. *Journal of Child Language, 11,* 81–88.

Hollos, M. (1977). Comprehension and use of social roles in pronoun selection by Hungarian children. In S. Ervin-Tripp & C. Mitchell-Kernan (Eds.), *Child Discourse.* New York: Academic Press.

Hull, C. (1943). *Principles of behavior.* New York: Appleton-Century-Crofts.

Jackendoff, R. (1975). Morphological and semantic regularities in the lexicon. *Language, 51,* 639–671.

Jackendoff, R. (1977). *X-bar syntax: A study of phrase-structure.* Cambridge, Mass.: MIT Press.

Jakobson, R., Fant, G., & Halle, M. (1963). *Preliminaries to speech analysis.* Cambridge MA: MIT Press.

Karmiloff-Smith, A. (1979). *A functional approach to child language: A study of determiners and reference.* New York: Cambridge University Press.

Katz, N., Baker, E., & Macnamara, J. (1974). What's in a name? A study of how children learn common and proper names. *Child Development, 45,* 469–473.

Keil, F. C. & Batterman, D. (1984). A characteristic-to-defining shift in the development of word meaning. *Journal of Verbal Learning and Verbal Behavior, 23,* 221–236.

Klatt, D. (1980). Speech perception: a model of acoustic-phonetic analysis and lexical access. In R. Cole (Ed.), *Perception and production of fluent speech.* Hillsdale, N.J.: Lawrence Erlbaum Associates.

Köpcke, K., and Zubin, D. (1983). Die kognitive Organisation der Genuszuweisung zu den einsilbigen Nomen der deutschen Gegenwartssprache. *Zeitschrift fur germanistische Linguistik, 11,* 166–182.

Kuczaj, Stan A. II. (1981). Factors influencing children's hypothetical reference. *Journal of Child Language, 8,* 131–137.

Kurtzman, H. (February 1985). *Studies in syntactic ambiguity resolution.* Doctoral dissertation, Massachusetts Institute of Technology,

Ladefoged, P. (1975). *A course in phonetics.* New York: Harcourt Brace Jovanovich.

Ladefoged, P. (1980). What are linguistic sounds made of? *Language, 56,* 485–502.

Macken, M. A. & Ferguson, C. A. (1983). Cognitive aspects of phonological development: Model evidence and issues. In K. Nelson (Ed.), *Children's language: Vol. 4.* Hillsdale, NJ: Lawrence Erlbaum Associates.

Macnamara, J. (1982). *Names for things.* Cambridge: MIT Press.

MacWhinney, B. (1975a). Pragmatic patterns in child syntax. *Stanford Papers and Reports on Language Development, 10,* 153–165.

MacWhinney, B. (1975b). Rules, rote, and analogy in morphological formations by Hungarian children. *Journal of Child Language, 2,* 65–77.

MacWhinney, B. (1977). Starting points. *Language, 53,* 152–168.

MacWhinney, B. (1978a). Conditions on acquisitional models. *Proceedings of the 1978 Annual Conference.* New York: Association for Computing Machinary.

MacWhinney, B. (1978b). The acquisition of morphophonology. *Monographs of the Society for Research in Child Development, 43,* Whole no. 1.

MacWhinney, B. (1982). Basic syntactic processes. In S. Kuczaj (Ed.), *Language acquisition: vol 1. Syntax and semantics.* Hillsdale, N.J.: Lawrence Erlbaum Associates.

MacWhinney, B. (1984a). Grammatical devices for sharing points. In R. Schiefelbusch (Ed.), *Communicative competence: Acquisition and intervention.* Baltimore: University Park Press.

MacWhinney, B. (1984b). Where do categories come from? In C. Sophian (Ed.), *Origins of cognitive skills.* Hillsdale, N.J.: Lawrence Erlbaum Associates.

MacWhinney, B. (1986). Hungarian language acquisition as an exemplification of a general model of grammatical development. In D. Slobin (Ed.), *The cross-cultural study of language acquisition.* Hillsdale, N.J.: Lawrence Erlbaum Associates.

MacWhinney, B., & Anderson, J. (1986). The acquisition of grammar. In M. Gopnik & I. Gopnik (Ed.), *From models to modules: Studies in cognitive science.* Norwood, N.J.: Ablex.
MacWhinney, B., Bates, E., & Kliegl, R. (1984). Cue validity and sentence interpretation in English, German, and Italian. *Journal of Verbal Learning and Verbal Behavior, 23,* 127–150.
MacWhinney, B. Pleh, C., & Bates, E., (1985). Case-marking and the development of sentence comprehension. *Cognitive Psychology, 55,* 178–209.
MacWhinney, B., & Snow, C. (1985). The child language data exchange system. *Journal of Child Language, 12,* 271–296.
Maratsos, M. P. (1976). *The use of definite and indefinite reference in young children.* Cambridge: Cambridge University Press.
Maratsos, M. (1982). The child's construction of grammatical categories. In E. Wanner, & L. Gleitman (Ed.), *Language acquisition: The state of the art.* New York: Cambridge University Press.
Maratsos, M., & Chalkley, M. (1980). The internal language of children's syntax: The ontogenesis and representation of syntactic categories. In K. Nelson (Ed.), *Children's language: Volume 2.* New York: Gardner.
Marcus, M. (1980). *A theory of syntactic recognition for natural language.* Cambridge, Mass.: MIT Press.
Markman, E. (1984). The acquisition and hierarchical organization of categories by children. In C. Sophian (Ed.), *Origins of cognitive skills.* Hillsdale, N.J.: Lawrence Erlbaum Associates.
Marslen-Wilson, W., and Tyler, L. (1981). Central processes in speech understanding. *Philosophical Transactions of the Royal Society of London, 290,* 34–66.
Martin, J., & Molfese, D. (1971). Some developmental aspects of preferred adjective ordering. *Psychonomic Science, 22,* 219–220.
Martin, J., & Molfese, D. (1972). Preferred adjective ordering in very young children. *Journal of Verbal Learning and Verbal Behavior, 11,* 287–292.
Massaro, D., & Cohen, M. (1983). Consonant/vowel ratio: An improbable cue in speech. *Perception and Psychophysics, 33,* 501–505.
Massaro, D. (1985). *Speech perception by ear and eye: A paradigm for psychological inquiry.* (Unpublished manuscript)
Mazurkewich, I., & White, L. (1984). The acquisition of the dative alternation: Unlearning overgeneralizations. *Cognition, 16,* 261–283.
McClelland, J. L. (1985). Putting knowledge in its place: A scheme for programming parallel processing structures on the fly. *Cognitive Science, 9,* 113–146.
McClelland, J., & Kawamoto, A. (1986). Mechanisms of sentence processing: Assigning roles to constituents. In J. McClelland & D. Kumelhary (Eds.), *Parallel distributed processing* (Vol. 2). Cambridge: MIT Press.
McClelland, J. (1985). Putting knowledge in its place: A scheme for programming parallel processing structures on the fly. *Cognitive Science, 9,* 113–146.
McClelland, J., & Rumelhart, D. (1981). An interactive activation model of context effects in letter perception: Part 1. An account of the basic findings. *Psychological Review, 88,* 375–402.
McDonald, J. (August 1984). *Semantic and syntactic processing cues used by first and second language learners of English, Dutch, and German.* Doctoral dissertation, Carnegie-Mellon University,
McDonald, J. L. (1986). The development of sentence comprehension strategies in English and Dutch. *Journal of Experimental Child Psychology, 41,* 317–335.
Medin, D., & Smith, E. (1984). Concepts and concept formation. *Annual Review of Psychology, 35,* 113–138.
Menn, L., & MacWhinney, B. (1984). The repeated morph constraint: Toward an explanation. *Language, 19,* 519–541.
Mervis, C. (1984). Early lexical development: The contributions of mother and child. In C. Sophian (Ed.), *Origins of cognitive skills.* Hillsdale, N.J.: Lawrence Erlbaum Associates.

Miller, G., & Johnson-Laird, P. (1976). *Language and perception*. Cambridge: Harvard University Press.

Ninio, A. (1986). Negative feedback on very young children's grammar.

Palermo, D., & Eberhart, L. (1968). On the learning of morphological rules: An experimental analogy. *Journal of Verbal Learning and Verbal Behavior, 7*, 337–344.

Perkins, E. (1978). *The role of word order and scope in the interpretation of Navajo sentences*. Doctoral dissertation, University of Arizona,

Peters, A. (1983). *The units of language acquisition*. New York: Cambridge University Press.

Piaget, J. (1966). *The child's conception of physical causality*. London: Routledge & Kegan Paul. originally publishe in 1930.

Pinker, S. (1979). Formal models of language learning. *Cognition, 7*, 217–283.

Pinker, S. (1982). A theory of the acquisition of lexical-interpretive grammars. In J. Bresnan (Ed.), *The mental representation of grammatical relations*. Cambridge, Mass.: MIT Press.

Quine, W. V. O. (1960). *Word and object*. Cambridge, Mass.: MIT Press.

Quine, W. (1974). *The roots of reference*. LaSalle, Ill.: Open Court Press.

Richards, M. (1979). Adjective ordering in the language of young children: An experimental investigation. *Journal of Child Language, 6*, 253–278.

Rosch, E. (1977). Human categorization. In N. Warren (Ed.), *Studies in cross-cultural psychology*. New York: Academic Press.

Rosch, E., & Mervis, C. B. (1975). Family resemblances: Studies in the internal structure of categories. *Cognitive Psychology, 7*, 573–605.

Rumelhart, D., & Norman, D. (1982). Simulating a skilled typist: A study of skilled cognitive-motor performance. *Cognitive Science, 6*, 1–36.

Sachs, J. (1983). Talking about the there and then: The emergence of displaced reference in parent-child discourse. In K. E. Nelson (Ed.), *Children's language, Vol. 4*. Hillsdale, N.J.: Lawrence Erlbaum Associates.

Saussure, F. de. (1966). *Course in general linguistics*. New York: McGraw-Hill.

Scheffelin, M. (1971). Childrens' understanding of constraints upon adjective order. *Journal of Learning Disabilities, 4*, 264–272.

Schieffelin, B. (1981). A developmental study of pragmatic appropriateness of word order and casemarking in Kaluli. In W. Deutsch (Ed.), *The child's construction of language*. London: Academic Press.

Schlesinger, I. M. (1977). *Production and comprehension of utterances*. Hillsdale, N.J.: Lawrence Erlbaum Associates.

Schlesinger, I. M. (1982). *Steps to language: toward a theory of native language acquisition*. Hillsdale, N.J.: Lawrence Erlbaum Associates.

Schwenk, M., & Danks, J. (1974). A developmental study of the pragmatic communication rule for prenominal adjective ordering. *Memory & Cognition, 2*, 149–152.

Scott, D. R. & Cutler, A. (1984). Segmental phonology and the perception of syntactic structure. *Journal of Verbal Learning and Verbal Behavior, 23*, 450–466.

Seidenberg, M., Tanenhaus, M., Leiman, J., & Bienkowski, M. (1982). Automatic access of the meanings of ambiguous words in context: Some limitations of knowledge-based processing. *Cognitive Psychology, 14*, 489–537.

Siegler, R. (1986). Unities across domains in children's strategy choices. In M. Perlmutter (Ed.), *Minnesota symposium of child psychology, Vol. 19*. Hillsdale, N.J.: Lawrence Erlbaum Associates.

Siegler, R., & Shrager, J. (1984). Strategy choices in addition and subtraction: How do children know what to do? In C. Sophian (Ed.), *Origins of cognitive skills*. Hillsdale, N.J.: Lawrence Erlbaum Associates.

Smith, N. V. (1973). *The acquisition of phonology: A case study*. Cambridge, England: Cambridge University Press.

Sokolov, J. L. (1985). *Free radicals not allowed: A lexicalist model of acquisition of syntax*. Unpublished master's thesis, Carnegie-Mellon University.

Sokolov, J. L. (1986). Que validity on Hebrew sentence construction. *Journal of Child Language*, submitted.

Sophian, C. (1984). Developing search skills in infancy and early childhood. In Sophian, C. (Ed.), *Origins of cognitive skills*. Hillsdale, N.J.: Lawrence Erlbaum Associates.

Stemberger, J. (1981). Morphological haplology. *Language, 57,* 791–817.

Stemberger, J. (1982). *The lexicon in a model of language production*. Doctoral dissertation, University of California, San Diego,

Stemberger, J., & MacWhinney, B. (1985). Frequency of the lexical storage of regularly inflectd forms. *Memory and Cognition, 14,* 17–26.

Stemberger, J., & MacWhinney, B. (1986). Form-oriented inflection errors in language processing. *Cognitive Psychology. 18,* 329–354.

Swinney, D. (1979). Lexical access during sentence comprehension: (re) consideration of context effects. *Journal of Verbal Learning and Verbal Behavior, 18,* 645–659.

Tanenhaus, M., & Leiman, J., & Seidenberg, M. (1979). Evidence for multiple stages in the processing of ambiguous words in syntactic contexts. *Journal of Verbal Learning and Verbal Behavior, 18,* 427–440.

Tanz, C. (1980). *Studies in the acquisition of deictic terms*. Cambridge: Cambridge University Press.

Tesniere, L. (1959). *Elements de syntaxe structurale*. Paris: Paris Klincksieck.

Thibadeau, R., Just, M., & Carpenter, P. (1982). A model of the time course and content of reading. *Cognitive Science, 6,* 157–203.

Vennemann, T. (1972). Rule inversion. *Lingua, 29,* 209–242.

Wanner, E., & Maratsos, M. (1978). An ATN approach to comprehension. In M. Halle, J. Bresnan & G. Miller (Ed.), *Linguistic theory and psychological reality*. Cambridge, MA: The MIT Press.

Warren, R., & Warren, N. (1976). Dual semantic encoding of homographs and homophones embedded in context. *Memory and Cognition, 4,* 586–592.

Weist, R., Wysocka, H., Witkowska-Stadnik, K., Buczowska, E., & Konieczna, E. (1984). The defective tense hypothesis: on the emergence of tense and aspect in child Polish. *Journal of Child Language, 11,* 347–374.

Werner, H., & Kaplan, E. (1950). Development of word meaning through verbal context: An experimental study. *Journal of Psychology, 29,* 251–257.

Wexler, K., & Culicover, P. (1980). *Formal principles of language acquisition*. Cambridge, MA: MIT Press.

Whorf, B., & Carroll, J. (Ed.). (1967). *Language, thought, and reality*. Cambridge, MA: MIT Press.

Wittgenstein, L. (1953). *Philosophical investigations*. Oxford: Blackwell.

Wolff, J. G. (1975). An algorithm for the segmentation of an artificial language analogue. *British Journal of Psychology, 66,* 79–90.

III CONSTRAINTS ON THE FORM OF GRAMMAR

9 The Acquisition of Implicit Arguments and the Distinction Between Theory, Process, and Mechanism

Thomas Roeper
University of Massachusetts

INTRODUCTION

The acquisition literature (e.g. papers in this volume) make frequent use of the terms *theory, process, mechanism,* and *account*. These terms are often assumed to mean the same thing, but I shall argue that they are different. To begin with, language acquisition is a process so broad that inevitably every aspect of human behavior (and a good deal of biology) is connected to it. Therefore, everyone's "theory" will inevitably describe some of the facts. For instance, there can be little doubt that rote memory, analogy, social aspects of pragmatics, individual differences and currently unknown aspects of neurology are central aspects of language.[1]

But from the perspective of current linguistic theory,[2] **grammar** and **language** are radically different though intimately connected. Grammar is exclusively a set of **principles** while language includes the interaction of principles with many other aspects of mind. Understanding the role of auxiliary language systems may allow us to isolate principles of grammar.

Explanations, which represent the principles behind a description of facts, are crucial to the understanding of a creative organism. A crude analogy may be helpful at the outset. It is where the whole is greater than its parts that we can see the work of a principle. A cake is not described by a list of ingredients. We need

[1]See work by Bates (1976) and MacWhinney (1982) and references therein.

[2]We will operate within the Government-Binding framework, although most of what we say would probably suit other perspectives as well.

to state the exact fashion in which it is cooked. It is the combination of heat and certain ingredients which causes a cake to rise, which makes it more than its ingredients. The icing may be the best part to a child, but in essence, the icing (perhaps like meaning in language) is actually extraneous to the central principle, namely, cooking from which the term "cake" comes.

THEORY, PROCESS, MECHANISM, AND ACCOUNT

We will use the term **theory** to refer to a set of deductive principles that state the relationship between innate knowledge and a representative sample of input sentences from any human language. The generative power in language ability comes from combining a set of inputs with grammatical principles. A theory has only principles in it. A theory may or may not be successful. It may fail to capture the domain of fact which, pre-theoretically, appeared to be relevant. Then, either the enterprise as a whole collapses, or the domain is redrawn. In fact, over the years the domain of grammar has been redrawn and narrowed repeatedly to enable linguistic principles to become successful. For instance, many features that were once written into transformational rules are now removed to other parts of grammar or other parts of mind.

Unfortunately, the term *theory* is used loosely to describe any programmatic account. It is unfortunate because a confusion between theory and process can easily become a blockade to insight. I will illustrate this with a biological analogy.

I will use the term **process** to refer to the interaction between a theory and the world, or what one might call *orthogonal theories*. If a child requires a kind of motivation, personality disposition, or exposure to a certain context, these features might be crucial to a real-world description of what occurs, but they lie outside a theory. Nevertheless it is quite possible that a theory cannot be successful without reference to these phenomena. They are then essential prerequisites.[3]

I use the term **mechanism** to refer to *deterministic* interactions within and beyond the theory. We might have one parameter which is set by the presence of a particular sentence. Another parameter might be set not simply by the syntax of the sentence but by features of its interpretation which are partially defined beyond language. I will illustrate such a case with the notion of "affectedness."

The fundamental hypothesis of linguistic theory is that such deterministic interactions exist. If a child has some knowledge X, then Y must occur. Some linguists make a stronger assumption: principles of grammar and representative sentences are exhaustively sufficient. I argue that it is the deterministic character

[3]For instance, it is important to know if improved lighting will improve reading, but it does not reveal how a child reads.

of acquisition, not the homogeneity[4] of linguistic theory, which is the crucial feature. Chomsky (1981) takes a position similar to mine; he argues that some universals have an ''extra-linguistic dimension'' which triggers linguistic knowledge. I believe that the extra-linguistic component can be completely non-linguistic and still function as a linguistic trigger. The widely-used notion of ''affectedness,'' as we shall see, is crucial to syntactic analysis but it has no syntactic character.

It is often difficult to separate deterministic relations from non-deterministic pre-requisites. To use a metaphor: must one blush if embarrassed? For some people, blushing is automatically triggered by certain emotions, for others it seems not to be. Likewise, one can ask, must one have a clear notion of ''definiteness'' in order to recognize the definite article? Or can it be recognized simply as a syntactic entity that marks nouns? Knowledge of ''definiteness'' might be positively correlated with recognition of an article, but not logically (or biologically) necessary. This is an empirical question.[5]

I will use the term **Account** to refer to the full picture of what occurs in acquisition: the deterministic interaction between linguistic principles, non-linguistic triggers, and their relation to non-deterministic processing and pragmatic pre-requisites. One goal of a linguistic theory, if it is ultimately to be a part of biology, is to provide a description of language ability that will serve as an input into a theory of neurology. The fulfillment of such a goal will require a fairly acute grasp of the context of language acquisition as well as the deductive principles behind it. The relation between maturation and nutrition is perhaps the appropriate analogy. To understand growth, one should not confuse food with genes. Toward that end, let us consider the role of environment more closely.

ENVIRONMENT

Excessive reference to non-deterministic interactive factors can undermine the insights of a theory. For instance, in biology, the theory of reproduction can be defined genetically. In addition, there is a theory of mutation which supposedly interacts with an orthogonal environmental factor, namely, the *survival of the fittest*. The latter concept involves a real-world concept that is totally unmeasureable: *environment* itself is infinitely varied. According to the theory, mutations are random and survivability causes a beneficial mutation to dominate.

---

[4]The vision of notational homogeneity has been implicitly abandoned with the advent of modularity in syntax. Whereas transformations were all written in a single notation, no one supposes that there is a single notation for thematic roles, case theory, and logical form. (An ambitious mathematician might develop such a notation, but in order to insure that it was not epi-phenomenal, he would have to be sure that the primitives of the theory functioned biologically.)

[5]See Nishigauchi and Roeper (1985) for an extensive discussion of the triggering role of referential information.

Current controversies in biology center on whether the emphasis on process may not be overstated. Perhaps other factors besides survivability determine how mutations occur. It could be non-random and, therefore, genetically principled. It is difficult to "disprove" the survivalist theory because it is intrinsically vague. But it appears that such a theory cannot account for numerous peculiarities of evolution. Consequently one must posit a more complex theory of *mutation*. In other words, current theories return to principles which govern mutation and which are contained within genetic structures that do not significantly interact with the world.[6] It has taken 50 years to confront the survivalist aspect of the theory of evolution partly because its claim of interaction was so vague that it could not be disproven (and partly because new insights came from molecular structure of DNA).

The relationship between theory and environment is the same in language acquisition as it is in evolution. It could be that certain patterns of acquisition are dictated by environment rather than structure. It could be that an independent factor like *recognition of authority* is crucial to the use of imperatives. Exposure to imperative sentences themselves would not elicit the analysis that the subject "you" is missing. The notion of authority, emerging independently, would trigger the analysis of you-deletion. Therefore an extraneous factor could be relevant to the learning of imperatives. In this sense an orthogonal component could bear a deterministic relation to the theory. The "process" alternative is that the notion of authority contributes to an understanding of the context in which a sentence is uttered. Grasping its context may incline a child to choose an imperative sentence to undergo syntactic analysis, but the syntactic analysis itself occurs in its own terms.

The "pragmatic" approach to language has often shown that contextual factors can facilitate acquisition.[7] I am unaware of any evidence that it has a deterministic role. The postulation of non-deterministic contextual explanations should be the last option selected because, in effect, it abandons the possibility of a principled understanding, and it is intrinsically beyond either proof or disproof. In what follows, I will show that a partially pragmatic property of "affectedness" plays a deterministic role in the acquisition of certain syntactic structures.

How can one tell the difference between deterministic and non-deterministic interactions? It is not necessarily easy. A non-deterministic interaction can easily have a gradualistic appearance. A deterministic interaction should not, but the interaction of other factors can produce the appearance of gradualism. As we shall see, there is one advantageous consequence of determinism: it makes straightforwardly falsifiable predictions.

---

[6]For instance, food can have an effect on genetic expression, but it is distinctly minor. We might grow an inch less because of poor nutrition, but one cannot suddenly grow an extra arm by eating an apple a day nor will the intricacies of facial appearance change.

[7]See Hamburger and Crain (1982), Bates (1976), Clark and Clark (1977) and references therein.

Our goal should be: to state the *mechanism* of interaction (between principles, sentences, and interpretations) with a precision that allows us to map in detail the course of language acquisition. This goal is hampered by the fact that we know very little about the course of acquisition even in English. Most of the structures of the language remain completely unexplored.

We know virtually nothing about wh-movement in complex sentences, one of the central features of modern grammar. One can imagine twenty steps in the acquisition of wh-words. In what order do children allow the following structures to emerge?

1 a. possessive: Whose hand can I hold __?
b. Object extraction: What did I think you said __?
c. Subject extraction: What did you say __ fell down?
d. Extraction over that: What did you say that you ate __?
e. Free relatives: Do you know what I want __?
f. Bound Variables: Who_i thinks he_i has a hat?
g. Variables excluded: Who_x does he_y think __ has a hat?
h. Pied Piping: To whom did you talk __?
i. Bridge Verbs: When did you say __? that Bill was coming __?
k. Non-Bridge: When did you agree __ that Bill was coming?
l. Parasitic Gaps: $What_i$ did you eat $\_\__i$ without cooking $\_\__i$?
m. Double-Wh: What did you play __ where?
n. Extraction Constraint: *Where did you play why?

Furthermore, we do not know how the restricted/unrestricted relative clause contrast emerges or when children learn that both that and which mark relatives. These sentences occur readily in the environment of the child although parents are not generally conscious of uttering them.

These questions precede more interesting ones: how and when are comparatives learned? Current theory argues that comparatives involve wh-movement although no wh- element appears? When do children learn the difference in interpretation between I know a lawyer smarter than Bill and I know a smarter lawyer than Bill. Only in the latter sentence must Bill also be a lawyer. As in any science, the crucial data and sentences are often obscure and sometimes quite exotic.

Nonetheless, there is a notable absence of attention to central domains of structural variation, like wh-movement, in acquisition research. We should function more in the manner of field linguists. A field linguist makes an extensive overview of language before he tries to fix its details.

This is not the pattern of acquisition research. There must be hundreds of experiments on the passive. Everything is varied (age, sex, verb classes, pragmatics) except the passive structure itself. I am unaware of any experiment that deals with the crucial cases of passives from "believe" sentences: John was believed to have taken drugs or John was made to eat his lunch.[8] And yet believe and make are in the vocabulary of 5-yr-olds. Without the believe and make sentences, where the subject comes from another clause, it is difficult to discern the difference between passives (John was hurt) and adjectives (John was big).

Another example: there is no real study of the emergence of *adverbs*. It is my impression that children do not use real adverbs until quite late.[9] What is complex about a sentence like: he played with me angrily? A recent theory suggests that adverbs assign independent thematic roles. Thus we can have a sentence like: John was arrested voluntarily where John is the object of arrest but the subject of voluntarily. This provides a possible explanation: (a) certain adverbs add a second thematic role to a nounphrase, and (b) in the unmarked case nounphrases have only one thematic role. Therefore, children do not initially use them. This simple, but perhaps important, theory cannot be evaluated currently because we lack a basic description of how sentential, verbphrase, and verbal adverbs emerge.

METHODOLOGY

The full range of data is unexplored in my estimation partly because of an experimental methodology in which we get inconsistent results from a domain that is too narrow. One cannot follow the "correct" methodology unless very little is explored. Linguistic theory, using intuitions, would slow down enormously if one did a psychological test for each intuition (or even if we just standardly asked ten speakers to judge every intuition in a linguistics article). It is more profitable to get a wide range of data than to purify intuitional data; errors in intuition (which are frequent in the literature) become themselves isolated by the theory in time.[10]

---

[8]Crucially, the latter sentence does not entail the meaning John was made. Do children know that fact? The same distinction arises in non-sentential environments: the house was made beautiful by John does not entail that John made the house.

[9]They are noticeable with six-year-olds. Verb intensifying adverbs like fast, or well occur earlier.

[10]Backwards anaphora is an interesting case in point. The sentences which form the core of recent work in theory work and acquisition (John saw im; after Bill; ran around) was judged ungrammatical initially by Langacker. This misjudgement delayed theoretical insight for a number of years, but the delay is much smaller than if all intuitional experiments followed psychological methodology. Obtaining intuitions is an experiment which is subject to all of the contextual effects, response biases, order biases, and so forth that any experiment is subject to plus one more: theoretical bias of the linguist. Nevertheless large agreement on subtle principles of grammar has emerged in many domains.

But in effect psychology requires the purification of each piece of data before a wider range of structures is examined. Its consequences are that the data is often uninterpretable because it's too narrowly focused and then often leads to an understatement of children's abilities. Heavy-handed, non-conversational experiments may not be the way to elicit a child's knowledge of subtle structures. The child reverts to less adult but simpler strategies of response.

What makes psychological data confounded? The problem is that *inference* is very powerful. If we hear a sentence like this book fills a much-needed gap in the literature it will often be understood, using inference, to mean that much-needed applies to book and not to gap. Nevertheless, upon reflection, a speaker knows that the *grammar* allows only the gap reading.

In such examples, inference overwhelms grammar. There is no such thing as a "neutral" context. Therefore, if there is a pragmatic bias *toward* the correct interpretation, then the child may use inference to arrive at what looks like the correct result *without* using grammar. (You can understand the milk was drunk without understanding the passive.) If there is a bias *against* the grammatical interpretation, then the child may use inference to overrule the grammar. (You might misunderstand the man was cut down by the tree even though you do have the passive.) One cannot be sure that the child has used the grammar, unless he uses the grammar against the pragmatics. However, most young children children resist anti-pragmatic interpretations.

The ultimate effect of this observation is that it is impossible to control adequately for pragmatic effects in experiments. This calls into question many experiments where the emphasis has been placed on control of context and not on surveying a broad range of structures. Such experiments, are still interpretable (particularly if they are addressed to subtle issues in grammatical theory where extraneous cognitive effects are impossible). Experiments in which the "controls" cannot be met may still have a powerful and natural interpretation within a theory. It is noteworthy that naturalistic data (like those of Bowerman) continues to provide a disproportionately large number of the central observations in the acquisition literature. We would lose a great deal if we excluded all naturalistic data simply because it is non-replicable, and the context is uncontrolled.

Our focus is upon minimal grammatical contrasts (like the ball bounced compared to the ball was bounced) which are explored in uniform environments in a conversational style. The goal is to generate new data in a fashion that is as naturalistic as possible.

THE SHIFTING DOMAIN OF GRAMMAR

A further reason for the failure to map the course of acquisition in detail is unavoidable: the boundaries of grammar and its internal content constantly evolve as linguistic theory evolves. The microscopic structural detail that is involved means that gross impressions of language can be quite misleading. A large number of the structural contrasts in (1) have been discovered within the last decade, and yet they are central to current versions of putative innate structure. If analogies to microbiology are apt, then it must be in terms of these microscopic variations that language grows.[11]

A related domain which remains untouched is quantifiers. Why is it impossible to say *2a* but possible to say *2b:*

2a. everyone$_i$ thinks and he$_i$ knows it (unless he is not everyone)
b. everyone$_i$ thinks he$_i$ knows it

If a child allows bound variables on both of these structures, then there is a strong chance that he is using inference and not grammar because no grammar allows bound variables across coordinated structures. It is only recently that it has become clear that there is a difference between pragmatic bound variables and true bound variables. There must be a point at which the child knows this distinction.[12]

NATIVISM

It is a fact that language acquisition does not occur at once. It takes several years and as our knowledge of what language is deepens, we may discover that it takes even longer. The deductive theory suggests that learning a language should be instantaneous. I suggested many years ago that the best operative assumption is that all of the relevant data is always present in the environment of the child.[13] Then the question becomes: why is acquisition not literally instantaneous?

There are several possible theories, all of which, in my estimation, could be partially correct. The answers await the detailed study to which I alluded above.

PROCESSING ACCOUNT

The processing limitations of a young child, though ill-understood, seem to have a profound impact upon a child's grammar, although this notion is based largely on children's obvious difficulties with production. The argument here, in effect,

---

[11]See Hamburger (1980) for an interesting discussion of six stages through which a child goes in learning relative clauses.

[12]See Roeper (1986) for extensive discussion of the acquisition of bound variables. A good example of pragmatic bound variable interpretation comes in a sentence like people have noses. We tend to assign one nose to a person, but this is not dictated by the grammar.

[13]Roeper (1978).

is that children do not register a large amount of the data, and therefore acquisition is not instantaneous. Whatever exceeds processing capacity is excluded.

This proposal differs from the proposal in Roeper (1978, 1981) that children have an input filter which systematically excludes portions of the data in order to guarantee that the grammar proceed through certain logical steps.[14] The latter suggests that the permissible input is structured by the child's grammar itself and not by processing capacity.

MATURATION

A second theory is that the child undergoes maturation, either in terms of cognitive ability or in terms of linguistic ability itself. Cognitive growth could be a barrier to acquisition. If we do not understand cognitively the notion of ''possibility'' then we might not be able to learn the subjunctive.

A variant of this proposal is that the child's initial generalizations are in a different notation. It could, for instance, be the case that a child begins with a cognitive definition of a thematic role before he has a linguistic one (see below).

A third proposal, recently promoted by Borer and Wexler (to appear) is that linguistic ability itself matures. The capacity to assign two grammatical roles to one NP is entailed in NP movement. This ability may be delayed.

GRAMMATICAL STAGES

It is logically possible that no stages result from the acquisition of grammar itself. There are facts, however, which make this strong hypothesis seem improbable. The persistent failure of children, over years, to learn the obligatory nature of subject-verb inversion in sentences like What I can do (instead of what can I do) cannot be attributed to parsing difficulty, an inability to perform transformations, or semantic obscurity. Therefore, it stands as an example of a part of language acquisition where grammatical analysis itself reflects a temporal dimension. Klein (1982) has some interesting proposals about the re-analysis of the COMP node which might lead to an explanation of the delay.

PREMATURE COMPARISONS

These theories provide a valuable backdrop to acquisition analysis. There is no reason to prefer any of them on *a priori* grounds. Comparisons seem premature.

[14]See Nishigauchi and Roeper (1985) for a brief discussion of the possibility that backwards anaphora might be initially excluded.

In fact they could all be true about different aspects of the acquisition process. There is little point in arguing about which is correct because they are all extremely crude postures toward a complex and intricate process. These theories are valuable insofar as they can be formulated with sufficient precision to make intricate predictions about structural growth. The refinement of these theories will only come with the refinement of our analysis of how language structures grow.

A CENTRAL QUESTION: HOW TO PREDICT UNGRAMMATICALITY

There is a curious disjunction between acquisition work motivated by linguistic theory and work which comes from other cognitivist perspectives. The emphasis in cognitive approaches is on the achievement of a cognitive representation for what a child can produce. The emphasis from a linguistic perspective is on explaining why a child does *not* produce certain structures.

The linguistic perspective presupposes the assumption that general cognitive abilities are *overpowerful* with respect to language. It is cognitively possible to represent numerous kinds of languages and generalizations which are not a part of natural language. Therefore it is no surprise that we can find cognitive representations for any structure. The problem is to explain the absence of generalization.[15]

AGENT/PATIENT IN A DEDUCTIVE ACCOUNT

Let us consider a particular problem in this regard. Our problem can be seen from a "process" perspective or a "theory" perspective. It has been noted that **Agent/Patient** structures play a prominent role in many languages of the world and in acquisition.[16] There is a cognitive theory which utilizes the idea as a part of the process of acquisition [Pinker (this volume), Bates and MacWhinney (this volume)]. One could state the idea in this fashion. The child recognizes Agent/Patient relations in the real world. He is therefore able to recognize structures which have the same relationships articulated, even if those structures fail to fit the most frequent and hence canonical forms. Therefore a child's first passives will be concrete. That is, he will recognize Bill was kicked more easily than Bill was liked. This is precisely what acquisition research has revealed.

---

[15]See Roeper (to appear) for discussion.

[16]This is discussed in literature emanating from the Universals project. See also Carlson and Roeper (1980) for discussion with reference to productive morphology. Jill deVilliers (1980) has pointed out that "concrete" objects are easy to acquire. See discussions in Brown (1973) along these lines, Pinker (1984) and notes therein.

David Lebeaux (1985) has examined the same issue from a deductive perspective. I will present essentially his argument. M. Anderson (1979) observed that there is an asymmetry between passives and nominalizations. She noted that passives, but not nominalizations, allowed a "non-affected object" to move (that is, a non-concrete object):

3a. the enjoyment of a play	*d.* the destruction of the city
b. the play was enjoyed	*e.* the city was destroyed
c. *the play's enjoyment	*f.* the city's destruction

The problem from a theoretical point of view, which is not addressed by the cognitive perspective, is why (3c) is impossible, but (3f) is possible. How can we prevent a child from extending all passives in sentences (3b,e) to all passives in nominalizations (3c,f)? The problem extends to other structures. We find middle forms like (4a) but not with unaffected objects (4b):

4a. Greek transcribes easily
b. *plays enjoy easily

Compounds also exhibit the distinction. Note that we can use the world illustrate in two ways, onc as an action (5a) and also as an equative (5b):

5a. the man illustrated the book
b. the man illustrated the problem (= he is the problem)
6a. a book-illustrating man
b. *the problem-illustrating man

How does the child learn that nominalizations, middles, and compounds all share this restriction against moving non-affected objects?

It would be simple to explain these phenomena if the passive also obeyed the constraint on affected objects. Instead we must motivate the child's shift from a stage where passive obeys the constraint to a stage where the passive is liberated from the affectedness constraint but other forms are not.

Lebeaux proposes an intuitively simple idea as a universal:

7. affected objects are internal arguments of a verb.

Therefore the apparent subject must somehow be represented in the verbphrase. In other words, the child initially uses a semantic device to establish the existence of a *trace* in a passive. An internal argument must occur within a verbphrase, and therefore the representation of passive is this:

8. the boy$_i$ was kicked *trace*$_i$

The critical point comes in the partial generalization of passive, but not other structures, to non-affected objects.

Why are affected objects excluded in nominalizations but permitted in passives? Lebeaux's central idea in intuitive terms is this: both a verb and a nominalization may require an object semantically. The verb *also* requires an object syntactically. In nominalizations the verb-object relation is semantically construed while in verb phrases it can be syntactically or semantically construed. The syntactic analysis allows passive to occur without a semantic trigger while the nominalization requires the semantic trigger of an affected object. In effect, then, the difference comes down to the fact that verbs have syntactic objects, but nouns have only semantic objects. The concept that verbs have objects is expressed in current theory through the idea that verbs *assign case*. This intuitive account contains some misleading simplifications.

We will now advance the same idea in technical terms. Our goal here is to provide a precise mechanical role for what has been treated as a vague semantic preference for concrete objects. A theory both achieves elegance and provides a deductive ladder for a child when seemingly unrelated phenomena possess a mechanical interaction.

A central tenet of current linguistic theory is this: *all NPs must receive case*. It is notable that the object in a passive receives nominative case when it is in subject position. Note the contrast between passive and topicalization:

9a. I was liked *trace*
b. *Me was liked *trace*
c. Me, he likes *trace*

In (9c) the object <u>me</u> continues to receive accusative case from the verb. This is impossible for passives (9b) where the former object now receives nominative case. What defines the difference between passive and topicalization? The topicalization operation keeps accusative case alive while the passive loses it.

It is interesting to note that topicalization appears very early in children's grammars. This supports the notion that children know (a) that NPs can be moved from their Deep structure position next to the verb, and (b) NP's receive case.[17] I will argue, as others have,[18] that the full comprehension of passives is not immediate.

---

[17]Gruber (1965). There needs to be a careful study of pronouns and topicalization in acquisition. I do not have, at the moment, anything beyond anecdotal evidence that children produce forms like "me, she likes."

[18]See Pinker (1984), Borer and Wexler (1987), deVilliers (1980) for evidence that children first learn concrete passives. Further research might overturn this result. This would mean that the two steps in acquisition which we argue are logically necessary would happen at the same time. The learnability sequence whether or not acquisition evidence happens to provide a temporal reflection of the process.

The explicit feature associated with the passive that makes it unlike TOPIC is the -ed affix. The failure of the object to retain accusative case is expressed in linguistic theory via an attribute of affixes; the passive participle -ed *absorbs accusative case*. The absorption of case requires an object position (from which case is absorbed) with *trace*. In effect, the passive participle continues to be a verb so there continues to be an object position. In technical terms, principles of Universal Grammar state: (1) transitive verbs assign case, and (2) case must be phonetically realized. Therefore we must put the case somewhere. The affix is the natural repository for case since it is part of what triggers the passive. The central point is that the theory of case assignment entails the existence of an object position.

Case-absorption then triggers a deductive chain. The object NP, lacking case, is forced to move to subject position to acquire case. Therefore, predictably, it has nominative and not accusative case. We now have a mechanical interaction between three modules of grammar: case-assignment, morphology, and syntactic movement. I can now advance a developmental interpretation.

We have now generated two different ways to identify a *trace* in the object position of the verb: (a) semantic recognition of an internal argument, or (b) recognition that -ed absorbs case. Case absorption is only possible if a verb projects an object position to assign case to. Now one can make the argument that the child first projects passives in terms of the notion of affected, hence internal, object. Then he learns that there is a second device to identify the object position: the -ed absorbs case, marking an object. He can now delete the first criterion or make it optional.[19] It follows that passive at first will be limited to affected objects.

NOMINALIZATIONS

Now let us approach the essence of our problem: explaining why nominalizations do not allow non-affected objects to prepose. Note that nominalizations do not have the power to generate case-assignment (10a). They must generate a preposition to assign case (10b):

10a. *the destruction the city
b. the destruction of the city

Nouns do not assign case and therefore there is no alternative mechanism for the generation of a trace in object position.[20] (Since of does not absorb case, a

[19]Thus, the affected object becomes a *disappearing trigger* in the sense of Nishigauchi and Roeper (1985). Nouns might first be identified as "things." Then article is recognized as a noun-marker and thing can be deleted, i.e. disappears. Consequently we can have nouns like the hope.

[20]See also Borer and Wexler (1987) for alternative deductive strategy.

phrase like *the city's destruction of is also ungrammatical.) In effect then, the nominalization system has only one option: it must use Lebeaux's principle (7) to establish a *trace,*[21] namely, affected objects are internal arguments. Therefore the child can never take the next step with nominalizations. They always are constrained by the use of principle (7) in the projection of traces. If the prenominal noun is not an affected object, it is interpreted as an ordinary possessive that is not an internal argument of the verb. For instance, yesterday's destruction does not mean *the destruction of yesterday.

There is no overgeneralization of nominalizations in children's grammars toward cases like *the play's enjoyment to my knowledge. The argument which Lebeaux advances provides a precise mechanical explanation of why this occurs. Such a mechanical explanation is crucially different from a "cognitive preference" which could only predict that there are more "affected object" cases than other cases.

THE "ACTIVITY" TRIGGER

One can now predict that a child cannot generalize from passive to nominalizations in the use of non-affected objects. Two stages exist:

Stage 1: Use of internal argument to fix a *trace* in the VP
Stage 2: Use of case-absorption on -ed to identify *trace*.

This theory works deductively but I still need to explain what triggers case-absorption. Why does a child not simply give an adjectival reading to all participles, treating John was hurt as if it were John was big?

Wasow (1979) pointed out that passives like the door was closed have a stative reading where no activity is possible and an activity reading where "closing" takes place. Other passives in fact have no stative reading; for example, the door was slammed. A child could easily see that such a sentence was not referring to a result or a property of the door. Therefore, an "activity" reading should be fairly perceptible[22] as a trigger for the presence of a verb within the participle from which the deductive chain then follows.

The concept of "activity" as a verbal trigger is not fully clear. We can

[21]We are simplifying a complex account. Many other interesting questions arise. Why, for instance, is it not possible to do of-insertion in passives, generating forms like "there was hit of the boy. Questions like this of course point again to the necessity of a deductive system. The child must be prevented from generalizing from the nominalization to the passive by some principle.

[22]Unless there is some sophisticated notion of "activity" that associates with passive that no one has yet discerned. Such a sophisticated notion would seem to require a refined innate sensitivity since it is obviously not accessible to ordinary cognition.

certainly say John was active or lively where "activity" is denoted, and no verb is involved. Therefore it is not the case that a child can recognize activity and conclude that a verb and not an adjective is present. Nevertheless, in the unmarked case, where no adjectival endings are present, some notion of activity could serve as a trigger.[23]

What kind of a concept is "affectedness"? I do not believe that it has a linguistic definition, but, like the notion of activity, it is not easy to see how it is defined cognitively. For instance one can say the discovery of America and America's discovery, and we can say the discovery of our common interests but not *our common interests' discovery. Now America is less likely to be affected by its discovery than our common interests are. It is unclear where the affect lies. Nonetheless from the perspective of linguistic theory, the notion of affectedness has a very clear and delimited role. One can use the concept in a deductive scheme without a full cognitive explanation of its origins.

In sum the child can use "internal argument" to trigger the presence of a trace in an adjectival phrase. Then he uses the notion of "activity" to trigger the case assigning properties of the verb which must then be absorbed by the -ed.

I have argued that the child passes through three phases in the analysis of passives. In the first phase, passives are simple adjectives where no verbal properties are recognized: John was hurt is like John was large. In the second phase the verb is recognized within the adjective, and therefore a trace can be assigned, but no case-assignment occurs.[24] In the third phase, when the activity property of the verb is recognized, then case-assignment occurs.

This theory is successful in a technical sense: it predicts exactly the data I have brought to bear and no more than that data. I predicted that nominalizations will not be generalized to include non-affected objects. Without a mechanical explanation, process accounts cannot provide a principled reason for such a limitation on generalizations.[25] This seems to be an intrinsic defect which all non-innatist theories must confront.

This theory, though, is not entirely homogeneous. I cannot explain the limitations on a syntactic operation entirely in syntactic terms. One must allude not only to a different module but, it seems, to a partially non-linguistic parameter. This kind of interaction does not disturb the idea that linguistic ability is genet-

---

[23]See Borer and Wexler (to appear) for an analysis that children do initially treat passives as adjectival. See Fabb (1984) and Lightfoot (1977) for arguments that adjectives can assign a trace which does not receive case.

[24]Note that adjectives take objects in other contexts and more frequently in other languages. We have forms like proud of his children (where non-case-assigning properties force Of-insertion).

[25]One might view the process accounts as a research strategy. They constitute part of a two step process: 1) identify a range of factors which affect a child's progress in acquisition, then (2) identify which features are involved in a deductive mechanism. To achieve explanatory power in acquisition, one must not fail to take the second step. With an explanatory theory in hand we can begin to ask questions about the neurological organization of the human being.

ically determined. The claim is that the interaction between specific linguistic abilities and non-linguistic abilities is itself innately determined and limited to very specific points.[26]

The crucial difference between process approaches and theory approaches lies not in reference to extra-linguistic ability, but in the function of those abilities. Theory approaches allow an extra-linguistic capacity, the capacity for cognitive determination of affectedness, to play a specific role in a deductive system. Process approaches identify the factor involved but do not state what role it plays.[27]

COGNITIVE ROLES AND THEMATIC ROLES

I will turn now to a related domain: the connection between cognitive and thematic roles. What are thematic roles and how does a child acquire them? The acquisition literature offers a straightforward answer; notions like *agent, patient,* and *goal* are fundamentally cognitive. I believe that they are fundamentally cognitive, but their cognitive character has a specific role: they trigger duplicate formal notions in linguistic theory. The cognitive definition covers too much territory and, once again, fails to predict ungrammaticality.

Consider the following contrasts:[28]

11a. the robber of the bank
b. *the thief of the bank (bankthief)
c. stewcook
d. *the cook of stew
e. a taxer of property
f. *a taxman of property

There can be little doubt that both robber and thief are agents. Why can one appear with an of-PP, but the other cannot? Why would a child, having heard

---

[26]The same argument might be reproduced at a subtler level with respect to neurology. We may discover that the notion of *movement rules* will decompose at the neurological level into several components one of which is used for other neurological actions. The innate component is still determining that the interaction occurs in this fashion and not some other one. See Chomsky (1975) for discussion along the same lines.

[27]See Koster (1978a) for discussion of the role of auxiliary systems in the history of science. The concept of gravity could not be isolated without a vision of extraneous factors causing friction which interfere with the pure expression of gravity. A neurological vision of language will probably be unattainable without a fairly clear vision of cognitive and pragmatic factors that interact with the deductive system.

[28]See Finer and Roeper (to appear) and Roeper (1985) for extensive discussion of both acquisition and theoretical aspects of these constructions.

''robber of a bank'' then *not* generalize to produce ''thief of a bank''? No careful study of the matter has been done, but no examples of children producing such sentences are prominent in the literature.[29]

The answer is that the status of agent in (11a,b) is different. The word thief involves agency as a part of its meaning, while robber represents agency as a part of its form (-er). In other words there is a formal AGENT and a cognitive agent. The notion of ''agency'' in the word thief is just like any other feature of meaning. The -er on a word means that the thematic projections of an underlying verb are maintained.[30] In effect, there is a ''duplicate'' formal notion of agency.

The generalization here is part of a larger one:

12a. Affixes maintain the formal thematic relations of a verb.
b. Formal Objects (THEMES) must be linked to formal AGENTS.[31]

An affix is distinct from another word when forming a compound (like taxman) which does not maintain the thematic roles of the verb.

Chomsky (1981) has proposed a syntactic ''Projection Principle'' which prevents deletion of thematic roles through syntactic movement. I propose that the same principle operates in the lexicon with respect to affixation: verbal affixes maintain thematic roles. Therefore we find that we do not have of without an affix:

13a. *the poet of a book (author of a book)
b. *the make of money (the making of money)
c. *the rake of leaves (the raker of leaves)
d. *a photographer of weddings.

In (13d) the -er is present but it has been incorporated into the noun. If we give a different stress pattern which articulates the -er as an affix, then there is a subtle improvement: a PHOtoGRAPHer of weddings. In (13b,c) a verb is but no affix present and therefore the of-phrase is excluded.

There are counter-examples, but they tend to have an idiomatic character as if the whole phrase is lexically represented. Thus we have:

14a. the roll of the dice
b. the pick of the crop

---

[29]If children commonly said things like ''I'm the cook of stew,'' the ungrammaticality is sufficiently egregious that it would be rapidly noted by both researchers and parents.

[30]See Randall (1982) for extensive discussion of the notion of *inheritance* and its acquisition.

[31]See Roeper (1985) for a more technical discussion of these observations. The generalization can be captured in terms of a notion that thematic roles are carried by affixes and thus bear a sister relation to the PP. Where a sister relation is broken, then ungrammaticality results. Note the contrast between the grammar is learnable by the child and *the child's learnability of grammar.

c. the run of the store
d. the push of a button (*the push of a child).[32]

The existence of counter-examples is interesting: why doesn't the child take them as a basis for generalization? In effect, the child does not make a generalization for which he *does* have evidence.

The answer is that the principles of UG are powerful enough to identify these structures automatically as exceptional. Consequently the grammar can tolerate these exceptions because the system immediately identifies them as exceptions (and attaches non-compositional or idiomatic readings to them). Exceptions do not generalize. How does the child recognize the system?

One can state the answer in a simple way:

15. A cognitive agent, an affix, and a verb trigger a formal thematic grid (a grid = set of thematic roles on a verb).

In effect, there is a cross-modular trigger in which the cognitive notion of agency is necessary. However it must be combined with the phonological isolation of an affix like -er and with recognition of the underlying verb. The fundamental trigger here is concrete: the affix. The system is therefore much more straightforward than proposals which require the simultaneous computation of several syntactic factors, as transformational systems often do.

IMPLICIT AGENTS

The generalization above states not only that affixes like -er will maintain thematic roles, but it also makes the (too strong) claim that all affixes will. The -er explicitly makes the noun it attaches to an agent. Other affixes carry thematic roles, but the thematic role remains *implicit:*[33]

16a. the ball rolled
b. the ball was rolled.

In (16b) there is an implicit agent while in (16a) there is none. Agency is neither referred to nor necessarily excluded in (16a). How does a child know that there is

---

[32]Where there is an interpretation we find the of-phrase receives a subject interpretation: the walk of a dog has the dog as the subject of walk, and it refers to the style of movement. See Roeper (1985) for extensive discussion.

[33]Other affixes may not maintain them at all. It has been noted by Williams that we have proud of his children but not *proudly of his children. There are categorial effects here as well, namely, the fact that words in -ly are adverbs. See Roeper (1985) for discussion.

an implicit agent in (16b)? The problem is as significant as the problem of how a child identifies invisible gaps or traces in syntax.

Implicit agents are present in a variety of constructions:

17a. the ship sank
b. the ship is sinkable
c. ship-sinking is fun.

Unlike (17a), we find that (17b,c) both contain implicit agents. They derive from the transitive form: someone sank the ship. The child must learn not only that there can be an implicit agent in (17b,c) but that it is obligatory.[34] The intransitive reading (17a) is ruled out. The problem, once again, is to explain the *absence* of a reading and not the presence of one, i.e. to explain why a child would not use (17b,c) to mean (17a). Occasionally children do misanalyze an affix ("Don't tickle me, I'm laughable"). How then do they learn to re-analyze the affix excluding the reading which they had allowed?

THE ACQUISITION OF IMPLICIT ARGUMENTS

It should be clear that we are faced with a substantial acquisition problem. How does the child learn the thematic properties of affixes? How does he learn to prevent intransitive readings for passivized verbs which, in the active, allow intransitives (e.g., the ball was rolled)?

Our answer is that the principle of preservation of thematic roles by affixation is innate. Therefore the child should simply have to recognize affixes, and the preservation of thematic roles is automatic. !t follows that as soon as a child can divide between a verb and an affix, she will know that the thematic roles are present. The solution is correct, I believe, but vastly oversimplified. It does not confront the fact that -ed is ambiguous between a past tense marker (John walked) and an adjective marker (the three-legged chair).

There are a number of empirical questions to be asked here: (1) When are affixes productive? (2) When do children understand the explicit lexical meaning of affixes? (3) When do children understand the implicit thematic meaning? (4) When do children understand the categorical properties of affixes? (5) When do they sort out ambiguities in the different meanings of affixes?

Since we are dealing with a single phonological object, an affix, we cannot directly invade its substructure. In effect, not all of these questions may be open to direct empirical investigation. Experiments are therefore constructed from a

---

[34]Again we are presenting a simplified form of the argument. Further details about distinctions among affixes that do or do not preserve thematic information is contained in Roeper (1985).

combination of assumptions and empirical data points. Assumptions are benign if they are a part of a deductive system and could not be otherwise.[35]

The first logical step is to seek a correlation between productivity of affixes and preservation of thematic roles. Randall (1982) has pursued the issue with -er affixation. She showed that when children used -er productively, they also preserved instrumental readings on a verb where adults would not (e.g. a skier on an airplane is someone who skis on an airplane).[36] Now we need to see if implicit thematic roles are preserved when other affixes (-ed, -ing, -able) are productive.

Productivity and the Instantaneous Model

We have come to a juncture where one can examine the character of the instantaneous model. If affix analysis is sufficient, then productive uses of affixes and recognition of implicit arguments should occur instantaneously. Therefore one can predict virtually no stage where children are aware of passive sentences (the boat was rolled) but unaware of implicit agents.

This approach, if true, solves the trigger problem. However it is possible that productivity can exist with *minimal* knowledge rather than complete knowledge of the behavior of an affix. I have argued above that children learn the -ed affix in three stages: adjective, deverbal adjective, and passive participle. We have not directly examined the productivity of these forms in children. It is commonly reported, however, that children use agentless passives from before the age of three.[37]

IMPLICIT ARGUMENT PREDICTIONS

I will make two general (opposite) predictions and then try to subdivide the predictions in light of experimental evidence:

19. I. +*Thematic Hypothesis:* When affixes are productive, all thematic roles are maintained.

---

[35]A great deal of empirical research on theoretical questions is based on the erroneous asumption that a successful theory supports each assumption with independent data. Evasion of strong but interesting assumptions causes attention to be directed to less interesting hypotheses. The most interesting experiments emerge from the top of a long but tight set of assumptions.

[36]Children occasionally say spontaneous utterances of the form: ''there's a bikerider without hands'' where the child does not suppose that the rider lacks hands altogether. Randall found the same interpretation in much subtler environments using sentences like a diver without goggles.

[37]It would, of course, be useful to know exactly what the character of early productive use of -ed is like. See Berwick and Weinberg (1984) for an analysis of the acquisition of -ed that also utilizes the notion that UG forces the child to project a trace. Their account also works under the assumption that there is an automatic projection of the verbal properties onto the affix.

II. *-Thematic Hypothesis:* When affixes are productive, thematic roles are not maintained. Under II there are a variety of possibilities.

A. Semantic Trigger: It could be that only when the perception of "activity" occurs, are thematic roles triggered, which triggers subcategorization, which triggers case assignment, which triggers a trace analysis, which then triggers case absorption. These are all modular subparts of the notion of "direct object." It is likely that they involve instantaneous mutual implication. The question I am attempting to answer is where the entry point is.

B. Hypothesis-Chain: It could be that there exist links between the formal properties of various affixes. Therefore the trigger to the passive analysis could be that the child discovers compounding and then seeks to analyze other structures as involving lexical object movement. In effect this proposal follows the concept of the "hypothesis-chain" discussed in Roeper et al (1981).

C. Lexical Bias: Children may first treat an affix as if it were an independent word. Then the two elements would be treated like a compound. That is, show+er would be like show+man. One piece of evidence in behalf of this view is that children first say things like "shirter" (See Clark (1982)).[38] Here there is no interpretation at the formal level and therefore the -er can attach anywhere, not just to verbs, because it carries its own meaning. How do children learn *not* to say "shirter"? Presumably at the moment when they realize that -er acquires its AGENT reading from the verb and does not mean "agent" as its lexical content, then they will eliminate "shirter," "mistaker," "storier."[39]

20. 1. *+Thematic:* predicts that when children use agentless passives productively, they will always know there is an implicit agent.

2. *Semantic:* predicts that when children discriminate *active* from *stative* readings, they will know that the former has an implicit agent.

3. *Hypothesis-Chain:* predicts that all affixes that involve implicit agents will appear in a logical sequence.

4. *Lexical:* predicts that implicit arguments will appear when the connection between verbs and affixation is realized.

Our experiments do not address all of these questions. They should be seen as a first pass in delineating an intricate map of acquisition. It will probably be

---

[38]There is no evidence to my knowledge that children ever use of-phrases with these created forms (*"he's a shirter of funny shirts"). It is not known when they begin to use of-phrases in any kind of nominalizations. The prediction here is that they will not begin to use them until they use -er as a productive *affix*.

[39]There are counter-examples in the adult language, like New Yorker, Detroiter. The fact that these exist but do not freely generalize, such that we recognize "shirter" as odd, indicates that a language-learner must also arrive at such a conclusion. The issue is minorly complicated by the fact that nouns can also become verbs. If, however, the child does not use an expression like *to shirt or *to story, then it does not seem that the -er is attaching to a verb.

necessary to follow individuals, using experimentation, to obtain a real vision of growth in morphology.

EXPERIMENTAL EVIDENCE

Our first task is to establish a test that reveals children's knowledge of implicit thematic roles. A very simple and distinctive demonstration of children's knowledge can be obtained through asking them to draw pictures.

EXPERIMENT 1: PICTURE DRAWING (SIX- AND SEVEN-YEAR-OLDS)

We asked a group of ten six- and seven-year olds to illustrate phrases like: the breaking stick, stick-breaking, a baby sitting, baby-sitting, a sinking ship, a sunk ship, a watching bird, bird-watching and other examples. We found that every child exhibited the distinction on some examples (see pages 332–333).

Then we asked a group of twenty-five six- and seven-year-olds to draw the contrast between (a) the pulled dog and (b) the pulling dog. These phrases involve the same thematic roles but in different arrays, in (a) the dog is the THEME while in (b) it is the AGENT. We found that twenty-three of twenty-five children exhibited the distinction perfectly. Therefore in a prenominal environment it is clear that children understand the passive nature of -ed.

EXPERIMENT 2: PICTURE IDENTIFICATION

We asked a group of sixteen children (between the ages of six and seven) to respond to twenty-five sentences.[40] The sentences were counter-balanced in two lists so that the same picture appeared with opposite sentences on each list. The sentences were read by the teacher to the children who listened in a group (but roughly separated at different tables). Each child was given a set of xerox copies to mark. Each page had three picture choices for each sentence. The pictures were of three types (see insert):

21a. agent and theme involved in an action (e.g. someone cooks food),
b. just one agent or a theme (food is cooking) involved in the action,
c. the mentioned noun involved in no action (food).

---

[40]These experiments were carried out in collaboration with Al Huettner who is primarily responsible for their design.

The third picture served as a control.[41]

22. *Sentence Types:*
Transitive passive: 1. the bear is being held (96% Agent)
Ergative passive: 2. the flag is being waved (ergative) (91% Agent)
Ergative active: 3. the bells are ringing (91% Theme and no Agent)
Transitive active: 4. the elephant is pushing (95% Subject = Agent).

These sentence types involve a contrast between passive and active progressive and transitive and ergative. The ergative sentences are those whose verbs can be either transitive or intransitive, such as wave, while the transitive sentences are only transitive, and serve as a control. The import of this contrast is, once again, that a child is not compelled by the cognitive structure of the ergative verb to include both a subject and an object. A flag can be seen waving with no perceptible agent or even cause. Therefore the choice of a transitive interpretation on (22.2) can only come from a perception of syntactic form.

Results: The results are indicated in parentheses in (22). The children clearly exhibit knowledge of the relevant distinctions. They project the missing THEME in the progressive cases and the implicit AGENT in the passive cases. The projection is syntactically forced in the ergative cases. It is cognitively (and syntactically) forced in the transitive cases. However in the transitive cases it is only the syntax which determines whether the missing element will be an AGENT or a THEME.

EXPERIMENT 3: PRENOMINAL STRUCTURES

This experiment is identical to Experiment (2) except that the structures used were all prenominal adjectives, except for four sentences which were, two each,

[41]One might object that an agent could be implied but not present on the second (21c) picture. This objection does not explain the contrast between adults and children (reported below) where adults clearly choose a single person picture to correspond to sentences like the food is cooking as opposed to the food is being cooked which calls for an AGENT. One can do an interesting thought experiment to show how pictures are interpreted contrastively. Imagine two pictures, one of which has Mary cooking food, and the other has Mary and John cooking food. If asked to show the one where Mary is cooking food, one gets a clear sense that the former picture should be chosen. Therefore the fact that Mary is also cooking in the second picture, with contrastive analysis, fails to make it a natural choice.

the sinking boat
boat sinking
the watching bird
bird watching
the breaking stick
stick breaking

Show me babysitting

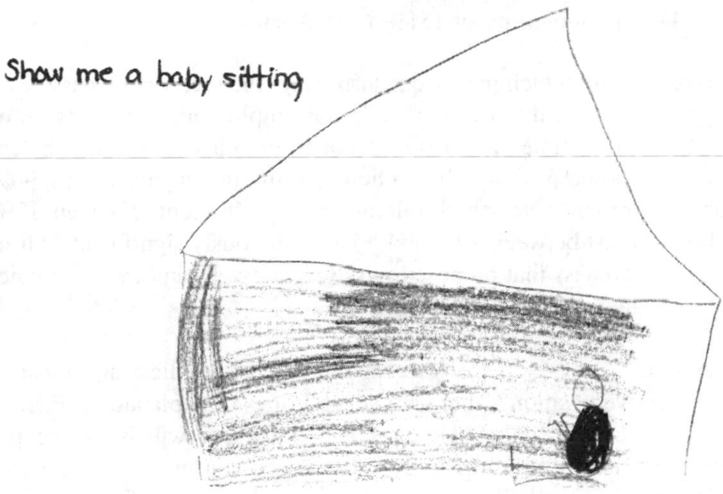
Show me a baby sitting

like the passive and progressives of the previous experiment. There were eight children who were seven years old.[42]

23. *Sentences:*

1. the pushing elephant	*2.* the watched bird
the dropping plant	the climbed man
the waving flag	the ridden pig
the bouncing ball	the drawn doll

---

[42]Thanks to helpful teachers, Doug Roupp and Susan Benedict, and the Amherst Public School System for their active involvement in these projects.

The primary contrasts are between transitive (push) and ergative (bounce) and between progressive and passive. I have provided several examples of each kind to illustrate some of the subregularities which we included. First, we included ergatives for which there was no clear result reading: a waved flag, unlike a sunken ship, has no special appearance after the action is over. Second, we included a variety of past tense suffixes. Third, we included examples where idiomatic factors might play a role. Therefore we might get the same reading for the watching bird and the watched bird because of the possible idiomatic status of bird-watching. In practice none of these subregularities made any difference.

24. *Results:*
   A. the pulling dog (91% N = Agent)
   B. the sinking ship (89% N = Theme)
   C. the pulled dog (85% N = Theme)
   D. the burned paper (51% N = Agent)

There is one result, which may seem surprising: the prenominal passive ergatives (the dropped plant) did not reliably elicit an implicit agent reading. It occurred roughly 50% of the time. This result is not random because it must be compared to the non-preposed passive which elicits the implicit agent reading 90% of the time and the progressive which elicits an implicit agent less than 10% of the time. The contrast between 10% and 50% is obviously significant.[43] It indicates significant awareness that preposed passive ergatives can have an implicit agent while true ergatives cannot.

Discussion: Why is there less recognition of implicit agents in the prenominal ergative position? There are several lines of explanation. First the child must know that it is only adjectives and not verbs which can be preposed. Therefore the participle in the ball was bounced can move, but not the simple intransitive verb in the ball bounced. Hence we do not have forms like *the died man. *the sung man. *the run boy. This knowledge one can expect to be delivered by innate mechanisms. The evidence is generally compatible with that view, particularly in light of the 10/50% contrast just discussed.

However there appears to be an additional operation which can give an intransitive interpretation to the adjective. It has a minor morphological representation. A contrast exists between the burned paper and the purely adjectival the burnt paper, where the latter has no implications of agency. There are a set of exceptions which exhibit the same characteristics: the escaped criminal, the departed

[43]Unfortunately we lack the desirable exact parallel sentences of the form the bounced ball (+ agent) and the ball bounced (− agent). But it is unlikely that the ball bounced will be more likely to elicit an implict agent than the ball is bouncing.

guest, (*the left guest), etc. The fact that these exceptions do not license generalizations reveals that they are defined as exceptional by UG.

The same experiment was performed with a group of 18 undergraduates at the University of Massachusetts. The results were comparable: over 92% of the prenominal *transitive* passives involved an implicit agent. While 91% of the prenominal progressives involved no agent and, sometimes, an implied object (if the verb was transitive).[44] However the prenominal *ergative* passives elicited only 59% implied agents. That is, the students were happy to point to a piece of charred paper, with no agent present, for the burned paper.

THE HYPOTHESIS-CHAIN

The hypothesis-chain is perhaps the most interesting hypothesis but the least easily studied using group experimental techniques. In Roeper et al. (1981) we found that there was a correlation between knowledge of passive, -able, and compounds in the six- to eight-year-old range for individuals. The most interesting result was the finding that the dative passive (John was given a hat), which is not open to analysis as an adjective, followed the acquisition of -able (The elephant is pushable). Children were able to comprehend the anti-pragmatic interpretation of -able before passive for 59/61 children tested.[45]

EVIDENCE FROM YOUNGER CHILDREN

We have carried out a series of pilot experiments using a variety of techniques from story-telling and picture identification, to toy-manipulation and the use of puppets. We seek just one experiment where children show unmistakable knowledge of implicit arguments. If other experiments fail to reveal the theoretically interesting result, then they may simply fail to elicit the child's deeper grammatical capabilities. The non-picture experiments have not revealed systematic behavior. This may mean that we have not found the subtle mix of semantics,

---

[44]One might ask why the results were not 100%. The answer probably has to do with the fact that the class was not composed entirely of native speakers of English and the latter were difficult to exclude systematically.

[45]The compound also seems to be correlated, but it is especially complex. Children of 3½ years will use novel compounds (''I'm the lunch-bringer''), but it is not clear that they will exclude the subject reading for sentence compounds like rat-biter (the rat cannot be the biter). The issue is complicated by the fact that contrastive stress allows an adjectival reading (see Solan 1983). For instance, a Gypsy driver can refer to a gypsy who drives and not someone who drives gypsies. See Schlerman (1981) who discusses the fact that children up to the age of eleven make errors on these compounds because they do not discern the subtle differences between contrastive stress and compound stress.

introductory environment, and sentence sequence that will allow children to avoid inferential heuristics.

Picture Experiment

The picture identification experiment described above was carried out with a group of eighteen 3 to 4-year-olds. The children were given 12 sentences in two counter-balanced lists. There were three "being" passives, three prenominal passives, three simple progressives, and three prenominal progressives. The gross results are mixed.

25a. active: the cat is chasing (87.5% correct)
b. passive: the bear is being washed (70.6% correct)

26a. transitive prenominal: the hitting boy (58.8% correct)
b. ergative prenominal: the spilling milk (56.3% correct)
c. ergative: the food is cooking (48.1% correct)
d. passive ergative: the cat is being hidden (46.7% correct)
e. transitive prenominal: the watched bird (43.8% correct)

In (26) the results are roughly those of chance. The contrast between (25b) the simple passive and (26d) the passive ergative suggests that children are using largely cognitive inference in the analysis of passive. An agent is inferred for (25b) because verbs like wash are transitive, while no agent is inferred in (26d) because verbs like hide can be interpreted intransitively. The simple passive in (25b) is clearly controlled by some children although the 70% success rate suggests less than complete mastery.

Individual Analysis: The more interesting questions pertain to individual analysis. Do individuals show mastery of the -ed affix? Do they show simultaneous (or temporally close) control of both passive and prenominal forms?

The tests were performed in counter-balanced fashion with 13 children between the ages of three and five. There were eight children who did not miss more than ⅙ of the -ed forms. The five children who showed more than one error exhibited errors on *both* the passive and the prenominal form. In other words, there were no children who showed mastery of the passive but not the prenominal form. This is precisely what the model predicts: when the argument properties of the affix are learned they extend to all syntactic contexts where the affix appears.[46]

---

[46]The generalization has to be modified slightly to say that the affix is marked both by its phonology and its syntax. An adjectival -ed does not collapse with a verbal -ed. We need this provision, once again, to account for the fact that a child will not allow the man died to generate *the died man.

The -ing forms were more difficult. Only three children met the ⅙-error criterion. The ten children who failed the criterion also exhibited errors on both the simple ergative and preposed forms. The errors were generally in the direction of choosing a picture with an agent for sentences like the food is cooking. I will discuss this result in light of another experiment.

Why should the -ing affix be more difficult? There are two features of the adult grammar which may begin to give an answer. First it is not clear that preposed transitives are fully grammatical. They are generally given an intransitive interpretation where there is an option. This follows from what Williams' calls the *Head Final Filter*.[47] We cannot say *the persuading men, and it is marginal to say *the buying boys. Second, where there is a preposed transitive, it generally has a compound interpretation. We find forms like the eating apples, a coloring book, etc. If we create a novel form, with stress on the first element, it is paraphrasable with a for-phrase: a throwing ball (= a ball for throwing).

Experiment 4: Prenominal -ing

We have performed a small experiment on prenominal -ing forms with children, four to six years, who fall between the seven-year-olds, who show complete mastery, and the three- to four-year olds, some of whom show no control of the argument structure of the -ing forms. These children exhibit clear knowledge of the Head Final Filter. They take prenominal ergatives which have both a transitive and an intransitive interpretation and reliably supply the intransitive.

Sixteen children, five four-year-olds and eleven six-year-olds, were asked to say what certain phrases meant. The conversational experiment is straightforward and revealing. The argument structure was very clear in over 90% of the responses. Questions were of the form: "what is a shoving tractor." The answer would be "a tractor that can shove dirt around" or, in contrast, "a tractor you can shove." All of the ergatives are potentially ambiguous. One boat can sink another, and therefore a transitive interpretation is possible.[48]

The results show that both groups know the distinction in argument assignment between transitive and intransitive adjectives. In addition, they show that ergatives uniformly receive the intransitive interpretation which is predicted by the Head Final Filter. One example is extremely anti-pragmatic: the throwing ball. This was the only transitive that did not assign AGENT to the mentioned noun (i.e., the ball throws something). This, not surprisingly, is further evidence that inference can overwhelm grammar.

In sum, the -ing affix appears to come in shortly after the -ed. The difference can be attributed to the compound reading and the questionable grammaticality of prenominal transitives.

---

[47] Williams states the constraint as prohibiting a trace after a preposed element. Therefore the Head of the X-bar phase must be final. A deeper explanation for this phenomenon is still needed.

[48] This experiment was carried out by Betty Schlerman.

	4yrs AGENT	THEME	6yrs AGENT	THEME
Ergatives				
bending wire		4		11
breaking glass		5		11
sinking boat		5		11
Transitives				
shoving tractor	3		9	3
hitting branch	3	2	7	3
throwing ball		5	1	9
Unclear				
feeding bird	3	2	7	4
Transitives	**74%**	**13%**	**82%**	**15%**
Ergatives	**0%**	**93%**	**0%**	**100%**

Conclusion

The analysis of younger children reveals support for the view that the argument structure of the affix is learned for passives and prenominals simultaneously. This result fits the instantaneous model. Nevertheless passive exhibits temporal stages: the case-absorbing character of passive -ed is acquired after children use the "affected" object criterion to establish a VP trace (following Lebeaux).

The grammar projects information from several modules onto an affix. Syntactic subcategorization is affected by the categorial character of the affix, case-assignment may be changed, thematic roles may be changed, and word-like lexical meaning may be added. It is not surprising that such a diverse bundle of information may be acquired in stages.

INFERENCES OF AGENT

Let us reconsider for a moment how a grammar-free approach might treat the combination of words and pictures. If we conjoined the words plant and dropping, then a picture that had just those two elements would be the natural choice. There would be no reason to include a person who was a dropper.

Our entire set of experiments, where two nouns are never mentioned, should show a strong bias toward single-object pictures. We have found to our surprise that this is not the case. There is a distinct bias toward the inclusion of an agent in the interpretation of transitive sentences. This bias showed up most distinctly in another experiment which we performed with six three-year-olds.

Experiment 5: Agent/Patient Bias with Three-Year-Olds

A group of five young three-year-olds and one 2.9-year-old were given a combination of 24 sentences using the same pictures with a variation of passives and ergatives:

27*a*. normal passive: the elephant is being pushed (40%)
b. ergative passives: the ship is being sunk (85.6%)
c. ergatives: the ship is sinking (31%)
d. normal actives: the elephant is pushing (45%)

The results are initially quite surprising (shown in parentheses above). Individual tabulations are all roughly the same (5/6 above 80% for ergative passives and 4/6 below 30% for ergatives). The simple ergatives proved to be surprisingly difficult and the passive ergative was much simpler. This is a very counter-intuitive result when seen from a purely grammatical perspective. In addition, we find that the ergative passives (27b) appear to be easier than the transitive passives (27a).

One factor renders these results compatible:

28. Children prefer sentences that include agents.

They mis-analyze the ergatives by selecting sentences with agents and they succeed in the analysis of ergative passives because they must have agents. They fail on the normal passives because they allow the first noun to function as the agent rather than the object (elephant), but still the interpretation contains an agent. The ergative passives cannot be analyzed as reversible passives because the first noun is an implausible agent (the food was being cooked). Therefore the agent-bias plus simple inference supplies the correct analysis of the ergative passives but not the normal passives.

What kind of principle is (28)? There is simply no reason to regard it as a principle of grammar. There is nothing in the grammar about the sentence the food is cooking that requires a person hovering over the stove. It is only an inference on typical situations or perhaps a preference for a complex notion of action that makes such a preference emerge.

My argument, once again, is that an extra-linguistic cognitive notion may be involved in the interpretation of sentences. Once again, the concept resembles *transitivity*, which ultimately plays a central role in grammar: It is not equivalent to transitivity, but it could be a precursor to it. The experiment does not force the child to seek agentive interpretations. Therefore it seems that the children are looking for agency and not simply recognizing it contextually.

I have delineated three notions each of which could be regarded as a portion of a primitive notion of *action:* affected object, agent, and activity. The argument claims that "affected object" triggers a *trace* in a VP, a cognitive notion of agent triggers the formal analysis of -er, a cognitive notion of activity may trigger the case-absorbing characteristics of -ed. The critical point is that these concepts have a *deterministic* role in triggering structural features of language that are not inherent in the cognitive notions.

I have argued that a child must be able to project the argument structure, implicitly, onto affixes. Therefore -ed must carry an AGENT. At this point one has to imagine the posture of the child before the rule is projected. In what form does he hold the ingredients of the passive in mind?

The typical answer to this question is that he has a combination of awareness of form and interpretation of context. I would argue that he has:

29. *Passive Trigger*

a. an *interpretation* in mind which equals *action,*

b. a phonological analysis which divides stems and affixes,

c. a canonical form from which he can detect deviations, for instance, subject-verb-object,

d. the canonical form is filled with canonical thematic projections (affected object) based on the particular transitive verb: agent-action-object.

These factors trigger, first, a movement transformation and a projection of the contents of the passive affix -ed. The affix can be interpreted in both normal passive and prenominal position.

Second, the case-assigning properties of the verb must be accounted for. Consequently she projects the affix as case-absorbing. The specific affix is the location of the generalization because it does not extend to nominalizing affixes. Case-absorption provides a second means to identify *trace:* it is now possible to project non-affected objects as the result of passive (John was liked).

THE NEXT STAGE

These experiments vary radically in the amount of structure and in the number of both sentences and subjects that are involved. Nevertheless fairly distinctive patterns have emerged in the recognition of implicit arguments. One now has a choice about how to proceed.

One might try to replicate those experiments which involve fewer subjects. One can only welcome replications of extant experimentation. It is not the only choice, however. One can also assume that the results are correct and then seek to answer the next logical question: How are other forms of affixation learned and how does a child reveal knowledge of the argument structure of affixes? If the same pattern recurs, then we have not only confirmed our early results but deepened our grasp of the language as a whole. If the patterns do not recur, then they may allow us to re-analyze the earlier work.

CONCLUSIONS

Returning now to the initial predictions:

1. We have found that children possess passives, prenominals, and implicit agents at the same time. This is consistent with the instantaneous model. What occurs before this stage remains an open question.

2. There is evidence that the notion of ''agency'' is spontaneously projected onto the interpretation of sentences. This could be a subpart of the notion of *activity,* and it functions as a prerequisite to the analysis of passive. It may also be a specific trigger for case-absorption in -ed. There is evidence for a second stage in the acquisition of passive in which case-absorption places the affected object as a trace-marker. This feature of passives is not instantaneously acquired.

3. There may be an hypothesis-chain. The object-to-subject affixes all seem to be analyzed within the five to seven age range. Closer study of individuals is needed.

4. There is an argument and anecdotal evidence that children may initially analyze -er as an independent word. When it becomes productive as an affix (i.e., not part of a compound), then all of the properties of the lexical projection principle should be in place. Only at that point will phrases like the robber of the bank appear in productive environments.

The research questions we have addressed here are connected to the exploration of a broad series of structures and experiments (which we discuss elsewhere[49]). In each case, there appears to be a cognitive notion that is either a prerequisite or a specific trigger to linguistic knowledge. In each case, the linguistic knowledge cannot be reduced to the cognitive pre-requisite. In work elsewhere (see note 49) I have argued that there is a pragmatic notion of:*bound variable, precede, agency,* and *definite reference* which participate in the instantiation of linguistic structure.

I have also argued for a certain style of research. The concepts of linguistic theory are woven into the analysis of child data in a fundamental way. I have not sought to treat theory and acquisition studies of adult grammar as an experimental domain where one can subject the theory to proof or disproof. In this approach, one assumes the correctness of insights from adult grammar to see if they lead to insights into child grammar. The strength or weakness of the theory lies in its deductive power with respect to the facts drawn from both child grammar and what one should call final child grammar, i.e., the adult grammar.

---

[49]See Roeper (1985), Solan (1983).

The central question remains: how do we explain why certain principles do not overgeneralize? How do children know that they cannot say *showman of hats, or *the play's enjoyment? I see no alternative to the argument that children must have innate knowledge of linguistic principles.

ACKNOWLEDGMENTS

Thanks to Dan Finer who originally pursued implicit arguments with me. Also to Al Huettner who helped me pursue acquisition implications and develop numerous experiments. In addition, Hagit Borer, Noam Chomsky, Charles Clifton, Lyn Frazier, Jay Keyser, Howard Lasnik, Brian MacWhinney, David Pesetsky, Janet Randall, Luigi Rizzi, Gert Webelhuth, Ken Wexler and Edwin Williams have contributed to either the theoretical or experimental work here. I would also like to thank many different audiences before which parts of this work have been presented. They include lectures at: McGill, UCLA, Irvine, U of Washington, British Columbia, MIT, Dutch Linguistics Society, BU Acquisition Conference, NYU. This work was supported in part by grants from the Sloan Foundation and NSF-BNS8014326.

REFERENCES

Anderson, M. (1979). *Nounphrase structure*. Doctoral Dissertation, University of Connecticut.

Bates, E. (1976). *Language and Context*. New York: Academic Press.

Berwick, R. and Weinberg, A. (1984). *The Grammatical Basis of Linguistic Performance*. Cambridge, MA: MIT Press.

Brown, R. (1973). *A First Language*. Cambridge, MA: Harvard University Press.

Borer, H. & Wexler, K. (1987). "The Maturation of Syntax" in T. Roeper and E. Williams, eds. *Parameter-setting*. Dordrecht, Holland: Reidel.

Carlson, G. & Roeper, T. (1980). "Morphology and Subcategorization: case and the unmarked complex verb". In T. Hoekstra, H. Van der Hulst, and M. Moortgat, (eds), *Lexical Grammar*. Foris, Dordrecht, Holland.

Chomsky, N. (1975). *Reflections on Language*. New York: Pantheon.

Chomsky, N. (1981). *Lectures on Government and Binding*. Dordrecht, Holland: Foris.

Clark, E. (1982). "The young word-maker: a case study of innovation in the child's lexicon". In E. Wanner and L. Gleitman, (eds), *Language Acquisition: the state of the art*. Cambridge, England: Cambridge University Press.

Clark, H. & Clark, E. (1977). *Psychology and Language: an introduction to psycholinguistics*. New York: Harcourt, Brace, Jovanovich.

deVilliers, J. (1980). "The process of rule learning in child speech: a new loo." In K. Nelson, (ed)., *Children's language*. Vol. II New York: Gardner Press.

Fabb, N. (1984). *Syntactic affixation*. Doctoral Dissertation, MIT.

Finer, D. & Roeper, T. (to appear). "From Cognition to Thematic Roles: the projection principle and language acquisition." In R. May and R. Matthews, eds., *Proceedings of the Ontario Conference on Learnability* Dordrecht, Holland: Reidel.

Gruber, J. (1965). *Studies in Lexical Relations*. Doctoral Dissertation, MIT

Hamburger, H. (1980). "A Deletion Ahead of its Time." *Cognition,* 8, 389–416.
Hamburger, H. & Crain, S. (1982). "Relative Acquisition." in S Kuczaj II (ed.), *Language Development* Hillsdale, NJ: Lawrence Erlbaum Associates.
Klein, S. (1982). *Syntactic Theory and Development Grammar.* Doctoral Dissertation, UCLA.
Lightfoot, D. (1977). "On traces and conditions on rules." In P. Culicover, A. Akmajian, & T. Wasow, eds., *Formal Syntax* New York: Academic Press.
MacWhinney, B. & J. Anderson (1982). "The Acquisition of Grammar." To appear in E. Gopnik (ed), *Cognitive Science.* Ablex.
Koster, J. (1978a). *Locality Principles in Syntax.* Dordrecht, Holland: Foris.
Lebeaux, D. (1985). "The Acquisition of Passive and Affectdness." Ms., U. of Mass.
Nishigauchi, T. & Roeper, T. (1985). "Deductive Parameters and the Growth of Empty Categories." T. Roeper and E. Williams, *Parameter-setting* Holland: Reidel, Dordrecht.
Maratsos, M. (1971). *The acquisition of the definite and indefinite article.* Cambridge: Cambridge University Press.
Pinker, S. (1984). *Language Learnability and Language Development.* Cambridge, MA: Harvard.
Randall, J. (1982). *Morphological Structure and Language Acquisition* Doctoral Dissertation, U. of Mass.
Roeper, T. and Bing, J., La pointe, S., and Tavakolian, S. (1981). "A Lexical Approach to Language Acquisition." In S. Tavakolian, ed., *Language Acquisition and Linguistic Theory.* Cambridge, MA: MIT Press.
Roeper, T. (1981a). "The Deductive Model and the Acquisition of Morphology." in C. L. Baker and J. McCarthy *The Logical Problem of Language Acquisition.* Cambridge, MA: MIT Press.
Roeper, T. (1981b). "Introduction." In V. Burke and J. Pusteovsky, (eds), *Markedness and Learnability.* Amherst, MA: U. of Mass. Occasional Papers.
Roeper, T. (1986). "How children acquire bound variables." In B. Lust, (Ed.), *Studies in the Acquisition of anaphona.* Dordrecht, Holland: Reidel.
Roeper, T. (1987). "Implicit Arguments and the Head-Complement Relation." *Linguistic Inquiry* Cambridge, MA: MIT Press. 18.2
Roeper, T., M. Rooth, L. Mallis, and S. Akiyama (1985). "On the Probelm of Empty Categories in Language Acquisition." Ms. U. of Mass.
Roeper, T. (1978). "Linguistic Universals and the Acquisition of Gerunds." In H. Goodluck and L. Solan *Papers in the Acquisition of Language* Amherst, MA: U. of Mass. Occasional Papers.
Roeper, T. (to appear). "The Modularity of Meaning in Language Acquisition." In E. Modgil, (ed)., *On Noam Chomsky.* Oxford, England: Farmer Press
Solan, L. (1983). *Pronominal Reference: on the Acquisition of Anaphora.* Dordrecht, Holland: Reidel.
Wasow, T. (1977). "Transformations and the Lexicon." In P. Culicover, A. Akmajian, and T. Wasow, (eds), *Formal Syntax.* New York: Academic Press.

10 Parsability and Learnability

Robert C. Berwick
Massachusetts Institute of Technology

INTRODUCTION: MODELS FOR LEARNING AND PARSING LANGUAGE

Natural languages must be learnable. They must also be parsable and producible. These three functional demands place clear constraints on the shape of natural language. With rare exception, there has been little work connecting these key constraints on natural languages, even though linguistic researchers usually assume that learnability somehow plays a dominant role in "shaping" language, while computationalists usually assume that efficient parsability is dominant. In this paper, I will examine the relation between learnability and parsability, seeking to explore overlaps in the way each constrains language.

The problem of language acquisition is to select a target grammar from a class of grammars based on a finite sample of sentences drawn from the language generated by the target grammar. There are a number of basic variants on this theme (Gold, 1967; Feldman, 1972; Hamburger and Wexler, 1973; Wexler and Hamburger, 1975). In the learnability framework, some families of grammars are learnable, and others are not. The learnability framework can be modified to capture the notion of "ease of learning" where "ease of learning" can involve limits on input data (limited embedding), computational resources of the acquisition procedure, and so forth.

The problem of parsability is, given a set of rules (a grammar) and a sentence, to find those rules that can be used to derive the sentence. Some classes of grammars generate languages that are easily parsable, while other classes of grammars do not. By "easily" I refer to the definition used in computability theory—namely, the amount of time that is polynomially proportional to the size of the input being processed.

There is no necessary connection between the constraints demanded for easy learnability and those needed for easy parsability. After all, learnability is a property of a family of grammars, while efficient parsability is a property of a single grammar. For example, if there were only one grammar, or language, it could be easily selected, yet it could be of arbitrary recognition complexity. Likewise, it is well known that there are families of languages that are not identifiable from positive evidence, even though each member of the family is easily parsable (e.g., a collection of all the finite languages plus an infinite, finite-state language that covers them all). This leaves us with the question of how learnability and parsability constraints are connected. Do these dual functional demands conflict or reinforce one another?

A related question concerns the developmental process of acquisition itself. Presumably, at each point in acquisition, the child can process some sentences of the target language, and cannot process others. As knowledge of grammar develops, more sentences of the target will be parsable (with other factors intervening to fix this developmental envelope, of course). At each stage, what we can parse is related to what we know about the grammar. This, then, is another place to look for the parsing-learning connection.

Learnability research (Wexler and Culicover, 1980) has demonstrated the need for a particular set of learnability constraints within one grammatical framework. Parsability research (Marcus, 1980) has argued that several particular locality conditions are required to faithfully model the efficiency of human sentence processing. The computer model of language acquisition developed by Berwick (1982, 1985) independently identified several ''locality principles'' as essential aids to learning. Table 1 summarizes this comparison between the parsability constraints of Marcus and Berwick and the learnability constraints of Wexler and Culicover.

The obvious question is why should this similarity of constraints hold. Why should two different streams of research—one concerned with language learning and one concerned with language processing—yield highly detailed solutions that are so similar? If the problems of learnability and parsability were in fact functionally independent, one would hardly expect such a close relationship. This confluence of constraint calls for an explanation.

Our first step is to look at the constraints on grammars advanced by other models. Then we'll turn to the computer model itself, so that we can compare its constraints to these.

Wexler and his colleagues have developed a specific mathematical model of the acquisition of transformational grammar. The aim of the theory is to define constraints such that a family of transformational grammars (Chomsky, 1965) will be learnable from ''simple'' data; the learning procedure can receive positive grammatical example sentences of depth of embedding of two or less. That is, simple sentences are allowed as are sentences with embedded sentences

TABLE 1
Learnability Constraints Compared to Parsability Constraints

Learnability Constraints	*Parsability Constraints*
Deterministic rule application	Deterministic rule application
Small number of new rule hypotheses	Small number of new rule hypotheses
Simple sentences establish learning context	Simple sentences establish parsing context
Binary Principle Freezing Principle Raising Principle	Determinism plus locality restrictions imposed by parser context

(*I know John likes ice cream*) and one more level of embedding (*I know John thinks Mary likes ice cream*) but no more complex sentences than these.

A sufficient condition for the learnability of a family of transformational grammars is *Bounded Degree of Error* (BDE). Roughly and intuitively, BDE is a property related to the "separability" of languages and grammars on the basis of simple data. If there is a way for the learner to tell that a currently hypothesized language (and grammar) is incorrect, then there must be some simple sentence that reveals this. All languages in the family must be separable by simple, positive example sentences.

A learner ascertains that a currently hypothesized grammar is inadequate on the basis of some sample sentence by testing whether the current sentence can be derived from a deep structure by means of the current grammar. That is, the learner is fed a sequence of base (deep structure) surface sentence **(b, s)** pairs. If the learner's currently hypothesized transformational component, T_l, can map from *b* to *s*, then all is well. The acquisition computer model has a somewhat different job, since it must *parse* an input sentence and come up with an underlying representation, corresponding to the deep structure, *b*, in the Wexler and Culicover model. Still, both models are assumed to have access to an independently constructed representation of the thematic structure of simple sentences. Both models do nothing at all if this recovery of thematic structure can be carried out by current syntactic knowledge—a forward generation of the sentence for Wexler and Culicover and an inverse parse of the sentence in the computer model.

What if the learner's transformational component is not yet correct? Then $T_l(b) = s' \neq s$. A detectable error has been revealed. The Wexler/Culicover learning procedure knows that something is wrong; it adds or deletes a transformational rule at random (with uniform probability over the class of rules) from its current transformational component and proceeds. Eventually, as Wexler and Culicover show, if certain conditions on transformational rules are met, this learning procedure converges to the right transformational component with probability one. The key property that is sufficient to guarantee convergence is BDE:

> A family of transformationally-generated languages *L* possesses the BDE property if for any base grammar *B* (for languages in *L*) there exists a finite integer *U*, such that for any possible adult transformational component *A* and learner component *C*, if *A* and *C* disagree on any phrase-marker *b* generated by *B*, then they disagree on some phrase-marker *b*′ generated by *B*, with *b*′ of degree at most *U*. (Wexler and Culicover 1980:108)

If we substitute 2 for *U* in the theorem, we get the Degree 2 constraint, the one actually established by Wexler and Culicover. Once BDE is established for some family of languages, then convergence of a learning procedure is easy to prove. Wexler and Culicover (1980) have the details, but the key insight is that given BDE, there can be at most a finite number of different kinds of errors on structures of bounded depth. Given enough sentences of this complexity, after some finite amount of time, the learner will hit upon the right transformational rules even if the acquisition procedure picks them at random.

The question then becomes how BDE may be ensured. Wexler and Culicover have found that in order to guarantee learnability one must impose a number of principles on transformations. These are summarized in Table 2. Wexler and Culicover propose two kinds of constraints: *1*. constraints on the application of a single rule, and *2*. constraints on the interaction of rules from one s domain to the next.

The constraint on single rules is easy to understand; no single rule can refer to

TABLE 2
Wexler and Culicover Constraints
Compared to the Berwick Computer Model

Wexler and Culicover Constraints	*Berwick Constraints*
Incremental rule acquisition	Incremental rule acquisition
No negative evidence	No negative evidence
No memory for past sentences (only current sentence used as data)	No memory for past sentences (only current sentence used as data)
Small number of new rule hypotheses	Small number of new rule hypotheses
Simple sentences used	Simple sentences used
Deterministic generation	Deterministic parsing
Binary Principle Freezing Principle Raising Principle No Bottom Context	Determinism plus locality restrictions imposed by buffer and pushdown stack context

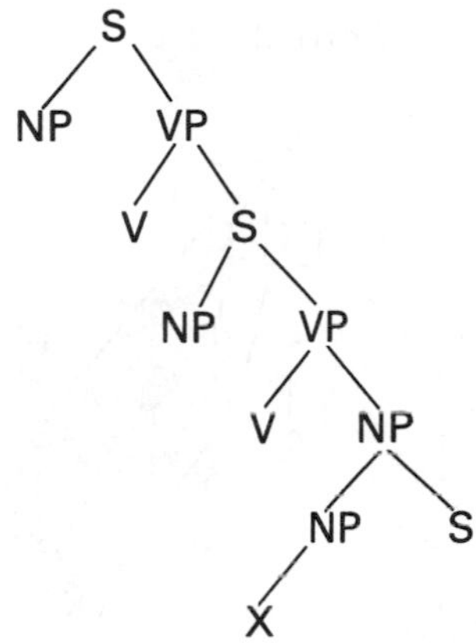

FIGURE 10.1. The Binary Principle blocks unbounded single rules

unbounded context. Specifically, no single rule can refer to more than two s domains, the current s and the next higher s. Wexler and Culicover call this the Binary Principle. It is clear why this constraint is necessary. If the constraint were not imposed, then a single rule could refer to an unbounded context, in terms of the number of s domains. Not only would this be a difficult situation for parsing; but since an arbitrary context would have only a small chance of appearing in the input data, the rule context would not be encountered with high enough probability, and the rule would not be acquired. Figure 1 illustrates the Binary Principle. The Binary Principle is essentially the Subjacency Constraint (cf., Wexler and Culicover, 1980, for discussion) though Wexler and Culicover discovered this principle independently.

The constraints on multiple rule interactions are more complex and make up the bulk of Wexler and Culicover's work. Basically, one must guarantee that an error made in one s domain cannot be propagated indefinitely as a "hidden" error only to be revealed in some large, hence rare, sentence structure. Since natural languages evidently do not contain such rules, Figure 2 gives only an abstract, schematic picture of what such a case would look like. Figure 2 shows how the correct decision to attach an *A* to node *X* (on the left) rather than to node *Y* (on the right) is undetectable in the domain where the rule is executed because the surface strings of tokens are the same for both rules. The error is revealed when this error-containing context is altered by moving it several sentences up the tree and then pulling *X* and *Y* apart so that the surface sentence is different for the correct and the incorrect versions of the rule. Note that no single movement violates the Binary Principle.

There are two possible classes of such interactions: *1*. an interaction of *material*—a transformation can move an entire lower context into a higher context, and *2*. an interaction of *context*—a transformation can be triggered or inhibited by the context of another cycle. How could a series of rules interact? A multiple

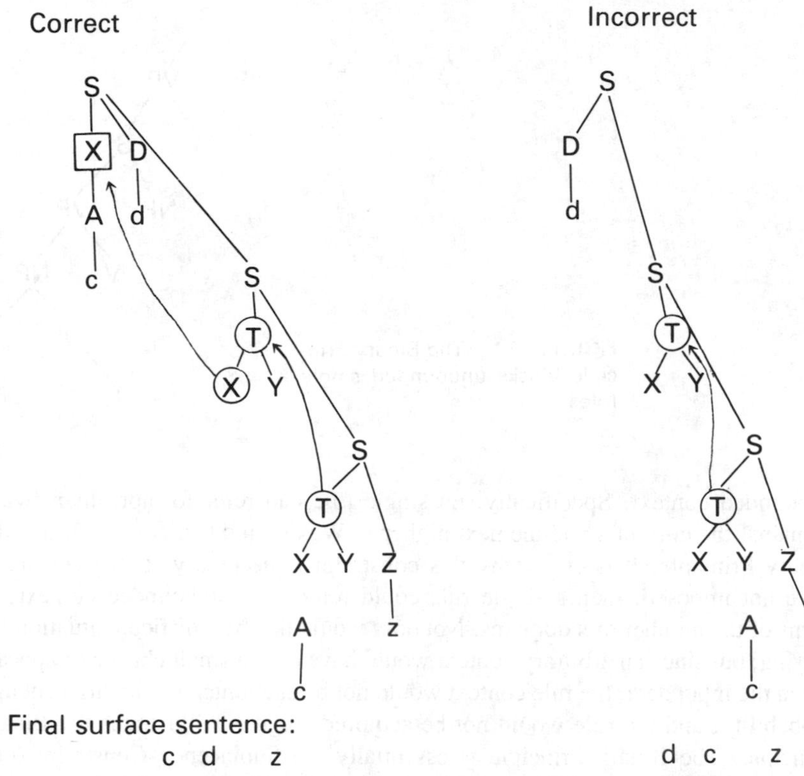

FIGURE 10.2. Multiple rules interactions can hide errors for long distances

rule chain could be arbitrarily long and hence provide unbounded context to trigger or inhibit a rule arbitrarily far away. Clearly this would have the same undesirable effect as a single unbounded context. Thus one aims to limit the amount of material that can be passed from one s domain to the next; several constraints are required here.

First, since a transformation can move an entire tree, an arbitrary context could be moved in a series of jumps, only to be torn apart later on. To rule out the movement of arbitrary context, the Degree 2 theory advances constraints that, in effect, render a phrase inaccessible to further syntactic action after it has been moved across an s boundary. Again, there are two senses of "accessible" here: the tree itself might be torn apart or syntactically manipulated, or it might be used as the context for some other rule. These two possibilities are ruled out by separate constraints posited by the Degree 2 theory. The *Raising Principle* plays a key role in eliminating such manipulation. Roughly speaking, it states that after a tree has been moved across an s boundary, its internal syntactic constituents cannot be moved by any later rules.

Acquisition Procedure | **Parser**

Input Positive example sentence:

1. Attempt to parse sentence
2. Successful parse; input next sentence
3. Failure: construct new rule at point of failure; add rule & continue parse if successful; else, → Add/Modify Rule ↑ Rule database
4. End current parse and input next sentence.

FIGURE 10.3. Outline of the acquisition procedure

Let us now turn to the computer acquisition model (Berwick 1982, 1985) and compare it to the Degree 2 constraints. Figure 3 outlines the model, which is based on the Marcus parser. For our purposes here, we may think of the Marcus parser as a variant of a standard bottom-up parser. It is in two parts: first, an *interpreter* along with a *pushdown stack* to hold partially completed phrases and an *input buffer* to hold upcoming words or phrases, and second a set of *grammar rules* written in an *if-then* form. The grammar rules carry out the actual construction of the parse tree under interpreter control. The *if* portion of a grammar rule specifies a predicate that must hold the items currently in the stack and buffer them in order for the *then* portion of the rule to be carried out. For example, a rule to attach Subject NPs to their proper position might look like this:

If first item in the buffer is an NP
top of the stack holds a bare S
Then attach the first item in the buffer to the top of the stack

Given this simple parser format, the way to turn it into a learning system is straightforward. We fix the interpreter and remove all the grammar rules. Learning now involves building new grammar rules. The basic idea is that we construct a sequence of parsers of increasingly greater sophistication. Acquisition is incremental: we add, one at a time, or generalize the *if-then* action rules of a Marcus parser on the basis of positive evidence. Figure 4 gives a flowchart of the procedure.

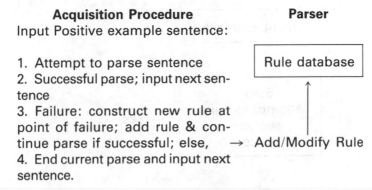

At each step, the system attempts to parse a given sentence with the grammar rules it currently knows. If it gets stuck because no rule applies, it tries to build a single new rule using the parser configuration at the point of failure as the pattern of a new grammar rule, and selecting a single new action as the candidate rule action. If an action succeeds (according to a simple success criterion we won't cover here), the new rule is saved after possibly generalizing the new rule with an already-known rule with the same action and context. Here, "context" refers to the machine configurations used by the Marcus parser: the *left context* consists of

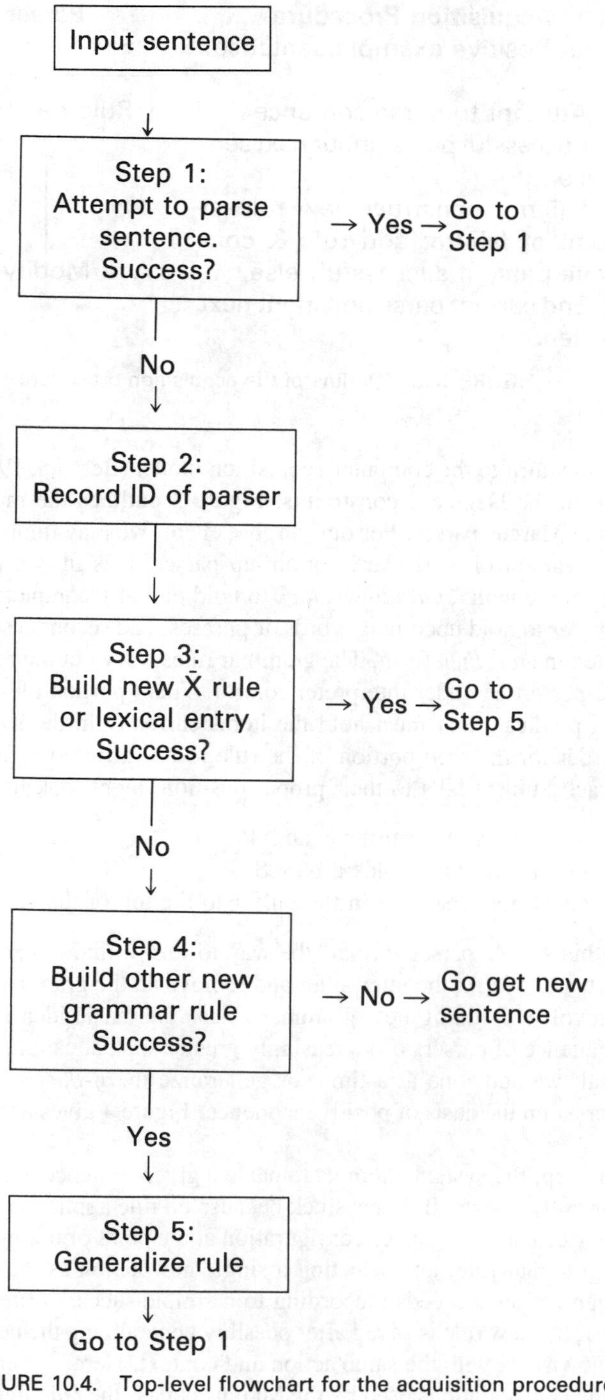

FIGURE 10.4. Top-level flowchart for the acquisition procedure

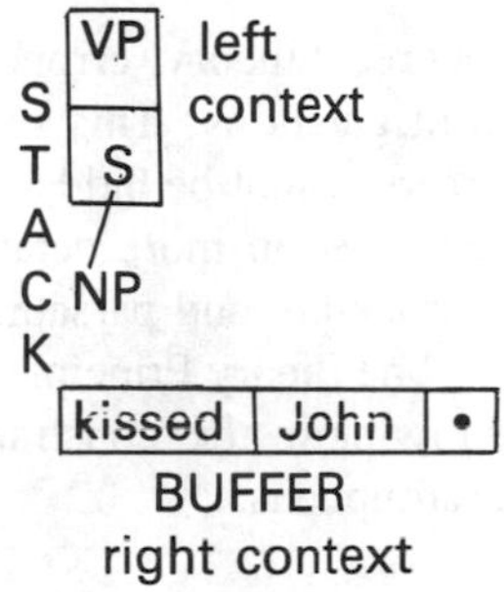

FIGURE 10.5. Left and right context in the parser

the top element of a pushdown stack plus one additional S or NP element; while the *right context* of a parse consists of items in a two-cell lookahead buffer. A final part of the machine configuration is the *currently scanned item* (which in Marcus's terminology occupied the first buffer position, see Figure 5).

We can now ask how the constraints of this procedure match with those of the Degree 2 theory. Let us get one bit of spadework out of the way. Williams (1981) showed that the Raising Principle can be strengthened to do nearly all the work of a second principle advanced by Wexler and Culicover to eliminate unbounded syntactic manipulation—the Freezing Principle. Let us adopt that suggestion here, since it greatly simplifies our task. Given Williams's proposal, there are three main Degree 2 constraints: the Binary Principle, the Raising Principle, and the No Bottom Context. We will now cover each of these in turn and investigate how the computer model reproduces them.

The Binary Principle (or Subjacency) has a natural and direct interpretation in the acquisition parser. Grammar rules can refer only to their current active node (possibly an S) and the current cyclic node above that (also possibly an S).[1] The result is that grammar rules cannot refer to unbounded context. In fact, grammar rules must trigger precisely the same domain as the operations spelled out by the Binary Principle.

To put the same point another way, the parser literally cannot distinguish between sentence configurations more than one sentence deep. This does not imply that the system cannot parse sentences of Degree 2 or more; rather, it implies only that all such complicated sentences are functionally equivalent in parsing terms to some less embedded sentence. Further, the consequences for learning theory are as follows: in the Degree 2 theory, errors can only be *created* on sentences at most one degree deep and *detected* on sentences at most one more S deep. Error detectability here means *string* error detectability. The resulting string of words must be different for correct and incorrect rules. The parser, however, has a stronger notion of detectability: as in the Degree 2 approach, errors can only be *created* on structures at most one degree deep; but, unlike

[1]We have modified the original Marcus definition so that Subjacency is, in effect, enforced directly by the parser.

Degree 2 theory, errors are assumed to be *detected* in terms of different parsing configurations. This means, as Wexler and Culicover (1980) show, that the errors cannot be hidden for one extra level of sentence embedding. This topic is discussed in more detail just below, when we discuss the connection between learnability and parsability in detail.

The Binary Principle has a parsing motivation. Berwick and Weinberg (1984) show how the constraint of Subjacency follows directly from three simple assumptions:

- Parsing is *deterministic,* in the sense that once information about the structure of a sentence is written down, it is never retracted. This means that the information about a sentence is monotonically preserved during analysis.
- Grammatical representations are embedded *directly* in parsers without intervening derived predicates or multiplied-out rule systems. This is an assumption of *transparency*.
- The human brain is finite.

The key idea is that wherever a syntactic construction could lead to an ambiguity that would require unbounded, left context to structurally resolve, that construction is bounded by some locality constraint. It must be so bounded, because if it were not, then the correct parsing rule for it would have to be infinitely long, an impossibility. For example, consider a rule whether or not to place a dummy object after *eat* in constructions such as:

Did John eat?
What did John eat?

In the first sentence, the parser should not place a dummy object after *eat,* which is intransitive; in the second sentence, a dummy object is required as a marker of the questioned thing eaten. This is a parsing ambiguity that is resolved by local, left context. The presence of the *wh* signals the parser to insert a dummy object or not. If grammar rules must be written in finite pattern-action form, then such a pattern can refer only to a bounded number of nodes in the left context (the stack); it is simply impossible to write down an unbounded number of nodes as a triggering pattern, since it would not fit in either brain or machine. This constraint is Subjacency, or the Binary Principle.[2]

We can contrast this situation with a construction that causes no local ambiguity at all. If there is no parsing ambiguity, then there is no need to refer to left context at all. Therefore, in this situation, there need be no bound whatsoever on

[2]The assumption of transparency is crucial here: we must assume that a coding of the left context as, e.g., a regular set, is not allowed. See Berwick and Weinberg (1984) for further details, in particular, for reasons why the apparent constraint is *one* sentence node rather than, say, seventeen.

the connection between left and right. For example, consider Verb Phrase deletion:

Mary kissed Sally and Harry did too.

From the parser's point of view, there is ample information to insert some kind of marker after *did,* which unambiguously marks the start of a Verb Phrase. The parser need not look to its left. Thus, we expect no bound comparable to Subjacency here, and we find none; VP deletion operates over unbounded domains.

This pattern is repeated in case after case. At its left context, where the parser must look in order to figure out what to do, there is a locality constraint; but where parsing is unambiguous, there is no such constraint. Consider some examples (for details, see Berwick and Weinberg, 1984).

Overt pronouns are syntactically and locally unambiguous from a parsing standpoint. Since they are actually present in the input stream, the parser need not look at its left context in order to decide how to build the parse tree. (Of course, finding the antecedent may require processing of left context, but that is presumably not a syntactic parsing problem.) We predict and confirm then that pronouns won't follow a locality constraint like the Binary Principle.

To take another example, consider gapping where there is no auxiliary verb, as in:

Harry fished in the ocean and I think John in the sea.

This is ambiguous: one must check the verb to see whether or not there is a small clause, as in **I believe Frank a liar* vs. *I consider Frank a liar.* (For the discussion here, a small clause is just a predicate with *to be* elided, e.g., *I consider Frank to be a liar.*) That is, if the verb is *believe,* then the sentence is bad; but if it is *consider,* then the sentence is OK. Therefore, the parser must refer to the left context in order to see what verb has been encountered and whether a smaller clause should be built. Following the logic of the argument, gapping with no auxilliary verb should obey a locality constraint, and it does.

Harry fished in the ocean and John in the sea.
**John fished in the ocean and I think Harry in the sea.*

In contrast, gapping where there is an auxiliary verb is unambiguous, since small clauses can't have auxiliaries. There is no parsing decision to reconcile in such cases. Therefore, there should be no locality constraint for such examples, and this too is confirmed:

Harry has fished in the ocean and I think Bill said that Harry has in the sea.

This last example shows that this functional constraint cuts across natural grammatical lines since the same grammatical construct, gapping, has subvarieties that either obey or do not obey locality constraints, depending on their respective parsing implications.

To summarize so far, bounded context parsing is essential to the deterministic design; it leads directly to Subjacency, which is simply the Binary Principle.

Let us turn now to the Raising Principle. It too is reflected in the Marcus parser, though it's not so clear whether it has as strong an independent motivation.

What goes on in the Marcus parser after a node is lowered into another S? By assumption, a node can be lowered into another clause only by first dropping that node into the input buffer, then creating the new clause node, an S, and finally attaching the node to be lowered to the new clause node. Figure 6 illustrates how the stack and input buffer changes between these steps. Note that since we are parsing, the analog of raising a node is lowering a node.

If we study the example in figure 6, we see that the node that was lowered had to have been completed, as is always the case in the Marcus parser design, so that it could be dropped into the input buffer. All the internal details of the node so lowered cannot be altered; that material has already been attached to the NP. By the determinism hypothesis, this material cannot be changed. But this means that once lowered, the internal structure of a phrase is not accessible; this is the parsing analog of the Raising Principle.

Again, we'd like some independent motivation for this machinery in the parser; otherwise, we could just be accused of simulating the Raising Principle. First, one can propose that completed nodes are "opaque" to further syntactic manipulation because they are shipped off to another module of sentence processing for semantic interpretation. The idea is that once an NP, for instance, is completely built (in phrase structure terms, that we've completely expanded the NP context-free rule), then we can call any semantic actions routines and replace that node with its interpretation. This is exactly the way that semantic interpretation is carried out in programming language design. Any such "replaced" node

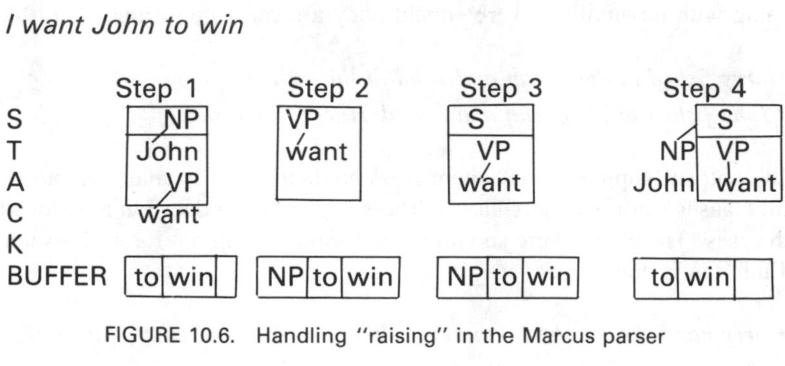

FIGURE 10.6. Handling "raising" in the Marcus parser

has no internal syntactic detail. Such a proposal is also compatible with many recent designs for compositional, on-line semantic interpretation suggested by Generalized Phrase Structure Grammar.

What in turn motivates this design? The constraint on replaced nodes automatically enforces the c-command restriction, where c-command is defined in terms of branching nodes; (α c-commands β if the first branching node that dominates α dominates β). This is because of the "opacity" effect: as soon as a branching subtree is completely built, its details are lost, and so the branching material beneath it is no longer accessible. This leads to an interesting functional account of indexing of pronouns, as outlined in Berwick and Wexler (1982) and Berwick and Weinberg (1984), and has some suggestive psycholinguistic support (see Berwick and Weinberg, 1984).

We're now well along the way in showing that all the Degree 2 constraints are reflected in the computer model. We've got one major constraint to explain, the one limiting *interacting* contexts. Wexler and Culicover dubbed this No Bottom Context. It says, roughly, that if a transformation acts across an s domain, moving an element from a lower s to a higher s, then it cannot refer to context in the lower s in order to act. Only the target s can have a context restriction. (Transformations operating *within* an s are obviously unaffected.) This requirement is imposed so that material raised from yet another previous (lower) s cannot be used as a triggering context, thereby creating a situation where context material can be successively "cascaded" from one domain to the next.

Because parsing is the inverse of generation, just as before we must be careful in seeing how this constraint might be reflected in parsing. The analog of "raising" in the original Marcus parser is the following "lowering" action sequence: *1.* create and bind an NP trace, *2.* insert the trace into the buffer, *3.* create an s, and *4.* attach the trace somewhere in the lower s. Note that all operations are clausebound; that is, no single grammar rule acts across an s using context in the higher domain (see Marcus, 1980, for additional discussion). Of course, this is not enough to force something like No Bottom Context. It might still be possible to write a grammar rule that violates this principle, however unnatural that rule might be, because we can use the second or the third buffer cells of Marcus's design in order to look into the next lower S (of course, this S won't have been built yet, so there is some question of whether we are violating NBC).

This suggests that in order to get NBC, we must engage in more radical surgery. We can eliminate the second and third buffer cells—the lookahead—in Marcus's design. We retain the first buffer cell, the currently scanned token. (Marcus refers to this as *lookahead* but it's really not.) Now No Bottom Context is directly enforced. Have we lost anything? Wasn't *lookahead* crucial to the success of the Marcus design? No. As it turns out, we can still parse deterministically with this scheme, if we are willing to adopt some variant of the X-bar theory and take "deterministic" to mean "monontonic refinement." That is, we are allowed to add to the features of the analysis we've built so far, but we can't delete any features or structure once built. Under this interpretation, the cases that Marcus claimed required *lookahead* (such as, *I know that blocks support the pyramid,* where *that* must be diagnosed as a complementizer or determiner or a pronoun) can be resolved by feature undetermination without *lookahead*. We first project *that* as an XP of some kind (probably a +N XP). Then, when we see *blocks* we can add to *that* and refine it as COMP or DET. Further examples would take us afield at this point. But the bottom line is that no *lookahead* seems necessary.

So far so good. We've got the three central Degree 2 restrictions—the Binary Principle, the Raising Principle, and No Bottom Context. There are other restrictions advanced by the Degree 2 theory that play a role in establishing the learnability of a transformational system. Most of these have to do with the data input to the learning procedure rather than constraints on the form or function of grammar rules themselves. Most are reflected in the computer model as well. The first six entries of the table summarize this relationship. Both models rely on simple data and positive-only evidence. Both analyze one sentence at a time, operate deterministically, and lack memory for past sentences.

LEARNABILITY, PARSABILITY, AND LOCALITY

It is clear that the constraints of the Wexler and Culicover model lie close to those of the Berwick computer model. A deeper question remains: why should the computer model, grounded on the goal of efficient parsability, reflect these learnability constraints so directly? How are the constraints of parsability and learnability linked?

For this comparison to make sense at all, one must precisely define efficient parsability and learnability. We already have good candidates for each of these. As a working definition of what is efficiently parsable, we shall take the class of Bounded Context Parsable (BCP) grammars which we define as bottom-up deterministic grammars restricted to use literally bounded left and right contexts for parsing decisions. Intuitively, a grammar is BCP if it is backwards deterministic given a radius of *k* tokens around every parsing decision. That is, it is possible to find deterministically the production that applied at a given step in a derivation by examining just a bounded number of tokens (fixed in advance) to the left and right at that point in the derivation.

Figure 7 depicts the situation. We fix some context in advance, say *m* symbols on the left and *n* symbols on the right. Suppose we have two candidate expansions of a tree, $A \rightarrow \alpha$ and $B \rightarrow \beta$. If a bounded context of *m,n* symbols about the point of this expansion is the same in both cases, where this context might extend outside of α or β itself, then we can conclude that $A = B$. (That is what is meant by "backwards determinism"—the reduction of the fringe of some subtree to *A*

FIGURE 10.7. A bounded context derivation

or B is determined.) If, whenever any such case of equal context arises, the two nonterminals in question are equal, then we say that the grammar as a whole is bounded context. This condition ensures that if we have two competing rules, (2) the real rule and (1) the false one, we can tell them apart by examining just a bounded number of tokens around the current point of the parse. Note that a BCP grammar must be unambiguous; that is, there cannot be *two* distinct derivations associated with the same surface sentence. If there were, then we would have one and the same context associated with (at least) two different rule productions, a contradiction.

Some examples should make the relationship between the bounded context and the Marcus parser design clearer. Consider the following simple grammar.

(1) $S \rightarrow aBc$ (2) $B \rightarrow Bb$ (3) $B \rightarrow b$

The language generated by this grammar requires one token of left context to parse correctly. When we see the sequence . . . *bb* . . . , we know to apply rule (2) instead of rule (3) depending on one token of left context. If that is a *b*, we know that rule (3) had to have applied; if the context is *B*, then it is rule (2). In Marcus parser terms, we would have either an s with a *b* attached on the node stack, or else we would have a *B*. Note how this is a transparent reflection of the grammatical rules. (Genitive constructions in English exhibit this pattern.)

Now consider the following grammar, which is not bounded context parsable.

(1) $S \rightarrow aA$ (2) $S \rightarrow bB$
(3) $A \rightarrow 0A$ (4) $A \rightarrow 1$
(5) $B \rightarrow 0B$ (6) $B \rightarrow 1$

The problem is that when se see a 1, in order to figure out whether rule (4) or (6) applied, we must see whether there is an *a* or a *b* at the front of the sentence. But this distinguishing context could be arbitrarily far away, separated by a long stretch of 0's. Therefore, the grammar is not bounded context. Some rules require unbounded literal context for their disambiguation. In contrast, this grammar is deterministically parsable by a nontransparent machine. It is simple for a finite state machine to "remember" that it has seen an *a* or a *b*. Once remembered, it can take appropriate action when it gets to the 1. If it has seen an *a* before, then it applies rule (4); otherwise, if it has seen a *b*, it applies rule (6). Note how this information is "compiled out" in the parser's finite control; it is not a part of the grammar itself. In other words, we must finitely *encode* a property of the derivation sequence nontransparently. The fact "if an *a* has been seen then do . . ." can't otherwise be finitely represented.

This example is not so far from the real world as it might seem. If we have a *wh* item at the front of a sentence, then this may be used as a trigger to decide whether to insert an empty element after an amiguously transitive verb like *eat*—if we are willing to encode left contexts. (This is what is done in Generalized Phrase Structure Grammar.) Note that we now can have rule effects extending over unbounded distances—precisely the learnability problem that we were trying to avoid.

The key idea, then, is to tie the bounded context effect to learnability. We want to block interaction effects—even if finitely encodable—so that any rule's domain of effect is limited. This is what the bounded context condition enforces. Once we do this, we want to show that BDE follows.

To actually demonstrate this, we must lay some technical groundwork.

First, to extend the bounded context definition to the original Marcus parser, we drop the requirement that the derivation is rightmost and use instead noncanonical derivation sequences. This permits us to place nonterminal names in the stack before the phrases to which they correspond are completely built. (In a pure bottom-up design, we can't put NP in the stack until it is completely built; in the Marcus design, we can put an NP there as soon as we know for certain that there is one.) This does not affect bottom-up recognition order, as Berwick (1985) demonstrates (following a discussion originally in Hammer, 1974).

As our definition of what is easily learnable, we shall simply take the families of grammars that meet the BDE condition, as defined earlier.

We can now at least formalize our problem of comparing learnability and parsability. The question now becomes: What is the relationship between the BDE property and the BCP property? Intuitively, a grammar is BCP if we can always tell which of two rules applied in a given bounded context. Also intuitively, a family of grammars is BDE if, given any two grammars in the family G and G' with different rules R and R' say, we can tell which rule is the correct one by looking at two derivations of bounded degree with R applying in one and yielding surface string s and R' applying in the other yielding surface string s', with s not equal to s'. This property must hold with respect to all possible adult and learner grammars. So a *family* of possible target grammars must be considered. The way we do this is by considering some "fixed" grammar G and possible variants of G formed by adding variant rules to the production rules in

G. This family of variant grammars contains all possible combinations of competing rules, including those where the rule R is absent. For example, suppose that the rule $X \rightarrow \alpha B\delta$ is in G. Then one variant G' is formed by addiing to G the rule $X \rightarrow \alpha C\delta$, a "competing" rule. We also require that this family of variants be finite—otherwise, we can clearly get an unlearnable family, as the Gold examples demonstrate. (This is not a necessary condition for learnability, but it is a natural one within the current model.) The resulting *finite, variant target family* is the original target grammar plus this finite set of variants.

The theorem we want to prove is this.

> If all the grammars in a finite, variant target family are BCP, then that family is also BDE.

The theorem is established by using the BCP property to directly construct a small-degree phrase marker that meets the BDE condition. Select two grammars G, G' from the finite family of target grammars. Both are BCP by assumption. To show that BDE holds, we must suppose that if there is a rule, R' in G', that causes a detectable error on some structure of arbitrary complexity, then that same error must be detectable on a small phrase marker. Let's suppose that R is the correct rule in this case, i.e., G has rule R and G' rule R', with $R \neq R'$. Finally let us suppose that rule R is of the form $A \rightarrow \alpha$; R' is $B \rightarrow \alpha'$[3]

Since R' creates a detectable error, there must be a derivation $S \Rightarrow \Phi$ such that R applies to Φ and eventually derives sentence s, while R' applies to Φ and eventually derives s', different from s. The number of steps in the derivation of the two sentences may be arbitrary, however. What we must show is that there are two derivations bounded in advance by some constant that yield two distinct sentences. This is very nearly the BDE property. We need only translate a bounded number of derivation steps into a bounded degree of error to finish things off. Thus, our proof will have three steps:

- First, show that BCP implies error detectability on a bounded (m,n) context;
- Second, show that error detectability on a bounded context implies error detectability at the surface sentence level;
- Third and last, show that this error detectability at the surface sentence level is of bounded degree (the BDE property).

To begin, let us see how to establish the first step of the proof. The BCP conditions state that identical (m,n) (left and right) contexts imply that nonterminals A and B are equal. See Figure 8.

Taking the contrapositive, if A and B are unequal, then the (m,n) context must

[3]More generally, we should write this rule in Marcus parser form with a bounded left and right context.

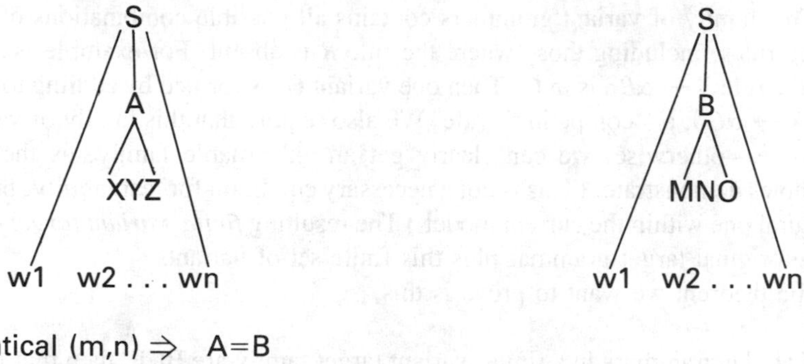

FIGURE 10.8. Bounded context equality implies identical rules

be non-identical. That is, we should be able to tell the two rules apart from (m,n) context. This establishes that the BCP condition implies (m,n) context error detectability. In other words, a rule R and any finite variant R' are distinguishable based on local context.

Let us now consider the second step. An (m,n) context detectable error could consist of terminal *and* nonterminal elements, not just terminal words as required by the detectable error condition. We must show that we can extend such an example to an error detectable at the sentence level. An easy lemma establishes this:

> If R' is an (m,n) bounded context detectable error, then R' is bounded degree of error detectable (at the surface sentence level).

The proof (by induction) is omitted; only a sketch will be given here. Intuitively, the reason is that we can extend any nonterminals in an error detectable (m,n) context to some valid surface sentence and bound this derivation by some constant fixed in advance and depending only on the grammar. This is because unbounded derivations in a grammar are possible only by the repetition of nonterminals via recursion.[4] Since there are only a finite number of distinct nonterminals, it is only via recursion that we can obtain a derivation chain that is arbitrarily deep. As is well known (compare the proof of the pumping theorem for context-free grammars), any such arbitrarily deep derivation producing a valid surface sentence also has an associated truncated derivation, bounded by a constant dependent on the grammar, that yields a valid sentence of the language. (We simply excise the repeated nonterminal sequence.) So, no matter how large

[4]Strictly speaking, this is obviously true only of a context-free grammar, but it is also true if deletions are bounded—as they are—in a more complex grammar. In any case, this property holds in the Marcus parser.

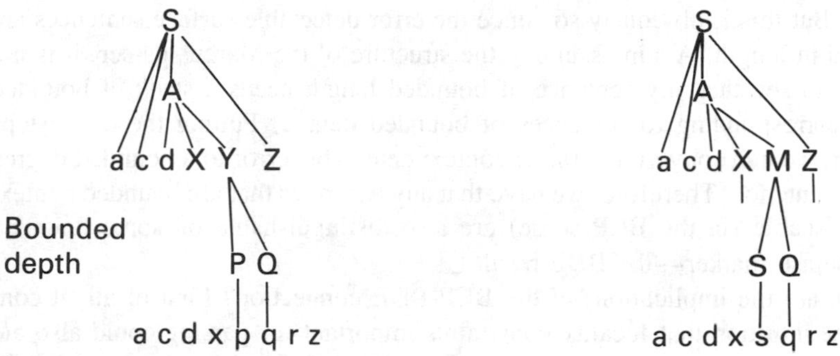

FIGURE 10.9. Bounded (*m,n*) context can be extended to a full sentence

the distinguishing (*m,n*) context, there must be some bounded (fixed in advance) context on which the same distinguishing condition holds, that also ultimately yields a sentence. Figure 9 gives an example.

Further, since by assumption the (*m,n*) contexts in the two cases are different, either *some* of the terminals in these contexts or *some* of the nonterminals must be distinct. If it is some of the terminals, then we are done, because we have produced two distinct surface sentences and, therefore, a surface sentence detectable error. If it is two nonterminals that are distinct, then consider the extension of these nonterminals to a surface sentence, as in Figure 9. Here the first sentence is *acdxpqrz* and the second is *acdxsqrz*. In this second case, we claim that such an extension *must* yield two distinct sentences. For otherwise, we would have a single surface sentence with two distinct derivations, i.e., an ambiguous sentence. But this possibility is barred by the original BCP condition. From the learner's standpoint, the effect of this condition is to assume a filter such that the correct underlying target parse is independently reconstructable, perhaps using semantic information. Situations where an input sentence could be analyzed in two different ways, one way by the learner and one way in the correct target grammar, are barred. Note that Wexler and Culicover also assume these conditions: a transformational derivation is assumed to be unambiguous, and the learner always knows what the correct unique underlying structure associated with a surface sentence should be.[5]

Since in either case the (*m,n*) context can be extended to a surface sentence detectable error, we have established the second step in our three step demonstration.

For the third and final step we must show that our extension is of bounded

[5]Note that this does *not* imply that natural languages are unambiguous, which is clearly false; it only implies that the sentences used to *learn* language are unambiguous, in the sense described in the text.

degree. But this is obviously so, since the error detectable surface sentences are bounded in length. Again assuming the structure of the Marcus parser, it is not difficult to see that any sentence of bounded length needs a stack of bounded depth, corresponding to sentences of bounded degree. Putting the three steps together, we can convert any (m,n) context detectable error to a bounded degree of error sentence. Therefore, we have that any two rules that are bounded context distinguishable (in the BCP sense) are also distinguishable on some bounded depth phrase marker—the BDE result.□

What are the implications of the BCP-BDE connection? First of all, it confirms the intuition that locality constraints important for parsing could also aid learning. Once a finite family of grammars as defined above meets the BCP condition, it already meets the BDE condition. Thus we might use the BCP condition as a touchstone for the BDE property, without resort to Wexler and Culicover's combinatorial demonstration. Second, the result demonstrates that the acquisition model described earlier is, in fact, quite closely related to the Wexler-Culticover BDE model. Both models give a single locality principle—a distinguishability criterion—that suffices to "scatter" grammars in such a way that they become learnable from bounded data.

Third, one can extend the result to other language subsystems. Just one application will be mentioned here. Consider morphological rule systems. Several recent models have suggested finite state transduction as a way to pair lexical (surface) and underlying word forms (Koskenniemi, 1983). However, it is known that easy learnability does not follow directly from this formalism. Gold (1978) shows that finite state induction is NP-hard: in some cases, one must examine an exponential number of examples. Without additional constraint, even finite state induction is intractable. What is needed is some way to localize errors. Is there an analog of the BCP condition for finite state systems that also implies easy learnability? The answer is yes. Angluin (1982) defines a notion of *k* reversibility: a finite state automaton is *k* reversible if it is backwards deterministic over *k* tokens. Such automata are polynomial-time learnable (from data of limited complexity). Berwick and Pilato (1985) shows that this condition is met by many natural linguistic subsystems—including the auxiliary verb system of English, and morphological subsystems. Here, too, the bounded context constraint may play an important role, just where "brute force" induction is required.

To summarize: from a computational point of view, the language acquisition faculty and the language processing faculty appear particularly well-designed. Under one reasonable model of what it takes to learn a language, budding learners must process input sentences in their environment and select from a scattered space of target grammars. The connection between the Wexler and Culicover model and the Berwick computer model shows informally that this scattering of grammars may aid both parsing and learning. The demonstration of the previous section suggests formally that easy learnability and easy parsability are in fact closely related—a surprising and happy result. Natural languages must be both learnable and parsable, and the same constraints aid both goals.

REFERENCES

Angluin, D. (1982). Inference of reversible languages. *Journal of the Association for Computing Machinery* 29:741–765.

Berwick, R. (1979). Learning structural descriptions of grammar rules from examples. *Proc. 6th international joint conference on artificial intelligence,* Cambridge, MA.

Berwick, R. (1982). Locality principles and the acquisition of syntactic knowledge. PhD dissertation, MIT Department of Electrical Engineering and Computer Science.

Berwick, R. (1985). *The acquisition of syntactic knowledge,* Cambridge, MA: MIT Press.

Berwick, R., and S. Pilato (1985). Reversible automata and the induction of the English auxiliary system. *Proc. of the 23rd meeting of the association for computational linguistics,* Chicago.

Berwick, R. and A. Weinberg. (1984). *The grammatical basis of linguistic performance.* Cambridge, MA: MIT Press.

Berwick, R., and K. Wexler. (1982). Parsing and c-command. *Proc. 2nd west coast conference on formal linguistics,* Stanford, CA.

Feldman, J. (1972). Some decidability results on grammatical inference and complexity. *Information and Control* 20:244–262.

Gold, E. (1967). Language identification in the limit. *Information and Control,* 10:447–474.

Gold, E. (1978). Complexity of automation identification from given data. *Information and Control,* 37.

Hamburger, H. and K. Wexler. (1975). A mathematical theory of learning transformational grammar. *Journal of Mathematical Psychology,* 12:137–177.

Hammer, M. (1974). A new grammatical transformation into deterministic top-down form. Cambridge, MA: MIT Project MAC TR-119.

Koskenniemi, K. (1983). Two-level model for morphological analysis. *Proc. eighth international joint conference on artificial intelligence,* 683–685.

Lasnik, H. and J. Kupin. (1977). A restrictive theory of transformational grammar. *Theoretical Linguistics* 4:173–196.

Marcus, M. (1980). *A theory of syntactic recognition for natural language.* Cambridge, MA: MIT Press.

Wexler, K. and P. Culicover. (1980). *Formal principles of language acquisition.* Cambridge, MA: MIT Press.

Williams, E. (1981). A readjustment in the learnability assumptions. In *the logical problem of language acquisition,* C. Baker and J. McCarthy, eds. Cambridge, MA: MIT Press, pp. 64–78.

11 Representation, Rules, and Overgeneralization in Phonology

Marlys A. Macken
Stanford University

1. INTRODUCTION

This paper takes as its starting point a theory that views the learner of a phonology or syntax as actively constructing rules and grammars by forming hypotheses and abstract rules over available data. The evidence for this theory is only briefly given here. Rather the focus in on the critical questions, under such a theory, of (i) why the learner succeeds so quickly, given the standard Chomskyan assumption that any grammar is radically underdetermined by the data, and on the related question of (ii) how the learner unlearns overly-general or incorrect rules. Let's call this the learning riddle and acknowledge at the outset that it is deeply connected to the theory's hypothesis testing mechanism, its abstract representational structure, a powerful and expressive formalism for that representation, and the assumption of an extensionally complex and variable world.

The typical solution to this riddle, within generative linguistics, is to invoke strong claims about the specific content of universal grammar, perhaps with asides about maturation or syntactic triggers dispersed through a corpus. In contrast, the solution here depends first on the semantically and informationally structured domains to which the formal system refers and within which acquisition actually takes place and, second, on the mathematical structure of those domains, structure that is here argued to be quite distinct from the algebraic structure of formal phonology and syntax.

The proposals thus challenge key, although tacit assumptions, behind formal linguistics and, derivatively, in learnability models. Formal theory, because so closely tied to classical logic and mathematics, inherits problems from tacitly assuming the standard Tarskian logic of truth in an arbitrary, consistent or monotonic, and atemporal domain. But natural language, unlike any set-theoretic world in mathematics, is not fully arbitrary, atemporal or consistent. The *non*arbitrariness of its structures across *time* and in linguistic, semantic space is *crucial* to language learning: several different structures are proposed that mutually constrain the learner's potentially untractable hypothesis space, each constraining weakly, yet in conjunction quite strongly. The *non*monotonicity of linguistic systems is a function of the *ceteris paribus* character of natural rules, generalizations over a variable domain . . . the problem of *exceptions*. Not surprisingly, learnability and acquisition models associated with formal linguistics stumble on this just as standard logic models for adult human reasoning do. Given the problems of exceptions, indeterminacy and certain empirical evidence, the proper direction is in pairing the formal, algebraic grammar with a stochastic representation, or grammar, that admits *probabilistic reasoning*. Inferencing mechanisms associated with the stochastic grammar then permit the unlearning of overly-general rules, especially a particularly difficult class of such rules—namely those for which no positive evidence exists that would disconfirm the rule. This is accomplished by allowing the learner to make inferences from a particular kind of implicit negative input, namely the *absence* of information.

Yet the formal system is nonetheless partly arbitrary and crucially characterized by levels and combinatorial properties that, it is argued, cannot be inductively inferred from even complex informational and semantical systems. Therefore, certain elements and paradigmatic structures are assumed to be antecedently given, and it is the deductive character of the algebraic structure that is largely responsible for the speed of acquisition. A key point is that the existence of other informational domains radically reduces the specifically linguistic content of the innate grammar—to the point that it only weakly determines the acquisition sequence for any particular language. This is a desirable result in view of the significant variation to language acquisition across languages and individuals acquiring the same language.

This paper is constructed in two parts, the first being the theory of the structure acquired and the second being the theory of the acquisition of that structure, specifically rules of a particular type. Section 2 distinguishes algebraic and stochastic models and sets up the thesis that *both* models are required for explaining linguistic and acquisitional phenomena, and therefore a "grammar" is a paired algebraic representation and stochastic representation. Section 3 defines the type of algebraic and stochastic representations used and argues that each representational type handles certain linguistic phenomena well, others not at all, and that each type is associated with a particular reasoning or inferencing model. Next are defined the basic set of inferencing mechanisms required by each structure, mechanisms that figure in the acquisition model. A topic in this section is the issues of combinatorial explosion and indeterminacy and how pairing representational types solves problems either one alone entails. Section 4 summarizes the theoretical points crucial to the acquisition model in section 5.

Also in (5) are the data on which the acquisition model is based, a discussion of the difference between rules and overgeneralizations, and certain characteristics of the representations, the learner and the input. Section 6 further relates the grammar of section 3 and the acquisition model of section 5 by discussing how the posited representations, inferencing algorithms and semantic/informational domains, work in conjunction to constrain the learner's hypothesis space. Section 7 covers the way in which the model accounts for the unlearning of the overgeneralizations and other incorrect rules. Concluding remarks on the implications of this work for acquisition research, learnability, and formal theories are in section 8.

2. REPRESENTATION

Given that the topic is the "learning riddle," one might think the key issue to be nature-nuture. Though whether language is innate is certainly central to the topic and decidedly distinguishes among competing models, this issue is surprisingly uninflamatory these days. Most researchers appear to accept some innate structure and some learning, regardless of their epistemological banners. What does polarize the field is the dispute over the models taken by each side to be the representational structures of the mind and language, but the current and earlier disputes are similar.

The earlier debate over nature-nurture is most often cast as the debate between invariant/universal structure, free of context or time, unfolding in a passive mind on the one hand, and variable/learned structure, tied to context and time, elicited by active environmental sources or constructed by an active mind on the other. The first constellation of ideas is typically associated with rationalism, the second with empiricism—irreconcilable views of the world and mind as determinate or nondeterminate, each at its extreme leading, in the twentieth century, to a metaphysical core of either Fregean certainty or Quinean scepticism. Yet, history shows us that these constellations can be partitioned differently as in the bridge philosophy of Kant.

Today's conflict over representation yields a dichotomy of models that also splits along the nature-nurture lines, and the property sets of the two contrasting models also are frequently redrawn, giving rise to both hybrid models and situations in which the same datum is argued as evidence for each of the opposing models. Yet, on this representation issue, two broad categories must also be distinguished, namely algebraic models and nonalgebraic models, here called stochastic models. By algebraic I mean various *determinate,* boolean models associated with strong universalist theories, e.g., formal, analytic, set-theoretic models, typically syntactic models (Chomsky, 1963; Chomsky, 1965; Chomsky and Halle, 1968). Under stochastic I include *nondeterminate,* nonboolean models typically associated with theories that deal with variable, incomplete, context-bound, or vague phenomena (e.g., geometrical, vector space, statistical, synthetic, prototype, distributed network, or Boltzmann models, frequently lexical or semantic models, or pattern recognition models). While the fields in which these models figure (e.g., linguistics, AI, and psychology) polarize easily in a binary way, the models themselves on objective grounds are not as simply dichotomized. An example relevant to subsequent discussion would be geometric vector space models; pure models of this type—though nondiscrete—are nonstochastic, using linear algebra techniques to transform variable data at one level into invariants at another. A particular geometry is always defined with respect to a set of tranformations for particular equivalence classes. Thus, though there will be differences, a fundamental similarity across these ''stochastic'' models is then the ways in which they are non-algebraic, and this will be made clear in section 3.0. Within acquisition, algebraic theories underlie the work of, for example, Berwick (this volume); Pinker (1984); Smith (1973); Wexler and Culicover (1980); while nonalgebraic theories characterize the models of, for example, Bates, Braine, McClelland and Rumelhart, and Pinker's implementation component (all from this volume); Olmsted (1966); Olmsted (1971), and Timm (1977).

The argument here is that phonology and syntax are fundamentally similar in that both are formal systems that, primarily, manipulate uninterpreted symbols and fall appropriately within algebraic models, and that, secondly, run afoul of projection puzzles largely as a consequence of their expressive power. Overgeneralization is then the *concomitant* of the learner's ability to generalize. The close, janus-relation of generalization and overgeneralization is a function of the nature of the formal system. Thus, the pruning of interim, overly general grammars requires a *different* mechanism. Next, it is argued that phonetics and semantics are fundamentally similar in that each provides *interpretation* functions for a formal system and both characterize structured, nonformal content domains and thus are best modelled by what are referred to here as stochastic models.[1] This parallelism does not force both members of a pair (phonology and syntax or phonetics and semantics) to be modelled identically. Rather, the claim has to do with which broad class of models is appropriate for each pair *and* with the properties that will hold of the relation between each formal system and its interpretive system. Thus, certain solutions to the projection puzzles in phonology are assumed to hold at a type level for syntax as well. Under this account, the tension between determinate and nondeterminate theories and representation models reflects a basic paradox of cognition and language, because both seemingly contradictory properties hold of the *same* objects and systems. This is in contrast to views that partition invariant/variant phenomena into dichotomies

[1]This could be quite controversial, particularly in the case of semantics, but the possibility that semantics may be a set-theoretic domain at some level of abstraction does not affect the claim being made here for the lower level.

like "competence/performance" or "grammatical/extragrammatical," where only one member of the pair is the locus of solutions (such as learnability) or for that matter, proper study. Furthermore, while some aspects of phonology or syntax may be studied independently, any reduction of phonology to phonetics or syntax to semantics leads to certain characteristic problems, most notably a failure to capture the higher order regularities and an inability to account for the speed of acquisition.

3. ALGEBRAIC AGAINST STOCHASTIC MODELS

The algebraic models common to formal grammars, set theory, formal logic, and automata theory all manipulate and combine discrete entities rather than continuous objects like lines or spaces, in structures where: the assignment of entities to categories is determinate, where complex categories are boolean functions of primitives, and the categories enter into hierarchical relations. Under standard interpretation, such systems are fully compositional, arbitrary (in that the content of a symbol is irrelevant to the rules that manipulate that symbol), context independent, and atemporal. All instances of a given category are fully equivalent, and categories at a given level are equal. Full compositionality refers to the absorption of the properties of the lower components by a higher predicate. syntactic rules for combining these symbols into well-formed (i.e., grammatical) actual syntactic or phonological system of human language fully meets these requirements. In practice, of course, phonologists and syntacticians spend a great deal of rule- and grammar-time dealing with context effects, noncompositionality, exceptions of all kinds, and so on. Yet, inspite of this, their implicit beliefs about their subject matter—which is what they use when constructing and evaluating theories—derive from a model of language as a formal system.

But what does it mean to claim that the phonology is a formal system? At a simple level, a phonology is a grammar that characterizes the set of strings on a particular finite alphabet. The grammar gives the vocabulary of symbols, the syntactic rules for combining these symbols into well-formed (i.e., grammatical) strings or formulas, and the semantic rules for assigning meanings or interpretations to such formulas. There is a close relation between natural language and grammar seen in this way and formal languages of symbolic logic, a relation that allows precise definition of "formal." The basic claim here is that what's referred to as the "formal" phonological (or syntactic) component is indeed a formal deductive system, in particular a logical calculus that is an algebra. A formal system is one in which some of the system's primitive, undefined terms are arbitrary, uninterpreted symbols. A calculus is a deductive system in which discrete elements are unambiguously defined or computed by means of other elements and rules of combination and manipulation. An algebra is a calculus in which the elements are expressed as uninterpreted symbols meaning general terms and general relations and where there is a set of algebraic operations over those elements. The natural algebraic structure that corresponds to the propositional calculus is the algebra of classes or Boolean algebra. For first-order theories, quantifiers introduce more algebraic structure. By deductive is meant a system in which a small number of propositions implies the truth of all other elementary propositions with certainty equal to the certainty of the axioms on which the deductive consequences are based. (An inductive system is, in contrast, one in which truth values are assigned separately by information outside of the system and where premises give only some evidence for their conclusions; such inductive arguments differ in degree of likelihood or probability which their premises confer on the conclusions.) Formal deductive systems must have certain precisely defined properties. This requirement of good deductive systems is crucial to the model developed here. One of these properties is consistency, which is defined over axioms and theorems and is closely related to the concept monotonicity. Monotonicity is defined over changes in states and means that the number of statements is strictly increasing over time such that, for example, information once added is not later taken away or contradicted.

In the real world, such linguistic systems are partly nonarbitrary with much nonequivalence of tokens and frequent many-to-many mappings. Phonological or syntactic operations on the types or categories are rarely total functions (due to lexical exceptions, for example), and the interpretive function from symbol-to-content is not fully determinate (i.e. may be incomplete, inexact, overlapping or indeterminate). Where rules have exceptions, reasoning over such systems is nonmonotonic. Algebraic models for actual phonological or syntactic systems encounter problems handling exceptions, some types of variation, true novelty and change across time, gradedness within a system, clustering that is not a subset relation, and dynamic phenomena generally. Exceptions then are characteristic of linguistic rules and comprise one formidable "natural" source of inconsistency or nonmonotonicity. If linguistic statements perforce require in certain instances both a formula and its negation, the latter must be separated from the formal system for the formal system to maintain consistency and its deductive character. The needed partitioning is here accomplished by pairing the formal system with a stochastic grammar.

A phonological representation that is algebraic requires a 'learning' algorithm that can create hierarchical structures of appropriate levels, construct tree parses through subareas of the hierarchy, and abstract from the complete hierarchy the constituent paradigms. I refer to such formal processes under the cover term "*grid algorithm*" and assume that they construct rule schemata that comprise a minimal, abstract subset of those found in current formal phonology (metrical structures, autosegmental tiers, etc.). Standard arguments concerning linguistic generalizations support the necessity for an algebraic grammar here as well (cf. Anderson, 1981). The precise form and operation of the grid algorithm are not immediately crucial. This algorithm is discussed below in the context of "inferencing mechanisms," although it is likely to be highly domain-specific and antecedently given. An algebraic inferencing mechanism that would be quite useful to the learner would be an *evaluation metric,* yet there has been very little work done on what such a metric would be like (apart from early work on an arithmetic symbol counter). None of the work that has been done has been of any significance—perhaps a telling indication of the difficulty of the task.

While algebraic models are the cornerstone of generative theory, stochastic models are not as familiar to linguists. Such models are taken here to be a superset of basically statistical models that depend on numerical algorithms for determining and/or representing the structure of a domain. A stochastic language is a language together with a probability distribution over its elements. A stochastic grammar, then, has probabilities associated with alternative productions which are used to define the probability that the grammar derives a given string. If a sequence of strings is generated at random according to probabilities associated with its elements, then the frequency of a given value in an input can be used to estimate its probability in the language.

Stochastic in the present context does not mean completely random (though there is some randomness in the system) but, rather, refers to probabilities that while often quite high are still typically less than one. Also included here is the concept of a geometric perceptual space where the *model* is some abstraction over an n-dimensional domain—a parameter or vector space in the world—where objects can be described in terms of geometric parameters or a point in the n-dimensional vector space defined by the n-describing parameters or parameter space. In the model, the numerical algorithms (e.g., linear transforms) extract features and enhance relevant classificatory properties to inductively determine the objects or categories of the space. A hierarchy of parameter spaces can be constructed on the basic space for complex objects, and a number of different geometries exist for characterizing the sameness of objects under different transformations, from Euclidean geometry where objects are metrically equivalent but rotated to the weakest but most abstract geometry—topology—where complex transforms change all but the connectivity of the object (e.g., Shepard, 1974; Shaw and Pittenger, 1977). If such a model corresponds to some aspect of human cognition, then the numerical algorithms correspond to the relevant perceptual mechanisms.

Such nonalgebraic models are well suited for handling variable data and recognizing patterning of certain types such as that of phonetic equivalence classes. But these models have trouble with induction of hierarchy (in fact, as will be argued, require an a priori hierarchy to constrain the search through complex spaces) and with 'learning' the combinatorial properties of a hierarchy (i.e., the rules that determine interrelations, arrangements, organization of primitives at each level in higher parameter spaces). A first, quite basic problem with such a model as a direct mental *representation* of objects in the world, for example, is infinity of representation: the partial answer to this is that the mind has certain limits on its resolution powers. Thus, for example, the human ear has lower bound restriction of approximately 2 db, 15 ms and 20 hz. In the case of temporal resolution the ear can only sequence two events if they are separated by more than 15 ms (milliseconds). Two points are important here. First, in human perceptual domains information is not densely packed (as in pure geometrical vector spaces) but is concentrated in "subspaces" that are relatively widely spaced. For example, in the perceptual domains for vocalic systems (cf. Liljencrants and Lindblom, 1972) and for consonantal systems (a la Shepard, 1972). Second, existing algebraic phonological models (e.g., their associated feature systems and theory) only capture a portion of the information in the *structure* of these domains.

This type of clustering of categorial information in cognitively relevant vector spaces is crucial to the following discussion: the so-structured perceptual spaces will be referred to as "*structured domains,*" the processing mechanisms that operate over the domains as "*distance metrics* over a similarity space," and the set as the "semantics" of the vector space. However, a fully bottom-up system would still work well only on perfectly pre-processed objects, and the human system works well on noisy, incomplete information. Such models typically assume then that the categories are partly statistically determined, such that the objects in these perceptual spaces are basically probability densities. Thus, the *representation* associated with such a model would require some format that preserves the numerical, graded character of the categories and the information that is contained in the particular ways the categories cluster and distribute throughout the space of the domain, as in prototype categories or in a network configuration approximating the topology of the domain. The inferencing mechanisms needed to operate over such a representation must, therefore, include a *stochastic algorithm* for tracking frequencies and computing probabilities, as well as appropriate geometric distance metrics. Phonetic and semantic domains have such properties and thus are appropriately modelled by what are referred to here as stochastic models. What the precise representation in the mind is is not crucial to discussion *provided* that the representational format meets the characterization just given. Also included here is a low-level "alignment metric" that makes use of the chunking of information across time. This mechanism makes a preliminary segmentation of a string that, while requiring no higher level information, eliminates a number of improbable alternations.

Dual representations

A phonology is, under this account, a single system that pairs an algebraic representation and a stochastic one. This pairing partly solves problems of combinatorial explosion and indeterminacy that either alone entails. In a system with both an algebraic representation and a stochastic representation and the necessary algebraic and stochastic inferencing mechanisms, the hierarchy of the algebraic system constrains the ''lower'' level, and the principled semantics of the stochastic system constrain the ''higher'' system. Further, the stochastic character of inferencing inherited at the algebraic level will ease certain induction problems, in particular, those associated with extraction of certain phonetic categories and with exceptions to phonological rules.[2]

Combinatorial explosion. Learning either an unconstrained stochastic system or an unconstrained algebraic system is difficult because of the combinatorial explosion in the search space associated with either system. Numerically defined categories in a completely nonhierarchical stochastic system have an impossible search space. There must be planes of some sort through the vector space to help organize that space for the learner (see Ladefoged, 1985, for a discussion of the large number of potentially independent entities even at the ''segment'' abstraction). In a phonological system, while some requisite dimensions or categories are stochastic, many appear to be purely algebraic; these latter are levels that are coherent with respect to the properties of the rules that operate at that level and not necessarily with respect to the phonetic identity of the symbols being manipulated by those rules. However, the algebraic system can have its own size problems. For example, a small—by current standards phonological feature set would include 20 binary features, yielding in principle, a million possible segments (2-20th), but most of these are impossible on phonetic rather than formal grounds. Similarly, metrical theory has seven parameters for determining tree formation [headedness; level of structure—rime, foot, word, phrase, etc.; branching; directionality; iterativity—iterate or branch only once; quantity sensitive (nonhead must be ''light''); and obligatory branching]. Many of these are implicitly or explicitly multivalued, and the system also allows extrametricality and destressing/shifting; determining possible trees over even small numbers of strings gets difficult. Without further constraints, the system is infeasible (cf. Hayes, 1984 on overgeneration). The hierarchy is crucial here to avoiding combinatorial problems, but while part of this hierarchy is purely formal (e.g., there is not obvious phonetic reason for ruling out ''iteration'' steps of two or three, etc.), part of it again is substantive (e.g., what counts as quantity).

---

[2]With complex informational sources, a mechanism is needed for tracking information, else the complex system has its own version of combinatorial explosion. In human systems, one component of such a mechanism is ''attention,'' where again an important, but poorly studied, factor is informational structures across particular stretches of *time—not* in the representation *nor* in the idealized, atemporal language, but rather in the learner's environment and in the language-qua-time . . . in the world. This structure in time and context—with the learner's existing knowledge/grammar—helps direct attention to crucial foci, integrate the information flow, and thus constrain the hypothesis space currently at hand.

Indeterminacy. One particular type of indeterminacy—that which occurs at the level of terminals—must be discussed, but a far more difficult problem exists at the level of our theories. For Quine (1960) linguistics is completely undetermined by the data because there is no fact of the matter (an argument that is less easy to forge in the case of phonology). In one of Chomsky's (1967) several replies to Quine, the situation is no worse in linguistics than in any other science: the problem is simply that all theories are underdetermined by the data. Our task of explaining acquisition would be much simpler if there *were* an accepted theory of the structure of phonology or syntax and, in particular, if the mapping between linguistic formalisms and the formal language hierarchy were straightforward. Partly due to the profileration of theories of phonological structure (and partly because only the earliest stages of acquisition have been well studied), no arguments are presented here that crucially depend on the status and properties of the *full* phonological armamentarium such as whether phonological rules have the power of context-sensitivity (which they do not, despite appearances), whether they do or do not operate over variables and unbounded rule contexts [e.g., Kenstowicz and Kisseberth, 1977) on Chimwinyi and Poser (1982) on Chumash sibilant harmony], or any number of other issues (n.b., most work of the last seven to ten years has been toward restricting phonology). As to the generative capacity of phonology, it is clear that, whatever the outcome of these other controversies, a phonological system is *not* finite (cf., Pullum 1983); it is a symbolic, formal, productive system requiring a grammar at least in the finite state class (e.g., Johnson, 1970), thus in the class of Gold text unlearnable (Gold, 1967).

The particular indeterminacy problem that is of concern is as follows. For certain primitives, it appears that *no* invariant features serve to select *all* members of the set. Thus decades of extensive research by many peope have failed to identify a set of necessary and sufficient features that serve to identify place of articulation in stop consonants (i.e., categorize all instances of /d/ across all vowel environments and in particular across [di] and [du]). Shifting even to complex computations over relatively large portions of the consonant *and* the vowel has achieved only about 80% to 90% categorization (cf., Stevens and Blumstein, 1981; Lahiri, Gewirth and Blumstein, 1984). A purely algebraic solution to this problem, if a reasonable one exists, would require at least disjunctive categories, and this would seriously complicate the learning procedure. Where phonological primitives do not have a unique type-token mapping, the stochastic grammar categorizes those primitives. The stochastic metrics associated with the stochastic grammar are particularly good at manipulating local properties that are variable at the boundaries and sensitive to noise. If mapped from a structured vector space with geometrical similarity functions for relating forms under transformations or in planes in the space, the stochastic grammar can correctly categorize tokens that *cluster* together in a perceptual space even though these elements may share no defining, discrete feature or property.[3]

Mutual constraints. Previously defined was the general nature of the ways in which the dual representations provide mutual constraints. Now added is that the stochastic representation solves what would be a problem of category indeterminacy for a purely algebraic grammar. These stochastic algorithms also handle noise, randomness, partially overlapping categories, etc., thus eliminating other types of indeterminacy. The need for a stochastic algorithm for categorization of terminals provides a *prima facie* case for a *general* stochastic algorithm. This mechanism can both eliminate hypothesized rules where confirming evidence fails to appear and select among grammars that on purely algebraic, structural grounds may be equivalent. This is in effect a stochastic variant of an evaluation metric and, similarly, reduces indeterminacy at the level of the grammar. (Further evidence for such a frequency tracker in human cognition comes from the sociolinguistic literature on variable rules and the psychological literature on the role of frequency in recognition and parsing tasks.)

Abstraction and losing information

It is crucial to the expressive power of the formal system that it be freed from the variability of the content domain where the symbols hold it. However, that abstraction is accomplished by losing much structured information as well. For example, establishing a level in a hierarchy requires establishing equivalence between categories that function at that level; information about how those categories differ must perforce be lost in the hierarchy, but it is that information that can be crucial to the identification of those categories. The structure in the semantic domain associated with the formal categories is preserved here in the stochastic representation and then is available for the learning process.

Properties of the stochastic representation

The key requirement of the stochastic representation is that it be annotated with frequency information (and that it be paired with an associated mechanism that properly uses this information). Independent of this is the proposal that the format of the stochastic representation be quite different in character from that of algebraic representation. In particular, it must preserve some of the properties of

[3]This solution, then, provides for a type of prototype category structure and thus resembles Stevens' early proposals for solving the problem of the lack of invariance (e.g., Stevens 1975); his recent work, however, is again aimed at finding a unique, though complex feature or features (e.g., Stevens and Blumstein 1981).

the structured domain subserving the algebraic representation. For argument, assume that some aspect of this representation is an acoustic analogue of an image, crucially containing more potential information than a formal phonological representation (say, in features) would contain and preserving information over which the distance metrics operate. Thus, for example, at points in development, children use unanalyzed wholes (e.g., acoustic word 'images') for which they have a representation and on which they later 'superimpose' an algebraic rule-governed representation (section 5.1). Clearly, such an 'image' representation is an abstraction and not a direct or faithfully iconic translation of the source of the 'image,' and no isomorphism is required by the present arguments.

The next section summarizes aspects of the framework thus far constructed that are important to the learning model that follows.

4. REPRESENTATIONS, INFERENCING AND DOMAINS

On this account, then, a phonology (or a syntax) consists of an algebraic grammar of a standard generative type and a stochastic grammar.

Two classes of inferencing algorithms operate over the two representations. For the algebraic representation the crucial mechanism is one that provides the necessary tree levels or paradigms on which particular types of symbols are combined and/or manipulated—the "grid algorithm," a cover term for several mechanisms. This class may include an algebraic evaluation metric to select among alternative rules, change rules, and contribute to the construction of a 'correct' grammar. For the stochastic representation, at least three crucial mechanisms are required: a stochastic algorithm that includes a frequency tracker and a means of computing probabilities; distance metrics for utilizing information within spatial/temporal domains; and a (preliminary) alignment metric that makes use of the chunking of information across short stretches of time. The stochastic algorithm solves what would be a problem of category indeterminacy in a purely algebraic grammar (and, as will be shown, explains certain empirical evidence). A similar mechanism is used at many levels for weighting variable rules generally. This generalized, perhaps domain-independent, induction mechanism is needed to track several types of relevant distributional information that will be of use to the learner, and its probabilistic character helps solve the learning riddle. Both the stochastic algorithm and the distance metric figure in how the learner un-learns overly-general and incorrect rules, because both provide the learner with sources of negative input by allowing the learner to make inferences from the *absence* of information.

Finally, "structured domains" were identified. They provide the content for the symbols at the algebraic level and are *not* densely packed, *not* random, *not* arbitrary. Rather they are highly structured and with sufficient dispersal of the objects in the space as to provide negative areas that indirectly contribute to categorization. The specific domain described was the acoustic vector space domain associated with the phonological stochastic representation. In addition, information distributed across the language as a whole comprises a structured domain: a language's lexicon can be partitioned and in fact is partitioned across time for the learner (''sublanguages,'' section 5.5). Thus, the input is partly ''sequenced'' with respect to complexity for the learner; the frequency of certain crucial types of phonological information is increased in particular stretches of time, and the probability that alternating forms will be paired within an appropriately small time window greatly increases. It is possible that the formal grammar ''space'' is similarly structured, that the structure is reflected in a 'spatial' domain of real languages, and that such formal space/structure of a given language is similarly sequenced across time for the learner. If so, such a (formal) informational domain would be another, quite powerful constraint on the learner's hypothesis space.

These points have thus far been largely theoretically motivated, and empirical data are presented below that strengthen the arguments. It should be noted that each of the above points changes Gold-learnability assumptions about the input, the language, the learner and the criteria for learning.

5. LEARNING A PHONOLOGY

With the notable exception of a few early diary studies, most linguistically oriented work on phonological acquisition[4] has been done since 1970. This work carries the imprint, one way or another, of Jakobson (1941) and Chomsky (1965), classic works of a rationalist, universalist linguistic theory. Most of this work is on children under the age of three and hence covers only the simplest of phonological systems and phenomena, and the majority is on the acquisition of English and related Indo-European languages. Given the zeitgeist and the subject, the expectation would be for great uniformity. While some of this literature is limited or flawed in various ways, one conclusion is quite incontrovertible: the acquisition of phonology is surprisingly underspecified by its innate component. Children acquiring the same dialect of the same language vary: they vary in the kinds of rules they use, how they organize their grammars, even how they solve very low level phonetic articulation problems; they go through different stages in

[4]Phonology, like all other language components, is a complex, not fully understood domain, and so too, the process by which it is acquired. This section attempts to make best use, in a broad and theoretically coherent fashion, of what is known including even that for which the evidence, though suggestive, is not conclusive. To keep the information in its proper perspective, particularly for the nonspecialist, pointers are included throughout to specific issues where key research is needed.

sometimes different order, and at any one point in time, their lexicons mix rule-governed and exceptional forms. Yet, there are certain broad similarities of a Jakobsonian type, and there are virtually no 'crazy' rules. The conclusion I draw is that phonology, while rule-governed, is nonetheless a remarkably flexible system. It can be started up at many different points and pursued in many different directions, and the ease with which it is acquired is not due to a highly specific innate grammar (though there is an innate component) but to a representational system with formal deductive properties and to a potentially powerful learning mechanism that is good at discovering patterns and that is *quite* unlike an empiricist reinforcement schedule. The emergence of cognitive, hypothesis-testing models (see Kiparsky and Menn, 1977; Macken and Ferguson, 1983) may be seen as partly a reaction to the overly-narrow construal of 'universal' in earlier works like those of Jakobson and Chomsky. The more recent works resemble rationalist theories quite a bit more than empiricist theories.[5] But in stressing the creativity of the learner and rule-system, these models share with more standard Chomskyan models the problem of constraining the acquisition system sufficiently to solve the projection problem yet with enough degrees of freedom to allow the learning of correct generalizations and the unlearning of ultimately incorrect ones.

Hypothesis-testing model

Hypothesis testing here means rule discovery and does not entail the systematicity or consciousness of scientific enquiry. Crucial evidence includes the following: *1.* widespread individual differences, especially of the type where several children acquiring the same language generalize different rules over the same data, *2.* "experimentation" where in a short period of time a child will vacilate between several forms for a word, each of which is governed by a different "rule," *3.* "isolated accuracy" of progressive idioms, forms that occur "before" a rule is added to a grammar and that show a complexity well in advance of the current system, a complexity that is lost when certain new rules are added,[6] *4.* "regressive phenomena," cases where correct rules are "lost" under the force of a new rule, *5.* "overgeneralizations," cases where new rules are applied

[5]The nonlinearity of development was taken by these hypothesis-testing models as key evidence against empiricist (cf., Olmsted 1971) and template type nativist (cf., Jakobson 1941) theories. Chomsky's early work characterized language acquisition as hypothesis testing (cf., Chomsky 1965), but by at least 1980 Chomsky had switched to a biological, rather than a psychological model; both the nonlinearity and the range of variation that is found are at odds with a maturation type mechanism though not with a more complex nativist account. A claim of Chomsky (1980a) is that there are strong similarities between a biological 'mental organ' account and a weak hypothesis testing account, namely abduction (cf., Pierce . .); at best, the argument as given is unconvincing.

[6]Child lexicons also include frozen forms, forms that fail to undergo a new rule and thus persist in an earlier simplified shape.

to incorrect environments, *6.* ''child grammar generalizations,'' rule additions that are lawful generalizations with respect to properties of the child's current internal grammar and *not* with respect to the grammar being acquired, *7.* ''selectiveness,'' phenomena showing selective attention to particular parts of the phonology and lexicon being learned, *8.* ''inventions,'' novel forms ranging from segments to words. These all instantiate novelty, the creation of knowledge, the nonautomatic nature of the child's responses, and the nonlinear nature of the progress to the adult grammar. (See Macken and Ferguson, 1983 for examples and sources.)

The picture of acquisition that emerges from current research is one in which the young child—one just learning to talk—acquires a small set of word forms that are not integrated into a conventional rule-governed system, but rather form a system in which word shapes are analyzed on an individual basis. Over time the child gradually develops rules manipulating successively smaller phonological units and constructs a succession of grammars or rule-systems. The early forms appear to be represented as wholes (see, for example, Ferguson and Farwell, 1975; Mean, 1978; Peters, 1977; MacWhinney, 1978; and Chiat, 1979). In the present context this stage is stochastic in that the lexical entries are in a nonsegmented, more ''image-like'' representation, the structures are highly affected by the frequency and distributional facts of the input, and the structures of the next stage are partly determined by these earliest forms. Modelling the grammar with two distinct representational formats accounts for the phenomenon of correct forms (or idioms) followed by later incorrect forms. These correct forms are not actually ''lost'' later but, rather, are temporarily replaced in production by incorrect forms when the relevant algebraic rules emerge. (How much of the information implicit in such stochastic representations the child actually ''knows'' is an open though crucial question.) The child then recognizes similarities between classes of sounds and contexts, constructing rules for relating similar phenomena. That the process is not automatic as template theories predict (cf., Jakobson, 1941; Stampe, 1969; and Stampe, 1973; Donegan and Stampe, 1979; etc.) can be shown in the variable experimentation forms that children produce as they search for solutions, in the creativity of their invented forms, and in the range and diversity of their solutions (cf., in particular, the discussion in Kiparsky and Menn, 1977; also Goldin-Meadow and Felman, 1977). Through a constrained, basic hypothesis-forming and testing process, rules are discovered and then applied to other related items in categories constructed partly by the child. Newly discovered rules are sometimes *overgeneralized,* as they are integrated into the system. Often, the formation of a rule and/or its overgeneralization results in *regression*—or a superficial loss of ability. These cases of regression are particularly important as they demonstrate that the process is not simply an unfolding of abilities or a linear progression toward some mature grammar. As new or relevant information is recognized, hypotheses or 'theories' are changed, and new rules are created. Some new rules depend not only on properties of the system being learned, but also on properties of the child's own current 'grammar'.

Under this account, acquiring a phonology looks similar to the development of other cognitive abilities, in particular, the account given in Karmiloff-Smith and Inhelder (74/75) of the acquisition of physical weight and balance knowledge: piecemeal single item match; gradual recognition of a pattern; period of exploration; construction of a theory or rule followed by overgeneralization and "loss" of ability; gradual recognition of the regularity of counterexamples; construction of a new, distinct theory or rule; gradual development of a single, unifying theory or grammar. (For more information on the points raised in this section see Macken and Ferguson, 1983; Kiparsky and Menn, 1977; Macken, 1979; Fey and Gandour, 1982; and Menn, 1985.)

Rules, generalizations, and overgeneralizations

The rules of early phonologies are of several distinct types, as noted early by Ingram, 1974 (cf. also, Menn 1976b). The rules that are of present interest are generalizations that go beyond the input data in particular ways. These rules are different from two following types of rules that are common during particular stages: perception rules that operate in some fashion between the auditory input and the lexical representation and production rules that operate downstream of the lexical representation. Perception rules are characterized by lexical exceptions, errors (i.e., sometimes change superficially similar segments in what had been correct, underlying representations) piecemeal spread across the lexicon and a long time period between start and completion. Production rules, on the other hand, are across-the-board in only correct environments and completed in a very short amount of time (Macken, 1980). Unlike either the perception rules or the production rules, overgeneralization rules start by manipulating, across-the-board, a well-defined class and then spread, also across-the-board, to *other* well-defined classes, thus causing errors.

It is important to keep the wider context of the whole rule system in mind partly because much learning is by comparison a more straightforward matching process (cf., Kiparsky and Menn who suggest that the lower articulatory levels also require the same cognitive processing) but also because the "motivation" for the overgeneralization rules is not exactly clear. The position taken here is that such rules are crucial windows on acquisition: they show rather directly how the child is *learning* the system; thus, a crucial issue is how these rules are *un*-learned. But given independent evidence for separate perception and production systems, one could take the view that the child's *knowledge* is always very directly tied to the input (i.e., that children do *not* overgeneralize) and that the cases of apparent overgeneralizations were a type of low level *production* phenomena associated with the development of a *skill,* for instance—a way to boot a faster system. Some interim phonological rules are in fact related to 'streamlining' the production system (e.g., by stabilizing new forms, Macken, 1978), and these rules do resemble overgeneralizations (e.g., by causing regression of certain forms). The problems of distinguishing perception, production, and grammar and of determining the particulars of the rule typology seem to be more central in phonology than in syntax, but whether that is more an accident of history than a substantive difference between the systems is not clear.

Simple examples of overgeneralization can be found in very young children, children engaged in learning some of the most basic types of phonological rules. Thus, for example, a child acquiring English went through the following stages when learning [obstruent + *r*] clusters: initially, [*r*] was deleted (1;6 − 1;10); then /tr/ and /dr/ were produced as [f] for two to three weeks while /pr/ was still [p] and /kr/ was still [k]; beginning at about 1;11.28, the "f-rule," which initially made highly plausible sense given the acoustics of /tr/ in English, was *overgeneralized* to /pr/ and /kr/. At this later stage, a not too unlikely story could perhaps be given for why [f] should be a token for /pr/, but similarly accounting for an independent relation between [f] and /kr/ tampers seriously with phonetic theory and would license a whole host of alternations that do not occur. These are, in fact, not independent phonetic changes, rather an overgeneralization that is fundamentally *phonological*. (The rule started to pull back by 2;6, when /pr/ words appeared as [pw]. See Macken and Ferguson, 1983.) Another similar example is found in Smith (1973):

	i	ii	iii
side	[dait]	[dait]	[lait]
light	[dait]	[lait]	[lait]
	2;2	2;4	2;5

In stage (iii), we see two types of regression: first, the contrast between two lexical items is lost, and second, in *side* the production of [l] is less close to adult /s/ that was [d]. Smith describes this change as a change in the child's hypothesis about how to pronounce /s/:

> What appears to be happening is that the child is confronted with a number of perceptually discrete but for him unpronounceable sounds and proceeds to formulate hypotheses as to their nature in terms of the distinctive features already available to him. Having mastered the sonorant continuant [l] he presumably hypothesized that [continuant] rather than [fricative] was the crucial feature characteristic of /s/ . . . as well as of /l/. . . . In fact, there was a very slight tendency to generalize beyond the examples given here, and extend the rule to /th/—*thank you* appeared briefly as [lɛŋku:]—and to all occurrences of /s/ irrespective of environment (p. 153).

Exceptions and going beyond the data

Rules like the ones we have just seen are explicable under the assumption of a representational language or formalism that allows abstraction and generalization across sets of related though physically distinct symbols. Such a formalism, by definition, allows overgeneralization. If we look at a child's phonological grammar at a given time, we find that certain rules represent a generalization over a proper set and an *overgeneralization* over an incorrect set, that is, given the rules of the language being learned (but, n.b., proper from the point of view of the child's current knowledge). The learner must then recognize exceptions to those generalizations—recognize the *discrepancy* between the internalized grammar and the input. Because only the youngest children have been well studied to this point, the exceptions in question are all with respect to some class of phenomena. Thus, to take the example just given, a rule can properly be constructed over the set of all /t/'s (in a given environment) and can be generalized to other members of a category, say to /p/ and /k/, as there are many phonological rules that manipulate precisely the set /ptk/. But in the case of English and the particular environment, such an *over*generalized rule must be unlearned, as the learner recognizes exceptional cases, here two entire classes. More restricted classes of exceptions—lexical sets with only one member—are simply special cases of the general phenomenon, and for these positive evidence would be lacking. Research on older children or children acquiring other languages would show a rule process operating on particular, more narrow exceptional cases (e.g., English stress rules for latinate vocabulary or tone rules for particular diacritically marked individual words). The task is taken here to be providing a general account that covers the full range of cases.

The learner

Basically, the child learning a phonology appears to be quite conservative. There appear to be few overgeneralizations of the extreme kind like those given in section 5.[7] Some children appear to not produce many such overgeneralizations. And, for those children who do, the overgeneralizations stay within what is an intuitively 'small' distance from their current grammar and from the grammar being learned. Research is needed on each of these points to answer the following questions for *both* phonology and syntax: how typical of particular children and across children is the phenomenon; are there other explanations that would more easily account for the near absence of the phenomenon in certain children and in doing so, radically change the theory of acquisition; and what accounts for the limitations on the occurring overgeneralizations. Clearly the answers to such questions could reside in domains other than the "learner" per se; thus, an answer to the last question could tell us more about an implicit 'simplicity' metric over rules than about the general learning process. In addition, information is needed in two areas that is unlikely to change the general acquisition

[7]This partly is a consequence of the restrictive definition used in Macken and Ferguson (1983) and partly of the nongrammar orientation of most of the literature.

theory: age of overgeneralizations of particular structures (most examples come from children of particular ages, probably as a result of the skew in published research) and complete time course of overgeneralizations (e.g., to answer the question of how much the learner actually *knows* in the stage immediately preceding the overgeneralization).

Finally, the learner uses her existing grammar (i.e., past knowledge) to guide the discovery process and to formulate new hypotheses (cf., section "Hypothesis-testing model" and references in Macken and Ferguson, 1983). What is not known is *how* frequently or what the effect of this is on the learning process. While research is needed in both of these crucial issues, even the existing evidence is important to learnability arguments. We subsume—under "existing grammar metric"—all such evidence showing the role being played by the child's current grammar.

Input

One consistent and surprising characteristic of early phonological grammars is their close relationship to frequency and distributional characteristics of not the whole language being learned but the specific input. First, the *order* in which rules are acquired and the structural properties of interim rules often are correlated with particular distributional characteristics of rules in the input. Note that while order of acquisition may only show the stages to (passively) reflect the input characteristics, the properties of interim rules tend to show that the learner uses some aspects of the frequency information to construct hypotheses about relations among elements. Second, features of the input do not hold for the language as a whole, but rather for "sublanguages" that can be ranked in complexity.[8] The particulars of these facts rarely are identical across languages but can be crucial to accounting for cross-language differences in acquisition (see, for example, Ingram, 1979a on French; Itkonen, 1977 on Finnish; Macken, 1980 on English and Spanish). Each of these sublanguages shows great redundancy for a small number of categories and rule types. For example, the simplest of these sublanguages—the first encountered by the child and basically the core vocabulary of the first 100 to 200 words—has certain properties in Spanish and certain, though different, properties in English. So the initial grammars of children learning Spanish or English are correspondingly different. The sublanguage of English or Spanish learned by the child in the second year has somewhat greater complexity and much repetition of certain kinds of phenomena, somewhat different from those in the first encountered sublanguage.

Such sublanguages are not absolute: each sublanguage includes some of the

[8]Sublanguages can be seen as instantiating a type of Praguean markedness, partially relativized to particular languages, where the position of a primitive in a hierarchy determines its relative frequency, combinatorial capacity and assimilative power.

forms or strings associated with the complex categories and rules of a higher sublanguage and probably has the full range of the language. The definition of each sublanguage depends on the *statistical* characteristics of the category and rule distributions, yet the differences in frequencies for particular categories and rule types are typically large. As noted before, a phonology and its associated learning process are remarkably flexible. This is also true of the *effect* of sublanguages on the acquisition process. It is as if languages can vary greatly in *how* the size (or complexity) of each subset is accomplished. The learning process can make use of *any* subset provided it is sufficiently redundant, as each of the sublanguages is. One caveat is in order: the particular time relation between some change in the input and an associated change in the learner's rule set is not fixed in any simple way; other than that the latter follows the former by a small but variable amount of time. In historical change, this is called the "riddle of actualization" (see Labov Yaeger and Steiner, 1972); for similar reasons, this phrase describes the phenomenon of rule change here. An argument often given against input having an effect (particularly negative input or correction) is that the learner may acknowledge in some way the relevance of the new information but doesn't *immediately* change the relevant rule. This is only a problem under a conception of the learner as a perfectly efficient logic machine, something that children are decidedly not. As it turns out, adults are *not* such logic machines either: changes in their rule systems lag behind and can lag quite a bit behind their first recognition that a rule is 'incorrect' even when they also recognize *how* the rule is wrong (Wason and Johnson-Laird, 1972); cf. also Schachter, 1984).[9] Certainly, both children and adults base rule changes on some *level* of evidence greater than single events.

Research on this sublanguage model is needed. If these findings continue to hold, there are at least four important implications. First, the input shows distributional characteristics of the type required by a general stochastic learnability model ("stochastic algorithm" below). Second, the input is "sequenced" across set of input or what we have called sublanguages that increase in complexity across time for the learner ("grammar scaling" below). Third, within any sublanguage, the learner's hypothesis space is reduced given the smaller set of items to consider, the concentration of evidence on the rules appropriate to that set, and the increased probability that relevant alternating forms will be paired within a necessary small time window. Finally, since the complexity of each sublanguage is partly in terms of a probability distribution and since the correlation with acquisition is not perfect, we infer that the learner in some way tracks these frequencies and uses this information in constructing rules. Note that the information contained in the distributions over the input and the information in

[9]It may be significant that most of the examples of children failing to immediately incorporate a correction comes from children aged two and three, a stage not well known for flexibility.

the grammar scaling yield structured domains (section 3.0) that depend on an extension in *time* and that are *nonarbitrary*.

As will be argued stochastic, probabilistic reasoning alone is sufficiently powerful in principle as to account for the unlearning of overgeneralizations and the logical problem of acquisition without recourse to explicit, negative evidence or to linguistic constraints on the class of languages and without the other constraints implicit in the algebraic and stochastic metrics (the 'existing grammar metric' and the grammar scaling). However, the issue of negative evidence is in great need of careful study. Many years of personal observation of children from age one on, and their caretakers, show *both* explicit correction of phonology (possibly only on extreme errors) and a great deal of negative information that is the equivalent of explicit correction (a possibility indeed noted by Gold). This indirect negative evidence includes many aspects of how parents and children negotiate successful communication (though not as much as is expected by hermeneutic, interpretivist theories, like those of Shafer, Bruner, etc.). Children do respond to such information. Once again, however, simple "all-or-none" models though fundamental to logic and mathematics, are inadequate for human reasoning.

6. THE RULE-LEARNING MODEL

Representations. Pairing a stochastic representation and an algebraic representation permits complete categorization where phonological primitives do not have, for example, a unique type-token mapping. It also partly eliminates the need for an algebraic mechanism for handling free disjunction of features. Eliminating disjunction enormously simplifies the learner's hypothesis space and the rule *induction* processes and may be required by any feasible learning procedure. Free disjunction would license many improbable alternations, precisely the kind of crazy rules that evidence shows basically do not occur. A stochastic representation accounts for a type of knowledge representation (cf., the early appearing phonological idioms, section 5) and a type of change over time that are highly problematic within a purely algebraic system. The formal, algebraic grammar, particularly the abstract paradigms, is crucial to the rule construction process: the paradigms control the rules, organize the frequency information produced by the stochastic metrics, and—because of their *deductive* character—are largely responsible for the speed of the process.

Inferencing algorithms. Evidence that the learner comes 'equipped' with an algebraic grid algorithm for constructing paradigms and rule schemata includes the virtual absence of crazy rules, the general patterns of similarity across children and across languages, and the abstract character of the invented rules. More to the point, no stochastic model has been able to show how equivalence classes could be learned (at all, much less relatively quickly) by a purely bottom-up system from distributional data without *some* a priori anchoring of the coordinate system. Second, no model has been able to show how such a system could induce the relationships that hold between primitives at requisite *levels,* relationships that are fundamental to phonological systems. To meet this initial requirement, the grid algorithm need only set an initial *two* categories and/or two levels (but the expectation is that the innate component is more detailed than this). Any purely stochastic system—purely phonetic or purely semantic—must be able to learn both the primitives and the levels, their combinatorial properties, and learn them in a plausible amount of time. While history and the state of the relevant fields do not lead to optimism about such a program, it should be noted that the current work of Lindblom and colleagues (e.g., Lindblom, 1984) is just such an attempt to find a 'self-organizing' phonetic system that could completely induce phonological structures. This approach is canonically stochastic in the present sense (and, not surprisingly, returns in spirit to the 50's work on self-organizing learning systems and the perceptron), and has focused to date on phonetic questions like categorization and *not* on higher level phonological issues.

In the "stochastic" set, a simple alignment grid takes advantage of the temporal separation of elements in the input. Such a grid provides an initial coordination that simplifies the number of alternations a learner would have to compare, if just given two strings. Most crucial, however, is the general stochastic algorithm tracking frequencies of various primitives and computing probabilities useful in constructing categories, rules and grammars. Such an algorithm is *required* at the lowest level of constructing the primitives, where it is highly particular to the properties of the primitives in question. If available at higher levels, such an algorithm can easily handle exceptions to rules and the unlearning of overly general rules (section 7). But what evidence have we for this generalized stochastic algorithm? First, the function of this algorithm at the higher level of rules is identical to its function at the lower level of primitives. Second, I argue that some such mechanism is required by any model to rule out effects of random errors, to handle exceptions and to prune rules, because exceptions are characteristic of the rules of language, learners overgeneralize at all levels of the grammar, and purely formal considerations rule out permitting the formal deductive grammar to encode exceptions and prune rules in the necessary way. Third, there is a parallelism between frequency and distributional characteristics of the sublanguage being learned and aspects of the learner's current grammar, these sublanguages scale in increasing complexity across time for the learner, and this grammar scaling differs in part from language to language. These data provide support for an algorithm that is sensitive to nonalgebraic—largely statistical and distributional —properties of the language being learned. However, the parallelism is partly a correlation and, as with any correlation, there are many possible interpretations. Several have implicitly been ruled out: that there is no relation, that both phenomena derive from a third factor that is completely algebraic in character (as this would amount to an ad hoc relabelling of something that still remains graded and nondeterminate), that there is a weak relation such that high frequency only effects the order in which rules are acquired (as this ignores the nonrandomness and the partly algebraic aspects of the scaling and the evidence that the learner uses this information in constructing hypotheses). The argument here is that there is a significant, causal relation between the interim grammars of the learner and properties of these sublanguages and, further, that the direction of effect is from the sublanguage to the learner (with the reverse direction ruled out as implausible). Note that the absolute *form* of the sublanguages is an independent issue: a linguistically interesting complexity measure across the sublanguages could fail to hold without affecting the correlation within a particular period of time, provided distributions did differ across sublanguages and were reflected in the learner's associated hypotheses.

The procedures by which the learner evaluates new information with respect to her existing grammar and uses the rule structure of the present grammar to generate hypotheses about the grammar being learned were referred to under the heading "existing grammar metric." Not enough is known about this process, and this is one area in particular where the non-grammar orientation of the field severely limits the evaluation of theories.

Domains. A phonological system contains much information not captured in its algebraic rule system, notably the frequency and distributional characteristics of primitives and rules, one effect of which is a partitioned lexicon. The evidence suggests that these partitioned sublexicons are temporally sequenced across time for the learner such that the learner is faced with a sequence of sublanguages. This "grammar scaling" functions as a constraint on the rule formation process, by reducing the size of the possible alternations to be considered and by increasing the likelihood that correctly alternating forms will be paired, given that both the scaling and the frequency facts create, as it were, a "figure-ground" perspective for the learner. It is likely that the regular contingencies of discourse (e.g., talking about a simple topic, repeatedly naming and describing the participants and the events, and—especially with young children—defining the terms and relations, etc.) also produce temporally local informational structures that function like sublanguages. *Anytime,* information is redundantly "packed" in such a fashion, the attention of the learner is focused on the relevant areas of the "search space." Note that this packing of relevant information in discourse is not dependent on any formal aspects of the rules or on any intention by the speaker to structure the information; rather, it is simply a consequence of talking in meaningful ways about meaningful topics.

A learner benefits from the structure of these domains, without there being any formal relation holding across the sequence of sublanguages. The in-general increase in complexity across time of these sublanguages and the broad cross-language similarities are suggestive, however, of a formal grammar space—or "formal grammar scaling'—that by virtue of *its* domain structure constrains the learner's hypothesis space. A significant research question is whether or not a learner could learn, or 'induce', a more complex grammar from a simpler grammar, one lower on the Chomsky hierarchy. (See Fodor, 1980 for a negative view on a similar hypothesis regarding logics.)

In conclusion, the above constraints in *conjunction* materially reduce the learner's hypothesis space. The learner does *not* randomly generate and test hypotheses, considering all possible alternations or the cartesian product of all primitives. Prior knowledge (encoded in the existing grammar) and information in both local and larger domains (across time as sublanguages in the input), as well as the constraints on the algebraic and stochastic grammars, limit the types of rules considered by the learner at any given point in *time*.

7. UNLEARNING INCORRECT AND OVERLY-GENERAL RULES

Several of the mechanisms of section 3 provide a means for unlearning incorrect rules. First, a learner can use information in other areas of a particular paradigm for correcting rules which function within that paradigm but for which the crucial evidence is not directly available. This is basically an algebraic form of positive evidence. Second, within the stochastic component, geometric distance metrics over the structure of perceptual domains can be used to change predictions or induce a type of negative evidence where dispersal of information allows the learner to infer from the absence of information in a particular subspace of the domain what the correct "analysis" (or linearization) of the overall space or domain is. However, it is the stochastic algorithm that is of most flexible use in unlearning the overly-general rules, and it too permits use of a type of negative evidence.

In the present model, the learner tracks and uses frequency of types of forms and structures (and, as already noted, in ways similar to what's seen in other areas of language, like sociolinguistic variable rule domains and some lexical recognition and parsing tasks). Crucially, the learner attends to the discrepancy between her existing rules and the presence or absence of relevant forms in the input, modulo certain restrictions to insure that probabilities are computed over quite a large sample. The latter is inferred partly from the fact that these overgeneralized errors are corrected over an unusually long time period, sometimes in fact over years. Such rules are discarded when the discrepancy between the learner's existing rules and the input has held for x period of time and when the input has reached a sufficiently "large" and "diverse" threshold. The precise time value and input threshold that such a rule-pruning mechanism uses are not known, but clearly the mechanism is quite conservative: for example, not only do the input-discrepant, overly general rules stay an unusually long time in the learner's productive system, some correct rules are retained during time periods when they temporarily are themselves input-discrepant.

This algorithm thus provides a simple solution to the problem of unlearning incorrect rules: the learner infers from the absence of confirming information over a critical time and information span that a rule is incorrect, and no explicit negative evidence or correction from an informant/parent is needed. The necessary stochastic metric can be used in two, related ways: for simply throwing out rules for which no confirming evidence occurs (i.e., the overgeneralized rules just discussed), a weak stochastic system; and, also, given the work of Horning (1969) and others, for selecting among grammars, the best grammar for the strings that have been presented, a strong stochastic system. The weak stochastic system would play a minor role overall in acquisition if it were responsible for weeding out only a relatively small number of errors.

The Horning model requires that the language be stochastic (i.e., provide a probability distribution over elements) and that the input presentation of strings be stochastic (i.e., generated by random selection according to the probabilities associated with the elements). This insures that every string will be generated at least once and that the frequency of some element can be used to estimate its probability of being in the language. Using a Bayesian enumerative procedure and an a priori distribution over grammars (for which several plausible weighting techniques exist), Horning proved that, if the input is stochastically generated, this algorithm leads to correct identification of at least the context free languages in the limit with probability 1.[10] The a priori distribution over all possible grammars allows the learner to choose the most probable *grammar* consistent with the language input. Overall, the procedure, though slow, is about as good a solution to the notoriously difficult, grammar inference problem as others that have been proposed (e.g., Wexler and Culicover, 1980), but there is a price to be paid (section 8). As to its slowness, its efficiency can be improved by any of the constraints that have been proposed here, and each must be investigated further. One factor, however, falls outside standard learnability models and thus is difficult to assess. That is the learner's use of her existing grammar, essentially learning a grammar not by adding rules but by building up chunks of a grammar, and where the grammar at any time T+1 is partly determined by the learner's prior knowledge, the grammar at T.

8. CONCLUSIONS

This paper attempts to establish the theoretical requirement and framework for integrated algebraic and stochastic representations and integrated operation of their associated inferencing mechanisms. Further work is required of key points.

---

[10]The Horning algorithm can be extended to include the indexed languages. References on stochastic grammatical inferencing include Cook, Rosenfeld and Aronson, 1976; Gaines, 1976; Maryanski and Booth, 1977; Wetherell, 1980 and VanderMude and Walker, 1978; see also Oehrle, 1985.

Yet, if the thesis proves true in its fundamental sense, there are at least four important consequences.

First, acquisition research must examine, for each phonological and syntactic rule or domain, the intertwined development of its abstract algebraic component and its stochastic interpretive component. At the outset of this paper, two issues were identified as the learning riddle. I argued first that the *speed* of acquisition is largely a function of the deductive character of the formal, algebraic component of the grammar and not, as is often claimed, a function of detailed, apriori full specification of linguistic structures (and, given the arguments, clearly not a consequence of purely inductive learning procedures). The generative and acquisition literatures often conflate and/or are ambiguous between the (first) two, quite distinct mechanisms. Typically, even the accounts that deal explicitly with the "rich deductive structure" of grammar fail adequacy criteria for a true formal deductive system. While the algebra does require a number of axioms defined independently of the system, deduction or inferencing over this system is made possible by specific properties of the system, properties like consistency. A further advantage of such a formal deductive system is that it would be over-all order-independent and thus predictably consonant with the empirical data showing a virtual absence of invariant orders of acquisition. With respect to the second issue, the unlearning of *overly general rules,* the arguments depart further from standard assumptions. On this point, I argued that overly general rules are a natural consequence of the *ceteris paribus* character of linguistic rules and that a *non*-monotonic structure and process must be introduced as a general system for handling the problem of exceptions. The structure proposed was a representational format that reflected the geometry and statistical content of the perceptual or informational space, the "structured domain," that interprets the algebraic grammar. This was called the "stochastic grammar," and the crucial inferencing mechanism the "stochastic algorithm." The key word is "interpret." This part of the solution is a semantic one and accordingly makes use of the *non*arbitrariness of the stochastic component. A second type of structured domain was identified and claimed to play a role. This is the informational structure that exists in the speaker/learner's environment, in the input-across-*time,* and this too is a semantical notion (but is not taken to be part of the representation). Under this account, even the simplest phonological or syntactic rule will be acquired with different types of information crucial at the same and at different times, and any analysis that ignores either the algebraic or stochastic dimension will be incomplete with respect to the single dimension under study. The principled integration of phonological form and phonetic interpretation (and syntactic form and semantic interpretation) is then fundamental to an adequate theory of acquisition. Yet no less fundamental are the distinct formal, mathematical structures that distinguish the domain of form and the domain of meaning.

Second, much greater attention must be paid within the field of child phonology to the development of rules and *grammars.* A deep division between phonetics and phonology is not unique to child phonology, yet here the asymmetry is considerably more pronounced than even in other relevant areas. Inspite of its name, the field has been to date largely concerned with early phonetic questions.

Third, learnability loses the special status it currently is considered to have—status, that is, as a heuristic tool for uncovering linguistic constraints and generalizations. The line of argument through the paper relevant to this point has been as follows. (i) Of the work done within the Gold paradigm in computer science (called there "inductive inference"), stochastic models, particularly Horning (1969), show that grammars can be learned for certain classes of languages without explicit informant presentation (i.e., without negative evidence) under a set of probabilistic assumptions. This approach is equally as good (or bad) a solution to a notoriously difficult problem as is the linguistic work using linguistic constraints (e.g., Wexler and Culicover 1980). (ii) With respect to actual acquisition, I argued first that certain acquisition data in conjunction with an interpretation of the relevant evidence and correlations show that there are stochastic aspects to language acquisition, like sensitivity to frequency information; and, secondly, that in order to prune overly general rules learners need to be able to infer from the *absence* of confirming evidence (after *n* length of time) that a hypothesized rule is ungrammatical and that the appropriate mechanism for handling nonmonotonicity of this type is a stochastic metric of a very simple kind, namely one that tracks the occurrence *and* nonoccurrence of hypothesized structures. The absence of information is, then, implicit negative evidence, and stochastic inferencing from such evidence insures learnability of at least the context free languages and, by extension, the indexed languages. (iii) Arguments (i) and (ii) provide prima facie plausibility to the stochastic inductive inference literature as relevant to grammar learning in humans. (iv) Thus, any linguistic constraint—like those associated with degree-2—used in linguistic learnability work requires *independent* justification as a plausible linguistic generalization since it becomes under (i) - (iii) only one of an *arbitrarily large* set of "moves" that work. Any proposed solution must be independently evaluated in terms of success, efficiency, domain relevance, and tradeoffs with other relevant factors like errors, memory, background knowledge and time. This dependence on independently determined facts largely accounts for why learnability results have contributed so little to theories of language and language acquisition.

Fourth, the difficult problems of nondiscrete, variable phenomena and dynamic change over time must be addressed by formal linguistic theories. A fundamental observation that has informed the analysis of this paper is that there is a structure of a very specific type underlying formal theories in phonology (and syntax), and that an examination of this structure, in effect the meta properties of these theories, makes clear the principled relationship between those theories and how much of their putative domain of application they can in fact explain. Two main results obtain. First, contrary to the implicit logic underlying algebraic theories, a significant portion of a phonology is variable, incomplete, and changing over situations, rule-contexts, time, domains within the lexicon, and so on. Nonmonotonicity exists both within the system at any given point in time and also is crucial to the speaker/learner's revision of hypotheses along time as information changes. There are several formal systems for handling nonmonotonicity, e.g., nonmonotonic logics as well as probability theory (which was used here), but theoretical work in linguistics should pay close attention to this issue. Certain devices used currently within algebraic theory, such as default mechanisms or full specification with feature changing rules, *introduce* nonmonotonicity; if overall consistency and monotonicity of the algebraic grammar is crucial to achieving the speed of acquisition as argued here, then these formal devices must be either not used or constrained so as to maintain general overall monotonicity. Second, with respect to incomplete and nondiscrete phenomena, I argued that the stochastic grammar is crucial to solving certain problems accruing to a purely algebraic system, such as (i) indeterminacy of those phonological predicates where there is no necessary and sufficient set of features that categorizes all members of the set and where the boundaries of categories crucially depend on the geometry of the total category space and (ii) where restrictions on possible strings are not due to restrictions on the formal grammar but to constraints at the content, interpretive level. Issues like these and others raised in the text are basic to an adequate theory of even the algebraic grammar but have been neglected by contemporary formal phonological theory.

In phonological theory, as well as in acquisition theory, the standard partitioning of the field is wrong. If integration of the two 'grammars' is crucial to solving the problems of combinatorial explosion and indeterminacy that either alone entails and thus is crucial to materially constraining the learner's hypothesis space, then the reason that language and language learning do not require a universal theorem prover is not because the abstract symbol system is strongly constrained by formal properties but because the objects manipulated by the formalism constitute highly structured domains that in effect constrain mathematical relations holding over the formal symbols. This paper's opening challenge to the thesis that a classical logical calculus defines language (both its phonology and its syntax) is at the conclusion of this paper a challenge to develop a unified, Kantian theory that takes seriously the fact that language *is* and *is not* arbitrary, atemporal, consistent.

ACKNOWLEDGMENTS

This research was made possible through an award from the Sloan Cognitive Science Program and a gift from the Systems Development Foundation to the Center for the Study of Language and Information. For helpful suggestions and stimulating discussion of this paper at many junctures in its preparation, many thanks to Eve Clark, Ron Kaplan, Lise Menn, Stanley Peters, Bill Poser and Kelly Roach. All errors are, of course, my own.

REFERENCES

Anderson, S. R. (1981). Why phonology isn't "natural." *Linguistic Inquiry, 12*, 493–539.

Chiat, S. (1979). The role of the word in phonological development. *Linguistics, 17*, 591–610.

Chomsky, N. (1963). Formal properties of grammars. In R. Luce, R. Bush & E. Galanter (Eds.), *Handbook of Mathematical Psychology*. New York: John Wiley and Sons.

Chomsky, N. (1965). *Aspects of the theory of syntax*. Cambridge, MA: The MIT Press.

Chomsky, N. (1967). Quine's empirical assumptions. In D. Davidson & J. Hintikka (Eds.), *Words and Objections*. Dordrecht: Reidel.

Chomsky, N. (1980a). *Rules and representations*. New York: Columbia University Press.

Chomsky, N. & M. Schutzenberger. (1963). The algebraic theory of context free grammars. In P. Braffort & D. Hirschberg (Eds.), *Computer Programming and Formal Systems*. Amsterdam, Holland: North Holland.

Cook, D. M., A. Rosenfeld, & A. R. Aronson. (1976). Grammatical inference by hill-climbing. *Information Sciences, 10*, 59–80.

Donegan, P. J. & D. Stampel (1979). The study of natural phonology. In D. A. Dinnsen (Ed.), *Current Approaches to Phonological Theory*. Bloomington: Indiana University Press.

Ferguson, C. A. & C. B. Farwell. (1975). Words and sounds in early language acquisition. *Language, 51*, 419–439.

Fey, M. & J. Gandour. (1982). Rule discovery in phonological acquisition. *Journal of Child Language, 9*, 71–81.

Fodor, J. A. (1980). Fixation of belief and concept acquisition. In M. Piattelli-Palmarini (Ed.), *Language and Learning: The Debate between Jean Piaget and Noam Chomsky*. Cambridge, MA: Harvard University Press.

Gaines, B. R. (1976). Behavior/structure transformations under uncertainty. *International J. Man-Machine Studies*, 1976, *8*, 337–365.

Gold, E. M. (1967). Language identification in the limit. *Information and Control, 10*, 447–474.

Goldin-Meadow, S. & H. Felman. (1977). The development of language-like communication without a language model. *Science, 197*, 401–403.

Hayes, B. (1984). The phonology of rhythm in English. *Linguistic Inquiry, 15*(1), 33–74.

Horning, J. J. (1969). *A study of grammatical inference*. Doctoral dissertation, Stanford University.

Ingram, D. (1974). Phonological rules in young children. *Journal of Child Language, 1*(1), 49–64.

Ingram, D. (1979a). Cross-linguistic evidence on the extent and limit of individual variation in phonological development. In *Proceedings of the 9th International Congress of Phonetic Sciences*. Copenhagen: Institute of Phonetics, U. of Copenhagen.

Itkonen, T. (1977). Notes on the acquisition of phonology. English summary of Huomiota lapsen äänteistön kehityksetä. *Virittäjä*, 279–308. English summary 304–308.

Jakobson, R. (1968). *Kindersprache, Aphasie und Allgemeine Lautgesetze*. The Hague: Mouton, 1941. Trans. by Allen R. Keiler, *Child Language, Aphasia and Phonological Universals*.

Johnson, C. D. (1970). *Formal aspects of phonological description*. UCB Project on Linguistic Analysis. Second Series, No. 11. J1-J144.

Karmiloff-Smith, A. & B. Inhelder. (1974/75). If you want to get ahead, get a theory. *Cognition, 3*(3), 195–212.

Kenstowicz, M. J. & C. W. Kisseberth. (1977). *Topics in Phonological Theory*. The Hague: Mouton.

Kiparsky, P. & L. Menn. (1977). On the acquisition of phonology. In J. Macnamara (Ed.), *Language Learning and Thought.* New York: Academic Press.

Labov, W., M. Yaeger, & R. Steiner. (1972). *A quantitative study of sound change in progress.* Philadelphia: U.S. Regional Survey.

Ladefoged, P. (1985). Redefining the scope of phonology. *UCLA Working Papers in Phonetics, 60,* 101–108.

Lahiri, A., L. Gewirth, & S. E. Blumstein. (1984). A reconsideration of acoustic invariance for place of articulation in diffuse stop consonants: evidence from a cross-language study. *Journal Acoustical Society of America, 76,* 391–404.

Liljencrants, J. & B. Lindblom. (1972). Numerical simulation of vowel quality systems: the role of perceptual contrast. *Language, 48,* 839–862.

Lindblom, B. (1984). Can the models of evolutionary biology be applied to phonetic problems? In M. Broecke & A. Colin (Eds.), *Proceedings from the 10th International Congress of Phonetic Sciences.* Dordrecht: Foris, 1984.

Macken, M. A. (1978). Permitted complexity in phonological development: one child's acquisition of Spanish consonants. *Lingua, 44,* 219–253.

Macken, M. A. (1979). Developmental reorganization of phonology: a hierarchy of basic units of acquisition. *Lingua, 49,* 11–49.

Macken, M. A. (1980). Aspects of the acquisition of stop consonants. In G. Yeni-Komshian et al (Eds.), *Child Phonology.* New York: Academic Press.

Macken, M. A. & C. A. Ferguson. (1983). Cognitive aspects of phonological development: model, evidence, and issues. In K. Nelson (Ed.), *Children's Language.* Hillsdale, New Jersey: Erlbaum Publishers.

MacWhinney, B. (1978). Processing a first language: the acquisition of morphophonology. In *Monographs of the Society for Research in Child Development.* Chicago, Ill.: Society for Research in Child Development.

Maryanski, F. J., and T. L. Booth. (1977). Inference of finite-state probabilistic grammars. *IEEE Transactions on Computing, C-26,* 521–536.

Menn, L. (1978). Phonological units in beginning speech. In A. Bell & J. Hooper (Eds.), *Syllables and Segments.* Amsterdam: North Holland.

Menn, L. (1985). Phonological development: learning sounds and sound patterns. In J. Berko Gleason (Ed.), *The Development of Language.* Columbus, Ohio: Charles E. Merrill Publishing Company.

Menn, L. (1978). *Pattern, control, and contrast in beginning speech, a case study in the development of word form and word function.* Doctoral dissertation, U. of Illinois, 1976b. Reprinted Indiana University Linguistics Club.

Oehrle, R. (1985). Implicit negative evidence. University of Arizona, Tucson.

Olmsted, D. L. (1966). A theory of the child's learning of phonology. *Language,* 1966, *42*(2), 531–535.

Olmsted, D. L. (1971). *Out of the Mouths of Babes.* The Hague: Mouton.

Peters, A. M. (1977). Language learning strategies. *Language, 53*(3), 560–573.

Pinker, S. (1984). *Language Learnability and Language Development.* Cambridge, MA: Harvard University Press.

Poser, W. J. (1980). Locality constraints on phonological rules. Paper presented at the CSLI N. Smith (Eds.), *The Structure of Phonological Representations, Part II.* Dordrecht, Netherlands: Foris.

Poser, W. J. (1980). Locality constraints on phonological rules. Paper presented at the CSLI Workshop on Finite State Morphology and Phonology. Stanford University. July 30, 1985.

Pullum, G. (1983). How many possible human languages are there? *Linguistic Inquiry, 14,* 447–467.

Quine, W. V. (1960). *Word and Object.* Cambridge, MA: M.I.T. Press.

Schachter, J. A. (1985). Universal Input Condition. In W. E. Rutherford (Eds.), *Language Universals and Second Language Acquisition.* Amsterdam: John Benjamins Publishing Company.

Shaw, R. E. & J. B. Pittenger. (1977). Perceiving the face of change in changing faces: Implications for a theory of object perception. In R. E. Shaw & J. Bransford (Eds.), *Perceiving, Acting, and Knowing.* Hillsdale, N.J.: Lawrence Erlbaum Associates.

Shepard, R. (1972). Psychological representation of speech sounds. In E. E. David & P. B. Denes (Eds.), *Human Communication: A Unified View.* New York: McGraw-Hill.

Shepard, R. (1974). Representation of structure in similarity data: Problems and prospectus. *Psychometrika, 39,* 373–421.

Smith, N. V. (1973). *The Acquisition of Phonology.* Cambridge, MA: University Press.

Stampe, D. (1973). *A dissertation on natural phonology.* Doctoral dissertation, University of Chicago.

Stampe, D. (1969). The acquisition of phonetic representation. Paper presented at the 5th Regional Meeting of the Chicago Linguistic Society, Chicago, IL, 443–454.

Stevens, K. N. (1975). The potential role of property detectors in the perception of consonants. In G. Fant & M. A. A. Tatham (Eds.), *Auditory Analyses and Perception of Speech.* London, England: Academic Press.

Stevens, K. N. & S. E. Blumstein. (1981). The search for invariant acoustic correlates of phonetic features. In P. D. Eimas & J. L. Miller (Eds.), *Perspectives on the Study of Speech.* Hillsdale, NJ: Erlbaum.

Timm, L. (1977). A child's acquisition of Russian phonology. *Journal of Child Language,* 1977, *4,* 329–339.

Van der Mude, A. & A. Walker. (1978). On the inference of stochastic regular grammars. *Information and Control, 38,* 310–329.

Wason, P. C. & P. N. Johnson-Laird. (1972). *Psychology of Reasoning: Structure and Content.* London: Batsford.

Wetherell, C. S. (1980). Probabilistic languages: a review and some open questions. *Computing Surveys, 12*(4), 361–379.

Wexler, K. & P. Culicover. (1980). *Formal Principles of Language Acquisition.* Cambridge, MA: MIT Press.

[illegible]

[illegible]

[illegible]

[illegible]

[illegible]

[illegible]

[illegible]

[illegible]

[illegible]

[illegible]

[illegible]

[illegible]

[illegible]

[illegible]

[illegible]

[illegible]

12 The Bootstrapping Problem in Language Acquisition

Steven Pinker
Massachusetts Institute of Technology

INTRODUCTION

Why is language acquisition such an impressive feat? Why has it been so difficult to explain how it happens? Everyone agrees that language is extremely complex, but so are other domains of expertise whose mastery seems less of a singular accomplishment.

One reason for the impressiveness of language acquisition is that there is a formal chasm between the input and the output of language learning. This can be seen by considering, in turn, what the input and output is. The *input* to the child consists of sentences heard in context. If we are charitable about the child's perceptual abilities, we can assume that he or she can extract a variety of types of information from that input: the set of words contained in the sentence; their order; prosodic properties, such as intonation, stress, and timing; the meanings of individual content words, insofar as they can be acquired before grammar learning begins; crude phonological properties of words, such as the number of syllables; the semantics of the utterance inferred from the nonlinguistic context, including its predicate-argument structure and relations of co-reference and predication; and finally, pragmatic information inferred from the discourse context, such as topic versus focus.

The *output* of language learning is a rule system for the adult language. This rule system, or grammar, consists of rules, principles, and parameter settings couched in a formal vocabulary, including syntactic categories (noun, verb, etc.), grammatical relations and cases (subject, object, oblique object, nominative, accusative, etc.), and phrase structure configurations (''daughter of,'' ''sister of,'' ''precedes''). Grammars are subject to universal constraints hypothesized to be innate but subject to parametric variation. That is, different languages allow these entities to behave in different ways. Language acquisition thus consists of the child attending to the arrangement of these entities in the input to determine which combinations of them the language permits.

The problem is that there is no direct relation between the types of information in the input and the types of information in the output: tokens of grammatical symbols are not perceptually marked as such in parental sentences or their contexts. Let's say the child wants to determine the relative order of nouns and other constituents. To do this, he or she must find some nouns in parental speech. But how does one do this if one doesn't know anything about the language yet? Since nouns do not have a unique serial position, affix, modifier, or intonation contour across all languages, the child is left with a dilemma. If he creates rules that generalize patterns of those features of the input that *can* be perceived, such as the serial positions of individual words or co-occurrences of pairs of individual words, he will have learned the wrong rules. Languages dictate the order of phrases, not the absolute or relative order of words or their simple co-occurrences. On the other hand, the *correct* grammatical generalizations involve abstract elements not perceivable in the input prior to language learning.

This dilemma shows that loose talk of "innate constraints" on the one hand and "distributional analysis" on the other, though popular in informal discussions of language acquisition, do not by themselves shed much light on how the acquisition process works. Distributional learning can identify nouns based on their occurring in noun contexts or with noun affixes, but how are noun contexts and noun affixes learned to begin with? Innate constraints dictate that there exist noun phrases, that they are subject to parametric variation (e.g., position within verb phrase), and that they have certain universal properties (e.g., NPs function as bounding nodes). But the child still must *find* noun tokens in the input so that their observed language-specific behavior can be used to fix parameters or apply universal principles (e.g., to determine whether the language orders its verbs before its nouns or vice-versa or to determine whether a given phrase in the language functions as a bounding node.)

This chapter is about the fundamental problem of getting the child started in forming the correct types of rules for natural languages. This "bootstrapping problem" is the first problem one must solve in designing models of language acquisition. I first discuss three proposed solutions that clearly will not work. Then I review a solution that worked well enough to lie at the foundation of an explicit theory of language acquisition I outlined in Pinker, 1984a *(Language Learnability and Language Development),* henceforth called the "LLLD" theory. This theory was to a reasonable degree computationally explicit, consistent with the facts of language development, and compatible with contemporary linguistic theory. But the solution assumed in that theory, too, gets its share of criticism. Then I try to diagnose the fundamental problem that seems to torpedo all the solutions discussed. I sketch out an alternative class of language acquisition mechanisms, based on "constraint satisfaction" models taken from artificial intelligence research, and show how these models might solve the bootstrapping problem. Finally, I spell out the implications of this class of models for the debate over language bootstrapping.

MUST THE CHILD LEARN FORMAL RULES?

A question that many people raise at this point is: why worry about the formal nature of the output of language acquisition? In modeling child language acquisition, why not simply equip the child to form generalizations in terms of properties that *are* perceptible, such as the order of specific words or the order of semantic categories? The result may not be identical to adult linguistic competence, but perhaps it is a useful approximation.

The answer is that a viable theory of language acquisition must show how the child acquires what we know to be true about languages, including their *abstractness* and their *constraints*. The regularities of language pertain to abstract categories. *Passivization,* for example, affects *grammatical objects,* virtually without regard to their semantic or logical status (see *1a–1g*). That is, a passivized object does not have to be a patient of an action (see *1b*), a perceptual "thing" (*1c*), an argument of the passivized verb (*1d–1f*), or a member of a particular list of words (*1g*). And not only does passivization *not* care about the semantic properties of grammatical objects, as long as they are objects, but it *does* care that the entities it affects are *exactly* objects and not simply entities that have properties in common with typical objects, such as being a noun phrase following a verb (see *1h*) or a patient of an action (see *1i*).

1. *a.* John elbowed Bill./ Bill was elbowed by John.
b. John pleased Bill./ Bill was pleased by John.
c. Early oiling prevents permanent rheumatism./ Permanent rheumatism is prevented by early oiling.
d. John thought unicorns to be fictitious./ Unicorns were thought by John to be fictitious.
e. John believes it to be snizzling./ It is believed to be snizzling by John.
f. John took advantage of Dick./ Advantage was taken of Dick by John.
g. Tom ate all the schnoogles./ All the schnoogles were eaten by John.
h. John finally became a movie mogul./ *A movie mogul was finally become by John.
i. John received a beating from Bill./ *John was received a beating by Bill.

Languages also have "eccentric" constraints, ones that do not appear to be epiphenomena of semantics, processing, or discourse (though they can assist functioning in these domains). Here is a random sample of sentences that are semantically and pragmatically interpretable, and reasonable generalizations from related sentences, buf not part of English:

2. *a.* John saw Mary with her best friend's husband./ Who did John see Mary with?
John saw Mary and her best friend's husband./ *Who did John see Mary and?
b. Irv drove the car into the garage./ Irv drove the car.
Irv put the car into the garage./ *Irv put the car.
c. Susan paid attention to the soldiers./ Susan gave all her attention to the soldiers.
Susan paid heed to the soldiers./ *Susan gave all her heed to the soldiers.
d. I expect the fur to fly./ I expect the fur will fly.
The fur is expected to fly./ *The fur is expected will fly.
e. The baby seems to be asleep./ The baby seems asleep.
The baby seems to be sleeping./ *The baby seems sleeping.
f. It is impossible that someone will win./ It is impossible to win.
It is certain that someone will win./ *It is certain to win.
g. That Sy was a spy was widely believed./ It was widely believed that Sy was a spy.
Sy was widely criticized for being a spy./ *It was widely criticized Sy for being a spy.
h. John liked the pictures of Bill that Mary took./ John liked Mary's pictures of Bill.
John liked the pictures of himself that Mary took./ *John liked Mary's pictures of himself.

This is just a small sample of the effects of constraints on languages that all children grow up to respect (for many more see, e.g., Chomsky, 1981; Bresnan, 1982). Any theory of language acquisition must account for how this happens. Ideally, a theory should show how the child acquires full competence as characterized by linguistic theory. Of course, it may not be reasonable in practice to expect a theory of acquisition plus an input corpus to predict *all* the aspects of grammar, (e.g., all the facts reported in all the linguistics journals), but it *is* reasonable to expect a theory to show how the child acquires the right *types* of entities for these constraints to work. The constraints operating in (2) refer to syntactic categories, grammatical and case relations, phrase structure configurations, finiteness, subcategorization, anaphora, and so on. Therefore, a good theory of language acquisition is one that shows how the child can acquire rules couched in those terms. Details can then be plugged in when one wants to account for the full richness of language. Such a theory, even if simplistic, would be *upward-compatible* with theories of grammatical universals. Alternative theories positing acquisition of nongrammatical rules (order of individual words, semantic categories or roles, discourse functions, etc.) might be equally simple but not compatible with the acquisition of language as a whole, given the formal nature of adult grammar. Such theories would require hand-waving when required to show how the child ever acquires full language competence. It must be stressed that this is not a frill but an integral part of the scientific problem called "language acquisition." For this reason, I would argue that many of the contemporary computer simulation models of language acquisition, though representing major advances in explicitness, have fundamental defects as theories of human language acquisition.

PROPOSED SOLUTIONS TO THE BOOTSTRAPPING PROBLEM

In this section I review proposed solutions to the bootstrapping problem. I associate each solution with a set of authors who have espoused a version of it. To make issues clearer I discuss "pure" versions of each hypothesis even though all the cited investigators have actually proposed various kinds of hybrids.

Correlational bootstrapping (e.g., Maratsos & Chalkley, 1981). According to this hypothesis, the child is sensitive to a set of "distributional" properties, such as serial position; position relative to other words, inflections, and to certain semantic notions encoded in sentences. The child begins by recording which words have which properties in the input. When a sufficiently large set of words are noted to have highly overlapping sets of properties, the equivalent of a grammatical category exists, and the child can now generalize. Specifically, any subsequent word observed to have one property in the intersection set is assumed to have the remaining properties automatically.

Hypotheses of this sort present a dilemma. What is the set of properties that the child attends to? It certainly cannot be *all* noticeable, distributional properties. For one thing, there are too many of them (e.g., occurring in seventh serial position, occurring in the same sentence as the word *mouse,* occurring to the left of the words sequence *the cat in*). Worse, the number of potential categories grows exponentially with the number of such properties. Also, most such properties are useless because languages don't contain generalizations that hinge upon them. Thus seeming generalizations based on simple distributional commonalities can do more harm than good (e.g., *John ate fish* and *John can fish* could lead to *John can rabbits;* see Pinker, 1979; 1982). On the other hand, under this hypothesis the set of properties the learner attempts to correlate cannot be the set of linguistically relevant properties such as phrase structure configuration, abstract case relations, affixation, binding, and so on. Because these are not perceptual properties, they themselves are dependent on the child knowing some fragment of the language, and that is what we are trying to explain to begin with.

In addition, many of the properties of grammatical entities exert their effects by ruling out sentences, as in (2). For example, noun phrases are deemed "bounding nodes" because they forbid dependencies between *wh-* words and gaps to span them (see, for example, *2a*). But the result of this constraint is sentences that children never hear, and would not be corrected for if they produced them (Brown and Hanlon, 1970). Thus it is difficult to see how children could use "being a bounding node" as one of the distributional properties that defines a noun phrase; it is more likely that they would use "being a noun phrase" to deduce automatically that it must be a bounding node.

Prosodic bootstrapping (Morgan & Newport, 1981; Wanner & Gleitman, 1982). According to this hypothesis, the child records the intonation contour, stress pattern, relative timing of elements, and pauses in input sentences. Cooper and Paccia-Cooper (1980) have found that phrase boundaries in English sentences have several acoustic effects on the speech wave such as lengthening, pausing, and falling pitch. According to the prosodic bootstrapping hypothesis, the child uses these regularities to infer the phrase structure tree for the sentence. Such a tree carves the sentence into roughly the correct units of analyses, and the child can couch generalizations about order and agreement in terms of these units.

There has been no explicit model on how the child would actually accomplish these analyses, so it is hard to evaluate this hypothesis. But Cooper and Paccia-Cooper's research is a shaky empirical foundation for it. First, Cooper and Paccia-Cooper only showed that in pairs of English sentences in which all irrelevant factors are held constant (e.g., syllable structure of words, emotional tone, contrast, word frequency, speakers' decision processes, serial position) there are differences in acoustic properties contingent on differences in phrase structure. Thus phrase structure is *one* determinant of prosody. That is not good enough for the child, who must go in the *opposite direction,* inferring phrase structure from prosody. To do that, either *a.* phrase structure must be the *only* determinant of prosodic properties (we know this is false); *b.* phrase structure effects on prosody must be large relative to other effects (also false; see Cooper and Paccia-Cooper, 1980); or *c.* the child must be able to subtract out the irrelevant influences first, then extract phrase structure from the normalized residue (this is possible in principle, but it is hard to see how it actually could be done). In addition, it must be true that the correlations observed by Cooper are true *in all languages;* if the correlations are due merely to rules of English phonology, they don't buy the child anything.

Prosody is surely important in language bootstrapping, but we need explicit proposals about the psychophysics that the child would exploit; Cooper and Paccia-Cooper's findings are not enough.

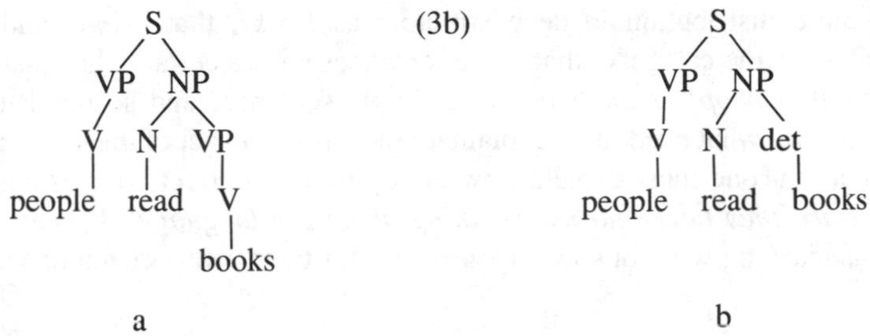

FIGURE 12.1.

Syntactic bootstrapping (Lasnik, in press). According to this argument, possible grammars are subject to so many innate constraints that a small amount of distributional analysis is sufficient to yield correct categorizations of linguistic elements—any incorrect hypotheses will at some point run afoul of some constraint. Consider, for example, the sentence *people read books*. Grimshaw (1981) and Pinker (1982) had argued that innate constraints on syntactic form would not be enough to prevent a hypothetical child from mistakenly analyzing the input sentence *people read books* as Figure 12.1a or b. This would be bad for the child when he or she applied innate constraints or further learning procedures that referred explicitly to NPs or VPs. Lasnik, however, points out that the child might avoid making or retaining such errors because of the following constraints and observations: *a.* If *read books* was really an NP for the child, then in the sentence *what do people read?*, *what* and the trace following *read* would span two bounding nodes, S and NP. Since subjacency rules out such configurations, *read books* could not be an NP and the child could recover from his or her error. *b. What* and *books* have the same "abstract distribution" (presumably, in deep structure), but *what* undergoes *wh*-movement. VP's cannot undergo this process; therefore, *what* is not a VP; therefore, *books* cannot be a VP either. *c. People* and *books* have the same distribution across sentences. Hence *people* cannot be a verb at the same time as *books* is a determiner. *d.* Because sentences must consist of a subject NP and a predicate VP, a simple sentence cannot contain two verbs and one noun. If *people* and *books* have the same categorization [see (c)], *read* must be a verb and the other two words nouns.

Lasnik did not intend to outline a theory of acquisition; he only presented these examples as a caution not to underestimate the potential power of inborn syntactic constraints in preventing misanalyses by the child (and not to overestimate the need for semantic information). Though I agree completely with his cautions and general approach, I also think the examples do not give much hope that innate constraints on syntactic form alone will solve the bootstrapping problem. For Lasnik's examples all hinge on the child already knowing certain facts about the language: that *what* is a *wh*-word, that *wh*-words in complementizer position are moved from or co-indexed with gaps in other positions, that *what* has the same distribution in deep structure as *books*, that *people* and *books* belong to the same category, that these sentences have a certain phrase-structure geometry, that *people read books* is a simple sentence, and so on. But these acquisitions are what need to be explained; the whole impact of the bootstrapping problem is that one must explain how children draw correct conclusions about syntax *before they have learned anything about the language*. Appeals to distributional learning will not solve the problem for the reasons mentioned above.[1]

THE SEMANTIC BOOTSTRAPPING HYPOTHESIS

This hypothesis was assumed by Wexler and Culicover (1980), made explicit by Grimshaw (1981) and Macnamara (1982), and defended at length by Pinker (1982, 1984). As outlined in Pinker (1984), the hypothesis requires four background assumptions:

1. The child can learn the meanings of many common content words independently of learning grammatical rules.
2. The child can construct a semantic representation of the input sentences with the help of the context and the meanings of the individual words in the sentence (see Macnamara, 1972; Slobin, 1977).
3. Substantive linguistic universals (the symbols mentioned in statements of universal grammar, such as "Noun," "SUBJECT," "sister-of") are universally used as the preferred way of expressing certain semantic concepts and relations (or at least there must be a distinguished subset of the language, its "basic sentences," in which this is true.) For example, Keenan (1976) has argued that agents of transitive action verbs, or cause arguments of causative verbs, are universally expressed as subjects in basic sentences. Grammatical objects are the preferred way of expressing discrete entities that are directly and totally affected by an action (Hopper and Thompson, 1980). Likewise, names for concrete objects and for people are universally nouns (Macnamara, 1982). Phrases serving as arguments are universally sisters of the node dominating the word expressing their predicate (Jackendoff, 1977). Auxiliaries express notions related to

[1]There is another problem with Lasnik's examples: given the discovery that a constraint is violated, how does the child know which way to change his or her grammar to eliminate the violation? For example, when faced with an input that would violate subjacency according to the child's current categorizations, how does he or she know that relabeling nodes is the proper way to restore grammaticality? Why not change the geometry of the tree, or declare that NP is not a bounding node in the language (an option that parameterized theories of subjacency must allow the child in any case)? Furthermore, in the absence of semantic information how can the child assume that an as-yet unanalyzed sentence has two nouns and one verb rather than a single noun and conjoined intransitive verbs (e.g., *Mary sang and danced*)?

truth, modality, tense, and obligation (Steele, 1981). A simplified table of such correlations, taken from Pinker (1984, p. 41), is reproduced in Table 1.

4. The "basic sentences" in which these correlations hold are either *a.* accompanied in the input by nonsyntactic cues such as special intonation, discourse context, or amount of perceptually salient affixation, and hence are identifiable independently of learning the complete grammar of the language; or *b.* used by parents to the exclusion of nonbasic forms in "motherese." As for identifiability, Keenan argues that the "basic sentences" in which his universal subject properties hold have special telltale properties. They are pragmatically neutral, minimally presuppositional, uttered with declarative intonation, and have minimally inflected main verbs. As for motherese, Hochberg and Pinker (1987) have found that American mothers largely avoid passives, deverbal nominalizations, deadjectival nominalizations, and several other constructions in which canonical syntax-semantics correlations do not hold.

Given these assumptions, the claim of the Semantic Bootstrapping Hypothesis is that the child uses the presence of *semantic* entities such as "thing," "causal agent," "true in past," and "predicate-argument relation" to infer that the input contains tokens of the corresponding *syntactic* substantive universals such as "noun," "subject," "auxiliary," "dominates," and so on. In the theory outlined in Pinker (1984a) this knowledge is used by several sets of *procedures* to build rules for the target language. Each set of procedures corresponds to a grammatical subcomponent (e.g., phrase structure, inflection, lexicon), and uses the arrangement of (semantically-inferred) grammatical tokens in the input and knowledge of universal grammar to create the appropriate rules. These rules are couched in the "correct" vocabulary for a natural language grammar; that is, they look like adult rules, though they may be incomplete or distorted at various stages.

Here is an example of how the perception of semantic entities in the input is used to posit syntactic phrase structure rules, according to the LLLD theory (Pinker, 1984a). Figure 12.1 illustrates the data structures created during the application of these procedures.

Bootstrapping of the first syntactic rules. Lexical entries are created by virtue of two sets of syntax-semantics correlations. The lexical category of a word in an input sentence is inferred from its semantics, according to the Syntactic Categories entry in Table 1 (e.g., name for a thing = Noun). For a word encoding an argument-taking predicate, the child must also determine which grammatical relations should be listed in the word's lexicon entry as encoding those arguments. These are inferred by noting the thematic relation that the argument bears to the predicate and by associating thematic relations with gram-

TABLE 1
Canonical Syntax-Semantics Pairings that Can Be Used in Semantic Bootstrapping
(from Pinker, 1984a)

Grammatical Element	*Semantic Inductive Basis*
	Syntactic Categories
Noun	Name of person or thing
Verb	Action or change of state
Adjective	Attribute
Preposition	Spatial relation, path, or direction
Sentence	Main proposition
	*Grammatical Functions**
Subject	Agent of action; cause of causal event; subject of an attribution of location, state, or circumstance; argument with "autonomous reference"
Object & Object 2	Patient or theme, affected entity
Oblique	Source, goal, location, instrument
Complement	Proposition serving as an argument within another proposition
Topic	Discourse topic distinct from the arguments of the main predicate
Focus	Discourse focus
	Cases
Nominative or Ergative	Agent of transitive action
Accusative or Absolutive	Patient of transitive action
Nominative or Absolutive	Actor of intransitive action
Dative	Goal or beneficiary
Instrumental	Instrument
Etc.	Etc.
	Grammatical Features
Tense	Relative times of event, speech act, and reference point
Aspect	Durativity
Number	Number
Human	Humanness
Animate	Animacy
Etc.	Etc.
	Tree Configurations
Sister of X	Argument of X
Sister of X′ (Aunt of X)	Restrictive modifier of X
Sister of X″ (Great aunt of X)	Nonrestrictive modifier of X

*The universals relating grammatical relations to thematic relations are not really one-to-one links; they probably involve hierarchies of thematic and grammatical relations that must be mapped onto one another in a way that preserves their relative orderings. See Pinker (1984a; Chapter 8).

matical relations according to the Grammatical Functions entry of Table 1 (e.g., agent of action = Subject).

Phrase structure rules are learned with the help of the lexical entries of the words in the sentence plus the syntax-semantics correlations pertaining to phrase structure. The lexical category nodes for words in the input sentence (N, V, etc.) are taken from the lexical entries of those words. These lexical category nodes are in turn assigned their mother nodes by virtue of the constraints that compose "X-bar theory" (Chomsky, 1970; Jackendoff, 1977), in particular, the constraint that all lexical category nodes are daughters of phrasal category nodes of the same phrasal type (e.g., N must be a daughter of NP; NP must be a daughter of NP').[2] To connect a string of lexical nodes into a hierarchical tree-structure, the child notes the logical and semantic relations among the words and exploits the canonical associations between logical/semantic relations and phrase structure configurations. If X is the lexical category node of a predicate, and Y is a node of one of its arguments, and Z is a node of one of its modifiers, then YP' is connected as a daughter of XP, and ZP' is connected as a daughter of XP'. The main predicate of the sentence, and its subject, are connected as daughters of S. The grammatical relation (SUBJ, OBJ, etc.) that labels each NP position is inferred by observing which of the main predicate's arguments is expressed in that position and by reading the corresponding grammatical relation off of the predicate's lexical entry. See Figure 12.2 for an illustration of the data structures a child creates using these procedures; once the tree is complete, the rules listed underneath Figure 12.2 can be read off it.

It is important to note that the semantic bootstrapping hypothesis does *not* claim that certain semantic elements are necessary conditions for use of syntactic symbols in either motherese or early child speech. Rather, it claims that semantic elements are *sufficient* conditions for use of the syntactic symbols. That is, not all subjects must be agents, but all agents must be subjects. Similarly, it does not claim that the child starts off with a grammar couched in a vocabulary of semantic symbols. It is designed, on the contrary, to account for the ability to acquire rules couched in a formal syntactic vocabulary despite the fact that the elements of such a vocabulary do not have universal perceptual correlates. In fact, the syntactic nature of the rules acquired is the basis for the real power of the bootstrapping theory, which is found in the *consequences* of positing the first set of rules.

Consequences of initially using semantics to learn syntax. Once the first set of rules is learned, it is used to guide future learning and language use in three ways. First, each rule defines distributional contexts that can be used to

[2]In the notation of X-bar theory, for a major category X (standing for N, V, A, and P), $X^0 = X$, $X^1 = X' = XP$ (X-phrase), $X^2 = X'' = XP'$ (superordinate X-phrase, i.e., one that includes an XP as its head.

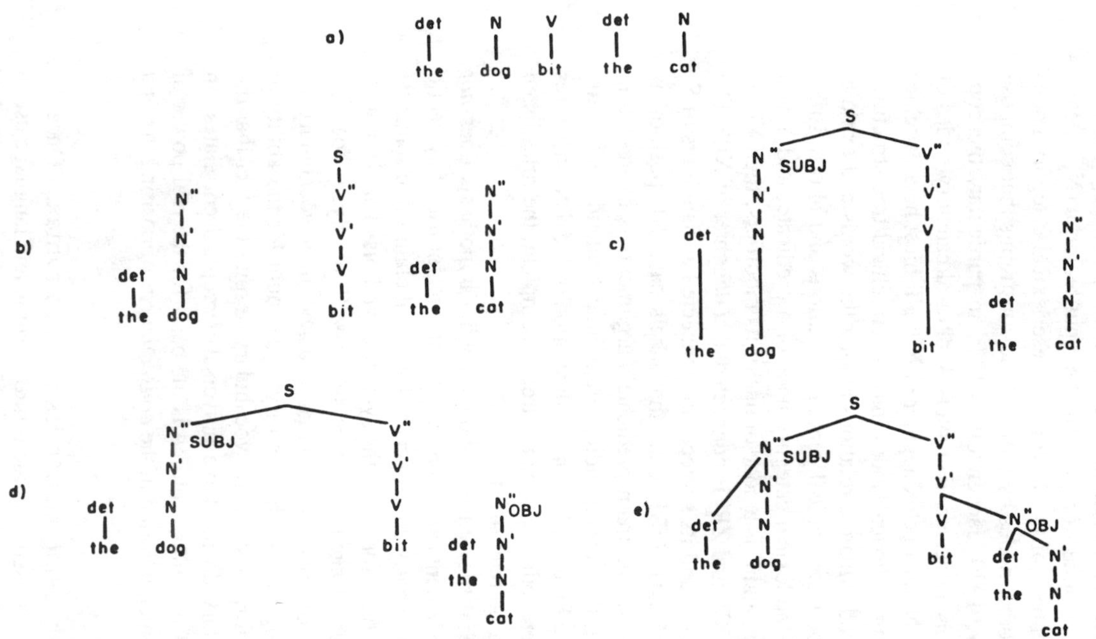

$S \rightarrow N^2_{SUBJ}\ V^2$ (analogous to $S \rightarrow NP_{SUBJ}\ VP$)

$N^2 \rightarrow det\ N^1$

$N^1 \rightarrow N$ (analogous to $NP \rightarrow det\ N$)

$V^2 \rightarrow V^1$

$V^1 \rightarrow V\ N^2_{OBJ}$ (analogous to $VP \rightarrow V\ NP_{OBJ}$)

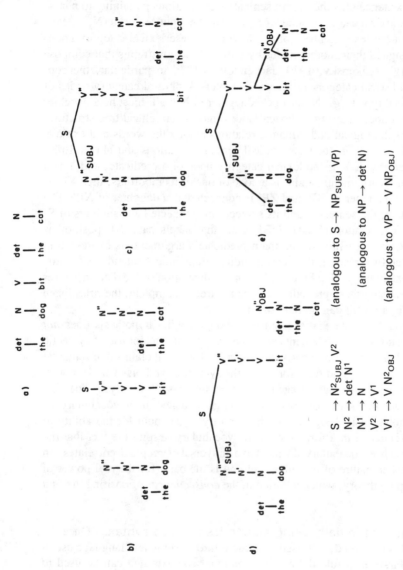

FIGURE 12.2. Illustration of the data structures computed by the child as he or she learns the first phrase structure rules and lexical entries according to the semantic bootstrapping theory of Pinker (1984a). It is assumed that the child has learned the meanings of the words and hears the sentence in a context in which it is clear that the dog is the agent. (a) shows the initial assignment of grammatical categories to words (based on their meanings); (b) shows the assignment of mother nodes (based on X-bar theory); (c) and (d) show the assignment of grammatical relations to nodes (based on thematic relations) and the attachment of the subject to the S-node (based on a universal); (e) shows the remaining attachments (based on X-bar theory and predicate-argument relations). Phrase structure rules are then read off of (e) and added to the grammar.

learn words and phrases that do not contain the triggering semantic features mentioned above. For example, once the rule S → NP_{SUBJ} VP is learned from examples like *the dog bit the cat,* the rule itself can be used to infer that the word *situation* is a noun in the sentence *the situation scares the dog,* even though *situation* is not the name of an object or person. This is how the large number of abstract words in the language are categorized.

Note that unlike "pure" distributional analysis, this type of learning defines distributions in terms of (earlier-acquired) structural contexts such as phrase structure positions rather than in terms of absolute serial positions, adjacencies to particular words, and so on. Thus, the child will be in no danger of making incorrect generalizations from adventitious surface regularities, e.g., from *this is a hand* and *this is a gift* and *hand me the phone* to *gift me the phone;* nor will he or she miss the generalization that the verb *amuse* takes a NP subject just because the set of words that can immediately precede it has no common property (e.g., *JOHN amuses me; Babies who SING amuse me; The museum we went TO amuses me; Singing in the shower LOUDLY amuses me;* etc.).

The second consequence of the bootstrapping hypothesis is that the learning of other rules and features can be made far more efficient. For example, only a subset of the logically possible dependencies among features and inflections are ever exemplified in languages. That is, there are languages in which determiners agree with their nouns but no languages in which nouns agree with the last morpheme in the sentence. If a child knows that a word is a noun and in a noun phrase, and is innately prepared to look for the permissible types of agreement but not the impermissible types, he or she can test whether the noun's features (number, humanness, animacy, gender, etc.) are encoded by its inflections, inflections on its open-class modifiers, and its determiners. This is a far smaller number of hypotheses to test than the cross-product of the features of *all* the words in a sentence times *all* the inflectable elements of a sentence, which is what would have to be examined by a child who lacked the innate constraints or who did not know where to apply them. In other words, once a child has identified syntactic categories and relations in the first, bootstrapping stage, his or her search for other rules of grammar can be constrained to the linguistically-possible subsets of a large space that would otherwise have to be searched exhaustively.

The third consequence of identifying syntactic symbols is that universal conditions for rules and sentences (e.g., subjacency, projection principle, case filter) can automatically apply. For example, because he or she knows the correct phrase structure of the English noun phrase, the child will automatically be able to say *the governor of Vermont from New Hampshire* while rejecting **the governor from New Hampshire of Vermont* (since the latter would require crossing branches in the tree according to the rules learned, and crossing branches are prohibited). Likewise, because he or she knows that the first NP under S is a

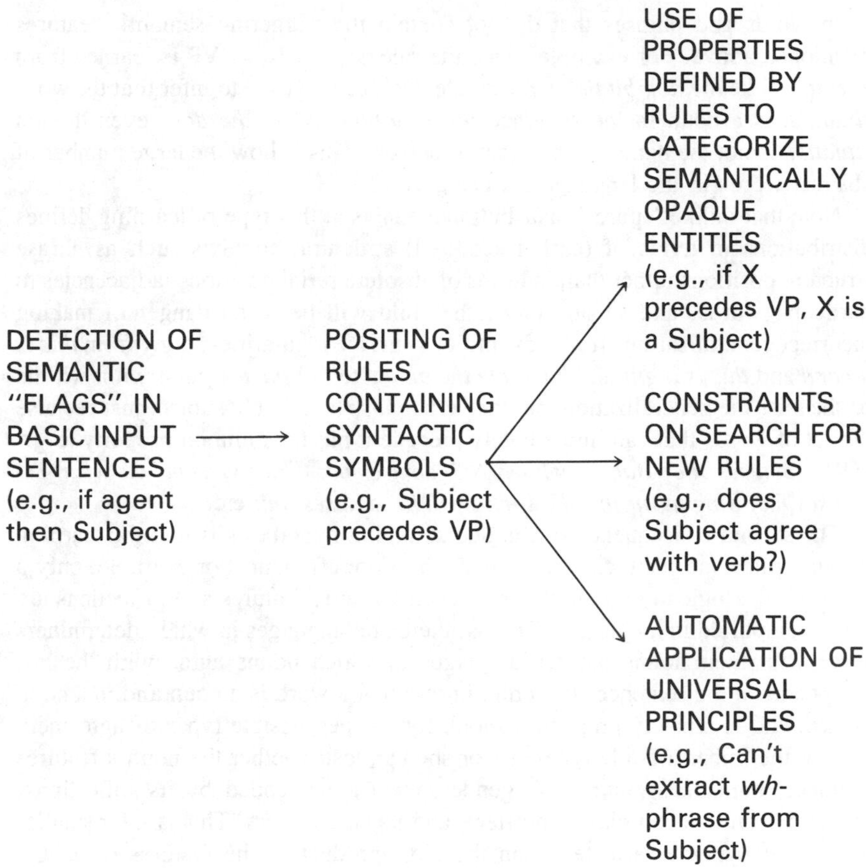
DETECTION OF SEMANTIC "FLAGS" IN BASIC INPUT SENTENCES (e.g., if agent then Subject)
POSITING OF RULES CONTAINING SYNTACTIC SYMBOLS (e.g., Subject precedes VP)
USE OF PROPERTIES DEFINED BY RULES TO CATEGORIZE SEMANTICALLY OPAQUE ENTITIES (e.g., if X precedes VP, X is a Subject)
CONSTRAINTS ON SEARCH FOR NEW RULES (e.g., does Subject agree with verb?)
AUTOMATIC APPLICATION OF UNIVERSAL PRINCIPLES (e.g., Can't extract *wh*-phrase from Subject)

FIGURE 12.3.

subject, the child could allow *who did you read a book about?* while rejecting **who did a book about please you?* (since the latter involves extraction from a subject, also prohibited). Since the rules learned are couched in the same vocabulary as the universal principles, there is no problem of knowing what the universal principles apply to. Thus principles that are not learnable from positive evidence alone (e.g., subjacency and bounding nodes) needn't be learned at all.

The semantic bootstrapping hypothesis thus assumes the chain of events shown in Figure 12.3.

This schema is used in Pinker (1984a) as the basis for seven sets of learning procedures. Each consists of a set of algorithms that take word strings plus structures representing semantic interpretations as inputs and yield grammatical rules as outputs. Three of the sets of procedures (for phrase structure rules, lexical entries, and inflections) have been successfully implemented as LISP programs (Walsh, 1981; Kaaret, 1984). Other sets of procedures, for the acquisition of auxiliaries, complementation, control, and lexical rules, have not been simulated but easily could be. See Pinker (1984a) for full treatment of the operations of these procedures, plus relevant developmental evidence.

PROBLEMS WITH THE SEMANTIC BOOTSTRAPPING HYPOTHESIS

Though I have argued that the procedures listed in Pinker (1984a) do a good job at acquiring correct rules on selected inputs and at accounting for developmental data, there are also several severe problems. Some of these are noted in Chapter 9 (pp. 354–357) of Pinker (1984a). They all hinge on a key property of the semantic bootstrapping hypothesis: its use of *unique sufficient conditions* for the positing of syntactic rules. I will refer to this as the ''smoking gun'' hypothesis: the child waits for irrefutable semantic evidence that an input contains a token of a substantive universal, and when it is found, he or she uses it to make maximally powerful and far-reaching conclusions about the grammar. Here are the problems:

1. The semantic regularities appealed to are not completely universal. It has been claimed that in ''true ergative'' languages such as Dyirbal and Central Arctic Eskimo, themes and patients, rather than agents, have the privileges of occurrence usually associated with subjects, such as being absent in complements, taking oblique case-markers in the passive, and behaving in certain ways in the dative and reflexive constructions (Dixon, 1972; Marantz, 1984). The semantic bootstrapping procedures would have the child predict that agents have the properties of subjects, and hence the procedures should be unable to learn such languages properly.[3]

2. ''Nonbasic sentences,'' such as passives, in which many of the syntax-semantics correspondences do not hold, may not invariably be filtered out of the proximal input to the bootstrapping mechanisms by the parent or by the child. Full passives, for example, though quite rare (Hochberg and Pinker, 1987), are not nonexistent in Motherese, and it is unlikely that all such cases could be rejected by the child. For example, it is not clear how the fact that the verb is inflected or that the agent is prepositionally case-marked could be recognized by the child so as to filter out passive inputs before inflections have been learned. Similarly, the child is probably not invariably so attuned to the discourse context

[3]Of course, if true ergative languages exist, they are rare (Marantz, 1984), and we do not know whether children err in the direction of accusative languages while learning them. Nonetheless, if true ergative languages *are* learned, it would pose a problem for the theory.

of the sentence that he or she can always recognize when a sentence has presuppositions or encodes a question or command. If the child treats a nonbasic sentence as basic, chaos could ensue. For example, a child unknowingly processing a passive sentence in English would conclude that English phrase structure order is OVS, that *by* is a nominative case marker, that there is a null accusative case marker, and so on. Subsequent learning that depends on knowing where the subjects go (e.g., control) would then go awry, mistakenly giving subject privileges to prepositional objects. Similarly, future distributional learning would spread the incorrect analysis to nonaction verbs.

3. The assumption that the child can infer the semantic interpretation of a parental input from its context is widely accepted (e.g., Wexler and Culicover, 1980; Anderson, 1977; see Macnamara, 1972; Slobin, 1977), but it must be acknowledged that such inferences fall short of telepathy and hence are fallible. The child might assume that the parent is referring to a participant acting as an agent, whereas in fact the parent is speaking of it as a patient (e.g., reciprocal actions, actions not immediately present). Again, incorrect conclusions would be made, and distributional learning based on them would spread the damage.

4. The theory predicts that learning must go in a particular direction for all children. Yet individual differences in the path of development of different children acquiring a variety of constructions have been documented (e.g., Bloom, Lightbown, & Hood, 1975; Bowerman, 1973; Bretherton, McNew, Snyder, & Bates, 1983; Nelson, 1981). Of course, virtually all contemporary theories of language acquisition suffer here, and there are many uninteresting ways to build individual differences into a model, such as building a disjunction of two or more different models. But clearly the best theory would allow the learner latitude in the aspects of language development where individual differences are observed but would have some kind of ''pull'' exerted by the end state that is strong enough so that children taking slightly different paths nonetheless approach a common destination.

5. In the sort of model I argued for, one must posit that one critical input feature is used as the premise in positing some rule with the others ''falling out'' deductively as conclusions. However, in many cases there is no basis for distinguishing premise from conclusion within the theory. The problem is that there is often a set of mutually predictive features across languages, and finding any one in the input could be used to predict the rest (or at least to acquire it with less evidence than would be needed otherwise). For example, in ''exceptional case-marking'' or ''raising-to-object'' verbs (e.g., *John considered Mary to be a genius*), the semantic subject argument of the embedded complement acts like the surface grammatical object of the main clause. It takes accusative case-marking *(John considered her/*she to be a genius);* it is passivizable *(Mary is considered by John to be a genius);* it can occur as the sole postverbal argument of the verb *(John considered the problem);* and it is excluded from syntactically being the overt subject of the embedded complement because it occurs in a non-

case-marked position (subject of a nonfinite clause: **John considered Mary is a genius*). In Chapter 6 of LLLD I examined the input to children and their first uses of such verbs, trying to determine which of these four properties was used by the child to predict the other three. All four logically possible hypotheses seemed equally plausible given the evidence.

6. There are other cases where there are mutually predictive relations among rules in the grammar and where there is also developmental evidence that actually provides information about what the child uses as premises and what he or she infers as conclusions. The problem is that the evidence suggests that children use *each* of the possible predictions. In the English lexicon, various facts about a verb are to a large extent mutually interpredictive. Consider the set of properties of a given transitive verb, such as *tickle,* listed in (3).

3. *a.* the verb has agent and theme arguments (e.g., the tickler and tickled)
b. it has an active lexical entry [e.g., *tickle* (SUBJ, OBJ)]
c. it has a passive lexical entry [e.g., *tickled* (*by*-OBJ, SUBJ)]
d. it can be used with a subject and object expressing its two arguments (e.g., *John tickled Mary*)
e. it can be used with an oblique object and subject expressing its two arguments. (e.g., *Mary was tickled by John*)

By definition in a mature grammar property, *3b* predicts *3d* and *3c* predicts *3e*. In addition, *3a* can be used to predict *3b, 3c* can be used to predict *3b, 3d* can be used to predict *3b, 3a* can be used to predict *3c, 3e* can be used to predict *3c,* and 3b can be used to predict *3c*. In Pinker (1984a) I examined evidence consisting of children's spontaneous creations of ungrammatical verb constructions and their willingness to generalize from one type of verb usage to another in controlled teaching experiments (e.g., Pinker, Lebeaux, and Frost, 1987). I discovered that there is reasonably good developmental evidence that children perform *all* of these inferences. This required me to posit five separate learning procedures, some of which required subprocedures. It would seem more economical to posit a single representation for a verb paradigm, spelling out the morphological, semantic, and syntactic properties of its alternative forms, and let it be implicit that any property can be used to infer any other property.

7. The predictions of the semantic bootstrapping hypothesis for counterfactual situations all make the child sound too "stupid." These difficult cases are needed to show that the hypothesis is falsifiable, but they have a strange ring to them. For example, consider the following thought experiment from LLLD (p. 54–55):

> Imagine exposing a child to an input sequence beginning with passive sentences only. According to the [semantic bootstrapping] hypothesis, the child would mistakenly conclude that English is an OVS language, since he uses patienthood as

> evidence for OBJ, agenthood as evidence for SUBJ (the *by* in the agent phrase could be conceived of as an optional nominative case marker, the various forms of *be* as obligatory tense-carrying auxiliaries). Then active sentences could be introduced, which the child would interpret as OVS sentences containing an alternative, "passive" lexical entry for the main verb. . . . Though to a casual observer the child might appear to be doing fine at that point, any subsequent learning that uses mechanisms that invoke SUBJ and OBJ should go awry. For example, when the child hears *John told Bill to kiss Mary,* he or she would use a procedure that allows a missing complement subject to be equated with the matrix object if there is one, the matrix subject otherwise. Our experimental child would be unable to analyze this sentence, since as far as he or she is concerned, it is not the subject that is missing from the complement but the object. If somehow the child did manage to analyze the complement phrase, he or she would interpret it incorrectly (or have trouble learning the correct interpretation if it was pointed out to him or her): the child would interpret *John,* the object according to his or her grammar, as the intended kisser, rather than *Bill,* the object for a real-life child. And if the child somehow overcame that problem, [then] unlike real-life learners, he or she should accept as grammatical the sentence *John was promised by Bill to leave,* since *by Bill,* analyzed as the subject by this child, is then allowed to be a controller, whereas its real-life analysis as an oblique object precludes it from having that role. . . .

One senses that a real child in such a situation would not be so dense. For example, it's pretty unusual for an active verb to be more inflected than its passive participle and for it to be nonfinite while its passive is finite. It's also unusual for there to be a zero accusative case-marker together with a morphologically-realized nominative case-marker; it's usually the other way around. The *tell* sentence, as mentioned, is unanalyzable under the assumption that the postverbal noun phrase in the main clause is a subject. If and when the child did manage to figure it out somehow, and the first time such a sentence was used in a context in which it was clear who was doing what to whom, the child's interpretation of the sentence and his interpretation of the world would be at odds. All of this information should tell the child that his semantically-inferred assignment of subject and object positions are unlikely to be correct.

However, the LLLD mechanisms do not give the child this option. The disconfirmatory information, taken as an aggregate, certainly points to a probable conclusion, but none of the individual pieces of information is valid enough itself to serve as the trigger for a learning mechanism. For example, though passive sentences tend to be more inflected than active sentences, it is hard to imagine a useful learning procedure that would say "if a sentence has some inflection, assume it is passive," or vice-versa; or "if a NP has no morphologically overt case-marking, assign it the grammatical relation of SUBJECT." The problem is that the nonsemantic contingencies are only weakly predictive and many of them rely on prior grammatical learning (e.g., knowing whether a word is composed of a stem plus an inflection, or just a long stem).

It is possible to revise the mechanisms to be able to backtrack when the weight of evidence appears to go against an earlier decision, but such mechanisms would be complicated. Each piece of potentially disconfirming evidence would have to be mentioned in a procedure for each decision it weighed against. And how would the child *un*learn the distributionally-learned words and phrases mistakenly acquired as a result of the earlier miscategorization?

8. Related to this, partially predictive evidence is hardly used at all in LLLD. For example, Greenberg showed that subjects tend to (but do not invariably) precede objects. Since there are OSV languages, I did not posit a mechanism exploiting this regularity for fear of its making mistakes in such languages. Likewise, head-argument order in one phrasal category (e.g., N-PP order in NP) is partially, though not perfectly, predictive of head-argument order in other phrasal categories (e.g., V-NP/PP/S order in VP). The prosodic correlates of phrase structure, downplayed earlier in this chapter, might fall into this category as well. Again, it is easy to see why one would not want to build in a procedure that triggered some change to a grammar based on poor diagnostic inputs. But it is also easy to see why a smart learner should be able to draw conclusions from an aggregate of individually nondiagnostic but mutually consistent evidence.

9. For what it is worth, there is something esthetically unpleasing about positing a set of innate procedures whose sole function is to create a set of grammatical rules (like the installation programs that come with software packages). Furthermore, it is unclear how such procedures could have evolved. Why would one need a language acquisition device if successive generations spoke the same language, and how could successive generations speak different languages unless there had already evolved a set of language acquisition procedures? Neither of these considerations is a strong argument, but they point to a conceivable, though vague, alternative: an innate universal grammar parts of which are underspecified and plastic. Linguistic diversity is a consequence of these underspecified parameters being fleshed out in different ways. And that would occur as a consequence of the child trying to create a consistent and complete representation for ambient sentences as he or she tried to comprehend them, despite insufficient inborn information. Such a notion, vague though it is, perhaps could also be made consonant with the claims of Bickerton (1981) and Slobin (1986) that children make errors that are not a consequence of the structure of the target language but due to a regression toward a central tendency defining a default "universal child grammar." With language-acquisition algorithms as the embodiment of grammatical universals (as in LLLD), impoverished input (as in Bickerton's Creole-forming societies) should lead to no output or degenerate output. In more standard input environments, errors should reflect the irregularities in the language to be acquired, or the scarcity of certain inputs, rather than a universal "central tendency."

10. Despite the overall lawfulness of language, grammarians frequently encounter odd areas of grammar that look like the products of weary compromises rather than master blueprints. For example, if anything is predictable about grammar, it is that words' phrase-structure privileges correlate with their morphological privileges (indeed, such correlations are often used as definitions of grammatical categories). Nonetheless, in English we find the word *near* whose phrase structure behavior is prepositional in that it takes direct objects (e.g., *near the house/ *fond the house*) but whose morphology is adjectival in that it takes comparative suffixes like *-er* and *-est* (e.g., *the fire department is nearest the blue house/ *John ran byest the blue house;* Maling, 1983). Similarly, in the English poss-*ing* construction (e.g., *John's giving Mary a gift will start a lot of gossip*), the specifier of the head and the external distribution of the phrase are identical to those of noun phrases whereas the stem, complements, and inflection of the head are identical to those of verb phrases. This is true despite the fact that external distributions, internal complement structures, specifiers, word classes, and inflections are usually correlated with each other. A mechanism that rigidly used one set of privileges of an element to predict the remainder, using universal definitions of grammatical categories, would either be unable to learn such exceptional cases, or once having learned them, could proceed to obliterate the distinctions between the conflicting categories throughout the grammar. (For example, if being inflected with *-est* is diagnostic of adjectivehood, and *near* can be inflected with *-est,* then *near* is an adjective. *Near* can take a direct object, thus adjectives can take direct objects; hence, *I am angry Mary* is a possible sentence—contrary to fact.) These examples suggest that grammars may be the product of conspiracies—and occasionally compromises—among local rule-forming processes, rather than the product of an aggressive exploiter of potential generalizations.

WHAT THESE PROBLEMS TELL US ABOUT THE CHILD'S BOOTSTRAPPING MECHANISMS

If one buys all my arguments thus far, *none* of the proposed solutions to the bootstrapping hypothesis is viable. At the same time, each of the sources of information invoked by the various hypotheses would seem to have some contribution to make in the overall solution to the bootstrapping problem. I think these problems point to the "smoking gun" assumption as the problem—the assumption that grammatical development is driven by a distinguished set of cues that are perceivable in the input and uniquely diagnostic of syntactic rules, which in turn serve as the premises of a powerful set of deductive generalizations yielding the rest of the grammar. Instead, the problems raised above call for a model of acquisition that would have the following properties:

- The child's inferences need not flow from a specially-designated subset of an innate set of correlated phenomena, serving as premises, to the remaining members of the set, serving as conclusions. Rather, inferences can flow opportunistically from any member of the set that is found to be exemplified in the input to the remaining members.
- Fallible but partially diagnostic input cues should be usable to make guesses about the language, especially when several of them point to the same conclusions and a single, ordinarily diagnostic cue, points to the opposite conclusion.
- Rule hypotheses should be tentative, so that if decisions made consequent to them turn out to be nonviable, they can be revised. Distributional analyses made on the basis of tentative rules should be even more tentative.
- Decisions about rules are consequences of a competition of different sources of information. The decision that is favored by the most input cues and that leads to the greatest degree of successful further learning is retained.

At the same time, the problems listed above do not give reason to abandon the original assumptions that the child possesses innate constraints on possible grammars, that possible grammars are couched in a formal vocabulary, or that semantic cues (among others) are used to make inferences about syntactic rules. What we need is a type of mechanism that can satisfy all these requirements.

CONSTRAINT SATISFACTION MODELS

Inferences without any clear distinction between premises and conclusions are not unique to language acquisition. In speech perception, for example, the identity of a phoneme with given spectral/temporal properties depends on the speaking rate, idiosyncratic properties of the speaker's voice, and the immediate context of the phoneme, among other things; idiosyncratic properties of the speaker's voice can often only be determined by noting the spectral/temporal properties of known phonemes uttered by that speaker; the unidentified phoneme may itself serve as a context influencing spectral/temporal properties critical to identifying both of its neighbors. If any piece of this puzzle could be solved, the remaining ones would fall into place, but none can be solved independently of the others. Similarly, in stereopsis, one can determine the retinal disparity (and hence depth) of a real-world visual feature if one knew which projected feature in one eye corresponded to which projected feature in the other. But this information is not generally available and is itself a perceptual problem to be solved (and could be solvable, if one antecedently knew the disparities involved).

These chicken-and-egg problems are often solvable, nonetheless, because only a subset of the logically possible *global* solutions to the problem are possible given certain constraints inherent in the problem. For example, the coherence of matter implies that neighboring points on one retina are much more likely to have similar disparities associated with them than greatly differing disparities. Thus not *every* set of choices of corresponding points in the two retinas plus disparity values for those pairs is equally likely. Those choices that consist of neighboring points with similar disparities are ecologically far more likely in terrestrial environments (excluding swarms of gnats on a foggy day, etc.).

This type of problem, and a possible solution to it, is often discussed in terms of an analogy with the "soap film" problem in physics. For example, Pinker (1984b) describes an example from Attneave (1982), concerning

> the problem of determining the shape of a film formed when an irregularly shaped loop of wire is dipped in soapy water (the shape can be characterized by quantizing the film surface into patches and specifying the height of each patch). The answer to the problem is constrained by the 'least action' principle ensuring that the height of any patch of the film must be close to the heights of all its neighboring patches. But how can this information be used if one does not know beforehand the heights of all the neighbors of any patch? One can solve the problem iteratively, by assigning every patch an arbitrary initial height except for those patches touching the wire loop, which are assigned the same heights as the piece of wire they are attached to. Then the heights of the other patches are replaced by the average of the heights of its neighbors. This is repeated through several iterations; eventually the array of heights converges on a single set of values corresponding to the shape of the film, thanks to constraints on height spreading inward from the wire. The solution is attained without knowing the height of any single interior patch a priori, and without any central processor.

"Relaxation" models (see Ullman, 1979; Davis & Rosenfeld, 1981) are implementations of this sort of computation consisting of a network of simple processors working iteratively. Each processor is wired to its neighbors and each processor computes a value for iteration i that is a function of its value on iteration $(i - 1)$ and the value of its neighbors on iteration $(i-1)$. For example, Marr and Poggio (1977) developed a model of stereopsis in which each point on the retina is represented by a unit that can assume a given disparity value. Neighboring units strengthen each other's choice of disparity values if and only if they are similar; in addition, each point is constrained to have a unique corresponding point in the other retina. Marr and Poggio showed that such models could converge to a unique set of joint values for disparities and pairings after several iterations. Waltz (1975) developed a program for interpreting the 3-D shape of line drawings of prismatic solids, in the face of the inherent problem that any junction of lines in the 2-D drawing (e.g., a "T," "X," or "L") could be the projection of more than one three-dimensional configuration of surfaces (e.g., convex corner, concave ridge). The solution was obtained by exploiting the constraint that many of the possible solutions for a given vertex were inconsistent with some of the solutions for a vertex at the other end of one of its lines. By having each vertex unit pass a "message" to the vertex units connected to it (one for each vertex that is joined to it by a line segment in a drawing) where each message states the possible 3-D configurations that the originating vertex could be a projection of, and having each vertex unit "know" which 3-D configurations were consistent with which other ones, a unique global solution could be arrived at despite the local ambiguities.

Relaxation models are typically used when there is a huge amount of information coming into a system at one time, such as in early visual processing, so that neither serial processing nor exhaustive interconnections among parallel units is feasible. This is not a problem of the same magnitude in language acquisition, and relaxation models as they are typically designed in vision research with large numbers of simple units with hardwired connections are not obviously needed. But more generally, chicken-and-egg problems (where one must find a global solution that satisfies many local constraints) and the use of iterative adjustment of parameters among interconnected elements may be common to perception and language learning. I loosely refer to such problems as "constraint satisfaction" problems. Similarly, I loosely use the term "constraint satisfaction network" to refer to devices designed to solve such problems that consist of a network of elements whose values on one iteration are determined by their values and the values of their neighbors on the previous one.

In the rest of the paper, I explore the possibility that language acquisition is accomplished by a constraint satisfaction network with some of the properties of devices proposed for perceptual problems. Then I explore the consequences of this hypothesis for the debate over the bootstrapping problem.

WHAT MIGHT A CONSTRAINT SATISFACTION MODEL FOR LANGUAGE ACQUISITION LOOK LIKE?

In this section I flesh out the conjecture that language acquisition is a term of constraint satisfaction just enough to highlight its consequences on the bootstrapping debate. I do *not* present an explicit theory of language acquisition; rather, I outline some modest steps that might bridge the theory of LLLD and its possible successor. Needless to say, many details are left imprecise.

To create an analogy between a language acquisition model and the perceptual models summarized above, three parallels have to be sketched out: the *constraints* that ensure a single overall solution despite massive local indeterminacies, the *boundary conditions specified by the input* that serve as "seeds" to get the network started, and the *local links* that serve to propagate constraints between one local data structure and its "neighbors." Basically, what I will propose is that the child's parser sets up incomplete representations of the input that serve as boundary conditions, that Universal Grammar provides a set of constraints that the analysis of input sentences and the acquired rules of grammar must satisfy, and that processes of pattern matching and parameter adjustment enforce consistency between the input, universal grammar, and the developing language-particular grammar.

Constraints. The analogue of constraints in a constraint satisfaction model of language acquisition (e.g., of the constraint in stereopsis that matter is coherent) comes from Universal Grammar: for example, constraints that subjects have certain properties in their interaction with rules of word order, phrase structure, anaphora, control, and so on. I model these constraints as networks of *rule prototypes*. Each network consists of a set of unmarked, default, or prototypical rules referencing a common substantive universal (e.g., SUBJ, N). Actually, it is the mention of common universal symbols in the different rule prototypes that makes a collection of prototypes a "network": all rule prototypes are implicitly linked with all other rule prototypes with which they share symbols. Different rule prototypes have different weights with respect to a given symbol, higher weights being associated with less marked prototypes.

The following is a fragment of the network of rule prototypes referencing "SUBJECT." In this diagram and the rest of the paper, I use the notation of Lexical Functional Grammar (Kaplan & Bresnan, 1982) for grammatical rules and the same set of universals appealed to in the LLLD model. However, the general points I am making about the architecture of the language acquisition device are mostly independent of the choice of particular contemporary theories of generative grammar or of grammatical universals.

Other grammatical relations will have their own networks of rule prototypes with varying degrees of overlap with the SUBJECT prototype. For example, the prototype network for OBJECT will contain a line exactly analogous to the first line specifying that the OBJECT function can be assigned to phrase structure positions. Other rule prototypes mentioning OBJECT will be distinct from those in the SUBJECT network, of course. For example, there is no entry in the OBJECT network corresponding to the PRO-drop phenomenon, and there would be no entry in the SUBJECT network that would be analogous to the one specifying that object markers are typically conflated with definiteness (Hopper & Thompson, 1980). As we shall see, these prototype networks are the source of local constraints within the acquired grammar, and they pushed and pull the acquired rules to be as close to those in the prototype as possible.

Boundary Conditions from the Input. The analogue of the "seeds" from the input that get the network started consists of information about particular

	Comments:
Phrase Structure:	
$XP \rightarrow \ldots NP_{SUBJ} \ldots$ [+tense]	—NP positions in tensed clauses can be subjects
$S = \{ VP, NP_{SUBJ} \}$	—subject NP is a daughter of S[4]
$NP_{SUBJ} > NP_{OBJ}$	—subject precedes object
Lexical	
<word>: pred (SUBJ, OBJ) agent theme; affix = ϕ; + tense; focus = unspecified	—subject is agent in basic lexical entry of transitive agent/patient verb
<word>: pred (OBL/ϕ, SUBJ) agent theme; affix = x; + participle; focus = theme	—subject is theme in passive entry of verb
Inflectional:	
<affix>: V affix; SUBJ's feature=value	—features of subject can be encoded in verb affix
<affix>: N affix; case=nom; SUBJ	subject encoded as nominative case-marker in noun affix
<ϕ>: N affix; case=nom; SUBJ	—zero case marking more likely in nominative case
<affix>: V affix; SUBJ's PRED = PRO; TENSE = x; SUBJ's feature=value	—in "PRO-drop" languages, the subject can be omitted with certain finite verb affixes
Control:	
<word>: pred (SUBJ, OBJ, XCOMP); OBJ = XCOMP's SUBJ	—lexical entries of control verbs specify that matrix argument can control understood subject of complement (XCOMP)
<word>: pred (SUBJ, XCOMP); SUBJ = XCOMP's SUBJ	

FIGURE 12.4. Fragment of a Universal Prototype Network involving "Subject"

[4]The notation is based on Gazdar, Klein, Pullum, & Sag's (1985) "linear precedence/immediate dominance" format. The elements within braces are immediate constituents of the left-hand-side symbol, with their order left unspecified. Orders of constituents, including partial orderings, can be specified in a separate part of the rule: for example, "X > Y" means that X must precede Y.

input sentences. This information must be created in a form that is compatible with the information in the rule prototype networks. I will assume that the child is equipped with a parser that attempts to do the same things as the adult parser: assign words to their lexical categories, group sequences of adjacent lexical categories into phrases, group phrases into larger phrases and clauses, unpack the features encoded in affixes and verify that they are mutually consistent, construct a representation of the predicate-argument relations defined by the subcategorization of the verb and the grammatical relation-bearing phrases in the sentence, and so on. The adult parser ordinarily does this by a pattern-matching process that finds the grammatical rules and lexical entries that are matched by properties in the input. At the beginning of language learning, however, there are no complete rules, and so there is nothing that properly matches. So let us assume that the parser at first constructs *underspecified* representations of the input properties. Such underspecified input representations contain a mixture of the linguistically-relevant features that are discernible in the absence of acquired rules (e.g., linear precedence, semantic properties of words, predicate-argument relations, prosodic properties) and variables substituting for the constants that rules of grammar would ordinarily provide. That is, the parser is built to assign every word a lexical category, every lexical category a phrasal category, every phrasal category a mother phrase, etc.. When the requisite grammatical information is absent, abstract and uncommitted representations are created instead.

For example, before the parser knows *which* grammatical relation (SUBJECT, OBJECT, etc.) to assign to a given noun phrase, it could still know that it must be assigned *some* relation. It could put a variable for a grammatical relation, symbolized by GR1, GR2, etc., in the place that ultimately must be filled with a constant for a particular relation. I will assume that such variables are actually vectors consisting of the current strengths (in the interval [0-1]) of each of the possible labels that could serve as constants for that variable. (This is an example of "fuzzy labeling" used in relaxation models; see Davis & Rosenfeld, 1981.) For example, at the start of learning, the GR variable assigned to a subcategorization frame or phrase structure position would look like Figure 12.5a. ("OBJ2" refers to the second object in dative constructions; "OBL" refers to oblique objects.) This data structure, for example, might be appended to a phrase structure position (e.g., the NP dominated by VP, as in Figure 12.5b), to a lexical entry (e.g., in the part of a subcategorization frame dictating how the second argument of a verb is expressed), or to a case-marker. Possessing a phrase structure rule such as 12.5b would correspond to the state of knowledge in which it is known that the postverbal NP in the language bears *some* grammatical function to the verb, but it is not known which one (e.g., subject or object). Knowing which formal types of symbols occur in which types of rules is equivalent to knowing what sorts of correlations a grammar can sanction and is a precursor to knowing the *actual* correlations that are implicit in a language's grammatical rules (e.g., knowing that accusative pronouns are correlated with

a. GR1

$$\begin{bmatrix} \text{SUBJ} & .0 \\ \text{OBJ} & .0 \\ \text{OBJ2} & .0 \\ \text{OBL} & .0 \end{bmatrix}$$

b. VP → V NP
GR1

$$\begin{bmatrix} \text{SUBJ} & .0 \\ \text{OBJ} & .0 \\ \text{OBJ2} & .0 \\ \text{OBL} & .0 \end{bmatrix}$$

FIGURE 12.5.

the first NP in a VP, both of which are correlated with the theme argument of causative verbs).

This data structure, of course, changes as the child accumulates evidence as to what the grammatical function listed in a rule actually is. For example, at some intermediate point in the learning process (to be described shortly), when the child has accumulated a certain amount of information about what that grammatical relation is likely to be, the GR vector in the rule might look like Figure 12.6a.

Since adult grammars are in general not "squishy," (i.e., an NP is either a subject or it isn't), these vectors would have a positive feedback mechanism that would push the highest-valued label to 1.0 if it had already surpassed some threshold of strength and if the other labels were significantly less than the highest-valued one. Thus, I assume that Figure 12.6a, under the influence of such a "rich-get-richer" scheme, would soon internally reorganize to Figure 12.6b. At this point the variable would be set to a constant value (i.e., a single label, in this case "OBJ"), and the structure containing it would yield a permanent rule of the grammar. As in LLLD, this is accomplished by recovering rules from phrase structure trees via a reverse derivation.

Variables similar to "GR" would exist for other portions of an input parse that cannot be fixed because the requisite rules had not yet been learned. For example, there would be a major category or CATG vector with strengths (ini-

GR1

$$\begin{bmatrix} \text{SUBJ} & .2 \\ \text{OBJ} & .7 \\ \text{OBJ2} & .0 \\ \text{OBL} & .2 \end{bmatrix}$$

GR1

$$\begin{bmatrix} \text{SUBJ} & .0 \\ \text{OBJ} & 1.0 \\ \text{OBJ2} & .0 \\ \text{OBL} & .0 \end{bmatrix}$$

FIGURE 12.6. a b

tially zero) associated with labels for N, V, A, and P. There would also be variables expressing partial knowledge about phrase structure configurations and rules. These would include assertions about two nodes being phrasemates, being in sister-sister or mother-daughter connectedness relations, being in certain linear precedence relations, being at phrase boundaries, being projections of particular lexical categories with level of projection unspecified, and so on. Examples of these structures will be provided in the next section.

Local links. Finally, the analogue of the *links* among units in perceptual constraint-satisfaction networks is a pattern-matching process. This is the aspect of the model I am proposing that makes it different from relaxation models in vision where the links among units are hardwired. It gives the model commonalities with ''pattern-directed systems'' (Waterman & Hayes-Roth, 1978) of which production systems (e.g., Anderson, 1983) and schema instantiation models (e.g., Bobrow & Winograd) are examples.

The pattern matching process works in two directions. The first direction is bottom-up. Configurations of symbols in an input representation (e.g., a sequence of category symbols, a set of thematic relations belonging to a verb's arguments, a prosodic pattern) will match corresponding configurations in rule prototypes *and* in already-acquired language-specific rules. This is followed by a spread of activation from rule to rule within the partially acquired grammar, from rule prototype to rule prototype within the prototype networks, and from actual rules to rule prototypes along paths defined by mentions of the same symbol in different rules.

In addition, pattern matching goes in a top-down direction: portions of rules that match previously activated rule prototypes are themselves activated, and portions of the underspecified input representation that match activated rules or rule prototypes are activated.

The actual learning is accomplished by a process associated with this top-down matching that can be called *adjustment*. If an underspecified rule or representation is matched by an activated rule or rule prototype, the vector of label strengths in its underspecified variables altered in the direction of the corresponding label strengths in the active rules or rule prototypes. Since more than one rule or rule prototype can be activated at a given time and can match an underspecified variable, variables will be adjusted by several sources at a time—some cooperating, some competing.

The degree of modification effected in this adjustment process would be monotonically related to the strength of the labels in the influencing rule or to the weight of the rule prototype with respect to that variable. It is possible that strength increases nonadditively with the number of concurrent consistent adjustments (perhaps multiplicatively) since converging evidence might be given a weight that is greater than the sum of its parts. It is also possible that strength increases in a nonlinear way with the number of adjustments over time (possibly according to the exponential or hyperbolic learning curves from classical mathematical learning theory). Finally, and crucially, strong settings of labels in acquired rules would inherently outweigh adjustments by innate rule prototypes. This feature is necessary to ensure that the distributional regularities of the language should be the final arbiter when they disagree with universal tendencies. (A similar feature was built into the LLLD distributional learning mechanism.)

EXAMPLES OF HOW A CONSTRAINT SATISFACTION MODEL MIGHT WORK

Unlike the semantic bootstrapping hypothesis as it is outlined in LLLD, it is difficult to illustrate the constraint satisfaction mechanism by tracing the child's operations while processing his first sentence. Instead, consider a child who has acquired some of the phrase structure rules of the language (how, you will see later) but has not yet formed any hypotheses about grammatical relations. For example, the child may hear a sentence like *the dog bit the man*. As before, we will assume that the child has inferred its overall meaning and knows the meaning of the individual content words. The parser, using learned rules (without specification of grammatical relations) and the cognitively induced representation of the predicate-argument structure of *hit*, sets up the underspecified input representation shown in Figure 12.7.

The co-indexing of the phrase structure positions in the parse tree and the slots in the subcategorization frame for *hit* is done with the help of the contextually-inferred semantic information and knowledge of the meaning of "dog" and "man." However, there is not yet a full subcategorization frame for *hit* specifying how its arguments should be expressed grammatically, only for the cognitive/semantic entry specifying how many and what kinds of arguments it has.

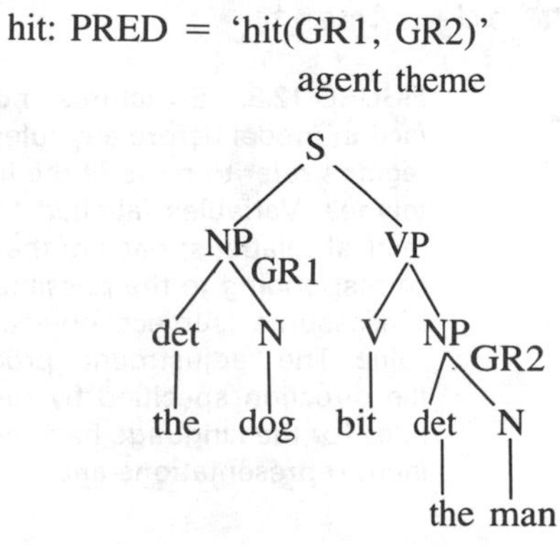

FIGURE 12.7.

Now the system uses a critical property of the prototype representation: it can be indexed by any of its entries using the pattern-matching operations of the parser. That is, if the input representation has a part that matches a prototype, the entire prototype network sharing symbols with the matched one is activated. If the input matches several prototypes, they are all activated to an extent proportional to the goodness of the match multiplied by the weight (unmarkedness) assigned to the matched prototype. Of course, if there are any rules in the developing grammar that are matched, they are activated as well; that is simply the adult parsing process.

In the current example, we are assuming that no rules mention SUBJ or OBJ yet, so these relations cannot be assigned by the parser. However, several parts of the currently underspecified input representation match parts of the prototype

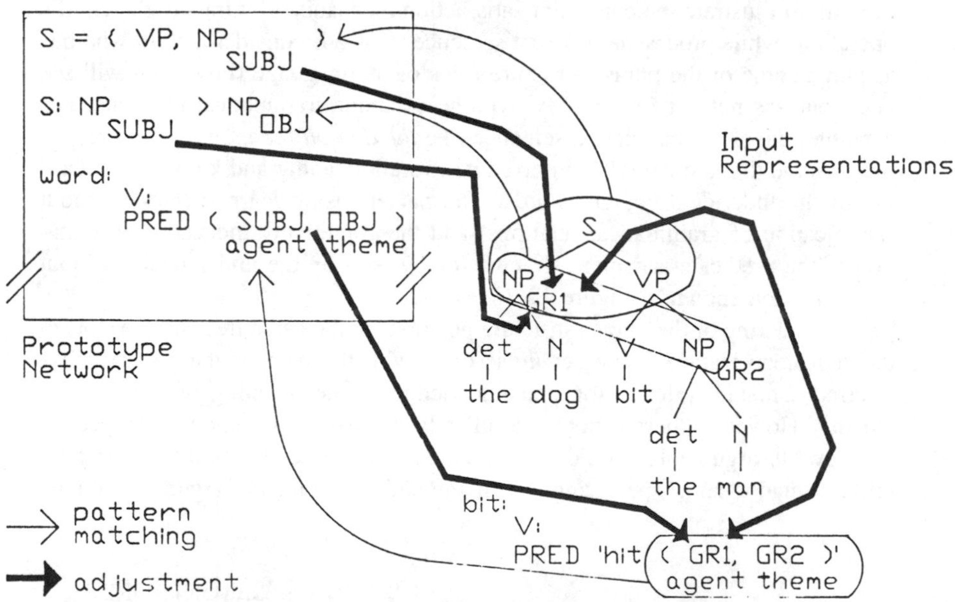

FIGURE 12.8. Structures and processes used in the constraint satisfaction model before any rules of grammar have been learned. Circled regions refer to parts of the input representation that match rule prototypes. Variables labelled "GRn" refer to as-yet unspecified grammatical relations; each of these variables is actually a vector of labels corresponding to the possible grammatical relations that the variable can assume (subject, object, etc.), each associated with a strength value. The "adjustment" process alters the values of these labels in the direction specified by the matched rule prototype. When some rules for the language have been learned, they too can match parts of input representations and can adjust the variables in them.

networks for grammatical relations. *1*. The lexical entry, with its 'agent-theme' structure, matches a line in the "lexical" section of the SUBJECT prototype. *2*. The first NP matches the very first rule prototype in the network, the one that states that certain NP positions can be assigned grammatical functions. The OBJECT network has a similar line and it is matched, too. *3*. The first NP is a daughter of S, so it matches a line in the SUBJECT network. *4*. There are two NP's in the sentence, so they (weakly) match the $NP_{SUBJ} > NP_{OBJ}$ entry. Some of these matches are illustrated in Figure 12.8 by the circled portions of the input and the thin arrows pointing to the rule prototypes they match.

Now the learning process begins. If an active rule prototype contains a GR constant (SUBJ, OBJ, etc.) that matches a GR variable in the input, it increments the corresponding label of that variable in the input representation. Hence, in the current example, the *pred*(SUBJ, OBJ) prototype lexical entry is activated, and its GR constants SUBJ and OBJ match the GR variables in the first and second argument slots of the lexical entry for *hit*. The same is true of the SUBJ and OBJ symbols in the prototypical order rule $NP_{SUBJ} > NP_{OBJ}$, also activated by the input. These matches would then cause the strengths of the SUBJ label in the first argument slot of the lexical entry for *hit* to be incremented, and likewise for the OBJ label in the second slot.

In addition, since this label in the lexical entry for *hit* and the GR vector in the phrase structure rule generating the first NP under S are co-indexed, they would mutually adjust each other. For example, the difference between corresponding element strengths would be reduced by adding or subtracting a small value to or from each element; the value would be related to the difference between their strengths and to the absolute strength of the stronger element. In other words, if the child hasn't learned part of one rule and hasn't learned part of another, but knows that the two parts must be set to the same value (because of formal consistency requirements in the grammar), evidence for the subjecthood of one part increases the strength of subjecthood for the other, and vice versa. These various adjustment processes are illustrated by the thick lines in Figure 12.8.

Figure 12.9 is a possible representation of the lexical entry for the verb *hit* following this episode of learning:

$$\text{bit(GR1} \begin{bmatrix} \text{SUBJ} & .13 \\ \text{OBJ} & .01 \\ \text{OBJ2} & .00 \\ \text{OBL} & .00 \end{bmatrix} \text{, GR2} \begin{bmatrix} \text{SUBJ} & .01 \\ \text{OBJ} & .12 \\ \text{OBJ2} & .00 \\ \text{OBL} & .00 \end{bmatrix} \text{)}$$

FIGURE 12.9.

The numbers are arbitrary. The OBJ label in the variable for the first argument and the SUBJ label in the variable for the second argument are incremented somewhat because the first argument NP, though possessing many of the hallmarks of a subject, is also in a possible (though unlikely) object position, and vice versa.

This example, of course, was a bit of a cheat, for two reasons. First, the example begs the question of how the syntactic categories and phrase structure configurations were assigned to begin with. I will deal with this problem in the next section (in a similar way). Second, all adjustments conspired to set SUBJECT as the most likely value for the unknown grammatical relation. Thus the same conclusion would have been reached under the single-sufficient-cue or ''smoking gun'' hypothesis.

There is a difference, though. In other types of inputs, especially when some rules have already been learned, a given decision will be affected by several possibly conflicting adjustments. For example, a very early passive sentence such as *the boy was kissed by the girl* would probably not send this learner very far down the garden path (unlike the smoking gun model), because the 'agent, therefore subject' inference could be attenuated by a number of factors, depending on the state of the learner. If the learner had acquired the uninflected form of *kiss,* the extra phonetic material at the end of *kissed* could support the hypothesis that it was inflected, activating the prototypical passive lexical entry somewhat, to the detriment of the active one. Similarly, if the child were sensitive to any of the following, they would decrease the effect of the top-down adjustment of the active prototype as it tried to make the *by*-phrase the subject: the greater (prepositional) case-marking of the putative subject as compared to the object, the nonfiniteness of the main verb (requiring an auxiliary to provide tense), the focus on the theme in the discourse context, or the object-subject order. Even if the child incorrectly assigned the grammatical roles after processing this sentence, all is not lost. The suboptimal match to the active prototype entry and the conflicting partial match to the passive prototype entry would ensure that the strength of those assignments would be low. As such, they would have little influence on future rule learning, because the adjustments of a learned rule on future learning is proportional to that rule's strength.

Another example showing the effects of competition in this model involves the distributional learning of noncanonical verbs, such as *receive,* whose subject is a goal and whose oblique *from*-object is its agent or source. As long as *receive* sentences (e.g., *John received a letter from Reagan*) are not the first ones heard, the consistency enforcing mechanisms will push and pull the goal argument in the subcategorization frame in two directions. The prototypical lexical entry for three-argument verbs states that goals are OBLIQUE, and accordingly it increments the OBLIQUE label in the GR vector in the lexical entry of *receive*. But the sequence of nouns and verbs created by the parser will also match the previously acquired S $\rightarrow$ NP_{SUBJ} VP rule. This activated rule will then adjust the subject label in the GR vector in the goal slot for *receive* by virtue of the word *John* heading the clause-initial phrase and the concept 'John' in the goal slot being bound to it. Thus the activated rule will increment the SUBJECT element.[5] Since adjustment by learned rules is greater than adjustment by prototypes, the 'distributional' conclusion, namely that the goal argument is subject, will win out. This is not terribly different from the LLLD mechanism where it was also stipulated that distributional inferences must override semantic ones. However, there are two advantages to having the distributional adjustment be graded and compete against the semantic adjustment. First, the distributional adjustment is related to the strength of the learned rule (so incorrect rules will not proliferate further incorrect conclusions throughout the grammar via distributional analyses); second, different learned rules that match the input but disagree over the grammatical relation appropriate to the unspecified rule compete against each other so that ambiguous contexts (e.g., *she called him blicket,* where *blicket* could be a proper noun, adjective, or particle) do not lead to incorrect conclusions (this was a major worry in LLLD).

Now let me redeem the promissory note I issued several paragraphs ago. As mentioned, for expository purposes I had to appear to break my own ground rules in the bootstrapping debate by not starting at the beginning of language acquisition. That is, part of my scenario for how subjects were learned assumed that phrase structure geometry and syntactic category labels had already been learned. At this point we are ready to see how this is done. Basically, I posit a similar account for the acquisition of category labels and phrase structure rules, have the three sets of mechanisms operate in parallel, and predict that they converge to a mutually consistent set of rules even though none of these three kinds of information is resolved in final form prior to the acquisition of the other two kinds.

Let us start with category labels. As before, I assume that the parser tries to build structures for incoming sentences, including a lexical category for every word. The parser is capable of inserting variables when existing rules do not allow critical decisions to be made. In this case, assume that there is a variable called CATG which is a vector with N, V, A, and P labels and which is assigned to words whose lexical entries have no categorization information yet. Assume also that there is a prototype network for nouns akin to Figure 12.10.

---

[5]Actually, the pattern matching and adjustment processes are a bit smarter than I have been letting on here. The problem is that the same semantic element can be bound to two grammatical functions; for example, in "equi" sentences such as *John told Bill to leave, Bill* is the matrix object and complement subject. Thus if the mechanism isn't careful, the agent role of Bill in the complement could trigger the SUBJ prototype and incorrectly assign it as the subject of the matrix clause. Thus the mechanism must ensure that the pattern-matching process and the adjustment process are confined to operate over the same domain in the input. That is, since Bill is the agent of the action denoted by *leave,* the top-down adjustment of the subject prototype must be constrained to adjust only the lexical entry of *leave* and the first NP position of the complement S, not the lexical entry of *tell* or the last NP position of the matrix S.

	Comments:
Phrase structure:	
NP → . . .N. . .	—nouns introduced in NPs
$NP'_{GR} \rightarrow NP$	—NPs introduced as daughters of NP′; NP′ can bear a GR
NP = { N, (det), (Adj) }	—NPs can contain adjectives & determiners
Lexical:	
<word>: N + {person, thing, place}	—persons/places/things denoted by nouns
Inflectional:	
<affix>: N affix CASE=nom/acc/gen/dat NUMBER=sng/pl/dual GENDER=m/f/n DEFINITE=+/− HUMAN=+/− CLASS=I/II/III/. . .	—noun affixes can be sensitive to the noun's case, number, etc.
Phonological:	
<word>: N [+stress]	—nouns are stressed (also other major categories)
Bounding:	
Bounding nodes = { NP′, S′, S }	—NP′ is a bounding node

FIGURE 12.10. Fragment of a Prototype Network for "Noun":

Similar structures, *mutatus mutandis,* would exist for verbs, adjectives, and so on. The parser would try to build a tree with the correct geometry for an input sentence, using CATG vectors for the category labels for the nodes and lexical entries. At first, phonological or semantic patterns, and later, acquired rules would be set up, and they would activate corresponding parts of the noun (or verb, etc.) prototype networks. Once activated, category variables in matched portions of the input would be adjusted in a tug of war among the different matched prototype categories and learned rules. For example, the categorization of the word *fight* in the sentence *he started four fights* would be adjusted (incorrectly) by the verb prototype network if the child construed it as the name of an action, but it would also be pushed toward nounhood if the child had previously acquired the rule V → NP or NP → Number N, both of which could match the input. Other possible adjustments would arise if the child had learned the meaning of *four* and if the prototype for NPs but not VPs allowed number modifiers expressing arbitrary numbers (i.e., other than single, dual, plural).

Finally, Figure 12.11 shows a fragment of a network for phrase structure rules.

	Comments:
$X^n \in \{N^n, V^n, A^n, P^n\}$	—N, V, A, P are major categories
XP → . . . X(head) . . .	—lexical categories are heads of phrasal categories of same type
XP′ → . . . XP . . .	—phrasal categories are heads of maximal projection categories of same type
YP = { . . ., Y [PRED], XP'_{GR} [ARG] }	—maximal projections which are arguments of a predicate are sisters of lexical category denoting predicate and are annotated with GR's
YP′ = { . . ., YP, XP′ [MOD] }	—maximal projections which are modifiers of heads are attached as daughters of the maximal projection of the head (YP′)
XP → . . . X [stress] . . . . . . [lengthened] [falling f_0]	—head is stressed; phrase-final words are lengthened with falling fundamental frequency
[X(head) > YP′ (comp)] OR [YP′ (comp) > X(head)]	—head tends to precede or follow its complements consistently across phrases
S = { NP_{SUBJ} , VP }	—subject is daughter of S

FIGURE 12.11. Fragment of Prototype Network for Phrase Structure Rules:

$$\begin{bmatrix} 0 & .2 \\ 1 & .7 \\ 2 & .1 \end{bmatrix}$$

FIGURE 12.12. $YP \rightarrow \ldots X^p \ldots$

Once again, it is assumed that the parser tries to build standard representations for the input sentence, using variables when there is not enough information in the set of acquired rules to do so completely. For example, there would be a variable p standing for the level of projection of a category to be used when a rule is uncommitted as to level. In Figure 12.12 for instance, the hypothesis that the category X mentioned in the rule is a lexical category (X^0, or equivalently, X) has a strength of .2; the hypothesis that it is a first-projection phrasal category (XP, or X′, or X^1) has a strength of .7; and the hypothesis that it is a maximal projection phrasal category (XP′, or X″, or X^2) has a strength of .1. There could also be variables for directions of attachment (i.e., for adjacent phrases X and Y, a variable that stands for whether X is a daughter of some projection of Y, or vice versa) and for levels of attachment between adjacent phrases (i.e., whether X is a daughter of YP or of YP′). Patterns that match existing rules activate those rules and cause the corresponding tree to be built (normal parsing); patterns that match prototypes cause the matching prototype entries to adjust those variables in the ways specified in the prototypes. For example, in *John kissed the dog last Tuesday,* the predicate-argument semantic relation between *kiss* and *dog,* the falling intonation and lengthening of *dog,* and the head-modifier semantic relation between *kiss* and *last Tuesday* all conspire to group *the dog* with *kiss,* and to group *last Tuesday* with *kiss the dog*. Once such phrase groupings have been converted into the corresponding rules, the rules can be matched to future inputs by the parser, giving the groupings and inputs the opportunity to influence the formation of new phrase structure rules. For example, in the sentence *I detest the illegal dumping of trash,* the rule NP′ → det Adj NP would be matched by the sequence *the illegal . . .* (assuming the categorizations of those words had been acquired), and thus the rule would try to adjust the choice for mother of the phrase *dumping of trash* to be NP (perhaps resulting in the rule NP → VP[+gerund]).

What do we have so far? We have three cross-referenced networks of rule prototypes (of course, there would also be prototype networks for inflection, anaphora, and so on) plus whatever language-specific grammatical rules have been learned at a given point. They are all invoked by partial matches with underspecified input representations set up by the parser, and all try to exert an influence on the matching uncommitted variables in the input representation. The strength of the adjustment is proportional to the weights of the prototype rules or the strengths of the acquired rules. Any part of the network can act as premise or as conclusion; the order of activation of parts of the network depends on whatever the parser can match, which will in turn depend on a combination of what has been acquired, what parts of the prototype network can be matched in the absence of acquired rules (more on this later), and whatever input properties the child can tentatively identify through whatever perceptual mechanisms work. One must then make the following conjecture: *The constraints that are inherent in the innate prototype networks and the constraints that accumulate as language-specific rules are acquired are jointly sufficient to cause the system to converge to unique correct settings for all variables even in the face of noisy or misconstrued inputs and fallible first guesses.*

Up to this point I have not provided much reason to believe that this conjecture is true. Nor have I really provided a genuine model. All of the following mechanisms must be specified in some detail before one can begin to evaluate the viability of the constraint-satisfaction picture that I have sketched out: what sorts of uncommitted, variable-laden representations the parser can compute in the absence of learned rules; exactly how the pattern matching functions operate; the shapes of the learning curves; the notation for rule prototypes; what the prototype rules are and how many grammatical components have prototypes; and many other things.

Nonetheless, I think there are good reasons to believe that a model along these lines could be made to work. If so, what would be the consequences for the language bootstrapping debate? I conclude by spelling out these implications, but first briefly compare the present proposal with others in the language acquisition literature that superficially resemble it.

PROPERTIES OF THE CONSTRAINT SATISFACTION MODEL AND ITS RELATION TO OTHER MODELS

All too often, models of cognitive processes (especially computer simulation models) are presented in a "take-it-or-leave-it" fashion, without any unpacking of the theoretical assumptions that lie behind the model's successes or failures. Thus, it is important to state exactly what theoretical claims are being made in the class of models advocated here, so that the success of such a model, if any, can teach us something about language acquisition. It would also aid in comparing one model to another in order to search for consensus or to highlight differences. The constraint satisfaction model involves theoretical commitments along at least five independent dimensions which must be kept distinct in discussions of its implications and comparisons to other models.

One property of the model is that rules are assigned graded strength values and can be acquired in an incremental fashion. This might help to account for the slow and noisy nature of children's language acquisition in comparison to the quick and direct rule-formation processes of the LLLD model. However, *incre-*

mental learning of graded rules is one of the less interesting innovations in the current proto-model because it would be simple to add this feature to the earlier LLLD mechanisms to slow it down, leaving its basic mode of operation intact. There are two more radical modifications that define the core of the new approach. The first is the use of *multiple partially-informative cues* in learning, as opposed to single sufficient cues. The second is *multidirectional inference*, where premises and conclusions are not defined a priori, but any property in a family of correlated properties can be used to predict any other property so long as one of the properties can be activated by a match in an input.

As far as I can see, these three claims are independent of one another, and are also independent of *task-specificity*—whether the innate mechanisms are specific to language, as I have been assuming, or serve a variety learning tasks. Furthermore, each of these dimensions can apply either to models of how the child uses universal grammar to acquire particular grammars (the concern of this chapter) or to models of how the adult uses particular grammars to parse input sentences during sentence comprehension. One must be careful not to assume that the constraint satisfaction proto-model is equivalent to other models simply because they use graded rules or multiple partially-informative cues.

The "competition model" of Bates and MacWhinney (1982) also posits multiple cues in deciding, say, whether something is a subject, but it differs in significant ways from the present proposal. For one thing, there does not seem to be an analogue of multidirectional inference in their model. More important, they show prototypes for grammatical functions like "subject" *within individual adult grammars* which are used in a competition over how to interpret elements in input sentences during comprehension. For example, agents and topics are more likely to be interpreted as subjects when a sentence is processed by adults. In contrast, I am proposing that prototypes for rules involving subjects and the use of multiple partially-informative cues exist primarily at the level of universal grammar (and hence in the child's language acquisition mechanisms). They are used in the acquisition of rules pertaining to subjects in individual languages (for example, the child might posit that phrases expressing agents and topics should be assigned as "subjects" in the rules recording the ordering of those phrases). However, I argue that in the acquired grammar, "subject" is an autonomous formal category regardless of which cues were used to acquire it. In contrast to the proposal of Bates and MacWhinney, it makes little sense in my model to talk of some phrases in a given adult grammar as being "better" subjects than others; there is simply the "SUBJECT" symbol and rules that refer to it. (In the present model one can, of course, compare the "goodness" of subjects in one *language* to that in another. For example, English might be said to have more prototypical subjects than Dyirbal.) By restricting prototypes, family resemblance structures, and "goodness" of subjecthood to acquisition, rather than adult competence, the current proposal is consistent with the facts of English such as those exemplified in (1) where it was shown that rules like passivization apply indiscriminately to all subjects regardless of their semantic properties.[6]

Since both Bates and MacWhinney and I appeal to "prototypes," a distinction drawn in the literature on categorization can illustrate the differences between our approaches. Smith, Medin, and Rips (1984) and Armstrong, Gleitman, and Gleitman (1983) distinguish between gradedness or prototypicality effects that are relevant to the perceptual task of identifying an element as an exemplar of a category on the basis of its perceivable features and prototypicality or gradedness effects that are part of the core of the concept itself and which are used in inference. (Armstrong, et al. deny that there is evidence for the latter; see also Smith, et al. for discussion.) For example, it is easier to identify a gray-haired kindly woman than a youthful-looking woman as a grandmother, and it is easier to identify the number "3" as odd than the number "47," but in terms of reasoning, all mothers of parents are equally good grandmothers, and all numbers yielding a remainder of 1 when divided by 2 are equally odd. Likewise, I would maintain that phrases referring to agents are easier for the child to identify as subjects during learning than phrases referring to abstract arguments, but in terms of the "core" notion of subject that is relevant to the application of adult grammatical rules, all elements in subject positions or bearing subject affixes are equally good subjects.

A final issue in the construction of language acquisition models is the use of *symbol-manipulating* versus *connectionist architecture* (e.g., McClelland and Rumelhart, this volume). Though the model I am proposing involves constraint-satisfaction methods that are often easily effected in parallel connectionist architectures (Marr, 1982; Hinton and Anderson, 1983), it is important to note that the model uses traditional symbol-manipulating computations rather than direct connections among simple hardware units. That is, the interconnected units (in my case, rules, rule prototypes, and input representations) do not simply send an on-off signal or even a graded value to one another; articulated symbolic messages, which are decomposed at each end, are communicated and are crucial to the bottom-up and top-down pattern matching process. (It is only the adjustment process, subsequent to matching, that can get by with only the communication of a scalar value.) In developing this model I tried to see if it was possible to use the connectionist architecture of the sort advocated by Feldman (1982), McClelland and Rumelhart (1980; see also their contribution to this volume), and the contributors to Hinton and Anderson (1983). However, it proved virtually impossible to construct the model in this way. The problem was that the top-down and bottom-up pattern matching processes had to be sensitive to the internal structure of the input and the rule prototypes so that when a prototype was activated, it did not

[6]This is not to deny that there is competition among cues in the parsing of sentences: indeed, the existence of local and global ambiguities in parsing make competition virtually a logical necessity.

just strengthen the input structures willy-nilly. Rather, selected parts of the prototypes each had to strengthen their corresponding parts of the inputs. Indeed, this process of ''schema instantiation'' is considered to be one of the current deficiencies of connectionist models (J. McClelland, personal communication; see also McClelland, 1985, for an attempt to address the problem).

IMPLICATIONS OF CONSTRAINT SATISFACTION MODELS FOR LANGUAGE ACQUISITION THEORY

If a nativist constraint satisfaction model can be made to converge in psychologically plausible ways, several things would have been accomplished. Most important, one would have a solution to the problem of how the child acquires a formal, constrained rule system despite the perceptual opacity of the formal elements involved and without the problems that I raised against the ''smoking gun'' assumptions of the LLLD theory. Languages with marked syntax-semantics correspondences would be learnable if enough of the other members of the correlated families of phenomena were exemplified in the language and if some of those phenomena were identifiable perceptually or through the influence of cross-referenced rules in other components. The same is true for environments in which nonbasic sentences are presented early, or not identified as such by the child, or in which the nonlinguistic contexts of parental utterances are not redundant enough to ensure correct semantic interpretations. Learning would be multidirectional and opportunistic with every ounce of predictiveness being exploitable. Children could learn the language via slightly different paths depending on order of input, attention to different aspects of the input, and so on, but the constraints among cross-referenced rules inherent in the prototype networks would propel them all to a common destination.

Furthermore, if the constraint satisfaction model is viable, the language bootstrapping debate would be altered in three ways. First of all, suggestions about which perceptual cues the child uses (semantic, prosodic, word-order) could no longer be impugned by pointing to isolated counterexamples within English or in other languages. In principle, any perceptual input with nonzero cue validity could play a role in language acquisition by nudging a rule variable in the right direction more often than not and could even be sufficient to fix certain rules if there were enough of them pushing in the same direction.[7]

---

[7]For that matter, simplistic distributional properties such as word order and co-occurrence, much maligned earlier in this chapter and in Pinker (1984a), could have a role to play. Perhaps prototypes for phrase structure rules have associated with them templates standing for frequently adjacent words, which would strengthen to a certain degree any analysis that would lump those words into a phrase. Then the child's records of adjacent or cooccurring words could add their voice to the competition over which way to flesh out a rule. Because of the problems mentioned in the discussion of

Second, computer simulation would have a crucial role to play in evaluating the utility of perceptual cues in language acquisition. In an interactive, iterative model, it is virtually impossible to use hand-simulation to determine whether a given source of information is crucial or even helpful in acquiring rules. One would have to implement a network such as the one described above, and allow it to run under many ranges of assumptions about learning curves, types of information in prototype rules, prototype weights, input orders, input noise, and so on, to see what such a language acquisition model would be sensitive to. In the worst case, the model would behave in very different ways depending on different arbitrary choices of parameter values, but one can only tell by trying.

Third, I think that syntax-semantics correlations will continue to play a crucial role in the process of bootstrapping a grammar, but for slightly different reasons than those assumed in the LLLD model. In that model, semantic cues had special, designated roles as the triggers of rule-learning procedures as befit their status as perceptually available and linguistically diagnostic features. In a constraint satisfaction model, they are simply one out of a network of mutually predictive attributes. Nonetheless, since many of those attributes cannot be matched by inputs until a certain amount of learning has already taken place (for example, the fact that passives tend to be inflected, which must await the analysis of verbs as stems plus inflections), whereas recognizing many of the semantic features depends only on learning word meanings and perceptually categorizing events in coarse ways, the semantic information could continue to function in practice as the most important "seeds" that get the network started.

ACKNOWLEDGMENTS

Preparation of this manuscript was supported by NSF grant BNS 82-09450, by NIH grant 1 R01 HD18381 and by a grant from the Sloan Foundation to the MIT Center for Cognitive Science. I thank Edward E. Smith for helpful comments on an earlier draft.

REFERENCES

Anderson, J. R. (1977). Induction of augmented transition networks. *Cognitive Science, 1,* 125–157.

Anderson, J. R. (1983). *The architecture of cognition.* Cambridge, MA: Harvard University Press.

"correlational bootstrapping," this contribution would be given a low weight, and it would have an effect on formal phrase structure rules rather than yielding adjacency templates that would actually serve in the grammar. But conceivably there are circumstances in which their contribution would make a difference.

Armstrong, S. L., Gleitman, L. R., & Gleitman, H. (1983). What some concepts might not be. *Cognition, 13,* 263–308.
Attneave, F. (1982). Pragnanz and soap bubble systems: A theoretical exploration. In J. Beck (ed.) *Organization and representation in perception* 11-29 Hillsdale, NJ: Lawrence Erlbaum Associates.
Bickerton, D. (1981). *The roots of language*. Ann Arbor, MI: Karoma.
Bloom, L., Lightbown, P., & Hood, L. (1975). Structure and variation in child language. *Monographs of the society for research in child development,* 40.
Bobrow, D. G. & Winograd, T. (1977). An overview of KRL, a knowledge representation language. *Cognitive Science, 1,* 3–46.
Bowerman, M. (1973). *Early syntactic development: a cross-linguistic study with special reference to Finnish*. Cambridge: Cambridge University Press.
Bresnan, J. (1982). *The mental representation of grammatical relations*. Cambridge, MA: MIT Press.
Bretherton, I., McNew, S., Snyder, L., & Bates, E. (1983). Individual differences at 20 months: analytic and holistic strategies in language acquisition. *Journal of Child Language, 10,* 293–320.
Brown, R., & Hanlon, C. (1970). Derivational complexity and order of acquisition in child speech. In J. R. Hayes (Ed.), *Cognition and the development of language*. New York: Wiley.
Chomsky, N. (1970). Remarks on nominalization. In R. Jacobs and P. Rosenbaum (Eds.), *Readings in English transformational grammar*. Waltham, MA: Ginn.
Chomsky, N. (1981). *Lectures on government and binding*. Dordrecht, Netherlands: Foris.
Cooper, W. E. & Paccia-Cooper, J. (1980). *Syntax and speech*. Cambridge, MA: Harvard University Press.
Davis, L. S. & Rosenfeld, A. (1981). Cooperating processes for low-level vision: A survey. *Artificial Intelligence, 17,* 245–263.
Dixon, R. M. W. (1972). *The Dyirbal language of North Queensland*. Cambridge: Cambridge University Press.
Feldman, J. (1981). A connectionist model of visual memory. In G. E. Hinton & J. A. Anderson (Eds.), *Parallel models of associative memory*. Hillsdale, NJ: Lawrence Erlbaum Associates.
Gazdar, G., Klein, E., Pullum, G., & Sag, I. A. (1985). *Generalized phrase structure grammar*. Cambridge, MA: Harvard University Press.
Gleitman, L. R. & Wanner, E. (1982). *Richly specified input to language learning*. Unpublished manuscript, University of Pennsylvania.
Grimshaw, J. (1981). Form, function, and the language acquisition device. In C. L. Baker & J. J. McCarthy (Eds.), *The logical problem of language acquisition*. Cambridge, MA: MIT Press.
Hinton, G. E. and Anderson, J. A. (Eds.). (1981). *Parallel models of associative memory*. Hillsdale, NJ: Lawrence Erlbaum Associates.
Hochberg, J. & Pinker, S. (1987). *Syntax-semantics correspondences in parental speech*. Unpublished manuscript, MIT.
Hopper, P. J. & Thompson, S. A. (1980). Transitivity in grammar and discourse. *Language, 56,* 251–299.
Jackendoff, R. (1977). *X-bar syntax: A study of phrase structure*. Cambridge, MA: MIT Press.
Kaaret, P. (1984). *A computer simulation of the acquisition of inflection*. Unpublished manuscript, MIT.
Kaplan, R. M. & Bresnan, J. (1982). Lexical Functional Grammar: A formal system for grammatical representation. In J. Bresnan (Ed.), *The mental representation of grammatical relations*. Cambridge, MA: MIT Press.
Keenan, E. O. (1976). Towards a universal definition of "subject." In C. Li (Ed.), *Subject and topic*. New York: Academic Press.
Lasnik, H. (in press). On certain substitutes for negative data. In W. Demopoulos & R. May (Eds.), *Learnability and linguistic theory*. Dordrecht, Netherlands: Reidel.

Macnamara, J. (1972). Cognitive basis of language learning in infants. *Psychological Review, 79,* 1–13.

Macnamara, J. (1982). *Names for things: a study of child language.* Cambridge, MA: Bradford Books/MIT Press.

Maling, J. (1983). Transitive adjectives: A case of categorial reanalysis. In F. Heny & B. Richards (Eds.), *Linguistic categories: auxiliaries and related puzzles.* Dordrecht, Netherlands: Reidel.

Marantz, A. P. (1984). *On the nature of grammatical relations.* Cambridge, MA: MIT Press.

Maratsos, M. P., & Chalkley, M. (1981). The internal language of children's syntax: the ontogenesis and representation of syntactic categories. In K. Nelson (Ed.), *Children's language,* Vol. 2. New York: Gardner Press.

Marr, D. (1982). *Vision.* San Francisco: Freeman.

Marr, D. & Poggio, T. (1977). Cooperative computation of stereo disparity. *Science, 194,* 283–287.

McClelland, J. L. (1985). Putting knowledge in its place: A scheme for programming parallel processing systems on the fly. *Cognitive Science, 9,* 113–146.

McClelland, J. L. & Rumelhart, D. E. (1981). An interactive activation model of context effects in perception: Part 1: An account of basic findings. *Psychological Review, 88,* 375–407.

Morgan, J. & Newport, E. L. (1981). The role of constituent structure in the induction of an artificial language. *Journal of Verbal Learning and Verbal Behavior, 20,* 67–85.

Nelson, K. (1981). Individual differences in language development: Implications for development and language. *Developmental Psychology, 17,* 170–187.

Pinker, S. (1979). Formal models of language learning. *Cognition, 1,* 217–283.

Pinker, S. (1982). A theory of the acquisition of lexical interpretive grammars. In J. Bresnan (Ed.), *The mental representation of grammatical relations.* Cambridge, MA: MIT Press.

Pinker, S. (1984). *Language learnability and language development.* Cambridge, MA: Harvard University Press. (a)

Pinker, S. (1984). Visual cognition: An introduction. *Cognition,* 18, 1–63. (b)

Pinker, S., Lebeaux, D. S., & Frost, L. A. (1987). Productivity and constraints in the acquisition of passivization.

Slobin, D. I. (1977). Language change in childhood and in history. In J. Macnamara (Ed.), *Language learning and thought.* New York: Academic Press.

Slobin, D. I. (1986). Crosslinguistic evidence for the language-making capacity. In D. I. Slobin (Ed.), *The crosslinguistic study of language acquisition.* Hillsdale, NJ.: Lawrence Erlbaum Associates.

Smith, E. E., Medin, D. L., & Rips, L. (1984). Reply to Rey. *Cognition, 17,* 265–274.

Steele, S. (with Akmajian, A., Demers, R., Jelinek, E., Kitagawa, C., Oehrle, R., & Wasow, T.) (1981). *An encyclopedia of AUX: A study of cross-linguistic equivalence.* Cambridge, MA: MIT Press.

Ullman, S. (1979). Relaxation and constrained optimization by local processes. *Computer Graphics and Image Processing, 9,* 115–125.

Walsh, R. W. (1981). *A computer model for the acquisition of lexical interpretive grammar.* Unpublished Bachelor's thesis, Harvard University.

Waltz, D. (1975). Understanding line drawings of scenes with shadows. In P. H. Winston (Ed.), *The psychology of computer vision.* New York: McGraw-Hill.

Waterman, D. A. & Hayes-Roth, F. (1978). *Pattern-directed inference systems.* New York: Academic Press.

Wexler, K. & Culicover, P. (1980). *Formal principles of language acquisition.* Cambridge, MA: MIT Press.

13 Commentary: Mechanisms of Language Acquisition

Melissa Bowerman
Max Planck Institute for Psycholinguistics
Nijmegen, The Netherlands

Investigators who study language acquisition from widely different theoretical perspectives rarely talk to one another. This is unfortunate but understandable. In part, they are separated by their subject matters. Learnability theorists, along with other modern-day nativists who stress the role of children's innate linguistic endowment, have typically focused on abstract syntactic constraints that have no obvious connection to semantics or pragmatics. In contrast, their empiricist counterparts—researchers who emphasize the role of general learning heuristics—more often concentrate on aspects of language with clear functional correlates, such as morphology, word meaning, and the ordering of major sentence constituents. If they think about constructs like 'bounding node' or 'c-command' at all, they tend to view them with suspicion.

Investigators have also been divided by their attitudes toward child language data. Empiricists pay close attention in their theory construction to what children actually say and how their utterances change over time. Nativists are typically guided more by theoretical considerations of how the ultimate goal of learning must be described and what kind of learning system could arrive at this goal. Of course, it is not incidental to these postures that data bearing on the acquisition of morphology, word meaning, and word order is abundant in almost every transcript of spontaneous speech, whereas evidence relevant to children's grasp of subjacency, for example, is much harder to come by. But despite good reasons for differences in attitude toward child language data, each camp is impatient with the other—the one is criticized for engaging in abstract, intellectual exercises that have little relationship with what children actually do and the other is accused of seriously underestimating the discrepancy between the input available to the child and the complex and strongly constrained system that must be acquired.

This is at least how it has been in recent years. But the present volume, and the conference on which it is based, suggest the welcomed onset of a new phase of investigation in which researchers of diverse orientations begin to pay more attention to each others' work. Beneficial exchange has been encouraged by at least two developments. One is the increasing reliance of investigators of different theoretical persuasions on computer modelling of language acquisition. The demands of successful computer simulation force an explicitness about what is learned and how it is learned that brings underlying assumptions into the open and facilitates comparison and evaluation. The second development is the emergence of a small set of basic questions about language acquisition that investigators from very different research traditions can agree are important. To the extent that we are focused on the same problems, we can assess the adequacy of each others' attempts to solve them.

This discussion is organized around two such shared problems to which participants in the conference returned again and again.[1] First is the question of how children avoid ending up with an overly general grammar if they receive little feedback about what is not a possible sentence. Second is the puzzle of what drives *change* in children's grammars—what causes the learner to move from one level of knowledge or representation to the next. Given the range of strongly-held views on these and other topics represented at the conference, it is a tribute to the manners of the participants that they did not come to blows. There may be another, less complimentary reason for the general mood of good will: as Mike Maratsos rightly pointed out in discussion, the data are often compatible with everyone's position. One problem for the future will be to become more precise about what would or would not constitute counterevidence to particular proposed solutions. In the interests of promoting the necessary evaluations and revisions, I raise certain issues that I think present problems for just about everyone's theory.

WHY DON'T CHILDREN END UP WITH AN OVERLY GENERAL GRAMMAR?

The problem of how children avoid an overly general grammar was first raised in 1971 by Martin Braine, who used it to argue against the nativist position espoused by Chomsky and in favor of the idea that language is learned largely from scratch. It was later revived by Baker (1979) who, in an interesting turn-around,

[1]Some of the papers in this volume are naturally more concerned with these problems than others. Because the problems are so fundamental I have decided to go into them in some depth, which means, unfortunately, that I cannot discuss the many other interesting hypotheses and issues covered in these proceedings.

made it the cornerstone of the argument that children must be guided by innate constraints in their acquisition of language. That nativist theorists have been able to adapt Braine's puzzle to their own use suggests that the problem transcends party lines. Indeed, I believe it constitutes one of the most intriguing and difficult challenges for all students of language acquisition.

The Problem

According to Chomsky (1965), children construct an internalized grammar by using incoming language data, together with innate linguistic knowledge, to formulate hypotheses about possible grammatical rules. Braine pointed out that in order for a hypothesis-testing procedure to work, learners must get feedback about the correctness of their predictions. In particular, they need to know when their predictions are incorrect so that they can revise hypotheses that are *overgeneral*—that generate not only all acceptable sentences but ill-formed sentences as well. However, language learners get little negative feedback, argued Braine. He concluded that the hypothesis-testing approach cannot be right and that children must acquire language with procedures for which positive evidence (i.e., exposure to possible sentences) is sufficient.

Baker agreed with Braine that children receive little information about what is not a possible sentence and must be prepared to learn from positive evidence only. However, he argued that this situation is not damning to the innatist program in general, but only to grammatical frameworks that allow types of rules that children apparently could not acquire on the basis of the evidence available to them. Baker's proposal was to constrain linguistic theory so that it excludes such rules. Put differently, Baker suggested that children are constituted in such a way that they will not entertain any rule that, if incorrect, could not subsequently be corrected on the basis of positive evidence alone.

Since Baker's article, hypotheses about how to solve the "no negative evidence" problem have proliferated. I do not attempt a detailed critique of every proposal, but I raise some general problems that affect many of the approaches that are pursued in the chapters of this volume.

The Appeal to Subsets

Initial restriction to a subset. Several investigators have suggested solutions that exploit the fact that candidate grammatical rules, constraints, or parameters may stand in a subset-superset relation to each other. For example, Berwick (1985; Berwick & Weinberg, 1984) proposes that since learning must proceed from positive instances only, children must first hypothesize the *narrowest possible rule* compatible with the evidence observed so far. If the rule is too narrow, positive evidence (i.e., sentences in the input that the rule will not cover) will eventually reveal this to the learner, who then moves on to the next larger rule compatible with the data as he now perceives it. What the learner must not do is start with or ever hypothesize a rule that is too general, since in the absence of negative evidence there seems to be no way he could then cut back to the correct, more narrow rule. (See also Dell, 1981, for a general statement of this principle; Wexler and Manzini, in press, for an application to parameter-setting; and Smith, 1981, for an application to rules with semantic constraints.)

Fodor and Crain (this volume) rightly point out an unattractive corollary to this approach to the "no negative evidence" problem. When the output of one rule is a proper subset of the output of another rule, then the more narrow rule is typically more complex than the broader one since it is annotated for one or more constraints on application that the broader rule does not respect. This means that if children always start out by hypothesizing the narrowest rule possible, their first rules are routinely more complex than their later ones. But it clashes with our intuition to imagine that children move consistently from more complex to less complex rules—that language acquisition proceeds by the successive removal of constraints on rule application.

We do not have to rely on theoretical considerations alone to question the subset principle as a general solution to the "no negative evidence" problem. There are also empirical grounds for rejecting it: evidence, in the form of children's errors, that learners do *not* always start out with the most restrictive rule compatible with the evidence. Some sample errors are shown in Table 1; see also Mazurkewich and White, 1984, for comparable overgeneralizations in children's judgments of the grammaticality of sentences with "shifted" datives.[2]

An alternative: Cutting back to a subset. Aware of such errors, some investigators (e.g., Mazurkewich & White, 1984; Pinker, 1984, Chapter 8) have proposed another way of exploiting subset relationships among certain types of rules to solve the "no negative evidence" problem. According to this approach it is not essential to block overgeneralizations before they occur. Retreat from overgeneralization can be triggered later, where necessary, when the child discovers that all the lexical items observed to undergo a given rule in adult speech *share certain semantic, morphological, or phonological properties*. Once these properties are recognized (i.e., once the appropriate subset is identified) the child will limit productive use of the rule to lexical items of the right class and errors will cease.[3]

---

[2]Such errors also go counter to Baker's (1979) proposal for solving the "no negative evidence" problem: that children do not form general rules for regularities with lexical exceptions but wait to see, for every item, which syntactic frames it can appear in (see Bowerman, 1983).

[3]This approach might also be extended to more complicated situations, if they exist, where a rule applies not to a single subset of lexical items but to two or more disjunctively defined subsets. Of course, a critical question for this general approach is *how* children identify the properties shared by a subset of lexical items subject to a rule; for relevant discussion see Maratsos and Chalkley (1982), Pinker (1984) chapter 8, and my later section on "Does change take place on-line or off-line?"

TABLE 1
Some Overgeneralizations of Rules with Lexical Exceptions[a]

A. Dative Alternation		
1.	C 3;1	*I said her* no.
2.	C 2;6	Don't *say me* that, or you'll make me cry.
3.	C 2;6	I want Daddy *choose me* what to have. (Re: what kind of juice to have at breakfast.)
4.	M 5+	*Choose me* the ones that I can have.
5.	C 3;4	*Button me* the rest. (Request to have remaining snaps on her pyjamas fastened.)
6.	— 6;0	Mommy, *open Hadwen* the door. (Mazurkewich and White, 1984.)
7.	— 2;3	I'll *brush him* his hair. (Mazurkewich and White, 1984.)
B. Lexical Causatives. (The regularity to which the verbs below are exceptions is exemplified by intransitive/transitive pairs like *The stick broke/I broke the stick.*)		
8.	J 6+	Do you want to see us *disappear* our heads? (Then, with a friend, she ducks down behind couch.)
9.	—2;8+	I don't want any more grapes; they just *cough* me. (Braine, 1971.)
10.	R 5;9	I want to *comfortable* you. (R lying on sofa cuddling her mother.)
11.	E 3;0	Don't *giggle* me. (As father tickles her.)
12.	E 3;2	Will you *climb* me up there and hold me? (Wants mother to help her climb a pole.)
13.	C 3;6	Did she *bleed* it? (After her sister falls and hits head on edge of table.)
14.	C 4;3	It always *sweats* me. (Refusing sweater.)
15.	M 5;8	M: These are nice beds. Mother: Yes, they are. M: Enough to *wish* me that I had one of those beds.
C. Reversative *un-* prefixation.		
16.	E 3;11	How do you *unsqueeze* it? (Coming to mother with clip earring dangling from ear; wants it off.)
17.	E 3;10	Mother: I have to capture you. (Grabbing E in a game.) E: *Uncapture* me!
18.	C 4;7	C: I hate you! And I'm never going to *unhate* you or nothing! (Angry after request is denied.) Mother: You're never going to unhate me? C: I'll never like you.
19.	C 4;5	(C has asked mother why pliers are on table): Mother: I've been using them for straightening the wire. C: And *unstraighting* it?
20.	C 5;1	He tippitoed to the graveyard and *unburied* her. (Telling ghost story.)
21.	C 7;11	I'm gonna *unhang* it. (Taking stocking down from fireplace.)

[a]Child's age is given in years; months. Sources as indicated, plus Bowerman, 1983, for dative alternation; 1982a,b,c, 1983 for lexical causatives; 1982b for reversative *un*-prefixation.

For dative alternation, for example, the child must learn that "shiftable" indirect objects must be "prospective possessors" of the entity named by the direct object and that the verb itself must be of "native stock," not Latinate (Mazurkewich & White, 1984, drawing on Green, 1974; Stowell, 1981; among others). For causativization of an intransitive verb or adjective, the causation must be direct (e.g., physical), and the agent, manner, and goal of causation must be stereotypic or conventional for the act in question (Pinker, 1984, drawing on Shibatani, 1976; Gergeley & Bever, in press; among others). And for reversative *un-* prefixation, a "covert semantic class" identified by Whorf (1956) is relevant: verbs that can be *un*-ed share "a covering, enclosing, and surface-attaching meaning . . . hence we say 'uncover, uncoil, undress, unfasten, unlock, unroll, untangle, untie, unwind,' but not 'unbreak, undry, unhang, unheat, unlift, unmelt, unopen, unpress, unspill'" (p. 72).

Although this alternative approach to exploiting subsets has the advantage of allowing for overgeneralizations that children actually make, and although there is evidence that children are indeed capable of restricting a rule that is initially overly general to verbs of the "right" semantic class (see Bowerman, 1982b, on *un-* prefixation), I do not think it is the right answer to the "no negative evidence" problem, at least for rules with lexical exceptions. (I leave open whether it is the solution for rules or constraints of other kinds.) The problem is that many of the subsets associated with rules with lexical exceptions are themselves dotted with gaps: items that fully conform to the semantic/morphological restrictions on candidates for the rule, as best we can identify them, but that still do not undergo the rule.

For dative alternation, such an item is *choose*. Many speakers find something distinctly odd about "shifted" indirect objects with *choose,* as in "I chose you a book at the library sale."[4] Yet *choose* satisfies the putative semantic/morphological restrictions on verbs that allow dative alternation, since (a) it is of native stock and (b) the beneficiary of an act of choosing is the "prospective possessor" of the object named by the direct object. (Many speakers who regard "shifted" indirect objects with *choose* as unacceptable find them perfectly normal with *pick out,* which is semantically almost identical to *choose.*)

For *un-* prefixation, the verb *squeeze* is an inexplicable exception. You can squeeze somebody's hand but you can't **unsqueeze* it, even though *squeeze* falls into Whorf's covert class of "centripetal" verbs. (Note, for example, that you can both clench *and* unclench your teeth or fists; *squeeze* is similar to *clench* in specifying a continuous pressure toward a center point.)

---

[4]I base this claim on an informal survey of about 20 native speakers of English, most of whom rejected examples like these. Failure to find 100 percent agreement is not surprising: for every rule with lexical exceptions there are items about which speakers disagree or are uncertain. This is not important for my argument. As long as there are mature speakers who find such examples odd, we must explain how in their grammars the lexical item involved came to be excepted from the rule under examination.

For lexical causatives there are gaps in English like 'to **cough*/**laugh* /**comfortable*/**vomit* someone.' There seems to be no principled reason why a too-big bite can *choke* or *gag* us but not *cough* us, why we can *cheer* someone *up* but not *laugh* or *giggle* her (e.g., with tickling or a joke), and why we can *quiet* or *burp* a baby but neither *comfortable* (or *comfy*) her nor *vomit* her when she is nauseated (e.g., with a finger). The acts of causation specified by the latter verbs do not seem any less 'direct' or 'conventional' than those specified by the former.

Gaps like these—let's call them "negative exceptions"—have gone largely unnoticed in discussions of the "no negative evidence" problem. In contrast, *positive* exceptions—items to which a rule *does* apply even though they do *not* belong to the right class—have been widely discussed. Positive exceptions are generally regarded as tractable, since in principle they could be learned on the basis of positive evidence. For example, children could learn that *assign* allows dative alternation—even though it is Latinate—through hearing sentences like "The teacher assigned John a desk in the back row." However, there is no comparable evidence to mark *squeeze, choose, cough,* etc., as exceptions that *cannot* undergo rules whose conditions they otherwise satisfy. They are invisible holes within their subsets.

How do speakers identify such holes? How do children learn to stop constructing sentences with *unsqueeze,* '*choose* + indirect object', and causative *cough* (cf. Table 1)? It would be handy, of course, if we could invoke the principle of preemption. If every negative exception just happened to have an exact irregular counterpart, the way *foots* has a counterpart in *feet,* children would eventually give up their rule-governed form in favor of the form they consistently heard. Unfortunately, many negative exceptions lack such counterparts—e.g., there are no forms that preempt *unsqueeze,* '*choose* + indirect object', and causative *cough,* nor do phrasal alternatives always do the trick. (I come back to this in more detail in the next subsection.)

Perhaps, however, there really are no "negative exceptions." Steve Pinker (personal communication) suggests that where there appear to be such exceptions, we might simply have failed to adequately pin down the semantic/morphological/phonological constraints on the class of items that can undergo a rule. This raises an important question about the nature of the lexicon. The regularities reflected in the errors shown in Table 1 should, according to Pinker and many other investigators currently interested in the "no negative evidence" problem, be characterized as lexical rules, not as syntactic transformations. (And *un-* prefixation is a lexical rule under almost everyone's treatment.) Do there have to be systematic principles governing which lexical items do and do not undergo a lexical rule? No, according to Wasow (1977):

> I assume that if a tree satisfying the structural conditions of a transformation is prohibited from undergoing the structural change, then some explanation is called

> for, but a lexical item that *does not undergo a lexical rule whose conditions it satisfies is perfectly normal.* Transformations are crucial to the generation of all and only the sentences of the language (and hence have infinite domains); in contrast, lexical rules express subregularities within a finite lexicon . . . Hence, I assume (following Jackendoff, 1975) that lexical rules . . . *will typically have unsystematic exceptions.* (p. 331, emphasis added)

Unsystematicity in lexical rules is of course recognized by most theorists; in fact this has been one important basis for arguing that certain regularities should be handled in the lexicon rather than in the syntactic component of grammar. However, as I have noted, investigators concerned with the "no negative evidence" problem have worried about only one kind of unsystematicity: items that *do not* satisfy the conditions on a rule and yet *do* undergo the rule. There seems to be no reason to rule out the opposite kind of unsystematicity: items that *do* satisfy the conditions and yet *do not* undergo the rule. I believe that Wasow's view of the lexicon is correct and that no matter how hard we try to pin down the conditions that correlate with the candidacy of lexical items to undergo a given rule we are always going to be able to find unexplained negative exceptions as well as positive ones.

If so, children must have techniques for identifying them. And if they do have such techniques, they could presumably apply them directly to *all* lexical items to which a rule has been overgeneralized, rather than first eliminating some items through discovery of the appropriate subset before bringing in stronger methods to detect any remaining stragglers. In sum, it is not clear that children's discovery of semantic/morphological/phonological subsets plays any necessary role in their retreat from an overly general grammar—although, of course, their identification of such subsets is an interesting phenomenon in its own right (see Bowerman, 1982b), and it raises interesting issues for the problem of what drives change in children's grammars, as discussed later.

Preemption

Almost every investigator who worries about the "no negative evidence" problem has assumed that at least part of the answer lies in preemption: when children formulate overly general rules, they eventually give up overgeneralized forms if they are consistently faced with positive evidence for other forms expressing the same meanings. For example, a child with general rules for forming plural and past tense forms will for a time say *foots* and *breaked*. However, in the contexts where she uses these forms she hears only *feet* and *broke* from others. Eventually, therefore, she abandons her own forms in favor of those that are conventional. Baker (1979) called rule exceptions that could be corrected in this way "benign" exceptions; in contrast, exceptions for which there is no exact irregular counterpart he termed "embarrassing."

How does preemption work? Investigators differ in their assumptions about why children give up their rule-governed forms in the face of evidence for conventional alternatives. On one side are theorists who propose that there is some property "in the child" that rejects the idea that two forms should have exactly the same meaning. For example, Pinker (1984) postulates a "Unique Entry" principle, according to which children resist having more than one entry in an inflectional or derivational paradigm (e.g., both *breaked* and *broke;* both 'to *die* (someone)' and 'to *kill* (someone)'. Clark (this volume) proposes a more general "Principle of Contrast," according to which children assume that every two forms differ in meaning, and resist acquiring or retaining two forms that seem synonymous unless they are faced with strong positive evidence that both forms exist.

In contrast to those who rely on some version of Uniqueness or Contrast, "competition" or "connectionist" theorists (MacWhinney & Sokolov, Bates & MacWhinney, Rumelhart & McClelland, all in this volume) explain preemption as the outcome of *competition* among alternative forms for expressing the same meaning. According to this approach, children do not come with any built-in assumptions about whether or not forms should contrast in meaning, or how many entries a cell in a paradigm should have. They simply use the forms that they associate with the meanings they want to express. At some point in the acquisition of an inflectional or derivational paradigm children may have several forms for the same meaning (e.g., *breaked, broke, broked*), and use them all. Over time, however, the activation strength of some forms increases and that of others decreases, both as a function of what the learner says and what he hears from others. Eventually the forms heard consistently from fluent speakers become so strong that they overwhelm the child's overregularized forms, and these weakened competitors fade out.

How shall we evaluate these two assumptions about how preemption works? This seems to be one of those situations alluded to earlier, where much of the available evidence is compatible with either view; where it is not, there are persuasive arguments either way (compare, for instance, Clark, this volume with Gathercole, to appear).

For example, we might assume that if childen start out with the expectation that two forms should not have the same meaning—and especially that there should not be two entries for a single cell in a paradigm—they should not use forms like *breaked* and *broke* or *bringed, brang,* and *brought* all interchangeably in the same speech context. They ought to decide on one and reject the others. But such alternation is in fact common (e.g., Kuczaj, 1977; Maratsos, 1979). This looks on the face of it like grist for the competition mill. However, Clark (this volume, note 8) argues that "instances of over-regularization may well linger on after children have begun to produce the appropriate, irregular past tense forms just because children have become used to saying the past-tense form of a verb that way. After all, they have been doing so for three or four years."

Thus, alternation between regular and irregular forms is interpretable on either account.

A point against Clark's interpretation and in favor of the competition account is that the simultaneous embrace of more than one form for the same meaning does not seem to be limited to spontaneous speech. Kuczaj (1978) found that when young children are asked to judge the acceptability of (for example) *eated, ate,* and *ated* as past tense versions of *eat,* they often find two or more forms equally acceptable. This outcome cannot be explained by appeal to automated routines for speaking. If the Uniqueness/Contrast approach were correct, we would expect that children should accept only *one* form for any given meaning.

However, the balance between the two approaches is again righted when we consider the following problem: where do intuitions of ungrammaticality come from? According to the competition account, the decline of *breaked, foots,* and the like is a matter of gradually decreasing activation strength. Presumably, activation strength never hits zero, since even adults occasionally produce forms like these and they certainly hear them from children. Where in the downhill slide of *breaked* and *foots* do these forms pass over the boundary from being possible but simply less robust instantiations of the notions of '*break* + PAST' and '*foot* + PLURAL' to being actively rejected as ungrammatical and unacceptable? (Note, for example, that adults and even relatively young children often correct such "slips" in their own speech when they detect them; see Clark, 1978.) Why should there be any such thing as a sense of ill-formedness, as opposed to simply a feeling of "low likelihood"? I do not know what the competition theorist's answer to this problem is. But clearly advocates of Uniqueness/Contrast have no trouble with it.

How much can preemption account for? Although it is not clear *how* preemption by existing forms works, I do not dispute that it does work. But how much of the "no negative evidence" problem can it handle? In general, I have the impression that investigators are often oversanguine about its potential.

A precondition for preemption is that for a child's overgeneralized word or construction there must exist a conventional adult counterpart that means what the child's form means and that occurs consistently in the contexts in which the child would use her own form. This precondition is met in most cases of inflectional overgeneralization. However, it is only spottily met in the case of overgeneralizations of derivational morphology and other lexical rules (e.g., *un*-prefixation, dative alternation, causativization; see Bowerman, 1983), and as Fodor and Crain (this volume) point out, it is not met at all for certain important syntactic phenomena, including extraction ("There is no well-formed competitor, for instance, for the ungrammatical sentence **Who did John overhear the statement that Mary kicked*?")

The notion of "preemption" is somewhat flexible, and several researchers have suggested what amounts to stretching it to cover certain otherwise problematic overgeneralizations. For example, Clark (this volume) suggests that children will give up their overgeneralized causative form 'to *disappear* (something)' (which lacks an exact suppletive counterpart) in favor of 'to *make* (something *disappear*', since in every context where they would say the former, they hear adults say the latter.

A stretch is involved here because *make disappear* is not a perfect semantic match to causative *disappear* (as *kill,* for example, is to causative *die*). In general, lexical causatives and their periphrastic counterparts differ with respect to the directness and conventionality of the act of causation specified (compare, for example, *John stood the baby up* [direct physical causation] with *John made the baby stand up* [indirect causation, e.g., through giving an order]). The weight of this meaning distinction, pervasive throughout English, ought to work somewhat against children's willingness to let periphrastic causatives like *make disappear* preempt nonexistent lexical causatives like *disappear*. Still, we might be willing to accept this solution, if only for lack of a better idea. (See also Pinker, 1981; Maratsos & Chalkley, 1982; and Bowerman, 1983 for the related proposal that children may identify items that are exceptions to their overly general rules through continually failing to encounter those items in discourse contexts where they "expect" them; this is sometimes called "indirect negative evidence," following Chomsky, 1981:9.)

But this extended view of preemption buys us only a little more help with the "no negative evidence" problem, not a cure. For the approach to work, there must at least be a *consistent relationship* between the child's overgeneralized form and an adult counterpart, even if that counterpart is not identical in meaning to the overgeneralization it will eventually come to replace. This condition is indeed met with causative *disappear* and its periphrastic counterpart. But what about, for example, errors with reversative *un-*? Here the child meets with no consistent alternatives in the adult input. For instance, in contexts where *unsqueeze* would be appropriate, if it existed, adults might say *loosen, ease up, release, let go, remove,* and so on. None of these is in direct semantic competition with *unsqueeze,* since none of them specifies or requires that the event referred to is the reversal of an act of "squeezing." Nor should the child take the existence of such forms as having any bearing on the possibility of *unsqueeze*: reversative *un-* forms coexist harmoniously with various related constructions, e.g., *unwrap* and *take the wrapper off, unzip* and *pull the zipper down, unload* and *empty*.

For overgeneralizations of the type shown in Table 2, the problem is even more complicated. This construction pattern is highly productive in English to express combinations of a causing event and a resulting change of state or location, but it is subject to constraints that are still poorly understood (Green, 1972; McCawley, 1971; Randall, 1983). How do children come to appreciate that there are any restrictions at all, much less what these restrictions are?

The difficulty is that novel utterances of this type, whether acceptable or

TABLE 2
Overgeneralizations of the 'Effect Complement' Sentence Pattern[a]

(The models for overgeneralizations of this type include shoot dead, pat dry, wipe clean, eat (oneself) into a stupor, pull up/ down/in/out, etc., *cut off/down,* etc.)		
1. C	3;8	I *pulled* it *unstapled.* (After pulling stapled booklet apart.)
2. C	3;10	*Untie* it *off.* (Wants mother to untie piece of yarn and take it off tricycle handle.)
3. C	4;0	I'm *patting* her *wet.* (Patting sister's arm after dipping her own hand into a glass of water.)
4. E	6;3	His doggie *bited* him *untied.* (Telling how tied-up man in a T.V. show was freed.)
5. M	5;6	Are you *washing* me *blind*? (As mother wipes corners of her eyes.)
6. M	5;10	Feels like you're *combing* me *baldheaded.* (As mother combs her hair.)
7. A	4;3	When you get to her, you *catch* her *off.* (A is on park merry-go-round with doll next to her. Wants a friend, standing nearby, to remove doll when it comes around to her.)
8. R	4;9	I'll *jump* that *down.* (About to jump on bath mat M has just put on top of water in tub.)

Sources: Bowerman, 1982b,c.

peculiar to adult ears, are usually "one time only" constructions—designed to fit a certain passing configuration of cause and effect such as pulling on a book and the book's becoming unstapled, or combing the hair and becoming bald. This means that learners do not have the opportunity to observe "the way other people express this particular meaning." Even if a particular configuration of cause and effect should arise quite frequently (say, "untying a rope" so that it "comes off" of something, as in example 2), so that a child has a chance to hear other ways of expressing it (e.g., "untie the rope and take it off," "take the rope off by untying it," or just plain "take the rope off"), these alternatives have no bearing on the grammaticality of the child's version. As Fodor and Crain (this volume) point out, a learner cannot take every sentence he hears as precluding all sentences that express somewhat related messages; natural languages are too rich for this.

To summarize, children make a number of overgeneralizations for which preemption, even if interpreted liberally, fails to provide a correction. This is a problem for everyone, but I think especially for the competition approach to language acquisition. This is because this model explicitly rejects the need for innate linguistic constraints on the child, and instead tries to solve the "no negative evidence" problem by reference to the successful resolution of competition between alternative ways to express the same meaning.[5] To the extent that

[5]This resolution can come about either by automatic adjustment of the relative activation strengths of overgeneralized and conventionally correct forms or by children's detection of discrepancies between the way they express a given meaning and the way others express it; see MacWhinney et al., this volume.

"alternative ways" do not battle it out—either because all of them normally coexist happily or because the particular message to be expressed is so rare that alternatives are never modeled—the child seems to be left with a rampant capacity for overgeneralization and very little to keep it in check.

Innate Constraints

Fodor and Crain (this volume) and Roeper (this volume) propose handling the "no negative evidence" problem by appeal to innate knowledge, although they do this in different ways.

Formal knowledge. Fodor and Crain's approach is to equip the child with a "metalanguage" for constructing grammatical rules. This metalanguage constrains learners in such a way that they hypothesize only very narrow phrase structure rules that are justified by the data already observed. If two narrow rules are formally related, they can be collapsed to create a single, broader rule. However, the broader rule is based on fully instantiated, narrower rules, so children will not make syntactic overgeneralizations.

Fodor and Crain recognize that children produce lexical overgeneralizations of the types shown in Table 1. They suggest that these might be dealt with through preemption. In essence, then, they assume that syntactic and lexical overgeneralizations are inherently different, with the former requiring prevention and the latter being amenable to correction.

I have argued earlier that preemption, along with "retreat to a subset," is insufficient to correct many errors involving lexical exceptions and that children must have other techniques for retreating from overly general rules of these types. Whatever these techniques are, it is possible that they can also be applied to overly general syntactic rules, which would make it unnecessary to constrain the child at the outset. However, children seem to make fewer syntactic than lexical overgeneralizations, and Fodor and Crain present some reasons for doubting even those syntactic ones that have been documented. So it may be desirable after all to somehow constrain children from the beginning in their construction of syntactic rules.

The success of Fodor and Crain's approach will hinge critically on how they spell out their notion of "rule collapsing" beyond its schematic introduction in this volume. Their problem will be to define the circumstances under which rule collapsing takes place in such a way that the new, broader rules can never accidently be too broad. What kinds of sentence representations will children rely on to determine "formal relatedness" between rules? Description at the level of the actual sentences instantiated in the input is clearly too limited, but the moment that more abstract representations are brought in (e.g., $VP \rightarrow V$; $VP \rightarrow V + NP$, as in a hypothetical example by Fodor and Crain), there is the risk that rule collapsing will result in overly powerful rules. I look forward to more concrete proposals from Fodor and Crain about the level of representation at which all the desired generalizations can be captured without concomitant overgeneration.

Substantive knowledge. In this volume and elsewhere, Roeper proposes that children's grammars are held in check by knowledge of substantive principles of grammar. His specific hypotheses are rather complex, and each one requires separate evaluation (for example, see Smith, 1981 for a careful consideration of proposals in Roeper, 1981). Without going into too much detail, I would like to suggest that at least one of the hypotheses he puts forward in this volume may be vulnerable to a criticism I raised earlier for the "retreat to subset" approach.

According to Roeper, children know, without having to learn it, that although they can say things like (1a) *the city's destruction* they should not say things like (1b) **the play's enjoyment*. (1a) is allowed while (1b) is not because children have innate knowledge that only "affected objects" can be preposed in nominalizations. (This follows from more complex considerations about the establishment of case; see Roeper's discussion, this volume.)

This constraint has the effect of defining a subset within which nominalization can comfortably operate: nominalizations of the form "the X's Y" are all right as long as X specifies an affected object. Any positive exceptions could be learned from positive evidence, e.g., possibly "*China's recognition* by the United States," where China is not in any clear sense an "affected object." But what about negative exceptions, as discussed earlier? Such "invisible holes" include **John's hitting* (=the hitting of John), **the wine's drinking* (=the drinking of the wine) and **the hair's brushing* (=the brushing of the hair). Here, the preposed nouns are clearly "affected objects," yet the constructions are felt to be strange.

To be sure, Roeper could point to some differences between negative exceptions like **John's hitting* and acceptable nominalizations with gerunds like *John's trouncing* (=the trouncing of John) and *John's mugging* (=the mugging of John): the more strongly established the verb-*ing* form is as an independent noun, the better the construction sounds. However, these distinctions are not specified in the innate constraint proposed by Roeper. Unless he can find a principled solution (one that does not, as an accidental byproduct, rule out perfectly acceptable constructions in languages other than English), I am inclined to think that whatever techniques children use to determine the ungrammaticality of negative exceptions like **John's hitting* they can also apply to items like **the play's enjoyment*. If so, Roeper's innate constraint on what can be preposed would be unnecessary.

Does the "No Negative Evidence Problem" Really Exist?

In view of the difficulties I have raised for various approaches to the "no negative evidence" problem, the reader might wonder by now whether children must not receive negative feedback after all. Several investigators have argued that they do, probably not in the form of explicit corrections but as misunderstandings, requests for clarification, repetitions, and recastings (e.g., Hirsch-Pasek, Treiman & Schneiderman, 1984; Demetras & Post, 1985). But I do not think the answer lies in this direction for the following reasons.

First, researchers who argue that children do get negative evidence from their speaking partners do not, in the studies I have seen, distinguish in the necessary way among responses to different categories of ungrammaticality on the child's part. Whenever negative feedback is observed for child utterances that are imperfect by adult standards, it is indiscriminately taken to count against the seriousness of the "no negative evidence" problem. But most of this feedback is simply irrelevant.

Many utterances, especially among younger children, are ungrammatical not because the speaker's rules are overly general but because the speaker hasn't yet constructed the necessary rules at all. (Omissions of grammatical morphemes are a case in point.) Adult misunderstandings, recastings and the like might or might not hasten rule construction in these cases, but they do not bear on the problem of how children cut back on overly general rules. Even when such feedback does follow upon errors resulting from overly general rules, these errors often involve "benign" rule exceptions, which, as noted earlier, can in principle be corrected *without* negative feedback. I do not know how much negative evidence remains after we eliminate these two types of irrelevant feedback, but I suspect it is not very much, especially since overgeneralizations of the types discussed in this chapter are produced by relatively old children and rarely cause misunderstanding (as noted also by Mazurkewich and White, 1984).

Second, listener misunderstandings, requests for clarification, repetitions, and recasts are not reliably diagnostic of ungrammaticality on the speaker's part: they follow well-formed utterances as well as those that are ungrammatical (Hirsch-Pasek et al., 1984; Demetras & Nolan, 1985). If a child's first impulse on hearing such responses is to question the adequacy of her grammar, she would continually be trying to revise perfectly acceptable rules. It seems unlikely that children are so readily led astray. Even if a child does on occasion question her grammar, only recasts give any information about where the problem lies—misunderstandings, repetitions and "what" questions are silent about what is wrong.

In sum, I conclude that the "no negative evidence" problem is not a myth, but a real and serious challenge for the construction of an adequate theory of language acquisition. I do not think this challenge has yet been satisfactorily met, but investigators are getting more ingenious in their ideas about it all the time.

WHAT DRIVES CHANGE IN CHILDREN'S GRAMMARS?

For many years a typical goal of research on children's developing grammars has been to provide a series of descriptions of what a child knows about language at successive stages of development. This goal was in part encouraged by the "grammar-writing" methodology that dominated the field in the mid-'60s and early '70s: a grammar is in essence a static portrait of a linguistic system at a single point in time. The goal of successive descriptions is now making way for a new set of concerns, as investigators, many of them inspired by the demands of computer simulation of language acquisition, struggle to identify the factors that lead to *change* in children's grammars.

Failure-Driven Determinants of Change

According to Berwick (this volume), change takes place when the child's current grammar cannot parse an incoming string. If the string can be successfully parsed, the grammar remains as it was. MacWhinney et al. (this volume) sketch a more comprehensive set of circumstances under which change can take place, but, like Berwick's (and like Wexler & Culicover's, 1980; see Berwick, this volume) their approach is essentially failure-driven. For example, change takes place when the child reaches an impasse in comprehending or producing a sentence, or when the child's monitoring system detects a discrepancy between the way the child would express a given message and the way it is expressed in an incoming string.

Failure-driven mechanisms are surely necessary to account for the child's progression to a full adult grammar, but it seems unlikely that they are enough. Karmiloff-Smith (1979a,b, 1986) and I (Bowerman, 1982b,c, 1985) have both documented the emergence of errors that seem to reflect changes taking place in children's grammatical systems long after the learners are fully capable of parsing incoming sentences of the sorts in question, and are producing sentences that are indistinguishable from those of adults. These errors often suggest that the speaker has discovered relationships among lexical items that were not previously seen as related, or deep regularities linking grammatical subsystems that were earlier represented independently of each other in the learner's developing grammar. These relationships and regularities are sufficiently abstract that children do not need to be sensitive to them in order to understand others or to construct their own perfectly adequate sentences. What drives them on to find structure in language when that structure has no direct consequences for their ability to use language fluently?

A further problem for which failure-driven mechanisms do not provide enough help is how children cut back on overly general rules. If a child has formulated such a rule, he is capable of parsing or generating every utterance of the relevant type he will hear from adults, so no further change would be expected (except in cases where there is a preempting adult form). This is why Berwick (1985; Berwick & Weinberg, 1984) relies so heavily on the subset principle: within a model that makes changes only upon parsing failure, it is critical that the child should never formulate an overly general rule, since he would never be able to correct it. But, as discussed earlier, children do formulate overly general rules that cannot be corrected by preemption. These are also a problem for MacWhinney et al.'s competition model, since when there is no conventional adult counterpart for a child's overgeneralization, the child's monitor can detect no mismatch and hence sees no reason to make a change.

In sum, change mechanisms that bring about only accurate parsing and adult-sounding utterances are not enough. Our theory of language acquisition is going to have to explain what causes grammars to change even when children receive no overt evidence that there is anything wrong with their current grammars.

Does Change Take Place On-line or Off-line?

Failure-driven mechanisms of language acquisition spring into action when the child is having trouble processing an incoming sentence or producing one himself, or when he detects a mismatch between his own utterance and an adult utterance. Let us term this the "on-line" theory of change: change takes place when the child is actually *using* language. This approach is particularly compatible with acquisition theories based on computer modeling, since computer programs require some clear-cut stimulus to jolt the grammar that is being constructed out of its current state and into a new one.

The on-line theory may be contrasted with another approach that for years has been assumed implicitly by the many researchers who view language acquisition as the construction of a grammar by a cognitively active, involved child. This is the idea that children (unconsciously) compare forms, extract regularities, and deepen their analyses "off-line," such that their grammars continue to develop even when they are not using them to process or produce speech. This approach is quite comfortable with evidence that children's grammars become more differentiated, better integrated, and more abstract even when children meet with no overt indications of trouble. (Of course, off-line theorists would not deny that change can take place on-line as well.)

Several authors in the present volume explicitly criticize the idea of off-line processing in language acquisition. For example, Fodor and Crain reject the hypothesis that children compute *nonoccurrences* of constructions their rules would predict on grounds that there is no plausible evolutionary reason why children should engage in this labor "on the side," when they are not actually exercising their rules to comprehend or to speak. And both Braine's and Fodor and Crain's chapters (this volume) criticize Pinker (1984) for assuming that children engage in complex, off-line surveying and analysis of inflectional and derivational paradigms. Braine argues that it is unlikely that children have the requisite long-term memory with a self-editing capability for carrying out such analyses, and Fodor and Crain don't see "why human beings should be designed to go to all this trouble, given that languages would be just as learnable without it as long as all generations of learners abjured it equally."

Although my own work on language acquisition clearly falls into the off-line camp, I must confess to growing discomfort with our collective difficulty in casting off-line hypotheses in more precise terms that would explain exactly how, when, and why change takes place in the child's system. When Herb Clark, despite my best efforts at defense, suggested that we should call the off-line approach the "theory of immaculate conception," the joke hit too close to home for comfort.

Two solutions for the problem seem possible. One is that more rigorous theories will be developed that fill in the missing details about when and how changes take place off-line in a child's language system (see Karmiloff-Smith, 1986, for a start on such a theory). The other is that the off-line approach is in fact wrong, and that all children's language processing does take place in the context of using language.

If the off-line approach is wrong, any on-line approach that replaces it should be sensitive to those aspects of language development that failure-driven, on-line approaches have typically ignored. I think the parallel distributed processing model discussed by Rumelhart and McClelland (this volume) might have promise in this respect. The advantage of this model is that it provides a mechanism, spreading activation, that allows relatively remote corners of the child's grammar to be "contacted" and brought into communication with each other while the child is actually only engaged in comprehending or trying to produce a single utterance. This means that the processes described by off-liners in terms of the child's "comparing of related forms" can take place more or less automatically as the child uses language. Let me try to suggest how this mechanism might account for a kind of learning that failure-driven, on-line approaches have trouble with: the child's gradual restriction of productive prefixation with reversative *un-* to the class of verbs sharing a "centripetal" meaning (covering, enclosing, surface-attaching, etc.).[6]

According to a parallel distributed processing explanation, every time the child hears or uses a particular verb prefixed with *un-*, all the other *un-* verbs in her vocabulary are activated as well, although more weakly. Let us assume that the child's lexical entries for "legitimate" verbs like *uncover* and *untie* contain features like [+reversative] (for the *un-* segment) and [+centripetal] (for the base verb). In this case each time the child hears or uses an *un-* verb, all these entries are activated and the connection between the features [+reversative] and [+centripetal] has an opportunity to get strengthened. Assuming that *un-* verbs of the right semantic class predominate in the child's lexicon (even though she

[6]Failure-driven on-line mechanisms are insufficient here for two reasons: (1) the child who is not yet sensitive to the associated semantic class can still parse and understand any verb prefixed with *un-* that she meets in the input, and (2) she will not be able to detect her own errors, since, as noted earlier, *un-* errors do not compete with preempting forms in adult speech. Negative evidence is also not the answer. Any explicit corrections, misunderstandings, etc. from adults would presumably be general across all children's errors with *un-* prefixation. This feedback cannot explain why errors involving verbs of the "wrong" semantic class (e.g., *unhate, unstraight(en),* die out while those with verbs of the "right" class continue unabated for a time (Bowerman, 1982b).

may have stored a few odd items of her own, like *unhate;* cf. Table 1), this connection will eventually get so strong that novel words constructed with *un-* will respect it, i.e., reversative *un-* will not be selected together with a verb that lacks the feature [+centripetal].

This account can in principle explain children's ability to home in on covert semantic, morphological, or phonological classes associated with particular rules. But it comes with a high cost. For the process to work, each lexical item would have to be entered into the child's mental lexicon tagged ahead of time with all the features that could possibly be relevant, in any language, to a semantically, morphologically, or phonologically constrained rule involving such a lexical item. Otherwise there would be no assurance that the activation process would contact and strengthen the features that are relevant to a particular rule in the particular language the child happens to be learning. But the number of such "possibly relevant" features, even if finite, is surely vast. It seems unlikely that children routinely mark their lexical items for the entire universal set (see also Pinker, 1984:168–171, who presents strong evidence that children do *not* engage in exhaustive *a priori* marking of this kind in the acquisition of inflections).

More plausible is that children enter at least some features into their lexical representations on the basis of evidence that these features are important in their language. But if this is so, parallel distributed processing loses much of its explanatory power and we are left with the same puzzle as before: how does the child identify these features as important if they are not present ahead of time to be strengthened through repeated activation?

The parallel distributed processing account would also, I think, have trouble with rules that are *negatively* constrained, i.e., that can apply *unless* such-and-such a condition obtains. For example, one of the constraints on "effect-complement" sentences of the type shown in Table 2 is that, as Green (1972) has pointed out, the "effect" must not be expressed with a past participle (compare, for example, *She combed her hair SMOOTH* and **She combed her hair UNTANGLED; She cooked the roast DRY* and **She cooked the roast BURNED/OVERDONE*).[7] When a constraint involves something that existing instantiations of a rule do *not* have rather than something they *do* have, this property would not get activated during use of the rule. How could it then get strengthened and come to participate in a block against novel words or sentences that do have that property?

In summary, the opposition between on-line and off-line approaches has yet to be resolved. Both have their strengths and weaknesses, and both may ultimately play necessary roles in an adequate theory of language acquisition. But the work of comparing the approaches has barely begun. From my own perspective, I would especially like to encourage on-line theorists to inspect acquisitional

[7]*Closed* and *shut* seem to be the only exceptions to this constraint (cf. Green, 1972).

phenomena that seem resistant to treatment within failure-driven and possibly also activation frameworks.

The Child as Sleuth: In Pursuit of Elusive Meaning Distinctions

As a final problem for our theory of what brings about change in children's grammars, let us consider what happens when a child is confronted with two forms that seem to have the same meaning. According to Clark's (this volume) Principle of Contrast, discussed earlier, the child should immediately begin trying to figure out how these words differ. If she finds a difference, all is well. If she cannot find a difference but only one of the forms is actually attested in the input (e.g., the other form is an overregularization produced only by her), she throws out the nonattested form and keeps the one she hears. Finally, if she cannot find a difference but both forms are clearly attested, she concludes (reluctantly, one imagines) that in this exceptional case there simply are two forms with the same meaning. Pinker's (1984) Unique Entry principle works similarly but for the more limited case of multiple entries competing for the same cell in an inflectional or derivational paradigm.

Each outcome is appropriate for some situations. For example, a child who at first thinks that 'to *break* something' and 'to *make* something *break*' are synonymous eventually discovers that they differ with respect to the directness, conventionality, etc., of the act of causation they specify (Bowerman, 1982a,c; Pinker, 1984:335–338). A child faced with *goed* and *went* eventually gets rid of *goed* since he or she doesn't hear evidence for it in the input. And a child who continually hears both *dived* and *dove* comes to accept both of them as instantiations of *dive* + PAST.

Now, the problem is this: When faced with uncontrovertable evidence in the input for two apparently synonymous forms, how do children know whether they should carry on in their attempt to discover a meaning difference or whether positive evidence entitles them to conclude that in this case there are two forms with the same meaning? More concretely, how do they know whether this is a case like causative *break* and *make break* or a case like *dived* and *dove*? This is an important question because the child's "decision" determines whether her grammar is still pushing toward change or has in a sense closed down, declaring itself done with this corner of the grammar.[8]

---

[8]These questions are most critical for Clark and others who believe that children have a generalized resistance to synonymity. For Pinker the problem does not arise as often since, according to his model, the child only resists synonymity when he finds more than one entry for a single cell in a paradigm. Pinker's child will also try harder to find a distinction between causative *break* and *make break* than between *dived* and *dove,* as is appropriate, since in the former case there is a doubling up of entries in a single cell across a large number of verbs (which leads the child to try to split the paradigm), whereas in the latter case doubling is restricted to only a handful of items (see Pinker, 1984:198).

Some meaning differences are no doubt so salient that children will recognize them quickly. Others, however, are subtle and are known to give children trouble (e.g., the distinction in Turkish between two forms of the past tense, one for past events known through direct perception and the other for those known only through inference or hearsay; Aksu, 1978). How long do children go on trying to find a meaning difference between two attested forms before they give up and accept the forms as synonymous? What happens if a child should give up on a tough meaning distinction too early?

So far I have considered this problem from the perspective of the Uniqueness/Contrast principle. But it is even more problematic for those who do not suppose that children have any *a priori* expectations that two forms should contrast in meaning. If children lack such a bias, they should be perfectly happy to treat two observed forms as synonymous. Their problem will be that they routinely stop looking for nonobvious meaning distinctions too early (see also Pinker, 1984:201–202). What sets the search into motion again?

Notice that an appeal to ''mismatch'' between what the child says and what adults say will not work here, since the child will associate both forms with the same meaning, so for her they can be used interchangeably. A child's own misunderstandings of what adults say might serve as clues that something is amiss, but true comprehension errors must be rare, since the meaning the child associates with the two forms will typically be underdifferentiated and so will comfortably subsume either of the adult's intended meanings. (For example, the Turkish child for whom the two past tense forms are synonymous will associate them both simply with ''past time''; if she misses the adult's more refined intention this will normally pass unnoticed by both speaker and listener.) Children might soon shape up if they were corrected for using the wrong forms in their own speech (e.g., the ''direct experience'' past tense form for an event only heard about), but, for reasons discussed earlier, it seems unlikely that there is enough of this kind of feedback to push children down all the paths they must follow in search of difficult meaning distinctions.

These are difficult problems, and I am not certain what the right approach to them is. But solving them is clearly essential to arriving at a satisfactory understanding of what drives change in children's developing grammars.

CONCLUSIONS

In this chapter I have concentrated on two challenging issues for students of language acquisition: the ''no negative evidence'' problem and the question of what motivates change in children's grammatical systems. I have pointed out some difficulties with hypotheses that are currently being explored and certain phenomena that still need to be accounted for.

The perspectives reflected in the chapters of this volume suggest that the extreme polarization between nativist and empiricist approaches to language acquisition is diminishing. Although there are certainly advocates of each camp represented, there seems to be a refreshing recognition on the part of those invoking innate knowledge that it is important to account for what children actually do and, on the part of those adopting data-driven approaches, that we must outfit the learner with special sensitivity to those features of language that lead to desirable generalizations. A new type of model is starting to appear: Braine, Macken, and Pinker (all in this volume) propose hybrid approaches, borrowing ideas from both ends of the theoretical continuum and weaving them into novel configurations designed to capitalize on the strengths of each approach while minimizing associated weaknesses.

In closing, I want to mention a remaining obstacle to an adequate theory of language acquisition with which we seem to have made little progress, despite advances in other areas. This is the representation of *meaning* in the language learner.

Without certain assumptions about children's meaning representations, no theory can get off the ground. For example, the models of Berwick (this volume), Wexler and Culicover (1980), and Pinker (1984) all depend on children's constructing, independent of what they know about syntax, a correct representation of the thematic structure of simple sentences. Similarly, MacWhinney et al.'s simulation procedures give the learner a set of semantic features that are tailored to the characteristics of the sentences whose structure is to be learned. Langley and Carbonell, this volume, give a to-the-point critique, noting that all existing modeling systems cheat by "hand-crafting" the input to the model. The input contains exactly the right features for the language being learned, and often *only* those features, which reduces the learner's search problem.

How to get around this problem is not at all clear, but it is too important to neglect or push aside until other problems are solved. No model of how children learn to talk can make a strong claim to success until it is firmly rooted in a plausible theory of where children's meaning representations come from and how they are called on in the course of acquisition.

ACKNOWLEDGMENT

I am grateful to Lee Ann Weeks and Jürgen Weissenborn for their comments on a draft of this chapter.

REFERENCES

Aksu, A. Aspect and modality in the child's acquisition of the Turkish past tense. Unpublished Ph.D. Dissertation, University of California at Berkeley, 1978.

Baker, C. L. "Syntactic theory and the projection problem." *Linguistic Inquiry,* 1979, *10,* 533–581.

Berwick, R.; Weinberg, A. *The grammatical basis of linguistic performance*. Cambridge, MA: M.I.T. Press, 1984.

Berwick, R. *The acquisition of syntactic knowledge*. Cambridge, MA: M.I.T. Press, 1985.

Bowerman, M. "Evaluating competing linguistic models with language acquisition data: Implications of developmental errors with causative verbs." *Quaderni di Semantica*, 1982, *3*, 5–66. (a)

Bowerman, M. "Reorganizational processes in lexical and syntactic development." In E. Wanner & L. R. Gleitman (Eds.), *Language acquisition: The state of the art*. Cambridge, England: Cambridge University Press, 1982. (b)

Bowerman, M. "Starting to talk worse: Clues to language acquisition from children's late speech errors." In S. Strauss (Ed.), *U-shaped behavioral growth*. New York: Academic Press, 1982. (c)

Bowerman, M. "How do children avoid constructing an overly general grammar in the absence of feedback about what is not a sentence?" *Papers and Reports on Child Language Development* (Stanford University), 1983, *22*.

Bowerman, M. "Beyond communicative adequacy: From piecemeal knowledge to an integrated system in the child's acquisition of language." In K. E. Nelson (Ed.), *Children's language*, Vol. 5. Hillsdale, NJ: Lawrence Erlbaum Associates, 1985.

Braine, M. D. S. "On two types of models of the internalization of grammars." In D. I. Slobin (Ed.), *The ontogenesis of grammar*. New York: Academic Press, 1971.

Chomsky, N. *Aspects of the theory of syntax*. Cambridge, MA: M.I.T. Press, 1965.

Chomsky, N. *Lectures on government and binding*. Dordrecht, Holland: Foris, 1981.

Clark, E. V. "Awareness of language: Some evidence from what children say and do." In A. Sinclair, R. J. Jarvella, & W. J. M. Levelt (Eds.), *The child's conception of language*. Berlin: Springer-Verlag, 1978.

Dell, F. "On the learnability of optional phonological rules." *Linguistic Inquiry*, 1981, *12*, 31–37.

Demetras, M. J., & Post, K. N. Negative feedback in mother–child dialogues. Paper presented at the biennial meeting of the Society for Research in Child Development, Toronto, April, 1985.

Gathercole, V. M. "The contrastive hypothesis for the acquisition of word meaning: A reconsideration of the theory." To appear.

Gergely, G. & Bever, T. "The mental representation of causative verbs." *Cognition*, in press.

Green, G. "Some observations on the syntax and semantics of instrumental verbs." *Papers of the Chicago Linguistic Society*, 1972, *8*, 83–95.

Green, G. *Semantics and syntactic regularity*. Bloomington, IN: Indiana University Press, 1974.

Hirsch-Pasek, K., Treiman, R., & Schneiderman, M. "Brown & Hanlon revisited: Mothers' sensitivity to ungrammatical forms." *Journal of Child Language*, 1984, *11*, 81–88.

Jackendoff, R. "Morphological and semantic regularities in the lexicon." *Language*, 1975, *51*, 639–671.

Karmiloff-Smith, A. *A functional approach to child language*. Cambridge, England: Cambridge University Press, 1979. (a)

Karmiloff-Smith, A. "Micro- and Macrodevelopmental changes in language acquisition and other representational systems." *Cognitive Science*, 1979, *3*, 91–118. (b)

Karmiloff-Smith, A. "From meta-processes to conscious access: Evidence from children's metalinguistic and repair data." *Cognition*, 1986, *23*, 95–147.

Kuczaj, S. "The acquisition of regular and irregular past tense forms." *Journal of Verbal Learning and Verbal Behavior*, 1977, *16*, 589–600.

Kuczaj, S. "Children's judgments of grammatical and ungrammatical irregular past-tense verbs." *Child Development*, 1978, *49*, 319–326.

Maratsos, M. "How to get from words to sentences." In D. Aaronson & R. Reiber (Eds.), *Perspectives in psycholinguistics*. Hillsdale, NJ: Lawrence Erlbaum Associates, 1979.

Maratsos, M. & Chalkley, M. "The internal language of children's syntax." In K. E. Nelson (Ed.), *Children's language*, Vol. 2. New York: Gardner Press, 1981.

Mazurkewich, I. & White, L. "The acquisition of the dative alternation: Unlearning overgeneralizations." *Cognition*, 1984, *16*, 261–283.

McCawley, J. D. "Prelexical syntax." In R. J. O'Brien (Ed.), *Georgetown University round table on languages and linguistics*. Washington, D.C.: Georgetown University Press, 1971.

Pinker, S. "Comments on the paper by Wexler." In C. L. Baker & J. J. McCarthy (Eds.), *The logical problem of language acquisition*. Cambridge, MA: M.I.T. Press, 1981.

Pinker, S. *Language learnability and language development*. Cambridge, MA: Harvard Press, 1984.

Randall, J. "A lexical approach to causatives." *Journal of Linguistic Research*, 1983, *2*, 77–105.

Roeper, T. "On the deductive model and the acquisition of productive morphology." In C. L. Baker & J. J. McCarthy (Eds.), *The logical problem of language acquisition*. Cambridge, MA: M.I.T. Press, 1981.

Shibatani, M. "The grammar of causative constructions: A conspectus." In M. Shibatani (Ed.), *Syntax and semantics, Vol. 6: The grammar of causative constructions*. New York: Academic Press, 1976.

Smith, C. "Comments on the paper by Roeper." In C. L. Baker & J. J. McCarthy (Eds.), *The logical problem of language acquisition*. Cambridge, MA: M.I.T. Press, 1981.

Stowell, T. Origins of phrase structure. Unpublished Ph.D. Dissertation, M.I.T., 1981.

Wasow, T. "Transformations and the lexicon." In P. W. Culicover, T. Wasow, & A. Akmajian (Eds.), *Formal syntax*. New York: Academic Press, 1977.

Wexler, K. & Culicover, P. W. *Formal principles of language acquisition*. Cambridge, MA: M.I.T. Press, 1980.

Wexler, K. & Manzini, M. R. "Parameters and learnability in binding theory." In T. Roeper & E. Williams (Eds.), *Parameter setting*. Dordrecht: D. Reidel, in press.

Whorf, B. *Language, thought, and reality* (J. Carroll, Ed.). Cambridge, MA: M.I.T. Press, 1956.

Author Index

D

E

M

N

O

P

Subject Index

A

C

D

F

G

I